Business Mathematics

A Positive Approach

Second Edition

Instructor's Edition

Business Mathematics

A Positive Approach

Second Edition

Maryann Doe

Michael Warlum

Instructor's Edition

West Publishing Company

St. Paul   New York   Los Angeles   San Francisco

Credits

1, article based on Mark Vamos, Jonathan Levine, and Matt Rothman, "Marketing's New Look: Campbell Leads a Revolution in the Way Consumer Products are Sold," *Business Week,* January 26, 1987: 64–69. Photo courtesy of Campbell Soup Company; **51,** article based on Patricia Sellers, "The Rag Trade's Reluctant Revolutionary," *Fortune,* January 5, 1987: 36–38. Photo courtesy of Liz Claiborne, Inc.; **97,** article based on an advertisement in *Forbes,* November 17, 1986. Logo courtesy of Bankers Trust Company; **131,** article based on Faye Rice, "The King of Suds Reigns Again," *Fortune,* August 4, 1986: 130–34. Photo courtesy of the Procter & Gamble Company; **155,** article based on Brian Deemaine, "How Polaroid Flashed Back," *Fortune,* February 16, 1987: 72–76. Logo courtesy of Polaroid; **215,** based on Amy Dunkin, "Big Names are Opening Doors for Avon," *Business Week,* June 1, 1987: 96–97. Logo courtesy of Avon Products, Inc.; **255,** based on Joan Hamilton and Amy Dunkin, "Why Rivals are Quaking as Nordstrom Heads East," *Business Week,* June 15, 1987: 99–100. Photo courtesy of Nordstrom; **311,** based on Susan Caniniti, "Steering His Own Course to Success," *Fortune,* January 5, 1987: 95 and the Lands' End company brochure. Photo courtesy of Lands' End, Inc.; **351,** based on Mark Maremont, Dori Jones, and Amy Dunkin, "Toys Я' Them Too," *Business Week,* January 26, 1987: 71–72. Photo courtesy of Toys 'Я' Us; **397,** based on Joel Kotkin, "Mr. Iacocca, Meet Mr. Honda," *Inc.,* November, 1986. 37–40. Photo courtesy of The Honda Motor Company; **433,** based on Ronald Grover, Mark Vamos, and Todd Mason, "Disney's Magic," *Business Week,* March 9, 1987: 62–69. Photo © The Walt Disney Company; **465,** based on George Gendron, ed., " # 151 Kirk Horse Insurance, Inc.," *Inc.,* December, 1986: 64. Photo courtesy of Laurel Race Course; **495,** based on Gregory L. Miles and Matt Rothman, "Recycling Alcoa," *Business Week,* February 9, 1987: 56–58. Photo courtesy of the Aluminum Association; **539,** based on the 1986 Greyhound Annual Report. Photo courtesy of the Greyhound Corporation; **601,** based on Richard Brandt, "The Billion-Dollar Whiz Kid," *Business Week,* April 13, 1987: 68–76. Photo courtesy of Microsoft.

Copyediting: Martha Morong
Design: John Edeen
Composition: Interactive Composition Corporation
Cover Image: Comstock Inc./M. & C. Werner
Cover Design: Theresa Jensen

COPYRIGHT © 1988 By WEST PUBLISHING COMPANY
50 W. Kellogg Boulevard
P.O. Box 64526
St. Paul, MN 55164-1003

All rights reserved

Printed in the United States of America

Library of Congress Cataloging-in-Publication Data

Doe, Maryann.
  Business mathematics: a positive approach / Maryann Doe, Michael Warlum. — 2nd ed., instructor's ed.
    p. cm.

  Includes index.
  ISBN 0-314-63053-8
  1. Business mathematics. I. Warlum, Michael. II. Title.
HF5691.D63 1988b
513'.93—dc19

87-31956
CIP

About the Authors

Maryann Doe holds a bachelor of science degree from the State University of New York at Albany, and a master of science degree from Montana State University. She has taught at the university and community college levels. While a tenured member of the Business Division faculty at Shoreline Community College, Seattle, Washington, she acted as coordinator of the Business Mathematics Program. At Shoreline, she also taught courses in retailing, salesmanship, marketing, retail buying, human relations, introduction to business, and fashion merchandising. She also has a wide range of business experience. In addition to working in retail and wholesale sales, she has held management and buyer positions in both the fashion and florist industries and was a partner in a graphics arts firm. Currently a resident of Anaheim, California, she is a consultant specializing in small business development.

Michael Warlum holds bachelors, masters, and doctorate degrees from the University of Wisconsin, Madison, and has done post-graduate work at Harvard University. He has held positions in higher education, not-for-profit corporations, and government. As an assistant professor at the University of Wisconsin, Madison, and as a faculty member at Shoreline Community College, Seattle, he taught courses in business mathematics, introduction to business, fundamentals of arithmetic, English composition using the computer, arts administration, fund raising, and public relations. Author of a number of published fiction and non-fiction works, Dr. Warlum is currently employed by the Boeing Company, Seattle, where he is involved in technical writing and oral presentation development.

Contents

Preface xi

1
Basic Processes and Decimals 1
Business Takes a Positive Approach
Campbell Soup 1

1.1 The Reading of Numbers 2
   Marking Place and Verbalizing Numbers 2
1.2 Addition and Subtraction 7
   Adding 7
   Developing Speed and Accuracy 7
   Subtracting 8
   Borrowing 8
   Checking Subtraction 9
1.3 Multiplication 13
   Multiplying Decimals 13
   Using Shortcuts in Multiplication 14
   Checking Multiplication 15
1.4 Division 19
   Dividing Decimals 19
   Using Shortcuts in Division 22
   Checking Division 23
1.5 Estimation 27
   Rounding Whole Numbers 27
   Rounding Decimals 27
1.6 Narrative Problems 31
   Following a Plan 31
1.7 Averages 37
   Comparing the Mean, the Median, and the Mode 37

2
Fractions 51
Business Takes a Positive Approach
Liz Claiborne, Inc. 51

2.1 The Basics of Fractions 52
   Writing Fractions 52
   Reading Fractions 53
   Defining Fractions 53
   Converting Improper Fractions Into Whole or Mixed Numbers 53
   Understanding the Law of Fractions 54
   Raising a Fraction or Finding Equivalent Fractions 55
   Reducing a Fraction 55
   Rules of Divisibility 56

2.2 Addition and Subtraction of Fractions 61
   Adding Fractions 61
   Finding the Lowest, or Least, Common Denominator 61
   Adding Fractions with Unlike Denominators 62
   Adding Mixed Numbers 63
   Subtracting Fractions 64
   Borrowing 65
2.3 Multiplication and Division of Fractions 71
   Multiplying with Cancellation 71
   Multiplying Mixed Numbers 72
   Dividing Fractions 74
2.4 Calculations Involving Both Decimals and Fractions 81
   Converting Decimals to Fractions 81
   Converting Fractions to Decimals 82
   Converting Complex Decimals to Pure Decimals or Fractions 83
   Common Decimals and Their Fractional Equivalents 84

3
Bank Records 97
Business Takes a Positive Approach
Bankers' Trust 97

3.1 Checks, Deposits, and Check Records 98
   Records of Checks and Deposits 100
   Share Accounts and Interest-Bearing Checking Accounts 106
   Electronic Banking 107
3.2 Reconciliation 115

4
Ratio and Proportion 131
Business Takes a Positive Approach
Procter & Gamble 131

4.1 Ratio 132
   Writing and Reading Ratios 133
   Comparing Unlike Quantities 133

      Making a Ratio Comparison to One   *133*
      Making a Ratio Comparison of More Than Two Numbers   *134*
      Applying Ratios   *134*
4.2 Proportion   141

5

Base, Rate, and Percentage   155
Business Takes a Positive Approach   Polaroid   155

5.1 Percents and Conversion from Percents   156
      Converting a Percent to a Decimal   *156*
      Converting a Percent to a Fraction   *156*
5.2 Conversion to Percents   163
      Converting a Decimal to a Percent   *163*
      Converting a Fraction to a Percent   *163*
5.3 The Percentage Formula   167
      Finding a Percentage   *168*
      Finding a Rate   *169*
      Finding Percent More Than and Percent Less Than   *170*
      Finding a Base   *171*
      Finding a Base Using Amount and Difference   *172*
5.4 Solving Narrative Problems Using the Percentage Formula   179
      Reviewing Narrative Problems   *179*
      Solving Percentage Narrative Problems   *180*
5.5 Solving Rate Narrative Problems   185
5.6 Solving Base Narrative Problems   191
5.7 Solving Amount and Difference Problems   197
      Finding an Amount   *198*
      Finding a Difference   *199*

6

Trade and Cash Discounts   215
Business Takes a Positive Approach   Avon   215

6.1 Invoices and Trade Discounts   216
      Understanding Invoices   *216*
      Understanding Common Invoice Abbreviations   *218*
      Understanding Trade Discounts   *218*
      Finding Trade Discount and Net Price When a Single Trade-Discount Percent Is Given   *219*
      Finding Trade Discount and Net Price When a Series of Trade-Discount Percents Is Given   *220*
      Finding Single Equivalent Trade-Discount Percent   *221*
6.2 Cash Discounts   229
      Reading Terms and Using Ordinary Dating   *229*

6.3 Other Dating Methods   233
      End-of-Month Dating   *233*
      Extra Dating   *234*
      Receipt-of-Goods Dating   *234*
6.4 Returns, Shipping Charges, and Partial Payments   241
      Deciding to Which Charges the Discount Applies   *241*
      Determining Credit for Partial Payments   *241*

7

Retail Merchandising   253
Business Takes a Positive Approach
Nordstrom   253

7.1 Profit   254
      Finding the Net Profit Percent of Sales   *255*
      Finding the Percent Increase or Decrease in Profit   *256*
7.2 Pricing and Markup   263
      Finding Percent of Markup Based on Retail   *263*
      Finding Percent of Markup Based on Cost   *264*
7.3 Cost, Retail, and Markup   269
      Finding Cost When the Markup Is Based on Retail   *269*
      Finding Retail When the Markup Is Based on Retail   *270*
      Finding Markup When the Markup Is Based on Retail   *271*
      Finding Retail When the Markup Is Based on Cost   *272*
      Finding Retail and Markup When the Markup Is Based on Cost   *272*
      Finding Cost and Markup When the Markup Is Based on Cost   *273*
7.4 Markdown   279
      Finding Markdowns Based on Original Retail Price   *279*
7.5 Merchandise Inventory   285
      Finding Average Inventory   *285*
      Finding Stock Turnover   *286*
      Converting Average Inventory   *287*
7.6 The Value of Ending Inventory   293
      Applying the FIFO Method   *293*
      Applying the LIFO Method   *294*
      Applying the Average-Cost Method   *294*

8

Payroll   311
Business Takes a Positive Approach
Lands' End   311

8.1 Types of Compensation   312
      Finding Salary   *312*
      Finding Wages   *313*

   Finding Overtime   313
   Finding Piecework Pay   314
   Finding Commission   315
  8.2 Payroll Deductions   319
   Determining Federal Income Tax   319
   Exemptions   319
   Determining Federal-Income Withholding Tax Using the Wage-Bracket Method   320
   Determining Federal-Income Withholding Tax Using the Percentage Method   321
   Determining Social Security Tax   323
   Filing Employer's Returns   325

9

Interest   351
Business Takes a Positive Approach
Toys 'Я' Us   351

  9.1 Simple Interest   352
  9.2 Ordinary Interest, 30-Day Month Time   357
  9.3 Exact Time   361
  9.4 Exact Interest, Exact Time and Ordinary Interest, Exact Time   365
   Calculating Exact Interest, Exact Time   365
   Calculating Ordinary Interest, Exact Time   365
  9.5 Principal, Rate, and Time Calculations   371
   Finding Principal   371
   Finding Rate   372
   Finding Time   373
  9.6 Compound Interest   379
   Determining Accumulated Value   379
   Computing Interest Earned   379
   Calculating Interest on a Several-Times-A-Year Basis   379
  9.7 The Compound-Interest Table   385
   Using the Table to Figure Interest Compounded Annually   385
   Using the Table to Figure Interest Compounded Several Times a Year   387

10

Finance   397
Business Takes a Positive Approach   Honda   397

  10.1 Promissory Notes   398
   Reading a Promissory Note   398
   Determining Interest Due   400
   Finding Maturity Value   401
   Calculating Days in the Note Period   402
  10.2 Discounting Notes   407
  10.3 Consumer Loans   411
  10.4 Installment Buying   423
   Actual Total Cost   423
   Carrying Charges   423
   Effective Interest Rate   424

11

Real Estate   433
Business Takes a Positive Approach   Disney   433

  11.1 Real-Estate Loans   434
   Choosing a Mortgage   434
   Finding Mortgage Money   435
   Amortizing Mortgages   435
   Dealing with Other Costs   436
  11.2 Loan-Repayment Schedules   441
  11.3 Property Taxes   447
   Finding Assessed Valuation Using Assessment Rate   447
   Finding Property Taxes   448
   Finding Assessed Valuation   451

12

Insurance   465
Business Takes a Positive Approach
Kirk Horse Insurance, Inc.   465

  12.1 Life Insurance   466
   Selecting a Life Insurance Policy   466
   Determining the Premium Using a Schedule   467
   Figuring Annual Premiums   468
  12.2 Automobile Insurance   473
   Understanding Types of Automobile Insurance   473
   Figuring Automobile Insurance Premiums   473
   Reading Automobile Insurance Premium Tables   474
  12.3 Fire Insurance   479
   Figuring Fire Insurance Premiums   479
  12.4 Other Aspects of Fire Insurance   483
   Cancellation by the Policyholder   483
   Cancellation by the Insurance Company   484
   Calculating Coinsurance   485

13

Depreciation   495
Business Takes a Positive Approach   Alcoa Aluminum   495

   Introduction to Depreciation   496
  13.1 Depreciation by the Straight-Line Method   497
   Constructing a Depreciation Schedule   498
  13.2 Depreciation by the Units-of-Production Method   503

13.3 Depreciation by the Sum-of-the-Years'-Digits Method   507
13.4 Depreciation by the Declining-Balance Method   511
13.5 Depreciation by the Accelerated Cost Recovery System and the Modified Accelerated Cost Recovery System   517
Using the ACRS Method of Depreciation   517
Using the Recovery Rate for the 3-, 5-, and 10-Year Classes   518
Using the Recovery Rate for 15-Year Class   519
Using the Modified ACRS Method of Depreciation   521

14
Accounting and Analysis   539
Business Takes a Positive Approach
Greyhound   539

14.1 Financial Statements   540
Preparing the Balance Sheet   540
Preparing the Income Statement   543
Finding the Cost of Goods Sold   544
14.2 Comparative Analysis   551
Performing Horizontal Analysis   552
Performing Vertical Analysis   553
14.3 Financial Ratios   563
Finding Current Ratio   564
Finding Acid-Test Ratio   564
Finding Ratio of Plant Assets to Long-Term Liabilities   565
Finding Ratio of Owner's Equity to Total Liabilities   565
Finding Ratio of Net Income to Owner's Equity   565
14.4 Bar Graphs and Pictograms   571
Simple Bar Graphs   571
Component Bar Graphs   572
Pictograms   574

14.5 Circle Graphs and Line Graphs   579
Circle Graphs   579
Line Graphs   580

15
Annuities and Investments   601
Business Takes a Positive Approach
Microsoft   601

15.1 Present Value   602
15.2 Annuities   609
Finding the Amount of an Ordinary Annuity   609
Finding the Amount of an Annuity Due   611
15.3 Present Value of Annuities   621
Finding the Present Value of an Ordinary Annuity   621
15.4 Sinking Fund for Annuities   629
Finding a Sinking Fund   629
15.5 Stocks   637
Defining Types of Stock   637
Determining Stock Dividends   638
Finding Dividend Yield   640
Buying and Selling Stock   641
15.6 Bonds   647
Defining Types of Bonds   647
Buying and Selling Bonds   648
Finding Bond Prices, Premium, and Discount   648
Determining Bond Price with Accrued Interest   649
Finding Current Yield on Bonds   650

Appendix A   The Metric System   A-1
Appendix B   The Electronic Calculator   B-1
Appendix C   Glossary   C-1
Appendix D   Answers   D-1
Index   I-1

Preface

Objectives

Business Mathematics: A Positive Approach, Second Edition, is designed and written to help you:

- Develop competence in the basic mathematical skills required in business.
- Move toward more advanced applications of mathematics in specific business situations.
- Understand the importance of a working knowledge of mathematics in a business career.

How to Use This Book

Each chapter of *Business Mathematics: A Positive Approach*, Second Edition, is arranged to let you move step-by-step through your study of a particular group of business mathematics concepts. Every chapter includes:

- *Business Takes a Positive Approach* As you read these timely explanations of how successful corporations remain in the forefront by taking assertive and imaginative actions to meet significant challenges, think about fresh approaches you can take to make the most of your study of business mathematics.

- *Learning Objectives* This list of goals is headed by the statement, "After reading and studying this chapter and working the problems, you will be able to:". Review the objectives before you read further in each chapter. They serve as a road map, marking the important points you need to understand.

- *Explanatory Material* This book's conceptual explanations are very complete. When you study them, make an effort to read every word. Resist any temptation to skim. Reading quickly is not important here—understanding the ideas is. If you do not comprehend part of a sentence at once, take time to read it until its meaning is clear. Doing so helps you gain a higher level of understanding. This in turn leads to a firm overall grasp of the material.

- *Examples with Step-by-Step Solutions* Study carefully the many examples that have been worked out for you. Read through each step, making an effort to understand the mathematical processes involved and looking at the placement of the numbers. Next, perform the calculations without looking at the example. The step-by-step explanations are set up in such a way as to allow you to use an electronic calculator efficiently. Finally, check your work against the example, restudying any steps you may have missed. The energy you put into understanding the examples saves you time when you work the assignment problems.

- *Interest Boxes* Throughout this book are study hints, explanations of business terms and processes not covered in detail elsewhere, and interesting historical facts about certain business institutions and mathematical techniques. Reading them helps you see mathematics as a useful tool and a major means of communication in the business arena.

- *Self-Checks* These mini-quizzes follow the presentation of each concept or process. They are included to help you monitor your understanding of the ideas and examples. Test yourself, solving the self-check problems without reference to the explanation preceding them. The answers to the self-checks appear directly below the problems. This gives you immediate feedback, allowing you to pinpoint areas you need to restudy before going on.

- *Section Assignments* Each section of every chapter is followed by appropriate assignment problems. Read each problem completely before proceeding to solve it. In some instances, your instructor might choose to assign only some of the problems. When this is the case, you may want to pick out others to work on your own. The more practice you give yourself, the more adept you become at solving business mathematics problems. (See Appendix D where the answers to all the even-numbered problems are provided.)

- *Comprehensive Assignments* At the end of each chapter is a set of comprehensive problems covering each concept presented in the chapter. This comprehensive assignment helps you and your instructor assess your mastery of the material and prepares you for the chapter test. (See Appendix D.)

- *Cases* The two case studies near the close of each chapter are designed to challenge you. They bring together in a business-based setting several of the concepts presented in the chapter. Many include "why-type" questions to assist you in considering the implications behind the numbers.

- *Key Terms* Review this list of important business mathematics terms that are used in the chapter. Notice that each of the key terms has been highlighted at the location in which it is defined. The definitions of all key terms are included in Appendix C.

- *Key Concepts* This section summarizes the main ideas of each chapter. Go over it carefully when you complete your studies and compare concepts presented with the objectives at the opening of the chapter. Ask yourself whether you have grasped the key concepts. Go back to restudy those of which you are still unsure. Because repetition is an important tool in successful learning, it is helpful to reread the key concepts from previous chapters from time to time. Your understanding of them helps you master the material you are currently covering.

Appendices

At the end of *Business Mathematics: A Positive Approach* are a series of additional helps. They include:

- *Appendix A:* **Metrics** For your convenience, this discussion of a widely used system of weights and measures is set up exactly like the chapter explanations. It includes step-by-step examples, frequent self-checks, and a practice assignment.

- *Appendix B:* **The Electronic Calculator** This review of basic calculator functions is complete with illustrations and step-by-step examples. Working them carefully helps acquaint you with one of today's most useful mathematical aids.

- *Appendix C* **Comprehensive Glossary** Use this alphabetized list of key terms and their definitions as a handy reference and as a review of the concepts presented.

- *Appendix D* **Selected Assignment Answers**   Answers to the even-numbered problems of all assignments are given to provide you with immediate feedback on your mastery of the various concepts. Refer to this section for the correct answer only after you have finished working a particular problem. If your answer does not agree with the one in the back of the book, try again. If you are still unsuccessful, seek help from others.

Using the study aids provided in *Business Mathematics: A Positive Approach*, Second Edition, makes learning easier for you as you progress through the course.

Taking Tests

Some students believe they have grasped business mathematics concepts until it comes time to take an examination. Then they discover that they are not really prepared. Here are some suggestions that should help you exhibit your best efforts.

How to Study and Prepare for the Test

- *Keep up with the work.*   Complete assignments as they are given. Do not put them off. Business mathematics concepts build on one another. Take time to think through how an idea relates to the one that follows it and to the one that came before.

- *Resist any temptation to cram.*   Spending the last hours before an examination trying to comprehend material you ought to have mastered weeks before does not work. An organized, ongoing program of study is the most effective approach. Review the list of objectives, the key terms, and the key concepts in each chapter, rework some of the problems in each assignment, and read over the notes you have taken during class sessions.

- *Study with others.*   Other people taking the course can be of help, and you can help them as well. Talking to your fellow students about the course material lets you focus your thinking and identify those concepts that are not yet clear to you. Most important, studying with others does away with feelings of isolation.

- *Relax mentally.*   Immediately before a test, some students prefer to read over their notes quickly. Others like to concentrate on something entirely different, perhaps sending their thoughts to a past event or place filled with pleasant, relaxing memories. Experiment to find what technique works best for you, then use it.

- *Expect to be tense.*   When you approach an examination, you are prepared to deliver your best performance. To be nervous is normal. It is important, however, to guard against letting your tension escalate into panic. Remember that a test is a challenge, not a trap. Dress comfortably. Sit in a relaxed position. Breathe deeply and regularly. Project an image of calm. Our minds pick up cues from our bodies. If you appear relaxed, you will become relaxed. Remember that your best defense against panic is to come to the test thoroughly and systematically prepared.

How to Take the Test

- *Read it through.*   Skim the entire examination. This gives you the opportunity to assess the situation as a whole. Take special note of any general directions. Read them carefully to be sure you understand what you are expected to do. Decide how much time you will devote to each section of the test.

- *Solve the problems of which you are most certain.* This technique allows you to enter into the test format, to settle into the rhythm of taking it, and to find a level of personal comfort. Moreover, completing some of the solutions and going on to others builds confidence.

- *Move on to problems that are more difficult.* Approach them systematically, relating them to problems you have already solved. Do not dwell too long on any one question. You can come back to it later.

- *Complete the remaining problems.* Going through the entire examination once more, complete the examples you find most difficult. Concentrate on one at a time, relating it to what you have already done. Pause to conduct a mental review of what you have learned, applying it to the problem at hand.

Above all, when dealing with the test-taking process maintain a positive attitude. Business mathematics consists of a body of material, just like any other. You can not only master it, you can demonstrate to others that you have done so.

Special Note

Depending on how the course you are taking is planned, you may or may not be covering in class the basic arithmetic processes that underlie business mathematics. These include addition, subtraction, multiplication, division, and working with decimals and fractions. They are the foundation for everything that follows them. Therefore, it is vital that you understand them before proceeding to the more advanced concepts.

If your class is not set up to discuss these processes formally, review chapters 1 and 2 on your own to refresh your memory.

Acknowledgments

We express our thanks to the thousands of students who have already used this book, to the many individuals whose help, understanding, and encouragement have made this second edition possible, and to our reviewers for their many and enlightening suggestions. The reviewers are:

Karen Y. Anderson—Utah Technical College
Sharon Benson—Shoreline Community College
Marie Cochrane—Asheville Buncombe Technical College
Martha Duncan—Three Rivers Community College
Donald W. Ferguson—El Camino College
William N. Fuller—Lower Columbia College
Carolyn Henry—Shoreline Community College
Brenda Jennings—Lane Community College
Lynn G. Mack—Piedmont Technical College
Laurence Maher—North Texas State University
Lonnie Mock—Diablo Valley College
Gary Odegaard—Centralia College
Kenneth F. O'Brien—State University of New York
Louise A. Stevens—Golden West College

Business Mathematics

A Positive Approach

Second Edition

Instructor's Edition

1
Basic Processes and Decimals

Business Takes a Positive Approach

CAMPBELL SOUP

After over 100 years in business, Campbell Soup Company was slowly losing its share of the market to its competitors. Campbell's challenge was to adjust to meet the changing tastes of today's consumer. The firm took a look at its philosophy of mass marketing and decided to try something different. Campbell altered its products, advertising, and sales approach to meet the specialized needs and particular tastes of consumers in different regions of the country. For example, a food product with the same label might contain more or less of a certain spice depending on the section of the United States in which it is being sold. Through sophisticated research, Campbell introduced over 400 new products and varieties in a span of five years. New product areas include spaghetti sauce, frozen foods, natural soups, and packaged snacks. Using a basic approach, the firm changed its image from conservative to innovative, yet dependable. Today, Campbell's ads reflect the hurried lifestyle of the modern consumer while stressing the wholesome goodness of the company's products. As a result of these approaches, both sales and profits have increased.

Learning Objectives

After reading and studying this chapter and working the problems, you will be able to:

- Read and verbalize whole numbers and decimals.
- Add and subtract with speed and accuracy.
- Multiply and divide, using various shortcut techniques where appropriate.
- Estimate answers and round off whole numbers and decimals.
- Solve narrative problems, using a step-by-step plan.
- Find mean, median, and mode averages.

Let's begin the study of business math with the basis of mathematics itself—numbers. The same number can have a variety of names. It is a symbol, a means of communication. Though numbers seem abstract, when you think of them in terms of what they represent in a particular situation, you discover useful relationships and meanings. The number 29,630 may not mean much to you as it stands, but put $ in front of the figures and the word "your" in front of that, and your interest may be aroused—your $29,630!

1.1 The Reading of Numbers

The method of numbering we use is called the **decimal system.** It is based on ten and groups and multiples of ten. Decimals are especially important in business mathematics because our monetary system is based on decimals: **dollars** and **cents.**

The **decimal point** is the signpost that shows you where the whole number ends and the description of its remaining parts begins. In business math, when we talk about a number that contains a decimal point, we refer to the decimal point as "and." Thus, 10.8 is called ten and eight tenths. Note that we are also describing the number as a fraction, $10\frac{8}{10}$.

Marking Place and Verbalizing Numbers

Whole numbers are the digits to the left of the decimal point as you look at the page. Think of the numbers behind the decimal point, to the right of it, as a modified mirror image of those to the left. The ones or units column is the basis for the rest of the number. Therefore, it is not reflected elsewhere in the number.

Billions	Hundred millions	Ten millions	Millions	Hundred thousands	Ten thousands	Thousands	Hundreds	Tens	Units	and	Tenths	Hundredths	Thousandths	Ten thousandths	Hundred thousandths	Millionths	Ten millionths	Hundred millionths	Billionths
1	6	1	4	3	7	6	8	7	1	.	1	7	3	6	7	3	4	1	6

The number above is read: one billion, six hundred fourteen million, three hundred seventy-six thousand, eight hundred seventy-one and one hundred seventy-eight thousand, six hundred seventy-three million, four hundred sixteen billionths.

Example 1

12.05 is twelve and five hundredths.
1.205 is one and two hundred five thousandths.
.1205 is one thousand two hundred five ten thousandths.
.120506 is one hundred twenty thousand, five hundred six millionths.

NOTE: The *th* suffix used in reading decimals is the way we communicate the fact that we are discussing a part of a unit rather than a whole number. *Hundreds* and *hundredths* are very different things.

When reading whole numbers, note that the word "and" is not stated between columns. It is used only as the signal for the decimal point. When writing whole numbers, place a comma before every third number, counting from your right of the decimal point. The commas group the number into readable clusters. This is particularly helpful in reading dollar figures.

Example 2 Express this number in verbal terms: 872,001.5

Answer Eight hundred seventy-two thousand one and five tenths

Another way to read decimals is by referring to the decimal point as "point" and giving the numbers following it individual labels. Thus, 10.8 reads "ten point eight." The advantage of this method is that it can make verbal communication in the business world more clear.

Example 3 12.5 is twelve point five.
1.125 is one point one two five.
.125 is point one two five.

Self-Check

Express each of the following numerals in words.

1. 38.5
2. 2.98
3. .6321

Basic Processes and Decimals

Express each of the following in numeral form.

4. Three and five thousandths _____

5. Sixteen point three four _____

6. Forty-two hundred thousandths _____

ANSWERS **1.** Thirty-eight and five tenths or thirty-eight point five   **2.** Two and ninety-eight hundreths or two point nine eight   **3.** Six thousand three hundred twenty-one ten thousandths or point six three two one   **4.** 3.005   **5.** 16.34   **6.** .00042

Counting

Every system of enumeration has its own base. Many primitive peoples used ten as the basis of calculation because of its immediate convenience. Humans have a built-in calculator—ten fingers and ten toes!

This is probably the major reason the decimal system came into being. It describes equal parts of a unit—any unit—divided into ten pieces of the same size.

The Babylonians used sixty as the base in their system. This is how our time measures of sixty seconds to the minute and sixty minutes to the hour evolved.

Assignment 1.1

Basic Processes and Decimals

Write each of the following numbers in words.

1. 107.26 — One hundred seven and twenty-six hundredths
2. 39.119 — Thirty-nine and one hundred nineteen thousandths
3. .1101 — Eleven hundred one ten thousandths
4. 2.908 — Two and nine hundred eight thousandths
5. 854.8 — Eight hundred fifty-four and eight tenths
6. 413.008 — Four hundred thirteen and eight thousandths
7. 79.079 — Seventy-nine and seventy-nine thousandths
8. 812.230 — Eight hundred twelve and two hundred thirty thousandths
9. .2455 — Two thousand four hundred fifty-five ten thousandths
10. 16.70008 — Sixteen and seventy thousand eight hundred thousandths
11. 1,500.456 — Fifteen hundred and four hundred fifty-six thousandths
12. 816.006 — Eight hundred sixteen and six thousandths
13. 50.05 — Fifty and five hundredths
14. 7.8007 — Seven and eight thousand seven ten thousandths
15. 6,150.291 — Sixty-one hundred fifty and two hundred ninety-one thousandths

Express the following groups of words in numeral form.

16. Thirty-three and one tenth — 33.1
17. One hundred eleven and twenty-five hundredths — 111.25
18. Nine and fifteen thousandths — 9.015
19. Eight hundred seventy-five ten thousandths — .0875
20. Four and five hundredths — 4.05
21. Two thousand sixty-eight ten thousandths — .2068
22. One and one hundred eleven thousandths — 1.111

continued

Assignment 1.1 *continued*

23. Thirty-five and ninety-one ten thousandths _____35.0091_____
24. Nine thousand seven hundred and eighty hundredths _____9,700.80_____
25. Seventeen and seventeen ten thousandths _____17.0017_____
26. Two thousandths _____.002_____
27. Six hundred six and four hundredths _____606.04_____
28. Forty-eight and eighty-four hundred thousandths _____48.00084_____
29. Ninety and fifty-three thousandths _____90.053_____
30. One hundred and one ten thousandth _____100.0001_____

1.2 Addition and Subtraction

Adding

To perform **addition,** first align the columns properly. Place units under units, tens under tens, and so on, using the decimal points as the central base. Note that any whole number is understood to have a decimal point to the right of its units place.

Example 1 Manfred Dunsten, manager of a research program, must total the number of miles covered over a four-day period by one of the field workers he supervises. The distances are 46 miles, 201.4 miles, .623 mile, and 1.03 miles. What is the total mileage?

Add 46, 201.4, .623, and 1.03.

Step 1 Write the numbers vertically, aligning the columns on the decimal points. The numbers to be added are called **addends.**

```
  46.
 201.4
   .623
  1.03
```

Step 2 Find the **sum.** Be sure to add tens to tens, units to units, tenths to tenths, and so on.

```
    46.
   201.4
     .623
 +  1.03
   249.053
```

Answer The **total** mileage is 249.053 miles.

Developing Speed and Accuracy

Work situations demand quick thinking. To increase your speed in adding numbers, learn to recognize combinations of 10. Become so familiar with the following pairs of numbers that as soon as you see them, you think "10."

```
  9      8      7      6      5
+ 1    + 2    + 3    + 4    + 5
```

Make a habit of checking your work. Many a businessperson has experienced the frustration of working through a long series of calculations or a complex situational problem only to discover a mistake in addition or subtraction in the very first step. It's best to eliminate this type of error as you go along. You'll actually save time by stopping frequently to review your work for accuracy. The most convenient way to do this when adding is the reverse-order check. To accomplish it, add the columns in the opposite direction from the way in which you added them originally.

Example 2

```
        3,765  ↓              3,765  ↑  then
        1,892  If you         1,892     check in
          432  add in this      432     this
        9,216  direction . . . 9,216     direction.
Sum    15,305               15,305
```

Self-Check

Find each of the following sums and check your work.

1. .06 + .3 + .265 + .002

2. 86 + .0056 + 32 + 8.606

3. 1000.01 + .00001 + 1 + .1

ANSWERS **1.** .627   **2.** 126.6116   **3.** 1001.11001

Subtracting

In business math, apply the same rule to **subtraction** that you did to addition. Position the numbers by aligning on the decimal points.

You must have as many places in the **minuend,** the number from which you subtract, as in the **subtrahend**, the number being subtracted. You can accomplish this by adding zeros to the minuend as needed.

Example 3 Sarah Moses works in the testing division of Consumers' Weekly Newsletter. In a recent trial, one small car made 24.375 miles to a gallon of gasoline, while a second made 4.98654 fewer than that. Sarah must calculate the mileage of the second car.

Subtract: 24.375 − 4.98654.

Step 1 Arrange the numbers by columns.

$$\begin{array}{r} 24.375 \\ 4.98654 \end{array}$$

Step 2 Add zeros behind the decimal point of the minuend to allow subtraction.

$$\begin{array}{r} 24.37500 \\ 4.98654 \end{array}$$

Step 3 Subtract the subtrahend from the minuend. The answer is called the **difference,** or the **remainder.**

$$\begin{array}{r} 24.37500 \\ -4.98654 \\ \hline 19.38846 \end{array}$$

Answer 24.375 − 4.98654 = 19.38846 miles per gallon

Borrowing

Often in subtraction, you must borrow from one column in order to subtract in another.

Example 4 For use in your model-ship–building business, you purchase 6,773 tiny, hand-carved masts. Upon their arrival, you find that 1,884 of them are damaged. Once you have returned the damaged masts, how many remain?

Step 1 Arrange the numbers in columns.

$$\begin{array}{rl} 6{,}773 & \text{Minuend} \\ -\;1{,}884 & \text{Subtrahend} \end{array}$$

Step 2 Subtract, borrowing as necessary

```
  5 16 16 13
  6  7  7  3
- 1  8  8  4
  4, 8  8  9   Difference, or
                remainder
```

Answer The number of masts remaining is 4,889

NOTE: In this example, the numbers above the minuend indicate borrowing. You should do this mentally, not by crossing out and obscuring the minuend. Look at the units column. You cannot subtract 4 from 3, so you borrow 1 from the tens column. Actually, you are borrowing 1 ten, which equals 10 + 3, or 13. The result for the units column is 13 − 4. This gives a difference of 9. In the tens column, borrow from the hundreds column; in the hundreds column, borrow from the thousands; and so on.

Checking Subtraction

Accuracy is important in business transactions. To check a subtraction problem, add the remainder, or difference, to the subtrahend. The sum of these two should be equal to the minuend. You can check all subtraction problems automatically. It is not necessary to rewrite the problem.

Self-Check

Arrange the columns properly, subtract, and check your work.

1. 7,006 − 4,095
2. 8,163 − 687
3. 8,065 − 56

ANSWERS   1. 2,911   2. 7,476   3. 8,009

Assignment 1.2

Basic Processes and Decimals

Arrange each of the following groups of numbers in the proper columns and add.

1. 48.841; 3,792; 200.913; 1.9; .683 =

   4,044.337

2. 14.38; 2.174; .683; 64.56; 1.249; .382 =

   83.428

3. 214.591; 10.86; 329.876; .1314; 12.22; 9.064 =

   576.7424

4. .2974; 74.82; .0191; 18.146; 886.74; .4091 =

   980.4316

5. 82.261; .1714; 874.08; .921; 236.9; 32.013 =

   1,226.3464

6. 402; 38.903; 167.521; .287; 537.03; 78.79 =

   1,224.531

7. 102.09; 5.228; 89.75; .24; 36.28; 119.057 =

   352.645

8. 53.78; 756; 68.372; 5.073; .40; 26.59; 9 =

   919.215

9. 2.163; 69.478; 3.56; 18.76; 384.2; .251; .061 =

   478.473

10. 7.57; 152; 4.959; 6.358; .7259; 356.23 =

    527.8429

1. 48.841
    3,792.
    200.913
    1.9
    .683
    4,044.337

2. 14.38
    2.174
    .683
    64.56
    1.249
    .382
    83.428

3. 214.591
    10.86
    329.876
    .1314
    12.22
    9.064
    576.7424

4. .2974
    74.82
    .0191
    18.146
    886.74
    .4091
    980.4316

5. 82.261
    .1714
    874.08
    .921
    236.9
    32.013
    1,226.3464

6. 402.
    38.903
    167.521
    .287
    537.03
    78.79
    1,224.531

7. 102.09
    5.228
    89.75
    .24
    36.28
    119.057
    352.645

8. 53.78
    756.
    68.372
    5.073
    .40
    26.59
    9.
    919.215

9. 2.163
    69.478
    3.56
    18.76
    384.2
    .251
    .061
    478.473

10. 7.57
    152.
    4.959
    6.358
    .7259
    356.23
    527.8429

continued

Assignment 1.2 *continued*

Find the sum in each of the following problems by adding combinations of 10. Check your work.

11. 7	12. 2	13. 3	14. 26
4	1	7	83
<u>3</u>	<u>8</u>	6	<u>71</u>
14	11	<u>4</u>	180
		20	

15. 93	16. 26,432	17. 924,381	18. 1
14	14,576	183,429	23
<u>23</u>	58,393	438,192	391
130	<u>35,038</u>	<u>819,243</u>	8
	134,439	2,365,245	78
			245
			<u>81</u>
			827

19. 1,932,621	20. 3,927,421
396,218	4,246,831
4,394,380	7,356,241
221	8,323,321
2,341,652	2,162,561
<u>421,984</u>	<u>1,923,471</u>
9,487,076	27,939,846

Arrange the following numbers by column and subtract.

21. 3.175 − 2.531   .644

22. 9.4 − .351   9.049

23. 111 − 83.6   27.4

24. 6.5 − .624   5.876

25. 143.64 − .796   142.844

26. 14.023 − 13.983   .04

27. 180.12 − 79.629   100.491

28. 81.051 − 55.95   25.101

29. .8315 − .7926   .0389

30. 32.083 − .568   31.515

Find each of the following differences and check your work.

31. 61,847	32. 54,000	33. 47,821	34. 86,579
<u>25,957</u>	<u>48,794</u>	<u> 7,410</u>	<u>14,668</u>
35,890	5,206	40,411	71,911

35. 60,978	36. 79,436	37. 705,961	38. 450,000
<u>60,868</u>	<u>68,451</u>	<u>537,809</u>	<u>328,542</u>
110	10,985	168,152	121,458

39. 532,654	40. 5,694,251
<u> 2,867</u>	<u> 86,206</u>
529,787	5,608,045

1.3 Multiplication

The use of **multiplication** speeds business calculations. The numbers in multiplication are called **factors**. The number multiplied or increased is called the **multiplicand**. The number by which it is increased is called the **multiplier**.

Example 1 Bamberg Bamboo Furniture, where you work, has 62 salespeople in the field. Each is expected to make 53 sales calls per month. If all calls are completed on schedule, how many are made?

Step 1 Multiply the multiplicand by each number in the multiplier. The results are called partial products.

```
   62   Multiplicand
 × 53   Multiplier
  186 ⎫ Partial
  310 ⎭ products
```

Step 2 Add the partial products. Their sum is the **product**.

```
  186
+ 310
3,286   Product
```

Answer The number of calls completed is 3,286.

NOTE: The factors in multiplication are interchangeable. This can ease calculation. For instance, because

$$\begin{array}{r} 28 \\ \times\ 1{,}560 \end{array}$$

is the same thing as

$$\begin{array}{r} 1{,}560 \\ \times\ \ \ \ 28 \end{array}$$

you can obtain the correct result by totaling two partial products instead of four.

Multiplying Decimals

It is not necessary to align numbers according to their decimal points when you multiply. However, placement of the decimal becomes important in the product. Multiplication of decimals is done in this way.

Step 1 Multiply as with whole numbers.

Step 2 Count the number of places to your right of the decimal point in the multiplier.

Step 3 Add the number of places to your right of the decimal point in the multiplicand to the number found in step 2.

Step 4 Count the total number of places in the product from right to left and insert the decimal point.

Example 2 As manager of the floor covering department of Fimbles Department Store, you recommend a certain pattern of vinyl sheet goods at 40 cents a running foot. A customer buys 2.674 feet of the sheet goods. How much will you charge?

Find the product of 2.674 × .4.

Step 1 Multiply.

```
  2.674
×   .4
 10696
```

Basic Processes and Decimals 13

Step 2	Count the number of decimal places in the multiplier.	2.674 has 3 places
Step 3	Add the number of decimal places in the multiplicand.	.4 has 1 place 3 + 1 = 4 places
Step 4	Count off this number of places in the product, starting at your right.	1.0696
Answer	The total price of the sheet goods is $1.07 (rounded to the nearest cent).	

Example 3 Find the product of .945 × .00302.

Step 1	Multiply.	.945 .00302 ————— 1890 2835 ————— 285390
Step 2	Count the number of decimal places in the multiplier.	.945 has 3 places
Step 3	Add the number of places in the multiplicand.	.00302 has 5 places Total = 8 places
Step 4	Count off the number of places in the product.	.00285390
Answer	.945 × .00302 = .0028539	

NOTE: In this example, more places are needed than there are digits in the product. Therefore, zeros are added in front of the number to mark places.

Self-Check

Find each of the following products.

1. $42.63 × $1.42 = _____
2. 5.004 × 634 = _____
3. .246 × .001031 = _____

ANSWERS 1. $60.5346, or $60.53   2. 3,172.536   3. .0002536

Using Shortcuts in Multiplication

If either or both the multiplier and multiplicand end in zeros, you can save time in business calculations. Disregard the zeros during the multiplication process. Place the total number of final zeros shown in the factors at the end of the answer.

Example 4 During the last month, your employer, Custom Television Sales, Inc., has acquired 71,280 portable color television sets. The sets are marked to sell at $400 each. If all the sets are sold at this price, how much money will be taken in?

Step 1	Disregard the zeros and multiply.	7,128 × 4 ——— 28,512
Step 2	Place the total number of zeros shown in the original factors (3) at the end of the product.	28,512,000

Answer The amount taken in will be $28,512,000.

One of the most useful timesavers in business calculation is the shortcut used in multiplying any number by 10 or its powers: 100; 1,000; 10,000; 100,000; and so on. No calculation is necessary. It is a simple matter of shifting the decimal point to your right.

Step 1 Count the number of zeros in the power of 10 by which you are multiplying.

Step 2 Move the decimal point in the number being multiplied as many places to your right as there are zeros in the power of 10.

Example 5 Harley Baker processes orders for Precision Machine and Tool, Inc. He has a request for 100 stainless steel pins, each precisely 2.835 centimeters long. How much stainless steel rod must he buy to enable him to fill the order, with no allowance for waste?

Find the product of 2.835 × 100.

Step 1 Count the zeros in the power of 10.   100 has 2 zeros

Step 2 Move the decimal point in the multiplicand.   2 83.5

Answer The amount of rod needed is 283.5 cm.

To state what happens in the form of a rule, we can say: When multiplying a number by a power of 10, move the decimal point of the multiplicand to your right as many places as there are zeros in the multiplier, the power of 10.

Self-Check

Find each of the following products using the shortcut method.

1. 81,000
   × 50

2. 6,490
   × 600

3. 3.211 × 1,000 =

4. .00401 × 100,000 =

ANSWERS 1. 4,050,000   2. 3,894,000   3. 3,211   4. 401

Checking Multiplication

To check multiplication, interchange the factors and multiply. This method operates on the same principle as the reverse-order check in addition (see Section 1.2).

Example 6 Check the product of 62 × 53, which you have determined is 3,286.

Step 1 Reverse the factors.

$$\begin{array}{r}53\\ \times 62\end{array}$$

Step 2 Find the product.

Answer The product of 53 × 62 is the same as that found for 62 × 53. The answer is correct.

$$\begin{array}{r}53\\ \times 62\\ \hline 106\\ 318\\ \hline 3,286\end{array}$$

Basic Processes and Decimals

A second method of checking multiplication is to divide the product by either the multiplicand or the multiplier. The result should be the other factor.

Self-Check

Find each of the following products and check it.

1. 351
   × 8

2. 35,128
   × 348

ANSWERS 1. 2,808   2. 12,224,544

THE MULTIPLICATION TABLES

If you have not studied basic mathematics in some time, you may want to refresh your memory concerning the products of commonly used combinations of numbers.

On the chart shown here, fill in the products of the vertical and horizontal numbers. You may want to post the completed table in your study area for ready reference.

×	0	1	2	3	4	5	6	7	8	9	10	11	12	13	14	15
1		1														
2			4													
3				9												
4					16											
5						25										
6							36									
7								49								
8									64							
9										81						
10											100					
11												121				
12													144			
13														169		
14															196	
15																225

Assignment 1.3

Basic Processes and Decimals

Find each of the following products and check your work.

1. 25
    $\times3$
    75

2. 72
    $\times5$
    360

3. 68
    $\times4$
    272

4. 39
    $\times9$
    351

5. 42
    $\times8$
    336

6. 79
    $\times9$
    711

7. 348
    $\times6$
    $2,088$

8. 37
    $\times24$
    148
    74
    888

9. 78
    $\times56$
    $4,368$

10. 48
    $\times92$
    $4,416$

11. 71
    $\times34$
    $2,414$

12. 144
    $\times42$
    $6,048$

13. 907
    $\times36$
    $32,652$

14. 897
    $\times18$
    $16,146$

15. 9.38
    $\times6.07$
    6566
    56280
    56.9366

16. $.735$
    $\times91.5$
    67.2525

17. $.271$
    $\times.638$
    $.172898$

18. $.019$
    $\times2.5$
    $.0475$

19. 3.06
    $\times.73$
    2.2338

20. 208
    $\times156$
    1248
    1040
    208
    $32,448$

21. $3,624$
    $\times708$
    $2,565,792$

22. $4,628$
    $\times1,006$
    $4,655,768$

23. $7,006$
    $\times3,456$
    $24,212,736$

24. $9,461$
    $\times605$
    $5,723,905$

25. $8,904$
    $\times7,804$
    $69,486,816$

26. $.0037$
    $\times4.61$
    37
    222
    148
    $.017057$

27. $.0785$
    $\times3.171$
    $.2489235$

28. 53.91
    $\times.0068$
    $.366588$

29. $.0928$
    $\times.0502$
    $.0046586$

30. $.2008$
    $\times.0387$
    $.00777096$

continued

Assignment 1.3 *continued*

Find each of the following products, using the power-of-10 rule.

31. 716.2 × 10 = __7,162__   716.2̣→   32. 2.5 × 10 = __25__

33. 25.068 × 100 = __2,506.8__   25.06̣8→   34. 54 × 1,000 = __54,000__

35. .025 × 10 = __.25__   .0̣25→   36. 74.376 × 10,000 = __743,760__

37. 462 × 10,000 = __4,620,000__   462.0000→   38. 65.328 × 100 = __6,532.8__

39. 30 × 100 = __3,000__   30.00→   40. 47.6 × 1,000 = __47,600__

1.4 Division

Division is the process of finding how many <u>times</u> one number is contained within another. The symbols for division are ÷, ⟍ ‾‾ , or a horizontal or diagonal line, as in a fraction (see Chapter 2, section 1.).

Example 1 Mary Lou Harris's supervisor at the construction site where she works told her to divide a load of 1,283 cement blocks into stacks of 46 blocks each. How many stacks of blocks will Mary Lou have when she has finished the job?

Step 1 Find the **quotient** by dividing the **divisor** into the first figure of the **dividend,** or, if necessary, into the first two or more figures of the dividend. 46 is not contained in 1 or in 12, but it is contained in 128 about 2 times. The 2 is called a trial quotient and is placed over the 8 in the dividend. This trial quotient is found by estimating. 4 is contained in 12 three times but 3 is too high a number for use here.

$$\begin{array}{r} 2 \\ 46\overline{)1{,}283} \end{array}$$

Step 2 Multiply the whole divisor by the trial quotient. Write the product under the corresponding figures in the dividend. If this product is greater than the dividend, use as the trial quotient a figure one unit less than the figure first tried.

$$\begin{array}{r} 2 \\ 46\overline{)1{,}283} \\ 92 \end{array}$$

Step 3 Subtract this product from the corresponding numbers in the dividend. If the **remainder** is greater than the whole divisor, then use a trial quotient one unit higher than the figure tried.

$$\begin{array}{r} 2 \\ 46\overline{)1{,}283} \\ 92 \\ \hline 36 \end{array}$$

Step 4 Bring down the next figure of the dividend and place it beside the remainder. If the resulting number, called the partial dividend, is not higher than the whole divisor, then the next number in the dividend should be brought down.

$$\begin{array}{r} 2 \\ 46\overline{)1{,}283} \\ 92\downarrow \\ \hline 363 \end{array}$$

Step 5 Using the remainder and the number or numbers brought down as partial dividends, repeat steps 1 through 4 until the remainder is no longer divisible by a multiple of the divisor.

$$\begin{array}{r} 27 \text{ Quotient} \\ \text{Divisor } 46\overline{)1{,}283} \text{ Dividend} \\ 92 \\ \hline 363 \\ 322 \\ \hline 41 \text{ Remainder} \end{array}$$

Answer Mary Lou will have 27 piles of cement blocks, with 41 blocks left over.

NOTE: The quotient may be written as 27 with a remainder of 41, 27r41, 27 + 41, or $27\frac{41}{46}$ (making a fraction by putting the remainder over the divisor).

Dividing Decimals

Just as in multiplication, in dividing decimals you must be concerned with the placement of the decimal point in the answer.

When dividing a decimal by a whole number, use the following procedure.

Step 1 Set the numbers up in division format.

Step 2   Position the decimal point in the quotient above the decimal point in the dividend. It is best to do this at once, before you start dividing.

Step 3   Divide as with whole numbers.

Example 2   Fifteen boys and girls receive a total of $11.85 one Saturday for doing yard work in their neighborhood. They decide to divide it equally. How much will each receive?

Divide: 11.85 ÷ 15.

Step 1   Set up the numbers for division.   15)11.85

Step 2   Establish the decimal point in the quotient.   15)11.85

Step 3   Divide. In this example, there is no remainder.
$$\begin{array}{r} .79 \\ 15\overline{)11.85} \\ \underline{10\ 5} \\ 1\ 35 \\ \underline{1\ 35} \end{array}$$

Answer   Each child receives $.79.

Self-Check

Find each of the following quotients.

1. 3.965 ÷ 46 = _____

2. 68.324 ÷ 238 = _____

3. 27.409 ÷ 99 = _____

ANSWERS   1. .0861 = .086$\frac{9}{46}$ 2. .2870 = .287   3. .277

When a division calculation with a decimal point in its dividend does not come out even, add zeros to the right of this decimal point. Keep dividing until you have found a level of accuracy that satisfies you.

When dividing by a decimal, change the divisor into a whole number before your proceed. Do this by multiplying both the divisor and the dividend by the same number, a power of 10, to clear the divisor. Doing this has no effect on the quotient, so long as you remember to move the decimal point the same number of places in both the divisor and the dividend.

Step 1   Set the numbers up in division format.

Step 2   Clear the decimal point from the divisor, moving it to your right until the divisor is a whole number.

Step 3   Move the decimal point of the dividend the same number of places to the right that you moved the decimal point in the divisor. Position the decimal point of the quotient directly above this.

Step 4   Divide.

Example 3   Divide: 10.5 ÷ 3.5.

Set up the numbers for division.   3.5)10.5

Clear the decimal point from the divisor.   3 5.)10.5

Move the decimal point of the dividend the same number of places, positioning the one in the quotient accordingly.   35.)10 5.

20   Chapter 1

Step 4   Divide.

$$\begin{array}{r}3.\\35\overline{)105}\\\underline{105}\end{array}$$

Answer   10.5 ÷ 3.5 = 3

Often, in clearing the divisor, you will not clear the dividend completely. It is not necessary to clear the dividend, but remember to place the decimal point of the quotient directly above the new position of the decimal point in the dividend.

Example 4   Divide: 10.815 ÷ 3.5.

Step 1   Set the numbers up for division.   3.5)10.815

Step 2   Clear the divisor.   3̬5̬.)10.815

Step 3   Adjust the decimal point of the dividend and position the decimal point of the quotient.   35.)10̬ 8̬.15

Step 4   Divide.

$$\begin{array}{r}3.09\\35\overline{)108.15}\\\underline{105}\\315\\\underline{315}\end{array}$$

Answer   10.815 ÷ 3.5 = 3.09

You will sometimes need to add zeros to the dividend in order to move the decimal point a sufficient number of places to correspond to the change you have made in the divisor when clearing it.

Example 5   Divide: 105 ÷ .35.

Step 1   Set the numbers up for division.   .35)105

Step 2   Clear the divisor.   35̬.)105

Step 3   Move the decimal point in the dividend, remembering that it is understood that all whole numbers have a decimal point following the final digit. Place the decimal point for the quotient.   35)105̬ 00̬.

Step 4   Divide.

$$\begin{array}{r}300\\35\overline{)10500}\\\underline{105}\end{array}$$

Answer   105 ÷ .35 = 300

Self-Check

Find each of the following quotients.

1. 48.965 ÷ .361 = _____

2. 9,638.4 ÷ 1.6842 = _____

3. .06012 ÷ .321 = _____

ANSWERS   1. 135.6371   2. 5,722.8357   3. .1872

Basic Processes and Decimals

Using Shortcuts in Division

When both the divisor and the dividend end in zeros, drop the zeros from the divisor and then drop the same number of zeros from the dividend.

Example 6 At the factory where you work, you must pack 34,200 bottles into 600 cases. How many bottles will you put in each case?

Step 1 Divide 34,200 by 600. Set up the calculation, disregarding the same number of zeros in the dividend and in the divisor.

$$6\emptyset\emptyset\overline{)34,2\emptyset\emptyset}$$
$$6\overline{)342}$$

Step 2 Divide.

$$\begin{array}{r}57\\6\overline{)342}\\\underline{30}\\42\end{array}$$

Answer The bottles will fit into 57 cases.

In the situation above, you are actually dividing both the divisor and the dividend by a power of 10. Just as you can multiply by 10 or a power of 10 by shifting the decimal point in the multiplicand a certain number of places (see section 1.3), you can divide by 10 or a power of 10 by shifting the decimal point in the dividend. However, in division, the decimal point is moved to the left.

Example 7 Divide: 28 ÷ 10.

Step 1 Count the number of zeros in the power of 10.   10 has 1 zero.

Step 2 Move the decimal point in the number being divided to your left, according to the number of zeros in the power of 10.   2.8

Answer 28 ÷ 10 = 2.8.

Example 8 Divide: .2835 ÷ 10.

Step 1 Count the number of zeros in the power of 10.   10 has 1 zero.

Step 2 Move the decimal point in the dividend.   .02835

Answer .2835 ÷ 10 = .02835

NOTE: It is necessary in this case to add a zero to mark the place.

The rule for dividing by 10 or a power of 10 is: Move the decimal point in the dividend to your left as many places as there are zeros in the divisor, the power of 10.

Example 9 Divide: 2.8 ÷ 1,000,000.

Step 1 Count the number of zeros.   1,000,000 has 6 zeros.

Step 2 Move the decimal point in the dividend.   .0000028

Answer 2.8 ÷ 1,000,000 = .0000028

Self-Check

Find each of the following quotients using the power-of-10 rule.

1. 126.45 ÷ 10 = _____

2. 3.211 ÷ 1,000 = _____

3. .00401 ÷ 100,000 = _____

ANSWERS 1. 12.645   2. .003211   3. .0000000401

Checking Division

To check the accuracy of a quotient, multiply the divisor by the quotient and add the remainder, if any. The result should equal the dividend.

Example 10 Check this calculation: 988 ÷ 29 = 34 r2.

Step 1 Multiply the quotient by the divisor.

```
    34
  × 29
   306
    68
   986
```

Step 2 Add the remainder to the product.

```
   986
  +  2
   988
```

Answer 34 r2 is the correct quotient.

Self-Check

Find each of the following quotients and check.

1. 6)19,296   _____
2. 46)31,740   _____

ANSWERS 1. 3,216   2. 690

FEEL FREE TO USE YOUR MIND

A calculator may not always be handy when you are in a situation where you must add numbers. Many people take a rigid view of numbers and feel we can only work with them as they appear. However, you can devise your own system of calculation by using numbers that are easier to work with. For example, suppose you are adding 46 and 99, and you want to get an answer quickly without resorting to addition.

Picture "46 plus 100 equals 146 less 1, which is 145." You can also use this technique with numbers ending in 7 or 8 by remembering to subtract a 3 or a 2, respectively. You will be surprised at how many different ways there are to arrive at a correct answer.

You can use a similar technique for subtraction. For example, you can think of 104 minus 36 as 100 minus 36 equals 64 plus 4, which is 68. With practice, it can actually take less time to arrive at an answer in your mind than by figuring on paper or entering numbers into a calculator.

Assignment 1.4

Basic Processes and Decimals

Find each of the following quotients.

1. 671 ÷ 11 = __61__
2. 1,728 ÷ 12 = __144__
3. 2,924 ÷ 43 = __68__
4. 34,944 ÷ 56 = __624__
5. 60,424 ÷ 83 = __728__
6. 48,503 ÷ 51 = __951 r2__

7. 46)1,242 = 27
8. 78)4,368 = 56
9. 375)29,250 = 78
10. 57)1,311 = 23

11. 24)17,136 = 714
12. 75)23,624 = 314 r74
13. 36)7,308 = 203
14. 11)16,180 = 1470 r10

15. 58)4,291 = 73 r57

Find the quotients. Continue two places after the decimal point.

16. 84)63.29 .753 = .75
17. 3.5)36.48 10.422 = 10.42
18. .009).63124 70.137 = 70.14

19. 8.2)37.81 4.610 = 4.61
20. .045)6.7321 149.602 = 149.60
21. .68).00693 .0101 = .01

22. 4.7).03186 .00677 = .01
23. 7.06)73.0452 10.346 = 10.35
24. 568)211.79 .372 = .37

25. 26.7)92.008 3.4459 = 3.45
26. 48)27.851 .5802 = .58
27. .02).4826 24.13

28. 3.5)8.2635 2.361 = 2.36
29. 150).95482 636.5466 = 636.55
30. .094).926341 9.8546 = 9.86

31. 4,500)306,000 = 68
32. 900)229,400 = 254 r8
33. 570)131,100 = 230

continued

Assignment 1.4 *continued*

34. $\dfrac{25}{3{,}7\cancel{0}\cancel{0} \overline{)92{,}5\cancel{0}\cancel{0}}}$

35. 68.2 ÷ 10 = _____6.82_____   6.8.2

36. 4 ÷ 1,000 = _____.004_____   .004.

37. .039 ÷ 10 = _____.0039_____   .0.039

38. 7.281 ÷ 100 = _____.07281_____   .07.281

39. 893.6 ÷ 1,000 = _____.8936_____   .893.6

40. 5,831.25 ÷ 10,000 = _____.583125_____   .5831.25

1.5 Estimation

An important habit for the businessperson to develop is estimating answers to see if solutions are within a reasonable, logical range. This technique also comes in handy in your daily routine. It assures you that your thinking is logical. It is also invaluable for checking on the accuracy of the bill in a restaurant or supermarket. Estimating involves rounding numbers. Many whole numbers used in business or in newspapers and magazine articles are expressed approximately. They are adjusted to the nearest ten, or nearest hundred, or nearest thousand, depending on the degree of exactness the situation requires. You can estimate quickly by **rounding.**

Rounding Whole Numbers

After locating the place you want to round (tens, hundreds, thousands, and so on), look at the first number to the right of this place. If the number to the right is 5 or more, increase the digit in the place being rounded off by 1. Change the numbers to the right of it to zeros. Remember: *When you round, you sacrifice accuracy.*

> **Rules of Rounding**
> - If the digits you are dropping begin with 5 or more, add 1 to the final digit to be kept.
> - If the digits you are dropping begin with 4 or less, simply drop them and do not change the final digit to be kept.
> - In rounding, always judge by the first digit to be dropped, not by any number that comes after that digit.

Example 1 As manager of the Roxie Theater, you are estimating attendance for the year. Round the number attending during the month of July, 46,731 people, to the nearest thousand.

Step 1	Locate the place to be rounded.	46,731 ↑
Step 2	Determine whether the digit immediately to the right of that place is less than 5, 5, or more than 5.	46,731 ↑
Step 3	Adjust the place number so that it is increased by 1 or remains the same, depending on step 2, and add zeros.	47,000 (The 6 is changed to 7.)
Answer	An estimated 47,000 people attended in July.	

Rounding Decimals

In communicating through mathematics in business, we agree mutually on a certain **level of accuracy.** There is no reason to work with a decimal that has been carried out to more places than necessary for the calculation you are performing. Therefore, you round it. You must decide what level of accuracy is needed in each case.

In dealing with money, as you will be doing in most business situations, you usually round to the nearest cent, that is, to the hundredths place. In working with bank interest, you carry the decimal out several places to ensure an accurate exchange of funds for both the bank and its clients. The same holds true when preparing property tax statements and in numerous other situations.

Example 2 Penny Montlake is pricing her handwoven pillows for sale. She has kept track of time and materials to the nearest tenth of a cent. She now needs to round the total per pillow, $35.446, to the nearest cent.

Round $35.446 to the nearest cent.

Step 1 Find the hundredths digit because cent means hundredth. In this case, it is 4. $35.446

Step 2 Find the digit immediately to its right. Here the digit is 6. $35.446

Step 3 Since the digit is more than 5, round the hundredths digit up by 1 and drop the 6. $35.45

Answer The price, rounded to the nearest cent, is $35.45.

Example 3 As a member of your company's public relations department, you are preparing a brochure emphasizing how one plant's increased production has enriched the community. To make certain production measurements are understandable to the public, you round them to the nearest thousandth.

Round .00643 to the nearest thousandth.

Step 1 Find the thousandths digit. Here it is 6.   .00643

Step 2 Find the digit directly to its right. It is 4.   .00643

Step 3 This digit is less than 5. Drop it and any digits that follow it. The thousandths digit is unchanged.   .006

Answer The number, rounded to the nearest thousandth, is .006.

NOTE: Base the rounding only on the first digit to the right of the number being rounded.

Self-Check

1. Round to the nearest ten thousand: 156,804.

2. Round to the nearest ten: 74.

Round to the nearest hundredth.

3. 24.347

4. .0635

ANSWERS 1. 160,000   2. 70   3. 24.35   4. .06

Assignment 1.5

Basic Processes and Decimals

Round each number to the nearest ten.
1. 150 — 150
2. 19 — 20
3. 1,849 — 1,850

Round each number to the nearest hundred.
4. 862 — 900
5. 436 — 400
6. 304 — 300
7. 3,298 — 3,300
8. 6,059 — 6,100
9. 9,649 — 9,600

Round each number to the nearest thousand.
10. 2,938 — 3,000
11. 6,820 — 7,000
12. 30,543 — 31,000
13. 14,650 — 15,000
14. 39,150 — 39,000
15. 50,098 — 50,000

Round each number to the nearest hundred thousand.
16. 2,875,300 — 2,900,000
17. 1,956,129 — 2,000,000
18. 84,608,995 — 84,600,000
19. 70,253,100 — 70,300,000

Find the sums and check the following problems by estimating to the nearest hundred.

20.		21.		22.	
647	600	829	800	4,756	4,800
794	800	6,257	6,300	9,169	9,200
980	1,000	1,892	1,900	2,509	2,500
538	500	401	400	8,496	8,500
256	300	768	800	6,510	6,500
963	1,000	3,531	3,500	304	300
4,178 (ans.)	4,200 (est.)	13,678 (ans.)	13,700 (est.)	31,744 (ans.)	31,800 (est.)

continued

Assignment 1.4 *continued*

Round each number to the nearest tenth.

23. .8956 _____.9_____   24. 3.0531 _____3.1_____

25. 861.63 _____861.6_____   26. 51.449 _____51.4_____

Round each number to the nearest thousandth.

27. 28.6029 _____28.603_____   28. .07492 _____.075_____

29. 308.1365 _____308.137_____   30. 11.6258 _____11.626_____

Round each number to the nearest ten thousandth.

31. .163875 _____.1639_____   32. 65.007354 _____65.0074_____

33. 15.421959 _____15.4220_____   34. .707548 _____.7075_____

Round each number to the nearest hundredth.

35. 47.2809 _____47.28_____   36. 8.6513 _____8.65_____

37. .0099 _____.01_____   38. 95.60346 _____95.60_____

39. 112.79649 _____112.80_____   40. 9.9998 _____10.00_____

1.6 Narrative Problems

Mathematics evolved from the need to solve everyday problems. It is a method for finding answers in our physical, economic, and social environment. It is an art of exploration and discovery. Attitude and understanding go hand in hand.

The matter of putting labels on or giving meaning to numbers is of utmost importance in business mathematics. You are preparing yourself to function in the marketplace, not to excel at theories of abstract mathematics. Throughout this book, you will find an emphasis on practical business situations. The numbers used represent or symbolize something, whether units produced, distance traveled, or, in the majority of cases, dollars and cents. To help you visualize this representation, the numbers are presented in the context of situations—narrative problems.

Narrative problems, or word problems, are a stumbling block for many people. If you take the steps toward a solution one at a time, however, you will lead yourself to a solution.

Following a Plan

Although there are no fixed rules for solving mathematical problems, your skill in solving them can be imporved if you keep the following steps in mind.

Step 1 Read the problem carefully. Be sure you understand the meaning of the words and the numbers.

Step 2 Analyze the data. You must see exactly what the problem asks for, or what is *required*, and also what is *given*. As you study the data, new facts and fresh insights will be revealed. Has all the necessary information for finding the solution been given? Which, if any, facts can be disregarded?

Step 3 Decide which process or processes you must use to find a solution.

Step 4 Estimate the answer. This is a very important step that is frequently overlooked. Ask yourself, "What is a reasonable answer?"

Step 5 Solve the problem. Use the data given with their relationships in order to find an answer. Being disorganized when figuring the problem will not improve speed or accuracy. Neat work will help you see what you are doing and assist you in checking your figuring as you go along.

Step 6 Check the answer. Is it close to the estimate you made in step 4? Verify the result. Substitute the answer back into the problem and see if it completes the problem correctly. As a challenge to yourself, go back over your work to see if it could have been designed more efficiently. This will help you in solving problems in the future.

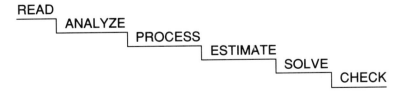

Basic Processes and Decimals **31**

Example Classic Poses, Inc., a ballet studio operated by Ivan Koski, sponsors 12 beginning ballet classes with 28 students to a class. What is the studio's total enrollment in beginning ballet?

Step 1 Read the problem. Here we are talking about a small business. It must have a certain number of paying clients in order to operate. The numbers included are:
12
28

Step 2 Analyze the data. What is needed? Look at the question being asked in the last line of the problem.
Total number of students in beginning ballet

What is given?
Number of classes: 12.
Students per class: 28.

Step 3 Decide what process(es) to use.
Multiplication

Step 4 Estimate the answer. What figure seems reasonable?
About 300+

Step 5 Solve the problem. Use the data given and the determined process.
$28 \times 12 = 336$
$336 \div 12 = 28$

Step 6 Check your work.

Answer The number of students in beginning ballet is 336.

NOTE: To solve almost any narrative problem, you must make certain reasonable assumptions. In this case we assumed that each of the 12 classes has full enrollment.

Self-Check

Solve each of the following narrative problems.

1. Harry Bumten buys several tools on sale at Daley Hardware Store. These include a heavy-duty wood chisel, $4; a bench grinder, $109; a twelve-inch lathe, $265; a ten-inch radial arm saw, $400; and a variable speed electric drill, $35. How much is his bill?

2. Parkwood Packaging Company can produce 673 boxes of cereal in one hour. How many boxes can it package at that same rate in 52 hours?

3. A television set retails for $648. This week it is on sale for $612. How much will you save if you buy 42 sets for your motel this week?

ANSWERS 1. $813 2. 34,996 3. $1,512

Assignment 1.6

Basic Processes and Decimals

Solve each of the following narrative problems.

1. Your latest inventory shows that the company where you work, Playclothes, Inc., has in stock 3,269 pairs of running shorts, 2,467 men's swimsuits, 312 athletic supporters, and 36 pairs of sunglasses. Find the total number of items listed.

   3,269
   2,467
     312
      36
   6,084

   6,084 items listed

2. First National Bank has several offices available for rent in its new tower. Each is a different size: 1,496 square feet, 480 square feet, 2,335 square feet, 786 square feet, 988 square feet, and 1,759 square feet. What is the total square footage available for rent?

   1,496
     480
   2,335
     786
     988
   1,759

   7,844

   7,844 square feet available

3. On a certain day, 20,315 vehicles passed a State Highway Department checkpoint. Of this number, 1,246 were semitrucks, 2,345 were pickup trucks, 598 were vans, and 368 were motorcycles. The rest were passenger cars. How many of them were passenger cars?

   1,246   20,315
   2,345   − 4,557
     598   15,758
     368
   4,557

   15,758 passenger cars

4. Allen Polaska, president of Fidelity Savings and Loan, noted that the day began with a cash balance of $15,265,789. During business hours the institution received deposits of $2,321,697 and paid out $3,475,890. What was the cash balance at the close of the day?

   $3,475,890 Paid out $15,265,789
   − 2,321,697 Deposits   − 1,154,193
     $1,154,193 $14,111,596

   $14,111,596 ending cash balance

continued

Assignment 1.6 *continued*

5. Mrs. O'Grady has a small apartment house. When all units are rented, she takes in $3,342 a month. At this time, one apartment, which rents for $325, is vacant. If Mrs. O'Grady receives rent payments of $450, $275, $425, $350, and $285, how much does she still have to collect?

```
   $450              $3,342
    275           −    325  Vacant unit
    425              3,017
    350           −  1,785  Rent received
    285             $1,232                        $1,232
 $1,785 Rent received                         to be collected
```

6. If an apartment rents for $324 per month, what is the gross rent per month for 823 units, assuming each rents for the same amount?

```
     823
  × $324
    3292
    1646
    2469
 $266,652                                     $266,652 gross
                                              rent per month
```

7. Mary Ann Andrews works as a buyer for a clothing manufacturer. If she buys 650 yards of fabric at $11 per yard, find the total cost of the fabric.

```
    650
  × $11
    650
    650
  $7,150                                       $7,150 total
                                              cost of fabric
```

8. Harold Bertoya travels for Tuffcover, Inc. If he averages 127 miles per day, how many miles will he travel in 26 days?

```
    127
  ×  26
    762
    254
   3,302                                       3,302 miles
```

9. If Alloyed Construction purchased three dozen sacks of cement at $5 each, 192 boxes of nails at $2 a box, and four dozen bags of decorative bark at $1 each, what was the total bill?

```
   36        192        48       $180
 × $5      × $2       × $1        384
  180        384        48         48
                                 $612          $612 total bill
```

continued

Assignment 1.6 *continued*

10. The Good Earth Theatre has 129 rows of orchestra seats and 38 rows of balcony seats. Each row contains 24 seats. If tickets for orchestra seats cost $8 apiece and those for balcony seats cost $6 apiece, how much money will the box office bring in if all the seats are sold?

```
    129            38
  ×  24          ×  24
    516           152
    258            76
   3096           912
```

```
     3,096            912          $24,768
   ×    $8         ×    $6        +  5,472
    $24,768         $5,472         $30,240
 (Orchestra seats) (Balcony seats)
```

$30,240 total gross receipts

11. Maurice Dongal manages an office building in which there is 12,925 square feet of rental space. The total monthly rental is $38,775. What is the monthly rent per square foot?

```
            $3
 12,925)38,775
        38 774
```

$3 per square foot

12. Ella Wagoner receives $296 for working a 37-hour week. What is her hourly pay rate?

```
       $8
  37)296
     296
```

$8 per hour

13. A factory that assembles power lawn mowers buys 3,125 circular blades for a total of $6,250. What is the cost per blade?

```
         $2
 3,125)6,250
       6,250
```

$2 per blade

14. Ernest Morris runs a stamping machine, that puts out 74 units per minute. If it put out 35,520 units, how many hours did it operate?

```
   74 Units/minute           8
 ×  60 Minutes         4440)35,520
 4440 Units/hour            3552
```

8 hours

continued

Assignment 1.6 *continued*

15. Liaw, Rollman, and Chetnik were in a partnership whose total sales amounted to $386,291. The cost of goods sold and expenses amounted to $254,468.

   a) Did the partnership make a loss or a profit?

   ```
   $386,291  Total sales
   - 254,468  CGS and expenses
   $131,823  Profit
   ```
   Profit _____

   b) If they decided to share losses and gains equally, what is each partner's share of the loss or gain?

   ```
        $43,941
     3)131,823
        12
        11
         9
         28
         27
          12
          12
           3
           3
   ```

   Each partner's share of gain _____$43,941_____

36 Chapter 1

1.7 Averages

Suppose you are preparing a business expense account. You want to state how much money you spent for lunches per day during the past two weeks. It might be hard to remember the amount you spent each day, but the average of these expenses serves to represent all of them. **Averages** have many uses in business. They show comparisons, goals, achievements, and any number of other indicators. Note that an average does not pretend to be exact in any one instance. It offers a close estimate or condition in a given situation.

To find the simple average of a group of values, divide the sum of the values by the number of values in the group.

Example 1 During a five-day work week, Cummings Assembly Plant turned out the following numbers of sewing machines on five different days: 173, 205, 190, 197, and 210. What was the average number of machines assembled per day?

Step 1 Find the sum of the set of values or items.

```
  173
  205
  190
  197
+ 210
  ---
  975
```

Step 2 Divide the sum by the number of values or items.

$$\frac{195}{5\overline{)975}}$$

Answer On the average, 195 machines were assembled per day.

Comparing the Mean, the Median, and the Mode

When reviewing business data and analyzing information, it is important to know what type of average has been used. There are three types: mean, median, and mode.

The **mean,** as described in the example above, is the type of average with which most people are familiar. It is the sum of the items divided by the number of items.

Example 2 Find the mean of the following departmental sales figures.

	Dept.	Sales
	A	$21,000
	B	23,000
	C	24,000
Mean	D	25,000
Median	E	25,500
Mode	F	26,500
	G	26,500
	H	26,500
	I	27,000

Step 1 Total the sales figures. $225,000

Step 2 Divide the sum by 9, the number of departments. $\frac{225,000}{9} = \$25,000$

Answer The mean is $25,000.

NOTE: Although the mean is easy to compute, it can be distorted by a high or low extreme.

The **median** is the number located at the midpoint when the items to be averaged are arranged in numerical order. In the example above, the numbers are arranged from the smallest to the largest. The number at the midpoint is $25,500. This is the median. There are four figures above it and four below it. If there were ten numbers instead of nine, the two central figures would be added and then divided by two to find the median. The median is not distorted by extremes, but sometimes it is awkward to arrange long lists of figures in numerical order.

The **mode** is the number that appears most often in a list of figures. In the example above, the mode is $26,500. The mode can be easier to find than the other averages and is not distorted by extremes. However, this average is not representative if only a small list of figures is involved.

If your test scores for a class were 88, 70, 91, 80, 10, 70, and 94, which type of averaging would you prefer your instructor to use?

Self-Check

1. Find the mean of the following group of numbers: 95, 102, 88.

2. The DeBucci family saved $104 in January, $113 in February, $109 in March, $95 in April, $99 in May, $105 in June, $96 in July, $100 in August, and $104 in September. Find the median and the mode of the amounts saved for this period.

ANSWERS 1. 95   2. $104 median; $104 mode

Assignment 1.7

Basic Processes and Decimals

1. During this year, the sales of J. D.'s Hobby Store were $176,846. They were $215,966 last year. What was the mean average monthly decrease in sales this year?

   ```
                                3260
   $215,966  Last year's sales   12)39,120
   - 176,846 This year's sales      36
   $  39,120 Difference             31
                                    24
                                    720
                                    720
   ```
   $3,260 average monthly decrease

Find the mean in each of the following situations.

2. 1,389 cars, 2,563 cars

   ```
   1,389      1976
   2,563    2)3,952
   3,952
   ```
   1,976 cars, average

3. 46 hours, 35 hours, 38 hours, 41 hours, 45 hours

   ```
   46         41
   35       5)205
   38
   41
   45
   205
   ```
   41 hours, mean average

4. 225 kilometers, 199 kilometers, 206 kilometers

   ```
   225       210
   199     3)630
   206
   630
   ```
   210 kilometers, average

5. 8 panels, 15 panels, 9 panels, 16 panels

   ```
    8         12
   15       4)48
    9
   16
   48
   ```
   12 panels, average

6. 28, 19, 23, 34, 20, 44

   ```
   28        28
   19      6)168
   23        12
   34        48
   20        48
   44
   168
   ```
   28

continued

Assignment 1.7 *continued*

7. Greenery Seed Company employs 43 people. One employee was absent on Monday, 2 on Tuesday, 3 on Wednesday, 1 on Thursday, and 3 on Friday. Find the median of daily attendance at the company for the week.

   42
   42
   ㊵ 41
   40
   40
                                                       41 people, median attendance

8. When you filled the tank of your company car with gasoline, the speedometer read 29,853. The next time you stopped for gasoline, it required 13 gallons to fill the tank. If the speedometer then read 30,074, how many miles did your car average on a gallon of gasoline?

   $$\begin{array}{r}30{,}074\\-\ 29{,}853\\\hline 221\end{array}\qquad \begin{array}{r}17\\13\overline{)221}\\\underline{13}\\91\\\underline{91}\\0\end{array}$$

                                           17 miles per gallon, average

9. a) What is your mode in a business math class if you received the following grades on your papers: 87, 94, 75, 65, 86, 100, 75, and 90?

   65
   ㊉ 75
   ㊉ 75   Mode
   86
   87
   90
   94
   100
   672
                                                     75 (mode)

   b) What is the mean?

   $$\begin{array}{r}84\\8\overline{)672}\\\underline{64}\\32\\\underline{32}\end{array}$$

                                                     84 (mean)

10. What is the mean daily production of grandfather clocks if the number of clocks produced in four, seven-day work weeks are as follows:

1st week	58	58	7	8
2nd week	62	62	4 Weeks	28)224
3rd week	59	59	28 Days	224
4th week	45	45		
		224		

                                                      8 clocks, average daily production

11. The delivery truck for Mom's Pies recorded the following mileage for a five-day work week:

Monday	86	a)	86
Tuesday	129		129
Wednesday	98		98
Thursday	117		117
Friday	95		95
			525 Total miles

continued

40   Chapter 1

Assignment 1.7 *continued*

a) What is the mean daily mileage?

$$\begin{array}{r}105\\5\overline{)525}\end{array}$$

105 average daily mileage

b) What is the median?

86
95
(98) Median
117
129

98 miles

12. Ford's Department Store is open every day of the week. If it did $1,243,920 in business for the month of September, what was its mean business per day?

```
       41464
30)1,243,920
    1 2
    4
    3
      13
      12
      19
      18
       12
       12
```

41,464 average daily business

13. Your company had monthly sales in the following amounts:

January $30,251
February   29,123
March   28,628
April   31,242
May   19,246

a) What are your mean monthly sales?

b) What is the median?

$19,246
28,628
(29,123) Median
30,251
31,242
$138,490 Total sales

$27,698 average monthly sales

$29,123 median sales

a) 27,698
   5)138,490
    10
    38
    35
    34
    30
    49
    45
    40
    40

continued

Basic Processes and Decimals **41**

Assignment 1.7 *continued*

14. Amanda Duckworth works as a bookkeeper at Belman Manufacturing. For the last ten months, the monthly sales figures were $12,850, $12,500, $12,000, $11,500, $12,500, $10,500, $12,500, $11,000, $11,050, and $10,900. What are (a) the mean, (b) the median, and (c) the mode?

$10,500
10,900
11,000
11,050
11,500
12,000
12,500
12,500
12,500
12,850
$117,300

a) 11,730
    10)117,300

b) 12,000   11,750
   11,500   2)23,500
   23,500

a) ____$11,730 mean____   b) ____$11,750 median____   c) ____$12,500 mode____

15. Mara Tillis, Teri Bames, and Maria Varquez work in the notions department of Fanford's Department Store. During the month of December, they sold a total of $9,582 worth of goods. What were the mean sales of each woman for the month?

$3,194
3)9,582

$3,194 average
sales each woman

16. As an insurance salesman, Hank Zeblaki made calls last Monday. Two of his clients were not at home, two were not interested, one increased his coverage by $20,000, and one bought a new policy for $10,000 in coverage. Find the mean dollar amount of insurance Hank sold per call.

$20,000 $5,000
 10,000   6)30,000
$30,000

$5,000 average
amount sold per call

Comprehensive Problems for Chapter 1

Basic Processes and Decimals

Write each of the following numerals in words.

1. $500,584 — Five hundred thousand, five hundred eighty-four dollars
2. $9,986,907 — Nine million, nine hundred eighty-six thousand, nine hundred seven dollars
3. 77,561 — Seventy-seven thousand, five hundred sixty-one
4. $793,500,000 — Seven hundred ninety-three million, five hundred thousand dollars
5. $3,038,033 — Three million, thirty-eight thousand, thirty-three dollars

Write each of the following words in numeral form.

6. Two hundred ten thousand, seventy-six — 210,076
7. Thirty million, two hundred thousand, one hundred — 30,200,100
8. Eight hundred thousand, eight hundred sixty — 800,860
9. Six thousand six — 6,006
10. Seventy-three million, twenty thousand, five hundred one — 73,020,501

Total each of the following.

11.	12.	13.
1,324	375	6,175
7,855	6,613	326
2,023	786	1,421
4,757	8,411	4,714
9,276	2,015	8,504
25,235	18,200	21,140

14. 8.57; 252; 4.858; 6.858; .7259; 866.28 = 1,139.2919

15. .039; 84.47; 2.492; 863.8; 46; 2.798; 3.89 = 1,003.489

Find each of the following differences.

16. 2,183,469
    92,547
    2,090,922

17. 62,483,581
    52,521,479
    9,962,102

18. 4.032 − .219 = 3.813

19. 65.875 − .008 = 65.867

20. 38.67 − 7.1982 = 31.4718

continued

Comprehensive Problems *continued*

Find each of the following products.

21.	146.3 × 3.795 = 555.2085	22.	20.71 × .0406 = .840826	23.	.6518 × .3829 = .24957422	24.	.0064 × .0038 = .00002432
25.	1.079 × .0091 = .0098189	26.	300 × 4 = 1,200	27.	3,200 × 40 = 128,000	28.	1,050 × 780 = 819,000

29. 3.426 × 100,000 = __342,600__   3.42600

30. 394,326 × 10,000 = __3,943,260,000__   394,326.0000.

Find each of the following quotients. Round to the nearest thousandth.

31. .39).84270   2.1607 = 2.161

32. .071)3.7962   53.4676 = 53.468

33. 5.5)21.659   3.938

34. 63)46.2   .733̄

35. 4.26).7638   .1792 = .179

36. 70)299,600   4,280

37. 3,716 ÷ 100 = __37.160__

38. 2,500)1,775,000   710

39. 26,544 ÷ 1,000 = __26.544__

40. 4,270)350,140   82

Find each of the following sums and check by estimating to the nearest ten thousand.

41.	59,609	60,000	42.	10,003	10,000	43.	33,000	30,000
	9,757	10,000		26,775	30,000		48,764	50,000
	71,496	70,000		84,456	80,000		122,117	120,000
	10,013	10,000		67,037	70,000		32,105	30,000
	11,251	10,000		49,074	50,000		8,633	10,000
	83,490	80,000		8,490	10,000		70,186	70,000
		240,000 (est.)			250,000 (est.)			310,000 (est.)
	245,616 (ans.)			245,835 (ans.)			314,805 (ans.)	

Round each of the following to the nearest hundredth.

44. 228.455 __228.46__

45. 10.86448 __10.86__

46. 57.54053 __57.54__

47. .0182 __.02__

Round each of the following to the nearest thousandth.

48. 956.0049 __956.005__

49. 14.3251 __14.325__

50. 77.17749 __77.177__

continued

44 Chapter 1

Comprehensive Problems *continued*

Solve each of the following problems.

51. If the total production cost for 219 toasters is $3,870.25, what is the production cost per unit?

$17.67 cost per unit

```
        17.672
219)3,870.250
    219
    1680
    1533
    1472
    1314
    1585
    1533
     520
     438
      82
```

52. A lighting store managed by Brian Yip received the following bill from a supplier. Calculate the amount owed.

24 pole lamps @ $72.49 each = $1,739.76
30 swag lamps @ $116.73 each = 3,501.90
19 desk lamps @ $39.98 each = 759.62
                              $6,001.28

$6,001.28 amount owed

53. Harry Bendix has sold 30 shares of stock in Fantus, Inc. When he sold, the stock was valued at $25 per share. The fee his broker charged was $75. Harry wants to divide the amount he received equally among his three sons. How much will each son be given?

$25 Value per share
× 30 Shares
750 Total value
− 75 Broker's fee
$675 To be divided equally

```
    $225
3)675
   6
   7
   6
  15
  15
```

$225 for each son

54. Cosmode, Inc., a dress manufacturer, calculates that 3 yards of orlon are required for a particular style of party dress. The fabric wholesales for $3 per yard. What will be the cost of fabric for 932 dresses?

932 Dresses
× 3 Yards
2,796 Total yards

2,796
× $ 3 Price per yard
8,388 Total cost

$8,388 total cost

55. As manager of Dilworth's Bookstore, you receive the following bill:

82 copies of *The Wind in the Willows* at $3 each, = $246
45 copies of *Alice in Wonderland* at $2 each, = $ 90
64 copies of *Dueling Through the Ages* at $2 each, = $128
38 copies of *Tarzan in Cincinnati* at $4 each. = $152

What is the total amount of the bill?

$616

$616 total amount of bill

56. Cecilia Webster needed 12.6 yards of material for curtains. If the price of the cotton she wanted was $2.98 per .5 yard, how much money would she spend?

$2.98 Per 1/2 yard
× 2
$5.96 Per yard

$5.96 Per yard
× 12.6 Yards purchased
3576
1192
596
75.096

$75.10 total cost

continued

Comprehensive Problems *continued*

57. You have $1,242.48 to spend for wood. If each piece of finished lumber you want costs $7.44, how many pieces can you buy?

```
         167.
7.44)1,242.48
      744
      4984
      4464
       5208
       5208
```

167 pieces of lumber

58. Bill Hatlow manages an agricultural combine. For irrigation purposes, he ordered 296.478 gallons of water to be placed in tanks that held 81.9 gallons each. How many tanks were filled? Give your answer to the nearest tenth of a tank.

```
          3.62
81.9)296.478
     2457
     5137
     4914
      2238
      1638
       600
```

3.6 tanks filled

59. Kevin Artures worked 49 hours a week and was paid at the rate of $5.7275 an hour. What were Kevin's gross earnings per week to the nearest cent?

```
$5.7275
    49
515475
229100
$280.6475
```

$280.65

60. The Besinford Arms Hotel has 579 rooms. Of these, 206 are singles and the rest are doubles. One hundred twenty-one of the single rooms rent for $38 per night; the remainder rent for $40. Two hundred thirty-six of the double rooms rent for $48 per night; the remainder rent for $52. How much profit will the hotel make on a night when it rents all its rooms, if its daily expenses are $18,347?

579 rooms
- 206 singles
  - 121 rooms @ $38 per night
  - 85 rooms @ $40 per night
- 373 doubles
  - 236 rooms @ $48 per night
  - 137 rooms @ $52 per night

All rooms rented $26,450
Less expenses 18,347
Net profit $ 8,103

```
121 × $38 = $ 4,598
 85 × $40 =   3,400
236 × $48 =  11,328
137 × $52 =   7,124
            $26,450  All rooms rented
```

$8,103 net profit

61. Harry Stans is payroll clerk at Bidwell Industries. For one year, his monthly payrolls are the following:

January	$9,836	May	$ 7,640	September	$9,254
February	8,325	June	8,982	October	9,999
March	9,425	July	10,056	November	9,546
April	8,213	August	9,984	December	8,756

continued

Comprehensive Problems *continued*

a) Calculate the annual payroll.   b) Find the mean.

The sum of monthly payroll equals annual payroll.

$110,016
annual payroll

$9,168 mean average

```
                9,168
            12)110,016
   Number   ↑ 108
   of months   20
                12
                81
                72
                96
                96
```

62. Taiwan Imports imported 182.986 feet of rope the first week, 264.23 feet the second week, 302.715 feet the third week, and 191.62 feet the fourth week. A mean of how many feet of rope were imported per week? Round your answer to the nearest hundredth.

```
                        235.387
182.986              4)941.551
264.23                 ↑ 8
302.715         Weeks 14
191.62                  12
941.551 Total feet of rope  21
                        20
                         1 5
                         1 2
                          35
                          32
                          31
                          28
                           3
```

235.39 mean average of feet of rope imported

Case 1

Marjorie Lord sold leather goods and worked on a salary plus commission basis. For sales up to and including $450 she received 1.25¢ per $1 sold. For sales between $451 and including $600, she received 2.5¢ per $1 sold, and for sales over $600, she received 3.5¢ per $1 sold. For the month of September she sold $829.39 worth of goods. For her salary, she received $4.21 for regular hours and time-and-a-half for overtime. (Overtime in this case is considered any time over 40 hours a week.) Her time schedule for each week in September was as follows:

1st week	41.6 hours
2nd week	45.89 hours
3rd week	43.5 hours
4th week	40.27 hours

What is her gross salary plus commission for the month of September?

Case 2

Since you are the office manager of Dabbington Parts Company, you have been assigned the task of submitting a supplies budget for the month of July. These are the figures you are working with:

Item	Unit Price	Inventory Level to be Maintained	Amount on Hand	Amount to Order	Total Price
Electronic calculator tape	$2	20	11	_____	_____
Box of ballpoint pens	$4	10	6	_____	_____
Typewriter ribbons	$2	35	18	_____	_____
Telephone pads	$1	50	29	_____	_____
Boxes of paper clips	$1	30	19	_____	_____
				Total	_____

Complete the form. If you are told to cut your budget, in what areas would you begin cutting? Why? What logic could you use with your employer, to convince her to drop the cut for your particular budget?

Key Terms

Addends	Divisor	Multiplier
Addition	Dollar	Product
Average	Factors	Quotient
Cent	Level of accuracy	Remainder
Decimal	Mean	Rounding off
Decimal point	Median	Subtraction
Decimal system	Minuend	Subtrahend
Difference	Mode	Sum
Dividend	Multiplicand	Total
Division	Multiplication	Whole numbers

Key Concepts

- A decimal describes part of a whole or a unit in terms of tenths, hundredths, thousandths, and so on.
- Addition: Addends are the numbers to be added. Align the columns vertically with decimal point under decimal point. The sum is the answer in an addition problem. Addition can be checked by reverse-order check.
- Subtraction: The minuend is the number subtracted from. The subtrahend is the number subtracted. The difference, or remainder, is the answer in subtraction. Subtraction can be checked by adding the subtrahend and the remainder.
- Multiplication: The multiplicand is the number multiplied. The multiplier is the number by which you multiply. In decimals, the product must contain the total number of decimal places that appear in the multiplier and the multiplicand. The product is the answer. Multiplication can be checked by dividing the product by the multiplier or the multiplicand or by interchanging the multiplicand and multiplier and multiplying again.
- Multiplication by Powers of Ten: Move the decimal point to the right in the multiplicand the same number of places as there are zeros in the power of ten in the multiplier.
- Division: The dividend is the number divided. The divisor is the number by which the dividend is divided. The quotient is the answer. When the division is not exact, and the quotient does not come out even, the number left is the remainder.
- Division of Decimals: Proceed as with whole numbers. The decimal point in the quotient is positioned above the decimal point in the dividend. If there is a decimal point in the divisor, move it to the right, converting the divisor into a whole number. Move the decimal point in the dividend to the right a corresponding number of places. To check a division problem, multiply the quotient by the divisor and add on the remainder.
- Rounding and Estimating: If the number to the right of the place being rounded is 5 or larger, the number being rounded is raised by 1. If the number to the right of the place being rounded is 4 or lower, the number being rounded remains the same. A decimal number is rounded to a higher digit, and the remainder dropped, when the first number to the right of it is 5 or more. Otherwise, the number to be rounded remains the same, and the remainder is dropped.
- Average: To find the mean average of a series of figures, divide the sum of the figures by the number of figures in the series. Other expressions of average are the median and the mode.

Addition

```
  1  Addend
+ 1  Addend
  2  Sum, or total
```

Subtraction

```
  2  Minuend
- 1  Subtrahend
  1  Difference, or
     remainder
```

Multiplication

```
  3  Multiplicand
× 2  Multiplier
  6  Product
```

Division

```
             2  Quotient
Divisor   3)6   Dividend
```

2
Fractions

Business Takes a Positive Approach

LIZ CLAIBORNE, INC.

Liz Claiborne, Inc., is one of the youngest companies ever to move into the Fortune 500 list of the largest industrial corporations in the United States. In only 11 years time and with an initial investment of under $300,000, Liz Claiborne transformed her firm into a business with annual revenues of over $750 million. She takes pride in the fact that her fashions are not designed for the runway model alone. At a time when the tailored suit was practically the uniform of the executive woman, Claiborne daringly premiered an apparel line featuring comfortable, colorful, and full-cut designs. Thus, she offered American women a welcome and refreshing reprieve from the norm. Liz Claiborne does not simply sit back and reap the rewards of success, however. Instead, she has become even more competitive, using a complex computer system to keep constantly informed as to what styles, colors, and sizes the consumer is buying. Her company is now expanding into the cosmetic field and opening its own retail stores, moving into position to command a greater fraction of the fashion market in the years ahead.

Learning Objectives

After reading and studying this chapter and working the problems, you will be able to:

- Write, read, and work with fractions and mixed numbers.
- Convert improper fractions to whole or mixed numbers.
- Convert whole or mixed numbers to improper fractions.
- Understand the law of fractions.
- Raise fractions to higher terms and reduce them to lower terms.
- Add and subtract fractions and mixed numbers, finding the lowest common denominator and borrowing if necessary.
- Multiply and divide fractions and mixed numbers, canceling if appropriate.
- Convert decimals to fractions, fractions to decimals, and complex decimals to pure decimals or fractions.
- Use common decimal–fraction equivalents.

Fractions, like decimals, are a way of talking about part of a whole number. Think of some object—a one-foot ruler, an apple, a share of stock, a plot of land, the gross monthly income of a corporation, the population of the earth, or anything else—as a complete whole, a unit. You can separate this unit into equal parts, as many equal parts as you want. The current value of a share of stock, for example, is quoted in points, representing dollars, and fractions of points, representing parts of dollars.

Look at a ruler. You can see it as 1 twelve-inch whole, as 2 six-inch pieces or halves, as 4 three-inch pieces or quarters, as 12 one-inch pieces or twelfths, or as a collection of parts of any other size. No matter what size pieces you visualize, all of them together equal the full length of the original ruler. The whole is equal to the sum of its parts. The parts are fractions.

Similarly, a group of individual things—a dozen rulers, for example—can be considered as a unit. Visualize 12 presidents of large corporations. Six of them represent $\frac{6}{12}$. This equals one half of the original—the group of 12. Three are $\frac{3}{12}$, which equals one fourth, a quarter of the whole group. Four are one third; and so on.

2.1 The Basics of Fractions

Writing Fractions

Fractions are written as two numerals, called **terms,** with a horizontal or diagonal line between them: 1/2, $\frac{6}{12}$, $\frac{264}{835}$, and 24/5 are all fractions.

The **denominator** is the number below or to the right of the line. It gives the total number of equal parts into which you have divided a whole—any whole.

The **numerator** is the number above or to the left of the line. It indicates the number of parts you are describing in this particular fraction.

The fraction $\frac{1}{2}$ tells you by its denominator that the unit—the one-foot ruler or the 12 corporation presidents—has been separated into 2 equal parts. It tells you by its numerator that you are working with 1 of these 2 parts—a 6-inch piece of ruler or 6 presidents. The fraction $\frac{264}{835}$ refers to 264 pieces of something that is being regarded as having 835 equal pieces.

The line between the terms of the fraction indicates division. A fraction is a division calculation waiting to happen. Thus, $\frac{1}{2}$ is the same thing as $1 \div 2$ or $2\overline{)1}$.

Reading Fractions

A fraction may be read three ways:

1. *In words*: 6/7 = six sevenths or six of seven parts;
2. *As a division problem*: 6/7 = six divided by seven or $6 \div 7$ or $7\overline{)6}$;
3. *Visually*: by a figure representing $\frac{6}{7}$ = six over seven.

Defining Fractions

There are three types of fractions.

1. A **proper fraction** has a numerator that is smaller than its denominator. It is less than the whole or less than 1. For example, $\frac{1}{2}$, $\frac{3}{8}$, $\frac{397}{398}$, and $\frac{596}{1003}$ are all proper fractions.
2. An **improper fraction** has a numerator that is equal to or larger than its denominator. It is equal to or greater than the whole or 1. For example, $\frac{2}{2}$, $\frac{19}{8}$, $\frac{398}{397}$, and $\frac{2596}{1003}$ are all improper fractions.
3. A **mixed number** combines units or whole numbers and partial units or fractions. For example, $1\frac{1}{2}$, $2\frac{3}{8}$, $398\frac{1}{397}$, and $11\frac{596}{1003}$ are all mixed numbers.

Converting Improper Fractions Into Whole or Mixed Numbers

Should your solution to a problem be an improper fraction, good business procedures call for converting it to a whole or mixed number when you present the final answer. You are not changing its meaning or value by doing this. You are simply expressing it in another way in order to communicate it to other members of the business community.

To carry out the conversion, follow these steps:

Step 1 Divide the numerator—in this case, the larger number—by the denominator.

Step 2 Place the remainder, if there is one, over the original denominator. This shows the number of parts remaining in addition to the whole.

Example 1 Marilee Ladislaw, comptroller of Rite-A-Lot Business Forms, Inc., performs a calculation that shows a result of $\frac{240}{8}$. How will she express this as a whole number?

Express $\frac{240}{8}$ as a whole number.

Step 1 Divide the numerator by the denominator.

$$\begin{array}{r} 30 \\ 8\overline{)240} \\ \underline{24} \\ 0 \end{array}$$

Fractions 53

Step 2   In this example, the calculation comes out even. There is no remainder.

Answer   The final answer is presented as 30.

Example 2   Later the same day, Marilee finds a result of $\frac{24}{7}$ for another calculation. How will she express it as a mixed number?

Express $\frac{24}{7}$ as a mixed number.

Step 1   Divide the numerator by the denominator.

$$\begin{array}{r} 3 \\ 7\overline{)24} \\ \underline{21} \\ 3 \end{array}$$

Step 2   Make a fraction by placing the remainder over the original denominator, now the divisor.

$$\frac{3}{7}$$

Answer   The final answer is presented as $3\frac{3}{7}$.

NOTE: This answer shows that the improper fraction, $\frac{24}{7}$, contains 3 whole units and an additional 3 parts. Each of these parts is equal to $\frac{1}{7}$ of the whole unit described.

Self-Check

Identify each of these fractions by type:

1. $\frac{4}{7}$ _____

2. $\frac{7}{4}$ _____

3. $1\frac{3}{4}$ _____

ANSWERS   1. Proper   2. Improper   3. Mixed number

Understanding the Law of Fractions

The *law of fractions* states that if both the numerator and the denominator of a fraction are multiplied or divided by the same number, the relative value of the fraction stays the same. Only its appearance is changed.

In completing certain business calculations, you will find yourself reducing or raising the terms of a fraction as you go along. So long as you remember to perform the same operation on both parts of the fraction, you will not run into trouble.

The tool that allows the law of fractions to work is the number 1. As you probably know, multiplying a number by 1 changes nothing: $1 \times 1 = 1$ and $2 \times 1 = 2$. The same is true in division: $2 \div 1 = 2$.

The number 1 can be separated into any number of equal parts. The total of these parts is represented by 1. Thus, $1 = \frac{1}{1}, \frac{2}{2}, \frac{3}{3}, \ldots \frac{999}{999}$, or whatever you decide. Each of them is the number 1 expressed in a different way. For instance, $\frac{1}{2} \times \frac{16}{16} = \frac{16}{32}$. The relative meaning of these fractions is the same; only their appearance is different. We have multiplied $\frac{1}{2}$ by 1, but it is 1 expressed as 16ths.

The law of fractions can be applied in both raising and lowering fractions.

Raising a Fraction or Finding Equivalent Fractions

Example 3   Hannah Sternberg, a cabinetmaker for Custom Kitchens, Inc., is cutting strips of decorative molding. One section is $\frac{3}{4}$ inch long, but because she wants an exact fit, Hannah is working in 32nds of an inch. How many 32nds will she find in the $\frac{3}{4}$-inch section?

$$\frac{3}{4} = \frac{?}{32}$$

Step 1   Determine how many 4ths there are in 32 by dividing. $4\overline{)32} = 8$

Step 2   Multiply this quotient by the number of 4ths in the original fraction. $3 \times 8 = 24$

Answer $\frac{3}{4}$ inch = $\frac{24}{32}$ inch

Self-Check

Raise each of these fractions as indicated.

1. $\frac{3}{8} = \frac{?}{40}$

2. $\frac{6}{7} = \frac{?}{77}$

3. $\frac{20}{27} = \frac{?}{216}$

ANSWERS   1. $\frac{15}{40}$ 2. $\frac{66}{77}$ 3. $\frac{160}{216}$

Reducing a Fraction

Just as you can raise a fraction by multiplying, you can reduce it by doing the opposite. Divide both the numerator and the denominator by the same number. Normally, in business, you reduce a fraction to its lowest terms, especially when presenting the final answer.

     To reduce to lowest terms, divide the terms of the fraction by numbers that go into each term evenly until no number other than 1 can be divided into them. Usually this can be done by inspection.

Example 4   Reduce $\frac{6}{18}$ to its lowest terms using inspection.

Step 1   Decide on a number that can be divided evenly into both 6 and 18.   6 is this number.

Step 2   Divide both terms by 6. $\frac{6 \div 6}{18 \div 6}$

Answer $\frac{6}{18} = \frac{1}{3}$

     Sometimes you may have to put the fraction through several stages of reduction before it is in its lowest terms. You might look on this as cutting the fraction down to size.

Example 5 Reduce $\frac{168}{252}$ to lowest terms using inspection.

Step 1 Decide on a number that can be divided evenly into both terms.
3 is this number.

Step 2 Divide both terms by 3.
$\frac{168 \div 3}{252 \div 3} = \frac{56}{84}$

Step 3 The terms are still divisible. Therefore, choose another divisor.
7

Step 4 Divide both terms by 7.
$\frac{56 \div 7}{84 \div 7} = \frac{8}{12}$

Step 5 The terms are still divisible. Choose another divisor.
4

Step 6 Divide both terms by 4.
$\frac{8 \div 4}{12 \div 4} = \frac{2}{3}$

Answer $\frac{168}{252} = \frac{2}{3}$

NOTE: You can also reduce $\frac{168}{252}$ by inspection using other sequences.

$$\frac{168}{252} \overset{(2)}{=} \frac{84}{126} \overset{(7)}{=} \frac{12}{18} \overset{(3)}{=} \frac{4}{6} \overset{(2)}{=} \frac{2}{3} \quad \text{or} \quad \frac{168}{252} \overset{(14)}{=} \frac{12}{18} \overset{(6)}{=} \frac{2}{3} \quad \text{or} \quad \frac{168}{252} \overset{(84)}{=} \frac{2}{3}$$

All are correct.

Rules of Divisibility

To help you in reducing fractions, here are some rules about dividing numbers. Keep them in mind when dealing with business transactions, and your task will be easier.

Any number can be divided by:	If:
2	The final digit is divisible by 2.
3	The sum of all digits is divisible by 3.
4	The final two digits are divisible by 4.
5	The final digit is either 0 or 5.
6	The number is even, and the sum of all digits is divisible by 3.
8	The final three digits are divisible by 8.
9	The sum of all digits is divisible by 9.
10	The final digit is 0.

Self-Check

Reduce each of these fractions to its lowest terms using inspection.

1. $\frac{8}{16}$

2. $\frac{45}{70}$

3. $\frac{261}{423}$

ANSWERS 1. (8) $\frac{1}{2}$ 2. (5) $\frac{9}{14}$ 3. (9) $\frac{29}{47}$

WHAT'S IN A ZERO?

The system or art of enumeration developed slowly over many centuries. We have evidence that the zero was used by the Babylonians as early as 300 B.C. Many other cultures did not make use of it until much later. The Chinese, for example, used a vertical system of numbering. This served their purposes even though it did not include the zero.

NAME _____ DATE _____ SECTION _____

Assignment 2.1

Fractions

Express each of the following fractions in writing.

	In Words	*As a Division Problem*
1. $\frac{4}{5}$ =	Four fifths	4 ÷ 5 or 5)4
2. $\frac{23}{25}$ =	Twenty-three twenty-fifths	23 ÷ 25 or 25)23
3. $\frac{75}{24}$ =	Seventy-five twenty-fourths	75 ÷ 24 or 24)75
4. $\frac{46}{13}$ =	Forty-six thirteenths	46 ÷ 13 or 13)46

Convert each of the following improper fractions into whole or mixed numbers.

5. $\frac{38}{33}$ $1\frac{5}{33}$
6. $\frac{123}{25}$ $4\frac{23}{25}$
7. $\frac{4}{1}$ 4
8. $\frac{18}{9}$ 2
9. $\frac{13}{7}$ $1\frac{6}{7}$
10. $\frac{54}{9}$ 6
11. $\frac{7}{7}$ 1

Raise each of the following fractions as indicated.

12. $\frac{3}{4} = \frac{27}{36}$ 4)$\overline{36}^{\,9}$ 3 × 9 = 27
13. $\frac{5}{8} = \frac{50}{80}$ 8)$\overline{80}^{\,10}$ 5 × 10 = 50
14. $\frac{1}{9} = \frac{5}{45}$ 9)$\overline{45}^{\,5}$ 1 × 5 = 5
15. $\frac{4}{11} = \frac{48}{132}$ 11)$\overline{132}^{\,12}$ 4 × 12 = 48
16. $\frac{3}{8} = \frac{33}{88}$ 8)$\overline{88}^{\,11}$ 3 × 11 = 33
17. $\frac{2}{7} = \frac{18}{63}$ 7)$\overline{63}^{\,9}$ 2 × 9 = 18
18. $\frac{1}{17} = \frac{5}{85}$ 17)$\overline{85}^{\,5}$ 1 × 5 = 5
19. $\frac{14}{15} = \frac{28}{30}$ 15)$\overline{30}^{\,2}$ 14 × 2 = 28

continued

Assignment 2.1 *continued*

20. $\dfrac{2}{11} = \dfrac{12}{66}$ $11\overline{)66}^{6}$ $2 \times 6 = 12$

21. $\dfrac{11}{18} = \dfrac{55}{90}$ $18\overline{)90}^{5}$ $11 \times 5 = 55$

Reduce each of the following fractions to its lowest terms by inspection.

22. $\dfrac{4}{8}$ $\dfrac{1}{2}$

23. $\dfrac{5}{15}$ $\dfrac{1}{3}$

24. $\dfrac{14}{21}$ $\dfrac{2}{3}$

25. $\dfrac{3}{12}$ $\dfrac{1}{4}$

26. $\dfrac{11}{77}$ $\dfrac{1}{7}$

27. $\dfrac{23}{46}$ $\dfrac{1}{2}$

28. $\dfrac{31}{93}$ $\dfrac{1}{3}$

29. $\dfrac{81}{189}$ $\dfrac{3}{7}$ (Divide each term by 27.)

30. $\dfrac{125}{175}$ $\dfrac{5}{7}$ (Divide each term by 25.)

31. $\dfrac{945}{963}$ $\dfrac{105}{107}$ (Divide each term by 9.)

32. $\dfrac{255}{340}$ $\dfrac{3}{4}$ (Divide each term by 85.)

33. $\dfrac{504}{658}$ $\dfrac{36}{47}$ (Divide each term by 14.)

2.2 Addition and Subtraction of Fractions

Adding Fractions

The process of adding fractions is not complicated. You merely find the sum of the numerators and place it over the common denominator, creating your answer.

Example 1 You are a painting contractor mixing $\frac{1}{5}$ gallon of one tint with $\frac{3}{5}$ gallon of another. What amount of paint will you have when you are finished?

Find the sum of $\frac{1}{5}$ and $\frac{3}{5}$.

Step 1 Add the numerators. $\hfill 1 + 3 = 4$

Step 2 Use the sum as the numerator. The common denominator is the denominator. $\hfill \frac{1}{5} + \frac{3}{5} = \frac{4}{5}$

Answer The amount of paint is $\frac{4}{5}$ gallon.

CAUTION: Find only the sum of the numerators, not the sum of the denominators. When you add fractions, you are determining how many parts there are of a particular size—in this case, fifths.

More often than not in business calculations, the denominators of the fractions you are adding or subtracting are different from one another. When this is the case, you cannot proceed without making some adjustments, namely, converting the fractions into like units. This is called finding the lowest common denominator.

Finding the Lowest, or Least, Common Denominator

To simplify calculation, determine the lowest whole number into which you can divide evenly all the denominators of the fractions to be added. This number is called the **lowest**, or **least, common denominator**. It is most commonly found by inspection.

By looking at the denominators of the fractions to be added, you may be able to determine the number into which all of them will divide evenly.

Example 2 Find the lowest common denominator for $\frac{1}{2}$, $\frac{1}{3}$, and $\frac{1}{4}$.

Step 1 Look at the denominators. $\hfill \frac{}{2}, \frac{}{3}, \frac{}{4}$

Step 2 Determine the number into which they will all divide evenly.
$\hfill 12 \div 2 = 6$
$\hfill 12 \div 3 = 4$
Answer The lowest common denominator $= \frac{}{12}$. $\hfill 12 \div 4 = 3$

Sometimes all the denominators divide evenly into the largest of the denominators. This, then, is the lowest common denominator.

Example 3 Find the lowest common denominator for $\frac{1}{4}$, $\frac{1}{8}$, and $\frac{1}{16}$. $\hfill \frac{}{4}, \frac{}{8}, \frac{}{16}$

Step 1 Look at the denominators.

Step 2 Consider whether the smaller denominators will divide evenly into the larger. They will.

Answer The lowest common denominator: $\frac{}{16}$. $\hfill 16 \div 4 = 4$
$\hfill 16 \div 8 = 2$

Fractions

In the event that you cannot be certain of the lowest common denominator by using inspection, multiply all denominators together to find a common denominator and reduce to lowest terms when you complete the problem.

Self-Check

Find the lowest common denominator.

1. $\dfrac{1}{3}, \dfrac{1}{6}, \dfrac{1}{4}$ _____

2. $\dfrac{5}{8}, \dfrac{1}{4}, \dfrac{11}{12}$ _____

3. $\dfrac{1}{6}, \dfrac{1}{9}, \dfrac{1}{12}, \dfrac{1}{16}$ _____

ANSWERS   **1.** 12   **2.** 24   **3.** 144

NUMERAL SIGNIFICANCE

In ancient times, four was considered an important number. It was thought of as representing the directions of the compass—east, west, north, and south—the way humans viewed the world about them. It also had ritual significance because of the fact that four is the smallest number of objects with which a square can be formed. To primitive peoples, the center of the square symbolized the center of the cosmos.

Adding Fractions with Unlike Denominators

Example 4   In taking inventory of the stock of his three taco stands, Hank Sarkian finds that $\frac{1}{2}$ the stock has been sold from stand one, $\frac{1}{4}$ from stand two, and $\frac{1}{8}$ from stand three. What fraction of the total stock has been sold?

Find the sum of $\frac{1}{2} + \frac{1}{4} + \frac{1}{8}$.

Step 1	Determine the lowest common denominator. Here, the denominators divide evenly into the largest denominator.	8
Step 2	Raise all fractions to eighths.	$\dfrac{1}{2} = \dfrac{4}{8}, \ \dfrac{1}{4} = \dfrac{2}{8}, \ \dfrac{1}{8} = \dfrac{1}{8}$
Step 3	Add the numerators.	$4 + 2 + 1 = 7$
Step 4	Place the sum of the numerators over the lowest common denominator.	$\dfrac{7}{8}$

Answer The common denominator is 8. The fraction of total stock sold is $\frac{7}{8}$.

NOTE: Adding fractional parts often results in an improper fraction. Remember that you convert this to a mixed number in your final answer, reducing the fraction to its lowest terms.

Self-Check

Find the sum of each of these groups of fractions.

1. $\frac{1}{7}$
    $\frac{3}{7}$
    $+ \frac{2}{7}$
    _____

2. $\frac{3}{5}$
    $\frac{4}{6}$
    $+ \frac{8}{15}$
    _____

ANSWERS 1. $\frac{6}{7}$ 2. $1\frac{4}{5}$

Adding Mixed Numbers

To add mixed numbers, combine the techniques that you have already reviewed.

Step 1 Add fractions to fractions, first determining the lowest common denominator, if necessary.

Step 2 If the sum of the fractions is an improper fraction, convert it to a mixed number.

Step 3 Add the sum of the fractions to the sum of the whole numbers.

Example 5 Marion Temkin, a plumbing contractor, needs two lengths of pipe, one $3\frac{5}{8}$ feet long and the other $4\frac{7}{16}$ feet long. How many feet of pipe does Marion need altogether?

Find the sum of $3\frac{5}{8} + 4\frac{7}{16}$.

Step 1 Find the lowest common denominator and add only the fractions.

$$\frac{5}{8} = \frac{10}{16}$$
$$+ \frac{7}{16} = + \frac{7}{16}$$
$$\frac{17}{16}$$

Fractions 63

Step 2 Convert the improper fraction to a mixed number.

$$\frac{17}{16} = 1\frac{1}{16}$$

Step 3 Add the sum of the fractions to the sum of the whole numbers.

Answer Marion needs $8\frac{1}{16}$ feet of pipe.

NOTE: It is easy to add the fractions and then forget to add the whole numbers and show them in the total. Be careful not to do this.

$$\begin{array}{r} 3\frac{3}{4} \\ + 1\frac{1}{16} \\ \hline 8\frac{1}{16} \end{array}$$

Self-Check

Find each of the following sums, converting answers to mixed numbers and reducing fractions to lowest terms.

1.
$$\begin{array}{r} 2\frac{5}{12} \\ 6\frac{3}{8} \\ + 10\frac{2}{3} \\ \hline \end{array}$$

2.
$$\begin{array}{r} 8\frac{9}{10} \\ 4\frac{5}{6} \\ + 3\frac{2}{3} \\ \hline \end{array}$$

ANSWERS
1. $2\frac{10}{24}$
   $6\frac{9}{24}$
   $10\frac{16}{24}$
   $18\frac{35}{24} = 18 + 1\frac{11}{24} = 19\frac{11}{24}$

2. $8\frac{27}{30}$
   $4\frac{25}{30}$
   $3\frac{20}{30}$
   $15\frac{72}{30} = 15 + 2\frac{12}{30} = 17\frac{6}{15}$

Subtracting Fractions

To prepare fractions for subtraction in business math, follow the same procedure that you used for addition.

Step 1 Find the lowest common denominator and convert both fractions, giving them the same denominator.

Step 2 Subtract the numerator of the bottom fraction (subtrahend) from the numerator of the top fraction (minuend), making a new fraction with the difference as numerator and the common denominator as denominator.

Step 3 Reduce this new fraction to its lowest terms.

Example 6 You are the attendance officer at Crestwood High School. This morning, $\frac{2}{3}$ of the student body was present. By noon, another $\frac{1}{6}$ of the student body had gone home with the flu. What fraction of the student body was left?

Subtract: $\frac{2}{3} - \frac{1}{6}$.

Step 1   Find the lowest common denominator and convert both fractions.

$$\frac{2}{3} = \frac{4}{6}$$

$$\frac{1}{6} = \frac{1}{6}$$

Step 2   Subtract the numerator of the subtrahend from the numerator of the minuend to make a new fraction showing the difference.

$$\frac{4}{6}$$
$$-\frac{1}{6}$$
$$\frac{3}{6}$$

Step 3   Reduce the difference to lowest terms.

$$\frac{3}{6} = \frac{1}{2}$$

Answer   The fraction of the student body remaining is $\frac{1}{2}$.

In business calculations, the same procedures apply when you subtract mixed numbers or improper fractions.

Example 7   Etta Petry, a research chemist for Longton Lawn Foods, Inc., is experimenting with fertilizers. The present mixture contains $6\frac{5}{6}$ parts of nitrogen. Etta removes $3\frac{1}{3}$ parts of nitrogen. How many parts are left?

Subtract: $6\frac{5}{6} - 3\frac{1}{3}$.

Step 1   Find the lowest common denominator and convert both fractions.

$$\frac{5}{6} = \frac{5}{6}$$

$$\frac{1}{3} = \frac{2}{6}$$

Step 2   Subtract the numerator of the subtrahend from the numerator of the minuend to make a new fraction.

$$\frac{5}{6}$$
$$-\frac{2}{6}$$
$$\frac{3}{6}$$

Step 3   Reduce the fraction to lowest terms.

$$\frac{3}{6} = \frac{1}{2}$$

Step 4   Subtract the whole numbers from one another.

$$6 - 3 = 3$$

Step 5   Add the fraction and the whole number.

$$3 + \frac{1}{2} = 3\frac{1}{2}$$

Answer   The amount of nitrogen remaining is $3\frac{1}{2}$ parts.

Borrowing

In subtracting mixed numbers, you will sometimes find that the numerator of the subtrahend (the number to be subtracted) is larger than the numerator of the minuend (the number subtracted from). In order to subtract, take one unit from the whole-number part of the mixed number, which is the minuend, convert it into a fraction, and add it to the fraction part. Proceed as in the examples above.

Example 8 Subtract: $6\frac{1}{7} - 5\frac{5}{14}$.

Step 1 Find the lowest common denominator and convert.

$$6\frac{1}{7} = 6\frac{2}{14}$$

$$5\frac{5}{14} = 5\frac{5}{14}$$

Step 2 Subtract the numerator of the subtrahend from the numerator of the minuend. This cannot be done as the numbers are expressed here.

$$\begin{array}{r}6\frac{2}{14}\\ -\,5\frac{5}{14}\\ \hline\end{array}$$

Step 3 Borrow 1 whole unit from the 6 in the minuend, and express it as a fraction. Remember that 1 can be expressed as any fraction whose numerator and denominator are the same number. (See Section 2.1.)

$$6\frac{2}{14} = 5\frac{14}{14} + \frac{2}{14} = 5\frac{16}{14}$$

Step 4 Subtract the numerators from one another.

$$\begin{array}{r}5\frac{16}{14}\\ -\,5\frac{5}{14}\\ \hline\frac{11}{14}\end{array}$$

Answer $\frac{11}{14}$

As in adding fractions, you may subtract fractions horizontally as well as vertically.

Self-Check

Subtract each of the following, reducing the difference to lowest terms.

1. $\begin{array}{r}\frac{5}{12}\\ -\,\frac{1}{16}\\ \hline\end{array}$

2. $\begin{array}{r}\frac{80}{50}\\ -\,\frac{3}{10}\\ \hline\end{array}$

3. $\begin{array}{r}35\frac{4}{7}\\ -\,6\frac{11}{12}\\ \hline\end{array}$

ANSWERS 1. $\frac{20}{48} - \frac{3}{48} = \frac{17}{48}$ 2. $\frac{80}{50} - \frac{15}{50} = \frac{65}{50} = \frac{13}{10} = 1\frac{3}{10}$ 3. $35\frac{48}{84} = 34\frac{132}{84}$
$6\frac{77}{84} = 6\frac{77}{84}$
$28\frac{55}{84}$

Assignment 2.2

Fractions

Determine the lowest common denominator and convert the fractions accordingly.

1. $\dfrac{3}{5}, \dfrac{7}{20}, \dfrac{3}{10}$ $\dfrac{12}{20}, \dfrac{7}{20}, \dfrac{6}{20}$

2. $\dfrac{7}{24}, \dfrac{3}{8}, \dfrac{5}{12}, \dfrac{1}{6}$ $\dfrac{7}{24}, \dfrac{9}{24}, \dfrac{10}{24}, \dfrac{4}{24}$

3. $\dfrac{2}{3}, \dfrac{5}{8}, \dfrac{1}{4}$ $\dfrac{16}{24}, \dfrac{15}{24}, \dfrac{6}{24}$

4. $\dfrac{2}{3}, \dfrac{5}{6}, \dfrac{8}{21}, \dfrac{5}{7}$ $\dfrac{28}{42}, \dfrac{35}{42}, \dfrac{16}{42}, \dfrac{30}{42}$

5. $\dfrac{5}{6}, \dfrac{2}{9}, \dfrac{1}{2}$ $\dfrac{15}{18}, \dfrac{4}{18}, \dfrac{9}{18}$

6. $\dfrac{1}{6}, \dfrac{2}{15}, \dfrac{3}{10}, \dfrac{2}{3}$ $\dfrac{5}{30}, \dfrac{4}{30}, \dfrac{9}{30}, \dfrac{20}{30}$

Find each of the following sums, converting answers to mixed numbers and reducing fractions to lowest terms.

7. $\dfrac{2}{3} + \dfrac{1}{3} =$ $\dfrac{3}{3} = 1$

8. $\dfrac{1}{17} + \dfrac{6}{17} + \dfrac{3}{17} =$ $\dfrac{10}{17}$

9. $\dfrac{1}{2} + \dfrac{2}{3} + \dfrac{3}{4} = \dfrac{6}{12} + \dfrac{8}{12} + \dfrac{9}{12} = \dfrac{23}{12} = 1\dfrac{11}{12}$

10. $4\dfrac{5}{8} + 6\dfrac{2}{5} + \dfrac{3}{4} =$ $\dfrac{25 + 16 + 30}{40} = \dfrac{71}{40} = 1\dfrac{31}{40}$ $4 + 6 + 1\dfrac{31}{40} = 11\dfrac{31}{40}$

11. $1\dfrac{2}{3} + \dfrac{21}{10} + 3\dfrac{4}{5} =$ $\dfrac{20 + 63 + 24}{30} = \dfrac{107}{30} = 3\dfrac{17}{30}$ $1 + 3 + 3\dfrac{17}{30} = 7\dfrac{17}{30}$

12. $23\dfrac{1}{2} + 18\dfrac{5}{16} + 9\dfrac{3}{4} =$ $\dfrac{8 + 5 + 12}{16} = \dfrac{25}{16} = 1\dfrac{9}{16}$ $23 + 18 + 9 + 1\dfrac{9}{16} = 51\dfrac{9}{16}$

13. Jim and Helen Colica worked as a team delivering boxes of wholesale flowers to local florist shops. Their delivery schedule for the four weeks of July was as follows:

     1st week $302\dfrac{7}{24}$ boxes $\dfrac{21 + 30 + 14 + 12}{72} = \dfrac{77}{72} = 1\dfrac{5}{72}$

     2nd week $295\dfrac{5}{12}$ boxes $302 + 295 + 306 + 300 + 1\dfrac{5}{72} = 1{,}204\dfrac{5}{72}$ boxes

     3rd week $306\dfrac{7}{36}$ boxes

     4th week $300\dfrac{1}{6}$ boxes

continued

Assignment 2.2 *continued*

How many boxes were they scheduled to deliver for the month of July?

$1{,}204\frac{5}{72}$ boxes delivered

14. Bret Harrington worked $47\frac{3}{20}$ hours the first week, $52\frac{1}{8}$ hours the second week, $43\frac{3}{5}$ hours the third week, and 45 hours the fourth week. How many hours did he work for the four weeks?

$$\frac{6+5+24}{40} = \frac{35}{40} = \frac{7}{8}$$

$$47 + 52 + 43 + 45 + \frac{7}{8} = 187\frac{7}{8} \text{ hours}$$

$187\frac{7}{8}$ hours worked

15. Sally Rollman owns investment property in three states. She has $170\frac{5}{6}$ acres in Ohio, $47\frac{1}{4}$ acres in Texas, and $89\frac{7}{12}$ acres in California. How much total acreage does she own?

$$\frac{10+3+7}{12} = \frac{20}{12} = 1\frac{8}{12} = 1\frac{2}{3}$$

$$170 + 47 + 89 + 1\frac{2}{3} = 307\frac{2}{3} \text{ acres}$$

$307\frac{2}{3}$ acres

Find each of the following differences, borrowing if necessary. Reduce the answer to lowest terms.

16. $\frac{5}{6} - \frac{1}{2} =$ $\frac{5}{6} - \frac{3}{6} = \frac{2}{6} = \frac{1}{3}$

17. $10\frac{5}{8} - 7\frac{1}{3} =$ $10\frac{15}{24} - 7\frac{8}{24} = 3\frac{7}{24}$

18. $\frac{19}{36} - \frac{2}{9} =$ $\frac{19}{36} - \frac{8}{36} = \frac{11}{36}$

19. $8\frac{5}{6} - \frac{3}{4} =$ $8\frac{10}{12} - \frac{9}{12} = 8\frac{1}{12}$

20. $\frac{8}{9} - \frac{1}{6} =$ $\frac{16}{18} - \frac{3}{18} = \frac{13}{18}$

21. $9\frac{1}{3} - \frac{4}{5} =$ $9\frac{5}{15} - \frac{12}{15} = 8\frac{20}{15} - \frac{12}{15} = 8\frac{8}{15}$

22. $\frac{7}{8} - \frac{2}{7} =$ $\frac{49}{56} - \frac{16}{56} = \frac{33}{56}$

23. $49\frac{7}{18} - 31\frac{11}{24} =$ $49\frac{28}{72} - 31\frac{33}{72} = 48\frac{100}{72} - 31\frac{33}{72} = 17\frac{67}{72}$

24. $\frac{1}{2} - \frac{5}{32} =$ $\frac{16}{32} - \frac{5}{32} = \frac{11}{32}$

25. $289 - 4\frac{7}{16} =$ $288\frac{16}{16} - 4\frac{7}{16} = 284\frac{9}{16}$

continued

Assignment 2.2 *continued*

26. At David's Restaurant, the special recipe for salad dressing calls for $1\frac{1}{2}$ cups of mayonnaise. If you have $\frac{2}{3}$ cup on hand, how much more mayonnaise do you need to make the recipe?

    $1\frac{3}{6} - \frac{4}{6} = \frac{9}{6} - \frac{4}{6} = \frac{5}{6}$ cup

    $\frac{5}{6}$ cup more mayonnaise needed
    _____

27. Rosalee Heacock, a manuscript typist, is proofreading $50\frac{1}{2}$ pages of her work. She has proofed $43\frac{5}{8}$ pages so far. How many pages of the manuscript remain?

    $50\frac{8}{16} - 43\frac{10}{16} = 49\frac{24}{16} - 43\frac{10}{16} = 6\frac{14}{16} = 6\frac{7}{8}$ pages

    $6\frac{7}{8}$ pages remain
    _____

28. In framing a window, a carpenter for Builders, Inc., finds that a board $42\frac{3}{8}$ inches in length is $2\frac{11}{16}$ inches too long. What is the length of board that she needs?

    $42\frac{6}{16} - 2\frac{11}{16} = 41\frac{22}{16} - 2\frac{11}{16} = 39\frac{11}{16}$ inches

    $39\frac{11}{16}$ inches
    _____

29. In Lincoln's Machine Shop, where Diana Gorman is the production supervisor, it took $36\frac{1}{3}$ hours to produce 3,872 metal bolts. After an overhaul of the bolt machine, it took $29\frac{4}{9}$ hours to produce the same number of bolts. How much time was saved?

    $36\frac{3}{9} - 29\frac{4}{9} = 35\frac{12}{9} - 29\frac{4}{9} = 6\frac{8}{9}$ hours

    $6\frac{8}{9}$ hours saved
    _____

30. A planer for Thompson Carpenters reduced the thickness of a board from $1\frac{7}{8}$ inches to $1\frac{11}{16}$ inches. By how much was the thickness of the board reduced?

    $1\frac{14}{16} - 1\frac{11}{16} = \frac{3}{16}$ inch

    $\frac{3}{16}$ inch reduction
    _____

2.3 Multiplication and Division of Fractions

To multiply fractions in business calculations, you need not find the lowest common denominator. That is done only in addition and subtraction. When multiplying, reduce all fractions to their lowest terms at the outset. This allows you to work with smaller numbers.

Step 1   Reduce the fractions to lowest terms.

Step 2   Multiply the numerator of the number being increased (multiplicand) by the numerator of the number of times it is increased (multiplier).

Step 3   Multiply the denominator of the multiplicand by the denominator of the multiplier.

Step 4   Place the product of the numerators over the product of the denominators, creating a new fraction.

Example 1   Find the product of $\frac{1}{8} \times \frac{3}{5}$.

Step 1   Multiply the numerators.

Step 2   Multiply the denominators. The fractions are already in lowest terms.

$$\frac{1}{8} \times \frac{3}{5} = \frac{3}{40}$$

Answer $\frac{3}{40}$

NOTE: Any number of fractions can be multiplied together.

Multiplying with Cancellation

Cancellation is a technique used in business to make multiplying fractions more manageable. As you know, you can divide both the numerator and the denominator by the same number without changing the value of the fraction. (See Section 2.1.) Thus, the cancellation procedure is related closely to reducing fractions to lowest terms. It differs only in that it is performed on the numerators and the denominators of a group of fractions rather than on the terms of one fraction.

Example 2   Find the product of $\frac{2}{3} \times \frac{1}{8}$ using cancellation.

Step 1   The number 2 divides evenly into the first numerator and into the second denominator.

$$\frac{\cancel{2}^{1}}{3} \times \frac{1}{\cancel{8}_{4}} =$$

Step 2   Multiply the canceled fractions, numerator by numerator and denominator by denominator.

$$\frac{1 \times 1}{3 \times 4} = \frac{1}{12}$$

Answer $\frac{1}{12}$

In some business situations, cancellation simplifies the calculation to the point where showing the actual multiplication is unnecessary. You can perform the calculation mentally.

Self-Check

Find each of the following products.

1. $\dfrac{4}{9} \times \dfrac{9}{5} =$ _____

2. $\dfrac{2}{5} \times \dfrac{5}{6} \times \dfrac{3}{8} =$ _____

3. $\dfrac{5}{12} \times \dfrac{4}{5} \times \dfrac{2}{3} \times \dfrac{10}{11} =$ _____

ANSWERS   1. $\dfrac{4}{5}$ 2. $\dfrac{\cancel{2}^{1}}{\cancel{5}_{1}} \times \dfrac{\cancel{5}^{1}}{\cancel{6}_{2}} \times \dfrac{\cancel{3}^{1}}{\cancel{8}_{4}} = \dfrac{1}{8}$ 3. $\dfrac{\cancel{5}^{1}}{12_{3}} \times \dfrac{\cancel{4}^{1}}{\cancel{5}_{1}} \times \dfrac{2}{3} \times \dfrac{10}{11} = \dfrac{20}{99}$

Multiplying Mixed Numbers

When performing business computations, you convert mixed numbers into improper fractions before proceeding.

Step 1 Multiply the whole-number part of the mixed number by the denominator of the fraction part to find the number of fractional units in it.

Step 2 Add the original fraction part.

Step 3 The result is an improper fraction with the original denominator.

Example 3 Convert $5\tfrac{3}{8}$ to an improper fraction.

Step 1 Multiply the whole number by the denominator of the fraction. $5 \times \dfrac{}{8} = \dfrac{40}{8}$ whole number $\times$ ─────────── denominator

Step 2 Add the original fraction. $\dfrac{40}{8} + \dfrac{3}{8}$ whole number $\times$ ─────────── denominator $+$ numerator

Step 3 The result is an improper fraction. $\dfrac{43}{8}$

Answer $\dfrac{43}{8}$

What you are actually doing here is determining how many fractional parts there are in the whole-number part of the mixed number that are of the same size as those expressed in the fraction part of the mixed number. You might think of the example above in this way: $\dfrac{5}{1} = \dfrac{?}{8}$.

Step 1 Determine the number of eighths in 5. (See Section 2.1.) $\dfrac{5}{1} = \dfrac{40}{8}$

Step 2 Add this to the fraction part of the mixed number. $\dfrac{3}{8} + \dfrac{40}{8} = \dfrac{43}{8}$

Answer $\dfrac{43}{8}$

Self-Check

Convert each of the following mixed numbers to an improper fraction.

1. $6\dfrac{5}{6} =$ _____

2. $12\dfrac{11}{12} =$ _____

3. $52\dfrac{5}{19} =$ _____

ANSWERS 1. $\dfrac{41}{6}$ 2. $\dfrac{155}{12}$ 3. $\dfrac{993}{19}$

Once you have converted the mixed numbers to improper fractions, multiply as before.

Example 4 Find the product of $7\dfrac{5}{6} \times 4\dfrac{4}{5}$.

Step 1 Convert the mixed numbers to improper fractions.

$$7\dfrac{5}{6} = \dfrac{47}{6}$$
$$4\dfrac{4}{5} = \dfrac{24}{5}$$

Step 2 Cancel if possible.

$$\dfrac{47}{\cancel{6}_{1}} \times \dfrac{\cancel{24}^{4}}{5} =$$

Step 3 Multiply numerator by numerator and denominator by denominator.

$$\dfrac{47 \times 4}{1 \times 5} = \dfrac{188}{5}$$

Step 4 Convert the improper fraction to a mixed number.

```
    37
5)188
    15
    38
    35
     3
```

Answer $37\dfrac{3}{5}$

Self-Check

Find each of the following products.

1. $7\dfrac{1}{2} \times 3\dfrac{2}{5} =$ _____

2. $1\dfrac{2}{9} \times 6\dfrac{1}{6} =$ _____

3. $5\dfrac{3}{4} \times 9\dfrac{4}{5} \times 3\dfrac{9}{10} =$ _____

ANSWERS 1. $\dfrac{\cancel{15}^{3}}{2} \times \dfrac{17}{\cancel{5}_{1}} = \dfrac{51}{2} = 25\dfrac{1}{2}$ 2. $\dfrac{11}{9} \times \dfrac{37}{6} = \dfrac{407}{54} = 7\dfrac{29}{54}$

3. $\dfrac{23}{4} \times \dfrac{49}{5} \times \dfrac{39}{10} = \dfrac{43,953}{200} = 219\dfrac{153}{200}$

Dividing Fractions

Division of fractions is merely multiplication with one important difference: the divisor is inverted. That is, when dividing, reverse the terms of the fraction that appears after the division sign.

Example 5 Find the quotient of $\tfrac{5}{8} \div \tfrac{3}{5}$.

Step 1 Invert the divisor. $\qquad\qquad \dfrac{3}{5}$ becomes $\dfrac{5}{3}$

Step 2 Change the sign and multiply. $\qquad\qquad \dfrac{5}{8} \times \dfrac{5}{3} = \dfrac{25}{24}$

Step 3 Convert the improper fraction to a mixed number if necessary, and reduce to lowest terms. $\qquad\qquad \dfrac{25}{24} = 1\dfrac{1}{24}$

Answer $1\dfrac{1}{24}$

If the divisor is a whole number, express it as a fraction with a denominator of 1. (See Section 2.1.)

Example 6 Bettina Columbro, office manager for Hardrock Insurance Company, estimates that work on the annual report is $\tfrac{1}{4}$ done. She wants to divide the remaining $\tfrac{3}{4}$ equally among six secretaries. how much of the work will she give to each of them?

Find the quotient of $\tfrac{3}{4} \div 6$.

Step 1 Invert the divisor. $\qquad\qquad 6 = \dfrac{6}{1}$ becomes $\dfrac{1}{6}$

Step 2 Change the sign and multiply. In this case, you can cancel. $\qquad\qquad \dfrac{\cancel{3}^{1}}{4} \times \dfrac{1}{\cancel{6}_{2}} = \dfrac{1}{8}$

Answer The amount of work to be given to each secretary is $\tfrac{1}{8}$ of the job.

As you did in multiplying fractions, convert mixed numbers to improper fractions before dividing.

Example 7 Find the quotient of $1\tfrac{1}{4} \div 6\tfrac{7}{8}$.

Step 1 Convert mixed numbers to improper fractions. $\qquad\qquad 1\dfrac{1}{4} = \dfrac{5}{4}$

$\qquad\qquad 6\dfrac{7}{8} = \dfrac{55}{8}$

Step 2 Invert the divisor. $\qquad\qquad \dfrac{55}{8}$ becomes $\dfrac{8}{55}$

Step 3   Change the sign and multiply. Cancel where possible.

$$\frac{\overset{1}{\cancel{3}}}{\underset{1}{\cancel{4}}} \times \frac{\overset{2}{\cancel{8}}}{\underset{11}{\cancel{55}}} = \frac{2}{11}$$

Answer $\frac{2}{11}$

Self-Check

Find each of the following quotients.

1. $\dfrac{6}{7} \div \dfrac{3}{5} =$ _____

2. $\dfrac{6}{7} \div 27 =$ _____

3. $6\dfrac{2}{5} \div 8\dfrac{1}{7} =$ _____

ANSWERS 1. $\dfrac{\overset{2}{\cancel{6}}}{7} \times \dfrac{5}{\underset{1}{\cancel{3}}} = \dfrac{10}{7} = 1\dfrac{3}{7}$ 2. $\dfrac{\overset{2}{\cancel{6}}}{7} \times \dfrac{1}{\underset{9}{\cancel{27}}} = \dfrac{2}{63}$ 3. $\dfrac{32}{5} \times \dfrac{7}{57} = \dfrac{224}{285}$

Fractions   75

Assignment 2.3

Fractions

Find each of the following products, reducing it to lowest terms. Use cancellation wherever possible.

1. $\dfrac{3}{4} \times \dfrac{1}{4} =$ _____ $\dfrac{3}{4} \times \dfrac{1}{4} = \dfrac{3}{16}$

2. $\dfrac{5}{12} \times \dfrac{3}{8} =$ _____ $\dfrac{5}{\cancel{12}_{4}} \times \dfrac{\cancel{3}^{1}}{8} = \dfrac{5}{32}$ or $\dfrac{5}{12} \times \dfrac{3}{8} = \dfrac{15}{96} = \dfrac{5}{32}$

3. $\dfrac{3}{4} \times \dfrac{5}{9} =$ _____ $\dfrac{\cancel{3}^{1}}{4} \times \dfrac{5}{\cancel{9}_{3}} = \dfrac{5}{12}$ or $\dfrac{3}{4} \times \dfrac{5}{9} = \dfrac{15}{36} = \dfrac{5}{12}$

Convert each of these mixed numbers to an improper fraction.

4. $9\dfrac{3}{8} =$ _____ $\dfrac{75}{8}$

5. $6\dfrac{1}{6} =$ _____ $\dfrac{37}{6}$

6. $5\dfrac{5}{16} =$ _____ $\dfrac{85}{16}$

7. $8\dfrac{7}{8} =$ _____ $\dfrac{71}{8}$

Find each of the following products and reduce fractions to lowest terms. Use cancellation where possible.

8. $3 \times \dfrac{1}{4} =$ _____ $\dfrac{3}{4}$

9. $\dfrac{2}{3} \times 1\dfrac{3}{4} \times 4 =$ _____ $\dfrac{2}{3} \times \dfrac{7}{\cancel{4}_{1}} \times \dfrac{\cancel{4}^{1}}{1} = \dfrac{14}{3} = 4\dfrac{2}{3}$

10. $1\dfrac{1}{2} \times 2\dfrac{3}{4} \times 6\dfrac{2}{3} =$ _____ $\dfrac{\cancel{3}^{1}}{2} \times \dfrac{11}{\cancel{4}_{1}} \times \dfrac{\cancel{20}^{5}}{\cancel{3}_{1}} = \dfrac{55}{2} = 27\dfrac{1}{2}$

11. $2\dfrac{14}{15} \times 3 \times \dfrac{2}{30} =$ _____ $\dfrac{44}{15} \times \dfrac{\cancel{3}^{1}}{1} \times \dfrac{\cancel{2}^{1}}{\cancel{30}_{\cancel{10}_{5}}} = \dfrac{44}{75}$

continued

Assignment 2.3 *continued*

12. A metal chain used by Koski Construction Company is $5\frac{3}{4}$ meters long. A second chain is $4\frac{1}{2}$ times as long. Find the length of the second chain.

    $5\frac{3}{4} \times 4\frac{1}{2} = \frac{23}{4} \times \frac{9}{2} = \frac{207}{8} = 25\frac{7}{8}$ meters

    $25\frac{7}{8}$ meters

13. Jo Anne Lucas, a land developer, paid $21,000 for a building lot and sold it 2 months later for $1\frac{6}{7}$ times what it cost her. For how much did she sell the lot?

    $\frac{21,000}{1} \times 1\frac{6}{7} = \frac{\cancel{21,000}^{3,000}}{1} \times \frac{13}{\cancel{7}_{1}} = \$39,000$

    $39,000

14. In stocking a shelf for a supermarket, Andy Simms has $123\frac{3}{4}$ feet of space to fill. Of the space, $\frac{2}{5}$ will be for boxed items and the rest for canned goods. How much space in feet will be used for canned goods?

    $123\frac{3}{4} \times \frac{2}{5} = \frac{\cancel{495}^{99}}{4} \times \frac{2}{\cancel{5}_{1}} = \frac{198}{4} = 49\frac{2}{4}$

    $123\frac{3}{4} - 49\frac{2}{4} = 74\frac{1}{4}$ feet

    $74\frac{1}{4}$ feet used for canned goods

15. Mary Malone, owner of Leisurewear, Inc., wanted to reduce her inventory. Six leather coats, which sold for $360 each at the regular price, were now marked down by $\frac{3}{20}$ of the regular price. What is the total dollar reduction of the six leather coats?

    $\frac{\cancel{\$360}^{18}}{1} \times \frac{3}{\cancel{20}_{1}} = \$54$ off per coat

    $54 \times 6 = \$324$ total

    $324 total reduction of the six coats

16. As an extra job, you type statistical manuscripts at $2\frac{1}{2}$ a page. Last week you typed $\frac{5}{8}$ as much as you typed this week. If you typed $17\frac{3}{5}$ pages this week:

    a) How many pages did you type last week?

    $17\frac{3}{5} \times \frac{5}{8} = \frac{\cancel{88}^{11}}{\cancel{5}_{1}} \times \frac{\cancel{5}^{1}}{\cancel{8}_{1}} = 11$ pages

    11 pages

    b) How much money did you make for the 2 weeks?

    $11 + 17\frac{3}{5} = 28\frac{3}{5}$ pages typed

    $28\frac{3}{5} \times 2\frac{1}{2} = \frac{143}{5} \times \frac{5}{2} = \frac{143}{2} = \$71\frac{1}{2}$

    $71\frac{1}{2}$ or $71.50 earned

continued

Assignment 2.3 *continued*

17. The Conway family spends $\frac{3}{4}$ of its income on food, rent, and utilities. They pay $\frac{4}{9}$ of this amount for food. What fraction of the family income goes toward food?

$$\frac{\cancel{3}^1}{\cancel{4}_1} \times \frac{\cancel{4}^1}{\cancel{9}_3} = \frac{1}{3} \text{ of income}$$

$\frac{1}{3}$ of family income goes toward food

18. The width of a skylight in the public relations office where you work is $\frac{1}{4}$ of its length. If the length is $36\frac{3}{8}$ inches, what is the width?

$$36\frac{3}{8} \times \frac{1}{4} = \frac{291}{8} \times \frac{1}{4} = \frac{291}{32}$$
$$= 9\frac{3}{32} \text{ inches}$$

$9\frac{3}{32}$ inches, width

Find the quotient for each of the following.

19. $\dfrac{8}{39} \div \dfrac{8}{21} = \quad \dfrac{\cancel{8}^1}{\cancel{39}_{13}} \times \dfrac{\cancel{21}^7}{\cancel{8}_1} = \dfrac{7}{13}$

20. $\dfrac{21}{44} \div \dfrac{7}{8} = \quad \dfrac{\cancel{21}^3}{\cancel{44}_{11}} \times \dfrac{\cancel{8}^2}{\cancel{7}_1} = \dfrac{6}{11}$

21. $3\dfrac{5}{16} \div \dfrac{7}{16} = \quad \dfrac{53}{\cancel{16}_1} \times \dfrac{\cancel{16}^1}{7} = \dfrac{53}{7} = 7\dfrac{4}{7}$

22. $\dfrac{7}{8} \div 14 = \quad \dfrac{\cancel{7}^1}{8} \times \dfrac{1}{\cancel{14}_2} = \dfrac{1}{16}$

23. A shipment of ceramic bowls arrived at the china shop where you are the receiving clerk. The total shipment weighed 66 pounds. If each bowl weighs $1\frac{3}{8}$ pounds, how many bowls were there in the shipment?

$$66 \div 1\frac{3}{8}$$
$$\frac{\cancel{66}^6}{1} \times \frac{8}{\cancel{11}_1} = 48 \text{ bowls}$$

48 bowls

24. The executive exercise group you are leading hikes at a rate of $3\frac{1}{5}$ miles per hour. How long will it take the group to hike 33 miles?

$$33 \div 3\frac{1}{5}$$
$$\frac{33}{1} \times \frac{5}{16} = \frac{165}{16} = 10\frac{5}{16}$$

$10\frac{5}{16}$ hours

continued

Assignment 2.3 *continued*

25. Harry Peters runs a gallery. The weight of a crate of picture frames that he purchased is 126 pounds. The weight of each picture frame is $2\frac{1}{4}$ pounds. How many picture frames are in the crate? (Disregard the weight of the crate itself.)

$126 \div 2\frac{1}{4}$

$\dfrac{\cancel{126}^{14}}{1} \times \dfrac{4}{\cancel{9}_{1}} = 56$ frames

56 frames

26. How many liters of imported olive oil can you buy for your pizzeria if each liter costs $\$5\frac{2}{3}$ and you have $\$6\frac{3}{8}$ to spend?

$6\dfrac{3}{8} \div 5\dfrac{2}{3}$

$\dfrac{\cancel{51}^{3}}{8} \times \dfrac{3}{\cancel{17}_{1}} = \dfrac{9}{8} = 1\dfrac{1}{8}$ liters

$1\dfrac{1}{8}$ **liters**

27. Helen Binky, a woodworker, knows that the length of a particular plywood board is $7\frac{1}{2}$ times its width. If the length is $13\frac{1}{8}$ feet, what is the width?

$13\dfrac{1}{8} \div 7\dfrac{1}{2}$

$\dfrac{\cancel{105}^{7}}{\cancel{8}_{4}} \times \dfrac{\cancel{2}^{1}}{\cancel{15}_{1}} = \dfrac{7}{4} = 1\dfrac{3}{4}$ feet

$1\dfrac{3}{4}$ **feet, width**

28. Ralph's Manufacturing Plant needs $\frac{7}{18}$ square yard of material to make each item in a special order of handkerchiefs. If a bolt of silk material is 2 yards wide by 41 yards long, how many handkerchiefs can be made from that bolt?

$2 \times 41 = 82$ square yards

$\dfrac{82}{1} \times \dfrac{18}{7} = \dfrac{1,476}{7} = 210\dfrac{6}{7}$

$210\dfrac{6}{7}$ **handkerchiefs**

29. How many complete circles can you make if you are given 29 parts that are each $\frac{1}{4}$ of a circle?

$29 \div 4$

$\dfrac{29}{1} \times \dfrac{1}{4} = \dfrac{29}{4} = 7\dfrac{1}{4}$ circles

$7\dfrac{1}{4}$ **circles**

30. Marion Hanpel is an upholsterer, specializing in overstuffed chairs. How many yards of trim can he purchase for $\$52\frac{1}{2}$ if each yard costs $\$1\frac{1}{4}$?

$52\dfrac{1}{2} \div 1\dfrac{1}{4}$

$\dfrac{\cancel{105}^{21}}{\cancel{2}_{1}} \times \dfrac{\cancel{4}^{2}}{\cancel{5}_{1}} = 42$ yards

42 yards of trim

2.4 Calculations Involving Both Decimals and Fractions

A decimal is similar to a fraction. A fraction can be expressed in decimal form. The two are **equivalent** to one another, unless the decimal is rounded off. (See Chapter 1, Section 1.5.) A decimal describes part of a whole or unit in terms of tenths or powers of ten.

DECIMALS AND FRACTIONS ARE EQUIVALENT

	Tenths	Hundredths	Thousandths	Ten Thousandths	Hundred Thousandths
Decimal	.3	.03	.003	.0003	.00003
Fraction	$\frac{3}{10}$	$\frac{3}{100}$	$\frac{3}{1,000}$	$\frac{3}{10,000}$	$\frac{3}{100,000}$

In Chapter 5, Base, Rate, and Percentage, you will see that numbers with percent signs are nothing more than decimals or fractions expressed in another way. It is important to learn to work with all three types of numerical expressions comfortably since they are used so often in business.

In business computation you will find yourself dealing with fractions and decimals in the same problem. When this happens, convert all the numbers to either fractions or decimals, remembering that they are simply different ways of expressing the same thing.

Because electronic calculators are so widely used in business today, you will convert the numbers from fractions to decimals in most situations. In some cases, though, you will convert decimals to fractions to ensure greater accuracy.

Converting Decimals to Fractions

The most convenient way to convert a decimal to a fraction is to read the decimal number literally, as shown in Chapter 1.

Example 1 To make fabrication specifications clear to the workers in his factory, Marcus Trilling expresses decimals as fractions. If a cabinet door requires a tolerance of .37 inch, how will Marcus convert this to a fraction?

Convert .37 to its fractional counterpart.

Step 1   Read the number literally, not as "point thirty-seven" but as "thirty-seven hundredths."

Step 2   Write this as a fraction. $\frac{37}{100}$

Answer   The tolerance expressed as a fraction is .37 or $\frac{37}{100}$ inch.

The same is true for decimals with any number of places. Thus,

.5 = five tenths = $\frac{5}{10}$;

.065 = sixty-five thousandths = $\frac{65}{1,000}$;

.5328 = five thousand three hundred twenty-eight ten thousandths = $\frac{5,328}{10,000}$.

Reduce the resulting fractions to lowest terms.

Fractions   **81**

A variation of this method of converting a decimal to a fraction is to remove the decimal point and use the number that remains as the numerator of a fraction. The denominator of this fraction is 1 followed by as many zeros as there were decimal places in the original number. Again, reduce the fraction to lowest terms.

Example 2   Convert .37 to its fractional counterpart.

Step 1   Remove the decimal point.   37

Step 2   Create a fraction, using the original number as the numerator. $\dfrac{37}{}$

Step 3   As the denominator, use 1 and the same number of zeros as there are places in the original decimal. In this example, there are 2 places. $\dfrac{}{100}$

Answer $.37 = \dfrac{37}{100}$

NOTE: This fraction is already in its lowest terms.

When whole numbers are involved, they are not affected by the conversion. You need be concerned only with what happens after the decimal point.

Self-Check

Convert each of these decimals to its fractional equivalent.

1. .575
2. 36.25
3. 274.00085

ANSWERS   1. $\dfrac{575}{1,000} = \dfrac{23}{40}$ 2. $36\dfrac{1}{4}$ 3. $274\dfrac{17}{20,000}$

Converting Fractions to Decimals

Converting fractions to decimals is a simple procedure. You will find yourself using it often in business. Divide the numerator of the fraction by the denominator, just as you did when converting an improper fraction to a whole or a mixed number. (See Section 2.1.)

Use the numerator of the fraction as the dividend and the denominator as the divisor. Place a decimal point after the numerator or dividend. Add the number of zeros you need to derive a decimal of as many places as you require.

Example 3   In order to add the figures on an invoice, Dalya DeVoe, comptroller of Potlatch Kitchen Supply, must convert $\frac{5}{8}$ to a decimal.

Find the decimal counterpart of $\frac{5}{8}$, carrying out the calculation to three places.

Step 1   Write the fraction as a divisor problem, with the numerator as dividend and the denominator as divisor. $8\overline{)5}$

Step 2   Show the decimal point in the dividend and add the needed zeros—in this instance, 4. $8\overline{)5.0000}$

82   Chapter 2

Step 3 Divide. Round back one place.

$$\begin{array}{r} .6250 \\ 8\overline{)5.0000} \\ \underline{4\,8} \\ 20 \\ \underline{16} \\ 40 \\ \underline{40} \end{array}$$

Answer $\dfrac{5}{8} = .625$

Self-Check

Convert each of these fractions to its decimal equivalent.

1. $\dfrac{4}{5}$ _____

2. $\dfrac{9}{25}$ _____

3. $\dfrac{19}{40}$ _____

ANSWERS 1. .8   2. .36   3. .475

Converting Complex Decimals to Pure Decimals or Fractions

We have established that in business math, fractions and decimals represent the same thing—parts of one, or less than whole units. Therefore, it may seem strange to see numbers such as $.62\tfrac{1}{2}$, $.02\tfrac{3}{7}$, or $.324\tfrac{1}{3}$.

The **complex decimal,** a decimal number with a proper fraction in its final place, is often an acceptable means of expression in business, but it must be modified for calculation. Convert it into either a pure decimal or a fraction. It is important to understand that the fraction does not occupy a full decimal place. It refers to and is part of the preceding place.

To convert a complex decimal to a pure decimal, convert its fraction part into its decimal equivalent. Place it next to the original decimal.

Example 4 Convert $.62\tfrac{1}{2}$ to a pure decimal.

Step 1 Divide the numerator of the fractional part by its denominator.

$$\begin{array}{r} .5 \\ 2\overline{)1.00} \end{array}$$

Step 2 Substitute the resulting equivalent, writing it in the appropriate decimal position—in this case, in the thousandths place.

.625

Answer $.62\tfrac{1}{2} = .625$

Converting to a pure decimal is fine in those cases where the fraction works out even or to a **terminating decimal.** If the fraction converts to a **nonterminating decimal,** one that never comes out even, either round off, sacrificing some accuracy, or convert the complex decimal to a fraction.

Example 5 Convert $.23\tfrac{1}{3}$ to a fraction.

Step 1 Write the decimal as a fraction with the appropriate denominator. Remember that the fraction does not occupy a full decimal place.

$\dfrac{23\tfrac{1}{3}}{100}$

Fractions 83

Step 2   Convert the numerator to an improper fraction. $\frac{\frac{70}{3}}{100}$

Step 3   Divide the numerator by the denominator, inverting the divisor. Reduce to lowest terms. $\frac{70}{3} \div 100 = \frac{70}{3} \times \frac{1}{100}$
$= \frac{7}{30}$

Answer $.23\frac{1}{3} = \frac{7}{30}$

NOTE: For purposes of calculation, $\frac{7}{30}$ is accurate. By contrast, .2333 is not.

Self-Check

Convert each of these complex decimals to a pure decimal or a fraction.

1. $.24\frac{1}{2}$ _____

2. $.120\frac{3}{4}$ _____

3. $.66\frac{2}{3}$ _____

4. $.8\frac{2}{7}$ _____

ANSWERS   1. .245 or $\frac{49}{200}$. Both are accurate.   2. .12075 or $\frac{483}{4000}$. Both are accurate.
3. $\frac{2}{3}$ or .6667. The common fraction is accurate. The decimal is accurate to 3 places.
4. $\frac{58}{70} = \frac{29}{35}$ or .82857. The common fraction is accurate. The decimal is accurate to 5 places.

Common Decimals and Their Fractional Equivalents

We began by saying that decimals and fractions are different ways of expressing a part of 1, or of a whole. In business math, every decimal has a fractional equivalent—a fraction with the same meaning—and vice versa. These are derived as shown on page 85.

Certain of these equivalents are so common in business that you probably use them without even thinking about it. For instance, twenty-five cents (.25) is a quarter ($\frac{1}{4}$) of a dollar ($1.00). In other words, .25 = $\frac{1}{4}$ of 1.

In order to increase your efficiency at business calculations, you will want to master those commonly used equivalents that you may not already know. Some of them are shown here.

Particularly important to note are decimals that do not terminate, that is, that do not come out even. Examples of these are marked with an asterisk (*) in the table on page 85. To get an accurate answer when calculating with them, you *must* use the fractional equivalent.

Decimal		Fraction of One	Decimal		Fraction of One
.25	=	$\frac{1}{4}$	*.16$\frac{2}{3}$	=	$\frac{1}{6}$
.50	=	$\frac{1}{2}$	*.83$\frac{1}{3}$	=	$\frac{5}{6}$
.75	=	$\frac{3}{4}$	*.14$\frac{2}{7}$	=	$\frac{1}{7}$
*.33$\frac{1}{3}$	=	$\frac{1}{3}$	.12$\frac{1}{2}$	=	$\frac{1}{8}$
*.66$\frac{2}{3}$	=	$\frac{2}{3}$	.37$\frac{1}{2}$	=	$\frac{3}{8}$
.20	=	$\frac{1}{5}$	.62$\frac{1}{2}$	=	$\frac{5}{8}$
.40	=	$\frac{2}{5}$	.87$\frac{1}{2}$	=	$\frac{7}{8}$
.60	=	$\frac{3}{5}$	.10	=	$\frac{1}{10}$
.80	=	$\frac{4}{5}$	*.08$\frac{1}{3}$	=	$\frac{1}{2}$
			.05	=	$\frac{1}{20}$

NAME _____ DATE _____ SECTION _____

Assignment 2.4

Fractions

Convert each of these fractions into its decimal equivalent. Round your answer after the third place, showing it as a complex decimal if necessary.

1. $\dfrac{3}{8}$ .375

2. $\dfrac{2}{5}$ .4

3. $\dfrac{6}{25}$ .24

4. $\dfrac{7}{50}$ .14

5. $\dfrac{7}{12}$ $.583\dfrac{1}{3}$

6. $\dfrac{19}{20}$ .95

7. $\dfrac{17}{40}$ .425

8. $\dfrac{11}{12}$ .917

9. $\dfrac{5}{8}$ .625

10. $3\dfrac{6}{11}$ 3.545

11. $7\dfrac{3}{16}$ 7.188

12. $13\dfrac{1}{12}$ 13.083

Convert each of these decimals into its fractional equivalent.

13. .25 $\dfrac{25}{100} = \dfrac{1}{4}$

14. .36 $\dfrac{36}{100} = \dfrac{9}{25}$

15. .275 $\dfrac{275}{1,000} = \dfrac{11}{40}$

16. .426 $\dfrac{426}{1,000} = \dfrac{213}{500}$

17. 2.45 $2\dfrac{45}{100} = 2\dfrac{9}{20}$

18. 5.2 $5\dfrac{2}{10} = 5\dfrac{1}{5}$

19. 15.25 $15\dfrac{25}{100} = 15\dfrac{1}{4}$

20. 127.705 $127\dfrac{705}{1,000} = 127\dfrac{141}{200}$

21. 20.3645 $20\dfrac{3,645}{10,000} = 20\dfrac{729}{2,000}$

22. .47628 $\dfrac{47,628}{100,000} = \dfrac{11,907}{25,000}$

23. 5.8246 $5\dfrac{8,246}{10,000} = 5\dfrac{4,123}{5,000}$

24. 28.548 $28\dfrac{548}{1,000} = 28\dfrac{137}{250}$

25. 3.39300 $3\dfrac{39,300}{100,000} = 3\dfrac{393}{1,000}$

26. 101.10001 $101\dfrac{10,001}{100,000}$

continued

Assignment 2.4 *continued*

Convert each of these complex decimals to its fractional equivalent.

27. $.12\frac{1}{2}$ $\frac{1}{8}$

28. $.83\frac{1}{3}$ $\frac{5}{6}$

29. $.13\frac{7}{15}$ $\frac{101}{750}$

30. $.8\frac{3}{5}$ $\frac{43}{50}$

31. $.72\frac{5}{8}$ $\frac{581}{800}$

32. $.14\frac{2}{7}$ $\frac{1}{7}$

33. $.17\frac{1}{6}$ $\frac{103}{600}$

34. $.14\frac{2}{31}$ $\frac{109}{775}$

35. $.83\frac{3}{7}$ $\frac{121}{140}$

36. $.238\frac{7}{8}$ $\frac{1,911}{8,000}$

37. $.92\frac{5}{6}$ $\frac{557}{600}$

38. $.536\frac{16}{17}$ $\frac{1,141}{2,125}$

39. $.193\frac{13}{16}$ $\frac{3,101}{16,000}$

29. $.13\frac{7}{15}$

$= 13\frac{7}{15} \div 100$

$= \frac{202}{15} \div 100$

$= \frac{\cancel{202}^{101}}{15} \times \frac{1}{\cancel{100}_{50}}$

Comprehensive Problems for Chapter 2

Fractions

1. How many fifths are there in a whole number 3?

   $3 \div \frac{1}{5} = \frac{3}{1} \times \frac{5}{1} = 15$ <u>15 fifths</u>

2. Convert $8\frac{5}{12}$ to an improper fraction.

   ```
      12        96 + 5 = 101
    ×  8
      96
   ```
            <u>$\frac{101}{12}$</u>

3. Expand $\frac{7}{10}$ to an equivalent fraction with a denominator of 50.

   $\frac{7}{10} = \frac{}{50}$ $\frac{7}{10} \times \frac{5}{5} = \frac{35}{50}$ <u>$\frac{35}{50}$</u>

4. Reduce $\frac{6}{32}$ to an equivalent fraction with a denominator of 16.

   $\frac{6}{32} = \frac{}{16}$ $\frac{\cancel{6}^3}{\cancel{32}_{16}} = \frac{3}{16}$ <u>$\frac{3}{16}$</u>

5. What fraction is largest: $\frac{11}{20}$, $\frac{5}{8}$, or $\frac{6}{10}$?

   $\frac{11}{20} \quad \frac{5}{8} \quad \frac{6}{10}$

   $\frac{22}{40} \quad \frac{25}{40} \quad \frac{24}{40}$ <u>$\frac{5}{8}$ is largest fraction</u>

6. Dale Murhow spends $\frac{1}{4}$ of his take-home salary for rent, $\frac{1}{3}$ for food, $\frac{1}{6}$ for clothing, and $\frac{1}{8}$ for auto expenses. He uses the remainder for personal expenses. If his monthly take-home salary is $1,240, how much money does he spend for clothing?

   $\frac{\cancel{1{,}240}^{620}}{1} \times \frac{1}{\cancel{6}_3} = \frac{620}{3} = \$206\frac{2}{3}$ <u>$\$206\frac{2}{3}$, or $206.67 spent on clothing</u>

7. You are the booking manager for Giles Stadium, which has a seating capacity of 67,000 persons. If 45,000 attended a game, what fraction of the stadium was not filled?

   $\frac{45{,}\cancel{000}}{67{,}\cancel{000}} = \frac{45}{67}$ filled

   $\frac{67}{67} - \frac{45}{67} = \frac{22}{67}$ not filled   <u>$\frac{22}{67}$ of stadium not filled</u>

   $\frac{22{,}000}{67{,}000} = \frac{22}{67}$ not filled

8. International Foods leases its unused warehouse space to three businesses. Tuffcraft leases $\frac{1}{8}$ of the space, Boren Inc., leases $\frac{2}{5}$, and Trupress leases $\frac{2}{10}$.

continued

Fractions   **89**

Comprehensive Problems *continued*

a) What fractional part of the warehouse space is used by International Foods?

$\frac{1}{8} + \frac{2}{5} + \frac{2}{10} = \frac{5}{40} + \frac{16}{40} + \frac{8}{40} = \frac{29}{40}$ used by others

$\frac{40}{40} - \frac{29}{40} = \frac{11}{40}$ used by International Foods

$\frac{11}{40}$ used by International Foods

b) If Tuffcraft leases 8,000 square feet, how much space is leased by Boren?

$8000 = \frac{1}{8}$ $8,000 \times 8 = 64,000$ total square feet

$\frac{\cancel{64,000}^{12,800}}{1} \times \frac{2}{\cancel{5}_1} = 25,600$ square feet

25,600 square feet leased by Boren

c) How much is leased by Trupress?

$\frac{\cancel{64,000}^{6,400}}{1} \times \frac{2}{\cancel{10}_1} = 12,800$ square feet

12,800 square feet leased by Trupress

9. What is the lowest common denominator for $\frac{5}{6}$ and $\frac{7}{16}$?

48 lowest common denominator

10. Which fraction is smallest: $\frac{2}{3}$, $\frac{7}{9}$, or $\frac{5}{6}$?

$\frac{2}{3}$ $\frac{7}{9}$ $\frac{5}{6}$
$\frac{12}{18}$ $\frac{14}{18}$ $\frac{15}{18}$

$\frac{2}{3}$ is smallest fraction

11. Reduce $\frac{108}{198}$ to lowest terms.

Use 18 to reduce the fraction.

$\frac{6}{11}$

12. Convert $23\frac{11}{12}$ into an improper fraction.

$\frac{347}{12}$

13. Are $\frac{13}{17}$ and $\frac{33}{34}$ equivalent?

$\frac{13}{17}$ $\frac{33}{34}$

34 is the common denominator $\frac{26}{34} \neq \frac{33}{34}$

No

continued

Comprehensive Problems *continued*

14. Tom Clowsky received a raise of $11\frac{1}{4}$ cents an hour. You received $\frac{1}{5}$ less of a raise than he did. How much of a raise did you receive?

    $11\frac{1}{4} \times \frac{1}{5}$

    $\frac{\cancel{45}^{9}}{4} \times \frac{1}{\cancel{5}_{1}} = \frac{9}{4} = 2\frac{1}{4}$ less

    $11\frac{1}{4} - 2\frac{1}{4} = 9¢$ raise received

    9¢ raise received

15. In the fund-raising office where Harian Hartley is employed, a shelf that measures 14 feet in length is to be divided into 7 spaces as follows: A $1\frac{1}{4}$-foot space is to be marked off at each end, and the remaining length is to be divided into 5 equal spaces. How long will each of these 5 spaces be?

    $14 - \left(1\frac{1}{4} \times 2\right) = 14 - 2\frac{1}{2} = 13\frac{2}{2} - 2\frac{1}{2} = 11\frac{1}{2}$ allotted for five equal spaces

    $11\frac{1}{2} \div 5 = \frac{23}{2} \times \frac{1}{5} = \frac{23}{10} = 2\frac{3}{10}$ feet per space

    $2\frac{3}{10}$ feet per space

16. What fraction of an hour is 36 minutes?

    $\frac{\cancel{36}^{3}}{\cancel{60}_{5}} = \frac{3}{5}$

    $\frac{3}{5}$ of an hour

17. In a class of 21 students, there are 8 males. What fraction represents the number that are females?

    $21 - 8 = 13$ females

    $\frac{13}{21}$ females

18. In the refrigerator of Gilowski's Mini-Market, there are 36 bottles of cola and 29 bottles of other types of soda. What fraction of the bottles are cola?

    $36 + 29 = 65$ total bottles

    $\frac{36}{65}$

    $\frac{36}{65}$ of bottles are cola

19. Seven is what fractional part of a dozen?

    $\frac{7}{12}$

20. Express the numeral 5 as a fraction with a denominator of 30. That is to say, how many thirtieths are there in 5?

    $\frac{5}{1} = \frac{}{30}$ $\frac{5}{1} \times \frac{30}{30} = \frac{150}{30}$

    $\frac{150}{30}$

continued

Comprehensive Problems *continued*

21. As an independent contractor renovating an authentic Victorian house, you purchase 12 windows at $28\frac{1}{3}$ each.

    a) What is the total cost of the windows?

    $$\frac{12}{1} \times 28\frac{1}{3}$$

    $$\frac{\cancel{12}^{4}}{1} \times \frac{85}{\cancel{3}_{1}} = \$340$$

    $340 total cost of windows

    b) If this represents $\frac{1}{5}$ of the total amount you set aside for renovation for the month, what is the total amount you set aside this month?

    $$\frac{340}{1} \div \frac{1}{5} = \frac{340}{1} \times \frac{5}{1} = \$1{,}700$$

    $1,700 set aside

22. The Hutchason family won $750,000 (after taxes) in the state lottery and were awarded a check for the full amount. With the help of a financial consultant, they decided to split the winnings in the following way: The three children would each receive $\frac{2}{15}$, the mother and father would each receive $\frac{1}{5}$, and the rest would be invested in stock.

    a) How much money will each child receive?

    $$\frac{\cancel{750{,}000}^{50{,}000}}{1} \times \frac{2}{\cancel{15}_{1}} = \$100{,}000$$

    $100,000 per child

    b) How much money will the parents receive together?

    $$\frac{\cancel{750{,}000}^{150{,}000}}{1} \times \frac{2}{\cancel{5}_{1}} = \$300{,}000$$

    $300,000 parent's share

    c) How much money will be invested in stock?

    $$3 \times \frac{2}{15} = \frac{6}{15} \quad 2 \times \frac{1}{5} = \frac{2}{5} \quad \frac{15}{15} - \frac{12}{15} = \frac{3}{15} \text{ invested}$$

    $$\frac{6}{15} + \frac{2}{5} = \frac{6}{15} + \frac{6}{15} = \frac{12}{15}$$

    $150,000 will be invested

    $$\frac{\cancel{750{,}000}^{50{,}000}}{1} \times \frac{3}{\cancel{15}_{1}} = \underline{\$150{,}000}$$

23. Jim Heacock was paid according to piece work. He was paid $3.75\frac{1}{4}$ for each small model airplane he assembled and $10.36\frac{3}{4}$ for each large model he assembled. If he assembled 84 small models and 91 large models, how much was he paid?

$3.7525	$10.3675
× 84	× 91
150100	103675
300200	933075
$315.2100	$943.4425

    $1,258.65 total paid to Jim

    $315.2100 Small models
    + 943.4425 Large models
    $1,258.6525 =
    $1,258.65 Total

continued

92   Chapter 2

| NAME | DATE | SECTION |

Comprehensive Problems *continued*

24. Sam Battersby is in charge of materials procurement for Stone Manufacturing Company. Glue, which originally cost 87.5¢ an ounce, was increased in price by $9\frac{1}{8}$¢ an ounce. If 219.34 ounces are needed in production, what is the total new cost of the glue?

```
  .875    Old price/ounce
+ .09125  Increase/ounce
  .96625  New price/ounce
```

$211.94
new cost of glue

```
      $.96625
×     219.34   Ounces needed
      386500
      289875
      869625
       96625
      193250
  $211.9372750
```

25. A building lot that measures $61.08\frac{1}{3}$ feet by 115.5 feet is sold for $31,890. What is the selling price per square foot?

$61\frac{1}{12} \times 115\frac{1}{2}$

$\frac{733}{12} \times \frac{231}{2} = \frac{169,323}{24} = 7{,}505.125$ square feet

$4.52 per square foot

```
              4.520
7,055.125)31,890.000,000
          28220500
          37595000
          35275625
           23193750
           14110250
            9083500
```

26. George Manfredis, owner of the Landmark Flower Shop, ordered the supplies listed here.

Item	Quantity Ordered	Unit Price	Total Price
Dried straw flowers	16 bunches	$.87½ a bunch	$14.00
Glass vase	20 vases	$1.19 each	23.80
Gravel	42 ounces	19.4¢ an ounce	8.15
Ceramic pot	19 pots	$15.62½ a pot	296.88

a) What was the total cost of the order?

$342.83 total cost of order

b) Two of the glass vases and one ceramic pot were damaged in shipment. Therefore, George does not have to pay for them. Once he has deducted the cost of them from the bill, what does he actually owe?

```
2 × 1.19 =    2.38
1 × 15.625 = 15.625
             18.005 = $18.01 damaged
  $342.83  Total cost
−  18.01   Damaged goods
  $324.82  Net cost
```

$324.82 net cost

Fractions

Case 1

Carl, Jackie, and Bill form a business that refinishes furniture. They decide to share loss or profit according to how much money each person has invested. Carl invested $36,000. Jackie invested $1\frac{1}{2}$ times what Carl invested, and Bill invested $\frac{1}{9}$ of what Jackie invested. The profit for the first year was $32,000.

a) What is the total investment?

b) How much of the total investment is Carl's fractional share?

c) How much of the total investment is Jackie's fractional share?

d) How much of the total investment is Bill's fractional share?

e) How much of the profit does Carl receive in dollars?

f) How much of the profit does Jackie receive in dollars?

g) How much of the profit does Bill receive in dollars?

Case 2

You hve decided to start a part-time business as a tailor and garment designer. The amount of material you used for a four-week period is as follows:

	Solid Material (in yards)	Tweed Material (in yards)
1st week	$18\frac{3}{4}$	$25\frac{5}{12}$
2nd week	$20\frac{1}{2}$	$27\frac{3}{8}$
3rd week	$18\frac{3}{5}$	$26\frac{1}{3}$
4th week	$21\frac{1}{4}$	$24\frac{1}{6}$

The cost of the tweed material is $2\frac{1}{4}$ for each $\frac{1}{2}$ yard of material. The cost of the solid material per $\frac{1}{2}$ yard is $\frac{1}{2}$ the cost of the tweed per $\frac{1}{2}$ yard.

a) How much solid material did you use for the four weeks?

b) How much tweed material did you use?

c) What was the total cost of the material?

d) If this cost represents $\frac{3}{4}$ of the amount you set aside for this project, how much money do you have left for other expenses?

e) What questions would you ask yourself in order to decide whether or not the business was sufficiently profitable?

Key Terms

Complex decimal
Denominator
Equivalent
Fraction
Improper fraction

Lowest, or least, common denominator
Mixed Number
Nonterminating decimal

Numerator
Proper fraction
Terminating decimal
Terms

Key Concepts

- Fractions are written as two numerals with a horizontal or diagonal line between them. The number above, or to the left of, the line is called the numerator; the number below, or to the right of the line is called the denominator.
- There are three types of fractions: a proper fraction, in which the numerator is smaller than its denominator; an improper fraction, in which the numerator is equal to or greater than its denominator; and a mixed number, in which a whole number is combined with a fraction.
- The Law of Fractions: If both the numerator and the denominator are multiplied or divided by the same number, the value of the fraction does not change.
- Addition of Fractions: Determine the lowest common denominator, convert the fractions, find the sum of the numerators, and place that sum over the common denominator. If the fractions to be added are mixed numbers, the whole numbers are also added. The final answer is the sum of the whole numbers presented with the sum of the fractions.
- Subtraction of Fractions: Determine the lowest common denominator, convert the fractions, find the difference between the numerators of the bottom fraction and the top fraction, and place that number over the common denominator. If mixed numbers are involved, the whole numbers are also subtracted from each other. It may be necessary to borrow from the whole number in order to complete the subtraction. The final answer is the difference of the whole numbers presented with the difference of the fractions, reduced to lowest terms.
- Multiplication of Fractions: Cancel where possible, multiply the numerators by one another, multiply the denominators by one another, and place the product of the numerators over the product of the denominators. If mixed numbers are involved, they must be converted into improper fractions before multiplying.
- Division of Fractions: Invert the divisor, change the division sign to a multiplication sign, and carry through as described under multiplication of fractions.
- In addition, subtraction, multiplication, and division of fractions, all final answers are normally expressed in lowest terms and in the form of proper fractions and/or mixed numbers.
- Convert a decimal to a fraction by reading the decimal number literally and writing it as a fraction. Another way is to remove the decimal point and place the number as a numerator over a denominator, which is 1 followed by as many zeros as there are decimal places in the original number. In both cases, reduce the fraction to lowest terms.
- Convert a fraction to a decimal by dividing the numerator of the fraction by the denominator.
- A complex decimal is a decimal with a proper fraction in its final place. Convert a complex decimal to a pure decimal by converting its fractional part into its decimal equivalent and placing it next to the existing decimal.

Proper fraction
$\frac{1}{2}$ Numerator
Denominator

Improper fraction
$\frac{2}{1}$ Numerator
Denominator

Mixed number
$1\frac{1}{2}$

3
Bank Records

Business Takes a Positive Approach
BANKERS TRUST COMPANY

In today's unpredictable marketplace, even the once formidable institution of banking is threatened. During the last few years, many banks have been forced to close their doors or to sell out to more powerful competitors. Nowadays, successful banking means much more than just offering solid savings and checking accounts. One bank to take notice of in this time of deregulation and change is Bankers Trust.

Bankers Trust has become a major force in the marketplace as a worldwide merchant bank—an institution that combines the lending capability and non-credit services of a commercial bank with the intermediary skills, flexibility, and entrepreneurial spirit of an investment bank.

As part of its merchant banking strategy, the bank has been organized for maximum effectiveness into two principal units. The first, Financial Services, brings together the principal credit and financing arms of the bank: corporate lending, investment banking, and money and securities markets activities. The second is PROFITC, which comprises the bank's trust, investment management, securities processing, cash management, and private banking businesses.

The success of Bankers Trust's merchant banking strategy has been demonstrated by the bank's strong earnings performance. Since 1979, when the strategy began to take form, net income has nearly quadrupled, from $114 million to $428 million in 1986.

> **Learning Objectives**
>
> After reading and studying this chapter and working the problems, you will be able to:
>
> - Deal successfully with checks, checking-account deposits, and checking-account records.
> - Reconcile a typical checking-account statement with the depositor's records.

Now that you have had the opportunity to review some basic mathematical processes, you are ready to apply them to the system most commonly used in carrying out financial transactions: the **checking account**. Few businesses, large or small, could operate without a business checking account. In most ways, it is similar to your personal checking account, but financial institutions generally offer more services to businesses than they do to individual customers. For example, they often accept payment of debts or notes owed to a company and deposit it to the company's account.

Today most financial dealings, both business and personal, involve the use of checks. Settling accounts by check is often safer and more convenient than paying cash. The canceled check, once returned to its author, acts as a receipt. In some systems, the check is not returned. Instead, the author keeps a carbon copy made when the check is written.

3.1 Checks, Deposits, and Check Records

A **check** is a written notice from you or your company to your banking institution, ordering it to pay to an individual or business some of the funds kept on deposit. A check includes important information. Note that some of the information appears twice, once for humans and once for machines.

Example 1 A typical check.

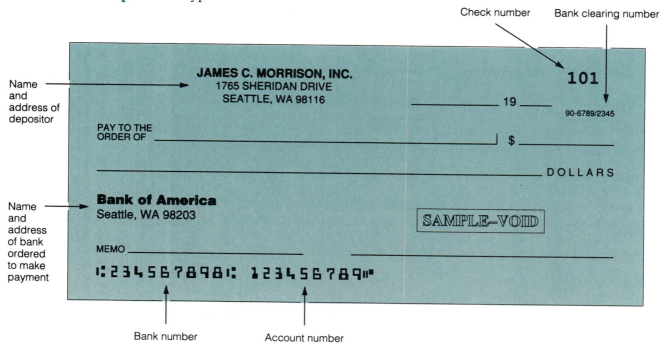

98 Chapter 3

When you make out a check—that is, when you fill in the blanks—you supply further information, as shown below.

Example 2 An authored check.

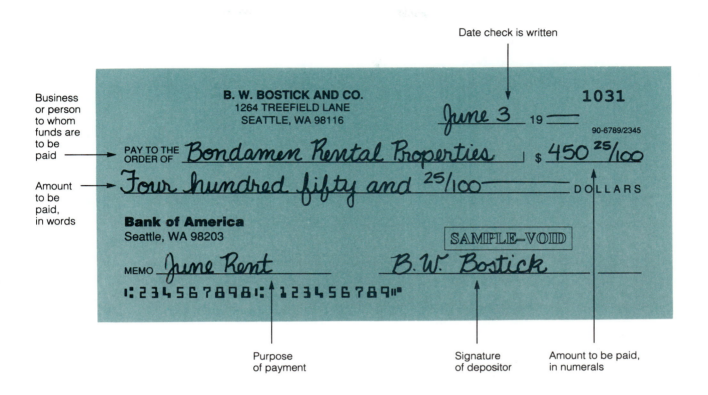

When writing checks that are drawn on a business or personal account, it is wise to follow these rules:

Always write legibly and in ink, or type everything but the signature.

When writing in words the amount to be paid, begin at the far left of the line provided. Express any cents as a fraction with a denominator of 100.

Draw a line to fill any space between the end of the written amount and the printed word *Dollars*.

Place the numerals of the check amount close to the printed dollar sign to prevent more numerals from being added after the check leaves your hands.

Always sign your checks the same way, with your legal signature.

Self-Check

Acting as an official of B. W. Bostick and Co., fill out this blank check in payment for a new desk chair. Use the current date and your own signature. Write the check to Wellington Office Supply, Inc., in the amount of $254.68.

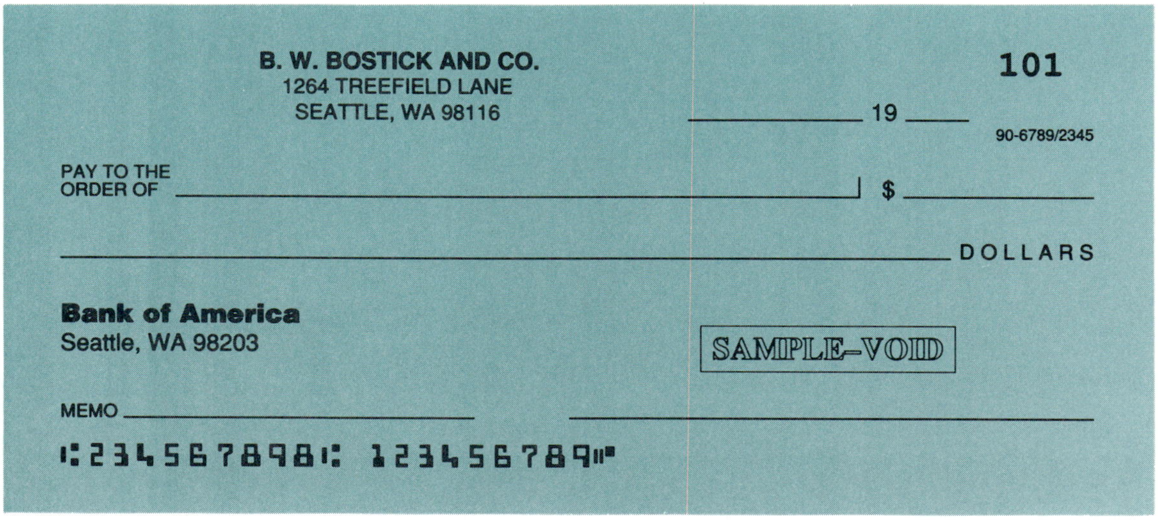

[blank check image]

ANSWER

[completed check image: Pay to the order of Wellington Office Supply, $254 68/100, Two hundred fifty-four and 68/100 DOLLARS, MEMO: Desk Chair, signed (Your legal signature), dated (current date)]

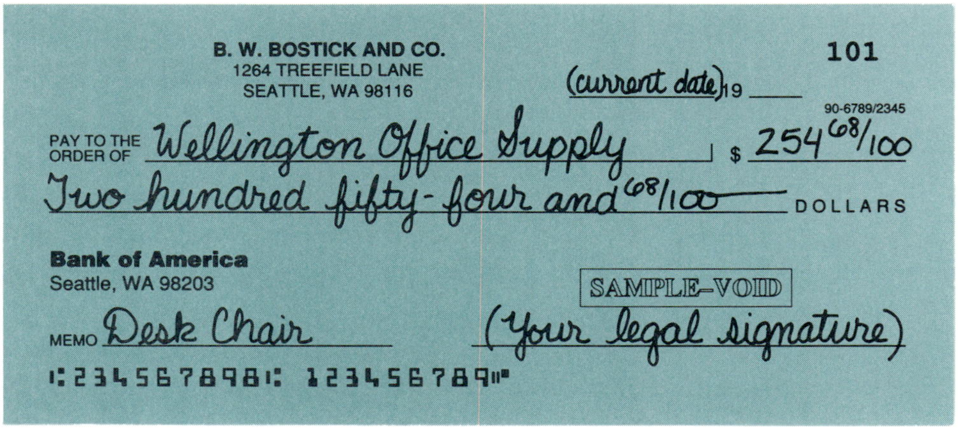

Records of Checks and Deposits

In some checking accounts, each check is attached to a **stub**. More and more frequently, however, a **check register** (a separate record sheet) is provided. The individual or business keeps track of each deposit made to the account and of each check written to draw funds from it. It is important to maintain such records accurately, keeping the stubs or register up to date, filling in necessary information as shown below.

Chapter 3

Writing Out Check Stubs

Example 3 A typical check stub.

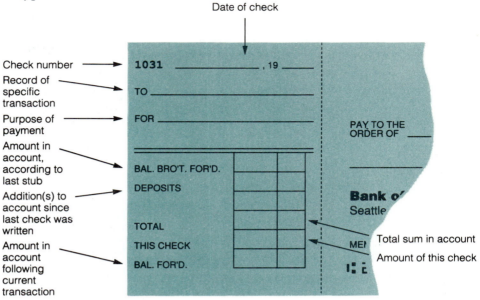

The upper part of the check stub contains space to record the current date, the business or individual to whom the check is written, and the purpose of payment.

The lower part provides room for:

Balance Brought Forward (abbreviated Bal. Bro't. For'd.): The amount that was in the account after the check immediately preceding this one was written.

Deposits: Any amount(s) added to the amount since the last check was written.

Total: The sum of the balance brought forward and any deposits, or the total amount in the account at this time.

This Check: The amount of the check currently being written.

Balance Forward (abbreviated Bal. For'd.): The difference between the total in the account and the amount of the check being written. It is the new balance in the account and should also be written on the next stub.

Example 4 The comptroller of B. W. Bostick and Co. must fill out the check stub for check 1031, shown on page 99. The balance forwarded from the stub for check 1030 is $225.28, and a deposit for $542.36 has since been made.

Step 1 Supply information on this transaction.

Step 2 Add new deposits to the previous balance, transferred from the last stub.

Step 3 Subtract the amount of this check from the total above.

Step 4 Write the new balance on the Bal. Bro't. For'd. line of the next stub.

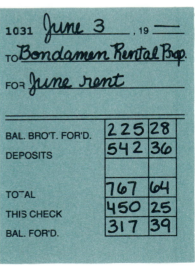

Bank Records 101

Keeping the Check Register

The check register, an alternative to the check stub system, has the advantage of showing the ongoing record of the account all in one place. This allows you to recheck figures and transactions more easily. A typical check register is shown here.

Example 5 A check register.

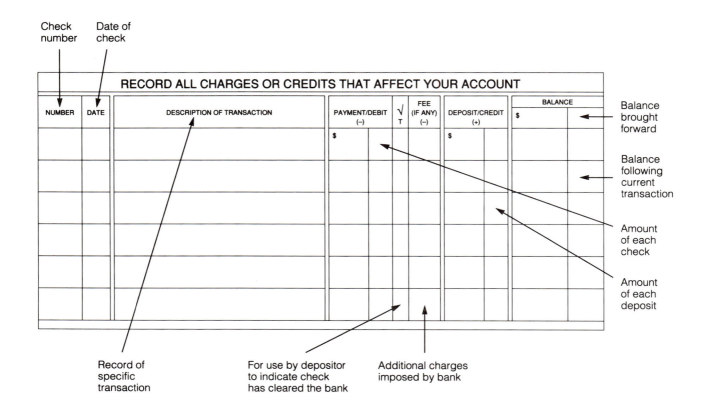

Example 6 As chief account for Computermax, Inc., Trudy Forbes must update the register of the company's checking account to reflect the following transactions: a payment of $4,245.25 on February 4, by check 1126, to Digital Corporation for 40 color monitors; and a payment of $574.38 on February 6, by check 1127, to Scrubber Associates for maintenance services. A deposit of $950 was made to the account on February 5, and the beginning balance was $5,284.30.

Step 1   Enter the balance brought forward from the previous page of the register ($5,284.30).

Step 2   Fill in the information regarding the first transaction—in this case, a check—subtracting its amount from the balance brought forward.

Step 3   Enter the second transaction—here, a deposit—adding it to the new balance.

Step 4   Fill in the information regarding the second check, subtracting the amount from the new balance to obtain the current balance in the account.

NUMBER	DATE	DESCRIPTION OF TRANSACTION	PAYMENT/DEBIT (−)	√ T	FEE (IF ANY) (−)	DEPOSIT/CREDIT (+)	BALANCE
							$ 5,284 30
1126	Feb. 4	Digital Corp. 40 Color monitors	$ 4,245 25			$	4,245 25
							1,039 05
	Feb. 5	Deposit				950 —	950 00
							1,989 05
1127	Feb. 6	Scrubber assoc. maintenance	574 38				574 38
							1,414 67

Self-Check

Fill out these two check stubs on behalf of Milsap Manufacturing Company, finding the balances to be forwarded in each case.

Stub 1: Check #1924, May 2, to Fairview Hardware Co., for drill bits totaling $90.27.

Stub 2: Check #1925, May 5, to Banyon Chemical, Inc., for cleaning solvents costing $325.82.

Deposits: $284.60 on May 2 (before #1924 was written); $133.18 on May 3; $168.42 on May 4.

Balance Brought Forward to stub 1924: $1,328.42.

Stub 1

```
1924 _____, 19___
TO _____
FOR _____

BAL. BRO'T. FOR'D.
DEPOSITS

TOTAL
THIS CHECK
BAL. FOR'D.
```

Stub 2

```
1925 _____, 19___
TO _____
FOR _____

BAL. BRO'T. FOR'D.
DEFOSITS

TOTAL
THIS CHECK
BAL. FOR'D.
```

Complete this check register, using the information given above.

NUMBER	DATE	DESCRIPTION OF TRANSACTION	PAYMENT/DEBIT (−)	√T	FEE (IF ANY) (−)	DEPOSIT/CREDIT (+)	BALANCE
							$1043 82
	May 2	Deposit	$			$ 284 60	+284 60
							1328 42

ANSWERS First Balance: Balance Brought Forward–$1,522.75   Second Balance: Balance Brought Forward–$1,498.53

THE ORIGIN OF THE CALCULATOR

The seventeenth century saw a surge of interest in mechanical computation devices. These machines were intended to assist people in solving higher-level mathematical problems more efficiently. The first successful mechanical calculator, other than the abacus, was developed in 1642 by Blaise Pascal, a Frenchman, who was 19 years old at the time. He invented the machine to help his father compute taxes. It added and subtracted using gears numbered from 0 to 9. An ingeniously designed ratchet was used to carry the 1.

Making Deposits

To put funds into a personal or business checking account, use a **deposit slip**. Deposit slips are usually supplied by the bank. They provide the bank with a record of the deposit. In return, you receive a deposit receipt, which is your record of the transaction. Record all deposits on your check stubs or register, as discussed above.

Writing Out the Deposit Slip

Example 7 A typical deposit slip.

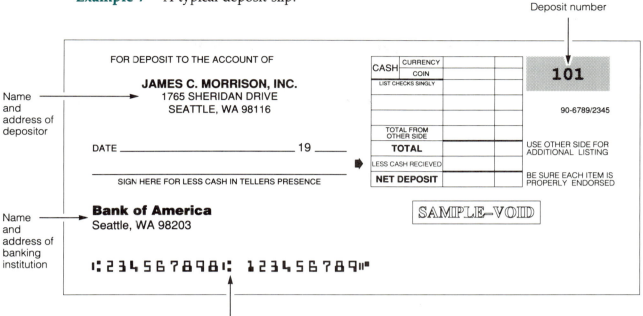

Example 8 On April 6, 19__, B. W. Bostick and Co., deposits three checks for $128.00, $75.63, and $26.41, respectively, and $42.68 in cash into its checking account. Complete the deposit ticket.

Step 1 Fill in the current date.

Step 2 Enter the total amount of cash to be deposited.

Step 3 Enter the amount of each check to be deposited.

Step 4 Total the amounts of cash and checks. Enter this on the Total line and on the Net Deposit line.

Step 5 Write the amount deposited in the check register.

Answer The completed slip is shown here.

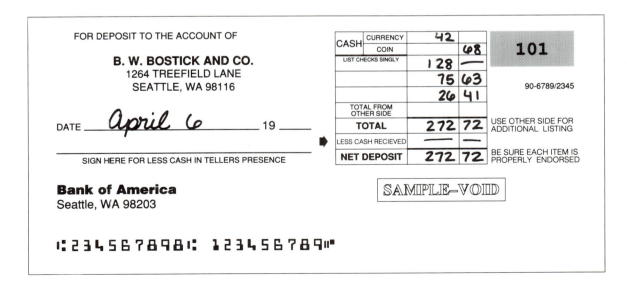

Bank Records 105

NOTE: In this transaction, the representative of B. W. Bostick and Co., did not request cash. Had cash been requested, the amount of cash desired would be entered on the Less Cash Received line and subtracted from the Total line. The difference would be written on the Net Deposit line. After receiving the cash from the bank teller, the depositor would sign for it in the space provided on the deposit ticket.

Endorsing Checks for Deposit

Checks deposited into your personal or business checking account should be signed on the back with the words "For deposit only" followed by your legal signature. By doing this, you ensure that, should a check be lost before it is processed by the bank, it is not negotiable by someone who might find it. An endorsement of this kind is called a **restricted endorsement**.

Self-Check

Maryann Trilling, president of Trilling Fabricating Company, prepares her March 8, 19__ , deposit ticket to Bellington National Bank. Included are checks in the following amounts: $3,784.58, $2,837.45, and $14.68. Maryann wants $250.00 in cash. Fill out her deposit ticket and determine the amount of her net deposit.

ANSWERS Total: $6,636.71   Net Deposit: $6,386.71

Share Accounts and Interest-Bearing Checking Accounts

Because of 1980 changes in federal banking laws, many savings and loans, credit unions, and other such institutions are now able to offer clients a service very much like the checking accounts available at most banks. Usually called a **share account,** it operates similar to the checking accounts described earlier, allowing the institutions that offer it to become more directly competitive with full-service banks.

In addition, funds in checking and share accounts can now draw interest. Using computers, financial institutions calculate interest on money kept in these accounts, adding it to the current balance as is done in compound interest-earning savings accounts. (See Chapter 9, section 9.6.)

Electronic Banking

Computers have made it possible to deposit and withdraw funds from business and personal checking accounts without the use of written documents or, indeed, without the owner of the account being physically present.

In many regions of the country, it is possible for a business to perform such functions as paying bills and issuing paychecks by simply informing the financial institution that funds are to be transferred from its account to that of a company with which it does business or of a particular employee, regardless of where these accounts are kept.

Also offered by a growing number of banks and savings and loan institutions are the services of Automatic Tellers, or computerized bank machines. These devices can be installed almost anywhere—outside the offices and branches of the institution itself, in downtown office buildings, even in supermarkets and shopping malls. They operate day and night, and customers of the bank can use them at their convenience to make deposits and withdrawals and carry out other financial transactions.

Assignment 3.1

Bank Records

Use the information below to fill in the checks and stubs for Delbert Smith of the D&S Construction Co. The balance brought forward from stub #380 is $238.46.

	Check Number	Date	To	For	Amount of Payment	Checks Deposited
1.	381	Oct. 2, 19__	Egbert Construction	Foundations	$165.63	$186.50
2.	382	Oct. 3, 19__	Bome Concrete	Cement	$121.36	$236.21, $1.78
3.	383	Oct. 5, 19__	Ditman Detailing	Finishing	$ 28.32	$123.00
4.	384	Oct. 7, 19__	Simon Hardware	Nails	$ 6.73	
5.	385	Oct. 9, 19__	Bardin Paints	Enamel	$ 64.32	$141.63, $26.41

1.

[Check stub #381: Oct. 2, 19__, To Egbert Construction, For Foundations. Bal. Brot. Ford. 238.46; Deposits 186.50; Total 424.96; This Check 165.63; Bal. Ford. 259.33]

[Check #381: October 2, 19__, Pay to the order of Egbert Construction $165.63, One hundred sixty-five and 63/100 Dollars, Memo: Foundations, signed Delbert Smith, SAMPLE—VOID]

continued

Bank Records 109

Assignment 3.1 *continued*

2.

Check stub 382:
- Oct. 3, 19__
- TO: Bome Concrete
- FOR: Cement
- BAL. BROT. FOR'D.: 259 33
- DEPOSITS: 236 21 / 1 78
- TOTAL: 497 32
- THIS CHECK: 121 36
- BAL. FOR'D.: 375 96

Check 382:
- DELBERT SMITH, D&S Construction Co., 622 Yancy Street, Detroit, MI 48214
- Date: October 3, 19__
- Pay to the order of: Bome Concrete — $121.36
- One hundred twenty-one and 36/100 DOLLARS
- Commerce State Bank, Detroit, MI 48244
- MEMO: Cement
- Signed: Delbert Smith
- SAMPLE—VOID

3.

Check stub 383:
- Oct. 5, 19__
- TO: Ditman Detailing
- FOR: Finishing
- BAL. BROT. FOR'D.: 375 96
- DEPOSITS: 123 00
- TOTAL: 498 96
- THIS CHECK: 28 32
- BAL. FOR'D.: 470 64

Check 383:
- DELBERT SMITH, D&S Construction Co., 622 Yancy Street, Detroit, MI 48214
- Date: October 5, 19__
- Pay to the order of: Ditman Detailing — $28.32
- Twenty-eight and 32/100 DOLLARS
- Commerce State Bank, Detroit, MI 48244
- MEMO: Finishing
- Signed: Delbert Smith
- SAMPLE—VOID

Assignment 3.1 continued

4.

Check stub 384:
- Oct. 7, 19___
- To: Simon Hardware
- For: Nails
- BAL. BROT. FOR'D.: 470 64
- DEPOSITS:
- TOTAL: 470 64
- THIS CHECK: 6 73
- BAL. FOR'D.: 463 91

Check 384:
- DELBERT SMITH
- D&S Construction Co.
- 622 Yancy Street
- Detroit, MI 48214
- Date: October 7, 19___
- Pay to the order of: Simon Hardware — $6.73
- Six and 73/100 DOLLARS
- Commerce State Bank, Detroit, MI 48244
- MEMO: Nails
- SAMPLE—VOID
- Delbert Smith
- ⑆1234567898⑆ 123456789⑊

5.

Check stub 385:
- Oct. 9, 19___
- To: Bardin Paints
- For: Enamel
- BAL. BROT. FOR'D.: 463 91
- DEPOSITS: 141 63
-             26 41
- TOTAL: 631 95
- THIS CHECK: 64 32
- BAL. FOR'D.: 567 63

Check 385:
- DELBERT SMITH
- D&S Construction Co.
- 622 Yancy Street
- Detroit, MI 48214
- Date: October 9, 19___
- Pay to the order of: Bardin Paints — $64.32
- Sixty-four and 32/100 DOLLARS
- Commerce State Bank, Detroit, MI 48244
- MEMO: Enamel
- SAMPLE—VOID
- Delbert Smith
- ⑆1234567898⑆ 123456789⑊

continued

Assignment 3.1 *continued*

6. Assuming that Delbert Smith of the D&S Construction Co., uses a check register instead of or in addition to keeping check stubs, fill out this register using the information from the checks above.

NUMBER	DATE	DESCRIPTION OF TRANSACTION	PAYMENT/DEBIT (−)	√T	FEE (IF ANY) (−)	DEPOSIT/CREDIT (+)	BALANCE $ 238 46
381	10/2	Egbert Construction Foundations	$165 63				−165 63 / 72 83
	10/2	Deposit				186 50	+186 50 / 259 33
382	10/3	Bome Concrete Cement	121 36				−121 36 / 137 97
	10/3	Deposit (2 checks)				237 99	+237 99 / 375 96
383	10/5	Ditman Detailing Finishing	28 32				−28 32 / 347 64
	10/5	Deposit				123 00	+123 00 / 470 64
384	10/7	Simon Hardware Nails	6 73				−6 73 / 463 91
385	10/9	Bardin Paints Enamel	64 32				−64 32 / 399 59
	10/9	Deposit				168 04	+168 04 / 567 63

112 Chapter 3

Assignment 3.1 *continued*

Harry Carilian has a dry cleaning business. He makes a series of deposits to his business checking account. Show how he will complete the deposit slips for his account during the period from August 1 to August 16, 19___.

Deposit Information

	Date of Ticket	Cash Deposited	Checks Deposited	Cash Received
7.	August 1	$ 23.32	$621.31 $123.36	
8.	August 6		$ 6.36 $725.18	$300.00
9.	August 15	$122.60	$ 90.64 $321.60 $ 21.46	

Deposit Slips

Complete these deposit slips using the information above.

7.

FOR DEPOSIT TO THE ACCOUNT OF

CARILIAN DRY CLEANING
1844 N. OAKLAND AVE.
MILWAUKEE, WI 53202

DATE *August 1* 19 ___

SIGN HERE FOR LESS CASH IN TELLERS PRESENCE

First Bank of Wisconsin
Milwaukee, WI 53252

|1:234567898|: 123456789|"

CASH	CURRENCY	23	
	COIN		32
LIST CHECKS SINGLY		621	31
		123	36
TOTAL FROM OTHER SIDE			
TOTAL		767	99
LESS CASH RECIEVED			
NET DEPOSIT		767	99

101

90-6789/2345

USE OTHER SIDE FOR ADDITIONAL LISTING

BE SURE EACH ITEM IS PROPERLY ENDORSED

SAMPLE–VOID

continued

Assignment 3.1 *continued*

8.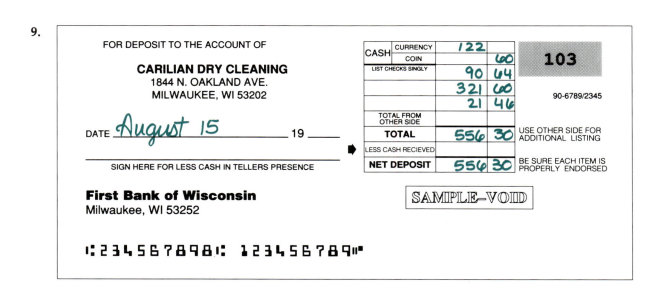

9.

3.2 Reconciliation

Your bank mails a monthly statement showing the activity of each personal and business checking account. This statement includes a listing of:

Deposits made during the period;

Checks honored and paid;

Any service or other charges imposed.

In order to keep your financial records current, it is important that you check the accuracy of the bank's figures against your own, comparing the two with one another using a process called **reconciliation**.

There are several reasons why your checking account records might not agree with those of the bank. Among them are:

A delay by either you or the bank in recording a particular transaction;

An arithmetical error by either you or the bank;

The deduction of service charges by the bank, such as for depositor overdraft, failure to maintain an agreed-upon minimum balance, and so on.

The reverse side of the bank statement often includes a printed reconciliation form for your use.

Example 1 The text of a typical bank statement.

```
                          C H E C K I N G

  YOUR LOWEST BALANCE DURING THIS PERIOD WAS        $285.25  ON  2/29/__
  BEGINNING BALANCE AS OF    2/26/__                   326.91+
     LESS      18 CHECKS                            1,356.22-
     LESS       3 OTHER DEDUCTIONS                      89.85-
     PLUS       3 DEPOSITS                          1,510.38+
     LESS         SERVICE CHARGE                         .00-

  ENDING BALANCE   AS OF   3/24/__                   [  391.22 ]
```

	CHECKS							
CHECK #	AMOUNT	PAID	CHECK #	AMOUNT	PAID	CHECK #	AMOUNT	PAID
851	22.95	02/27	857	40.00	02/28	863	29.96	03/06
852	40.00	02/27	858	150.00	02/28	864	61.00	03/07
853	26.69	02/27	859	260.00	03/17	865	14.87	03/20
854	37.56	02/29	860	38.00	03/10	866	73.48	03/21
855	85.50	02/27	861	20.04	03/19	868*	115.64	03/24
856	44.96	02/28	862	52.64	03/05	869	242.93	03/24

* INDICATES PRECEDING CHECK(S) MISSING FROM NUMERICAL SEQUENCE

OTHER CHECKING DEDUCTIONS

DESCRIPTION		AMOUNT	INITIATED	POSTED	ACCOUNT/ID.	TERMINAL LOCATION
CHARGE	DELUXE CHECK	4.85	800222	3/03	101	
WITHDRAWAL	BANKMACHINE	40.00	03/10	3/10	SERIAL #0320	030-NORTHGATE
WITHDRAWAL	BANKMACHINE	45.00	03/15	3/17	SERIAL #6875	048-WEST SEATTLE

CHECKING DEPOSITS

DESCRIPTION	AMOUNT	INITIATED	POSTED	ACCOUNT/ID.	TERMINAL LOCATION
DEPOSIT	406.00		2/26		
DEPOSIT	704.38		3/03		
DEPOSIT	400.00		3/19		

Note that the bank has listed the cashed checks in order by check number. This makes it easy for you to identify those that have not yet cleared, that is, the checks that have not been presented to the bank for payment by the time the statement is prepared.

Although there are no **service charges** listed on this particular statement, you will note a charge of $4.85 for the printing of personalized checks.

Comparing the information on the statement with your check stubs or check register allows you to reconcile your account.

Example 2 Assuming the statement shown above is for your business checking account, reconcile it with your records, which show the following:

Deposits since the date the statement was prepared: $ 75.00
$240.00
$571.60

Checks outstanding:	Number	Amount
	867	$ 68.54
	870	$ 40.00
	871	$224.10
	872	$ 5.00

Step 1 Compare the checks shown on the statement with your check stubs or register. The amounts of the checks should match.

Step 2 Total any deposits made since the statement was prepared.

$ 75.00
240.00
+ 571.60
$886.60

Step 3 Add the total of the deposits to the ending balance shown on the statement.

$ 391.22   Balance
+   886.60   Deposits
$1,277.82

Step 4 Total any checks and/or charges that are outstanding.

$ 68.54
40.00
224.10
+   5.00
$337.64

Step 5 Subtract the total of the checks and charges from the total of the deposits.

$1,277.82
−   337.64
$ 940.18

Answer The **adjusted**, or **current, balance** is $940.18.

NOTE: The adjusted or current balance should match the figure on the Balance Forward line of the stub of the last check you wrote (or the balance of your check register) minus any bank service charge.

It might be helpful to look at reconciliation in terms of a pair of formulas.

$$\text{statement balance} + \text{additional deposits} - \text{checks outstanding} = \text{adjusted bank balance}$$

$$\text{checkbook balance} - \text{service charges} + \text{credits (bank collections)} = \text{adjusted checkbook balance}$$

Self-Check

Determine the adjusted or current balance for each of the following.

	Balance Shown on Statement	Deposits Not Shown on Statement	Outstanding Checks
Account 1.	$ 238.60	$ 90.56	$ 33.14
		$194.26	$ 126.14
		$132.16	$ 231.22
			$ 2.36
			$ 52.61
Account 2.	$3,721.43	$124.62	$1,212.61
		$246.36	$ 394.68
		$536.28	$1,327.14
		$ 66.22	$ 36.28

ANSWERS Account 1: $655.58 Account 2: $4,694.91
− 445.47   − 2,970.71
$210.11 $1,724.20

A NOTE OF HISTORY

The concept of the checking account is not new. The first checks were issued in England in 1681, before the founding of the Bank of England, which was chartered on July 27, 1694. The charter was granted by the British government to a company of businessmen in return for a loan of £1,200,000. This loan saved the realm from bankruptcy.

Assignment 3.2

Bank Records

1. Calculate the current balance for Carilian Dry Cleaning's business checking account. The balance shown on the statement is $3,172.37. Since then, Harry Carilian has made deposits totaling $2,946.80. Checks are outstanding in the amounts of $2,400.00; $294.86; $434.00; $1,134.39; $220.20; $87.88; and $500.00.

    $3,172.37 Balance shown
 + 2,946.80 Total deposits
    $6,119.17
 − 5,071.33 Total checks outstanding
    $1,047.84 Current balance

$1,047.84 current balance

$2,400.00
294.86
434.00
1,134.39
220.20
87.88
500.00
$5,071.33 Total checks outstanding

2. Mary McReady, treasurer of the Buskirk Community Arts Council, receives a bank statement showing a balance of $924.36. Checking her record of the council's checking account, she notes that since the date of the statement she has made deposits in the amounts of $261.50 and $72.46. Checks are outstanding for $31.67, $236.18, and $52.30. What is the current adjusted blance of the account?

    $924.36 Balance shown
 + 333.96 Total deposits
    $1,258.32
 − 320.15 Total checks outstanding
    $938.17 Current adjusted balance

$938.17 current adjusted balance

$261.50
 + 72.46
$333.96 Total deposits

$ 31.67
236.18
52.30
$320.15 Total checks oustanding

Mary Jean Adamac is a personal financial manager. She is reconciling bank statements for some of her clients. Help her find the current balance for each account.

	Balance from Statement	Deposits since Statement	Outstanding Checks	Adjusted or Current Balance
3.	$8,325.62	$1,264.35 276.21	$ 547.68 $ 237.42 $1,954.28	$7,126.80
4.	$ 926.41	$ 136.18 $ 372.16 $ 221.28	$ 241.37 $ 622.14 $ 38.76	$ 753.76
5.	$1,621.89	$ 28.46 $ 124.32	$ 563.20 $ 27.60 $1,028.82	$ 155.05

3. $8,325.62 Balance shown
 + 1,540.56 Total deposits
    $9,866.18
 + 2,739.38 Total checks outstanding
    $7,126.80 Current balance

4. $926.41 Balance shown
 + 729.62 Total deposits
    $1,656.03
 − 902.27 Total checks outstanding
    $ 753.76 Current balance

5. $1,621.89 Balance shown
 + 152.78 Total deposits
    $1,774.67
 − 1,619.62 Total checks outstanding
    $ 155.05 Current balance

continued

Assignment 3.2 *continued*

6. $ 236.45 $1,672.00 $ 923.61
                 $ 231.62 $ 26.42 $ 868.88
                               $ 321.16   ―――――――――

7. $1,132.25 $ 22.56 $ 90.27
                 $ 37.81 $ 125.82 $ 468.50
                 $ 126.18 $ 634.21   ―――――――――

8. $9,468.21 $1,672.40 $8,621.42
                 $ 278.36 $ 176.28
                               $ 27.86 $2,593.41
                                           ―――――――――

6. $ 236.45 Balance shown
  + $ 1,903.62 Total deposits
    $ 2,140.07
  −   1,271.19 Total checks outstanding
    $ 868.88 Current balance

7. $1,132.25 Balance shown
  +   186.55 Total deposits
    $1,318.80
  −   850.30 Total checks outstanding
       468.50 Curent balance

8. $9.468.21 Balance shown
  + 1,950.76 Total deposits
    $11,418.97
  − 8,825.56 Total checks outstanding
    $2,593.41 Current balance

Comprehensive Problems for Chapter 3

Bank Records

Harry Carilian has a dry cleaning business. He makes a series of deposits to his business checking account and writes a number of checks. Show how he will fill out the checks and keep records for his account during the period August 1 to August 16, 19___.

Deposit Information

Date of Ticket	Cash Deposited	Checks
August 1	$ 23.32	$621.31
		$123.36
August 6		$ 6.36
		$425.18
August 15	$122.60	$ 90.64
		$321.60
		$ 21.46

Check Information

Fill in each of these checks and check stubs, using the information given below. The balance brought forward from stub #793 is $3,210.61.

	Check Number	Date	Written To	For	Amount of Check
1.	794	August 2	Albert Manufacturing Co.	Solvents	$2,525.00
2.	795	August 4	Manfridi Oil Co.	Heating oil	$ 194.36
3.	796	August 5	Ace Garage	Truck repairs	$ 425.00
4.	797	August 7	Peterson Insurance Agency	Liability insurance	$1,034.29
5.	798	August 9	Albert Manufacturing Co.	Plastic bags and supplies	$ 230.10
6.	799	August 16	Bonstein Tire Co.	New truck tire	$ 52.28
7.	800	August 16	Harry T. Abbott	Building rent	$ 500.00

continued

Comprehensive Problems continued

1.

Check Stub 794:
- Aug. 2, 19__
- TO: Albert Mfg. Co.
- FOR: Solvents

BAL. BROT. FOR'D.	3,210	61
DEPOSITS	767	99
TOTAL	3,978	60
THIS CHECK	2,525	00
BAL. FOR'D.	1,453	60

Check 794:
- CARILIAN DRY CLEANING
- 1844 N. OAKLAND AVE.
- MILWAUKEE, WI 53202
- Date: August 2, 19__
- 90-6789/2345
- PAY TO THE ORDER OF: Albert Manufacturing Co. — $2,525.00
- Two thousand five hundred twenty-five and 00/100 DOLLARS
- First Bank of Wisconsin, Milwaukee, WI 53252
- MEMO: Solvents
- SAMPLE–VOID
- Harry Carilian
- ⑈123456789⑈: 123456789⑈

2.

Check Stub 795:
- Aug. 4, 19__
- TO: Manfridi Oil Co.
- FOR: Heating Oil

BAL. BROT. FOR'D.	1,453	60
DEPOSITS		
TOTAL	1,453	60
THIS CHECK	194	36
BAL. FOR'D.	1,259	24

Check 795:
- CARILIAN DRY CLEANING
- 1844 N. OAKLAND AVE.
- MILWAUKEE, WI 53202
- Date: August 4, 19__
- 90-6789/2345
- PAY TO THE ORDER OF: Manfridi Oil Co. — $194.36
- One hundred ninety-four and 36/100 DOLLARS
- First Bank of Wisconsin, Milwaukee, WI 53252
- MEMO: Heating Oil
- SAMPLE–VOID
- Harry Carilian
- ⑈123456789⑈: 123456789⑈

Comprehensive Problems continued

3.

Check #796
Date: August 5, 19__
Pay to the order of: Ace Garage
Amount: $425.00
Four hundred twenty-five and no/100 DOLLARS
CARILIAN DRY CLEANING
1844 N. OAKLAND AVE.
MILWAUKEE, WI 53202
First Bank of Wisconsin
Milwaukee, WI 53252
Memo: Truck Repairs
Signed: Harry Carilian
SAMPLE—VOID
⑈⑈⑈⑈⑈⑈⑈⑈⑈: ⑈⑈⑈⑈⑈⑈⑈⑈⑈"

Check stub #796:
Aug. 5, 19__
To: Ace Garage
For: Truck Repairs

BAL. BROT. FOR'D.	1,259 24
DEPOSITS	
TOTAL	1,259 24
THIS CHECK	425 00
BAL. FOR'D.	834 24

4.

Check #797
Date: August 7, 19__
Pay to the order of: Peterson Insurance Agency
Amount: $1,034.29
One thousand thirty-four and 29/100 DOLLARS
CARILIAN DRY CLEANING
1844 N. OAKLAND AVE.
MILWAUKEE, WI 53202
First Bank of Wisconsin
Milwaukee, WI 53252
Memo: Liability Insurance
Signed: Harry Carilian
SAMPLE—VOID

Check stub #797:
Aug. 7, 19__
To: Peterson Ins. Agency
For: Liability Insurance

BAL. BROT. FOR'D.	834 24
DEPOSITS	431 54
TOTAL	1,265 78
THIS CHECK	1,034 29
BAL. FOR'D.	231 49

continued

Comprehensive Problems continued

5.

Check stub 798:
- Aug. 9, 19___
- To: Albert Mfg. Co.
- For: Plastic Bags + Supplies

BAL. BROT. FOR'D.	231	49
DEPOSITS		
TOTAL	231	49
THIS CHECK	230	10
BAL. FOR'D.	1	39

Check 798:
- CARILIAN DRY CLEANING
- 1844 N. OAKLAND AVE.
- MILWAUKEE, WI 53202
- 90-6789/2345
- Date: August 9, 19___
- Pay to the order of: Albert Manufacturing Co. — $230.10
- Two hundred thirty and 10/100 DOLLARS
- First Bank of Wisconsin, Milwaukee, WI 53252
- Memo: Plastic Bags + Supplies
- Signed: Harry Carilian
- SAMPLE—VOID

6.

Check stub 799:
- Aug. 16, 19___
- To: Bonstein Tire Co.
- For: New Truck Tire

BAL. BROT. FOR'D.	1	39
DEPOSITS	556	30
TOTAL	557	69
THIS CHECK	52	28
BAL. FOR'D.	505	41

Check 799:
- CARILIAN DRY CLEANING
- 1844 N. OAKLAND AVE.
- MILWAUKEE, WI 53202
- 90-6789/2345
- Date: August 16, 19___
- Pay to the order of: Bonstein Tire Co. — $52.28
- Fifty-two and 28/100 DOLLARS
- First Bank of Wisconsin, Milwaukee, WI 53252
- Memo: New Truck Tire
- Signed: Harry Carilian
- SAMPLE—VOID

Comprehensive Problems *continued*

7.

800		
	Aug. 16	, 19 ___
TO	Harry T. Abbott	
FOR	Building Rent	

BAL. BROT. FOR'D.	505	41
DEPOSITS		
TOTAL	505	41
THIS CHECK	500	00
BAL. FOR'D.	5	41

CARILIAN DRY CLEANING
1844 N. OAKLAND AVE.
MILWAUKEE, WI 53202

August 16 19 ___ 800
90-6789/2345

PAY TO THE ORDER OF Harry T. Abbott $ 500.00

Five hundred and no/100 ——————— DOLLARS

First Bank of Wisconsin
Milwaukee, WI 53252

MEMO Building Rent   SAMPLE—VOID   Harry Carilian

⑆123456789⑆: 123456789‖'

continued

Bank Records **125**

Comprehensive Problems *continued*

8. Assuming that Carilian Dry Cleaning uses a check register rather than or in addition to keeping check stubs, fill out this register using the information given above.

NUMBER	DATE	DESCRIPTION OF TRANSACTION	PAYMENT/DEBIT (−)	√T	FEE (IF ANY) (−)	DEPOSIT/CREDIT (+)	BALANCE
							$3,210.61
	8/1	Deposit				$767.99	+767.99
							3,978.60
794	8/2	Albert Manufacturing — Solvents	2,525.00				−2,525.00
							1,453.60
795	8/4	Manfridi Oil Co. — Heating Oil	194.36				−194.36
							1,259.24
796	8/5	Ace Garage — Truck Repairs	425.00				−425.00
							834.24
	8/6	Deposit				431.54	+431.54
							1,265.78
797	8/7	Peterson Insurance Agency — Liability Insurance	1,034.29				−1,034.29
							231.49
798	8/9	Albert Manufacturing — Plastic Bags & Supplies	230.10				−230.10
							1.39
	8/15	Deposit				556.30	+556.30
							557.69
799	8/16	Bonstein Tire Co. — New Truck Tire	52.28				−52.28
							505.41
800	8/16	Harry T. Abbott — Building Rent	500.00				−500.00
							5.41

Help Narci Espinosa, a financial consultant, in finding the current balance in the following checking accounts, each of which belongs to one of her clients.

	Balance from Bank Statement	Checks Outstanding	Deposits since Last Statement	Current or Adjusted Balance
9.	$3,794.12	$ 95.36 956.25	$ 523.39	$3,265.90
10.	$ 37.50	$ 327.95 536.27 14.67	$ 927.30 24.56	$110.47
11.	$9,586.02	$1,920.35 5,056.19 2,561.43	$ 35.82 1,004.26	$1,088.13
12.	$ 327.12	$ 234.57 225.96 32.66	$ 123.34	$−42.73 (Negative balance)

continued

Comprehensive Problems *continued*

13. $2,765.92 $1,356.22 $2,987.00 $3,625
                      1,234.66   462.96

14. Can you think of a reason why Ms. Espinosa might want to contact one of her clients at once? If so, what is it?

   Client in Problem 12 is overdrawn by $42.73

Case 1

Help Danie Montreat, who owns a fashion model agency, reconcile her checking account. The balance on her statement is $2,375.21.

Checks outstanding: $6,375.41

Deposits made since statement: $5,681.26

Service charges on bank statement: $5.50 for overdraft

Balance according to Danie's check register: $1,686.56

a) Find the current adjusted balance.

b) Do you think Danie is managing her business account adequately? Why or why not?

Case 2

Bern Hertzberg owns a small catering business. His bank statement shows a balance of $248.68. Since the date of his last statement, Bern has deposited $624.32, $321.18, and $246.81. He has written the following checks:

To	For	Amount
Banchek's Market	Beef roasts	$236.00
Tanford's Wholesale Foods	Flour	38.64
Jenrath Rentals	Cocktail glasses	84.26
Wiletta Morris	Services	124.50

Bern's records show a balance of $276.55. His bank statement shows a balance of $248.68 and notes the return of an uncollectible check deposited to his account for $24.37. Also, he has been assessed a service charge of $3.50 for falling below a minimum balance of $250.

a) Reconcile the balances.

b) State your opinion of Bern's banking abilities and explain it.

Key Terms

Adjusted, or current, balance
Balance brought forward
Balance forward
Check
Check register
Check stub
Checking account
Deposit
Deposit slip
Reconciliation
Restricted endorsement
Service charge
Share account

Key Concepts

- A check is a written order from the depositor to a banking institution, directing payment of some of the depositor's funds to another party.

- Checks should be written legibly and in ink. Precautions should be taken to prevent additional words or digits from being added at a later time before deposit.
- As it is written, each check is recorded on a stub or in a check register. Deposits are also noted. This information should be kept accurate and up to date.
- A deposit slip is a ticket that accompanies funds when they are turned over to the banking institution for placement in the checking account.
- When checks are deposited, they are endorsed on the back by the individual or business cashing them. Use of the words "for deposit only" assures that no one other than the party for whom it is intended can cash the check.
- A bank statement is sent to the depositor detailing deposits made, checks paid, and service charges assessed.
- When the statement is received, the depositor reconciles it with the check stubs or register, comparing the two sets of data and adjusting the balance accordingly.

4
Ratio and Proportion

Business Takes a Positive Approach
PROCTER & GAMBLE

In the early 1980s Procter & Gamble faced new challenges. Its position in the market place was dropping, and its earnings showed their biggest decline in over 35 years. Procter & Gamble bounced back, however, thanks to an energized approach and a forward-looking strategy. The firm discovered that its ratio of investment in established products as compared to research and development was too large. To correct this, it invested heavily in product development and in consumer and distribution research. The result was improved products with familiar names such as Tide, Pampers, and Crest. Tuning into dealer needs, Procter & Gamble offered new package sizes designed for ease of handling. The company made a major capital investment, modernizing machines and factory facilities to accommodate new technology. It also chose to support its products by expensive advertising: The company spent $1,297,000,000 to advertise more than 80 different brands of products. Procter & Gamble's comeback was phenomenal. The proportion of the market it captured, its earnings, and its profits have climbed dramatically. Maintaining this position is an ongoing commitment for the company as old and new competitors gather their forces to strike back. The battle will be a fierce one.

Learning Objectives

After reading and studying this chapter and working the problems, you will be able to:

- Write and read ratios.
- Compare unlike quantities in ratio form.
- Compare like quantities in ratio form.
- Calculate a comparison-to-one ratio.
- Figure a ratio comparison of more than two numbers.
- Determine a true proportion.
- Set up and apply the proportion principle in a variety of situations.

The concepts of ratio and proportion form an important bridge of understanding between the basic arithmetic processes, particularly fractions and decimals, which we considered in Chapters 1 and 2, and the concept of percentage, which we will discuss in Chapter 5.

Ratios can be regarded as a type of fraction. They also bear a close relationship to rate percents. Like percents, ratios are an important tool in the business world. They offer the businessperson a means of comparison that is easy to communicate to others.

As you will see in this chapter, proportions, or pairs of ratios, are principally useful as a practical method of solving narrative problems. Later, when you begin to study Chapter 5, note that the percentage formula is in fact merely a simplification of the proportion comparison.

4.1 Ratio

The one thing certain about life is that it is flexible. Situations and values change constantly in the business world. In order to put values in perspective, we make comparisons using expressions such as "more," "less," "farther," "sooner," and so on.

A **ratio** is the expression of a relationship between two numbers. We compare numerical values by either subtraction or division. For example, suppose Harry's Hardware House had a gain of $1,200 one year and a gain of $300 the next year. These gains can be compared in the following two ways:

By Subtraction

$1,200 gain for first year
−   300 gain for second year
$ 900 difference

By Division

$\frac{\$1,200}{\$300} = 4$ times the gain

$\frac{\$300}{\$1,200} = \frac{1}{4}$ the gain

Using subtraction, you are saying that the difference between $1,200 and $300 is $900, which means the business gained $900 less the second year than it did the first year.

Using division, you are saying that $1,200 is 4 times as large as $300, which means that the gain the first year was 4 times as large as the gain the second year. You can also say that $300 is $\frac{1}{4}$ as large as $1,200, which means that the gain the second year is only $\frac{1}{4}$ as large as the gain the first year. When you are setting up a ratio, the number to which a comparison is made is always the denominator of the fraction.

Writing and Reading Ratios

We call the comparison by division the ratio method. You can regard ratios as fractions because they compare two numerical values using division. Therefore, you can solve problems concerned with ratios by using the procedures that apply to fractions. (See Chapter 2.) For example, $\frac{36}{54}$ can be reduced to lowest terms, or $\frac{2}{3}$. The common ways to write the ratio of "36 to 54" are 2 : 3, 2 ÷ 3, 2 to 3, or $\frac{2}{3}$. When you compare more than two items, write the ratio in a similar form. For example, the ratio of 3 to 5 to 7 can be expressed as 3 : 5 : 7.

Though sometimes written as fractions, ratios are not read as fractions. Read the bar that separates the terms of the ratio as "to." Thus, you read $\frac{2}{75}$ as "2 to 75" or "2 out of 75."

You can use ratios to compare like and unlike quantities. When two quantities of the same kind, or like quantities, are compared, each quantity must be expressed in the *same units*. For example, the ratio of 6 inches to 1 foot is not $\frac{6}{1}$, but $\frac{6}{12}$, because 1 foot contains 12 inches. This can be reduced from $\frac{6}{12}$ to $\frac{1}{2}$ or 1 : 2.

Comparing Unlike Quantities

Many times we use ratios to compare unlike quantities, such as miles to gallons, houses to TV sets, acres to bushels, and so on. When you compare unlike quantities in business situations, it is important to keep the labels of the numbers in mind throughout the computation.

Example 1 In your role as market researcher, you are asked to find the ratio of the number of cars to households in the city of Enis, Nevada. Cars number 540; households number 360. Express the ratio in the form of a fraction and reduce it to lowest terms.

Step 1 Compare the numbers in the form of fractions as stated. In this instance, the number of cars is the numerator because it is mentioned first in the comparison. $\frac{540 \text{ cars}}{360 \text{ households}}$

Step 2 Reduce the ratio. $\frac{3}{2}$

Answer The ratio of cars to households is $\frac{3 \text{ cars}}{2 \text{ households}}$.

Making a Ratio Comparison to One

In business situations we often use ratios instead of percentages to express comparisons. A common form of ratio is the comparison to one. We achieve this by taking the ratio expressed as a fraction and dividing the numerator by the denominator. In ratio problems, the number following the word "to" is normally the denominator of the fractions.

Example 2 Alice Wilson, the store's buyer for children's wear, wanted to know the ratio of children per family. If there are 29 children to 10 families, what is the ratio to 1 family?

Step 1 Divide the numerator by the denominator. $\dfrac{29 \text{ children}}{10 \text{ families}} = 2.9$

Step 2 Place this result over 1. $\dfrac{2.9 \text{ children}}{1 \text{ family}}$

Answer The ratio of children per family is 2.9 children for every 1 family.

Making a Ratio Comparison of More than Two Numbers

Many ratios are concerned with the comparison of more than two numbers or quantities. In this case, the sum of the numbers compared is the denominator and each item is the numerator.

Example 3 Brownell Manufacturing produces 25 file cabinets a day. Of these, 4 are red, 12 are tan, and the rest are black. What is the ratio of red cabinets, tan cabinets, and black cabinets to the total number of cabinets produced?

Step 1 Use the total number of cabinets as the denominator. $\dfrac{}{25}$

Step 2 Place the number of each color cabinet produced over the total. Red $= \dfrac{4}{25}$

Note that the number of black cabinets is found by totaling the number of red (4) and the number of tan (12) and subtracting the sum from the total given in the problem (25): $25 - 16 = 9$.

Tan $= \dfrac{12}{25}$

Black $= \dfrac{9}{25}$

Answer The ratios of red, tan, and black cabinets to the total are $\dfrac{4}{25} : \dfrac{12}{25} : \dfrac{9}{25}$, respectively.

Applying Ratios

Now that you understand how to form ratios, the next step is to see how they can be used.

Example 4 Conrad, Boyle, and Winters decide to dissolve their partnership and divide their land assets of 408 acres in the ratio of 3 : 4 : 5, respectively. Find how many acres each of the partners will receive. Note that what is really being said is that one partner will receive three parts, another partner will receive four parts, and the last will receive five parts.

Step 1 Find the sum of the parts into which the land is divided. $3 + 4 + 5 = 12$

Step 2 Form a ratio expressing what part each partner will receive. Conrad $= \dfrac{3}{12} = \dfrac{1}{4}$

Boyle $= \frac{4}{12} = \frac{1}{3}$

Winters $= \frac{5}{12}$

Step 3   Multiply the item to be divided, the acreage, by the fractional equivalent for each part.

Conrad: $408 \times \frac{1}{4} = 102$

Answer   Conrad will receive 102 acres, Boyle will receive 136 acres, and Winters will receive 170 acres.

Boyle: $408 \times \frac{1}{3} = 136$

Winters: $408 \times \frac{5}{12} = 170$

NOTE: To check your calculation, note that the sum of acres that each partner receives should equal the total acreage: 102 + 136 + 170 = 408.

Self-Check

1. What is the ratio of Marilyn's earnings to Sebastian's earnings if Marilyn earned $240 and Sebastian earned $320?

2. There are 240 houses for every 9 newspaper stands. What is the ratio of houses to newspaper stands?

3. Extension A of a building is 36 months old. Extension B is 6 years old. What is the ratio of the age of extension A to the age of extension B?

4. For every 3 miles of roadway there are 87 reflectors. What is the ratio of reflectors to each mile?

5. Morris's Moorage held 37 boats. Of these, 4 were fishing boats, 8 were speedboats, 10 were sailboats, and the rest were cabin cruisers. What are the ratios of fishing boats, speedboats, sailboats, and cabin cruisers to the total number of boats?

6. Conklin, Juarez, and Peron were in a partnership with a ratio of 3 : 5 : 2, respectively. If a profit of $100,000 were realized, how much would each one receive of the profit?

ANSWERS   1. $\frac{240}{320} = \frac{3}{4}$ 2. $\frac{240}{9} = \frac{80}{3}$ or 80 : 3   3. $\frac{3}{6} = \frac{1}{2}$ or 1 : 2   4. $\frac{87}{3} = \frac{29}{1}$ or 29 : 1   5. Fishing boats, 4 : 37; speedboats, 8 : 37; sailboats, 10 : 37, cabin cruisers, 15 : 37   6. Conklin, $30,000; Juarez, $50,000; Peron, $20,000

APPROXIMATING WITH RATIOS

In many business situations a quick decision must be made. Many times an approximation of a condition can give clearer insight into a problem or discussion. The combination of estimation, rounding, and ratios can be a useful tool.

EXAMPLE: Last week Southsport, Inc., sold 97 pairs of running shoes and 195 pairs of aerobic shoes. What is the approximate ratio of the sale of aerobic shoes to the sale of running shoes?

SOLUTION: Set up the ratio first, round, and then reduce.

$$\frac{\text{aerobic shoes}}{\text{running shoes}} = \frac{195}{97} = \frac{200}{100} = \frac{2}{1} \text{ (after rounding)}$$

ANSWER: Approximately twice as many aerobic shoes were sold as running shoes.

Assignment 4.1

Ratio and Proportion

Write each of the following as a ratio and reduce.

1. 10 chairs to 8 people   5 : 4

2. 9 boxes to 27 component parts   1 : 3

3. 16 families to 48 children   1 : 3

4. 168 meters to 63 meters   8 : 3

5. 72 females to 180 males   2 : 5

6. 25 quarters to 5 cents (compare in pennies)   125 : 1

7. State what ratio to a total distance of 1,000 miles a cargo ship has covered at the end of (a) 100 miles; (b) 200 miles; (c) 250 miles; (d) 600 miles; (e) 875 miles.

$$\frac{100}{1{,}000} = \frac{1}{10} \qquad \frac{200}{1{,}000} = \frac{1}{5} \qquad \frac{250}{1{,}000} = \frac{1}{4} \qquad \frac{600}{1{,}000} = \frac{6}{10} = \frac{3}{5} \qquad \frac{875}{1{,}000} = \frac{35}{40} = \frac{7}{8}$$

a) $\frac{1}{10}$ b) $\frac{1}{5}$ c) $\frac{1}{4}$ d) $\frac{3}{5}$ e) $\frac{7}{8}$

8. On the night shift of Compo Assembly Plant, there are 20 females and 15 males.

   a) State the ratio of the number of males to the total number of people on the night shift.

   20 female
   + 15 males
   35 Total people

   $\frac{15}{35} = \frac{3}{7}$

   $\frac{3 \text{ males}}{7 \text{ people}}$

   b) State the ratio of the males to females.

   $\frac{15}{20} = \frac{3}{4}$

   $\frac{3 \text{ males}}{4 \text{ females}}$

continued

Assignment 4.1 *continued*

9. Coleman's Novelties, Inc., divided its inventory of 720 ballpoint pens in the following manner: 140 pens to gift sets, 180 pens to office supplies, 100 pens to individual sales, 240 pens to school supplies, and the remaining pens to bookstore supplies. Express the ratios of pens divided into gift sets, office supplies, individual sales, school supplies, and bookstore supplies to the total inventory of pens.

9. *Note:* If fractions are all kept in terms of 36^{ths}, the answer would be $7:9:5:12:3$.

```
140      720 Total inventory
180    - 660
240      60  Bookstore
100
660
```

$$\frac{7}{36}; \frac{1}{4}; \frac{5}{36}; \frac{1}{3}; \frac{1}{12}$$

Gift sets $\quad \frac{140}{720} = \frac{7}{36}$

Office supplies $\quad \frac{180}{720} = \frac{2}{8} = \frac{1}{4}$

Individual $\quad \frac{100}{720} = \frac{10}{72} = \frac{5}{36}$

School supplies $\quad \frac{240}{720} = \frac{8}{9} = \frac{1}{3}$

Bookstore $\quad \frac{60}{720} = \frac{1}{12}$

10. Package A weights 135 pounds, package B weighs 160 pounds, and package C weighs 105 pounds.

   a) What is the ratio of the weight of package A to the weight of package B?

   $$\frac{A}{B} = \frac{135}{160} = \frac{27}{32}$$

   $$\frac{27 \; A}{32 \; B}$$

   b) What is the ratio of the weight of package B to the total weights of the packages?

   ```
   135
   160
   105
   400 Total weight
   ```

   $$\frac{B}{Total} = \frac{160}{400} = \frac{2}{5}$$

   $$\frac{2 \; B}{5 \; Total\ weight}$$

   c) What is the ratio of the weight of package C to the weight of package B?

   $$\frac{C}{B} = \frac{105}{160} = \frac{21}{32}$$

   $$\frac{21 \; C}{32 \; B}$$

11. A lot measures 100 feet long by 720 inches wide. What is the ratio of the length to the width?

   $$\frac{100 \text{ ft long}}{720 \text{ in. wide}} = \frac{100 \text{ ft}}{60 \text{ ft}} = \frac{5}{3}$$

   Changed inches to feet

   $$\frac{5 \text{ ft long}}{3 \text{ ft wide}}$$

12. There are 26 supermarkets for every 20 miles. For a location study, what is the ratio of supermarkets to each mile?

   $$\frac{26 \text{ markets}}{20 \text{ miles}} = \frac{1.3}{1}$$

   $$\frac{1.3 \text{ markets}}{1 \text{ mile}}$$

13. In a recent survey, it was found that there were 408 radios for 120 households. What is the ratio of radios per household?

   $$\frac{408 \text{ radios}}{120 \text{ households}} = \frac{3.4}{1}$$

   $$\frac{3.4 \text{ radios}}{1 \text{ household}}$$

continued

Assignment 4.1 *continued*

14. The Whitney Wallpaper Store had a net income of $30,000 last year. Monthly mortgage payments are $500. What is the ratio of last year's net income to the total yearly mortgage payments?

    $$\frac{\$30,000 \text{ last year's income}}{\$500 \text{ mortgage payment for one month}} \qquad \frac{\$5 \text{ last year's income}}{\$1 \text{ total yearly mortgage}}$$

    $$\begin{array}{r}\$500 \text{ Mortgage for 1 month} \\ \times \quad 12 \text{ Months} \\ \hline \$6,000 \text{ Total yearly mortgage}\end{array}$$

    $$\frac{30,000}{6,000} = \frac{5}{1}$$

15. For Colica's Bakery recipe file, reduce the ratio of 22 cups of flour to 6 loaves of bread to a one-loaf comparison.

    $$\frac{22 \text{ cups}}{6 \text{ loaves}} = \frac{3.66\frac{2}{3}}{1} \qquad \frac{3.66\frac{2}{3}}{1} \text{ or } \frac{3\frac{2}{3} \text{ cups of flour}}{1 \text{ loaf}}$$

16. The estate of C. W. Powers is to be divided among his business creditors with a ratio of 4 : 3 : 5. If the total estate is valued at $492,000, how much money will each creditor receive before taxes?

    $$\begin{array}{c}\frac{4}{3} \\ \frac{5}{12}\end{array} \qquad \cancel{492,000}^{41,000} \times \frac{4}{\cancel{12}_{1}} = \$164,000$$

    $$492,000 \times \frac{3}{12} = \$123,000$$

    4 : 3 : 5
    $164,000; $123,000; $205,000

17. Dale Morgan earned $18,000 as a salesman. The sales manager, Howard Chung, earned $30,000.

    a) What is the ratio of Dale's earnings to Howard's?

    $$\frac{\text{Dale's}}{\text{Howard's}} = \frac{18,000}{30,000} = \frac{3}{5} \qquad \frac{\$3 \text{ Dale's earnings}}{\$5 \text{ Howard's earnings}}$$

    b) What is the ratio of Howard's earnings to Dale's?

    $$\frac{\text{Howard's}}{\text{Dale's}} = \frac{30,000}{18,000} = \frac{5}{3} \qquad \frac{\$5 \text{ Howard's earnings}}{\$3 \text{ Dale's earnings}}$$

4.2 Proportion

A statement of two fractions naming the same ratio is a **proportion**. It shows that the two ratios are equal. For example,

$$\frac{2}{7} = \frac{4}{14}.$$

This should look familiar to you. In Chapter 2, on fractions, these were called equivalent fractions. There are four numbers in a proportion. If three numbers are given, it is a simple task to find the fourth, or missing number.

In the example above, the numerators, 2 and 4, and the denominators, 7 and 14, are the four numbers, or *terms*, in the proportion. The first numerator, 2, and the second denominator, 14, are called the *extremes*. The first denominator, 7, and the second numerator, 4, are called the *means* of the proportion.

$$\begin{array}{c}\text{Extreme} \\ \text{Mean}\end{array} \frac{2}{7} = \frac{4}{14} \begin{array}{c}\text{Mean} \\ \text{Extreme}\end{array}$$

The **rule of proportion** is: The product of the means equals the product of the extremes. If the ratios were expressed in this form, $2 : 7 = 4 : 14$, the same principle holds true. The product of the means, the inner terms, equals the product of the extremes, the outer terms.

Outer terms

$2 : 7 = 4 : 14$ $2 \times 14 = 7 \times 4$

Inner terms $28 = 28$

Another way to express this relationship is to say that the cross products are equal.

$$\frac{2}{7} = \frac{4}{14}$$

$$2 \times 14 = 4 \times 7$$

$$28 = 28$$

This proportion is read, "2 is to 7 as 4 is to 14."

The rule of proportion applies to *any* proportion. You can use it either to test the correctness of a proportion quickly or to find any missing term of a proportion when the other three are given. We can represent the unknown, or missing term, with the letter N.

Example 1 $\dfrac{2}{7} = \dfrac{N}{14}$

Step 1   Cross multiply to form an equation. $7 \times N = 2 \times 14$

$7 \times N = 28$

Step 2   Divide to find the missing number. $N = \dfrac{28}{7}$

To find what number multiplied by 7 will give the product 28, you must divide 28 by 7.

Division undoes the process of multiplication so that the answer can be found.

$$\begin{array}{r}4\\7\overline{)28}\\\underline{28}\end{array}$$

Ratio and Proportion

Answer   The missing number is 4.

Example 2   If the A&G Farmer Cooperative processes 15 tons of wheat in 2 days, how many tons will it process in 6 days, assuming the co-op continues to work at the same rate?

Step 1   Set up the proportion.

$$\frac{15 \text{ tons}}{2 \text{ days}} = \frac{N \text{ tons}}{6 \text{ days}}$$

Step 2   Cross multiply and form an equation.

$$2 \times N = 15 \times 6$$
$$2 \times N = 90$$

Step 3   Divide.

$$\begin{array}{r} 45 \\ 2\overline{)90} \\ \underline{8} \\ 10 \\ \underline{10} \end{array}$$

Answer   The missing number is 45 tons.

NOTE: It is important to keep the quantities labeled and to place them in the correct order. If you label the first ratio tons to days, the second ratio must also be labeled tons to days, not days to tons.

Self-Check

Determine whether each of the following proportions is correct or incorrect.

1. $\dfrac{5}{9} = \dfrac{15}{27}$ _____

2. $2 : 1 = 60 : 180$ _____

3. 1 is to $1\frac{1}{2}$ as 3 is to $4\frac{1}{2}$ _____

Fill in the missing number.

4. $\dfrac{N}{3} = \dfrac{8}{12}$ _____

5. $\dfrac{30}{45} = \dfrac{2}{N}$ _____

ANSWERS   1. Correct   2. Incorrect   3. Correct   4. $N = 2$ 5. $N = 3$

IS EVEN EVEN BETTER?

In some parts of Africa, odd numbers are looked on unfavorably. Certain tribes once believed that a group is vulnerable and may even be cursed if it is made up of an odd number of people. This belief is not too far from some contemporary peoples' distrust of the odd number 13 or of inviting an uneven number of guests to a dinner party.

Assignment 4.2

Ratio and Proportion

Determine whether each of the following proportions is correct or incorrect.

1. $\dfrac{10}{3} = \dfrac{20}{6}$ _____ Correct

2. $\dfrac{5}{12} = \dfrac{7}{15}$ _____ Incorrect

3. $8 : 3 = 24 : 9$ _____ Correct

4. $\dfrac{5}{9} = \dfrac{15}{27}$ _____ Correct

5. $2 : 1 = 60 : 180$ _____ Incorrect

6. 1 is to $1\tfrac{1}{2}$ as 3 is to $4\tfrac{1}{2}$ _____ Correct

Solve for the unknown.

7. $\dfrac{1}{N} = \dfrac{5}{15}$ _____ $N = 3$ $\quad$ $5N = 15$; $N = 3$

8. $\dfrac{49}{7} = \dfrac{N}{1}$ _____ $N = 7$ $\quad$ $7N = 49$; $N = 7$

9. $108 : 9 = 1 : N$ _____ $N = \tfrac{1}{12}$ or $.08\tfrac{1}{3}$ $\quad$ $108N = 9$; $N = \tfrac{1}{12}$

10. $\dfrac{N}{14} = \dfrac{1}{7}$ _____ $N = 2$ $\quad$ $7N = 14$; $N = 2$

11. $\dfrac{10.5}{250} = \dfrac{N}{300}$ _____ $N = 12.6$ $\quad$ $250N = 3{,}150$; $N = 12.6$

12. $2 : N = 10\tfrac{1}{2} : 420$ _____ $N = 80$ $\quad$ $10\tfrac{1}{2}N = 840$; $N = 80$

13. $\dfrac{25}{N} = \dfrac{5}{3}$ _____ $N = 15$ $\quad$ $5N = 75$; $N = 15$

14. $18 : 23 = 36 : N$ _____ $N = 46$ $\quad$ $18N = 828$; $N = 46$

15. A trucker for Travel Movers, Inc. calculated that on a trip of 1,050 miles he used 70 gallons of gasoline. How many gallons would the trucker use on a trip of 1,575 miles if he carried the same weight and covered similar terrain?

    $\dfrac{1{,}050 \text{ miles}}{70 \text{ gallons}} = \dfrac{1{,}575 \text{ miles}}{N \text{ gallons}}$

    $1{,}050N = 70 \times 1{,}575$
    $1{,}050N = 110{,}250$
    $N = 105$

    $N = 105$ gallons

continued

Assignment 4.2 *continued*

16. Lola Sterns, a marketing representative for LDR Pharmaceuticals, had an annual income of $36,000 and spent $6,000 in income tax. How much would she pay in income tax if her salary was raised to $42,000, assuming she is taxed at the same rate?

    $$\frac{\$36,000 \text{ income}}{\$6,000 \text{ tax}} = \frac{\$42,000 \text{ income}}{N \text{ tax}}$$

    36,000N = 42,000 × 6,000
    36,000N = 252,000,000
    N = 7,000

    N = $7,000 paid in taxes

17. Jensen Repair Service can buy 2 large stove bolts for $1.38. At that rate, how much will the company have to pay for 6 bolts of the same size?

    $$\frac{2 \text{ bolts}}{\$1.38} = \frac{6 \text{ bolts}}{\$N}$$

    2N = 6 × $1.38
    2N = $8.28
    N = $4.14

    N = $4.14 for six bolts

18. One and one-half tons of rock chips from MacGilva's Landscaping is sold at the quarry for $900. At this rate, what is the cost of a 60-pound sack of chips?

    $1\frac{1}{2}$ tons = 3,000 lb

    $$\frac{1\frac{1}{2} \text{ tons}}{\$900} = \frac{60 \text{ lb}}{\$N}$$

    3,000N = 60 × 900
    3,000N = 54,000
    N = $18

    N = $18 for a 60-lb sack

19. At Vano Paviro's Hair Care Outlet, an eight-ounce bottle of cream hair rinse costs 77 cents. At this price, what would a quart of cream rinse cost?

    1 quart = 32 ounces

    $$\frac{8 \text{ oz}}{77¢} = \frac{32 \text{ oz}}{N¢}$$

    8N = 32 × .77
    8N = 24.64
    N = $3.08

    $3.08 per quart

20. In bidding for a job for Millcreek Land Developers you find that you need to cover 336 square feet of land with grass seed. If 5 pounds of seed will cover 210 square feet of land, how many pounds will you need?

    $$\frac{5 \text{ lb}}{210 \text{ sq ft}} = \frac{N \text{ lb}}{336 \text{ sq ft}}$$

    210N = 336 × 5
    210N = 1,680
    N = 8

    N = 8 lb

21. A holding tank at Morris Motorhomes Company holds 1,200 gallons of gasoline when filled to a depth of 8 feet. How much will the tank hold when filled to a depth of 3 feet?

    $$\frac{1,200 \text{ gal}}{8 \text{ ft}} = \frac{N \text{ gal}}{3 \text{ ft}}$$

    8N = 3 × 1,200
    8N = 3600
    N = 450 gal

    N = 450 gallons

22. Assume that a certain ratio of men to women is 5 : 3.

    $$\frac{5 \text{ men}}{3 \text{ women}} = \frac{35 \text{ men}}{N \text{ women}}$$

    a) How many women are there in a business that employs 35 men?

    5N = 3 × 35
    5N = 105
    N = 21

    21 women

    b) How many people are employed by the business?

    21 + 35 = 56

    56 people

continued

Assignment 4.2 continued

23. If a truck that is loaded to full capacity travels 276 miles on 12 gallons of diesel fuel, how many gallons will be used to travel 1,150 miles under the same conditions?

    $\dfrac{276 \text{ mi}}{12 \text{ gal}} = \dfrac{1{,}150 \text{ mi}}{N \text{ gal}}$

    276N = 1,150 × 12
    276N = 13,800
    N = 50 gal

    __N = 50 gal__

24. Averill and Larry make stained boxes every day of the week, and they sell the boxes at the local crafts market. They can make 18 boxes in 3 days. How many weeks will it take them to make 126 boxes?

    $\dfrac{18 \text{ boxes}}{3 \text{ days}} = \dfrac{126 \text{ boxes}}{N \text{ days}}$

    18N = 126 × 3
    18N = 378
    N = 21 days
    N = 3 weeks

    __N = 3 weeks__

25. As a driver for Travel Movers, Inc., you know that 4 crates hold a total of 112 books. How many crates of the same size will you need to hold 1,568 books?

    $\dfrac{4 \text{ crates}}{112 \text{ books}} = \dfrac{N \text{ crates}}{1{,}568 \text{ books}}$

    112N = 1,568 × 4
    112N = 6,272
    N = 56 crates

    __N = 56 crates__

QUICK MENTAL MULTIPLICATION

Instead of writing down each step of a math problem, try to picture in your mind what is happening. The trick to mental multiplication is in your perception of the numbers. For example, suppose you are asked to find quickly the total price of 96 flower pots at $4 each and you have no calculator handy. Instead of writing down the problem the long way, think of the number of flower pots as 90 plus 6 instead of 96. Multiply 90 by 4 and 6 by 4 and add the products together. In your mind you see:

90 × 4 = 360
+
6 × 4 = 24

Concentrating on the individual answers and then adding them together gives you the actual price, $384. Once you practice multiplying mentally a few times, you will be amazed at how quick and easy it can be. You can learn to do it with numbers of three or four digits.

Comprehensive Problems for Chapter 4

Ratio and Proportion

Write as a ratio and reduce.

1. 80 ounces to 8 pounds _____5 : 8_____

2. 176 athletes to 64 exercise machines _____11 : 4_____

3. 36 points lost to 40 points gained _____9 : 10_____

4. 52 hats to 68 display stands _____13 : 17_____

5. 108 dollars to 648 dollars _____1 : 6_____

6. 14 feet to 4 inches (compare in inches) _____42 : 1_____

Determine whether each of the following ratios is correct or incorrect.

7. $\dfrac{13}{17} = \dfrac{52}{68}$ _____Correct_____

8. $6 : \dfrac{3}{4} = 48 : 6$ _____Correct_____

9. $\dfrac{24}{13} = \dfrac{144}{98}$ _____Incorrect_____

10. 10.4 is to 6.3 as 31.2 is to 18.1 _____Incorrect_____

Solve for the unknown.

11. $N : 45 = 7 : 21$ _____N = 15_____ $21N = 315$; $N = 15$

12. $\dfrac{1\frac{1}{5}}{2.7} = \dfrac{3.4}{N}$ _____N = 7.65_____ $1.2N = 9.18$; $N = 7.65$

13. $\dfrac{5}{48} = \dfrac{2.5}{N}$ _____N = 24_____ $5N = 120$; $N = 24$

14. $12 : N = 5 : 3\frac{3}{4}$ _____N = 9_____ $5N = 45$; $N = 9$

15. $\dfrac{N}{17} = \dfrac{96}{102}$ _____N = 16_____ $102N = 1632$; $N = 16$

16. $21.3 : 5\frac{1}{5} = N : 15.6$ _____N = 63.9_____ $5.2N = 332.28$; $N = 63.9$

17. In a survey done by the Chamber of Commerce, it was found that for a total of 1,362 small businesses, 10,896 people were employed. How many people were employed per business? (Round to the nearest whole number.)

continued

Comprehensive Problems *continued*

$\dfrac{10.896 \text{ people}}{1{,}362 \text{ businesses}} = \dfrac{8}{1}$ __8 people__

18. In a steel production plant, a wheel made 75 revolutions in 5 seconds. At that rate, how many revolutions will the wheel make in one hour?

    $5N = 75 \times 3{,}600$
    $5N = 270{,}000$
    $N = 54{,}000$ revolutions/hr

    __$N = 54{,}000$ revolutions per hour__

    $1 \text{ hr} = 3{,}6000 \text{ sec}$
    $\dfrac{75 \text{ rev}}{5 \text{ sec}} = \dfrac{N \text{ rev}}{3{,}600 \text{ sec}}$

19. Brite's Dry Cleaning Service can wash and press 25 shirts in 1 hour and 15 minutes. How many can it handle at that rate in an 8-hour day?

    $1\dfrac{1}{4}N = 25 \times 8$

    $\dfrac{5}{4}N = 200$

    $N = 160$ shirts

    __$N = 160$ shirts__

    $\dfrac{25 \text{ shirts}}{1 \text{ hr, 15 min}} = \dfrac{N \text{ shirts}}{8 \text{ hr}}$

20. Connie, Nadene, and Heather were in a partnership with the ratio of 2 : 3 : 7, respectively. A loss of $64,800 was sustained by the business in the first year of operation. What is each woman's share of the loss?

    $\dfrac{2}{3}$
    $\dfrac{3}{12}$ ... er:

    $\cancel{64{,}800}^{5{,}400} \times \dfrac{2}{\cancel{12}_{1}} = \$10{,}800$ Connie

    $64{,}800 \times \dfrac{3}{12} = \$16{,}200$ Nadene

    __$\$10{,}800$ Connie's loss__
    __$\$16{,}200$ Nadene's loss__
    __$\$37{,}800$ Heather's loss__

    $\$64{,}800 \times \dfrac{7}{12} = \$37{,}800$ Heather

21. Dillon's Carpet Store charged a contractor $1,350 for 900 square feet of foam padding. At that rate, what would he be charged for 1,500 square feet of padding?

    $900N = \$1{,}350 \times 1{,}500$
    $900N = \$2{,}025{,}00$
    $N = \$2{,}250$

    __$N = \$2{,}250$__

    $\dfrac{\$1{,}350}{900 \text{ sq ft}} = \dfrac{N}{1{,}500 \text{ sq ft}}$

22. Water is being pumped from a reservoir into a holding tank for Browsberg's Chemical Plant at the rate of 85 gallons in 2 minutes. If the capacity of the holding tank is 7,650 gallons, how long will it take to fill the tank?

    $85N = 7{,}650 \times 2$
    $85N = 15{,}300$
    $N = 180$ min, or 3 hr

    __$N = 180$ min, or 3 hr to fill tank__

    $\dfrac{85 \text{ gal}}{2 \text{ min}} = \dfrac{7{,}650 \text{ gal}}{N \text{ min}}$

23. In a carload of 140,000 cans of vegetables, 56,000 cans were Grade A, 49,000 cans were Grade B, and the rest were Grade C.

    a) What is the ratio of the number of Grade A to the number of Grade B?

    $\dfrac{A}{B} = \dfrac{56{,}000}{49{,}000} = \dfrac{8}{7}$ __$\dfrac{8}{7}$__

continued

Comprehensive Problems *continued*

b) What is the ratio of the number of Grade C to the total number of cans?

56,000 Grade A
+ 49,000 Grade B
105,000

140,000 Total cans
− 105,000
35,000 Grade C

$\dfrac{C}{Total} = \dfrac{35,000}{140,000} = \dfrac{5}{20} = \dfrac{1}{4}$

$\dfrac{1}{4}$

24. Because of a special sale at the crafts store, 2 rolls of ribbon sold for $0.36. If you need 12 rolls, how much will you have to pay?

$\dfrac{2 \text{ rolls}}{36¢} = \dfrac{12 \text{ rolls}}{N¢}$

$2N = 12 \times 36$
$2N = 432$
$N = \$2.16$

$N = \$2.16$ for twelve rolls

25. A department store sold a waterbed for $640. The cost, including all expenses of the bed to the store, was $400. Find the ratios of each of the following.

a) Cost to selling price

$\dfrac{Cost}{SP} = \dfrac{400}{640}$

$\dfrac{5}{8}$

b) Profit to cost

$\dfrac{P}{C} = \dfrac{240}{400} = \dfrac{3}{5}$

$\dfrac{3}{5}$

c) Profit to selling price

$\dfrac{P}{SP} = \dfrac{240}{640} = \dfrac{3}{8}$

$\dfrac{3}{8}$

26. Separate 1,064 into four numbers in the ratio of 5 : 4 : 7 : 3.

5
4
7
3
19

$1{,}064 \times \dfrac{5}{19} = 280$ (with 56 shown above 1,064)

$1{,}064 = \dfrac{4}{1} = 224$

$1{,}064 \times \dfrac{7}{19} = 392$

$1{,}064 \times \dfrac{3}{19} = 168$

5 : 4 : 7 : 3
280; 224; 392; 168

27. If an 8-foot coil of rope at Dupré's Hardware Store costs $4.80, how much will a 10-foot coil cost?

$8N = \$4.80 \times 10$
$8N = \$48$
$N = \$6$

$N = \$6$ for a 10-ft coil

28. Connie DeMill is stocking gardening supplies at Sylvester's Department Store. Seed packets are priced at 5 for $1.00. At this rate, at what price should she mark a package of 12 seed packets?

$5N = 1200¢$
$N = 240¢$, or $2.40

$2.40 package of twelve

continued

Comprehensive Problems *continued*

29. Quick and E. Z. Freight Company is transporting a total of 6,498 mannequins of uniform size to distribution centers. If three trucks hold a total of 1,083 mannequins, how many more trucks are needed for this shipment?

    $\dfrac{1{,}083}{3} = \dfrac{6{,}498}{N}$ 18 Need
                            − 3 Have
    $1{,}083N = 19{,}494$ 15 More
    $N = 18$

    15 more

30. Greg Linderman, a travel agent for Time Travel Agency, is planning a trip across Canada. On his map $\tfrac{1}{4}$ inch represents 52 miles. How many miles are represented by $2\tfrac{1}{2}$ inches?

    $\dfrac{\tfrac{1}{4}\text{ in}}{52\text{ mi}} = \dfrac{2\tfrac{1}{2}\text{ in.}}{N\text{ mi}}$

    $\tfrac{1}{4}N = 52 \times 2.5$
    $\tfrac{1}{4}N = 130$
    $N = 520$ mi

    N = 520 mi

31. Last month's expenses for Carol's Cycle Shop amounted to $6,160. The expenses were divided into five categories: payroll, $3,360; utilities, $280; advertising, $1,120; insurance $560; miscellaneous, the remainder.

    ```
    3360          6160
     280        − 5320
    1120          840
     560        Remainder
    5320
    ```

    a) What is the ratio of each category to the total expenses:

    Payroll $\dfrac{3360}{6160} = \dfrac{12}{22} = \dfrac{6}{11}$

    Utilities $\dfrac{280}{6160} = \dfrac{1}{22}$

    Advertising $\dfrac{1120}{6160} = \dfrac{4}{22} = \dfrac{2}{11}$

    Insurance $\dfrac{560}{6160} = \dfrac{2}{22} = \dfrac{1}{11}$

    Miscellaneous $\dfrac{840}{6160} = \dfrac{3}{22}$

    $\tfrac{6}{11}$ payroll; $\tfrac{1}{22}$ utilities; $\tfrac{2}{11}$ advertising; $\tfrac{1}{11}$ insurance; $\tfrac{3}{22}$ miscellaneous

    (or if expressed in terms of 22nd's : 12 : 1 : 4 : 2 : 3)

    b) What is the ratio of payroll to advertising?

    $\dfrac{3360 \text{ payroll}}{1120 \text{ advertising}} = \dfrac{3}{1}$

    3 : 1

32. Betsy's Upholstery Store purchased 24 square yards of material for $204. The following week, the store needed to buy 16 square yards of the same material. How much did it cost if the price per yard has not increased?

    $\dfrac{24 \text{ sq yd}}{\$204} = \dfrac{16 \text{ sq yd}}{\$N}$

    $24N = 16 \times 204$
    $24N = 3{,}264$
    $N = 136$

    N = $136

continued

Comprehensive Problems *continued*

33. You are mixing a fruit punch that requires 3 cups of water to be added to the frozen concentrate, which makes $1\frac{1}{2}$ quarts of punch. If you need 12 quarts of punch for the office Christmas party, how many cups of water will you need?

    $$\frac{3 \text{ cups water}}{1\frac{1}{2} \text{ qt punch}} = \frac{N \text{ cups water}}{12 \text{ qt punch}}$$

    $1\frac{1}{2}N = 12 \times 3$

    $\frac{3}{2}N = 36$

    $N = 36 \times \frac{2}{3}$

    $N = 24$ cups

    $N = 24$ cups of water needed

34. In June Meadow Sun Dairy produced 5,433 half gallons of ice milk and 65,196 pints of ice cream. What is the ratio of ice cream to ice milk?

    4 pints = 1 half gallon

    $\frac{65,196}{4} = 16,299$ half gallons

    $\frac{16,299 \text{ half gallon of ice cream}}{5,433 \text{ half gallon of ice milk}} = \frac{3}{1}$

    3 : 1

35. Pete Paizano, general contractor, is figuring his work schedule. If it takes 7 workmen 12 hours to complete a section of a bridge, how many sections can they complete in 60 hours?

    $$\frac{1 \text{ section}}{12 \text{ hr}} = \frac{N \text{ section}}{60 \text{ hr}}$$

    $12N = 60$
    $N = 5$

    $N = 5$ sections

36. You are the clock repairer for the House of Clocks, Inc., for the city of London. If Big Ben has lost 2 seconds in 3 hours, how much time will it lose in 2 days?

    $$\frac{2 \text{ section}}{3 \text{ hr}} = \frac{N \text{ section}}{2 \text{ day}}$$

    $3N = 2 \times 48$
    $3N = 96$
    $N = 32$

    $N = 32$ seconds lost

Case 1

Mr. Cromwell refinanced his house and received $16,000 ten years ago. As a hedge against inflation, he decided to invest the money in the following way: three parts in real estate and five parts in stock. Mr. Cromwell met a farmer who was selling parcels of barren land. The land sold for $1,000 for $\frac{1}{5}$ of an acre.

a. At this rate, how many acres could Mr. Cromwell buy?

The stock that he wanted to purchase cost $125 for 3 shares.

b. At this rate how many shares could he buy?

At the end of five years, he sold all his real estate and stock holdings and made a total profit of $28,400. The profit he received from real estate represented three parts and that from stock, one part.

c. How much profit did he receive from the real estate and how much did he receive from the stock?

d. What is the ratio, to the nearest tenth, of total profit per $1 to total investment?

e. If you had $16,000 to invest, what would you invest in? Why?

Case 2

You are working as an assistant to the principal at Shelton High School. The policy of the school is to have 4 teachers for 92 students. The estimated enrollment for next year is 1,472, with a ratio of boys to the total enrollment of 1 : 1.5. The current teaching staff is 56 teachers. The principal asks you to find the following figures on the basis of the information above.

a. How many new teachers must be hired in order to maintain current policy?

b. How many girls and how many boys will be enrolled next year? (Round to nearest whole number.)

c. What will be the ratio of the number of new teachers to the total number of faculty?

Key Terms

Proportion
Ratio
Rule of proportion

Key Concepts

- A ratio is the expression of a relationship between two numbers.
- Ratio of Like Quantities: When quantities of the same kind are compared, each quantity must be expressed in the same units and then reduced to lowest terms.

- Ratio of Unlike Quantities: When quantities of different kinds are compared, label the quantities and then reduce to lowest terms.
- Ratio of Comparison to One: When expressing a comparison to one, write the original ratio in the form of a fraction and divide the numerator by the denominator.
- A proportion is the expression of two ratios that are equal to each other.
- Rule of Proportion: The product of the means, inner terms, equals the product of the extremes, outer terms.

5

Base, Rate, and Percentage

Business Takes a Positive Approach

POLAROID

Polaroid was suffering. Consumers appeared to be losing their fascination with instant photography. Even more serious, the corporation that produced the original Land camera seemed to have gone stagnant. Thanks to heavy investments in research and development and a new approach to marketing and management, however, Polaroid turned itself around. The company managed to revitalize interest in instant photography by introducing its Spectra camera. In addition to delivering immediate results, the Spectra produced high-quality pictures. Less volatile than the individual consumer market, the commercial market has also proved profitable for Polaroid. The firm's research and development funds were particularly well spent here. The investment led to the introduction of new equipment that makes an instant photographic print or slide from a videotaped scene. This has proven particularly valuable to newscasters and police investigators. Polaroid is currently developing other new products, such as an electronic camera that stores photographs on magnetic disk rather than on film. In addition to its new-product explorations, the company reorganized and also strengthened its marketing approach through increased consumer research. As a result, Polaroid has quintupled its profits. Its stock jumped 55% over a 12-month period. Polaroid is back on target, and its winnings show it.

> **Learning Objectives**
>
> After reading and studying this chapter and working the problems, you will be able to:
>
> - Convert a percent to its equivalent decimal and fraction.
> - Convert a decimal or fraction to its equivalent percent.
> - Define base, rate, and percentage along with the percentage formula.
> - Apply the percentage formula in a variety of short and narrative problems.
> - Solve amount and difference problems.

Advertisements may declare "20% off retail" or "10% below regular price." Labels may state "50% of recommended daily allowance of Vitamin A" or "20% less cholesterol than other leading brands." A person might say, "I have about 40% of my house left to paint" or "I'd need a 20% pay raise before I'd consider changing jobs." These are examples of how we use percents.

In business, we refer to percent of loss or gain, percent return on investments, percent of interest, or percent of discount, and the meaning is much the same as when we use the term in nonbusiness situations. There is no reason to feel uneasy about figuring percents or understanding what they mean, once you know a few simple facts about them.

By itself, a percent or rate does not provide much information. To have meaning, it must be expressed in relation to certain other numbers. For example, a store advertises a sale on tennis racquets, promising 25% off the regular price. Before you buy, consider that the dollar amount of the reduction depends completely on the regular price of the racquet. The regular price may be so much higher than that of other stores that the 25% reduction is not really much of a savings.

The term **percent** means *per hundred* and is defined as a fraction with a denominator of 100 or as a decimal with two places. In other words, 60%, 0.60, $\frac{60}{100}$ (reducible to $\frac{3}{5}$) all mean the same thing and are equal to one another.

When calculating, convert the percent into either a common fraction or a decimal and solve the problem.

5.1 Percents and Conversion from Percents

Converting a Percent to a Decimal

To convert a percent to a decimal, drop the percent sign and move the decimal point two places away from the percent sign, or to the left.

Example 1   Convert 32% to a decimal.

    Step 1   Cross out the percent sign.   32%

    Step 2   Move the decimal point two places to the left.   .32
Unless it is otherwise shown, assume that the

decimal point is after the last whole number before the percent sign. In this step you are actually dividing by 100.

Answer 32% converted to a decimal is .32.

Example 2 Convert 32.3% to a decimal.
- Step 1 Cross out the percent sign.   32.3%
- Step 2 The decimal point is already showing in the number. Move it two places to the left.   .323
- Answer 32.3% converted to a decimal is .323.

Example 3 Convert 3.2% to a decimal.
- Step 1 Cross out the percent sign.   3.2%
- Step 2 Place a 0 before the 3 to show that you moved the decimal point two places to the left.   .03 2
- Answer 3.2% converted to a decimal is .032.

Example 4 Convert 300% to a decimal.
- Step 1 Cross out the percent sign.   300%
- Step 2 Move the decimal point two places to the left.   3.00
- Answer 300% converted to a decimal is 3.

Example 5 Convert $32\frac{1}{4}$% to a decimal.
- Step 1 Convert the fraction to a decimal, keeping the percent sign. $32\frac{1}{4}$% = 32.25%
- Step 2 Cross out the percent sign.   32.25%
- Step 3 Move the decimal point two places to the left.   .32 25
- Answer $32\frac{1}{4}$% converted to a decimal is .3225.

Self-Check

Convert each of these percents to a decimal.

1. 62%
2. 62.4%
3. 6.2%
4. 624%
5. $62\frac{4}{10}$%

ANSWERS 1. .62   2. .624   3. .062   4. 6.24   5. .624

Converting a Percent to a Fraction

For a percent with no decimal point showing, cross out the percent sign and place the number over 100.

Example 6 Convert 30% to a fraction.

Step 1   Cross out the percent sign.   30%

Step 2   Place the number over 100. $\frac{30}{100}$

Step 3   Reduce the fraction to its lowest terms. $\frac{30}{100} = \frac{3}{10}$

Answer   30% converted to a fraction is $\frac{3}{10}$.

Example 7 Convert 350% to a fraction.

Step 1   Cross out the percent sign.   350%

Step 2   Place the number of over 100. $\frac{350}{100}$

Step 3   Reduce the fraction to its lowest terms, converting the improper fraction to a mixed number for the final answer. $\frac{350}{100} = \frac{35}{10} = \frac{7}{2}$, or $3\frac{1}{2}$

Answer   350% converted to a fraction is $\frac{7}{2}$ or $3\frac{1}{2}$.

Example 8 Convert $12\frac{1}{2}$% to a fraction.

Step 1   Cross out the percent sign. $12\frac{1}{2}$%

Step 2   Place the number over 100. $\frac{12\frac{1}{2}}{100}$

Step 3   Reduce the fraction to its lowest terms. (See Section 2.4.)

$12\frac{1}{2} \div 100$

$\frac{25}{2} \div \frac{100}{1}$

$\frac{\cancel{25}}{2} \times \frac{1}{\cancel{100}} = \frac{1}{8}$

Answer $12\frac{1}{2}$% converted to a fraction is $\frac{1}{8}$.

To convert a percent to a fraction when there is a decimal showing, first convert the percent to a decimal.

Example 9 Convert 42.5% to a fraction.

Step 1   Cross out the percent sign.   42.5%

Step 2   Convert to a decimal.   .425

Step 3   Convert to a fraction and reduce to lowest terms. (See Section 3.3.) $\frac{425}{1,000}$

$\frac{425}{1,000} = \frac{17}{40}$

Answer   42.5% converted to a fraction is $\frac{17}{40}$.

NOTE: Example 8 could have been solved as this one was by changing $12\frac{1}{2}$% to 12.5% first.

Self-Check

Convert each of these percents to a fraction.

1. 46%
2. 101%
3. $37\frac{1}{2}\%$
4. 2.25%

ANSWERS 1. $\frac{23}{50}$ 2. $1\frac{1}{100}$ 3. $\frac{3}{8}$ 4. $\frac{225}{10,000}$, or $\frac{9}{400}$

Assignment 5.1

Base, Rate, and Percentage

Convert each of the following percents to a decimal.

1. 25% .25
2. 37% .37
3. 125% 1.25
4. 274% 2.74
5. 66% .66
6. 426% 4.26
7. 38% .38
8. 528% 5.28
9. 78.5% .785
10. 10% .1
11. 1% .01
12. .0101% .000101
13. .0011% .000011
14. .004% .00004

Convert each of the following percents to a fraction.

15. 50% $\dfrac{50}{100} = \dfrac{1}{2}$
16. 43% $\dfrac{43}{100}$
17. 25% $\dfrac{25}{100} = \dfrac{1}{4}$
18. 76% $\dfrac{76}{100} = \dfrac{19}{25}$
19. 340% $\dfrac{340}{100} = \dfrac{34}{10} = 3\dfrac{2}{5}$
20. 262% $\dfrac{262}{100} = \dfrac{131}{50} = 2\dfrac{31}{50}$
21. 100% $\dfrac{100}{100} = 1$
22. $11\tfrac{3}{4}\%$ $\dfrac{1{,}175}{10{,}000} = \dfrac{47}{400}$
23. $16\tfrac{2}{3}\%$ $\dfrac{1{,}666}{10{,}000} = \dfrac{1}{6}$
24. $14\tfrac{1}{2}\%$ $\dfrac{145}{1{,}000} = \dfrac{29}{200}$
25. .002% $\dfrac{2}{100{,}000} = \dfrac{1}{50{,}000}$
26. 47.33% $\dfrac{4{,}733}{10{,}000}$
27. 102.6% $1\dfrac{26}{1{,}000} = 1\dfrac{13}{500}$
28. .5% $\dfrac{5}{1{,}000} = \dfrac{1}{200}$

5.2 Conversion to Percents

Converting a Decimal to a Percent

To convert a decimal to a percent, move the decimal point two places to the right. Then add the percent sign.

Example 1   Convert .78 to a percent.

Step 1   Move the decimal point two places to the right. In this step you are actually multiplying by 100.   .78.

Step 2   Add the percent sign.   78%

Answer   .78 converted to a percent is 78%.

Example 2   Convert 4 to a percent.

Step 1   Move the decimal point two places to the right.   4.00.

Step 2   Add the percent sign.   400%

Answer   4 converted to a percent is 400%.

Example 3   Convert .0982 to a percent.

Step 1   Move the decimal point two places to the right.   .09.82

Step 2   Add the percent sign.   9.82%

Answer   .0982 converted to a percent is 9.82%.

Self-Check

Convert each of these decimals to a percent.

1. .85   _____
2. 62   _____
3. .0001   _____

ANSWERS   1. 85%   2. 6200%   3. .01%

Converting a Fraction to a Percent

To convert a fraction to a percent, divide the numerator of the fraction by the denominator, finding the quotient to at least two decimal places. Convert the resulting decimal to a percent.

Example 4   Convert $\frac{3}{4}$ to a percent.

Step 1   Divide the numerator by the denominator. $\frac{3}{4}$, or $4\overline{)3.00}$ = .75

Step 2   Convert the decimal to a percent.   .75, or 75%

Answer $\frac{3}{4}$ converted to a percent is 75%.

Base, Rate, and Percentage

Example 5 Convert the mixed number $3\frac{1}{5}$ to a percent.

Step 1 Divide the numerator by the denominator in the fractional portion of the mixed number.

$\frac{1}{5} = .20$

Step 2 Place the whole number in front of the decimal point.

$3\frac{1}{5} = 3.20$

Step 3 Convert the decimal to a percent.

3 20.

Answer $3\frac{1}{5}$ converted to a percent is 320%.

Self-Check

Convert each of these fractions to a percent.

1. $\frac{1}{2}$ _____

2. $\frac{2}{3}$ _____

3. $3\frac{3}{8}$ _____

ANSWERS 1. 50%   2. $66\frac{2}{3}$%, or 66.67%   3. 337.5%, or $337\frac{1}{2}$%

THE MODERN ADDING MACHINE

William S. Burroughs of St. Louis, Missouri, patented the first successful key-set adding machine in 1888. When his initial design was not successful commercially, Burroughs and three partners organized and sold stock in the American Arithmometer Company. After another false start, in 1891 Burroughs finally produced a machine that automatically printed each entry and the answer to each calculation. It sold so well that eventually American Arithmometer became the highly successful Burroughs Corporation.

Assignment 5.2

Base, Rate, and Percentage

Convert each of the following decimals and fractions to a percent.

1. $\frac{6}{10}$ ____60%____
2. $\frac{3}{8}$ ____$37\frac{1}{2}$%____
3. $\frac{1}{10}$ ____10%____
4. $\frac{5}{6}$ ____$83\frac{1}{3}$____
5. 2.5 ____250%____
6. .001 ____.1%____
7. $\frac{1}{30}$ ____$3\frac{1}{3}$%____
8. $\frac{17}{20}$ ____85%____

Fill in the blanks.

	Percent	Decimal	Fraction
9.	50%	.5	$\frac{1}{2}$
10.	$12\frac{1}{2}$%	.125	$\frac{1}{8}$
11.	75%	.75	$\frac{3}{4}$
12.	5%	.05	$\frac{1}{20}$
13.	80%	.8	$\frac{4}{5}$
14.	87.5%	.875	$\frac{7}{8}$
15.	$33\frac{1}{3}$%	$.33\frac{1}{3}$	$\frac{1}{3}$
16.	$62\frac{1}{2}$%	.625	$\frac{5}{8}$
17.	3.25%	.0325	$\frac{325}{10,000} = \frac{13}{400}$
18.	.25%	.0025	$\frac{25}{10,000} = \frac{1}{400}$

continued

Assignment 5.2 *continued*

	Percent	Decimal	Fraction
19.	$14\frac{2}{7}\%$	$.14\frac{2}{7}$	$\frac{1}{7}$
20.	65%	$.65$	$\frac{65}{100} = \frac{13}{20}$
21.	$\frac{1}{2}\%$	$.005$	$\frac{5}{1,000} = \frac{1}{200}$
22.	5%	$.05$	$\frac{1}{20}$
23.	$66\frac{2}{3}\%$	$.66\frac{2}{3}$	$\frac{2}{3}$
24.	140%	1.4	$1\frac{2}{5}$

5.3 The Percentage Formula

As we have said, percents have meaning only as they relate to other numbers. This relationship is called the **percentage formula,** and it is expressed by a formula you will want to understand:

$$\text{Base} \times \text{Rate} = \text{Percentage}$$

Its importance in business cannot be overemphasized. You will find applications of the percentage formula throughout this text.

Go through the rest of this chapter slowly and carefully, reviewing the formula in its various forms. Each of the three elements of the percentage formula relates to the other two. You will soon grasp these relationships. Challenge yourself by expressing the same problem in different words. When you have mastered the percentage formula, you will have at your command a major principle of business mathematics.

Any percentage situation has three main elements: base, rate, and percentage. In most problems, two of these elements are given. The third, or missing quantity, is to be found.

Base: The whole number or the total of whatever quantity is dealt with in the situation. The base is the number to which the rate and the percentage are being compared.

Rate: The figure that determines how large a part of the base the percentage will be. It can be expressed as a percent (30%), a decimal (.3), a fraction ($\frac{3}{10}$), or other form such as $30 per $100. For our purposes in this chapter, we will use the percent form for rate.

Percentage: A part of the whole, or base, it is the product of the base times the rate. Depending on the rate, the percentage can be larger or smaller than the base.

The relationship among these terms is expressed by three formulas.

To find percentage:	Percentage = Base × Rate	$P = B \times R$
To find base:	Base = $\dfrac{\text{Percentage}}{\text{Rate}}$	$B = \dfrac{P}{R}$
To find rate:	Rate = $\dfrac{\text{Percentage}}{\text{Base}}$	$R = \dfrac{P}{B}$

To remember the formulas, you may want to draw a triangle with three compartments.

When looking for percentage, cover the P in the triangle with the tip of your pencil, and the remaining letters reveal the formula.

Base, Rate, and Percentage

Use the same technique to find the other formulas, remembering that P is always on top.

 $B = \dfrac{P}{R}$  $R = \dfrac{P}{B}$

To understand more about the relationship among the terms of the formula, you might regard it as follows:

Base × Rate = Percentage

Whole × % of whole = Part of whole

The key to solving percentage problems is to identify which elements are given in the problem.

To discover which number is the base, look for the word *of* or words that express the same concept, such as:

Compare to	Less than
As much as	Greater than
More than	Smaller than

The number or word directly following these words will, in most cases, be the base. It is the original amount, that is, the amount that occurred first in time.

The rate is usually the number followed by the percent sign (%).

is = P
of = B
% = R

Note: The words *percent* and *percentage* are not used interchangeably. They do *not* mean the same thing.

The percentage is the *number* expressing the percent or rate, but it appears as a numerical quantity or a dollar amount. It is usually closely associated with the words *is* or *equal to*.

You should also note that rate and percentage share a special affiliation. Both refer to the same thing but express it in different terms. Whatever label or name is placed on the rate, that same label is placed on the percentage, as shown here.

Rate	Percentage
% gain	gain in dollars
% commission	commission in dollars
% increase	increase in dollars
% deduction	deduction in dollars
% change	change in dollars

Percentage and rate must be labeled the same before a problem can be solved.

Finding a Percentage

Example 1 What is 25% of 80?

Step 1 Identify the elements.

	a. The number following *of* if the base.	B = 80
	b. The number with the percent sign is the rate.	R = 25%
	c. Through elimination, we know that the element missing is the percentage.	P = ?
Step 2	Apply the formula and solve.	
	a. Write the formula.	P = B × R
	b. Substitute the numbers.	P = 80 × 25%
	c. Solve by converting the percent to a decimal or fraction and multiplying.	80 × .25, or 80 × $\frac{1}{4}$
Answer	20 is 25% of 80.	

NOTE: If you are using a calculator there is no need to convert the percent; instead, use the % key for step 2(c).

Self-Check

1. _____ = $\frac{1}{2}$% of 35

2. _____ = 46% of 3,500

3. What is 210% of 150?

ANSWERS   1. .175, or .1$\frac{3}{4}$ 2. 1,610   3. 315

Finding a Rate

Example 2	20 is a what percent of 18?	
Step 1	Identify the elements.	
	a. The base follows the word *of*.	B = 18
	b. The percentage is 20, a part of the base.	P = 20
	c. The rate is the unknown.	R = ?
Step 2	Apply the formula and solve.	
	a. Write the formula.	R = $\frac{P}{B}$
	b. Substitute the numbers.	R = $\frac{20}{18}$
	c. Divide the numerator by the denominator and change the decimal to a percent.	R = 1.11$\frac{1}{9}$
		R = 111$\frac{1}{9}$%
Answer	20 is 111$\frac{1}{9}$% of 18.	

NOTE: Because the percentage is higher than the base, the rate is more than 100%.

Base, Rate, and Percentage

Example 3 18 is what percent of 20?

Step 1 Identify the key elements.

    a. The base is the number following *of*. $B = 20$

    b. The percentage is 18. Substitute the word *equals* for *is* to clarify the problem statement. 18 equals what percent of 20? $P = 18$

    c. The rate is the missing element. $R = ?$

Step 2 Apply the formula and solve.

    a. Write the formula. $R = \dfrac{P}{B}$

    b. Substitute the numbers. $R = \dfrac{18}{20}$

    c. Solve for the rate. $R = \dfrac{18}{20} = \dfrac{9}{10}$

    $R = 90\%$

Answer 18 is 90% of 20.

Substitute your answer in the original problem and you will see that it makes mathematical sense: 18 is 90% of 20.

NOTE: The percentage (18) is smaller than the base (20). Therefore, the rate must be smaller than 100%.

Self-Check

1. 45 = _____ % of 90.
2. 2.925 = _____ % of 65.
3. 54 is what percent of 36? _____

ANSWERS 1. 50%   2. 4.5%, or $4\tfrac{1}{2}\%$ 3. 150%

Finding Percent More Than and Percent Less Than

In situations containing words such as *more than, less than, greater than,* or *smaller than,* you must determine, *in units,* the quantity more or quantity less before solving the problem.

Example 4 20 is what percent greater than 18?

Step 1 Identify the elements.

    a. The base is the number following *greater than*. $B = 18$

    b. The percentage is the amount greater. You must, therefore, subtract. $20 - 18 = 2$
    $P = 2$ greater

Step 2 c. The rate is the missing element. $R = ?$

    Apply the formula and solve.

    a. Substitute the numbers. $R = \dfrac{P}{B}$

b. Divide.

$$R = \frac{2}{18} = \frac{1}{9} = 9\overline{)1.00}^{.11\frac{1}{9}}$$

$$R = 11\frac{1}{9}\%$$

Answer   20 is $11\frac{1}{9}\%$ greater than 18.

NOTE: How is this problem different from "20 is what % of 18" in Example 2?

Example 5   18 is what percent smaller than 20?

Step 1   Identify the elements.

a. The base is the number following *smaller than*.   B = 20

b. The percentage is the actual number of units   20 − 18 = 2
   that express how much smaller. It is found by   P = 2 smaller
   subtracting.

c. The rate is the missing element.   R = ?

Step 2   Apply the formula and solve.

a. Write the formula. $R = \frac{P}{B}$

b. Substitute the numbers. $R = \frac{2}{20}$

c. Solve. $R = \frac{2}{20} = \frac{1}{10}$

                             R = 10%

Answer   18 is 10% smaller than 20.

Substitute the answer into the formula to see if it is correct and makes sense.

Self-Check

1. 40 is what % greater than 30?   _____
2. 40 is what % of 30?   _____
3. 30 is what % less than 40?   _____
4. 30 is what % of 40?   _____

ANSWERS   1. $33\frac{1}{3}\%$ 2. $133\frac{1}{3}\%$ 3. 25%   4. 75%

Finding a Base

Example 6   20 is 25% of what number?

Step 1   Identify the elements.

a. The number followed by the percent sign is the   R = 25%
   rate.

b. The quantity associated with *is* and equal to   P = 20
   the rate is the percentage.

	c. The number following *of* is the base. It is not given.	B = ?
Step 2	Apply the formula and solve.	
	a. Write the formula.	$B = \dfrac{P}{R}$
	b. Substitute the numbers.	$B = \dfrac{20}{25\%}$
	c. Convert the percent to a decimal or a fraction and divide.	$B = \dfrac{20}{.25}$
Answer	20 is 25% of 80.	B = 80

Finding a Base Using Amount and Difference

Example 7 40 is 20% smaller than what number?

Step 1 Identify the elements.

a. The quantity associated with and equal to the rate is the percentage.

$P = 40$

$$\begin{array}{r} 100\% \\ -\ 20\% \\ \hline 80\% \end{array}$$

b. The number followed by the percent sign is the rate but since it is "% smaller than," the true rate is found by subtracting from 100%.

$R = 80\%$

c. The number following *smaller than* is the base. It is not given.

$B = ?$

Step 2 Apply the formula and solve.

a. Write the formula. $B = \dfrac{P}{R}$

b. Substitute the numbers. $B = \dfrac{40}{80\%}$

c. Convert the percent to a decimal or a fraction and divide. $B = \dfrac{40}{0.8}$

$B = 50$

Answer 40 is 20% smaller than 50.

NOTE: "40 is 20% smaller than 50" is the same as saying "40 is 80% of 50."

Example 8 48 is 20% greater than what number?

Step 1 Identify the elements.

a. The quantity associated with and equal to the rate is the percentage.

$P = 48$

b. The number followed by the percent sign is the rate but since it is "% greater than," the true rate is found by adding to 100%.

$$\begin{array}{r} 100\% \\ +\ 20\% \\ \hline 120\% \end{array}$$

$R = 120\%$

c. The number following *greater than* is the base. It is not given.

$B = ?$

Step 2 Apply the formula and solve.

a. Write the formula.

$$B = \frac{P}{R}$$

b. Substitute the numbers.

$$B = \frac{48}{120\%}$$

c. Convert the percent to a decimal or a fraction and divide.

$$B = \frac{48}{1.2}$$

$$B = 40$$

Answer 48 is 20% greater than 40.

NOTE: "48 is 20% greater than 40" is the same as saying "48 is 120% of 40."

Self-Check

Supply the missing element in each of the following.

1. $25 = 33\frac{1}{3}\%$ of _____.

2. $1{,}500 = .05\%$ of _____.

3. 1,300 is 325% of _____.

4. 104 is 20% smaller than _____.

5. 793 is 30% greater than _____.

ANSWERS   1. 75   2. 3,000,000   3. 400   4. 130   5. 610

WHY THE PERCENT SIGN?

Many of the abbreviations used in business come to us from the Italians, by way of the British. The concept of percentage, for example, was originally described by Italian businessmen as *Numero Per Cento*. Roughly translated, this means "to this number in a hundred." It was shown in business documents as *No/c*:

- No.   The Italian abbreviation for *number* (numero);
- /   A slash signifying *per* (on the basis of);
- c   Short for *cento* (hundred in Italian).

Over time, the "N" fell into disuse, and, through sloppy penmanship, the "c" became an "o," leaving us with the sign we use today, %.

Base, Rate, and Percentage

Assignment 5.3

Base, Rate, and Percentage

Solve for the percentage. $P = B \times R$

1. What is 80% of 620? __496__
2. 110% of $4.20 is __$4.62__.
3. What is $6\frac{1}{2}$% of 400? __26__
4. .09% of 894 is __.8046__.
5. What is $\frac{1}{4}$% of 3,981? __9.9525__

Solve for the rate. $R = \dfrac{P}{B}$

6. 94 is __47__ % of 200.
7. 130 is __130__ % of 100.
8. What percent of 3,500 is 1,750? __50%__
9. 4.5 is __75__ % of 6.
10. 9 is what % of 81? __$11\frac{1}{9}$%, or 11.11%__

Solve for percent more than or less than. $R = \dfrac{P}{B}$

11. 72 is what percent smaller than 108? __$33\frac{1}{3}$%__
12. 980 is what percent larger than 800? __$22\frac{1}{2}$%__
13. 50 is what percent more than 20? __150%__
14. 1,680 is what percent more than 1,550? __8.39%__
15. 876.86 is what percent larger than 873? __.44%__

Solve for the base. $B = \dfrac{P}{R}$

16. 60 is 2% of what number? __3,000__
17. 30 is 120% of what number? __25__

continued

Assignment 5.3 continued

18. 1,589 is 70% of what number? _____2,270_____

19. 39.25 is $\frac{1}{2}$% of what number? _____7,850_____

20. 192.06 is 33% of what number? _____582_____

Solve for the base using amount and difference.

21. 112 is 40% more than _____80_____.

22. 7.7 is 40% more than _____5.5_____.

23. 3,280 is 18% less than _____4,000_____.

24. 6,346 is 5% less than _____6,680_____.

25. 113.52 is 3.2% greater than _____110_____.

Solve each of the following problems.

26. What is 35% of $756? _____$264.60_____   27. 7% of _____$900_____ = $63.

28. 108 is what percent greater than 72? _____50%_____

29. 48 is 112% of what number? _____42.86_____

30. 13 is what percent of 156? _____$8\frac{1}{3}$%_____

31. 456 is 5% lower than _____480_____.

32. What number is 28% of 300? _____84_____

33. 400 is what percent of 500? _____80%_____

34. 150% of $150 is _____$225_____.

35. 8,008 is what percent more than 8,000? _____.1%_____

36. 19 is what percent of 114? _____$16\frac{2}{3}$%_____

37. $7\frac{1}{2}$% of 250 is _____18.75_____.

38. 1,054 is what percent greater than 692? _____52.31%_____

39. 24 is 70% less than _____80_____.

40. What is $\frac{1}{2}$% of $117? _____$.585_____

continued

176   Chapter 5

Assignment 5.3 *continued*

41. 25 is $12\frac{1}{2}$% of what number?   200

42. 1501.5 is $\frac{1}{10}$% more than   1,500 .

43. 91 is $43\frac{3}{8}$% of what number?   209.79827

44. $12\frac{1}{2}$% of 328 is   41 .

45. 400 is what percent of 400?   100%

46. $434.25 is what percent lower than $450? $3\frac{1}{2}$%

47. $12\frac{1}{2}$ % of $328 = $41?

48. 95 is $62\frac{1}{2}$% of what number?   152

49. 10 is 100% greater than   5 .

50. 48 is what percent more than 30?   60%

51. What is 8% of $2,500? $200

52. 110 is what percent less than 330? $66\frac{2}{3}$%

Base, Rate, and Percentage

5.4 Solving Narrative Problems Using the Percentage Formula

Reviewing Narrative Problems

In using percentage formulas and in working in the following chapters you will encounter mostly narrative problems. Now is the ideal time to review the steps involved in understanding narrative problems. This appears in Chapter 1, section 1.6. After you have reread that section, study the following example of how to apply those steps to a common type of narrative problem.

Example 1 You are in charge of shipping for the Atlantic Railroad. The full capacity of a freight car is 125 crates. If 25 crates are loaded in the car now, what percent of additional crates is needed to reach the full capacity of the car?

Step 1 *Read.* It's helpful to read through the problem quickly at first just to get the gist of the material. Then reread every word to make sure you understand the complete meaning. What is it about?

Step 2 *Analyze.* Break down the data to the given facts and what is asked for. Many times, where applicable, drawing a simple picture will help.

Given: Full capacity of freight car = 125 crates
Loaded crates = 25 crates

Find: The percent of additional crates needed for full capacity.

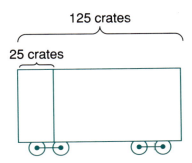

Step 3 *Process.* In deciding what process to use for this problem, you need to figure out which percentage formula you will use. Because this problem asks for a percent, you are looking for rate, so:

$$\text{Rate} = \frac{\text{Percentage}}{\text{Base}}$$

Before you can find the percent added, you first need to know exactly how many crates must be added. Thus the first process used is subtraction.

Applying the formula to find rate, we see that the next process is division.

Step 4 *Estimate.* You know that full capacity = 100%, so the percent needed would have to be less than that. Since 25 is less than $\frac{1}{4}$ or 25% of 125, the percent of additional crates needed must be more than 75%. A range of 76% to 85% seems probable.

Step 5 *Solve.*

125 crates for full capacity
− 25 crates loaded
100 additional crates needed

$$R = \frac{P}{B} = \frac{100}{125} = 80\%$$

Step 6 *Check.* Substitute the answer back into the problem and see if it makes sense.

Base, Rate, and Percentage

If 25 crates are loaded and full capacity is 125 crates, 80% more crates are needed.

$$B \times R = P$$

$$125 \times 80\% = 100 \text{ crates more}$$

$$\begin{array}{r} 25 \text{ crates loaded} \\ + \ 100 \text{ crates more} \\ \hline 125 \text{ crates total} = \text{full capacity (check)} \end{array}$$

NOTE: In examining the problem, as part of the check, see if you can find another way to solve it.

Step 7 Another method is to find the percent loaded and subtract this percent from the full capacity, which equals 100%.

$$R = \frac{P}{B} = \frac{25}{125} = 20\% \text{ crates loaded}$$

$$\begin{array}{r} 100\% \text{ full capacity} \\ - \ \ 20\% \text{ crates loaded} \\ \hline 80\% \text{ crates more} \end{array}$$

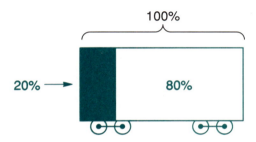

Solving Percentage Narrative Problems

Percentage represents a part of the whole. The size of the part (percentage) is determined by the size of the percent (rate). Percentage is better understood as it applies to business situations, as the following example shows.

Example 2 You are the manager of a toy department. One of your jobs is to allocate space for young children's toys and for older children's toys. If the total floor space available is 1,750 square feet, and you decide that 60% of the space will be for the young children's toys, how many square feet will you allocate for these toys?

Take the elements of the situation apart and see what is given. Remember that the base is the whole or the entire quantity. It represents 100%. It is the thing that will be divided into parts. It is the starting point. Here, the base is the total floor space, or 1,750 square feet.

The rate is the number with the percent sign. In this case, it is 60%. It indicates what percent of the space will be allocated to young children's toys.

The information not given is the square footage to be allocated to young children's toys. In other words, the percentage is the unknown.

In solving narrative problems, it is wise to highlight the facts by simplifying the language as we have done below.

In this situation there is 1,750 square feet of space available, and 60% is for younger children's toys. How much is this in square feet? What is 60% of 1,750?

Step 1 Identify the elements.

a. The base is the total amount.   B = 1,750 square feet

b. The rate is the number with the percent sign.   R = 60%

c. The part or percentage of the base that is equal to 60% is not given.   P = unknown

Step 2 Apply the formula.   P = B × R

a. Substitute the selected numbers.   P = 1,750 × 60%

b. Convert the percent to a decimal or a fraction.   P = 1,750 × .6, or $\frac{3}{5}$

c. Multiply and label the answer.   P = 1,750 × .6
P = 1,050 square feet

Answer   60% of 1,750 is 1,050. Thus, P = 1,050 square feet for younger children's toys.

Example 3 Your boss tells you that 30% of the company's workers are absent today. If there are 50 workers on the payroll, how many are absent?

Step 1 Identify the elements.

a. The base is the total number on the payroll.   B = 50 workers

b. The rate is the percent absent.   R = 30%

c. The percentage is the number absent.   P = unknown

Step 2 Apply the formula.   P = B × R

a. Substitute the known quantities.   P = 50 × .3

b. Multiply.   P = 15

Answer   30% of 50 is 15. Thus, P = 15 workers absent.

Remember the relationship between rate and percentage. They express the same subject in different terms, and that subject is a portion of the base. In identifying the elements, be certain that both rate and percentage are referring to the same thing. This is the only way the formula can work correctly. In the example above, 30% of the workers are absent and the percentage (15) represents the number of workers absent.

Self-Check

Find the percentage in each of the following situations.

1. You are the bookkeeper for the Weber Manufacturing Company. One of the wholesalers from whom you buy offers a 2% discount for prompt payment of bills. How much money will you save your company if you pay a bill of $555 within the discount period?

2. Last month, the notions department of Kimbal's Department Store sold 11,875 items. Of these items, 8% were paperweights. How many paperweights were sold?

3. Your employer at Weber Manufacturing Company where you work part-time deducts 24% of your gross pay for taxes and insurance premiums. If your gross pay is $186, how much money is deducted? _____

ANSWERS   1. $11.10   2. 950 paperweights   3. $44.64

Assignment 5.4

Base, Rate, and Percentage

1. A business math class of 36 students was given a test on the percentage formula. Seventy-five percent of the students received an A on the exam. How many students received A's?

   P = B × R
   P = 36 × 75%
   P = 27

   27 received A's

2. A shipment of candles ordered by Barbara's Gift Shop was damaged in transit. If the candles were valued at $250, and 35% of them were damaged, what was the value of the damaged candles?

   P = B × R
   P = $250 × 35%
   P = $87.50

   $87.50 value of damaged candles

3. In the Crestview Community College library, 24% of the books are classified as fiction. If the total book collection is 34,600 volumes, how many are fiction books?

   P = B × R
   P = 34,600 × 24%
   P = 8,304

   8,304 fiction books

4. Bill Vought, sales manager for Ace's Distribution Company, decided to increase his fleet of company cars by 30% because additional salespeople were being hired. If the company currently leases 60 cars, how many more cars are needed?

   P = B × R
   P = 60 × 30%
   P = 18

   18 more cars needed

5. In promoting a concert, Pop's Production Company found that in order for the concert to break even, the Civic Center must be filled to 65% capacity. If the Center holds 8,000 people, how many tickets must be sold in order to break even?

   P = B × R
   P = 8,000 × 65%
   P = 5,200

   5,200 tickets must be sold

6. Mina Brownell recently inherited $48,000 from her mother's estate. She invested it in a rental property and expects a return of 9% per year on this investment. What will this return be in dollars?

   P = B × R
   P = $48,000 × 9%
   P = $4,320

   $4,320 return on investment

continued

Assignment 5.4 *continued*

7. In processing your application for a loan, the bank informs you that your salary will have to be increased by 16% before you qualify for a loan. If you are currently making $7,000 a year part-time, how much more must you make if you want to take a loan from the bank?

   P = B × R
   P = $7,000 × 16%
   P = $1,120

   $1,120 increase in salary needed to qualify for loan

8. Stoneridge Central High School awarded 420 diplomas. In a survey of the graduating seniors, 60% of them said they planned to go on to higher education of some sort. How many of the graduates planned to go on to higher education?

   P = B × R
   P = 420 × 60%
   P = 252

   252 graduates going on to higher education

9. A marketing research study was conducted of 384 housewives in the United States. Sixty-six and two-thirds percent of these women felt that they should be paid for their housekeeping duties. How many thought they should be paid?

   P = B × R
   P = 384 × $66\frac{2}{3}$%

   $\left(66\frac{2}{3}\% = \frac{2}{3}\right)$

   $\frac{\cancel{384}^{128}}{1} \times \frac{2}{\cancel{3}_1} = 256$

   256 housewives thought they should be paid

10. Considering the rising cost of living, you decide to take 75% of the money you've saved and invest it in preferred stock. If you have saved $3,524, how much money will you invest?

    P = B × R
    P = $3,524 × 75%
    P = $2,643

    $2,643 to invest

11. Because of remodeling it is estimated that $33\frac{1}{3}$% of the inventory of five-gallon paint buckets would have to be moved. If the entire inventory of these buckets numbered 861, how many must be moved?

    B × R = P
    $\cancel{861}^{287} \times \frac{1}{\cancel{3}_1} = 287$

    287 buckets

12. Karl Westphal of Feed Industries, Inc., found that he could increase his yield per acre by 15% if he used an automatic irrigation system. If he has 1,528 acres and each acre currently yields 20 bushels of feed, what will be the total increase if the new irrigation system is used?

    1,528 Acres
    ×   20 Bushels
    30,560 Current yield

    B × R = P
    30,560 × 15% = P
    4,584 = P

    4,584 total increase

5.5 Solving Rate Narrative Problems

Rate or percent problems are perhaps the easiest type of percentage problems to solve. The fact that percent is missing from the explanation is usually obvious. Knowing this, determine which number is the base and make certain the percentage given and the rate you are seeking refer to the same thing.

Example 1 You sell cosmetics door-to-door and start out in the morning with 600 tubes of lip gloss. By noon, you have sold 30 tubes. What percent of your stock have you sold?

Base is the total number of tubes, 600, the figure with which you are comparing the number sold. Because you are solving for the percent sold, you must know the number sold. This is given. The percentage sold is 30 tubes. You can now say, "30 is what percent of 600?" In solving the problem, follow the steps below.

Step 1 Identify the elements.

    a. The base is the total number of tubes. $B = 600$ tubes

    b. The percentage is the number sold, reported in the same terms as the base. $P = 30$ tubes

    c. The rate is the number sold, expressed as a percent. It is not given. $R =$ unknown

Step 2 Apply the formula. $R = \dfrac{P}{B}$

    a. Substitute the known quantities. $R = \dfrac{30}{600}$

    b. Divide. $600 \overline{)30.00}\;\;.05$

    c. Convert the decimal to a percent. $.05 = 5\%$

Answer 30 is 5% of 600. Thus, $R = 5\%$.

This answer indicates that you sold 5%, or 30, of the 600 tubes of lip gloss.

Example 2 Your boss at Command Computer Company tells you that 15 of the company's workers are absent today. If 50 workers are on the payroll, what percent of them are absent?

Step 1 Identify the elements.

    a. The base is the total number of workers, the reference point. $B = 50$ workers

    b. The percentage is a part of the base expressed in the same units as the base. $P = 15$ workers

    c. The rate is a part of the base expressed as a percent. It is not given. $R =$ unknown

Step 2 Apply the formula. $R = \dfrac{P}{B}$

    a. Substitute the numbers. $R = \dfrac{15}{50}$

    b. Divide. $50 \overline{)15.0}\;\;.3$

c. Convert the decimal to a percent. $\qquad$ .3 = 30%

Answer 15 is 30% of 50. Thus, R = 30%.

This answer means that 30%, or 15, of the workers are absent.

Example 3 In your gift shop last year you sold $5,200 worth of greeting cards. This year you sold $5,980 worth of greeting cards. By what percent did your greeting-card sales increase from last year?

Step 1 Identify the elements.

    a. The base is the original amount, the amount that occurred first in time. In this case, the base is last year's figures.   B = $5200

    b. Since you are looking for a percent increase, the percentage is the actual increase in dollar form. You must, therefore, subtract first.

$$\begin{array}{r} \$5980 \text{ this year} \\ -\ 5200 \text{ last year} \\ \hline \$780 \text{ increase} \end{array}$$

P = $780

    c. The rate is the percent of increase. It is not given.   R = unknown

Step 2 Apply the formula. $R = \dfrac{P}{B}$

    a. Substitute the numbers. $R = \dfrac{780}{5200}$

    b. Divide. $5200 \overline{)780.00}^{\ .15}$

    c. Convert the decimal to a percent.   .15 = 15%

Answer 780 is 15% of 5200. Thus, R = 15%.

The answer indicates that greeting-card sales increased 15% from last year.

NOTE: The method used to solve this problem is similar to what you learned in section 5.3. Another way to state this problem is, "$5,980 is what % more than $5200?" When you are looking for the percent change between two numbers, you must first express that change in units or dollars before you can apply the formula to find rate. Hence, in step 1(b) it was necessary to subtract first to find the change in dollars, which in this case was an increase of $780.

Self-Check

Find the rate in each of the following situations.

1. Air Survey Company found that on flight 279 there were 48 vacant seats. If the total number of available seats amounted to 300, what percent were vacant?   _____

2. Coldwell Services, Inc., employs 2,150 employees. Eighty-six of these employees were selected for management training. What percent were selected for training?   _____

3. In one week 60,320 parts are assembled at Emerson Electronics Company. Out of

these, 1,508 parts are rejected. What is the rejection rate?

4. The report filed by your office manager stated that the Casper copying machine cost $605 and the Master copying machine cost $500. What percent more is the cost of the Casper brand compared to the Master brand?

ANSWERS 1. 16%   2. 4%   3. 2.5%   4. 21%

Assignment 5.5

Base, Rate, and Percentage

1. If a television set that retails for $285 is on sale for $68.40 less than the retail price, what is the rate of sale discount?

   $R = \dfrac{P}{B} = \dfrac{68.40}{285}$ .24 = 24%

   $R = .24$
   $R = 24\%$ **24% sale discount**

2. Good E. Chocolate Factory produces 125 pounds of chocolate every day. The manager announced that production must be cut by 20 pounds. What percent of the total production is this?

   $R = \dfrac{P}{B} = \dfrac{20}{125}$
   $R = .16$ **16% cut in production**
   $R = 16\%$

3. Your gold initial ring is insured in case of theft for $442. The current value of the ring is $613. For what percent of its total value is the ring insured?

                                                                 72.10% of total value insured
   $R = \dfrac{P}{B} = \dfrac{\$442}{\$613}$ .72104 = 72.10%

4. Find the rate of profit or loss, based on cost, on a wood stove that cost Jake's Woodstoves, Inc., $386 and sold for $219.

   386 B
   − 219 $R = \dfrac{P}{B} = \dfrac{167}{386}$ .4326 = 43.26%   **43.26% loss**
   167 P

5. Because of a change in company policy, your sales quota for the month will be increased by $7,855. If your current sales quota is $46,200, by what percent will it be increased?

                                                                 17% increase in quota
   $R = \dfrac{P}{B} = \dfrac{7,855}{46,200}$ .17002 = 17%

6. In the month just ended, there were $700 worth of customer returns in your store. In the previous month, there were $600 worth of customer returns. Compared to the previous month, what was the percent increase in the customer returns?

   $700
   − 600 B $R = \dfrac{P}{B} = \dfrac{100}{600} = \dfrac{1}{6} = 16\dfrac{2}{3}\%$ **$16\dfrac{2}{3}\%$ increase in dollar amount of customer returns**
   $100 P

7. Justin Andrews works for Payne Delivery Service. Today, his truck is loaded with 48 areca palm tropical plants. What percent of his job is done after he has delivered 16 plants?

                                                                 $33\dfrac{1}{3}\%$ of job done
   $R = \dfrac{P}{B} = \dfrac{16}{48} = \dfrac{1}{3} = 33\dfrac{1}{3}\%$

continued

Assignment 5.5 *continued*

8. A woolen scarf regularly selling for $23.75 is on sale for $20.36. Find the percent reduction, based on the regular price.

   $23.75 B
   −20.36
   $ 3.39 P

   $R = \dfrac{P}{B} = \dfrac{3.39}{23.75} = .142736 = 14.27\%$

   <u>14.27% reduction</u>

9. Berman's Department Store marked a group of men's jeans down to $10 a pair. As the buyer for the men's department, you know the jeans cost the store $12 a pair. What percent of loss, based on the store's cost, is the store taking on each pair of jeans?

   $12 B
   − 10
   $ 2 P loss

   $R = \dfrac{P}{B} = \dfrac{2}{12} = \dfrac{1}{6} = 16\dfrac{2}{3}\%$

   <u>$16\dfrac{2}{3}\%$ loss</u>

10. Both men and women responded to a newspaper poll. In all, 779 individuals responded. Of these, 643 were women. What percent of the responses were from women?

    $R = \dfrac{P}{B} = \dfrac{643}{779}$ .825417 = 82.54%

    <u>82.54% of responses from women</u>

11. In an electronics assembly plant, there were 540 employees in January. By the following June, only 459 persons were employed. What was the percent of decrease in the number of employees during that time?

    540
    − 459
    81 Decrease

    $R = \dfrac{P}{B} = \dfrac{81}{540} = .15 = 15\%$

    <u>15% decrease</u>

12. For the gift-wrapping service, Al Mondy, manager for Customer Service, ordered the following boxes:

Size	Quantity
1	280
2	156
3	74
4	119

    What percent of the total quantity ordered does each size represent? Round each answer to the nearest tenth of a percent.

    280 + 156 + 74 + 119 = 629 Total quantity ordered

    Size 1 = $\dfrac{280}{629}$ = .44515 = 44.5%

    Size 2 = $\dfrac{156}{629}$ = .24801 = 24.8%

    Size 3 = $\dfrac{74}{629}$ = .11764 = 11.8%

    Size 4 = $\dfrac{119}{629}$ = .1891 = 18.9%

    <u>Size 1 = 44.5%
    Size 2 = 24.8%
    Size 3 = 11.8%
    Size 4 = 18.9%</u>

5.6 Solving Base Narrative Problems

Remember that base refers to the whole figure or that which comes first. It is the basis for comparison. Consider the following example.

Example 1 You are a furniture salesperson, earning a commission of 8% on what you sell. Your commission last month was $864. You wonder how many dollars worth of actual merchandise you sold during the month.

What information is given? You know that your commission of $864 represents 8% of the total dollar amount sold. You want to know how much this was. Simply stated, the situation is, "$864 is 8% of what number?"

Before you could receive commission, you had to sell something. What came first is the base. In this case, it is the dollar value of the actual merchandise you sold, and it is the element for which you are looking.

Solve the problem as follows.

Step 1 Identify the elements.

a. The rate is the number with the percent sign. $R = 8\%$

b. The percentage is the part of the total sold that you receive as a commission. $P = \$864$

c. Check to be sure that the percentage and the rate are expressing the same thing. In this case, both are concerned with the commission.

d. The missing element is the base. $B = \text{unknown}$

Step 2 Apply the formula. $B = \dfrac{P}{R}$

a. Substitute the numbers. $B = \dfrac{864}{8\%}$

b. Convert the percent to a decimal or a fraction. $B = \dfrac{864}{.08}$

c. Divide.
$$.08 \overline{)864} = 10800$$

Answer $864 is 80% of $10,800. Thus, B = $10,800.

The answer tells you that the base is $10,800, meaning that you sold $10,800 worth of furniture last month to make your 8% commission of $864.

Example 2 Your boss tells you that 15 of the company's workers, or 30% of those on the payroll, are absent today. What is the total number of workers employed by the company?

Step 1 Identify the elements.

a. The rate is the percent absent. $R = 30\%$

b. The percentage is the number of workers absent. $P = 15 \text{ workers}$

c. The base is the total number employed. $B = \text{unknown}$

Step 2 Apply the formula. $B = \dfrac{P}{R}$

a. Substitute. $B = \dfrac{15}{30\%}$

Base, Rate, and Percentage

b. Convert from a percent to a decimal.

$$B = \frac{15}{.3}$$

c. Divide.

$$.3\overline{)15} \quad 50$$

Answer 15 is 30% of 50. Thus, B = 50 workers employed.

Example 3 The price you paid for office furniture was $2,568, which included a sales tax of 7%. What was the original price of the furniture before the sales tax was added on?

Step 1 Identify the elements.

a. The percentage is a part of the base.   P = $2,568 final price

b. The rate is the percent that is related to the percentage. In this case, the true rate is found by adding to 100%.

```
  100%  original price
+   7%  sales tax
  107%  final price
```

R = 107%

c. You are asked to find the original price, which means that the base is unknown.   B = unknown

Step 2 Apply the formula.

$$B = \frac{P}{R}$$

a. Substitute the numbers.

$$B = \frac{2{,}568}{107\%}$$

b. Convert the percent to a decimal.

$$B = \frac{2{,}568}{1.07}$$

c. Divide.

$$1.07\overline{)2568} \quad 2400$$

Answer $2,568 is 107% of $2,400. Thus, B = $2,400, which is the original price.

NOTE: The method used to solve this problem is similar to what you learned in section 5.3. Another way to state this problem is, "$2,568 is 7% more than what number?" In step 1(b) 7% is added to 100% because the price paid is 7% higher than the original price. The original price is the base, which is represented by 100%.

Example 4 This month's sales at Cook's Restaurant Supply Company are $40,420. If there was a decrease of 6% from last month, what were last month's sales?

Step 1 Identify the elements.

a. The percentage is a part of the base.   P = $40,420 this month's sales

b. The rate is the percent that is related to the percentage. In this case, the true rate is found by subtracting from 100%.

```
  100%  last month's sales
-   6%  decrease
   94%  this month's sales
```

R = 94%

c. You are asked to find last month's sales, which means the base is unknown.   B = unknown

Step 2 Apply the formula.

$$B = \frac{P}{R}$$

a. Substitute the numbers.

$$B = \frac{40{,}420}{94\%}$$

b. Convert the percent to a decimal.

$$B = \frac{40{,}420}{0.94}$$

c. Divide.

$$0.94 \overline{)40420} \; = 43000$$

Answer $40,420 is 94% of $43,000. Thus, B = $43,000, which is last month's sales.

NOTE: Another way to state this problem is, "$40,420 is 6% less than what number?" In step 1(b), 6% is subtracted from 100% because this month's sales are 6% lower than last month's sales. Last month's sales figure is the base, which is represented by 100%.

Self-Check

Find the base in each of the following situations.

1. Due to flooding 56% of the merchandise stored at Western Warehouse was damaged. If the damaged merchandise was valued at $535,360, what was the value of the total merchandise stored?

2. Last week Express Shipping transported 23% of its total number of crates by air, 41% by truck, and 36% by railroad. If the number of crates shipped by air amounted to 14,904, find the total number of crates transported by all three methods.

3. Because of a preseason sale, sweaters were sold with a discount of 15%. If the discount amounted to $3.90 on a particular sweater, what was the original price?

4. This year at your cycle shop you sold 161 unicycles. If you had an increase of 15% from last year's sales, how many unicycles did you sell last year?

5. A word processing system is priced at $2,116, which includes a discount of 8%. Find the original price of the system before the discount was taken.

ANSWERS 1. $956,000   2. 64,800 crates   3. $26   4. 140 unicycles   5. $2,300

Assignment 5.6

Base, Rate, and Percentage

1. Superstar Releasing Company, a sponsor of rock concerts, pays an entertainment tax of 10% on ticket proceeds. If the tax collected is $293, what were the total proceeds?

    $B = \dfrac{P}{R} = \dfrac{\$293}{10\%}$
    $B = \$2,930$

    $2,930 total proceeds

2. Olga Bechalis paid $86 on a debt. This payment was 20% of the total debt. What was her total debt?

    $B = \dfrac{P}{R} = \dfrac{\$86}{20\%}$
    $B = \$430$

    $430 total debt

3. Finestein's Discount Palace is offering a discount of 24% on a computer printer. The salesperson tells you that the discount amounts to $68.40. What was the original price of the printer?

    $B = \dfrac{P}{R} = \dfrac{\$68.40}{24\%}$
    $B = \$285$

    $285 original price

4. Mary Lou Luft, a customer of Lee's Gardening Supplies, made a 25% deposit on a greenhouse, Her deposit was $80. What was the total price of the greenhouse?

    $B = \dfrac{P}{R} = \dfrac{\$80}{25\%}$
    $B = \$320$

    $320 total price

5. Barry Dunsmore receives a discount of $15\tfrac{1}{2}\%$ on a shirt he buys on sale. He pays $9.25. What was the price of the shirt before the discount?

    1.000
    − .155
    .845 R

    $B = \dfrac{P}{R} = \dfrac{\$9.25}{.845}$ 10.946 = $10.95

    $10.95 price before discount

6. Crestview Community College has 1,576 male students this quarter. This represents 62% of the total enrollment. What is the total enrollment? Round your answer off to the nearest whole number.

    $B = \dfrac{P}{R} = \dfrac{1,576}{62\%}$ 2,541.93 = 2,542

    2,542 students

7. Because of a contract dispute, eighty percent of the employees at United Pulp Mill went out on strike. If 185 employees reported for work, what is the total number of workers employed?

    100%
    − 80%
    20%

    $B = \dfrac{P}{R} = \dfrac{185}{20\%}$

    925 total workers employed

continued

Assignment 5.6 *continued*

8. This year's sales at Textron Computer Software Company were down 6% from last year. If this year's sales were $919,733.60, what were last year's sales?

   $\begin{array}{r}1.00\\-.06\\\hline.94\text{ R}\end{array}$ $B = \dfrac{P}{R} = \dfrac{\$919,733.60}{.94} = \$978,440$

   $978,440

9. Victor Montebo discovers that Sears is offering 20% off the regular price on a telephone answering machine. If the Sears price is $119.95, what is the regular price?

   $\begin{array}{r}100\%\\-20\%\\\hline 80\%\text{ R}\end{array}$ $B = \dfrac{P}{R} = \dfrac{\$119.95}{80\%}$ $\$149.937 = \$149.94$

   $149.94 regular price

10. Lynn Momoto is keeping the petty-cash records for her office. If she has $46.50 left after spending 24% of the monthly petty cash allowance, how much petty cash was allowed for the month?

    $\begin{array}{r}100\%\\-24\%\\\hline 76\%\text{ R}\end{array}$ $B = \dfrac{P}{R}$ $\$61.184 = \$61.18$

    $\dfrac{\$46.50}{.76}$

    $61.18 petty cash for month

11. Of those taking the test for a real estate license, 63% receive a passing score. If 5,652 licenses are issued as a result, find out how many people took the test. Round your answer to the nearest whole number.

    $B = \dfrac{P}{R}$

    $\dfrac{5{,}652}{.63} = 8{,}971.42$

    $= 8{,}971$

    8,971 people

12. Virginia Tobias, an agent for Biz E. Bee Advertising Agency, found that readership of the local newspaper increased by 22% over last year. If the current readership is 1,050,420, what was the readership last year?

    $B = \dfrac{P}{R}$

    $\dfrac{1{,}050{,}420}{1.22} = 861{,}000$

    861,000 readership last year

5.7 Solving Amount and Difference Problems

The other important application of the percentage formula is in figuring **amount** and **difference.** Situations requiring these calculations are common in both business and consumer transactions. The formulas for amount and difference are:

> Amount = Base + Percentage   Difference = Base − Percentage
> A = B + P   D = B − P

Situations involving increase and decrease are common examples of amount and difference problems.

Example 1 20 increased by 25% of itself equals what number?

Step 1 Identify the elements.

a. The base is the original, or starting, number.   B = 20

b. The rate is the number with the percent sign.   R = 25%

c. The percentage will tell you how much the increase is, but you also need to find the amount.   P = ?

A = ?

d. The amount is B (20) increased by the P (unknown).

Step 2 Apply the formula and solve for the percentage.   P = B × R

a. Write the formula and solve for the percentage.   P = 20 × 25%

b. Substitute the numbers.   P = 5 (represents the increase)

c. Solve.

Step 3 Apply the formula and solve for the amount.

a. Write the formula.   A = B + P

b. Substitute the numbers.   A = 20 + 5

c. Solve.   A = 25

Substitute the answer in the original problem to see if it is correct and makes sense.

Answer 20 increased by 25% of itself is 25. Thus, A = 25.

Example 2 50 decreased by $\frac{1}{2}$% of itself equals what number?

Step 1 Identify the elements.

a. The base is the original, or starting, number.   B = 50

b. The rate is $\frac{1}{2}$%.   R = $\frac{1}{2}$%

c. The percentage is an unknown and will be the decrease in units.   P = ?

d. The difference is what the problem is actually asking for, which is B (50) minus P (unknown).   D = ?

Base, Rate, and Percentage

Step 2 Apply the formula for percentage and solve.

    a. Write the formula. $P = B \times R$

    b. Substitute the numbers. $P = 50 \times \frac{1}{2}\%$

    c. Solve. $P = 50 \times .005$
                                    $P = .25$

Step 3 Apply the formula for difference.

    a. Write the formula. $D = B - P$

    b. Substitute numbers. $D = 50 - .25$

    c. Solve. $D = 49.75$

Substitute the answer in the original problem as a check.

Answer   50 decreased by $\frac{1}{2}\%$ of itself equals 49.75. Thus, $D = 49.75$.

Self-Check

1. 50 increased by 2% of itself is
2. 120 decreased by 10% of itself is

ANSWERS   1. 51   2. 108

Finding an Amount

Example 3   You are the owner of a downtown stereo store. Your normal weekly sales bring in $20,000. Because of a new advertising campaign, you expect to increase your sales by 15%. What is your projected total sales?

    Current sales + Increase in sales = Projected sales
        Base   +   Percentage   =   Amount

You can solve the problem in two different ways and can use one method as a check for the other.

Method A

Step 1 Identify the elements.

    a. The base = the original figure or starting point. $B = \$20{,}000$

    b. The rate = the number with the percent sign. Note that this is the rate of increase. Thus the percentage will also refer to increase. $R = 15\%$

    c. The percentage = the missing element. $P =$ unknown

Step 2 Apply the formula for percentage. $P = B \times R$

    a. Substitute the numbers. $P = \$20{,}000 \times 15\%$

    b. Change the percent to a decimal or a fraction. $P = \$20{,}000 \times .15$

    c. Multiply. $\$20{,}000 \times .15 = \$3{,}000$

Answer $3,000 increase in sales.

This answer is the first phase of the solution. Remember, you are looking for the projected total sales.

Step 3 Find the amount.

a. Substitute the numbers.

b. Add.

$A = B + P$

$A = \$20{,}000 + \$3{,}000$

$\$20{,}000 + \$3{,}000 = \$23{,}000$

Answer $\$23{,}000$ projected sales.

NOTE: The amount ($\$23{,}000$) is greater than the original base ($\$20{,}000$).

Method B

Step 1 Express the projected total sales in terms of percent, remembering that the base always equals 100%.

$$\underset{100\%}{\text{Base}} + \underset{15\%}{(\text{Percentage})} = \underset{115\%}{\substack{\text{Amount} \\ (\text{Rate})}}$$

Base	+	Increase (Percentage)	=	Amount (Rate)
100%	+	15%	=	115%

$R = 115\%$ of current sales

Step 2 Apply the percentage formula.

a. Substitute the numbers.

b. Change the percent to a decimal.

c. Multiply.

$P = B \times R$

$P = \$20{,}000 \times 115\%$

$P = \$20{,}000 \times 1.15$

$\$20{,}000 \times 1.15 = \$23{,}000$

Answer $\$20{,}000$ increased by 15% is $\$23{,}000$. Thus, $A = \$23{,}000$ projected sales.

Because the rate used in method B represents the amount in terms of percent, the resulting percentage, $\$23{,}000$, is the projected total sales.

Self-Check

Find the amount in each of the following situations.

1. Your employer at Weber Manufacturing Company grants you a raise of 12%. What is your new weekly salary if you were making $486 before the raise?

2. Casper Jansen bought a lot for $4,250. Since then, it has increased in value by 132%. Calculate its present value.

3. This month's sales at Kimbal's Department Store are expected to be 15% more than last month's sales of $90,525. What sales figure is expected for this month?

ANSWERS 1. $544.32 2. $9,860 3. $104,103.75

Finding a Difference

Example 4 You purchased several shares of stock for $2,000. Reading the *Wall Street Journal*, you notice that your stock has declined in value by 8%. What is the present value of the stock?

You are not being asked how much the stock declined in value, but for the value of the stock now. The difference is the original price paid for the stock, the base, minus the dollar value of decline, the percentage.

$$\text{Original price} - \text{Dollar Decline} = \text{Present Value}$$
$$\text{Base} - \text{Percentage} = \text{Difference}$$

Note that the difference is smaller than the base. Again, there are two ways to solve the problem, and one method can be used as a check on the other.

Method A

Step 1 Identify the elements.

a. The original value of the stock, the value that came first, is the base.   B = $2,000

b. The rate is the number with the percent sign. Note that this is that rate of decline or decrease. The percentage will, therefore, also refer to decrease.   R = 8%

c. The percentage is the missing element.   P = unknown

Step 2 Apply the percentage formula.   P = B × R

a. Substitute the numbers.   P = $2,000 × 8%

b. Change the percent to a decimal.   P = $2,000 × .08

c. Multiply. $2,000 × .08 = $160

The stock has declined by $160. You want the present value, the difference.

Step 3 Find the difference.   D = B − P

a. Substitute the numbers.   D = $2,000 − 160

b. Subtract. $2,000 − 160 = $1,840

Answer $2,000 decreased by 8% is $1,840. Thus, D = $1,840 present value.

Method B

Step 1 Express the difference in terms of percent, knowing that the base equals 100%.

Base	−	Decrease (Percentage)	=	Difference (Rate)
100%	−	8%	=	92%

R = 92% of original value

Step 2 Apply the percentage formula.   P = B × R

a. Substitute the numbers.   P = $2,000 × 92%

b. Change the percent to a decimal.   P = $2,000 × .92

c. Multiply. $2,000 × .92 = $1,840

Answer $2,000 decreased by 8% is $1,840. Thus, D = $1,840 present value.

Self-Check

Find the difference in each of the following situations.

1. Weber Manufacturing Company lowers the price on certain items by 12%. If an item sold for $208.32 originally, how much does it sell for now?

2. Barry Musgrave earned $285 working part-time. If 24% of this were withheld, how much was his take-home pay?

3. In the month of July, sales at Kimbal's Specialty Store were down 17% from June, when sales totaled $86,754. Calculate the sales for July.

ANSWERS 1. $183.32   2. $216.60   3. $72,005.82

CROSS-NUMBER PUZZLE

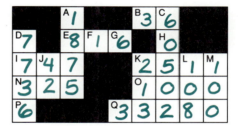

ACROSS

A) What percent of 795 is 7.95?
B) What number plus 10% equals $39.60?
D) $\frac{N}{49} = \frac{21}{147}$. N = _____.
E) What is 20% of 4,080?
H) Forty percent of $390 less $66\frac{2}{3}$% of $234 = _____.
I) What number minus .2% is 745.506?
K) Eight hundred thirty-seven is $33\frac{1}{3}$% of what number?
N) Two hundred sixty increased by 25% of itself is _____.
O) What is .001% of 100,000,000?
P) Thirty is to 35 as _____ is to 7.
Q) Nine thousand nine hundred eighty-four is 30% of what number?

DOWN

A) What is $18\frac{3}{4}$% in decimal form?
B) Eighty-seven point three is what percent less than 90?
C) Forty eight thousand four hundred one and six tenths is 20% less than _____.
D) Twelve and one-half percent of 61,888 is _____.
F) 11 : 121 as _____ : 11.
G) The decimal equivalent of 600% is _____.
J) Five hundred sixty-eight is what percent more than 400?
K) Three hundred nineteen point five is 50% more than _____.
L) Four hundred eighty-six is what percent of 450?
M) One thousand eighty-two is _____% of 1,082.
Q) Three-fourths percent is _____ times larger than $\frac{1}{4}$%.

Base, Rate, and Percentage

Assignment 5.7

Base, Rate, and Percentage

Solve for amount and difference.

1. 850 increased by 3% of itself is __875.50__.
2. 200 decreased by $\frac{1}{8}$% of itself is __199.75__.
3. 1,280 decreased by 50% of itself is __640__.
4. 789 increased by 100% of itself is __1,578__.
5. 40 increased by 120% of itself is __88__.
6. 6,468 decreased by .5% of itself is __6435.66__.
7. 98 decreased by 100% of itself is __0__.
8. 592 increased by $87\frac{1}{2}$% of itself is __1,110__.

Solve for amount.

9. During the month of December, the Embassy Unfinished Furniture Store increased its advertising budget by 18% over the previous month. If $300 was allowed for the month of November, how much was allocated for the December advertising budget?

   $300 Nov. allowance
   + 54 Allowance increase
   $354 Dec. allocation

   B × R = P
   $300 × 18% = 54

   $354 allocated for Dec. advertising budget

10. On a certain building tract, the contractors estimated that the cost of building a new home would be approximately 825% of the cost of the lot. If a lot cost $16,000, what is the estimated cost of a new home including the lot?

    $132,000 New home
    + 16,000 Lot
    $148,000

    B × R = P
    16,000 × 825% = $132,000

    $148,000 cost of new home including lot

11. The landlord at Walden Shopping Mall increased the monthly rent by 12%. If Victor's Shoe Store previously paid $1,225 rent, how much must he pay each month?

    $1,225 Original rent
    147 Increase
    $1,372 New rent

    B × R = P
    $1,225 × 12% = $147

    $1,372 per month

12. Fox E. Carpet Store sold a rug costing $388 at a gross profit of 40% of cost. What was the selling price?

    $388.00 Cost
    + 155.20 Markup
    $543.20 Selling price

    B × R = P
    388 × 40% = 155.20

    $543.20 selling price

    12. Alternative Method
    C + M = SP
    100% + 40% = 140%
    $388 + $155.20 = __$543.20__

continued

Assignment 5.7 *continued*

13. Barry Saraga put $900 into his savings account. If his money gathers 4% interest annually, how much does he have by the end of the year?

    B × R = P $900 Year's deposit total
    $900 × 4% = $36   +   36 Interest received   **$936 by the**
                         936   **end of the year**

Solve for difference.

14. A building tract was divided into 65 lots, all equal to one another in area. After 60% of the lots were sold, how many lots of the tract remained?

    B × R = P   65 Original lots
    65 × 60% = 39   − 39 Lots sold   **26 lots remaining**
                       26 Lots remaining

15. Sheila Dunsmore, a marketing representative for Happy Greeting Cards, takes home $2,600 a month and spends 85% of it on family expenses. How much does she have left?

    B × R = P $2,600 Monthly take-home
    $2,600 × 85% = $2210 − 2,210 Expenses   **$390 left**
                          $ 390 Left

16. James Blackmore's Men's Store ordered 150 dress shirts from a New York manufacturer. The order was checked by the shipping and receiving clerk, who found that 40% of the shirts were missing. How many dress shirts arrived at the store?

    B × R = P   150 Shirts ordered
    150 × 40% = 60   − 60 Shirts missing   **90 shirts arrived**
                         90 Shirts arrived

    16. (Ordered − Missing = Arrived)
        100% − 40% = 60%

    or   150 Shirts (B)
         × .60 % of shirts arrived (R)
           90.00 Shirts arrived (P)

17. A plastics factory molded 3,850 wall telephones. Quality control found that 8% were defective in some way. How many telephones passed the inspection?

    B × R = P   3,850 Molded
    3850 × 8% = 308   −   308 Defective   **3,542 telephones**
                        3,542 Passed   **passed inspection**

18. At a discount house in your neighborhood, television sets retailing for $285 are on sale for 24% off.

    a) If you buy one on sale, how much will you pay?

    B × R = P $285.00 Original price
    285 × 24% = $68.40 −   68.40 Sale discount   **$216.60 sale price**
                         $216.60 Sale price

    b) What is the amount of the sale discount?

                                                          $68.40 sale discount

Solve for difference or amount.

19. At last week's baseball game, 47,326 fans were in attendance. The announcer said that this week the number attending is about 15% higher than attendance the week before. How many attended this week?

    B × R = P
    47,326 × 115% = 54,424.9
                  = 54,425 fans   **54,425 fans attended**

continued

Assignment 5.7 *continued*

20. A theater building in the downtown district was purchased for $336,000 last year. During one year the property has increased in value by 20%. How much is the building worth now?

    B × R = P
    336,000 × 20% = $67,200

    $336,000 Last year's worth
      67,200 Increase in value
    $403,200 Current worth

    $403,200 building's current worth

21. Your labor union has just negotiated a contract that will give you a raise of 18% over last month's wage. What is your new wage if last month's wage was $1,762?

    B × R = P
    $1,762 × 18% = $317.16

    $1,762.00 Last month's wage   or $1,762 × 115% = $2,079.16
       317.16 Raise
    $2,079.16 New wage

    $2,079.16 new wage

22. Bierman's Department Store marks a group of sport shirts down 25%, based on their original retail price. If these shirts originally sold for $18.25, what is the new sales price?

    B × R = P
    $18.25 × 75% = 13.687
          = $13.69

      100%
    − 25%
       75%

    $13.69 new sales price

23. Tio Pepe's Restaurant advertises that its tacos contain 12% more ground beef than those of the Mexican restaurant down the street. If the tacos down the street contain 4 ounces of beef each, how much beef does each of Tio Pepe's tacos contain?

    B × R = P
    4 × 112% = 4.48 oz

      100%
    + 12%
      112%

    4.48 oz beef

Comprehensive Problems for Chapter 5

Base, Rate, and Percentage

1. 567 is $5\frac{1}{2}$% lower than __600__.
2. 101 equals $16\frac{2}{3}$% of what number? __606__
3. 15 is what percent of 10? __150%__
4. $25.50 is $37\frac{1}{2}$% of what number? __$68__
5. 624 is 4% greater than __600__.
6. 4,370 increased by 11% of itself is __4,850.7__.
7. 250% of __28__ = 70.
8. 9 is what percent less than 20? __55%__
9. 12 = $0.33\frac{1}{3}$% of __36__.
10. What percent of 26 is 26? __100%__
11. 14.8 is 80% less than __74__.
12. 800 is what percent more than 650? __23.1%__
13. What is $\frac{3}{8}$% of 980? __3.675__
14. What percent of 1,136 is 710? __62.5%__
15. $47.60 is what % higher than $28? __70%__
16. 0.815 decreased by 80% of itself is __.163__.
17. $3508.75 is $\frac{1}{4}$% more than __3,500__.
18. 8.1 is 8.1% of what number? __100__
19. $\frac{1}{4}$ of what number is 6.25? __25__
20. $3\frac{1}{4}$% of __2,000__ = 65.
21. $24.80 increased by 200% of itself is __$74.40__.
22. $1,487.40 is what % more than $1480? __.5% or $\frac{1}{2}$%__
23. 18 is what percent of 16? __$112\frac{1}{2}$%__
24. 400 is what percent less than 500? __20%__
25. 135 is $33\frac{1}{3}$% of what number? __405__
26. $8,928 is $\frac{4}{5}$% less than __$9,000__.

continued

Comprehensive Problems *continued*

27. 27 is what percent smaller than 36? __25%__

28. 32 is what percent of 160? __20%__

29. 20% of a number is 5. The number is __25__.

30. 0.1% of 1,500 is __1.5__.

31. 500 is 100% greater than __250__.

32. 656 decreased by $\frac{1}{8}$% of itself is __655.18__.

33. The population of Central City rose from 300,000 to 450,000 in ten years. What is the percent increase of population?

   $$\begin{array}{r}450,000\\-\;300,000\\\hline 150,000\end{array}$$ $\dfrac{150,000}{300,000}=\dfrac{1}{2}=50\%$ $\dfrac{P}{B}=R$ __50% increase in population__

34. Last year, the plant where Hank Morrison works had a total payroll of $534,926.16. This year, its payroll has increased to $623,542.06. What is the percent of payroll increase?

   $$\begin{array}{r}\$623{,}542.06\\-\;534{,}926.16\\\hline \$\;\;88{,}615.90\end{array}$$ $\dfrac{P}{B}=R$

   $\dfrac{88{,}615.90}{534{,}926.16}=.165660$

   $=.1657$ __16.57% payroll increase__

35. The head teller at Bank of Bentley, Mrs. Hughes, finds that the cost of rubber stamps is now $5.79 a stamp. This represents an increase of 9% over the price of the previous month. What was the price the previous month?

   1.00 Last month
   .09 Increase
   1.09

   $\dfrac{P}{R}=B$

   $\dfrac{\$5.79}{1.09}=5.311$

   $=\$5.31$ __$5.31 last month__

36. The company for which you work had sales of $56,207.98 this year. This is 5% below last year's sales. What were last year's sales?

   1.00 Last year's sales
   − .05 Decrease/rate
   .95 This year's sale

   $B=\dfrac{P}{R}$

   $\dfrac{\$56{,}207.98}{.95}=\$59{,}166.294$ __$59,166.29__

37. Rainier's Restaurant Supply prices a set of 4 chairs at $271. It is decided to raise the price by $6\frac{3}{4}$%. What will the new price be for the set of chairs?

   B × R = P
   271 × 6.75% = $18.2925

   $271.00 Old price
   18.29 Increase
   $289.29 New price

   __$289.29 new price of set__

continued

Comprehensive Problems *continued*

38. Cecilia Montez manages a small store. Her advertising expenses for the month of July were $1,562, and her total sales were $9,542.68. Find the percent of the total sales Cecilia spends on advertising.

    $R = \dfrac{\$1,562}{\$9,542.68} = \dfrac{P}{B} = .16368$

    $= 16.37\%$

    16.37% of total sales spent on advertising

39. Lake City has a population of 356,280. This is 8% more than the population last year, which is 6% higher than the population the year before that. Find the population of Lake City two years ago.

    $\dfrac{P}{R} = B$ Current population

    $\dfrac{356,280}{1.08} = 329,888.88$

    $= 329,889$ Last year's population

    $\dfrac{P}{R} = B$

    $\dfrac{329,889}{1.06} = 311,216.03$

    $= 311,216$ pop. Lake City two years ago

    311,216 pop. Lake City two years ago

40. Leroy Williams spends 25% of his income on rent, 22% on food, 16% on car payments, 12% on college expenses, and 8% on recreation. If he has $350 left, find his net income.

    ```
    25%          100%
    22         − 83% spent       B = P/R
    16           17% left
    12                        $350/.17 = $2,058.8235
     8
    83% spent
    ```

    $2,058.82 net income

41. A compact car retails for $7,785. The radio is worth $105.78. What percent of the price of the automobile covers the price of the radio?

    $\dfrac{P}{B} = R$

    $\dfrac{\$105.78}{\$7,785} = .013587$

    $= 1.36\%$

    1.36% of price covers radio

42. A hair dryer regularly selling for $23.75 is on sale for $20.36. What percent is the sale price of the regular price?

    $\dfrac{P}{B} = R$ $\dfrac{\text{Sale } \$20.36}{\text{Regular } \$23.75} = .85726$

    $= 85.73\%$

    85.73% of regular price

43. After taking inventory, J. P. Grocers discovered that $9\frac{1}{2}\%$ of its fresh produce had begun to spoil. If the total value of the fresh produce is $500, how many dollars worth has begun to spoil?

    $P = B \times R$
    $P = \$500 \times 9.5\%$
    $P = 47.50$

    $47.50 has begun to spoil

continued

Comprehensive Problems *continued*

44. Marie McNair receives $122.50 in overtime pay. This represents 14% of her gross pay. What is her gross pay? Round your answer to the nearest cent.

$B = \dfrac{P}{R}$

$B = \dfrac{122.50}{14\%}$

B = $875

_____ $875 gross pay

45. Catherine Bieber employs five clerks part-time at her antique store. If her total monthly payroll is $2,126, and she deducts $531.50 for fringe benefits, what percent of the total monthly payroll is she deducting for fringe benefits?

$\dfrac{P}{B} = R$

$\dfrac{\$531.50}{\$2,126} = .25 = 25\%$

_____ 25% deducted for fringe benefits

46. Pete Stripper's Furniture Refinishing Service did 23% more business this year than he did last year. His present sales are $16,281.48. What were his sales last year?

$\dfrac{P}{R} = B$

$\dfrac{\$16,281.48}{1.23} = \$13,236.975$

= $13,236.98

_____ $13,236.98 sales last year

47. Barry Ballard, a computer programmer, bought a duplex for $104,000 as an investment. Real estate in the city where he lives is appreciating at the rate of 2% a month. How much more will his duplex be worth at the end of three months if the rate remains the same?

① 104,000 × 2% = 2,080
104,000 + 2,080 = 106,080 end of first month
② 106,080 × 2% = 2,121.60
106,080 + 2,121.60 = 108,201.60 end of second month

B × R = P

_____ $6,365.63 increase in value

③ 108,201.60 × 2% = 2,164.03
108,201.60 + 2,164.03
 = 110,365.63 end of third month
$110,365.63 End of third month
− $104,000.00 Original value
 $ 6,365.63 Increase

48. Last year, Frank Oehl's gross pay was $19,820.68. This year, his gross pay was $20,342.26. What percent raise did he receive?

  $20,342.26
− 19,820.68
 $ 521.58 Raise

$R = \dfrac{P}{B}$

$R = \dfrac{521.58}{19820.68}$

R = .026314

R = 2.63%

_____ 2.63% raise

49. Jong Lee Restaurant must turn $4\frac{1}{2}\%$ of its income over to the state department of taxation as sales tax. If the restaurant takes in $4,056.79 one two-week period, how much must it pay the state?

B × R = P
$4056.79 × 4.5% = $182.55555

_____ $182.56 sales tax due

50. The final price for a four-poster waterbed is $543.20. This price includes a discount of 10% of the original price and a sales tax of 7%. Find the original price of the bed.

 10% Discount
− 7% Sales tax
 3% Effect of discount
   after sales tax

 100% Original
− 3% Discount
 97% Final price

(There is space provided for your work on the following page)

continued

Comprehensive Problems *continued*

$$B = \frac{P}{R}$$

$$B = \frac{\$543.20}{97\%}$$

B = $560 $560 original price

51. Tom's Bicycle Shop bought a used bike for $75. In repairing it, Tom spent $15 for new parts. He estimated that his other expenses in handling the bike were $5. He sold the bike for $120. What was his percent profit based on the total cost and expenses of the bike?

 $75 $120 SP $\frac{P}{B} = R$
  15   – 95 C
   5      $ 25 Profit
 $95 Total C + E $\frac{\$25}{\$95}$ = .26315

          = 26.32%   26.32% profit

52. You have insured your condominium for $56,000. If your insurance premium is $\frac{1}{8}$% of the face value of the policy, how much is your premium?

 $\frac{1}{8}$% = .00125   B × R = P $70
       $56,000 × .00125 = $70   amount of premium

53. A train car can hold 320 boxes of Type IV radio equipment. If the car currently has 89 boxes, what percent more boxes can it hold?

   320    $\frac{P}{B} = R$
 –   89
   231
     $\frac{231}{320}$ = .72187

     = 72.19%   72.19% more boxes

54. A display for women's accessories, which usually wholesales for $879, is on sale for the month of August at $770. What percent savings does this sale represent?

 $879 Regular price $R = \frac{P}{B}$
 – 770 Sale price
 $109 Savings
      $\frac{\$109}{\$879}$ = .124004

      = 12.4%   12.4% savings

55. Masque and Wig Community Theater sells 4% of the tickets for seats in its 750-seat theater for $6.00 each, 30% for $4.50 each, and the remaining tickets for $3.50 each. If the group completely sells out a performance, how much money will it take in?

   30 @ $6.00 =   180.00
  225 @ $4.50 = 1,012.50
  495 @ $3.50 = 1,732.50
         $2,925.00

   750   750   750   B × R = P
 × .04   .3   .66
 30.00 seats   225.0 seats 4500
   @$6.00   @ $4.50   4500
          495.00 seats @ $3.50 $2,925 if sold out

56. Able Books records the following breakdown of its inventory (each percent is based on the total inventory): romance 21%, fiction 29%, nonfiction 25%, children's 18%, and educational 7%.

continued

Comprehensive Problems *continued*

a) If fiction amounts to 12,673 books, find the total inventory.

$$B = \frac{P}{R}$$

$$B = \frac{12{,}673}{29\%}$$

B = 43700

43,700
total inventory

b) How many books are in the children's section?

B × R = P
43,700 × 18% = 7,866

7,866 in children's

57. You are the shipping clerk for Wondercraft, Inc. The roof of your company's warehouse sprang a leak during a torrential rainstorm, and 23% of the stock stored there was damaged beyond repair. If this damaged stock was valued at $64,528.78, and all the items in the warehouse were identical, how much is the remaining stock worth?

$280,559.91 Total stock
− 64,528.78 Damaged
 216,031.13 Remaining

$$\frac{P}{R} = B$$

$$\frac{\$64{,}528.78}{.23} = \$280{,}559.91 \text{ Total stock}$$

$216,031.13 worth of remaining stock

58. Because of a slowing trend in market conditions, there was a decrease of 802 new housing starts this year in Clayton County. This decrease is 16% of last year's new housing starts. Determine the number of new housing starts for this year.

$$B = \frac{P}{R}$$

5,012.5 Last year
− 802 Decrease
 4,210.5 This year

$$B = \frac{802}{16\%}$$

B = 5,012.5 last year

4,210.5 housing starts

59. Gross income of Andy's Lithuanian Restaurant this year is 134.4% of last year's income. This year's income is $108.542. How much did the restaurant take in last year?

$$\frac{P}{R} = B$$

$$\frac{\$108{,}542}{1.344} = \$80{,}760.416$$

= $80,760.42

$80,760.42 income last year

60. Jacob and Mary Silber talk to a real estate agent about selling their condominium. Jacob and Mary have completely paid for the condominium. The agent informs them that there will be a sales fee of 8% based on the selling price. Jacob tells her that he and Mary must clear $27,600 on the sale, the amount they must pay down on the house they want to buy. With this in mind, what is the lowest price the agent should put on the condominium?

100% Total selling price
−   8% Fee
  92% Clear

$$B = \frac{P}{R}$$

$$B = \frac{\$27{,}600}{92\%}$$

B = $30,000 lowest selling price

$30,000

Case 1

Bob Simins owned a small souvenir and gift shop located at a seaside resort. His total inventory amounted to $24,680. A fire broke out one evening and it was estimated that $6,663.60 worth of merchandise was completely burned or damaged beyond repair. The building was also damaged, and Bob decided the store would have to be closed for repairs during the month of August.

He was expecting a large shipment of beach towels from Beachwear, Inc. His original order was for 150 beach towels at a total price of $1,115. This price included a 10% quantity discount because Bob ordered over 100 towels. Because the store would be closed, Bob cut back the order to 50 towels, even though this meant foregoing the discount.

Bob needs to know what percent of the merchandise was ruined in the fire. He also needs to know the total price of his revised order from Beachwear, Inc.

Case 2

Mida Frances and Emma Fritz coauthored a detective novel. They negotiated with several publishers, each of whom made an attractive offer. Then they sat down with paper and pencil and listed the good and bad points of each.

"It looks to me," Mida said, "as though it boils down to the rate of royalty each of them is willing to pay."

Because she knew that the royalty was the compensation they would receive based on sales of the book, Emma agreed.

"Let me see," she said, looking at one of the contracts. "Crownly Publishing Company will pay us 12% on the first 10,000 copies based on the books sold at publisher's net and 19% on all sales over 10,000."

"What's publisher's net?"

"That's the amount they make after they give a 20% discount to the bookstores," Emma said.

"Then if the book sells for $12.95, our royalty is based on a figure 20% below that. Is that right?"

"Yes. That's what all the companies we're dealing with use as a basis. Branold Publishing offers 12% royalty on the first 5,000 copies sold, 15% on the next 5,000, and 17% on all sales over 10,000. Belling Publishers Limited, that English firm, offers a straight 15%."

"If we assume we'll sell 15,000 copies at a selling price of $12.95, which one is the best deal?" Mida asked.

a) Can you tell her the answer?

b) What other things should be considered before signing a contract of this nature?

Key Terms

Amount
Base
Difference
Percent

Percentage
Percentage Formula
Rate

Key Concepts

- **Converting a Percent to a Decimal:** Move the decimal point two places to the left and delete the percent sign.
- **Converting a Percent to a Fraction:** Move the decimal point two places to the left and place the number over 100. Reduce to lowest terms.
- **Converting a Decimal to A Percent:** Move the decimal point two places to the right and add the percent sign.
- **Converting a Fraction to a Percent:** Divide the numerator by the denominator. Find the quotient to at least two decimal places. Convert the decimal to a percent.
- **Base:** The basis of comparison; the starting the point; the initial figure. Always equal to 100%. Usually the figure or expression following "of," "less than," or "more than." Often labeled "last year," "gross salary," "original price," "principal," "total enrollment."
- **Rate:** A percent, decimal, or fractional part of base. Usually expressed as percent, followed by %.
- **Percentage:** A portion or part of the base resulting from multiplying the base by the rate. Often labeled "tax," "commission," "increase," "decrease," "more," "less," "deduction," "interest," "discount," "loss," "gain."
- **Percentage and Rate:** The same thing expressed in different terms.
- **Percentage Formulas:**

    Percentage = Base times Rate $\qquad P = B \times R$

    Base = Percentage divided by Rate $\qquad B = \dfrac{P}{R}$

    Rate = Percentage divided by Base $\qquad R = \dfrac{P}{B}$

    Amount = Base plus Percentage $\qquad A = B + P$

    Difference = Base minus Percentage $\qquad D = B - P$

6

Trade and Cash Discounts

Business Meets a Challenge
AVON

Changing times presented a challenge for Avon. With more and more women joining the workforce, there were fewer housewives at home to answer the doorbell when Avon called. As a result, the company's earnings began to decline. After considerable research, Avon became better able to tune into the changing needs and desires of its potential customers. It changed the style of its jewelry line from traditional to contemporary and added more colors to its makeup line in order to become more competitive with other cosmetics firms. The company also began to offer additional direction and more free training to its home sales force in order to improve proper invoicing, record-keeping and professional selling. Avon searched for areas of diversification, even entering the health services field. Its most impressive acquisition and one that is bound to have long-reaching effects was the Beverly Hills–based company, Giorgio, Inc. This purchase gives Avon access to prime selling space in prestige retail stores. With its revitalized sales and marketing efforts, Avon's revenues have now reached the $3 billion mark.

> **Learning Objectives**
>
> After reading and studying this chapter and working the problems, you will be able to:
>
> - Understand invoices and common invoice abbreviations.
> - Find the net price when a single trade discount or a series of trade discounts is given.
> - Find the single equivalent trade-discount percent for a series of trade discounts.
> - Calculate the amount of cash discount.
> - Determine the net amount due after trade and cash discounts have been allowed.
> - Figure the amount due when returns and shipping charges are involved.
> - Determine the amount of credit and amount still owed after a partial payment has been made.

As consumers we have a vast array of products available to us. Most often, the products we buy have traveled through many hands before reaching the retailer's shelf.

Trade sales are the sales between businesses. To study them, we must trace the path that a product takes from the point of origin to the final user. For example, the path may lead from the manufacturer to the wholesaler to the agent to the retailer to the consumer. A particular business that purchases the product along the path is not the ultimate consumer. Trade sales use documents called invoices. To talk about them, we use such terms as trade discount, cash discount, net price, dating, freight, and partial payment. All these important terms and the concepts behind them are explained in this chapter.

6.1 Invoices and Trade Discounts

Understanding Invoices

An **invoice** is a document prepared by the seller and presented to the buyer. A copy is either included with the merchandise when it is shipped or mailed to the buyer under separate cover. The invoice acts as a record of sale and is called a **sales invoice**. The information contained in an invoice is often printed by computer.

A typical invoice:

1. Identifies the seller and buyer by name and address.
2. Lists the items purchased.
3. Shows the quantity of each item, the unit price, and an *extension total*, that is, number of items × unit price.
4. Tells how the merchandise is shipped.
5. Details applicable trade discounts.

6. Shows terms of payment and cash discount allowances.
7. Lists shipping and insurance charges.
8. Gives an *invoice total*, that is, the sum of the extension totals.

Study the following invoices. Familiarize yourself with how they are set up and how information is presented.

Bargraves Hardware Company
924 South Dale Avenue
Seattle, Washington 98109

Invoice

Date	Number
Oct. 15, 19__	C216842

Sold to
Hank's Quality Hardware
4675 Banfield Drive
Astoria, Oregon 97103

Shipped to
Hank's Quality Hardware
4675 Banfield Drive
Astoria, Oregon 97103

Customer No. 2-4783-6

Shipped via	Salesperson	Terms
Truck	Thomas	2/10, n/30, E.O.M.

Quantity Ordered	Quantity Shipped	Unit	Stock No.	Description	Unit Pr.	Total Pr.
16	16	Ea	A240	Screwdriver	3.98	63.68
8	8	Ea	A362	Pliers	4.50	36.00
14	0	Ea	B023	Tape measures	18.50	*
12	12	Ea	B142	Power hammer	24.20	290.40
1	1	Ea	C531	Table saw	298.00	298.00
					Total Cost	**688.08**

*Back ordered—Merchandise to be shipped when available.

Gordon Sporting Goods, Inc.
536 Gordon Avenue
Indianapolis, Indiana 46204

Order Rcd:	5/1/__
Order Sent:	5/3/__
Invoice Date:	5/6/__
Invoice No:	0054605

Terms: 3/10, 2/30, N/60

Ship to/Charge to:
The Athlete's Foot
4216 Drover Avenue
Toledo, Ohio 43605

Quantity	Description	Unit Price	Extension Total
1 gro.	Running shorts 4 doz. ea. S, M, L	5.50 ea.	792.00
4 doz.	Shirts, basketball 1 doz. ea. S, M, L, XL	33.25 doz.	133.00
12 bx.	Shoe strings	22.50 bx.	270.00
		Total	**1,195.00**

Trade and Cash Discounts

Understanding Common Invoice Abbreviations

There are a number of abbreviations commonly used on invoices. The following table includes many of them. You may want to keep it for reference should you work in this area of business.

Abbreviation	Meaning
@	At, as in 16 items @ $5.00
bbl.	Barrel, usually a container holding 31.5 gallons
bx.	Box
C	One hundred: C is the symbol for *centum*, Latin
Cart./ctn.	Carton
c.o.d.	Cash on delivery
cpm.	Cost per thousand
cs.	Case
crt./ct.	Crate
ctn.	Carton
cwt.	Per hundredweight
doz.	Dozen, or 12 items
drm.	Drum
ea.	Each
e.o.m./EOM	End of the month. The discount period is calculated from the end of the month in which the invoice is dated.
f.o.b.—destination	Free on board—destination: the seller pays shipping charges
f.o.b.—shipping point	Free on board—shipping point: the buyer pays shipping charges
ft.	Foot, 12 inches
gal.	Gallon, 4 quarts
gro.	Gross, 144, or 12 dozen items
gr. gro.	Great gross: twelve gross, or 1,728 items
in.	Inch
lb/#	Pound
M	One thousand: M is the symbol for *mille*, Latin for 1,000
oz.	Ounce
pr.	Pair
prox.	Proximo: a synonym for EOM dating
qt.	Quart, 2 pints
R.O.G.	Receipt of goods: the discount period begins when the order arrives at the buyer's location
X	Extra dating: the discount period is extended by a specified number of days; for example, 90X means 90 additional days
yd.	Yard

Understanding Trade Discounts

Many wholesalers and manufacturers publish catalogues that include pictures, descriptions, and prices for their line of products. The price printed in the catalogue is called the **list price.** A reduction in the list price is called a **trade discount.** The trade discount may be a single discount or a series of discounts, such as "$420 list price less discounts 10%, 20%." The price paid by the customer—for example, a retailer—after the trade discount(s) have been subtracted from the list price is called the **net price.**

Because the list price may be reduced or increased over a relatively short period of time, it would be too expensive for the manufacturer or wholesaler to publish a new catalogue every time a price changes. Thus an additional printed sheet is usually available along with the catalogue, which states what discounts are allowed on the prices quoted in the catalogue.

When costs for the wholesaler or manufacturer rise, as during a time of inflation or a shortage of supply, a discount may be reduced or dropped. Trade discounts may be added or increased because of a decrease in costs for the supplier or changing competitive market conditions. They normally are not considered a price "savings," but rather a business practice of quoting prices based on list prices. Unlike cash discounts, which are explained later in this chapter, trade discounts generally are not a point of negotiation.

Trade discounts vary according to the type of buyer, not the actual quantity of goods ordered. For example, a 40% discount may be offered to the wholesaler and a 30% discount offered to the retailer for the same merchandise. Trade discounts do not apply to freight or delivery charges.

It is important for the buyer and/or owner of a business to keep up to date with price changes and trade-discount offerings since, particularly in today's economy, prices can change frequently without a major announcement from the supplier.

Finding Trade Discount and Net Price When a Single Trade-Discount Percent Is Given

The process used to calculate these problems is an application of the percentage formula as presented in Section 5.3. All you need do here is redefine the terms as follows:

HOW THE PERCENTAGE FORMULA APPLIES

List price = Base
Trade discount % = Rate
Trade discount = Percentage
Net price = Difference

List price × Trade discount % = Trade discount
B × R = P

List price − Trade discount = Net price
B − P = Difference

Example 1 The list price of a stove is $200 and the trade discount is 20%. Find the trade discount in dollars and the net price.

Step 1 Multiply the list price by the trade-discount percent to find the trade discount in dollars.

List price × Trade discount % = Trade discount
$200 × 20% = Trade discount
$40 = Trade discount

Step 2 Subtract the trade discount from the list price to find the net price

$200 List price
− 40 Trade discount
$160 Net price

Answer The trade discount is $40; the net price is $160.

NOTE: The net price could also be found in the case of a single trade-discount percent by multiplying the list price by the complement of the single trade-discount percent. The **complement** is the difference between 100% and the percent of the discount. In the example above, the net price can be found by multiplying the list price [$200] by 80% [100% − 20%].

$$\$200 \times 80\% = \$160 \text{ net price}$$

Self-Check

The list price of a display case is $800 less a trade discount of 30%. How much are the trade discount and the net price?

ANSWERS $240 = trade discount; $560 = net price

Finding Trade Discount and Net Price When a Series of Trade-Discount Percents Is Given

It is common in business to find two or more trade discounts given for the same merchandise. This is called a **series of discounts,** or **chain discounts.** More than one discount may be given for any number of reasons. An additional discount may be offered in order to change a supplier's prices for a particular line of merchandise or to stimulate business. Also, more than one discount may be quoted according to the different types of wholesalers and retailers buying the merchandise.

One method to use when a series of discounts is allowed is to apply the percentage formula separately for each discount in the series. It is important to understand that the discounts *cannot* be added together and then applied because the base changes with each discount. In other words, each discount must be subtracted from the balance that remains after the preceding discount has been subtracted.

Example 2 A set of living room furniture is listed at $1,200 and the dealer offers trade discounts of 20% and 10%. What are the trade discount and the net price?

Step 1   Multiply the list price by the first trade-discount percent in the series to find the first discount.

$1,200 × 20% = First trade discount
$240 = First trade discount

Step 2   Subtract the first trade discount from the list price to find the net amount after the first discount.

$1,200
−   240
$ 960 Net amount after first discount

Step 3   Multiply the net amount by the second trade-discount percent to find the second trade discount.

$960 × 10% = Second trade discount
$96 = Second trade discount

Step 4   Subtract the second trade discount from the net amount found in step 2 to find the net amount after the second trade discount.

$960
−   96
$864 Net amount after second discount

NOTE: Since there are only two discounts offered, the net amount after the second discount is the net price. If there were more trade discount percents offered, the same process would continue.

Step 5   Subtract the net price from the list price to find the total trade discount in dollars.

$1,200 List price
−   864 Net price
$336 Trade discount

Answer   The trade discount is $336; the net price is $864.

Example 3 A pool listed at $3,000 is allowed a chain discount of 20%, 10%, and 10%. Find the total trade discount and the net price.

Solution Instead of showing each step, we will work out this problem in a more compact manner.

$3,000 List price
− 600 First discount (20% of $3,000)
$2,400 Net amount after the first discount
− 240 Second discount (10% of $2,400)
$2,160 Net amount after the second discount
− 216 Third discount (10% of $2,160)
$1,944 Net amount after the third discount (net price)

$3,000 List price
− 1,944 Net price
$1,056 Trade discount

Answer The trade discount is $1,056; the net price is $1,944.

Self-Check

1. A chain saw listed at $500 is subject to trade discounts of 20% and 10%. What are the net price and total trade discount in dollars? _____

2. Weed Office Supplies offers trade discounts of 30%, 10%, and 10% on a file cabinet listed at $196. What is the total trade discount in dollars? _____

ANSWERS 1. $360 = net price; $140 = trade discount   2. $84.87 = trade discounts

Finding Single Equivalent Trade-Discount Percent

There is a simpler way to find the total trade discount and net price when a series of trade-discount percents is allowed: We find a percent that is equal to the series and apply this one rate to the list price. This is called the **single equivalent trade-discount percent.**

Example 4 Find the single equivalent trade-discount percent if a chain discount of 20%, 10%, and 5% is allowed.

Step 1 Determine the complement of each discount percent (subtract each percent from 100%).

Complements:
100% − 20% = 80%
100% − 10% = 90%
100% − 5% = 95%

Step 2 Express each complement in decimal form and multiply. This will give you the equivalent net price in decimal form.

$0.8 \times 0.9 \times 0.95 = 0.684$

Step 3 Subtract the net price equivalent from 1.00 (100%) and convert to a percent to find the single equivalent trade-discount percent. (It is important to keep all decimal places for accuracy.)

1.000
− .684
.316
31.6 = 31.6%

Answer 31.6% is the single equivalent trade-discount percent.

Example 5 Find the net price and trade discount for a grandfather clock that lists at $1,000 and is allowed trade discounts of 30%, 20%, and 10%.

Step 1 Find the single equivalent trade-discount in decimal form

a. Find complements in decimal form.   .7 .8 .9

b. Multiply.   .7 × .8 × .9 = .504
Equivalent net price in decimal form

c. Subtract from 1 (note that this "1" represents the list price, which equals base or 100%).

```
  1.000
−  .504
   .496  Single equivalent
         trade discount in
         decimal form
```

Step 2 Multiply the list price by the single equivalent trade discount in decimal form to find the trade discount in dollars.

```
  $1,000  List price
×   .496
  $  496  Trade discount
```

Step 3 Subtract the trade discount from the list price to find the net price.

```
  $1,000  List price
−    496  Trade discount
  $  504  Net price
```

Answer The trade discount is $496; the net price is $504.

In the example above, the net price could have been found first by multiplying the list price, $1,000, by the equivalent net price in decimal form, .504, which was found in step 1(b). The equivalent **net-price percent** could also be found by moving the decimal point two places to the right. In Example 5, this would be 50.4%. The net-price percent represents the net price in terms of percent rather than in dollars.

```
  $1,000  List price
×   .504
  $  504  Net price
```

Then the trade discount could be found by subtracting this number from the list price.

```
  $1,000  List price
−    504  Net price
  $  496  Trade discount
```

If the problem asks you to find the net price, all you need to use is the equivalent net price in decimal form. This is why it is important to label your work as you go along so that you do not become confused as to what each decimal equivalent represents. When finding single equivalent discounts, keep the decimal to four places, rounded for accuracy. For instance, 0.23625 = 0.2363 = 23.63%. Percents in this chapter should be rounded to the nearest hundredth of a percent where applicable.

Self-Check

1. Find the single equivalent trade-discount percent for each of the following series.
   a. 20%, 10%
   b. 10%, 5%, 5%

2. Find the net-price percent for each of the following series.

    a. 5%, 10%

    b. 5%, 10%, 10%

3. Jolly Camp Gear, Inc., offers a chain discount of 10%, 10%, and 5% on a tent that lists for $605. What are the total trade discount in dollars and the net price?

4. A cart that lists for $196 is allowed trade discounts of 25%, 20%, and 10%. Find the net price.

ANSWERS   **1.** (a) 28%; (b) 18.77%   **2.** (a) 85.5% (b) 76.95%   **3.** Trade discount = $139.45; net price = $465.55   **4.** $105.84

BEFORE INVOICES

Until the invoice was developed as a means of billing, creditors kept track of money owed them by using the tally system. The customer cut notches on a wooden rod, called a tally stick. This was then given to the shopkeeper, the creditor. The creditor later presented the tally stick to the customer for payment.

After dishonest shopkeepers began cutting additional notches in the sticks, a refinement to the tally system was developed. The rod was split down the center, and both the creditor and the debtor had to match or *tally* the notches on the stick before payment was made. The tally system was used well into the sixteenth century.

Assignment 6.1

Trade and Cash Discounts

Find the trade discount and the net price.

	List Price	Discount Percent	Trade Discount	Net Price	
1.	$ 350	20%	$ 70.00	$ 280.00	1. $350 × 20% = $70 TD $350 − $70 = $280 NP
2.	$ 579	33⅓%	193.00	386.00	2. $579 × ⅓ = $193 TD $579 − $193 = $386 NP
3.	$ 162.50	15%	24.38	138.12	3. $162.50 × 15% = $24.38 TD $162.50 − $24.38 = $138.12 NP
4.	$1,900	2½%	47.50	1,852.50	4. $1,900 × 2.5% = $47.50 TD $1,900 − $47.50 = $1,852.50 NP
5.	$ 647	21%	135.87	511.13	5. $647 × 21% = $135.87 TD $647 − $135.87 = $511.13 NP
6.	$ 52.48	8¼%	4.33	48.15	6. $52.48 × 8.25% = $4.33 TD $52.48 − $4.33 = $48.15 NP
7.	$2,470	40%	988.00	1,482.00	7. $2,470 × 40% = $988 TD $2,470 − $988 = $1,482 NP
8.	$ 870.75	25%	217.69	653.06	8. $870.75 × 25% = $217.69 TD $870.75 − $217.69 = $653.06 NP
9.	$5,000	37½%	1,875.00	3,125.00	9. $5,000 × 37.5% = $1,875 TD $5,000 − $1,875 = $3,125 NP
10.	$ 944.60	18%	170.03	774.57	10. $944.60 × 18% = $170.03 TD $944.60 − $170.03 = $774.57

Find the single equivalent trade-discount percent. Round to the nearest hundredth of a percent.

	Discount Series	Single Equivalent Trade-Discount Percent	
11.	30%, 10%	37 %	11. .7 × .9 = .63 1.00 − .63 = .37 = 37%
12.	20%, 10%, 5%	31.6 %	12. .8 × .9 × .95 = .684 1.00 − .684 = .316 = 31.6%
13.	25%, 10%	32.5 %	13. .75 × .9 = .675 1.00 − .675 = .325 = 32.5%

Find the net-price percent. Round to the nearest hundredth of a percent.

	Discount Series	Net Price Percent	
14.	10%, 5%, 3%	82.94 %	14. .9 × .95 × .97 = .82935 = .8294 = 82.94%
15.	12½%, 10%, 6%	74.03 %	15. .875 × .9 × .94 = .74025 = .7403 = 74.03%

continued

Assignment 6.1 *continued*

Find the single equivalent trade discount and the equivalent net price in *decimal form*. Round to four places.

	Discount Series	Single Equivalent Trade Discount	Equivalent Net Price	
16.	25%, 5%	$ .2875	$ .7125	16. .75 × .95 = .7125 ENP 1.0000 − .7125 = .2875 SETD
17.	20%, 10%, 10%	.352	.648	17. .8 × .9 × .9 = .648 ENP 1.000 − .648 = .352 SETD
18.	30%, 12½%	.3875	.6125	18. .7 × .875 = .6125 ENP 1.0000 − .6125 = .3875 SETD
19.	15%, 5%, 5%	.2329	.7671	19. .85 × .95 × .95 = .7671 ENP 1.000 − .7671 = .2329 SETD
20.	20%, 8%	.264	.736	20. .8 × .92 = .736 ENP 1.000 − .736 = .264 SETD

Find the trade discount and the net price in dollars.

	List Price	Discount Series	Trade Discount	Net Price	
21.	$ 300	10%, 5%	$ 43.50	$ 256.50	21. .9 × .95 = .855 ENP $300 × .855 = $256.50 NP $300 − $256.50 = $43.50 TD
22.	$10,800	8%, 2%	1,062.72	9,737.28	22. .92 × .98 = .9016 ENP $10,800 × .9016 = $9,737.28 NP $10,800 − $9,737.28 = $1,062.72 TD
23.	$ 850	20%, 10%, 10%	299.20	550.80	23. .8 × .9 × .9 = .648 ENP $850 × .648 = $550.80 NP $850 − $550.80 = $299.20 NP
24.	$ 631.50	14%, 4%	110.13	521.37	24. .86 × .96 = .8256 ENP $631.50 × .8256 = $521.37 NP $631.50 − $521.37 = $110.13 TD
25.	$ 788	25%, 5%	226.55	561.45	25. .75 × .95 = .7125 ENP $788 × .7125 = $561.45 NP $788 − $561.45 = $226.55 TD
26.	$ 552.50	15%, 10%, 10%	172.10	380.40	26. .85 × .9 × .9 = .6885 ENP $552.50 × .6885 = $380.40 NP $552.50 − $380.40 = $172.10 TD
27.	$ 4,730	12½%, 5% 5%	994.72	3,735.28	27. .875 × .95 × .95 = .7897 ENP $4,730 × .7897 = $3,735.28 NP $4,730 − $3,735.28 = $994.72 TD
28.	$ 372.00	10%, 5%	53.94	318.06	28. .9 × .95 = .855 ENP $372 × .855 = $318.06 NP $372 − $318.06 = $53.94 TD
29.	$ 400	20%, 5%, 5%	111.20	288.80	29. .8 × .95 × .95 = .722 ENP $400 × .722 = $288.80 NP $400 − 288.80 = $111.20 TD
30.	$ 87.75	10%, 10%, 3%	18.80	68.95	30. .9 × .9 × .97 = .7857 ENP $87.75 × .7857 = $68.95 NP $87.75 − $68.95 = $18.80 TD

31. A car battery that lists for $22 is allowed a trade discount of 20%. What is the net price for five batteries?

$22 × 5 = $110
$110 × 20% = $22 TD
$110 − $22 = $88 NP

$88 net price

continued

226 Chapter 6

Assignment 6.1 *continued*

32. Jebar Wholesale Furniture lists a matching set of baby furniture for $1,450 less 10% and 20%. What are the net price and the trade discount?

    .9 × .8 = .72
    $1,450 × .72 = $1,044 NP
    $1,450 − $1,044 = $406 TD

    $1,044 net price,
    $406 trade discount

33. Find the net price of a wood stove offered by Port Distributors if the list price is $450 with trade discounts of 25% and 5%.

    .75 × .95 = .7125
    $450 × .7125 = $320.625
              = $320.63

    $320.63 net price

34. What is the trade discount for a conveyor that lists for $2,780 and is allowed a trade-discount percent of $23\frac{1}{4}\%$? If the charge for delivery is $55, how much is the total bill?

    $2,780 × 23.25% = 646.35 TD
    $2,780 − $646.35 = $2,133.65 NP
    $2,133.65 + $55 = $2,188.65 Total bill
      (NP)   (Freight)

    $646.35 trade discount,
    $2,188.65 total bill

35. Oak doors that list for $168 are offered with trade discounts of 15%, 10%, and 5% from Posner's Supply House. What is the net price?

    .85 × .9 × .95 = .7268
    $168 × .7268 = $122.10 NP

    $122.10 net price

36. Atkin's Wood Works advertises ceiling fans in its catalogue for $225. An updated price sheet offers trade discounts of 20% and 10%. If Hunter's Department Store buys five fans, what are the trade discount and the net price?

    $225 × 5 = $1,125
    .8 × .9 = .72
    $1,125 × .72 = $810 NP
    $1,125 − 810 = $315 TD

    $315 trade discount,
    $810 net price

37. Brunswick Sporting Supplies offers a golf cart for $1,200 with trade discounts of 20%, 5%, and 5%. What is the trade discount in dollars?

    .8 × .95 × .95 = .722
    $1,200 × .722 = $866.40 NP
    $1,200 − $866.40 = $333.60 TD

    $333.60
    trade discount

38. As the buyer for Boro Home Builders, you order a hot water heater from Samuel Enterprises that lists for $458 with trade discounts of $10\frac{1}{2}\%$ and 4%. If you are charged a freight expense of $32.35, what is the total bill?

    .895 × .96 = .8592
    $458 × .8592 = $393.51 NP
    $393.51 + $32.35 = $425.86 Total bill

    $425.86 total bill

continued

Assignment 6.1 *continued*

39. The Royal Motor Inn orders 120 lamps listed at $56.50 each with trade discounts of 12%, 7%, and 5%. What is the total net price?

    $56.50 × 120 = $6,780
    .88 × .93 × .95 = .7775
    $6,780 × .7775 = $5,271.45 NP

    $5,271.45 net price

40. Lithographic blankets are listed in Davison's Printing Supply catalogue for $211. What is the trade discount in dollars for 35 blankets if a chain discount of 14% and 5% is offered?

    $211 × 35 = $7,385
    .86 × .95 = .817
    $7,385 × .817 = $6,033.55 NP
    $7,385 − $6,033.55 = $1,351.45 TD

    $1,351.45 trade discount

6.2 Cash Discounts

To encourage customers to pay invoices promptly, many manufacturers and wholesalers offer a **cash discount.** Sometimes a buyer will negotiate for a higher cash discount or a longer discount period. This incentive, based on the net price, is figured as follows:

> Cash discount = Net price × Rate of cash discount.

You will recognize this as another application of the percentage formula: P = B × R. In this case.

Cash discount = Percentage,	Net price × Cash discount % = Cash discount
Net price = Base,	B × R = P
Rate of cash discount = Rate,	Net price − Cash discount = Net amount due
Net amount due = Difference.	B − P = D

Example 1 Ms. Morrison is the bookkeeper for Hanford Electric Appliances. In examining an invoice from Jambow, Inc., one of Hanford's suppliers, she sees that the net price, after trade discounts are taken, is $300. Because she is paying promptly, her company is entitled to a 2% cash discount. Assuming she pays the bill in full, what will be the amount of the check Ms. Morrison makes out to Jambow, Inc.?

Step 1   Find the amount of the cash discount, using the net price as the base.
       B × R = P
       $300 × .02 = $6.00

Step 2   Subtract the discount from the net price.
       $300
       −   6
       $294

Answer   The amount of the check for full payment is $294.00.

Self-Check

1. Determine the amount of the cash discount on an invoice showing a net price of $525, if a 3% discount is allowed.   _____

2. Find the amount due to Danforth Publications, a wholesaler, on a bill with a net price of $800, if a 4% cash discount is allowed.   _____

ANSWERS   1. $15.75   2. $768

Reading Terms and Using Ordinary Dating

Clearly stated on many invoices, usually near the top, are the **terms** (see Section 6.1). The terms specify the percent of the cash discount and the number of days it applies. Each company has its own method of determining cash discounts. Terms can be adjusted, depending on the customer and on the circumstances surrounding a particular order. For example, if the retailer purchases seasonal merchandise in the off-season, the wholesaler may decide to extend the terms of the cash discount, making them apply until the retailer is able to sell some of the merchandise, thus putting him or her in a better financial position to pay the bill.

In the **ordinary-dating method,** the first number shown represents the percent of discount, and the second number indicates the number of days after the date of the invoice that the discount is allowed.

Example 2 Looking at an invoice, Ms. Morrison notes terms that read 2/10, n/30. What do these terms mean?

Answer 2/10 means that Ms. Morrison's company is entitled to a 2% cash discount if the bill is paid within 10 days after the date on the invoice. n/30 means that if the company pays between the eleventh and the thirtieth day after the date on the invoice, the full net price (n) is due. After the thirtieth day, payment is overdue and a late charge may be added.

In the reading of terms, exact dating is used. In other words, you must know the number of days in each calendar month and count accordingly, beginning with the date of the invoice.

Example 3 Looking at an invoice dated December 11, with terms reading 2/10, n/30, Ms. Morrison wants to know the last date the discount applies and the last date before payment is overdue.

Step 1 Add 10 to the date on the invoice.

```
  December 11
+         10 days
  December 21
```

Answer The last date of the discount is December 21.

Step 2 Subtract the date of the invoice from the number of days in the month.

```
  31 days in December
- 11th (date of invoice)
  20 days left in December
```

Step 3 Subtract the result from 30 to find the correct date on the following month.

```
  30 days to pay net
- 20 days in December
  10 January
```

Answer The last day before payment is overdue is January 10.

Ordinary terms may be more elaborate than those shown above. For instance, 5/10, 2/30, n/60 is read:

5% discount if paid within 10 days after the invoice date.

2% discount if paid within 30 days after the invoice date, that is, from the 11th to the 30th day.

The full amount is due if paid between the 31st and the 60th day. There may be a penalty after the 60th day.

Self-Check

Terms	Date of Invoice	Final Date of Discount	Final Date for Net Payment
1. 2/10, n/30	June 2	_____	_____
2. 3/15, net 60	November 15	_____	_____

3. On November 15, Charles Le Bow, who works in the accounting department of Zoom Cleaning Products, pays an invoice for $395, net price, which shows terms of 3/10, 2/30, n/60, and is dated October 30. What is the amount of the check? _____

ANSWERS 1. June 12; July 2   2. November 30; January 14   3. $387.10

NAME _____ DATE _____ SECTION _____

Assignment 6.2

Trade and Cash Discounts

Pembroke Trevanian is the bookkeeper for Teva's Toys, Inc. He reviews the invoices on his desk and determines the final date of discount and the last day of net payment. Given the following dates and terms, what are these dates?

	Date of Invoice	Terms	Final Discount Date	Final Net Payment Date
1.	November 1	2/10, net 30	Nov. 11	Dec. 1
2.	November 5	3/15, n/60	Nov. 20	Jan. 4
3.	November 13	net 30	None	Dec. 13
4.	November 14	3/10, n/30	Nov. 24	Dec. 14
5.	November 28	3/10, net 15	Dec. 8	Dec. 13
6.	December 1	2/15, n/60	Dec. 16	Jan. 30
7.	December 2	2/10, n/30	Dec. 12	Jan. 1
8.	December 12	2/10, net 60	Dec. 22	Feb. 10
9.	December 26	3/15, n/30	Jan. 10	Jan. 25
10.	December 30	3/5, n/30	Jan. 4	Jan. 29

11. Your model shop buys 500 tiny spaceships from Plastocraft Models, Inc. The net price is $468. The invoice is dated April 4, with terms of 2/10, 1/15, n/30. What is the amount of your discount if you pay the bill in full on:

   a) $468 × 2% = $9.36
   b) $468 × 1% = $4.68
   c) Net due

   a) April 13? $9.36
   b) April 15? $4.68
   c) May 1? No discount

12. Gimbo, Inc., bills the firm for which you work for five electric motors. The total net price is $5,656.80.

   Invoice Date: March 5   Terms: 2/10, 1/30, n/60

   a) $5,656.80 × 2%
       = $113.14 Discount
       $5,656.80 − $113.14
       = $5,543.66 Remittance
   b) $5,656.80 × 1%
       = $56.57 Discount
       $5,656.80 − $56.57
       = $5600.23 Remittance
   c) Same discount applied as in (b) Terms: 1/30

   Find: Amount of Discount   Total Remittance
   If paid by:
   a) March 13 $ 113.14 $ 5,543.66
   b) March 16   56.57   5,600.23
   c) March 30   56.57   5,600.23

continued

Assignment 6.2 continued

Pamela Conway is head of accounting for Broadway Bookstore. She must pay off the following invoices. What is the amount due for each of them?

	Invoice Amount	Date of Invoice	Terms	Date Paid	Amount Due	
13.	$ 42.50	April 2	2/10, n/30	April 10	$ 41.65	($.85 discount)
14.	$ 38.65	June 3	6/10, net 30	June 6	36.33	($2.32 discount)
15.	$ 101.46	May 6	net 30	June 1	101.46	(No discount)
16.	$ 82.50	July 19	3/10, net 30	August 6	82.50	(No discount)
17.	$1,165.30	March 1	2/8, n/40	March 10	1,165.30	(No discount)
18.	$2,406.36	Sept. 30	2/10, net 60	October 10	2,358.23	($48.13 discount)
19.	$3,426.00	Oct. 20	2/10, 1/20, n/30	November 2	3,391.74	($34.26 discount)
20.	$2,586.28	March 1	3/5, 2/10, n/30	April 1	2,586.28	(No discount)
21.	$ 680.52	August 23	3/20, 1/30, n/60	September 8	660.10	($20.42 discount)
22.	$5,624.48	Jan. 2	5/10, 3/20, net 30	January 15	5,455.75	($168.73 discount)

Barcraft Boats offers cash discount terms of 3/10, 1/20, n/30 on all purchases. Your company orders from Barcraft on a regular basis. What amounts will you pay for the following purchases?

	Net Price Amount	Date of Invoice	Date of Payment	Amount Paid	
23.	$ 384.68	January 2	January 10	$ 373.14	($11.54 discount)
24.	$2,924.16	October 12	November 5	2,924.16	(No discount)
25.	$ 948.36	March 15	April 1	938.88	($9.48 discount)
26.	$1,382.14	April 20	May 1	1,368.32	($13.82 discount)
27.	$ 236.82	February 3	February 5	229.72	($7.10 discount)
28.	$3,821.95	December 20	January 10	3,821.95	(No discount)

6.3 Other Dating Methods

Methods of granting cash discounts other than ordinary terms are sometimes used.

End-of-Month Dating

End-of-month dating is a way of lengthening the period during which a discount may be taken. The discount period begins after the end of the month of the date of invoice, not after the invoice date itself. The end of the month is designated in the terms by the initials e.o.m.

Example 1   Carla Montez works as a bookkeeper for Tudor Industrial Products. If an invoice dated November 5 has terms that read 2/10, n/30 e.o.m., what is the last day of the discount?

Step 1	Look at the terms.	2% discount if bill is paid within 10 days. Net due in 30 days.
Step 2	Note that the terms are e.o.m.	The discount period begins after the end of the month: November 30.
Step 3	Add 10 days to the month following the invoice month.	End of November + 10 days = December 10
Answer	The last day for the 2% discount is December 10.	

Example 2   Reading another invoice dated November 16, and in the amount of $568, Carla sees that it has terms of 3/15, net 60 e.o.m. If she pays the bill on December 15, what amount will she remit?

Step 1	Read the terms.	3% discount if paid within 15 days. Net due in 60 days.
Step 2	Note that the terms are e.o.m.	The discount period begins after November 30.
Step 3	Find the last discount day. Since the bill is paid on this date, the discount applies.	End of November + 15 days discount period = December 15 Last discount day = December 15
Step 4	Figure the discount.	$568 × .03 = $17.04
Step 5	Subtract the discount from the net price.	$568 − 17.04 = $550.96
Answer	The amount due is $550.96.	

NOTE: If an invoice is dated the twenty-sixth of the month or after, many firms allow the discount to apply for an extra month. For instance, an invoice dated October 26, with terms 2/10, n/30 e.o.m., has a final discount date of December 10.

Extra Dating

The **extra-dating method** allows even more time in the discount period. When the abbreviations X or ex or the word "extra" are added, followed by a designated number of days, the buyer has that many additional days after the date of the invoice to take advantage of the cash discount. Terms 2/10, n/30, 30-X means that the buyer has 40 days from the date of the invoice to take the cash discount. This allows the discount to be taken on merchandise bought during the off season, and thus improves the buyer's cash flow position.

Example 3 In July, Bill Chang purchases fifty pairs of boots for his ski shop. Both he and the manufacturer know that no one is apt to buy the boots until the ski season starts in September. Therefore, the terms on the invoice read 2/10, n/30, 60X. If the invoice is dated July 16, what is the last day of the discount?

Step 1 Read the terms.   2% discount if bill is paid within 10 days or July 26. Net is due in 30 days.

Step 2 Note the 60X.   The discount period is extended for 60 days after July 26.

Step 3 Find the last day of the discount period.

```
  31 days in July
− 26 July
   5 days left
+ 31 August
  36

  60 extra days
− 36 accounted for
  24 September
```

Answer   September 24 is the last day for the discount.

Receipt-of-Goods Dating

In some instances, the shipping period for merchandise may be a number of weeks, or even months. When this is so, there is no point in considering the date of the invoice in figuring the discount period. Instead, it is figured from the date the buyer receives the shipment. This process is known as **receipt-of-goods dating,** and is abbreviated r.o.g.

Example 4 At a gift show in April, Myrtle Heck orders a gross of miniature dolls, which are manufactured in South Korea. Because they are to be shipped by ocean freighter, the salesperson gives her terms of 3/15, n/30, r.o.g. If the dolls arrive at her shop on June 23, what is the last day of the discount period?

Step 1 Read the terms.   3% discount if paid within 15 days.

Step 2 Note r.o.g.   The discount period begins when the merchandise arrives—in this case, June 23.

Step 3 Find the last day of the discount period.

```
  30 days in June
− 23 June—goods rec'd
   7
```

$$\begin{array}{r} 15 \text{ days for discount} \\ -7 \text{ accounted for} \\ \hline 8 \text{ July} \end{array}$$

Answer July 8 is the last day for the discount.

Self-Check

Determine the last day of discount and the net due date.

1. Terms: 3/15, net 30, e.o.m.
   Invoice date: June 29

2. Terms: 2/12, n/30, r.o.g.
   Invoice date: December 12
   Arrival date: April 18

3. An invoice for Christmas ornaments is dated September 16, with terms of 3/10, n/40-50 ex. State the last day of the discount and the net due date.

ANSWERS 1. Discount: August 15 (because invoice is dated after the 26th, an extra month is allowed); net: August 30   2. Discount: April 30, net: May 18   3. Discount: November 15; net: December 15

Assignment 6.3

Trade and Cash Discounts

The bookkeeper at Teva's Toys, Pembroke Trevanian, is looking over a group of invoices, determining the final discount date and the last day of net payment. Using the data below, determine these dates.

	Date of Invoice	Terms	Date of Delivery	Final Discount Date	Final Net Date
1.	January 15	3/15, n/30, r.o.g.	February 10	Feb. 25	March 12
2.	May 11	2/10, n/60, e.o.m.	June 15	June 10	July 30
3.	September 15	3/12, n/30	October 30	Sept. 27	Oct. 15
4.	January 27	3/10, n/30, 60X	February 15	April 7	April 27
5.	May 26	3/20, n/60, e.o.m.	May 31	July 20	Aug. 29
6.	October 30	2/10, n/30, r.o.g.	December 14	Dec. 24	Jan. 13
7.	May 17	2/10, n/60, 10X	June 10	June 6	July 26
8.	November 1	5/15, 60 net	December 2	Nov. 16	Dec. 31
9.	April 11	2/12, n/30, 30X	May 1	May 23	June 10
10.	July 12	2/10, net 60, r.o.g.	October 5	Oct. 15	Dec. 4

11. Banjos, Inc., your music store, purchases one hundred tubas at $556.20 each. Because the salesperson cannot guarantee a shipment date, he gives you terms of 3/10, net 30, r.o.g. The horns eventually arrive on June 5. Find each of the following.

    a) Last date of discount   June 15
    b) Net due date   July 5
    c) Amount of discount $1,668.60
    d) Amount due if paid during discount period $53,951.40

$556.20 × 100 = $55,620
3/10, n/30 r.o.g. arrived June 5

a)   June 5
  +   10
    June 15 Discount date

b)   30 days in June
  −   5 June arrival
    25 days left

    30 days net due
  − 25 days left in June
    5 July net due date

c) $55,620 × 3% = $1,668.60
    Amount of discount

d) $55,620 − $1,668.60
    = $53,951.40

12. You buy an electrical generator and necessary accessories for use by your company. The invoice reads as follows:

Date of Invoice: March 8   Terms: 5/10, 2/15, n/30, e.o.m.

NO. SENT	ITEM	UNIT PRICE	TOTAL PRICE
1	#6834 Generator	$7,968.42	$7,968.42
6	#3254 Fittings	268.10	1,608.60
5	# 241 Clamps	5.15	25.75
1	#6214 Stand	538.24	538.24
	Total invoice		$10,141.01

continued

Assignment 6.3 continued

Find each of the following.

			Amount Due
a) Last day of first discount	April 10	b) $	9,633.96
c) Last day of second discount	April 15	d) $	9,938.19
e) Last day net can be paid without penalty	April 30	f) $	10,141.01

b) $10,141.01 × 5% = $507.05   d) $10,141.01 × 2% = $202.82
   $10,141.01 − $507.05 = $9,633.96 $10,141.01 − $202.82 = $9,938.19

At Broadway Bookstore, Pamela Conway, head of accounting, must pay off several invoices. Find the amount of the cash discount and the amount due.

	Invoice Amount	Date of Invoice	Date Goods Received	Terms	Date Paid	Amount of Discount	Amount Due
13.	$1,204.10	Aug. 1	Aug. 15	3/10–30X	Sept. 1	$ 36.12	$ 1,167.98
14.	836.42	Aug. 23	Aug. 30	5/10–60X	Nov. 6	None	836.42
15.	692.18	Nov. 24	March 1	2/20, r.o.g.	March 6	13.84	678.34
16.	95.44	Oct. 30	Nov. 15	2/10, e.o.m.	Jan. 5	None	95.44
17.	66.24	Jan. 14	Jan. 30	3/30, r.o.g.	Feb. 25	1.99	64.25
18.	1,234.38	May 16	May 30	3/10, e.o.m.	June 11	None	1,234.38
19.	9,421.82	Dec. 26	Dec. 31	1/10–20X	Jan. 16	94.22	9,327.60
20.	3,283.26	March 28	April 14	2/15, r.o.g.	April 29	65.67	3,217.59
21.	4,862.91	March 13	March 26	3/10–40X	May 29	None	4,862.91
22.	5,642.40	May 27	June 1	1/15, e.o.m.	June 10	56.42	5,585.98

23. Paul Farren, president of Paul's Runners' Supply, receives an invoice dated December 7, for shoes that reach his store the following May 16. The total list price shown is $1,675.80, with trade discounts of 20%, 10%, and 5% and cash discount terms of 2/30, r.o.g. What is the amount of Paul's check, if he pays the bill on June 1?

    31 days in May
  − 16 May goods received
    15
    30 days for discount
  − 15 accounted for
    15 July last day

.8 × .9 × .95 = .684 $1,146.25 − $22.93 = $1,123.32 Amount due $1,123.32
$1,675 × .684 = $1,146.25 NP   amount due
$1,146.25 × 2% = $22.93 Discount

24. Penny Sample, the billing clerk for Tufftone, Inc., sends out an invoice for $836.50, dated January 12, with terms of 3/10, e.o.m. If payment is made on February 9, and if Tufftone allows trade discounts of 25% and 40%, what amount is due?

    End of Jan. + 10 days =
    Feb. 10 last day of discount

.75 × .6 = .45
$836.50 × .45 = $376.43 NP
$376.43 × 3% = $11.29 Discount $365.14 amount due
$376.43 − $11.29 = $365.14 Amount due

continued

Assignment 6.3 *continued*

25. Ben Grover's Furniture Store receives an invoice for 6 sofas @ $395.00 each, with discounts of 10% and 5% and cash terms of 2/15, n/60, e.o.m. If the invoice is dated July 27, find each of the following.

   a) Date of cash discount __Sept. 15__

   b) Total net price before cash discount is taken __$2,026.35__

   c) Total due if paid within cash discount period __$1,985.82__

   a) End of August + 15 days =
      Sept. 15 last day
   b) $395 × 6 = $2,370
      .9 × .95 = .855
      $2,370 × .855 =
      $2,026.35 NP
   c) $2,026.35 × 2% = $40.53
      Discount
      $2,026.35 − $40.53 =
      $1,985.82

Find the missing amounts in each of the following problems.

26. Trade-discount series: 20%, 10%

   a) Single discount equivalent __28%__
      List Price: $950
      Terms: 3/10, 2/30, n/60
      Invoice date: May 14
      Date account paid in full: May 22

   b) Net price before cash discount __$684__

   c) Trade-discount amount __$266__

   d) Cash-discount amount __$20.52__

   e) Net amount due after cash discount __$663.48__

   a) .8 × .9 = .72
      1.00 − .72 = .28 =
      28% SDE
   b) $950 − $266 = $684 NP
   c) $950 × 28% = $266 TD
   d) $684 × 3% = $20.52
      Cash discount
   e) $684 − $20.52 = $663.48
      Amount due

27. Trade-discount series: 25%, 20%

   a) Single discount equivalent? __40%__
      List price: $338.75
      Terms: 5/10, 90X
      Invoice date: August 19
      Date account paid in full: September 10

   b) Net price before cash discount? __$203.25__

   c) Trade-discount amount? __$135.50__

   d) Cash-discount amount? __$10.16__

   a) .75 × .8 = .6
      1.00 − .6 = .4 = 40% SDE
   b) To find net price before cash discount:
      List price − TD amount
      $338.75 − $135.50 =
      $203.25 NP
   c) $338.75 × 40% =
      $135.50 TD
   d) $203.25 × 5% = $10.16
      Cash discount

28. Trade-discount series: 30%, 20%

   a) Single discount equivalent __44%__
      List price: $75.80
      Terms: 2/10, n/30, r.o.g.
      Invoice date: November 10
      Goods received: December 2
      Date account paid in full: December 12

   b) Net price before cash discount __$42.45__

   c) Trade-discount amount __$33.35__

   d) Cash-discount amount __$ .85__

   a) .7 × .8 = .56
      1.00 − .56 = .44 = 44%
      SDE
   b) $75.8 − $33.35 = $42.45
      NP
   c) $75.80 × 44% = $33.35 TD
   d) $42.45 × 2% = $ .85
      Cash discount

6.4 Returns, Shipping Charges, and Partial Payments

Deciding to Which Charges the Discount Applies

Trade and cash discounts apply only to the amount actually owed for merchandise. Some items may have to be returned to the wholesaler or manufacturer, perhaps because they have been damaged in shipment or are otherwise unsuitable for sale. The cost of goods returned is deducted before discounts are calculated.

The same holds true for freight or shipping charges. If they are included in the invoice, that is, f.o.b.—shipping point, deduct them before figuring the discounts. Remember, however, to add them in full when determining the final amount due.

Example 1 Pamela Hartman receives an invoice for $946, including $26 in shipping charges. When she unpacks the merchandise, she finds that $120 worth of it is damaged and must be returned. If she is entitled to a trade discount series of 20% and 10% and a cash discount of 3%, what amount must she pay?

Step 1 Subtract amounts not subject to discount.

$946.00 Total bill
− 26.00 Shipping
920.00
− 120.00 Returns
$800.00 Amount on which discounts are allowed

Step 2 Determine the percent of the net price.

100% − 20% = 80%
100% − 10% = 90%
0.8 × 0.9 = = 72%

Step 3 Find the net price before the cash discount.

$800
× 0.72
$576 Net price

Step 4 Find the cash discount and subtract from the net price.

$576 $576.00
× 0.03   − 17.28
$17.28 Cash discount $558.72

Step 5 Add the shipping charges.

$588.20
26.00
$584.72

Answer The total amount that Pamela must pay is $584.72.

NOTE: When solving these problems, be careful to see whether the freight charge is included in the bill or is listed separately. If it is listed separately, do *not* subtract the freight charge in step 1.

Determining Credit for Partial Payments

Often a customer will satisfy the total amount due with a series of partial payments. Many businesses practice the policy that partial payments made within the cash discount period are eligible for discount. Since the cash discount reduces the amount that must be paid, the partial payment is worth more than the actual dollar amount paid. This "extra worth" is shown in the form of a credit. The payer is credited as having remitted more than the actual dollar amount paid. The credit is determined by first finding the percent paid. Then this percent is used to figure the true value of the partial payment, which is the amount of credit. The formula is:

> 100% − Percent of cash discount = Percent paid
>
> $$\frac{\text{Amount of partial payment}}{\text{Percent paid}} = \text{Amount of credit}$$

Once the amount of credit is found, the final step is to determine how much is still owed on a bill. This is figured by subtraction:

> Total bill
> − Amount credited
> Amount still owed

Example 2   Delaner Zarole, bookkeeper for Bemberton Tire Shop, pays $200 on account on a $300 purchase during the cash discount period. If the cash discount rate is 2%, how much is still owed?

Step 1   Find the percent paid. Subtract the percent of discount from the total, 100%.   100% − 2% = 98% paid

Step 2   Find the amount of credit. Divide the amount of payment by the percent paid. $\frac{\$200}{0.98} = \$204.08$ amount credited

Step 3   Find the amount owed. Subtract the amount credited from the total of the bill.

$300.00
− 204.08
$ 95.92

Answer   The amount owed after payment on account is $95.92.

NOTE: To understand the concept further consider that if a cash discount of 2% is allowed and you pay the entire bill within the discount period, you would pay 98% of the bill but would receive full credit. So in the above example, if you paid the entire bill of $300 within the cash discount period you would pay $294 in cash ($300 × 98% = $294). For full payment within the cash discount period, you pay $294 but receive credit for $300. Similarly, for partial payment within the cash discount period, you pay $200 but receive credit for $204.08.

Self-Check

1. Denfurst Auto Parts receives an invoice for $255.00 in merchandise and $10.50 in freight charges. Also, $26.50 worth of parts were defective and had to be returned. No trade discount is involved, but Denfurst pays in time to be eligible for a 4% cash discount. What will be the amount of the check, if the bill is paid in full?

2. You receive a bill for $340.50 from Albert's Floral Supply that includes freight charges of $31.20. Three items that cost $16 each are damaged and must be returned. If you are entitled to receive a 5% cash discount, how much money should you send in payment of your bill?

3. You receive a bill from Hoser Wholesale Supply for $198, and make a payment of $95

during a period when you are entitled to a 3% cash discount. How much do you still owe?

ANSWERS 1. 229.86   2. $279.44   3. $100.06

BAD GRADES PUNISHABLE BY DEATH

In the Inca empire of Peru, scribes were responsible for recordkeeping. To do so, they used small stones and counting boards. Each scribe specialized in a particular category of records such as military supplies, housing, foodstuffs, and so on, and their techniques were handed down from father to son. Scribes were required to have expertly trained memories and were expected to perform mental calculations quickly and accurately. If they forgot facts or were proved inaccurate, the penalty was death.

Assignment 6.4

Trade and Cash Discount

1. Casey's Bookstore receives an invoice for bookcases totaling $1,378 with terms 2/10, n/60. The invoice includes a shipping charge of $52.40. If the discount is taken, what is the amount to be paid?

   $1,378.00 Total bill
   − 52.40 Shipping
   $1,325.60 Amt. allow. disc.

   $1,325.60
   × 2%
   $26.51 Cash discount

   $1,351.49 amount to be paid

   $1,325.60 Amt. allow. disc.
   − 26.51
   $1,299.09
   + 52.40 Freight
   $1,351.49 Amount paid

2. An invoice in the amount of $620.39 was received by U-Frame Company. After the merchandise had been unpacked, it was found that three frames listed at $12.59 each were damaged and had to be returned. If the terms are 2/30, n/60, how much money must be paid in order to take advantage of the discount?

   $12.59 × 3 = $37.77 damaged

   $620.39 Total bill
   − 37.77 Damaged
   $582.62 Amt. allow. disc.

   $582.62
   × 2%
   $11.65 Cash discount

   $570.97 amount to be paid

   $582.62 Amt. allow. disc.
   − 11.65 Discount
   $570.97 Amount paid

3. McCoy's Photography Studio receives an invoice for $476.80 on April 19 with terms 2/10, 1/30, n/60. A freight charge of $41 is included in the invoice. If McCoy returns $19.90 worth of goods to the seller and makes payment on May 2, how much must he pay?

   $476.80
   − 41.00 Freight
   435.80
   − 19.90 Returns
   $415.90 Amt. allow. disc.

   $415.90
   × 1%
   $4.16 Cash discount

   $452.74 amount to be paid

   30 days in April
   − 19
   11 April
   + 2 May
   13 days

   $415.90
   − 4.16 Discount
   411.74
   + 41.00 Freight
   $452.74 Amount paid

4. Berry Baby Furniture received a shipment of office supplies totaling $189.60. Returns amounted to $21.17. If terms are 2½/10, n/30 and the discount is taken, what is the amount of full payment?

   $189.60
   − 21.17 Returns
   $168.43 Amt. allow. disc.

   $168.43
   × 2.5%
   $4.21 Cash discount

   $164.22 full payment

   $168.43
   − 4.21 Cash discount
   $164.22 Amount paid

5. La Casita's Restaurant received an invoice dated June 2 for merchandise totaling $879.20. The freight charge listed separately was $54. The goods were received on June 27. After unpacking, it was found that four plates worth $8.08 each and three wine glasses worth $1.17 each had to be returned. The terms of the invoice were 2/10, 1/30, n/60, r.o.g. If payment is made on July 2, how much must be paid?

   4 × $8.08 = $32.32
   3 × $1.17 = 3.51
   35.83 Returns

   $879.20
   − 35.83 Returns
   $843.37 Amt. allow. disc.

   $880.50 to be paid

   Rec'd June 27
   30
   − 27
   3 left
   + 2 July
   5 days—2% discount

   $843.37
   × 2%
   $ 16.87 Cash discount

   $843.37
   − 16.87 Cash discount
   826.50
   + 54.00 Freight
   $880.50 Amount paid

6. Within the cash discount period, Barrister Corporation pays $650 on account on a $1,500 purchase of office equipment. If the discount rate is 5%, how much does the corporation still owe?

continued

Assignment 6.4 continued

$100\% - 5\% = 95\%$ paid

$\dfrac{\$650}{.95} = \$684.21$ credited

$\begin{aligned}&\$1,500.00 \text{ Total bill}\\&\underline{-\quad 684.21 \text{ Credited}}\\&\$815.79 \text{ Still owed}\end{aligned}$

$\$815.79$ still owed

7. If Manny Watkins, bookkeeper for Pancheek Industries, pays $550 during the period when a 3% discount is allowed, how much does his company still owe if the total bill was originally $980?

$\$980.00$ Total bill
$-\ \underline{567.01}$ Credited
$\$412.99$ Still owe

$100\% - 3\% = 97\%$ paid

$\dfrac{\$550}{97\%} = \$567.01$ credit

$\$412.99$ still owed

8. On April 14, Delbert Boris pays $450, which is one half of an invoice dated April 7, with terms of 3/10, n/30. How much does Delbert still owe?

$\$900.00$ Total bill
$-\ \underline{463.92}$ Credited
$\$436.08$ Still owe

$100\% - 3\% = 97\%$ paid   Total invoice = $900

$\dfrac{\$450}{97\%} = \$463.92$ credit

$\$436.08$ still owed

9.

Invoice

Toy Distributors, Inc.
136 Dale Avenue
Chicago, IL 60656

DATE: JUNE 18
TERMS: 6/10 $4\tfrac{1}{2}/20$ n/30

Sold to:

Sheila McDivot
Tots' Toys, Inc.
40 Hill Rd.
San Francisco, CA 94114

Item #	Description	Quantity	Unit Price	Total Price
B269	Stuffed baby bear	30	$ 8.50	_____
K40	Wooden monkey	12	12.55	_____
D157	Plastic penguin	6	5.45	_____
			TOTAL	_____

$30 \times \$8.50 = \$255.00$
$12 \times 12.55 = \ \ 150.60$
$6 \times \ \ 5.45 = \ \ \ \underline{32.70}$
$\$438.30$ Total bill

If Sheila McDivot makes a partial payment of $300 on June 30, how much does she still owe?

$\$438.30$ Total bill
$-\ \underline{314.14}$ Credited
$\$124.16$ Still owe

$100\% - 4.5\% = 95.5\%$ paid

$\dfrac{\$300}{95.5\%} = \$314.14$ credit

$\$124.16$ still owed

10. Jerry Johnson, an office manager, purchased a printing calculator for $95, paying $35 on account during the period when a 2% cash discount was allowed. How much does he still owe?

$\$95.00$ Total bill
$-\ \underline{35.71}$ Credited
$\$59.29$ Still owe

$100\% - 2\% = 98\%$ paid

$\dfrac{\$35}{98\%} = \$35.71$ credit

$\$59.29$ still owed

Comprehensive Problems for Chapter 6

Trade and Cash Discounts

Terry Kenwood is bookkeeper for Panford Bath and Bed Shop, Inc. He has a number of invoices to prepare for payment. They involve both trade and cash discounts. Help him by filling in the missing information.

	List Price	Trade Discount Rate	Trade Discount	Net Price	Date of Invoice	Terms	Date Paid	Cash Discount	Final Net Amount Due
1.	$ 78.40	20%, 25%, 10%	$ 36.06	$ 42.34	August 1	2/10, n/30	Aug. 9	$ .85	$ 41.49
2.	67.42	12½%, 10%	14.33	53.09	July 21	2/10, n/60	Aug. 1	none	53.09
3.	89.86	12½%, 10%, 5%	22.64	67.22	Feb. 15	2/10, 1/30, n/60	Feb. 25	1.34	65.88
4.	124.32	20%, 10%, 5%	32.29	85.03	Feb. 15	2/10, 1/30, n/60	Feb. 27	.85	84.18
5.	245.68	20%, 10%, 5%	77.63	168.05	June 6	6/10, n/30	June 12	10.08	157.97
6.	424.30	25%, 15%, 5%	167.34	256.96	Feb. 16	3/10, n/30, e.o.m.	Mar. 10	7.71	249.25
7.	560.80	25%, 10%, 5%	201.16	359.64	Jan. 25	3/10–90X	Mar. 22	10.79	348.85
8.	550.72	20%, 5%, 2½%	142.64	408.08	May 9	6/10–20X	June 9	none	408.08
9.	986.22	15%, 5%, 5%	229.69	756.53	Oct. 27	3/10, n/60, e.o.m.	Dec. 1	22.70	733.83
10.	876.43	10%, 5%, 5%	164.51	711.92	April 29	2/10, 1/20, n/60	June 1	none	711.92

continued

Comprehensive Problems *continued*

(Space for working problems 1–10 is provided here)

1. .8 × .75 × .9 = .54
 $78.40 × .54 = $42.34 NP
 $78.40 − $42.34 = $36.06 TD

 $42.34 × 2% = $.85 Cash discount
 $42.34 − $.85 = $41.49 Amount due

2. .875 × .9 = .7875
 $67.42 × .7875 = $53.09 NP
 $67.42 − $53.09 = $14.33 TD

3. .875 × .9 × .95 = .7481
 $89.86 × .7481 = $67.22 NP
 $89.86 − $67.22 = $22.64 TD

 $67.22 × 2% = $1.34 Cash discount
 $67.22 − $1.34 = $65.88 Amount due

4. .8 × .9 × .95 = .684
 $124.32 × .684 = $85.03 NP
 $124.32 − $85.03 = $39.29 TD

 $85.03 × 1% = $.85 Cash discount
 $85.03 − $.85 = $84.18 Amount due

5. .8 × .9 × .95 = .684
 $245.68 × .684 = $168.05 NP
 $245.68 − $168.05 = $77.63 TD

 $168.05 × 6% = $10.08 Cash discount
 $168.05 − $10.08 = $157.97 Amount due

6. .75 × .85 × .95 = .6056
 $424.30 × .6056 = $256.96 NP
 $424.30 − $256.96 = $167.34 TD

 $256.96 × 3% = $7.71 Cash discount
 $256.96 − $7.71 = $249.25 Amount due

7. .75 × .9 × .95 = .6413
 $560.80 × .6413 = $359.64 NP
 $560.80 − $359.64 = $201.16 TD

 $359.64 × 3% = $10.79 Cash discount
 $359.64 − $10.79 = $348.85 Amount due

8. .8 × .95 × .975 = .741
 $550.72 × .741 = $408.08 NP
 $550.72 − $408.08 = $142.64 TD

9. .85 × .95 × .95 = .7671
 $986.22 × .7671 = $756.53 NP
 $986.22 − $756.53 = $229.69 TD

 $756.53 × 3% = $22.70 Cash discount
 $756.53 − $22.70 = $733.83 Amount due

10. .9 × .95 × .95 = .8123
 $876.43 × .8123 = $711.92 NP
 $876.43 − $711.92 = $164.51 TD

11. Burns and Company offers trade discounts of 25%, 10%, and 2% to retail merchants, and 35%, 10%, and 5% to wholesalers. Assuming that each qualifies for a 2% cash discount, what is the net amount due to (a) a retailer and (b) a wholesaler for 612 sets of dishes with a list price of $485 per dozen sets?   612 ÷ 12 = 51 doz.   51 × $485 = $24,735 LP

 a) Retailer
 $16,034.96 due

 b) Wholesaler
 $13,472.76 due

 a) *Retailer* 25%, 10%, 2%
 .75 × .9 × .98 = .6615
 $24,735 × .6615
 = $16,362.20 NP
 $16,362.20 × 2%
 = 327.24 CD
 $16,362.20 − $327.24
 = $16,034.96 due

 b) *Wholesaler* 35%, 10%, 5%
 .65 × .9 × .95 = .5558
 $24,735 × .5558
 = $13,747.71 NP
 $13,747.71 × 2%
 = $274.95 CD
 $13,747.71 − $274.95
 = $13,472.76 due

12. The following invoice was paid on November 17 for merchandise that arrived on November 5.

Invoice Date: October 13   *Terms:* 2/10, 1/15, n/30, r.o.g.

Quantity	Item	Unit Price	Total
8	Food processors	@ $86.50 ea.	$ 692.00
18	Wooden spoons	@ 6.50 doz.	9.75 (18 ÷ 12 = 1.5)
4	Garlic presses	@ 3.25 ea.	13.00
6	Meat grinders	@ 45.35 ea.	272.10
		Invoice Total	$986.85

Note: All sales subject to 25%, 10%, 5%. T.D. (Trade Discount)

Find each of the following.
 a) Total invoice amount $986.85
 b) Net before cash discount $632.87
 c) Amount of cash discount $6.33
 d) Final net amount due $626.54

.75 × .9 × .95 = .6413
$986.85 × .6413
 = $632.87 NP
$632.87 × 1% = $6.33 CD
$632.87 − $6.33
 = $626.54 Amount due

continued

Comprehensive Problems *continued*

13. Two firms offer the same color television set for sale for $455.

Alpha Electronics

Trade discount 25%, 10%
Cash terms 2/10, n/30

Beta Enterprises

Trade discount 20%, 20%
Cash terms 3/10, n/60

Assuming you qualify for the cash discount, what will the set cost you at each of the two firms?

Alpha
.75 × .9 = .675
$455 × .675 = $307.13 NP
$307.13 × 2% = $6.14 CD
$307.13 − $6.14 = $300.99 Amount due

Beta
.8 × .8 = .64
$455 × .64 = $291.20 NP
$291.20 × 2% = $8.74 CD
$291.20 − $8.74 = $282.46 Amount due

Alpha $300.99 Amount due,
Beta $282.46 Amount due

14. Ian Nickles receives an invoice dated April 13 with cash terms of 3/10, net 30. It lists $695.30, $56.00 of which is freight charges, and the rest, glassware. He finds that $49.25 worth of glasses are broken. If he pays the bill on April 20, what is the amount he remits?

```
  $695.30
−  56.00 Freight
  $639.30
−  49.25 Damaged
  $590.05 Amt. allow. disc.
```

```
590.05
×   3%
$17.70 Cash Discount
```

$628.35 remitted

```
  $590.05
−  17.70 Cash discount
  $572.35
+  56.00 Freight
  $628.35 Amount paid
```

15. The invoice below was paid on February 9.

Terms: 3/10, net 30, e.o.m.   *Invoice Date:* 1/10

Quantity	Item	Unit Price	Extension Total
12	Salad bowls	@ $ 10.25 ea.	$123.00
24	Goblets	@ 25.00 doz.	50.00
144	Salt Shakers	@ 195.50 gr.	195.50
		Shipping Charges	$17.50
		Invoice Total	386.00

```
  $386.00 Total merchandise
−  17.50 Freight
  $368.50
−  14.41 Damaged
  $354.09 Amt. allow. disc.
−  10.62 Cash discount
  $343.47
+  17.50 Freight
  $360.97 Amount due
```

One salad bowl arrived cracked and two of the goblets were chipped. What was the total paid?

1 × $10.25 = $10.25
2 × $2.08 =   4.16
(25 ÷ 12)   14.41 Damaged

354.09 × 3% = $10.62 Cash discount
$360.97 amount due

continued

Comprehensive Problems *continued*

16. On July 15, Benny Sweetwater pays one third of an invoice totaling $1,200. The invoice is dated July 5, with terms of 5/10, net 30. How much does Benny still owe?

$1,200 ÷ 3 = $400 paid
100% − 5% = 95% paid

$\frac{\$400}{95\%}$ = $421.05 credit

$1,200.00 Total bill
−   421.05 Credited
$ 778.95 Amount still owed

$778.95 amount still owed

17. Fairview Furniture, Inc., owes payment on the following invoice.

Date: July 9			Terms: 2/10, e.o.m.	
Quantity	Item	Price	Total	
1	Sofa	@ $475 ea.	$	475
3	Chair	@ 78 ea.		234
6	Hassock	@ 34 ea.		204
12	Candles	@ 12 doz.		12
		Invoice Total	$	925

All sales subject to trade discounts of 10% and 5%.

The company pays $200 on August 8. How much does it still owe?

.9 × .95 = .855
$925 × .855 = $790.88 NP (total bill)

$586.80 still owed

100% − 2% = 98%

$\frac{\$200}{98\%}$ = $204.08 Credit

$790.88 Total bill
− 204.08 Credit
$586.80 Amount due

As bookkeeper at Pekwood Electronic Sales, Inc., John Sizemore has several invoices to be paid. What are the final net prices on them?

	List Price	Percent of Trade Discount	Date of Invoice	Terms	Date Paid	Final Net Amount Due
18.	$ 250.00	10, 5	Jan. 12	2/10, e.o.m.	Feb. 9	$ 209.47
19.	375.00	10, 5, 2	Feb. 14	4/15, 2/30, n/60	Mar. 10	307.93
20.	594.37	10, 20, 4	Mar. 16	2/10–40 ext.	June 1	410.83
21.	826.42	5, 15, 5	April 19	2/10, n/60	May 1	633.95
22.	473.28	25, 12½, 10	May 27	3/10, n/30	May 29	271.13
23.	684.29	2, 8, 37½	June 28	3/15, e.o.m.	August 14	374.03
24.	1,324.62	10, 40, 20	July 6	2/10, 1/15, n/30	July 21	566.52
25.	4,381.43	10, 10, 5	Aug. 6	3/10–30X	Sept. 10	3,270.36

continued

Comprehensive Problems *continued*

26.   9,264.25   5, 15, 25   Sept. 29   2/15–30 ext.   Oct. 15   <u>5,498.22</u>

18. .9 × .95 = .855
$250 × .855 = $213.75 NP
$213.75 × 2% = $4.28 CD
$213.75 − $4.28 = $209.47 Due

19. .9 × .95 × .98 = .8379
$375 × .8379 = $314.21 NP
$314.21 × 2% = $6.28 CD
$314.21 − $6.28 = $307.93 Due

20. .9 × .8 × .96 = .6912
$594.37 × .6912 = $410.83 NP/Due

21. .95 × .85 × .95 = .7671
$826.42 × .7671 = $633.95 NP/Due

22. .75 × .875 × .9 = .5906
$473.28 × .5906 = $279.52 NP
$279.52 × 3% = $8.39 CD
$279.52 − $8.39 = $271.13 Due

26. .95 × .85 × .75 = .6056
$9,264.25 × .6056 = 5610.43
$5,610.43 × 2% = $112.21 CD
$5.610.43 − $112.21 = $5,498.22 Due

23. .98 × .92 × .625 = .5635
$684.29 × .5635 = $385.60 NP
$385.60 × 3% = $11.57 CD
$385.60 − $11.57 = $374.03 Due

24. .9 × .6 × .8 = .432
$1,324.62 × .432 = $572.24 NP
S572.24 × 1% = $5.72 CD
S572.24 − $5.72 = $566.52 Due

25. .9 × .9 × .95 = .7695
$4,381.43 × .7695 = $3,371.51 NP
$3,371.51 × 3% = $101.15 CD
$3,371.51 − $101.15 = $3,270.36 Due

Case 1

You are the assistant director for the Infinity Math Institute and one of your many responsibilities is to purchase all office supplies. Now you are deciding from which supplier you will purchase typewriter ribbons.

IBM offers you ribbons listed at $210 with trade discounts of 10% and 5%.

Burroughs offers the ribbons at $245 with trade discounts of 20% and 5%.

Standard Brands lists their ribbons at $260 with trade discounts of 20%, 10%, and 5%.

All of the ribbons are of comparable quality.

a. Which company offers the lowest net price?

b. What other things should you consider before choosing the supplier for the ribbons?

Case 2

Andy Dubanowitz, the marketing representative for Mansfield's Menswear, received the following invoice with merchandise from Trim-A-Window, a display supplier.

Invoice

Trim-A-Window
325 7th Avenue
New York, NY 10268

Date: June 11, 19__
Terms: 3/10, 2/20, n/30–30X

Sold to:
Andy Dubanowitz, Mktg. Rep.
Mansfield's Menswear
Seattle Trade Center
Seattle, Washington 98133

Item Code #	Description	Quantity	Unit Price	Total Price
128-A	Display rack	4	$82.00	_____
463	White Christmas tree	2	56.40	_____
95-D	Red spotlight	4	14.50	_____
607-B	2' Cube	2	21.80	_____
607-C	3' Cube	1	29.00	_____
21	Green wreath	1	34.75	_____

A trade discount of 10% and 10% is allowed. Freight charges of $46.32 were prepaid by Trim-A-Window for which the supplier must be reimbursed. After close inspection, Andy finds that one of the red spotlights is damaged. He decides not to pay for it and instead to return it to Trim-A-Window. If on July 22 Andy sends a check to cover this bill, what should the amount be?

On September 15, Andy receives a late payment notice from Trim-A-Window for one red spotlight listed at $14.50. He decides to ignore it. Do you agree with his response? Why or why not?

Key Terms

Cash discount
Complement
End-of-month dating
Extra dating
Invoice, or sales invoice
List price

Net price
Net-price percent
Ordinary-dating method
Receipt-of-goods dating

Series of discounts, or chain discounts
Single equivalent trade-discount percent
Terms
Trade discount

Key Concepts

- An invoice is a record of sale prepared by the seller and presented to the buyer.
- The list price is the original price quoted in a catalogue or on a price list for merchandise.
- The net price is the amount that remains after the trade discount has been subtracted from the list price.
- The trade discount can be a single discount or a series of discounts.
- The cash discount is offered as an incentive to pay invoices promptly and is based on the net price.
- The different methods of dating are ordinary, end of month, extra, and receipt of goods.
- The formula for determining credit for partial payments is:

    100% − Percent of cash discount = Percent paid

    $$\frac{\text{Amount of partial payment}}{\text{Percent paid}}$$

- In final summary:

    $$\begin{array}{r} \text{List price} \\ - \text{ Trade discount} \\ \hline \text{Net price} \\ - \text{ Cash discount} \\ \hline \text{Net amount due} \end{array}$$

7

Retail Merchandising

Business Takes a Positive Approach

NORDSTROM

At one time it was questionable whether a specialty store based in the Pacific Northwest could compete nationally with established big-name retailers. Nordstrom not only competed but also caused its competitors to take note of its accomplishments in the marketplace. Although the company's secret is simple, it is one that has been all but ignored by many contemporary retailers: customer service. Nordstrom realizes that customer service goes much further than a smile. The motivated salespeople at Nordstrom truly believe that the customer comes first. They are attuned to individual needs, even going so far in some cases as to travel to shoppers' homes to help with wardrobe planning. If requested, a Nordstrom salesperson will accompany a customer from department to department to help decide which accessories look best with a particular ensemble. Nordstrom also has a "no questions asked" returns policy, turning a normally frustrating chore into a pleasant shopping experience. All Nordstrom sales executives start out on the selling floor. This practice helps them focus on how important the customer really is. Its commitment to customer service and its stock of quality merchandise have made Nordstrom a legend in its own time. By the late 1980s the company boasted the highest sales per square foot of any department store in the country. Its profits rose by 46%, and revenues were reported to have grown 25% since 1984. Projections are that this trend will continue through the early 1990s. Nordstrom has over 45 stores on the West Coast and is expanding rapidly in the East, a retailer that keeps its competitive edge well sharpened.

> ## Learning Objectives
>
> After reading and studying this chapter and working the problems, you will be able to:
>
> - Figure profit and loss in dollar amounts and as percents of total sales.
> - Find the percent of markup on the basis of both retail price and cost.
> - Determine the dollar amount of cost, retail, and markup in a variety of situations.
> - Find markdown, new retail price, and net sales.
> - Calculate average inventory, turnover at cost, and turnover at retail.
> - Convert average inventory at cost to average inventory at retail and vice versa.
> - Find the value of ending inventory using FIFO, LIFO, and average cost methods.

Retailing is a major industry, making an important contribution to our economy. In one way or another, it affects every consumer and business.

Merchandising involves the buying and selling of goods and products. A retail business sells to the general public. Although there are many different sizes of business, types of organization, and varieties of product sold, there is a common goal: to make a profit. To achieve this goal the use of effective pricing techniques and proper inventory methods is essential. Let's begin with a discussion of profit.

7.1 Profit

Although a business may have many different objectives, the most important of these is to make a profit. Without a fair profit, a business cannot stay alive over the long term. Many people have a negative viewpoint about profit and see it only as gain made at the expense of someone else. Actually, it is not uncommon for a retailer to make a profit of less than 3 percent. In reality, profit is an incentive for business to meet the demands and desires of the consumer.

If you were forced to go to the manufacturer directly for all your material needs, the price of goods would be so high that you could not afford many of the items you now possess. Take, for example, the variety of goods you are able to buy at a supermarket. If you had to purchase these items separately from their places of origin, you would spend more time and money than the goods are worth, or do without them. Instead, because of the profit incentive, retail businesses buy goods in volume, pack them, transport them, display them, and offer them for sale to you, usually in a pleasant shopping environment.

This chapter looks at profit, pricing, and inventory from the retailing point of view.

Profit is carefully planned. It is the amount that remains after all expenses have been paid. It is dependent on proper management of operating expenses, cost of goods sold, selling price, and sales volume. A change in any one of these variables will affect the amount of profit or loss.

Here are some definitions to help you understand these concepts:

Cost, or **cost of goods sold,** is the price the retailer pays to the supplier of merchandise. It is commonly referred to as the *wholesale price*.

Selling price is the price the consumer pays to the retailer for merchandise, or the *retail price*.

Gross margin is the difference between the cost and the selling price. The gross margin must be higher than the operating expenses in order to show a net profit or real profit. It is also called **gross profit,** or **markup.**

Operating expenses are the costs involved in running a business, such as rent, insurance, payroll, delivery charges, advertising, and so on. Through modern accounting methods, these expenses can be expressed in relation to the individual items.

The basic formula used to find a net profit or loss is:

Selling price
− Cost
Gross profit (gross margin)
− Operating Expenses
Net profit or loss

Profit is also discussed in Chapter 14, section 14.1, "Preparing the Income Statement."

Example 1   The Baby Boutique purchased 50 cribs at a cost of $76 each, and set the retail price at $125. If the boutique sells all the cribs during the year and figures the operating expenses for these items to be $2,180, what is the net profit?

Step 1   Find the total selling price (selling price × sales volume).

$125
×   50
$6,250 Selling price

Step 2   Find the total cost of the goods sold (cost × sales volume).

$76
×   50
$3,800 Cost of goods sold

Step 3   Subtract the cost of the goods sold from the selling price to determine the gross margin.

$6,250
− 3,800
$2,450 Gross margin

Step 4   Subtract the operating expenses from the gross margin to determine the net profit.

$2,450
− 2,180
$ 270 Net profit

Answer   The net profit is $270.

NOTE: A company would show a *loss* if the expenses were higher than the gross margin.

Finding the Net Profit Percent of Sales

Besides the dollar value of net profit or loss, another way to describe profit is as a percent of sales. The percent figure is an important tool to use because it indicates the return of investment on the basis of the actual amount of merchandise sold. Keep in mind that the total sales is the base in this situation because that is what the net profit or loss is being compared to. The procedure is as follows:

> **HOW THE PERCENTAGE FORMULA APPLIES**
>
> Total sales = Base
>
> Net profit (Loss) = Percentage
>
> Percent net profit (Loss) = Rate
>
> $\dfrac{P}{B} = R$
>
> $\dfrac{\text{Net profit (loss)}}{\text{Total sales}} = \text{Percent net profit (loss)}$

Example 2 Using the figures from Example 1, determine the percent profit of sales rounded to the nearest hundredth.

Step 1 Divide the net profit by the total sales. $\dfrac{\$270}{6250}$ $\left[\dfrac{P}{B} = R\right]$

Step 2 Change the decimal to a percent. $0.0432 = 4.32\%$

Answer The net profit percent of sales is 4.32%.

Finding the Percent Increase or Decrease in Profit

In order to give more meaning to the net profit figure, businesses will often compare the increase or decrease in profit between two periods or two different pricing situations. This increase or decrease is usually expressed in percent form and measures the change in net profit. This is found by applying the percentage formula to find rate.

> **HOW THE PERCENTAGE FORMULA APPLIES**
>
> Original profit = Base
>
> Increase or decrease in profit = Percentage
> Percent increase or decrease = Rate
>
> $\dfrac{\text{Increase or decrease in profit}}{\text{Original profit}} = \text{Percent increase or decrease}$
>
> $\dfrac{P}{B} = R$

Example 3 Last year Entertainment World sold $720,000 worth of party merchandise that had a wholesale price of $490,000. Operating expenses last year amounted to $128,000. This year the wholesale price was reduced to $470,000 while sales remained the same. Operating expenses this year amounted to $133,000. Find the percent increase or decrease in net profit to the nearest tenth.

Step 1 Determine the dollar amount of net profit (loss) for last year.

```
  $720,000  Selling price
−  490,000  Cost
   230,000  Gross profit
−  128,000  Expenses
  $102,000  Net profit (last year)
```

Step 2 Determine the dollar amount of net profit (loss) for this year.

```
  $720,000  Selling price
−  470,000  Cost
   250,000  Gross profit
−  133,000  Expenses
  $117,000  Net profit (this year)
```

Step 3	Subtract to find the increase (decrease) in profit in dollar amount.	$117,000 Net profit (this year) − 102,000 Net profit (last year) $ 15,000 Net profit increase
Step 4	Find the percent increase in net profit.	$\dfrac{P}{B} = R$
	a. Divide the increase in net profit by the net profit for last year.	$\dfrac{\$15{,}000 \text{ Increase}}{\$102{,}000 \text{ Net profit (last year)}}$
	b. Change the decimal to a percent.	$0.14705 = 14.7\%$
Answer	The percent increase in net profit is 14.7%.	

Self-Check

1. Silver King Jewelers purchased thirty silver rings for $140 each. It was figured that the operating expenses for these rings amounted to $1,300. If each ring sold for $210, determine each of the following:

   a. The net profit in dollars _____

   b. The net profit percent of sales to the nearest whole percent. _____

2. Last year Goodwin's Treats sold $540,000 worth of gourmet ice cream bars. Total cost amounted to $260,000, and operating expenses were $109,000. This year a price increase made sales total $580,000 while cost remained the same. Operating expenses totaled $114,000 for this year.

   a. Was there a net profit increase or decrease from last year? _____

   b. Determine the percent change in net profit to the nearest tenth of a percent. _____

ANSWERS   1. (a) $800; (b) 13%   2. (a) Increase; (b) 20.5%

A RETAILING FIRST

Montgomery Ward, established in 1872 with a capital investment of only $2,400, was the first mail-order house. Its initial catalogue consisted of a single-sheet price list. Soon Montgomery Ward became widely known for its money-back guarantee. This surprising and innovative offer was well received by the public, and Montgomery Ward grew into a mail-order empire.

Assignment 7.1

Retail Merchandising

Fill in the blanks, given the figures below.

	Selling Price	Cost	Gross Margin	Operating Expenses	Profit	Loss
1.	$ 12,980	$ 7,600	$ 5,380	$ 2,121	$ 3,259	$ _____
2.	87,600	62,050	25,550	15,746	9,804	_____
3.	34,280	29,300	4,980	8,500	_____	3,520
4.	154,590	159,400	(4,810)	30,760	_____	35,570
5.	58,250	30,197	28,053	11,825	16,228	_____

6. The following figures are available from Jeans Unlimited.

Style	Quantity	Cost	Selling Price
281	20	$20	$36
196	35	18	31
524	25	15	26
399	40	9	18
760	25	14	25

Cost Ext.	Retail Ext.
$ 400	$ 720
630	1,085
375	650
360	720
350	625
$2,115 Total Cost	$3,800 Total SP

Operating expenses amounted to $1,343.

a) Was there a profit or a loss if all the jeans were sold?

```
$3,800 SP        $1,685 GM
- 2,115 C      - 1,343 Op. Exp.
 $1,685 GM       $  342 Net profit
```

Profit _____

b) What is the dollar amount of the profit or loss?

$342 profit

c) What percent of profit or loss was made of the total selling price?

$$\frac{\$ 342 \text{ NP}}{\$3,800 \text{ SP}} = .09 = 9\%$$

9% profit

7. Scandinavian China Shop prices its china at $250 a set. The cost to the store is $150 a set. Operating expenses amount to $3,500. At $250, the shop estimates it can sell 40 sets of china. However, if the price were dropped to $200 a set, 55 sets can be sold.

continued

Assignment 7.1 *continued*

a) If the cost per set and operating expenses remain constant, would more or less net profit be made by reducing the price?

Step 1 $150 Unit cost
× 40 Volume
$6,000 Cost ext.

Step 2 $250 Unit retail
× 40 Volume
$10,000 Retail Ext/SP

Step 3 $10,000 SP
− 6,000 C
$ 4,000 GM
− 3,500 Op Exp.
$ 500 Net profit @ $250 set

Step 4 $200 Unit SP
× 55 Volume
$11,000 SP

Step 5 $150 Unit cost
× 55 Volume
$ 8,250 Cost

Step 6 $11,000 SP
− 8,250 C
$ 2,750 GM
− 3,500 Op Exp.
(750) Loss @ $200 a set

Less ──────

b) By what amount will the net profit revenue change if the lower sales price is used?

@ $200 per set $750 Loss   Change downward of 1250
@ $250 per set + 500 Profit
$1,250 Change

$1,250 change ──────

8. Last year, Franco's Furniture sold wooden rocking chairs for a price of $200 each. The chairs cost the store $100 each. Operating expenses amounted to $25,000. Three hundred rockers were sold. This year, a new supplier was found who quoted Franco's cost for the rockers at $10 less apiece. If the expenses, sales volume, and retail price remain the same, find each of the following.

a) Percent increase in net profit

Step 1 $100 Unit Cost
× 300 Volume
$30,000 Cost

2 $200 Unit Return
× 300 Volume
$60,000 SP

3 $60,000 SP
− 30,000 C
$30,000 GM
− 25,000 Op Exp.
$ 5,000 Net profit last year

4 $90 Unit Cost
× 300 Volume
$27,000 Cost

5 $60,000 SP
− 27,000 C
$33,000 GM
− 25,000 Op Exp.
$ 8,000 Net profit this year

6 This year's profit − last year's profit = Increase
$8,000 − $5,000 = $3,000

7 $\frac{\$3,000 \text{ increase}}{5,000 \text{ last year's profit}} = 60\%$

60% increase in profit ──────

b) Percent profit of sales for last year

$\frac{5,000 \text{ profit last year}}{60,000 \text{ sales last year}} = 8\frac{1}{3}\%$

$8\frac{1}{3}\%$ profit ──────

continued

262 Chapter 7

Assignment 7.1 continued

9. Last year, the Pro-Golf Shop sold $80,000 worth of goods at a cost to the store of $45,000. Expenses amounted to $29,000. This year it is estimated that expenses will rise by 18%. However, the cost and the selling price will remain the same.

   a) By what amount will net profit decrease this year?

   work below $6,000 Last year's profit
                 −   780 This year's profit
                   $5,220 Decrease

                                                                      $5,220 decrease

   b) What is the percent net profit of sales this year? Round to the nearest hundredth of a percent.

   $\dfrac{\$780 \text{ profit}}{\$80,000 \text{ sales}} = .975\%$

   $\phantom{\dfrac{\$780 \text{ profit}}{\$80,000 \text{ sales}}} = .98\%$ **.98% profit of sales**

Last year	This year	
$80,000 SP	$29,000 Op Exp., last year	$80,000 SP
− 45,000 C	× 1.18 Increase	− 45,000 C
$35,000 GM	$34,220 Op Exp., this year	$35,000 GM
− 29,000 Op Exp.		− 34,220 Op Exp.
$ 6,000 Net profit		$ 780 Net profit

10. K&L Appliance Store had 50 refrigerators priced at $600 each. The cost of each refrigerator was $350. Operating expenses amounted to $6,000. If the price were dropped to $500 each and all other factors remained the same, by what percent would the net profit decrease if all the refrigerators were sold? Round to the nearest whole percent.

$600 Unit rental	$350 Unit cost	$30,000 SP
× 50 Volume	× 50 Volume	− 17,500 C
$30,000 SP	$17,500 Cost	$12,500 GM
		− 6,000 Op. Exp.
		$ 6,500 Net profit

    Price drop:

$500 Unit retail	$25,000 SP
× 50 Volume	− 17,500 C
$25,000 SP	$ 7,500 GM
	− 6,000 Op. Exp.
	$ 1,500 Net profit

    $6,500 Net profit
    − 1,500 Net profit with price change
    $5,000 Decrease

    $\dfrac{\$5,000 \text{ difference}}{6,500 \text{ original net profit}} = .76923 = 77\%$

                                                                  77% decrease

7.2 Pricing and Markup

As explained earlier, *markup* is the difference between the selling price of merchandise and the price the retailer pays for the merchandise. It is also called gross margin or gross profit. Markup must be planned carefully so that a profit can be realized. The amount of markup *does not* equal the amount of net profit. Actual profit is only a small part of the markup:

$$\text{Selling price} \begin{cases} \text{Cost} \\ \left.\begin{matrix} \text{Operating expenses} \\ \text{Net profit} \end{matrix}\right\} \text{Markup} \end{cases}$$

The markup must be large enough to include operating expenses and retail reductions such as employee discounts, markdowns, and shortages, as well as a reasonable profit.

Markup can be based on selling price or on cost of goods sold. Most large retailers use the selling or retail price as the markup base because their records are kept and their inventory is figured on the basis of retail. Many of the business statistics that indicate industry standards and are available to retailers are based on retail prices, and helpful comparisons can be made from them if a store's records are kept at retail. Some small-volume merchants, however, use cost price as the base for markup because they find it more convenient or because they have been using that system for many years and do not want to convert to the retail method. Businesses that face frequent price changes, such as those selling fruits and vegetables, find that using the cost price as the markup base is a more stable method for them.

Markup is usually expressed as a percent or rate to aid in making meaningful comparisons and retailing decisions. The relationship to be used for problems dealing with markup is:

$$\text{Cost} + \text{Markup} = \text{Retail}$$

For convenience, use the initials: "C + M = R."
Remember:

Retail means the same thing as *selling price*.

Cost means the same thing as *wholesale price* and/or *manufacturer's price*.

The standard formulas for base, rate, and percentage, as explained in Chapter 5, will be applied here.

Finding Percent of Markup Based on Retail

Example 1 A chair that costs $30 is retailed at $40 at Morris and Moen Furniture. What is the percent of markup based on retail?

Step 1 Write the formula for markup and identify the key elements.

C + M = R
$30 + M = $40

Step 2 Find the missing element, which in this case is the amount of markup. To do this, subtract the cost from the retail to obtain the markup.

$40 R
− 30 C
$10 M

Before the percentage formulas can be used, you must have a rate and percentage expressing the same labeled quantity (see Section 5.3). Therefore, if you want to find the percent or rate of markup, you must first find the markup in dollars.

Step 3 Write the formula for rate and solve. In this case, the rate is the markup percent, the percentage is the markup in dollars, and the base is the retail price.

$$\text{Rate} = \frac{P}{B}$$

$$M\% = \frac{M}{R}$$

$$M\% = \frac{\$10}{\$40}$$

$$M\% = 25\%$$

Answer The percent of markup on retail is 25%.

Finding Percent of Markup Based on Cost

Example 2 A Wood stove sells for $800 and cost the Energy Store $500. What is the percent of markup based on cost?

Step 1 Write the formula for markup and identify the key elements.

$$C + M = R$$
$$\$500 + M = \$800$$

Step 2 Find the missing element in dollars. In this case, it is the markup.

$$\begin{array}{rl} \$800 & R \\ -\ 500 & C \\ \hline \$300 & M \end{array}$$

Step 3 Write the formula for rate and solve. In this problem, the rate is the percent of markup, the percentage is the markup in dollars, and the base is the cost.

$$R = \frac{P}{B}$$

$$M\% = \frac{M}{C}$$

$$M\% = \frac{\$300}{\$500}$$

$$M\% = 60\%$$

Answer The percent of markup on cost is 60%.

NOTE: In some problems, the amount of markup is given, which saves you from doing step 2. Simply use the rate formula to find the percent.

In summary:

> **HOW THE PERCENTAGE FORMULA APPLIES**
>
> **Finding the % markup *on cost***
>
> Cost = Base
>
> Markup = Percentage
>
> Markup % = Rate
>
> $$R = \frac{P}{B}$$
>
> $$M\% = \frac{\text{Markup}}{\text{Cost}}$$

266 Chapter 7

> **Finding the % markup *on retail***
>
> Retail = Base $\qquad R = \dfrac{P}{B}$
>
> Markup = Percentage $\qquad M\% = \dfrac{\text{Markup}}{\text{Retail}}$
>
> Markup % = Rate

Self-Check

1. A plastic ice bucket that costs $8 is sold for $12. Find the percent of markup on cost and the percent of markup on selling price.

2. At Hemple's Department Store, a coat that costs $60 has a markup of $60. What is the rate of markup on selling price?

3. A lawn mower sells at Dan's Hardware for $250. If the markup is $100, what is the percent of markup on cost?

ANSWERS 1. Markup on selling price, $33\frac{1}{3}\%$; markup on cost, 50%   2. 50%
3. $66\frac{2}{3}\%$

AN EMPIRE IS FORMED

In 1886, Richard Sears, a 23-year-old railroad station agent in North Redwood, Minnesota, bought a shipment of watches refused by a local jeweler. Making use of his railroad telegraph, he offered the watches, meant to retail for $25, to other station agents at $14 each. As a result, he quickly made $5,000. This inspired him to quit his railroad job and go into business for himself. The following year, he hired Alvah Roebuck, a watchmaker, and began selling watches through the mail. By 1893, Sears had diversified and was selling a wide variety of products through a 500-page catalogue. That year, operating under the name Sears, Roebuck & Company, the firm boasted sales of over $338,000

Assignment 7.2

Retail Merchandising

Fill in the blanks and carry percents to the nearest whole percent.

	Cost	Selling Price	Markup	% Markup of Selling Price	% Markup of Cost
1.	$ 350	$ 700	$ 350	50%	100%
2.	$ 40	$ 60	$ 20	33%	50%
3.	$ 125	$ 275	$ 150	55%	120%
4.	$ 100	$ 160	$ 60	38%	60%
5.	$ 18	$ 25.50	$ 7.50	29%	42%
6.	$ 1,200	$ 1,700	$ 500	29%	42%
7.	$ 28	$ 50	$ 22	44%	79%
8.	$ 16	$ 27	$ 11	41%	69%
9.	$ 89.20	$ 141.60	$ 52.40	37%	59%
10.	$ 240	$ 520	$ 280	54%	117%

11. The store where Sheldon Levy works sells a black-and-white television set for $150. If the set costs $95, what is the percent of markup based on retail?

    C + M = R $150 R
    $95 + M = $150   −   95 C
                      $ 55 M

    37% markup on retail

    Rate = $\frac{P}{B}$ M% = $\frac{M}{R}$
    M% = $\frac{$55}{$150}$
    M% = 37%

12. What is the rate of markup on retail on a coffee service, with a wholesale price of $50, which sells for $100?

    C + M = R $100 R
    $50 + M = $100   −   50 C
                      $ 50

    50% markup on retail

    Rate = $\frac{P}{B}$ M% = $\frac{M}{R}$
    M% = $\frac{$50}{$100}$
    M% = 50%

13. Meyer and Morgan Department Store buys 6 dozen scarves for $360. They retail for $7 each. Figure the percent of markup on retail for each scarf.

    $360 ÷ 72 = $5 cost for one scarf
    C + M = R $7 R
    $5 + M = $7   − 5 C
                    $2 M

    29% markup on retail per scarf

    Rate = $\frac{P}{B}$ M% = $\frac{M}{R}$
    M% = $\frac{$2}{$7}$
    M% = .2857
    M% = 29%

continued

Assignment 7.2 *continued*

14. Murray Nursery buys 16 dozen flats of Scotch moss for a total of $1,200. The nursery marks them to sell at $10.50 each. Calculate the percent of markup on cost per flat.

    16 × 12 = 192 flats
    $1,200 ÷ 192 = $6.25 cost per flat
    C + M = R $10.50 R
    $6.25 + M = $10.50   − 6.25 C
                          $ 4.25 M

    68% markup on
    cost per flat

    Rate = $\frac{P}{B}$ M% = $\frac{M}{C}$

    M% = $\frac{\$4.25}{\$6.25}$

    M% = 68%

15. A dozen short-sleeve sweaters cost $216 and retail for $30 each. What is the percent of markup based on retail?

    $216 ÷ 12 = $18 cost each
    C + M = R $30 R
    $18 + M = $30   − 18 C
                    $12 M

    40% markup
    on retail

    Rate = $\frac{P}{B}$ M% = $\frac{M}{R}$

    M% = $\frac{\$12}{\$30}$

    M% = 40%

16. At Barringer's Fireplace Shop, a set of hearth tools costs the store $18 and retail for $27. Give the percent of markup on retail.

    C + M = R $27 R
    $18 + M = $27 − 18 C
                   $ 9 M

    $33\frac{1}{3}$% markup
    on retail

    Rate = $\frac{P}{B}$ M% = $\frac{M}{R}$

    M% = $\frac{\$9}{\$27}$

    M% = $33\frac{1}{3}$%

17. Mario Pelligrini owns a fish market. He buys 120 pounds of halibut for $94.80 and sells it for $1.25 a pound. Find his rate of markup per pound based on cost.

    $94.80 ÷ 120 = $.79 cost per pound
    C + M = R $1.25 R
    $.79 + M = $1.25 − .79 C
                      $ .46 M

    58% markup
    on cost

    Rate = $\frac{P}{B}$ M% = $\frac{M}{C}$

    M% = $\frac{\$.46}{\$.79}$

    M% = 58%

18. Find the percent of markup based on cost if parakeets retail for $25 and it cost the Prid E. Kat Pet Store $15 each for the birds.

    C + M = R $25 R
    $15 + M = $25 − 15 C
                   $10 M

    67% markup
    on cost

    Rate = $\frac{P}{B}$ M% = $\frac{M}{C}$

    M% = $\frac{\$10}{\$15}$

    M% = 67%

7.3 Cost, Retail, and Markup

When determining amounts other than the percent of markup, you also use the markup formula, C + M = R, as well as the percentage formulas: Base × Rate = Percentage, and Base = Percentage ÷ Rate (see Section 5.3). In these situations, it is easy to identify the base because you are always told whether markup is *based on* cost or *based on* selling price. In many cases, the word "of" or "on" is used in describing the base. For instance, the problem may read "the markup is 60% *of cost*." The base in this problem is, therefore, cost. It is important to decide from the outset whether the base is cost or selling price.

The following problems are solved using the markup formula, C + M = R, except that the elements are expressed as percents. Remember: The base is always 100%. Once you express the percents, identify the dollar amounts given in the problem. Find the missing elements by applying one of the formulas for percentage. Which of them you use depends on whether you have the base in dollar amount or not. If so, then use B × R = P to find the missing element. If not, use B = P/R to find the base in dollars. Markup is actually an application of what you have learned earlier. Follow through with one step at a time. You are working with percentage.

Finding Cost When the Markup is Based on Retail

Example 1   A wall clock at Blevens Jewelry Store has a markup of $60, which is a 40% markup of retail. What is the wholesale cost of the clock?

Step 1   Write the markup formula and identify the key elements in terms of percents. Because the markup is on retail, the retail price is the base, or 100%. The percent, which is equal to cost, is found by subtracting.

     C + M = R
     ?% + 40% = 100%
     100% R
     − 40% M
     60% C
     60% + 40% = 100%

Step 2   Fill in any given dollar amounts under the appropriate label. The only dollar figure you have here is markup. Place it under the M.

     C + M = R
     60% + 40% = 100%
     $60

Step 3   Apply the percentage formula. To determine which formula to use, look under the 100% figure. If you have not placed a number there, find the base by using the formula B = P/R. Note that the only percentage and rate that represent the same element are in the markup column. Thus, P = $60 and R = 40%. Do not use the 60% under C because you have no corresponding dollar figure.

$$B = \frac{P}{R}$$

$$B = \frac{\text{Markup}}{\text{Markup \%}}$$

$$B = \frac{\$60}{40\%}$$

B = $150

Step 4   Place the result of step 3 in the markup formula and solve for the missing element. Because you found $150 to be the base, place it in the R column. Subtract $60 from the $150 to find the cost.

     C + M = R
     60% + 40% = 100%
     C + $60 = $150
     $90 + $60 = $150
     $150
     −   60
     $ 90

Answer   The cost of the wall clock is $90.

> **HOW THE PERCENTAGE FORMULA APPLIES**
>
> The following combinations are used in markup to find the base.
>
> $$\text{Base} = \frac{\text{Percentage}}{\text{Rate}}$$
>
> $$\text{Base} = \frac{\text{Cost}}{\text{Cost \%}}$$
>
> $$\text{Base} = \frac{\text{Markup}}{\text{Markup \%}}$$
>
> $$\text{Base} = \frac{\text{Retail}}{\text{Retail \%}}$$
>
> Which combination you use depends on what numbers are given in the problem.

Finding Retail When the Markup Is Based on Retail

Example 2 You are the buyer for the carpet department of Stallone's Furnishings Store. You purchase an Oriental rug, which costs $1,300. If the markup percent of retail is 60%, what will be the retail price of the rug?

Step 1 Write the markup formula and identify the key elements in terms of percents. Because this markup is based on retail price, R = 100%. The percent of cost is found by subtracting M% from R%.

C + M = R
?% + 60% = 100%

C + M = R
40% + 60% = 100%

Step 2 Fill in the dollar amounts given in the problem.

C + M = R
40% + 60% = 100%
$1,300

Step 3 Apply the percentage formula. Since the base is not given in dollar figures, find the base first. You have a quantity and a percent with the same label only in the cost column.

$B = \dfrac{P}{R}$

$B = \dfrac{\text{Cost}}{\text{Cost \%}}$

$B = \dfrac{\$1,300}{40\%}$

B = $3,250

Step 4 Place the result of step 3 in the markup formula.

C + M = R
$1,300 + M = $3,250

The retail price of the rug is $3,250.

Answer NOTE: To find the markup in dollars, subtract the cost price from the retail price. In this case, $3,250 − $1,300 = $1,950. The amount of markup equals $1,950.

In setting up this type of problem, some people prefer to use a grid layout:

$1,300	C	40%
	M	60%
	R	100%

Use the layout that suits your needs best, but remember to place the 100% where the base is. In Example 2, markup is based on retail; therefore, the 100% is next to the "R." If markup were based on cost, then the 100% would be placed next to the "C."

Finding Markup When the Markup Is Based on Retail

Example 3 At Brigand's Antique Shoppe, a table that retails at $129 has a markup of $33\frac{1}{3}\%$ based on retail. What is the markup of the table in dollars?

Step 1 Write the markup formula and identify the key elements in terms of percent.

$$C + M = R$$
$$66\frac{2}{3}\% + 33\frac{1}{3}\% = 100\%$$

Step 2 Fill in the dollar amounts given in the problem.

$$C + M = R$$
$$66\frac{2}{3}\% + 33\frac{1}{3}\% = 100\%$$
$$\$129$$

Step 3 Apply the percentage formula. In this case, the base is already expressed in dollars. Use it to find either the cost or the markup with the formula $B \times R = P$. Because this problem asks for markup in dollars, use the markup percent.

$$B \times R = P$$
$$\$129 \times 33\frac{1}{3}\% = M$$
$$\$43 = M$$

Answer The markup on retail is $43.

NOTE: You can find the dollar amount of the cost by using the cost percent; in the example above, it is $66\frac{2}{3}\%$. Depending on whether the base is cost or retail, here are the various combinations that can be used:

HOW THE PERCENTAGE FORMULA APPLIES

Base × Rate = Percentage
Base × Markup % = Markup
Base × Cost % = Cost
Base × Retail % = Retail

Self-Check

1. At La Mode Gallery, a portrait that costs $440 has a markup of 20% based on retail. What is the retail price?

Retail Merchandising

2. If the markup on a stereo system you want to buy is $200 and this is a 25% markup of retail, what is the retail price? What is the cost price?

3. In the store where you work, lawn furniture that retails at $385 has a markup of 40% based on retail. Find the cost and the markup in dollars.

ANSWERS 1. R = $550   2. R = $800; C = $600   3. C = $231; M = $154

The next few examples deal with finding cost, retail, and markup when the percent of markup is based on cost. These are solved in the same way as the previous examples, *except* that cost is the base and is, therefore, equal to 100%.

Finding Retail When the Markup Is Based on Cost

Example 4   A wall clock at Blevens Jewelry Store has a markup of $60, which is a 40% markup on cost. What is the selling price of the clock?

Step 1   Write the markup formula and identify the key elements in terms of percents. Remember, the base is cost, so cost is 100%. Retail equals C + M.

$$C + M = R$$
$$100\% + 40\% = 140\%$$

Step 2   Fill in the given dollar amounts.

$$C + M = R$$
$$100\% + 40\% = 140\%$$
$$ \$60$$

Step 3   Apply the percentage formula. Because the base (cost) is not given in dollars, you must find that figure first.

$$B = \frac{P}{R}$$

$$B = \frac{\text{Markup}}{\text{Markup \%}}$$

$$B = \frac{\$60}{.4} = \$150$$

Step 4   Place the result of step 3 into the formula and solve for the missing element.

$$C + M = R$$
$$100\% + 40\% = 140\%$$
$$\$150 + \$60 = \$210$$

Answer   The retail or selling price of the clock is $210.

Finding Retail and Markup When the Markup Is Based on Cost

Example 5   At Stallone's Furnishings Store, an oriental rug that costs $1,300 has a markup percent of cost of 60%. What are the retail price and the markup?

Step 1   Write the markup formula and identify the key elements in terms of percents.

$$C + M = R$$
$$100\% + 60\% = 160\%$$

Step 2   Fill in the dollar amounts given in the problem.

$$C + M = R$$
$$100\% + 60\% = 160\%$$
$$\$1,300$$

274   Chapter 7

Step 3   Apply the percentage formula. Because you have the base in dollars, use it to find a percentage.

$$B \times R = P$$
$$B \times \text{Retail}\% = \text{Retail}$$
$$\$1{,}300 \times 160\% = R$$
$$\$2{,}080 = R$$

Step 4   Place the result of step 3 into the markup formula and find the missing element.

$$C + M = R$$
$$100\% + 60\% = 160\%$$
$$\$1{,}300 + M = \$2{,}080$$
$$\$1{,}300 + \$780 = \$2{,}080$$

Answer   The retail price of the rug is $2,080, and the markup is $780.

NOTE: If you used 60% in step 3, you would find the markup of $780 first. By adding it to the cost of $1,300, you would find the retail price of $2,080. Use this alternative method to check your work.

Finding Cost and Markup When the Markup Is Based on Cost

Example 6   You want to buy a table that retails at $129. It has a markup of $33\frac{1}{3}\%$ on cost. What is the dollar markup on the table? What is the cost?

Step 1   Write the markup formula and identify the key elements in terms of percents.

$$C + M = R$$
$$100\% + 33\tfrac{1}{3}\% = 133\tfrac{1}{3}\%$$

Step 2   Fill in the given dollar amounts.

$$C + M = R$$
$$100\% + 33\tfrac{1}{3}\% = 133\tfrac{1}{3}\%$$
$$\$129$$

Step 3   Apply the percentage formula. Since the base in dollars is not given, find this figure first. You have a percentage and a rate labeled the same only in the "R" or Retail column. (Use the fractional equivalent of $\tfrac{4}{3}$ for $133\tfrac{1}{3}\%$.) Since the base equals the cost, C = $96.75.

$$B = \frac{P}{R}$$
$$B = \frac{\text{Retail}}{\text{Retail \%}}$$
$$B = \frac{\$129}{133\tfrac{1}{3}\%}$$
$$B = \$96.75$$
$$C = \$96.75$$

Step 4   Place the result into the markup formula and find the missing element.

$$C + M = \$$$
$$\$96.75 + M = \$129$$
$$\$96.75 + \$32.25 = \$129$$

Answer   The markup on the table is $32.25. The cost is $96.75.

Self-Check

1. If the markup percent on cost is 60%, find the retail price of a wood stove whose markup is $120.

2. If a canoe at Hank's Sporting Goods costs $480, what is the retail price when the markup on cost is $87\frac{1}{2}\%$?

3. What are the markup and the cost of a tool set that sells for $260 with a markup of 30% of cost?

ANSWERS   1. R = $320   2. R = $900   3. C = $200; M = $60

Assignment 7.3

Retail Merchandising

1. The furniture store where Harriette works buys a lounge chair for $125 and marks it up 40% on retail. Calculate the retail price.

   C + M = R
   60% + 40% = 100%
   $125

   $208.33 retail price

   Base = P/R   B = Cost/Cost %
   B = $125/60%
   B = $208.33 retail

2. A head of lettuce sells for 59 cents, with a markup of 30% based on cost. Find the cost to the supermarket of a gross (12 dozen heads) of lettuce.

   C + M = R
   100% + 10% = 130%
   $.59

   144 heads × $.45 = $64.80 cost/gross
   $64.80 cost/gross

   Base = P/R   B = Retail/Retail %
   B = $.59/130%
   B = .45

3. K & D Meats has a total markup on frozen meat patties of $200, which is a 10% markup on cost. What are the total retail price and total cost for the patties?

   C + M = R   C + M = R
   100% + 10% = 110% $2,000 + $200 = $2,200
   $200

   $2,200 total retail,
   $2,000 total cost

   Base = P/R   B = Markup/Markup %
   B = $200/10%
   B = $2,000 cost

4. At Pamela's Antique Shoppe, a crystal vase retails for $160. The markup is 45% on cost. Find the cost.

   C + M = R
   100% + 45% = 145%
   $160

   $110.34 cost

   Base = P/R   B = Retail/Retail %
   B = $160/145%
   B = $110.34 cost

5. Hanford Fabrics buys a 20-yard bolt of velvet for $145. The markup is 37½% on retail. What is the retail price per yard? $145 ÷ 20 = $7.25 cost/yd

   C + M = R
   62½% + 37½% = 100%
   $7.25

   $11.60 retail

   Base = P/R   B = Cost/Cost %
   B = $7.25/62.5%
   B = $11.60 retail

6. A buyer for Stewart's Department Store needs to find a line of coats that retail for $85 each and have a markup of 55% of retail. What is the most the buyer can pay for each coat?

   C + M = R
   45% + 55% = 100%
   $85

   $38.25 cost

   P = B × R   B × R = P
   $85 × 45% = C
   $38.25 = C

7. As the buyer for La Mode Fashions, Sara La Tour retails an evening gown for $600. If the markup on retail is 54%, what does the gown cost the store?

   C + M = R
   46% + 54% = 100%
   $600

   $276 cost

   P = B × R   B × R = P
   $600 × 46% = C
   $276 = C

8. At Toby O'Malley's Tobacco Shop, a calabash has a markup on cost of 55%. If the markup is $8, what does the pipe retail for?

   C + M = R   C + M = R
   100% + 55% = 155% $14.55 + 8 = $22.55 retail
   $8

   $22.55 retail

   B = P/R   B = Markup/Markup %
   B = $8/55%
   B = $14.55 cost

continued

Assignment 7.3 continued

9. Myra Sokol is employed at a kitchenware shop. She marks a Japanese cookbook up 36% on cost. If the amount of markup is $7.50, what is each of the following?

    $B = \dfrac{P}{R}$ $B = \dfrac{\text{Markup}}{\text{Markup \%}}$

    $B = \dfrac{\$7.50}{36\%}$

    $B = \$20.83 \text{ cost}$

    a) The wholesale price of the cookbook

    C + M = R
    100% + 36% = 136%
          $7.50

    $20.83 cost
    _____

    b) The retail price of the cookbook

    C + M = R
    $20.83 + $7.50 = $28.33

    $28.33 retail
    _____

    or

    B × R = P
    $20.83 × 1.36 = R
    $28.33 = R

10. Find the individual cost and the individual selling price of linen tablecloths, if the total markup for 14 of them is $537.60 and the percent of markup based on selling price is 30%.

    $B = \dfrac{P}{R}$ $B = \dfrac{\text{Markup}}{\text{Markup \%}}$

    $537.60 ÷ 14 = $38.40 each

    $B = \dfrac{\$38.40}{30\%}$

    $B = \$128 \text{ retail}$

    C + M = R $128.00 R
    70% + 30% = 100% − 38.40 M
        $38.40 $ 89.60 C

    $89.60 cost,
    $128 retail
    _____

11. Bronson Business Machines adds a markup of 40% of cost to its private-brand typewriter. If the typewriter sells for $966, what is the cost?

    $B = \dfrac{P}{R}$ $B = \dfrac{\text{Retail}}{\text{Retail \%}}$

    $B = \dfrac{\$966}{140\%}$

    $B = \$690 \text{ cost}$

    C + M = R
    100% + 40% = 140%
          $966

    $690 cost
    _____

12. At the men's store where Bob Ganzaga works, a tuxedo retails for $225 and is marked up 50% on retail. What is the cost of the suit?

    B × R = P
    $225 × 50% = $112.50 cost

    C + M = R
    50% + 50% = 100%
          $225

    $112.50 cost
    _____

13. At Playland Products, Inc., an electronic basketball game retails for $60, and is marked up 30% on retail. Find the total cost for 20 of the games.

    B × R = P
    $60 × 70% = $42

    C + M = R
    70% + 30% = 100%
          $60

    20 × $42 = $840 total cost
    $840 total cost
    _____

14. The markup on a small piece of gold jewelry is $20. If the mark-up based on selling price is 20%, what is the cost?

    $B = \dfrac{P}{R}$ $B = \dfrac{\text{Markup}}{\text{Markup \%}}$

    $B = \dfrac{\$20}{20\%}$

    $B = \$100 \text{ retail}$

    C + M = R $100 R
    80% + 20% = 100% − 20 M
        $20 $ 80 C

    $80 cost
    _____

15. Gibran's Book Store sells an atlas that costs $30 and is sold at a markup of 25% of the selling price. Find the total markup and total selling price if 25 of the atlases are sold.

    $B = \dfrac{P}{R}$ $B = \dfrac{\text{Cost}}{\text{Cost \%}}$

    $B = \dfrac{\$30}{75\%}$

    Retail = $40
    25 × $40 = $1,000
    Total selling price
    25 × $10 = $250 Total markup

    C + M = R
    75% + 25% = 100%
          $30

    $250 total markup,
    $1,000 total selling price
    _____

continued

Assignment 7.3 *continued*

16. A golf club that costs $25 will be sold at a markup of 25% based on cost. What are the total selling price and total markup if Rick's Recreation Shop sells 150 of these clubs? $25 × 150 = $3,750 total cost

    C + M = R
    100% + 25% = 125%

    $4,687.50 total selling price
    $937.50 total markup

    P = B × R
    $3,750 × 25% = M
    $937.50 = M
    $3,750 × 125% = R
    $4,687.50 = R

17. The retail price of a ceramic bowl is $56. If the markup is 40% of cost, find the cost of the bowl. If the housewares buyer has $720, how many of these bowls can the buyer purchase for the store?

    C + M = R $720 ÷ $40 = 18 bowls
    100% + 40% = 140%
    $56

    $40 cost, 18 bowls

    $B = \dfrac{P}{R}$ $B = \dfrac{\text{Retail}}{\text{Retail \%}}$
    $B = \dfrac{\$56}{140\%}$
    B = $40 cost

18. Dan Cortney, purchasing agent for Albertini Supermarket, buys six gross of zucchini for $196.50. What will each zucchini sell for if the store's markup is 35% of the cost?   144 × 6 = 864 zucchini, $196.50 ÷ 864 = $ .23 each

    C + M = R
    100% + 35% = 135%
    $ .23

    $ .31 retail per zucchini

    P = B × R
    $.23 × 135% = Retail
    $ .31 = R

19. Lola Freeman sells earthmoving equipment. If a tractor is offered for $48,000 with a markup of 40% on retail, what is its cost to Lola's company?

    C + M = R
    60% + 40% = 100%
    $48,000

    $28,800 cost

    P = B × R
    $48,000 × 60% =
    $28,800 = cost

20. Gail Lockerby customizes automobiles and offers them for sale. She buys an old Mustang, refurbishes it, and offers it for sale for $10,200, including a markup of 58% on the cost of the car plus materials. What did she pay for the wrecked car, if paint, chrome and other materials used cost her $1,200?

    C + M = R $6,455.70 Cost
    100% + 58% = 158%   − 1,200.00 Materials
    $10,200 $5,255.70 Paid for car

    $5,255.70 paid for wrecked car

    $B = \dfrac{P}{R}$ $B = \dfrac{\text{Retail}}{\text{Retail \%}}$
    $B = \dfrac{\$10,200}{158\%}$
    B = $6,455.70 cost

7.4 Markdown

In nearly all retail businesses, markdowns are an expected part of doing business. They can be taken for many reasons: The store may run a special sale; merchandise may be out of season, old, late, shopworn, or damaged; there may be simply too many items; or the cost of the merchandise to the store may have been reduced. Taking too many markdowns, however, has a negative effect on gross margin because the selling price is decreased too drastically to maintain a profit.

Some important terms are as follows.

New retail price is the amount at which merchandise is priced after it has been marked down.

Original retail price is the amount at which merchandise is marked when first offered for sale.

Amount of **markdown** is the difference between the original retail price and the new retail price.

Markdown percent is the rate of markdown based on the original price.

Net sales is the dollar amount of goods actually sold.

To find the dollar amount of markdown, multiply the original retail by the percent of markdown.

HOW THE PERCENTAGE FORMULA APPLIES

Original retail = Base
Percent of markdown = Rate
Markdown = Percentage
New retail price = Difference

B × R = P
Original retail × Percent of markdown = Markdown

B − P = Difference
Original retail − Markdown = New retail price

Finding Markdowns Based on Original Retail Price

Example 1 Maplewood Accessories, Inc., has 25 sets of stoneware dishes in its inventory. The dishes originally sold for $360 a set and were then marked down 25%. Five sets sold at the original price and 20 sold at the new retail price. Find the new retail price for each set and the total net sales.

Retail Merchandising **281**

Step 1	Write the percentage formula and identify the key elements. The base is the original retail and the rate is the markdown percent. The percentage is the amount of markdown.	B × R = P $360 × 25% = P
Step 2	Solve for markdown. (For conversion of 25% to $\frac{1}{4}$, see Section 5.1.)	$360 × 25% = P $360 × $\frac{1}{4}$ = $90
Step 3	Subtract the markdown from the original retail price to find the new retail price.	$360 Original retail price − 90 Markdown $270 New retail price
Step 4	Find the total net sales by multiplying the numbers sold by the prices and then adding the totals.	5 × $360 = $1,800 20 × $270 = $5,400 $7,200 Net sales
Answer	The new retail price is $270, and total net sales is $7,200.	

Self-Check

At Forest Spas, Inc., there were 50 redwood hot tubs to sell. Each tub was originally priced at $2,400 and was then marked 15% off the original price. Twenty sold at the original price and 27 sold at the new retail price. Find

a. the individual markdown; _____

b. the new retail price; and _____

c. the total net sales. _____

ANSWERS a) Markdown: $360; b) new retail price: $2,040; c) net sales: $103,080

AHEAD OF ITS TIME

The first bank in the world to make available an automatic teller machine was Chemical Bank of New York. Installed in 1969, their revolutionary system used a coded card similar in concept to the cards used today. Chemical Bank has long been noted for its progressive attitude toward customer service. In the 1970s, for example, the bank instituted the practice of showing movies to entertain waiting customers.

Assignment 7.4

Retail Merchandising

1. Hannah's Furniture Store has its annual sale in March. A contemporary sofa, priced at $895, is marked down 30% from the original price. What is its sale price?

    895 × 30% = $268.50 markdown
    $895.00 Original retail
    − 268.50 Markdown
    $626.50 New retail

    $626.50 sale price

2. Frederick's Department Store originally priced its designer jeans at $60 a pair. They had 150 pairs in inventory. Fifty-eight sold at this price. Three months later the rest of the jeans were marked down 25% and all were sold.

    a) What was the new retail price for each pair?

    B × R = P
    $60 × 25% = $15 markdown
    $60
    − 15
    $45 New retail price

    $45

    b) What is the total net sales figure?

    $60 × 58 jeans = $3480
    $45 × 92 jeans = $4140
    $7,620 Total net sales

    150
    − 58
    92 left

    $7,620

3. Adam Jameson needs a new suit. He is looking for the best value he can find on sale. One blue suit retails for $350 but has been marked down 26%. Another, a gray suit retails for $340 but has been marked down 24%.

    a) What is the sale price of each of the suits?

    Blue suit:
    $350 × 26% = $91 markdown

    $350
    − 91
    $259 New retail

    Gray suit:
    $340 × 24% = $81.60 markdown

    $340
    − 81.60
    $258.40 New retail

    $259 blue;
    $258.40 gray

    b) How much would he save by buying the less expensive suit?

    $259.00
     258.40
    $ .60 saved

    $ .60 saved

4. Kingstone Garden Supply has a dozen stone birdbaths marked to sell for $45 apiece. As part of an end-of-the-season sale, ten of the birdbaths are marked down 15% from this retail pirce. Calculate the total net sales, if two of the birdbaths sold at the original retail price and ten sold at the new price.

    $45 × 15% = $6.75 Individual markdown

    $45.00 Original retail
    − 6.75 Markdown
    $38.25 New retail

    $6.75 × 10 = $67.50 Total markdown
    $45 × 2 = $90.00
    $38.25 × 10 = $382.50
    $472.50 Total net sales

    $472.50

continued

Assignment 7.4 continued

5. A line of lace collars was not selling well at a retail price of $6.50 each. The buyer found that there were 40 of these collars on hand and decided to mark them down 20% off the original retail. Determine the markdown for each collar. If 30 collars sold at the sales price and none sold at the original price, what is the net sales figure for the merchandise?

    $6.50 × 20% = $1.30 Individual markdown

    $6.50
    − 1.30
    5.20 New retail

    $5.20 × 30 = $156 Total net sales

    $1.30 markdown;
    $156 net sales

6. Six pine chests original retailed for $875 each. None sold at this price. Now they are priced at 18% off the original price. If four of the chests are sold at the new retail price, what are the markdown for each chest and the total net sales figure?

    $875 × 18% = $157.50 Individual markdown

    $875.00 Original retail
    − 157.50 Markdown
    $717.50 New retail

    $717.50 × 4 = $2,870 Net sales

    $157.50 markdown;
    $2,870 net sales

7. Lucky's Luggage Store advertised in the paper, announcing "Tote bags—15% off original price." The tote bags were originally priced at $42. Thirty tote bags were offered for sale at the new retail price and 24 were sold. The remaining were sold at an additional 10% off the sales price and all were sold. Determine the total net sales.

    $42 × 15% = $6.30 Individual markdown

    $42
    − 6.30
    $35.70 New retail for first discount

    $35.70 × 24 = $856.80 Sales for first discount

    $35.70 × 10% = $3.57 Individual markdown

    $35.70
    − 3.57
    $32.13 New retail for second discount

    $32.13 × 6 = $192.78 Sales for second discount

    $ 856.80
    + 192.78
    $1,049.58 Total net sales

    $1,049.58

8. The shop where Danny Chu works ordered twenty-four Swis musical boxes that sell for $26 each. Only 5 sold at the original retail price. The rest were marked down 25% off to make room for new stock, seventeen were sold at the new price.

    a) What is the new retail price for each box?

    $26 × 25% = $6.50 Individual markdown

    $26.00
    − 6.50
    $19.50 New retail price

    b) What is the net sales amount?

    $19.50

    $26 × 5 = $130   Sales at original price
    $19.50 × 17 = $331.50 Sales at new price
    $461.50 Total net sales

    $461.50

7.5 Merchandise Inventory

The inventory tells a business how much stock it has on hand. As with markup, inventory can be evaluated either at retail or at cost. Small stores commonly base their inventories on the cost figure. Businesses that sell items whose retail price fluctuates often, such as fresh fruit and vegetable stands, also use this method. However, the retail method is most widely used, particularly by larger concerns.

Finding Average Inventory

One key figure is the average inventory. Inventory can be taken yearly, semi-annually, quarterly, monthly, or more often. The **average inventory** is the total inventory divided by the number of times the inventory has been taken during the year.

Example 1 On January 1, the beginning inventory at retail in the small-appliance department was $68,000. The ending inventory at retail, on December 31 of the same year, was $76,500. What was the average inventory at retail?

Step 1 Find the total inventory by adding all inventories taken.

$$\begin{array}{r}\$\ 68,000 \text{ Beginning inventory} \\ +\ 76,500 \text{ Ending inventory} \\ \hline \$144,500 \text{ Total inventory}\end{array}$$

Step 2 Divide the total inventory by the number of inventories taken. In this case, the number of inventories is 2.

$$\frac{\$144,500}{2} = \$72,250$$

Answer The average inventory at retail was $72,250.

Example 2 At Mary's Ceramic Shop, inventories taken at cost for a six-month period are as follows:

January 1	$16,500	May 1	$19,100
February 1	$21,200	June 1	$20,600
March 1	$20,900	June 30	$18,400
April 1	$16,300		

What is the average inventory taken at cost?

Step 1 Find the total inventory.

$$\begin{array}{r}\$\ 16,500 \\ 21,200 \\ 20,900 \\ 16,300 \\ 19,100 \\ 20,600 \\ \underline{18,400} \\ \$133,000 \text{ Total inventory}\end{array}$$

Step 2 Divide the total inventory by the number of inventories; in this case, 7.

$$\frac{\$133,000}{7} = \$19,000$$

Answer The average inventory at cost is $19,000.

NOTE: The total inventory is divided by 7, even though the time period is six months. Use the number of *inventories*, not the number of months, to find the average inventory. (See Section 1.7).

Self-Check

1. Starlight Gift Shop had a beginning inventory at retail of $34,600, and an ending inventory at retail of $29,700. What was the average inventory at retail? _____

2. The ABC Book Company had the following inventories taken at cost for a six-month period:

July 1	$38,300	November 1	$40,200
August 1	$31,700	December 1	$35,800
September 1	$42,400	December 31	$30,500
October 1	$34,100		

   What was the average inventory at cost? _____

ANSWERS 1. $32,150   2. $36,142.86

Finding Stock Turnover

The basic concept of retailing is to make merchandise available to the customer and to sell it as quickly as possible so that new merchandise can take its place. The cycle repeats itself. Stock turnover, also known as stockturn, is an important figure because it tells the retailer how quickly the merchandise is moving. By definition, **stock turnover** is the number of times the average inventory is sold and replaced during a certain time period. It is often figured on a yearly basis.

An annual stockturn of 3 in a toy department means that the average inventory of toys was sold and then replaced 3 times during the year. Note the use of the term "average." Turnover does not mean that every toy is sold. It is, instead, an estimate of sales and restocking.

Turnover varies with the type of merchandise and the type of retail business. For example, the turnover for jeans or dresses is normally higher or faster than the turnover for fur coats. The turnover for a gas station is higher than the turnover in a furniture store. Stock turnover is also used to evaluate performance by allowing for comparison of a business with other departments, with other firms, or with industry averages. It can be figured at retail or at cost, depending on what method a business uses for recordkeeping.

Guidelines have been established to indicate a "good" turnover for different types of merchandise and businesses. For example, a good turnover for cameras might be approximately 3.2, whereas a good turnover for grocery items might be 11.8. If turnover is much higher or lower than established standards for the industry and size of business, it could indicate that there are some serious problems. If turnover is too high, it may mean that the merchandise is priced too low for the market or that the inventory is not properly stocked. If turnover is too low, it may indicate that the retail price is too high, the salespeople are unproductive, or more effective displays and/or advertising are needed.

The formulas for stock turnover are:

$$\text{Stockturn at retail} = \frac{\text{Net sales}}{\text{Average inventory at retail}}$$

$$\text{Stockturn at cost} = \frac{\text{Cost of goods sold}}{\text{Average inventory at cost}}$$

Example 3 The Good Earth Ceramics Company had net sales for the month of April of $52,000. The inventory at retail was $12,000 in the beginning of April and $14,000 at the end of the month. What is the turnover at retail for the month of April?

Step 1 Find the average inventory at retail. $\dfrac{\$12,000 + \$14,000}{2}$

$\dfrac{\$26,000}{2} = \$13,000$ Average inventory

Step 2 Divide the net sales by the average inventory at retail.

$\dfrac{\$52,000 \text{ Net sales}}{\$13,000 \text{ Average inventory at retail}} = 4 \text{ Turnover}$

Answer The turnover at retail is 4 times for the month of April.

Example 4 Given the following information for Freddie's Fruit Stand, find the turnover at cost:

Net sales: $80,000
Cost of goods sold: $45,000

Inventories at Cost

January 1 $17,000
June 1 $24,000
December 31 $19,000

Step 1 Find the average inventory at cost. $\dfrac{\$17,000 + \$24,000 + \$19,000}{3}$

$\dfrac{\$60,000}{3} = $ Average inventory

$\$20,000 = $ Average inventory

Step 2 Divide the cost of goods sold by the average inventory at cost to find the turnover at cost.

$\dfrac{\text{Cost of goods sold}}{\text{Average inventory at cost}} = \dfrac{\$45,000}{\$20,000} = 2.25 \text{ Turnover}$

Answer The turnover at cost is 2.25 times.

NOTE: The net sales figure was not used to solve this problem. Pick out and use only the information needed to solve a narrative problem. Do not be led astray.

Converting Average Inventory

In some businesses, where inventory is taken at cost and the net sales figure is known, the approximate turnover at retail is determined by applying the overall percent of markup. This tool is especially useful for small businesses that want to check their performance with the statistics published by the retail industry. These problems involve using the markup formula (Cost + Markup = Retail) and the formula for turnover. Average inventory at retail also can be converted to average inventory at cost by applying the percent of markup.

Example 5 Harry's Hardware takes its inventory at cost. The beginning inventory was $42,000 and the ending inventory was $38,000. The Net sales for the period was $192,000. Find the turnover at retail if the markup on cost is 60%.

Step 1 Find the average inventory at cost.

$\dfrac{\$42,000 + \$38,000}{2} = \$40,000$ Average inventory at cost

Step 2 Convert the average inventory at cost to the average inventory at retail.

a) Write the markup formula and identify the key elements in terms of percents. Note that markup is based on cost, so C = 100%.

$$C + M = R$$
$$100\% + 60\% = 160\%$$

b) Fill in the dollar amounts given. Average inventory at cost = C.

$$C + M = R$$
$$100\% + 60\% = 160\%$$
$$\$40{,}000$$

c) Apply the percentage formula.

$$B \times R = P$$
$$\$40{,}000 \times 160\% = \$64{,}000$$

d) Place the result into the markup formula. Average inventory at retail = R.

$$C + M = R$$
$$\$40{,}000 + M = \$64{,}000$$

Step 3 Divide the net sales by the average inventory at retail.

$$\frac{\$192{,}000}{\$64{,}000} = 3 \text{ Turnover at retail}$$

Answer The turnover at retail is 3 times.

NOTE: This procedure can also be used to find turnover at cost if the inventory is taken at retail and the cost of goods sold and percent of markup are known.

Self-Check

1. The average inventory of Linda's Lace Shop is valued at a cost of $31,000. If the markup on cost is 45%, what is the average inventory at retail?

2. Given the following information, find the stockturn at retail and the stockturn at cost.

Net Sales:	$855,000
Cost of goods sold:	$512,000
Beginning inventory at retail:	$248,000
Ending inventory at retail:	$202,000
Average inventory at cost:	$128,000

3. The Leather Craft Shop's beginning inventory at retail is $36,000, and its ending inventory at retail is $44,000. The cost of goods sold is $120,000. If the markup is 40% of retail, what is the stockturn at cost?

ANSWERS   1. $44,950   2. 3.8 times at retail; 4.0 times at cost   3. 5 times

Assignment 7.5

Retail Merchandising

Where it applies, round turnover in these problems to the nearest tenth.

1. The beginning inventory at retail at the Village Shop is $143,600. Sales are $487,000. If the ending inventory at retail is $121,300, find the average inventory.

    Beginning inventory $143,600
    + Ending inventory   121,300
      Total inventory $264,900

    $\frac{264,900}{2} = \$132,450$ Average inventory

    $132,450

2. The following inventories were taken at cost at Fabulous Frames, Inc.

January 1	$72,000
February 1	$61,300
March 1	$64,400
April 1	$71,900
May 1	$74,700
June 1	$68,200
June 30	$66,500

    The total cost of goods sold is $360,000. What is the average inventory?

Jan.	$ 72,000
Feb.	61,300
Mar.	64,400
April	71,900
May	74,700
June	68,200
June 30	66,500
	$479,000 Total inventory

    $\frac{\$479,000}{7} = \$68428.57$ Average inventory

    $68,428.57

3. Find the stock turnover at cost for each of the following situations. Inventory is taken at cost.

	Cost of Goods Sold	Beginning Inventory	Ending Inventory	Turnover at Cost
a)	$48,000	$11,400	$ 8,200	4.9
b)	$65,000	$18,340	$ 7,250	5.1
c)	$94,000	$35,628	$25,355	3.1

    Beginning inventory
    + Ending inventory
      Total inventory

    $\frac{\text{Total inventory}}{2} = $ Average inventory

    $\frac{\text{Cost of goods sold}}{\text{Average inventory}} = $ Turnover

4. The children's swimwear section of Meyer's Department Store has retail sales of $12,000 for the year just ended. The swimwear had cost the store $4,800. The average stock of swimwear was valued at $2,000 at cost and $6,000 at retail.

continued

Assignment 7.5 continued

a) What was the stockturn at retail?

$$\frac{\text{Total sales}}{\text{Average inventory @ retail}} = \frac{\$12,000}{\$6,000} = 2$$

2 stockturn at retail

b) What was the stock turn at cost?

$$\frac{\text{CGS}}{\text{Average inventory @ cost}} = \frac{\$4,800}{\$2,000} = 2.4$$

2.4 stockturn at cost

5. You are an accountant for Palmeadow Frozen Foods. Figure the inventory turnover at cost, given the following information:

Sales:	$400,000	Merchandise on Hand at Cost	
Purchases:	340,000		
Cost of goods sold:	300,000	Beginning:	$ 60,000
		Ending:	100,000

Beginning inventory $ 60,000
Ending inventory 100,000
$160,000

$$\frac{\$160,000}{2} = \$80,000 \text{ Average inventory @ cost}$$

Inventory Turnover @ Cost:

$$\frac{\text{CGS}}{\text{Average inventory @ cost}} = \frac{\$300,000}{80,000} = 3.75 = 3.8 \text{ inventory turnover at cost}$$

3.8 inventory turnover at cost

6. You are a new employee at Christaman's Dry Goods Store. Jonah Christaman, the owner, hands you the ledger and asks you to figure the turnover at retail for the last six months. Here are the totals.

Sales		Inventory at Retail	
January	$24,000	January 1	$46,000
February	$18,000	February 1	$51,500
March	$27,500	March 1	$55,250
April	$38,200	April 1	$68,000
May	$44,625	May 1	$82,000
June	$62,650	June 1	$97,400
Total sales	$214,975	July 1	$88,000
		Total inventory	$488,150

Turnover at retail:

$$\frac{\text{Net sales}}{\text{Average inventory @ retail}} = \frac{\$214,975}{69,735.71}$$

Stockturn = 3.1

$$\frac{\$488,150}{7} = \$69,735.71 \text{ Average Inventory}$$

3.1 stockturn at retail

7. The following data are given for Bechtold's Stationery Store for the six-month period beginning February 1 and ending July 31. What is the stock turnover at retail?

Month	Stock on Hand at Retail	Net Sales
February 1	$14,000	$ 9,000
March 1	$17,000	$10,000
April 1	$17,000	$11,000

$$\frac{\text{Total Inventory @ Retail}}{\text{\# Inventories}} = \frac{\$105,000}{7}$$

Average Inventory @ Retail = $15,000

$$\frac{\text{Total sales}}{\text{Average Inventory @ Retail}} = \frac{\$57,000}{\$15,000}$$

Stockturn @ Retail = 3.8

continued

Assignment 7.5 *continued*

May 1	$16,000	$ 9,000
June 1	$14,000	$10,000
July 1	$15,000	$ 8,000
July 31	$12,000	$57,000
Total	$105,000	

3.8 stockturn at retail

8. Determine the rate of turnover at cost from the following statement:

Sales		$120,500	
Beginning inventory at cost	$ 21,000		
Added purchases	$ 88,000		
Total merchandise available for sale	$109,000		
Ending inventory at cost	$ 29,500		
Cost of goods sold		$ 79,500	
Gross profit on sales		$ 41,000	

Beginning inventory $21,000
Ending inventory   29,500
              $50,500

$$\frac{\$50,500}{2} = \$25,250 \text{ Average inventory @ cost}$$

$$\frac{CGS}{\text{Average Inventory @ cost}} = \frac{\$79,500}{\$25,250}$$

Stockturn @ cost = 3.1

3.1 turnover at cost

9. Currently inventory at Clyde's House of Clocks has a wholesale value of $46,000. If the markup based on cost is 49%, find the average inventory at retail.

C + M = R
100% + 49% = 149%
$46,000

B × R = P
46,000 × 149% = $68,540

$68,540 average inventory @ retail

10. The beginning inventory at cost at Shelton Photo Store is $40,000. The ending inventory at cost is $44,000.

a) If the cost of goods sold is $491,400, what is the turnover at cost?

Beginning inventory $40,000
Ending Inventory $44,000
               $84,000

$$\frac{\$84,000}{2} = \$42,000 \text{ Average inventory @ cost}$$

$$\frac{CGS}{\text{Average inventory @ cost}} = \frac{\$491,400}{\$42,000} = 11.7 \text{ turnover @ cost}$$

11.7 turnover @ cost

b) What is the average inventory at retail if markup on cost is 30%?

C + M = R
100% + 30% = 130%
$42,000

B × R = P
$42,000 × 130% = $54,600

$54,600 average inventory @ retail

continued

Assignment 7.5 *continued*

11. The Land of Leather Shop took the following inventories at retail:

January 1	$26,000
March 31	$30,000
June 30	$24,000
September 30	$24,000
December 31	$26,000

    If the cost of goods sold for the year is $90,000 and the markup is 25% based on cost, what is the turnover at cost?

    $ 26,000
    30,000
    24,000
    24,000
    26,000
    $130,000 Total inventory

    $\dfrac{\text{Total inventory retail}}{\text{\# Inventories}} = \dfrac{\$130,000}{5}$

    Average inventory @ Retail = $26,000

    $B = \dfrac{P}{R}$

    $\dfrac{\text{Retail}}{\text{Retail \%}} = \dfrac{\$26,000}{125\%}$

    Cost = $20,800

    C + M = R
    100% + 25% = 125%
          $26,000

    $\dfrac{\text{CGS}}{\text{Average inventories @ cost}} = \dfrac{\$90,000}{\$20,800}$

    Stockturn @ Cost = 4.3

    4.3 stockturn at cost

12. The inventories at retail taken at the Silent Stained Glass Studio are as follows:

January 1	$35,000
February 1	$29,000
March 1	$30,000
April 1	$34,000
May 1	$28,000
June 1	$32,000
June 30	$31,000

    $219,000 = Total inventory @ retail

    $\dfrac{\text{Total inventory @ retail}}{\text{\# inventories}} = \dfrac{\$219,000}{7}$

    Average inventory @ retail = $31,285.71

    The markup on cost is 55% and the cost of goods sold is $120,000. Find the turnover at cost.

    C + M = R
    100% + 55% = 155%
           $31,285.71

    $B = \dfrac{P}{R}$

    $\dfrac{\text{Retail}}{\text{Retail \%}} = \dfrac{\$31,285.71}{155\%}$

    Average inventory @ cost = $20,184.33

    $\dfrac{\text{Cost of goods sold}}{\text{Average inventory @ cost}} = \dfrac{\$120,000}{\$20,184.33}$

    Turnover at cost = 5.9

    5.9 turnover at cost

292   Chapter 7

7.6 The Value of Ending Inventory

Proper management of inventory is important to the profitability of a business. It is particularly important to know the cost value of inventory in stock. For accounting and tax purposes, the value of inventory must be figured at least once a year. This process may be complicated by the fact that since prices fluctuate, the cost of the same item may change over a year's time. When the same item is ordered at different times and at different prices, how do you know the value of the items remaining in stock? Which cost price do you choose in order to place a value on the ending inventory? There are three possible methods:

1. FIFO (First In, First Out)
2. LIFO (Last In, First Out)
3. Average cost

Applying the FIFO Method

FIFO means "first in, first out." This method assumes that the items purchased first by the business were the items that sold first. Therefore, the items in the ending inventory are the ones that were purchased most recently. In inflationary times, when prices are rising, the remaining inventory would include principally the items purchased at higher cost. From a tax perspective, this results in higher income and higher taxes. On the other hand, if a business were for sale and a change of ownership likely, valuing the ending inventory at the highest cost could be beneficial to the seller.

When figuring the value of inventory using FIFO, you must first subtract the total amount ordered in each price category from the ending inventory. The number of items remaining in inventory in each category is multiplied by the cost for these items. You start valuing the inventory from the items purchased most recently and move on to each preceding category until the total number of items in the ending inventory is reached.

Example 1 The Music Source Company had 188 blank cassette tapes in stock. The company uses the FIFO method of valuing inventory. Find the value of the ending inventory if the following purchases were made during the year:

Purchase Date	Number of Cassettes	Price per Cassette
January 1	140	$1.87
March 1	200	$2.10
August 1	150	$2.34
December 1	160	$2.61

Step 1   Multiply the number of units in the most recent purchase by the unit price.

$$160 \times \$2.61 = \$417.60$$

Step 2   Find the remaining inventory by subtracting the number of units above from the ending inventory.

```
  188
- 160
   28 left
```

Step 3   Multiply the number of remaining units in the previous category by the unit price. Note that not all the units in this price category remain in the ending inventory.

$$28 \times \$2.34 = \$65.52$$

Retail Merchandising

Step 4   Add the dollar value of the inventory in each price category used on the previous page to find the total value of the ending inventory.

$417.60
+ $ 65.52
$483.12

Answer $483.12 is the value of the ending inventory.

Applying the LIFO Method

LIFO means "last in, first out." This method assumes that the items purchased most recently by the business were the items that sold first. Therefore, the items in the ending inventory are the ones first purchased.

Because there are complex tax rules involved in using LIFO, a special statement must be filed with a business's tax return in order to apply this method. From a tax perspective, LIFO shows a larger cost of goods sold and thus a lower income in times of inflation than the other methods. The effect is lower taxes. (For a complete discussion of cost of goods sold, refer to Section 14.1.)

The earliest units with their corresponding prices are used to place a value on the remaining units in stock. Although the actual flow of physical goods is first in, first out, the opposite concept of last in, first out is permitted for accounting and tax purposes. In fact, a company may choose one method for accounting purposes and another for tax purposes. However, once chosen, the method of valuing inventory for tax purposes cannot be changed without the consent of the IRS.

Example 2   The Music Source Company uses the LIFO method of valuing inventory. Find the value of the ending inventory given the same figures used in Example 1.

Step 1   Multiply the number of units in the earliest purchase by the unit price.

$140 \times \$1.87 = \$261.80$

Step 2   Find the remaining inventory by subtracting the number of units above from the ending inventory.

188
− 140
48 left

Step 3   Multiply the remaining portion of the ending inventory by the next price category. Note that only some of the units in this price category are in the remaining ending inventory.

$48 \times \$2.10 = \$100.80$

Step 4   Add the dollar value of the inventory in each price category used above to find the total value of the ending inventory.

$261.80
+ $100.80
$362.60

Answer $362.60 is the value of the ending inventory.

Applying the Average-Cost Method

Average cost, another method used for evaluating inventory, involves finding the total cost of the items purchased and dividing it by the number of items purchased. This average cost per unit is then multiplied by the items remaining in inventory to find the value of the ending inventory. The average cost method is considered to be the closest to the actual cost of inventory. But, again, each company's situation dictates which method of valuing inventory is the most advantageous to use. The formula for average cost method is as follows:

$$\frac{\text{Total cost}}{\text{Total units purchased}} = \text{Average cost per unit}$$

$$\text{Ending inventory in units} \times \text{Average cost per unit} = \text{Total value of ending inventory}$$

Example 3 The Music Source Company uses the average-cost method of valuing inventory. Find the value of the ending inventory given the same figures used in Example 1.

Step 1 Multiply each price by the number of units purchased at that price to find the total cost for each price category.

$140 \times \$1.87 = \$261.80$
$200 \times \$2.10 = \$420.00$
$150 \times \$2.34 = \$351.00$
$160 \times \$2.61 = \$417.60$

Step 2 Add the dollar amounts together to find the total cost.

$\quad\$\ 261.80$
$\quad\ \ 420.00$
$\quad\ \ 351.00$
$\quad\ \ \underline{417.60}$
$\$1,450.40$ Total cost

Step 3 Add the number of units purchased in each price category to find the total number of units purchased.

140
200
150
$\underline{160}$
650 Total units

Step 4 Divide the total cost by the total number of units purchased to find the average cost per unit. Round to the nearest cent.

$\dfrac{\$1450.40}{650} = \$2.23$

Step 5 Multiply the number of units remaining in stock by the average cost per unit to find the dollar value of the ending inventory.

$188 \times \$2.23 = \$419.24$

Answer $419.24 is the value of the ending inventory.

Let's compare the answers for the value of the ending inventory for the Music Source Company using the three methods:

FIFO   = $483.12

LIFO   = $362.60

Average cost = $419.24

As you can see, the answers differ widely. Note that in a time of rising prices, as in this example, the LIFO method gives the lowest value of ending inventory, FIFO the highest and average cost the middle value.

The following diagram will help you summarize how the value of ending inventory is determined through use of the three methods.

LIFO: Start valuing ending inventory from the earliest purchase.

Purchase Date	Number of Units	Price per Unit
January 1	140 units @	$1.87
March 1	200 units @	$2.10
August 1	150 units @	$2.34
December 1	160 units @	$2.61

Earliest ↘ (January 1)
Latest ↗ (December 1)

Average cost: Value ending inventory by figuring the average of all costs.

FIFO: Start valuing ending inventory from the latest purchase.

Remember! FIFO: Earliest purchases are sold first.
LIFO: Latest purchases are sold first.

Self-Check

Custom Ceramics has an ending inventory of 58 kitchen cannister sets of design #A6. The company has made the following purchases:

Date	Number of Units	Price per Unit
February 11	25 units	$20.11
May 28	32 units	$19.60
August 30	20 units	$20.57
November 3	41 units	$21.29

Figure the value of the ending inventory by using each of the following methods.

1. FIFO
2. LIFO
3. Average cost

ANSWERS   1. $1,222.58   2. $1,150.52   3. $1,186.68

THE SPECIFIC-IDENTIFICATION METHOD OF INVENTORY

This inventory method requires that each item be tagged and coded individually with its original cost. (The original cost is the invoice price of the items less any discounts.) The units of stock on hand are valued at each individual cost figure. Obviously, this evaluation can be quite time-consuming. Furthermore, confusion can result should costs on identical items fluctuate frequently. However, for a small business with limited inventory, the specific-identification method can be a viable method of valuing ending inventory.

Assignment 7.6

Retail Merchandising

Assume that all purchases were made in the same calendar year.

1. Blackwell Industries had 1,200 industrial belts in stock at the end of the year. The company uses the FIFO method of inventory. Figure the value of the ending inventory if the following purchases were made.

Purchase Date	Number of Units	Price per Unit
January 14	1,800	$7.00
April 2	950	$7.28
July 28	1,400	$7.80
November 7	920	$8.40

   920 × $8.40 = $7,728   1200
   280 × $7.80 = $2,184 − 920
                           280 left

     $7,728
   + 2,184
     $9,912 $9,912

2. Tennis World uses the LIFO method of inventory and has an ending inventory of 210 rackets. Find the value of the ending inventory if the following purchases were made.

Purchase Date	Number of Units	Price per Unit
March 2	105	$17.50
June 10	80	$17.60
September 24	170	$18.70
December 1	140	$19.00

   105 × $17.50 = $1,837.50   210
   80 × $17.60 = $1,408   − 185
   25 × $18.70 = $467.50   25 left

     $1,837.50
      1,408.
   +   467.50
     $3,713. $3,713

3. Given the following purchase schedule, figure the value of an ending inventory of 240 wine glasses. Use the average-cost method.

Purchase Date	Number of Glasses	Price per Glass
January 4	120	$3.40
April 9	330	$3.16
July 21	180	$3.52

continued

Assignment 7.6 *continued*

Purchase Date	Number of Glasses	Price per Glass
October 18	250	$3.37
December 1	370	$3.61

```
       120 × $3.40 =   $  408.00
       330 ×  3.16 =    1,042.80
       180 ×  3.52 =      633.60
       250 ×  3.37 =      842.50
       370 ×  3.61 = +  1,335.70
Totals 1,250 units    $4,263.60 cost
```

$$\frac{\$4,262.60}{1,250} = \$3.41 \text{ Average cost per unit}$$

$3.41 × 240 = $818.40

$818.40

The following business situation applies to problems 4, 5, and 6.

Quality Frame Supplies found that they had 141 16″ × 20″ metal frames remaining in stock. The following purchases were made during the year.

Purchase Date	Number of Frames	Price per Frame
February 1	50	$9.10
May 11	61	$8.86
August 24	87	$8.54
November 5	63	$8.97
December 18	59	$9.56

Find the value of the ending inventory by applying each of the following methods.

4. FIFO

```
59 × $9.56 =   $564.04      141
63 ×  8.97 =    565.11    − 122
19 ×  8.54 = +  162.26     19 left
     Total   $1,291.41
```

$1,291.41

5. LIFO

```
50 × $9.10 =   $455.00      141
61 ×  8.86 =    540.46    − 111
30 ×  8.54 = +  256.20     30 left
     Total   $1,251.66
```

$1,251.66

6. Average cost

```
       50 × $9.10 = $  455.00
       61 ×  8.86 =    540.46
       87 ×  8.54 =    742.98
       63 ×  8.97 =    565.11
       59 ×  9.56 =    564.04
Totals 320 units    $2,867.59 Cost
```

$$\frac{\$2,867.59}{320} = \$8.96 \text{ Average cost per unit}$$

$8.96 × 141 = $1,263.36

$1,263.36

continued

Assignment 7.6 continued

7. Wilderness Outfitters took their end-of-year inventory and found that they had 180 sleeping bags, style #34C, in stock. The following purchases of these bags were made.

Purchase Date	Number of Bags	Price per Bag
February 2	146	$31.20
April 19	121	$30.86
July 8	138	$29.40
October 24	155	$28.92

   Determine the value of the ending inventory using each of these methods.

   a) LIFO

   ```
   146 × $31.20 =   $4,555.20        180
    34 ×  30.86 = + 1,049.24        -146
              Total $5,604.44        34 left
   ```
   $5,604.44

   b) FIFO

   ```
   155 × $28.92 =   $4,482.60        180
    25 ×  29.40 = +   735.00        -155
              Total $5,217.60        25 left
   ```
   $5,217.60

Learning Aids, Inc., had 136 blackboards in stock at the end of the year. Their purchase orders showed 102 at $24.25 in March; 86 at $25.30 in June; 131 at $26.50 in September; and 95 at $27.10 in December. Evaluate the ending inventory using each of the following methods.

8. LIFO

   ```
   102 × $24.25 =   $2,473.50        136
    34 ×  25.30 = +   860.20        -102
              Total $3,333.70        34 left
   ```
   $3,333.70

9. FIFO

   ```
   95 × $27.10 =   $2,574.50         136
   41 ×  26.50 = + 1,086.50         - 95
             Total $3,661.00         41 left
   ```
   $3,661

10. Average cost

    ```
    102 × $24.25 =   $2,473.50
     86 ×  25.30 =    2,175.80
    131 ×  26.50 =    3,471.50
     95 ×  27.10 = +  2,574.50
    Totals 414 units  $10,695.30 cost

    $10,695.30
    ---------- = $25.83 Average cost per unit
       414

    $25.83 × 136 = $3,512.88
    ```
    $3,512.88

continued

Assignment 7.6 *continued*

11. The ending inventory of smoke alarms for Safety Plus, Inc., is 106. Using the FIFO method, calculate the value of the ending inventory if the purchases included are as follows.

Purchase Date	Number of Units	Price per Unit
January 28	51	$48.59
April 10	42	$46.28
June 1	39	$47.04
August 31	54	$49.10
November 16	40	$51.83

    40 × $51.83 = $2,073.20   106
    54 × $49.10 =   2,651.40   − 94
    12 ×   47.04 = +   564.48   12 left
    　　　 Total $5,289.08

    $5,289.08

12. Pinnacle Learning Center uses the LIFO method of valuing inventory. Find the total value of the ending inventory of 127 calculators if the following purchases were made.

Purchase Date	Number of Units	Price per Unit
February 15	61	$7.84
May 21	52	$8.01
August 2	90	$8.48
December 11	83	$8.90

    61 × $7.84 = $ 478.24   127
    52 × 8.01 =   416.52   − 113
    14 × 8.48 = + 118.72   14 left
    　　　Total $1,013.48

    $1,013.48

13. Home Interiors has an ending inventory of 86 doorbells, model #21–L. The company uses the average-cost method of valuing inventory. Find the value of the ending inventory if the following purchases were made.

Purchase Date	Number of Units	Price per Unit
February 18	35	$19.20
May 21	49	$18.78
July 6	60	$18.33
October 1	55	$19.80
December 13	62	$18.40

    　　　35 × $19.20 = $ 672.00
    　　　49 ×   18.78 =   920.22
    　　　60 ×   18.33 = 1,099.80
    　　　55 ×   19.80 = 1,089.00
    　　　62 ×   18.40 = + 1,140.80
    Totals 261 units $4,921.82

    $4,921.82 / 261 = $18.86 Average cost per unit
    $18.86 × 86 units = $1,621.96

    $1,621.96

300   Chapter 7

Comprehensive Problems for Chapter 7

Retail Merchandising

1. At Trucolor Printers sales of brochures amounted to $158,300, total cost was $97,800, and operating expenses amounted to $39,000.

   a) What is the gross margin?

   $158,300 Sales
   − 97,800 Cost
   60,500 Gross margin

   a) __$60,500__

   b) Is there a profit or a loss? What amount?

   $60,500 Gross margin
   − 39,000 Expenses
   $21,500 Profit

   b) __Profit, $21,500__

   c) Find the percent profit or loss to the nearest tenth based on sales.

   $\frac{\$21,500}{\$158,300}$ = .135818 = 13.6%

   c) __13.6%__

2. The markup on stereo cabinets is $50. The percent of markup is 15% based on selling price. Find each of the following.

   a) The cost

   C + M = R
   85% + 15% = 100%
   $50

   $B = \frac{P}{R} = \frac{50}{15\%}$
   B = $333.33   Retail = $333.33

   a) __$283.33 cost price__

   b) The retail price

   C + M = R
   $283.33 + $50 = $333.33

   b) __$333.33 retail price__

3. Dolly's Miniatures advertised in the newspaper, "Victorian Doll Houses—20% off original price." The doll houses were originally priced at $180. Twenty-four houses were offered at the sale price and 21 of them were sold. Find each of the following.

   a) The new retail price

   $180 × 20% = $36 Unit markdown

   $180
   − 36
   $144 New retail

   a) __$144 new retail price__

   b) Total net sales

   $144 × 21 = $3,024

   b) __$3,024 total net sales__

4. Carla Andrews, an art teacher, has a small markup of $25 on the easels she sells to her art students. The percent of markup based on cost is 20%. Find the retail price.

   C + M = R $B = \frac{25}{20\%}$
   100% + 20% = 120%
   $125 + $25 = $150   B = $125

   __$150 retail price__

continued

Comprehensive Problems *continued*

5. At Carter Imports the retail price for an antique dresser from Wales is $725. The cost is $460. Find each of the following, giving answers to the nearest whole percent.

   a) The percent markup based on retail

   $725 Retail
   − 460 Cost
   $265 Markup

   $\dfrac{265\ M}{725\ R} = .365517 = 37\%$

   a) __37% on retail__

   b) The percent markup based on cost

   $\dfrac{265\ M}{460\ C} = .576086 = 58\%$

   b) __58% on cost__

6. The owner of Well Blooms Florist, Jennifer Chase, has a cost of $32 for each of her silk flower arrangements. The percent of markup on retail is 30%. Determine each of the following.

   a) The markup on one arrangement

   C + M = R
   70% + 30% = 100%
   $32 + $13.71 = $45.71

   $B = \dfrac{32}{70\%} = \$45.71$

   a) __$13.71 markup__

   b) The total selling price of eleven arrangements

   $45.71 × 11 = $502.81

   b) __$502.81 total selling price__

7. A department store takes inventory every three months, computing values at selling prices. The inventories taken last year were as follows.

January 1	$49,310
March 31	$73,300
June 30	$68,540
September 30	$101,860
December 31	$68,090

   If the sales for the year were $315,575, find each of the following.

   a) The average inventory

   $49,310
   73,300
   68,540
   101,860
   + 68,090
   $361,100 Total inventory

   $\dfrac{\$361,100}{7} = \$72,220$ Average inventory at retail

   a) __$72,220__

   b) The merchandise turnover at retail to the nearest tenth

   $\dfrac{\text{Sales}}{\text{Average Inventory}} = \dfrac{\$315,575}{\$72,220} = 4.369 = 4.4$ Turnover at retail

   b) __4.4__

continued

Comprehensive Problems *continued*

8. Harry's Ski Shop offers a pair of boots for sale at $85. These boots cost the shop $45. What is the percent of markup on retail to the nearest whole percent?

    $85 Retail
    − 45 Cost
    $40 Markup

    $\frac{40\ M}{85\ R}$ = .470588 = 47%

9. The percent of markup on cost for a set of dictionaries is 60%. If the markup amounts to $51.60, find each of the following.

    a) The cost

    C + M = R
    100% + 60% = 160%
    $51.60

    B = $\frac{51.60}{60\%}$
    B = $86
    Cost = $86

    a) __$86 cost price__

    b) The retail price

    $86.00 Cost
    + 51.60 Markup
    $137.60 Retail

    b) __$137.60 Retail price__

10. An appliance store had four dishwashers on hand that were slightly damaged and had been in stock for nearly 8 months. One of them originally retailed for $150 and the other 3 originally retailed for $120 each. The store marked them all down 30% off the original price and all were sold. What is the total net sales?

    $150 × 30% = $45 Markdown
    $150
    − 45
    $105 New retail price

    $120 × 30% = $36 Markdown
    $120
    − 36
    $ 84 New retail price

    $105 × 1 = $105
    $84 × 3 = + 252
    $357 Total net sales

    __$357 total net sales__

11. Sales of tables at Cook's Corner amounted to $478,300. Cost for this merchandise is $362,400. If operating expenses amount to $120,000, determine each of the following.

    a) Is there a profit or a loss?

    $478,300 Sales
    − 362,400 Cost
    $115,900 Gross Margin
    − 120,000 Expenses
    ($4,100) Loss

    a) __Loss__

    b) What is the dollar amount of the profit or loss?

    b) __$4,100__

continued

Comprehensive Problems *continued*

If operating expenses can be decreased by 15%, determine each of the following.

c) Is there a profit or a loss?

$120,000 × 15% = $18,000 decrease

$120,000
− 18,000
$102,000 New expenses

$115,900 Gross Margin
− 102,000 Expenses
$ 13,900 Profit

c) _____Profit_____

d) What is the dollar amount of the profit or loss?

d) _____$13,900_____

12. At Europa Boutique, a leather jacket costs $78 and sells for $138. What is the percent of markup on cost to the nearest whole percent?

$138 Retail
− 78 Cost
$ 60 Markup

$\dfrac{60\ M}{78\ C} = .7692307 = 77\%$

77% markup on cost

13. Chris Murray, a buyer for Clocks Unlimited, purchased 2 dozen paperweight clocks for a total cost of $3,120. If each clock will retail for $225, find the percent of markup on retail to the nearest whole percent.

12
× 2
24 clocks

$130 Unit cost
24)3120

$225 Retail
− 130 Cost
$ 95 Markup

$\dfrac{95\ M}{225\ R} = .42222 = 42\%$

42% markup

14. Solar Building Supply takes its inventory at retail. The beginning inventory is $68,000; purchases amounted to $29,000; and the ending inventory is $42,000. The cost of goods sold is $157,143, the markup on cost is 40%, and net sales are $218,900. Find each of the following.

a) The average inventory at cost

$ 68,000
+ 42,000
2)$110,000 Total inventory
    55,000 Average inventory at retail

C + M = R $B = \dfrac{P}{R}$
100% + 40% = 140%
           55,000

$B = \dfrac{55,000}{140\%}$

B = $39,285.71 Average inventory at cost

$39,285.71

continued

304 Chapter 7

Comprehensive Problems *continued*

b) The turnover at cost to the nearest tenth

$$\frac{\text{Cost of goods sold}}{\text{Average inventory at cost}} = \frac{\$157{,}143}{\$39{,}285.71} = 4.0000 \text{ Turnover at cost}$$

4.0

---

15. The cost on word processing software is $120. If the percent of markup on retail is 45%, determine the selling price.

C + M = R
55% + 45% = 100%
$120

$$B = \frac{P}{R}$$

$$B = \frac{120}{55\%}$$

B = $218.18
Retail = $218.18

$218.18

---

16. M. A. Wood Shop had an inventory of 120 cutting blocks. Eighty-four of these sold at the original retail price of $42. The rest were marked down 15% and were all sold out at the new retail price. Find each of the following.

a) The new retail price

$42 × 15% = $6.30 Unit markdown
$42.00
− 6.30
$35.70 New retail

$35.70

b) Total net sales

$42 × 84 = $3,528
$35.70 × 36 = $1,285.20
$4,813.20 Total net sales

120
− 84
36 left

$4,813.20

---

17. Shelly De Paul is the hosiery buyer for a large department store. Help her figure her merchandise inventory turnover at retail for the second half of the calendar year. Round your answer to nearest tenth.

Inventory at Retail		*Total Sales per Month*	
July 1	$16,000	$15,000	
August 1	$33,000	$19,000	
September 1	$39,000	$22,000	
October 1	$41,000	$24,000	
November 1	$37,000	$21,000	
December 1	$34,000	$18,000	
December 31	$11,000	Total $119,000	
Total	$211,000		

$$\frac{\text{Total inventory @ retail}}{\text{\# Inventories}} = \frac{\$211{,}000}{7}$$

Average inventory @ retail = $30,142.86

$$\frac{\text{Total sales}}{\text{Average inventory @ retail}} = \frac{\$119{,}000}{\$30{,}142.86}$$

Inventory turnover @ retail = 3.947 = 3.9

3.9 turnover

continued

Comprehensive Problems *continued*

18. As the accountant for Keeping Fit, Inc., you have the following information:

Beginning inventory	$84,200
Middle-of-the-year Inventory	$69,800
Ending inventory	$53,600

    The inventories are taken at retail. The markup is 28% of the selling price. Cost of goods sold is $350,340, and net sales amount to $485,000. Determine each of the following.

    a) The average inventory at cost

    $ 84,200
    69,800
    + 53,600
    3)$207,600 Total inventory
    $69,200 Average inventory at retail

    $69,200

    b) The turnover at retail to the nearest hundredth

    $$\frac{\text{Sales}}{\text{Average inventory @ retail}} = \frac{\$485,000}{\$69,200} = 7.01 \text{ Turnover at retail}$$

    7.01

    c) The turnover at cost to the nearest hundredth

    C + M = R   B × R = P
    72% + 28% = 100% $69,200 × 72% = $49,824 Average inventory at cost
    $69,200

    $$\frac{\text{Cost of goods sold}}{\text{Average inventory @ cost}} = \frac{\$350,340}{\$49,824} = 7.03 \text{ Turnover at cost}$$

    7.03

19. The percent of markup on cost for decorative pottery is 60%. If a large planter costs $210, determine each of the following.

    a) The individual dollar markup for each planter

    C + M = R   B × R = P
    100% + 60% = 160% $210 × 60% = $126 Markup
    $210

    $126 markup

    b) The total selling price for sixteen planters

    $210 Cost
    + 126 Markup
    $336 Selling price
    $336 × 16 planters = $5,376

    $5,376 total selling price

20. Eastsport prices its jogging suits at $45 each. The store purchased the suits for $30 each. Total operating expenses amount to $580. At the $45 price the store expects to sell 80 jogging suits. Find each of the following.

    a) The gross margin

    $45 × 80 = $3,600 Selling price
    $30 × 80 = − 2,400 Cost
                 $1,200 Gross margin

    $1,200

continued

Comprehensive Problems *continued*

b) The percent net profit of sales to the nearest hundredth.

$1200 Gross margin
− 580 Expenses
$ 620 Net profit

$\frac{620}{3600} = 17.22\%$

17.22%

c) The percent increase in profit if the suits can be purchased at $27 each and all other factors remain the same

$3600 Selling price
− 2160 ($27 × 80) Cost
$1440 Gross margin
− 580
$ 860 Net profit

$860 New net profit
− 620 Original net profit
$240 More profit

$\frac{240}{620} = .387096 = 38.71\%$

38.71%

21. Kelly's Office Furniture had an inventory of 54 metal desks in stock at the end of the year. The company made three purchases of these desks during the year:

Purchase Date	Number of Desks Purchased	Price per Desk
January 1	46	$120
June 1	61	$135
November 1	50	$138

Determine the value of the ending inventory using each of the following methods:

a) LIFO

LIFO
46 × $120 = $5,520
8 × $135 = $1,080
　　　　　$6,600 Ending inventory

54
− 46
　8 left

$6,600

b) FIFO

50 × $138 = $6,900
4 × $135 = $ 540
　　　　　$7,440 Ending inventory

54
− 50
　4 left

$7,440

c) Average cost

46 × $120 = $5,520
61 × $135 = $8,235
50 × $138 = $6,900
157 Total units　$20,655 Total cost

$\frac{\$20,655}{157}$ = $132.56 Average cost per unit

$132.56 × 54 = $7,158.24 Ending inventory

$7,158.24

22. Sound Stereo, Inc., has found 86 sets of JBL speakers, style #601, in stock at the end of the year. The following is a schedule of purchases for the speakers.

continued

Comprehensive Problems *continued*

Purchase Date	Number of Speakers	Price per Speaker
January 15	52	$183.40
April 4	67	$196.25
August 10	79	$201.57
November 22	63	$214.18

Determine the value of the ending inventory using each of the following methods.

a) LIFO

    a) LIFO
    52 × $183.40 = $ 9,536.80   86
    34 × $196.25 = $ 6,672.50   − 52
                                34 left
                  $16,209.30 Ending inventory

a)   **$16,209.30**

b) FIFO

    b) FIFO
    63 × $214.18 = $13,493.34   86
    23 × $201.57 = $ 4,636.11   − 63
                                23 left
                  $18,129.45 Ending inventory

b)   **$18,129.45**

c) Average cost

    c) 52 × $183.40 = $ 9,536.80
       67 × $196.25 = 13,148.75
       79 × 201.57 = 15,924.03
       63 × 214.18 = 13,493.34
      261 Total units $52,102.92 Total cost

$$\frac{\$52102.92}{261} = \$199.63 \text{ Average cost per unit}$$

    $199.63 × 86 = $17,168.18 Ending inventory

c)   **$17,168.18**

Case 1

You are the owner of the Good Earth Health Food Store. At the beginning of the year the inventory was at $84,200 based on selling price. Six months later, the inventory was valued at $69,800. At the end of the year, the inventory was valued at $53,600. The markup, on the average, was 28% of the selling price. The net sales for the year were $487,000, and the cost of goods sold was $350,340.

a) What is the estimated value of the average inventory based on cost?

b) What is the inventory turnover to the nearest hundredth valued at cost and at retail?

c) What suggestions do you have for increasing the turnover rate?

Case 2

As the merchandise manager for Klosner's Department Store, you are reviewing the following report submitted by Sandro Samuels, the buyer for lamps and lighting fixtures and supplies.

Item	Amount Purchased	Unit Cost	Percent Markup Based on Original Retail	Unit Markdown
Tiffany lamp	50	120	40%	$60

Thirty of the lamps were sold at the original retail, and the remainder were sold at the reduced price.

a) What is the total sales in dollars of Tiffany lamps?

b) What is the markdown "off" percent of original retail?

c) What advice can you give Mr. Samuels in order to keep his markdowns in check for the future?

Key Terms

Average-cost method
Average inventory
Cost
FIFO
Gross profit, or gross margin
LIFO
Markdown
Markdown percent

Markup
Net profit
Net sales
New retail price
Operating expenses
Original retail price
Selling price
Stock turnover

Key Concepts

- Gross margin is the difference between the total selling price and the cost of goods sold.
- Profit is found by subtracting the operating expenses from the gross margin.

- Markup is the difference between the selling price (retail price) of the merchandise and the cost. Markup can be based on either the retail price or the cost price.
- The markup formula is Cost + Markup = Retail.
- Markdown is the difference between the original retail price and the new retail price.
- Average inventory = $\dfrac{\text{Sum of the inventories}}{\text{Number of inventories taken}}$
- Turnover at retail = $\dfrac{\text{Net sales}}{\text{Average inventory at retail}}$
- Turnover at cost = $\dfrac{\text{Cost of goods sold}}{\text{Average inventory at cost}}$
- The average inventory at cost can be converted to the average inventory at retail and vice versa by applying the percent of markup with the markup formula (Cost + Markup = Retail).
- The ending inventory can be valued by one of the following methods.
  1. FIFO: First in, first out
  2. LIFO: Last in, first out
  3. Average cost
- The formula for valuing ending inventory by the average-cost method is:

$$\dfrac{\text{Total Cost}}{\text{Total Units Purchased}} = \text{Average Cost Per Unit}$$

$$\text{Ending Inventory in Units} \times \text{Average Cost per Unit} = \text{Total Value of Ending Inventory}$$

8

Payroll

Business Takes a Positive Approach

LANDS' END

Is it possible to turn your interest in a favorite sport into a profitable business? Gary Comer, pictured above, thought so and proved it. Comer's first love is sailing. In talking to others with similar hobbies, he discovered that people involved in outdoor sports have a need for long-wearing, rugged gear and clothing items that are not easy to find in conventional stores. Encouraged by friends, he started a mail-order business called Lands' End. Located in a small town in rural Wisconsin, Lands' End offers quality merchandise and specializes in natural-fiber items. Lands' End also features an unusual catalog aimed at solving one of the major problems of direct-mail merchandising: getting the customer to read the material. Comer's catalog is a monthly publication that resembles a magazine, complete with stories and a central theme. One feature article entitled "In person" gives a detailed portrayal of an employee complete with photographs and personal anecdotes. The reader is left with the impression that morale and goodwill among the employees themselves go far beyond just receiving a paycheck. There is also information in the catalog on how some of the merchandise is made and acquired from markets around the world. The fact that it is interesting to read ensures it a longer life in the home than the usual merchandise catalog. The catalog and the well-trained, polite telephone salespeople of Lands' End offer a winning combination, as shown by the fact that yearly sales currently exceed $250 million.

> **Learning Objectives**
>
> After reading and studying this chapter and working the problems, you will be able to:
>
> - Figure compensation for employees on the basis of salary, wages, overtime, and piecework pay.
> - Find earnings based on straight commission and salary plus commission.
> - Determine federal income tax using the wage-bracket method.
> - Determine federal income tax using the percentage method.
> - Figure social security withholding tax.
> - Complete a payroll register.
> - Become aware of the types of employer's tax reports.

8.1 Types of Compensation

Nearly all of us are interested in payroll, whether we are employer or employee. As an employee, we need to know how our gross pay is figured and why funds are withheld, reducing it to the net, or take-home, pay. As an employer, we need to understand the various methods of figuring payroll. Employers are legally responsible for following specific tax guidelines for figuring payroll taxes withheld. Payroll is a major portion of a business's operating expense. So whether you issue or receive a pay check it is important to know the steps involved in determining payroll.

Payroll is usually one of the largest expenses of a firm, and all businesses must keep accurate records of the earnings for each employee. There are several different methods for paying employees. Those discussed in this section are salary, wage, overtime, piecework, and commission.

Finding Salary

When an employee's earnings are a fixed payment, the compensation is called a **salary**. This fixed payment is made at different times during a year according to a specific schedule. The most common pay periods are as follows:

Type	Pay Periods During the Year
Annual	1
Semiannual	2
Monthly	12
Semimonthly	24
Weekly	52
Biweekly	26

Very often, management personnel are paid a salary. The hours worked may vary according to the type of work performed, but whether the time is under or over 40 hours a week, the salaried employee receives the same fixed amount. The services that the salaried employee performs are usually not associated with mechanical or manual operations. Often, at the time of initial employment, the salary is negotiated by the employer and employee.

Example 1 Emma Johnston earns an annual salary of $20,000 as a training supervisior at International Import Company. If she is paid on a monthly basis, what is her pay each month (to the nearest cent)?

Step 1 Divide the total salary by the number of pay periods (monthly = 12 pay periods).

$$12\overline{)20{,}000.000} = 1{,}666.666$$

Answer Her monthly pay is $1,666.67.

Finding Wages

If an employee's earnings are termed **wages,** they are paid according to the amount of time spent on the job. A wage is expressed as a certain amount of dollars per hour worked. According to the work laws passed in 1938—specifically, The Fair Labor Standards Act—employees earning wages and covered by the law must be paid a minimum of $1\frac{1}{2}$ times the hourly rate for all time worked over 40 hours a week. This is called *overtime pay*. Some employees are exempted from this provision. These include executive, administrative, and professional employees as well as outside salespeople.

Example 2 Ben Belmont works at Dundy's Restaurant and earns $4.10 an hour. If he worked 45 hours last week, what was his gross pay?

Step 1 Find the regular pay by multiplying 40 hours times the regular wage of $4.10 an hour. $4.10 × 40 = $164

Step 2 Find the overtime wage by multiplying the regular wage times $1\frac{1}{2}$. $4.10 × 1.5 = $6.15

Step 3 Find the overtime pay by multiplying the overtime wage times the number of overtime hours worked. $6.15 × 5 = $30.75

Step 4 Find the gross pay by adding the regular pay and the overtime pay.

$164.00 Regular pay
 30.75 Overtime pay
$194.75 Gross pay

Answer His gross pay was $194.75.

Finding Overtime

Some firms use other calculations to figure overtime pay, depending on the type of business and the incentives offered employees. For example, sometimes employees are paid overtime for all hours worked over 8 hours per day. Double time (twice the regular hourly wage) may also be paid to employees who work on Sundays or holidays. Often, this type of compensation can be found in retail stores. State laws usually have specific requirements concerning overtime pay.

Example 3 Ann Mazelis receives an hourly pay rate of $5.40 an hour. The department store where she works offers double time for Sundays. If she worked her regular 40-hour week and also 8 hours on Sunday, what was her gross pay for the week?

Step 1   Find the regular pay. $5.40 × 40 hours = $216.00

Step 2   Find the overtime pay ($5.40 × 2 = $10.80 overtime rate per hour). $10.80 × 8 hours = $86.40

Step 3   Add the regular pay and the overtime pay. $216.00 + $86.40 = $302.40

Answer   Her gross pay was $302.40.

Finding Piecework Pay

With **piecework pay** an employee's earnings are based on the number of units produced rather than the number of hours worked. The rationale behind this method is that employees will be motivated to work faster, hence, will be more productive. The gross earnings are found by multiplying the number of items produced by the pay per item. This is called the *straight-piecework method*.

Example 4   Ed Tronson, a part-time assembler at Flex Electronics Plant, finished 94 units in one week. If his pay is a set rate of $1.23 per unit, what is his gross pay?

Step 1   Multiply the number of units times the rate per unit. $1.23 × 94 = $115.62

Answer   His gross pay is $115.62

Bonus Rate

As an added incentive, some companies use a bonus-rate method, where a worker has a quota to reach and is paid a certain amount for each piece fulfilling the quota. All pieces finished above the quota are multiplied by a higher rate called the **bonus rate,** or the *differential-piece rate*.

Sometimes a worker may be given a series of quotas and wages are paid at a higher rate for the extra production at each level. This is similar to being paid on a sliding scale. For instance, a differential scale may be:

0–50 units produced	$1.00 per unit
51–75 units produced	$1.25 per unit
76–100 units produced	$1.50 per unit

In this case, up to and including 50 units produced, the pay is $1 each. If more than 50 units were produced, the next step on the pay scale ($1.25) is used for the portion over 50. At more than 75 units, the $1.50 rate is used for the portion over 75 units. Total earnings are then found by adding the amount of pay for each category.

Example 5   Kathy Eikoff is a garment worker. She receives 56¢ for each lace collar produced for the first 50 collars. Any additional collars will be paid at a rate of 79¢ each. Her output for the day was 88 collars. What is her gross pay for the day?

Step 1   Find the pay for the pieces fulfilling the quota. 50 × 56¢ = $28.00

Step 2   Subtract the quota from the total number of items produced.
88
−50
38

Step 3   Multiply the number found in step 2 by the bonus rate. 38 × 79¢ = $30.02

Step 4   Add the two pay amounts.
$28.00
+$30.02
$58.02

Answer   Her gross pay is $58.02.

Finding Commission

A common form of compensation for people involved in selling is commission. With this method, wages are based on the sales or the amount of business generated by the employee. Although commission plans vary from company to company, the two most common methods are **straight commission** and **salary plus commission**.

Straight Commission

An employee is paid a fixed percent for his or her total sales. In this case, the productivity of the worker dictates the pay received. This also can lead to a competitive spirit among the sales force and to a high salary for the successful salesperson. However, for the inexperienced salesperson, this can be a difficult position, particularly if there happens to be a slump in the industry such as has occurred, for example, in the construction and automotive trades.

Example 6 Diane Shane, a saleswoman for Precision Printing Company, receives an 8% commission on all sales. What is her commission if she generates $24,000 in sales?

Step 1 Multiply the total sales by the rate of commission. This is an application of the Base × Rate = Percentage formula. $24,000 × 8% = $1,920

Answer Her commission is $1,920.

Salary Plus Commission

An employee receives a minimum salary and, in addition, a commission based on total sales. The element of risk is less for the salesperson under this plan, although the incentive is also offered to achieve a high volume of sales. Sometimes this type of compensation, often used in retail saleswork, is also given to a salesperson in training; the employee is then switched to a straight-commission plan after a certain period of time. Since a base salary is guaranteed, the commission rate may be lower than that used for straight commission.

Example 7 Paul Robinson, working in the men's department of Belmont's Department Store, receives a monthly salary of $800 plus a commission of 6% of his total sales for the month. What are his gross monthly earnings if his total sales amount to $63,000?

Step 1 State the total base salary for the month.   Salary = $800

Step 2 Find the total commission by multiplying the total sales by the rate of commission. $63,000 × 6% = $3,780

Step 3 Add the pay amounts together. $800 + $3,780 = $4,580

Answer His total gross earnings are $4,580.

Self-Check

1. Kimiki Takedo receives an annual salary of $19,728. If she is paid on a semimonthly basis, what is her gross pay for each pay period?

2. Karl Justin, an employee for Joseph's Home Decorating Center, earns $4.20 an hour plus time and a half for any hours worked over 40. If he worked 43 hours last week, what is his gross pay?

3. Citation Model Company pays its part-time workers $2.00 for each of the first 70 units assembled and $2.50 for every unit over 70. What is the gross pay for a worker who assembles 89 units? _____

4. The salespeople at Town and Country Buildings are paid a salary of $600 per month plus a 2% commission on sales. What is the gross pay for the month for a salesperson who had a sales figure of $171,600? _____

ANSWERS 1. $822   2. $186.90   3. $187.50   4. $4,032

TAXATION WITH REPRESENTATION

On February 25, 1913, the Sixteenth Amendment to the United States Constitution went into effect. This amendment gave Congress the power to levy a graduated income tax on annual incomes of over $3,000.

Assignment 8.1

Payroll

Determine the gross pay for each of the following part-time employees of K. Hills Painting Company.

Name	\multicolumn{6}{c}{Daily Hours Worked}	Total Hours	Hourly Rates	Gross Pay
	M	T	W	Th	F	S			
1. Allen, P.	3	0	3	4	0	6	16	$6.80	$ 108.80
2. Amerson, J.	0	2	4	3	4	0	13	$4.75	61.75
3. Buckley, W.	2	3½	5	0	0	7	17.5	$9.50	166.25
4. Ennis, A.	0	4	0	5	7	3	19	$5.00	95
5. Hughes, R.	4½	0	6	3	3	4	20.5	$5.35	109.68
6. Manly, S.	5	0	2¼	8	0	3	18.25	$7.90	144.18
7. Peters, M.	0	5	0	5	5	6½	21.5	$4.45	95.68
8. Stevens, E.	2¼	4	2	0	0	8	16.25	$5.40	87.75
9. Tenneyson, A.	3	6	0	0	3¼	0	12.25	$8.25	101.06
10. Walters, B.	0	3½	2¾	4	2	0	12.25	$4.80	58.80

11. Total gross pay: $1028.95

Find the regular pay, the overtime pay, and the gross pay for each of the following employees of Mountain Design Ski Manufacturers. (Overtime rate is time and a half after 40 hours worked.)

Name	\multicolumn{6}{c}{Daily Hours Worked}	Reg. Hours	OT Hours	Hourly Rate	Reg. Pay	OT Pay	Gross Pay
	M	T	W	Th	F	S						
12. Rasp, P.	8	7	8	9	8	5	40	5	$ 9.40	$376	$70.50	$446.50
13. Reston, A.	6	8	10	8	10	0	40	2	6.50	260	$19.50	279.50
14. Richman, J.	8	0	9	8½	6	10¼	40	1.75	12.10	484	31.76	515.76
15. Rollman, S.	0	9	8	8	10	8	40	3	10.63	425.20	47.85	473.05
16. Russell, R.	9	8	7¼	10	10	0	40	4.25	8.28	331.20	52.79	383.99

continued

Assignment 8.1 continued

Ennis Metal Febrication Company pays its employees on a piecework basis. A quota-plus-bonus system is used. The weekly quota for each worker is as follows: Dept. A, 50; Dept. B, 70; Dept. C, 40. Complete the following pay record.

Name	Dept.	Pieces Completes M	T	W	Th	F	Total Pieces	Quota Rate	Bonus Rate	Quota Earning	Bonus Earning	Gross Pay
17. Adams	A	11	10	15	11	13	60	$8.30	$8.80	$415	$88	$503
18. Barnett	B	14	13	19	14	18	78	$7.25	$7.60	507.50	60.80	568.30
19. Delciello	A	12	10	13	15	16	66	$8.30	$8.80	415	140.80	555.80
20. Hunter	C	12	8	10	10	12	52	$9.10	$9.90	364	118.80	482.80
21. Kaiser	A	13	11	10	14	13	61	$8.30	$8.80	415	96.80	511.80
22. Mitchell	B	15	12	13	19	14	73	$7.25	$7.60	507.5	22.80	530.30
23. Moyer	C	14	10	13	13	15	65	$9.10	$9.90	364	247.50	611.50
24. Rice	B	19	15	19	17	16	86	$7.25	$7.60	507.50	121.60	629.10
25. Schwartz	A	8	14	12	10	14	58	$8.30	$8.80	415	70.40	485.40
26. Vinberg	C	11	12	13	14	12	62	$9.10	$9.90	364	217.80	581.80

Ben's Automart pays each of its salespeople a base salary of $200 a week plus a commission of $1\frac{1}{4}\%$ on sales. Calculate the total gross pay for each salesperson on a bi-weekly basis.

Name	Sales for the Pay Period	Commission	Base Salary	Gross Earnings
27. S. Benson	$140,000	$1,750	$400	$2,150
28. T. Caughe	185,000	2,312.50	400	2,712.50
29. A. Murray	156,000	1,950	400	2,350
30. D. Tolstoy	98,000	1,225	400	1,625
31. B. Warren	210,000	2,625	400	3,025

8.2 Payroll Deductions

The difference between an employee's gross earnings and his or her net earnings or take-home pay are the **payroll deductions.** These can be both required or optional. Some examples of optional deductions are medical, life, and disability premiums, savings bonds, union dues, credit union contributions, and donations to charitable organizations. Although individual states and/or cities may have required payroll deductions, the major required deductions are federal: the federal income tax and the social security tax.

THE FIRST U.S. INCOME TAX

The United States Congress levied the country's first income tax on August 5, 1861. Its purpose was to raise funds for the Union Army and Navy to wage the Civil War. The new tax affected those with annual incomes of over $800, assessing them at a rate of 3%. The Civil War income tax was abolished by Congress in 1872.

Determining Federal Income Tax

With passage of the Current Tax Payment Act of 1943, the collection of **federal income taxes** at the source of wages paid came into existence. This tax is collected by the employer and is usually the largest single deduction from an employee's paycheck. It is often referred to as the FIT tax. The employer is required by law to deduct and withhold the taxes. The employer then forwards the tax collected to the Internal Revenue Service. The employer is liable for payment of the tax whether or not it is collected from the employee. If less than the correct tax is withheld, the employer is still liable for the full amount of the correct tax.

Exemptions

In order to know how much income tax to withhold, the employer must have a completed W-4 form on file for each employee. The W-4 lists social security number, marital status, and number of exemptions allowed. An **exemption allowance** represents a certain amount of money that is deducted from the gross pay before the tax is figured. Exemptions are allowed for the wage earner as well as his or her dependents, such as a wife, husband, child, or parent, who are supported by the wage earner. An example of a W-4 form is shown on page 320.

If employees want to change the number of exemptions claimed or change marital status, they must file a new W-4 form. If a husband and wife both work, they may divide their exemptions in any way they wish, but one may not claim an exemption claimed by the other.

---------- Cut along this line and give this form to your employer. Keep the rest for your records. ----------

Form **W-4** Department of the Treasury Internal Revenue Service	**Employee's Withholding Allowance Certificate** ▶ For Privacy Act and Paperwork Reduction Act Notice, see instructions.	OMB No. 1545-0010

1 Type or print your full name	**2** Your social security number

Home address (number and street or rural route) City or town, state, and ZIP code	**3** Marital Status	☐ Single ☐ Married ☐ Married, but withhold at higher Single rate **Note:** *If married, but legally separated, or spouse is a nonresident alien, check the Single box.*

4 Total number of allowances you are claiming (from the Worksheet on page 3) . . . .

5 Additional amount, if any, you want deducted from each pay (see Step 4 on page 2) . . . . $

6 I claim exemption from withholding because (see Step 2 above and check boxes below that apply):
  a ☐ Last year I did not owe any Federal income tax and had a right to a full refund of **ALL** income tax withheld, **AND**
  b ☐ This year I do not expect to owe any Federal income tax and expect to have a right to a full refund of
       ALL income tax withheld. If both a and b apply, enter the year effective and "EXEMPT" here . . . . ▶ Year 19
  c If you entered "EXEMPT" on line 6b, are you a full-time student? . . . . ☐ Yes ☐ No

Under penalties of perjury, I certify that I am entitled to the number of withholding allowances claimed on this certificate or, if claiming exemption from withholding, that I am entitled to claim the exempt status.
Employee's signature ▶   Date ▶   , 19

7 Employer's name and address (**Employer: Complete 7, 8, and 9 only if sending to IRS**)	**8** Office code	**9** Employer identification number

Employees can claim additional allowances if they had a large amount of deductions, credits, or losses on the return filed for the previous year or if they expect this to happen during the current year. On the other hand, employees can also claim fewer exemptions than they are entitled to so that an extra amount of withholding tax is deducted from the paycheck. This minimizes any additional income taxes due at the end of the year. This "over-deduction" might be requested by a person who has other income, such as bank account interest, from which no withholding would have been deducted. The over-deduction from the paycheck can then offset the anticipated tax on other income. Other employees claim additional allowances because they enjoy anticipating a tax refund.

Regardless of whether employees claim more, fewer, or exactly the number of allowances to which they are entitled, the employer is not legally responsible for verifying the allowances claimed by employees.

Employers may use either of two methods in figuring the amount of income tax to withhold: (1) the wage-bracket method or (2) the percentage method. The employer has a choice of which method to use and can even use a different method for each employee and each paycheck. Detailed information about both these methods can be obtained from the Internal Revenue Service publication *Circular E, Employer's Tax Guide.*

Determining Federal-Income Withholding Tax Using the Wage-Bracket Method

Contained in *Circular E* are the withholding tables for federal income tax according to pay periods: monthly, semimonthly, weekly, biweekly, daily, and miscellaneous pay periods. There are separate listings for both single and married taxpayers, examples of which have been reproduced in this section on pages 330 through 333. These represent a partial listing and are used for a monthly or weekly pay period for single or married persons, according to the heading of the table. In order to use these tables, you must know (1) the pay period, (2) the marital status of the wage earner, (3) gross earnings, and (4) the number of exemptions declared. Follow through the steps of this example to see how these tables are used.

Example 1   Tom Klein has a gross weekly salary of $503, is married, and has three exemptions. Find the amount of withholding tax to be deducted, using the wage-bracket method.

- **Step 1**   Locate the table on page 330 for married persons—weekly payroll period.
- **Step 2**   Find the range in which $503 falls by looking at the first two columns of the table.

  Range = 500 – 510

- **Step 3**   Find the amount of withholding tax by moving across this line until you reach the column for 3 exemptions.

  $$\begin{array}{c} \textit{Exemptions} \\ \underline{0 \quad 1 \quad 2 \quad 3 \quad 4} \\ 68 \; 63 \; 57 \; 52 \; 46 \end{array}$$

- **Answer**   His withholding tax is $52.

Determining Federal-Income Withholding Tax Using the Percentage Method

This method also uses the tables published in *Circular E*. The table for the percentage method gives the payroll period and the amount of *one* withholding exemption. This amount is multiplied by the number of exemptions claimed, and the product is subtracted from the employee's wages. The remainder is the taxable wages. Tax is taken on this final figure according to the tax tables.

Actually, this method makes use of two tables. The first table is as follows:

Percentage-Method Income Tax Withholding Table

Payroll Period	One Withholding Allowance
Weekly	$ 36.54
Biweekly	$ 73.08
Semimonthly	$ 79.17
Monthly	$ 158.33
Quarterly	$ 475.00
Semiannually	$ 950.00
Annually	$1,900.00
Daily	$ 7.31

The above table is used to figure the allowance for exemptions. The actual withholding tax is found by using the tables or percentage method of withholding which appears on pages 334 and 335. (All figures in these tables were taken from *Circular E*.) If you follow through the steps in Example 2, this method will become clearer to you.

Example 2   Jonetta Lukin is single and claims 2 exemptions. She is paid $580 biweekly. What is her income withholding tax according to the percentage method?

- **Step 1**   Refer to the table above and find the allowance for the biweekly payroll period.

  $73.08

- **Step 2**   Find the total allowance for exemptions by multiplying one withholding allowance for the biweekly payroll period by the number of exemptions claimed.

  $73.08 × 2 = 146.16

Step 3	Subtract this amount from the employee's wages to find the taxable wages.	$580.00 Biweekly pay − $146.16 $433.84
Step 4	Determine the amount to withhold by using the tables for percentage method of withholding that follow.	
	a. Locate the table on page 000 for single person—biweekly payroll period.	
	b. Locate the wage range.	Over But not over 94 671
	c. Follow the line across to find the amount of income tax withheld.	$7.59 plus 15% (which means the tax is $7.59 plus 15% of any amount over $94).
	d. Find the amount "over $94" by subtracting $94 from the figure subject to withholding tax.	$433.84 − $ 94.00 $339.84
	e. Find the tax on this figure by multiplying by 15%.	$339.84 × 15% = $50.976
	f. Add the two taxes together to give the total income tax withheld.	$ 7.59 + $50.98 $58.57
Answer	The income tax withheld is $58.57.	

Self-Check

1. Using the wage-bracket method, determine the withholding tax for Eric Sorno, who is paid weekly. He is single, has 1 exemption, and is paid $903.

2. Using the percentage method, determine the withholding tax for Renita Keller, who receives a semimonthly salary of $1,800. She is married and has 3 exemptions.

ANSWERS 1. $220   2. $259.08

HIGH-TECH RED TAPE

The Interval Revenue Service has finalized regulations requiring that certain information be filed on magnetic media, such as computer disk or tape, rather than on paper forms. Employers who file 500 or more information returns on forms such as the W-2 must file via magnetic media. Beginning in 1988, employers who file 250 or more returns must also use magnetic media.

Determining Social Security Tax

The **social security tax** is also commonly known as *FICA*. Because of the hardships caused by the depression of the 1930s, the Federal Insurance Contributions Act was passed. Under this act, workers pay into a fund through a withholding tax. The fund is used to pay benefits to persons, such as retired and disabled workers, who are entitled to receive monthly financial help under the Social Security Act.

Through legislation the federal government decides what amount of gross earnings will be taxed, up to a fixed amount, and the rate or percent of tax. Employers are required to keep accurate records for this tax and to *match* each employee's tax with an equal amount, which is paid into a social security account.

The federal social security rate for 1987 was 7.15% up to $43,800 in earned wages. Once the limit of earned wages ($43,800) for an individual is reached and the taxes have been paid, no further payment of FICA taxes is required for the remainder of that calendar year. For our purposes in this text, the 7.15% rate will be used. Although the rate and the limit of taxable earned wages will probably continue to increase from year to year, the procedure for figuring the tax should remain the same. The current rate for each year can be found in *Circular E*.

To calculate the actual tax, the employer multiplies the gross wages times the withholding tax rate.

Example 3 Kelly Phelps works part-time for Photo Processing. Her gross earnings for the month are $89.30. How much will be deducted for FICA tax? (For these problems, assume that the employees have earned below the maximum amount to be taxed.)

Step 1   Multiply the gross earnings by the tax rate of 7.15%. $89.30 × 7.15% = $6.38

Answer   Kelly's FICA tax is $6.38.

A schedule of the social security tax is published in *Circular E*. To find it, locate the wage bracket of the employee. A section from this table appears at the end of this section. Example 3 also can be solved using the table.

Step 1   Locate the wage bracket for the gross earnings.   *From table* 89.17–89.31

Step 2   Follow across the line to the next column to find the FICA tax.   6.38

Answer   The FICA tax is $6.38.

For gross wages in multiples of $100, you need to look at the lower right-hand corner of the social security tax table.

Example 4 Find the social security tax withheld for Bob Iden, whose gross wages are $4,570.

Step 1   Find the tax on $4,000 by looking at the multiples of the withholding for FICA on $1,000 on the bottom of page 337. Multiply the taxes on $1,000 by 4. $71.50 × 4 = $286.00

Step 2   Find the tax on $500 by looking at that same section of the table. $35.75

Step 3   Locate the wage bracket for the remaining wages of $70. $5.01

Step 4   Add the taxes together for the total social security tax.

Answer   Bob's social security tax is $326.76.

Self-Check

1. By applying the tax rate, find the FICA tax withheld for an employee who earns $2,104.80.

2. By using the table, find the FICA tax for Karen Nelson, whose gross pay this week is $615.47.

3. Jay Jones earned a gross pay of $3,262.50. Use the table to find his social security tax.

ANSWERS   1. $150.49   2. $44.01   3. $233.27

DO YOU PAY FICA AND FIT TAXES IF YOU ARE SELF-EMPLOYED?

Since social security benefits are available to individuals who are self-employed just as they are to wage earners, people who work for themselves are also liable to be taxed. The self-employment tax is a social security tax for people who work for themselves. You must pay this tax if you have net earnings from self-employment of $400 or more.

You need not carry on full-time business activities to be considered self-employed. Part-time work either by itself or in addition to your regular job may also be considered self-employment. The wage limits and rates change from year to year. For 1987, for example, the tax rate was 12.3%, with the maximum taxable amount being $43,800.

In addition to the social security tax, you may be required to pay on estimated income tax. This depends on how much of your expected income will be subject to withholding tax. If you do not pay enough tax by the due date for each quarterly period, you may be charged a penalty even if you are due a refund when you file your regular income tax return.

Filing Employer's Returns

It is the employer's responsibility to become aware of the types of returns that must be filed and taxes that must be paid. These include the following.

1. Quarterly Return of Withheld Income and Social Security Taxes

Employers who pay FIT and FICA taxes must file Form 941, the Quarterly Return of Withheld Income and Social Security Taxes. This return must include figures stating the total taxable wages, the amount of income tax withheld, employees FICA taxes, employer FICA taxes, total taxes, and the number of employees and their social security numbers. If the return is not filed and the proper taxes are not paid, a penalty is charged. This makes it crucial that accurate and complete payroll records be kept. The due dates for returns and tax payments are as follows:

Quarter	Ending	Due Date
January–March	March 31	April 30
April–June	June 30	July 31
July–September	September 30	October 31
October–December	December 31	January 31

An example of this return appears on page 326.

2. Employer's Annual Federal Unemployment Tax Return

Another form that must be filed is Form 940, the Employer's Annual Federal Unemployment Tax Return. This tax is commonly referred to as FUTA. The federal and state unemployment tax systems provide for unemployment compensation for people who have lost their jobs. Most employers pay both a federal and a state tax. In 1986, for example, the unemployment tax was figured on the first $7,000 paid in wages to each employee. The rate was 6.2%. The employer is given a federal tax credit if a state also imposes an unemployment tax. The employer, however, must not collect the tax or deduct it from the wages of the employees. The return and payment are generally due one month after the calendar year ends. Since the rate and guidelines for this tax can change from year to year, it is important to check with the IRS for the most current information.

An example of this return appears on page 327.

3. Additional Tax Returns

Other returns that must be filed quarterly and/or annually, depending on which type of business a person owns, are those covering excise taxes, heavy vehicle use tax, taxes on wagering, and state, city, and county sales taxes. Besides being aware of the regular expenses of operating a business, it is pressing for the employer to carefully evaluate and estimate a business's tax responsibilities.

Form **941**
Department of the Treasury
Internal Revenue Service

Employer's Quarterly Federal Tax Return
▶ For Paperwork Reduction Act Notice, see page 2.
Please type or print

OMB No. 1545-0029

Type or print your name, address, employer identification number, and calendar quarter of return as shown on original. ▶

Name (as distinguished from trade name)　　　Date quarter ended

Trade name, if any　　　Employer identification number

Address and ZIP code

If you are not liable for returns in the future, check here . . . ▶ ☐　　Date final wages paid . . . . ▶

Complete for First Quarter Only

1a	Number of employees (except household) employed in the pay period that includes March 12th . . . ▶	1a
b	If you are a subsidiary corporation AND your parent corporation files a consolidated Form 1120, enter parent corporation employer identification number (EIN) . . ▶	1b —
2	Total wages and tips subject to withholding, plus other compensation . . . . ▶	2
3	Total income tax withheld from wages, tips, pensions, annuities, sick pay, gambling, etc. . . . ▶	3
4	Adjustment of withheld income tax for preceding quarters of calendar year (see instructions) . .	4
5	Adjusted total of income tax withheld	5
6	Taxable social security wages paid . . . . $ _____ X 14.3% (.143) . .	6
7a	Taxable tips reported . . . . $ _____ X 7.15% (.0715) . .	7a
b	Tips deemed to be wages (see instructions) . . $ _____ X 7.15% (.0715) . .	7b
c	Taxable hospital insurance wages paid . . . . $ _____ X 2.9% (.029) . . .	7c
8	Total social security taxes (add lines 6, 7a, 7b, and 7c)	8
9	Adjustment of social security taxes (see instructions for required explanation) . . . . . . ▶	9
10	Adjusted total of social security taxes (see instructions)	10
11	Backup withholding (see instructions) . . . . ▶	11
12	Adjustment of backup withholding tax for preceding quarters of calendar year	12
13	Adjusted total of backup withholding	13
14	Total taxes (add lines 5, 10, and 13) . . . . ▶	14
15	Advance earned income credit (EIC) payments, if any	15
16	Net taxes (subtract line 15 from line 14). **This must equal line IV below** (plus line IV of Schedule A (Form 941) if you have treated backup withholding as a separate liability) . . . . . ▶	16
17	Total deposits for quarter, including overpayment applied from a prior quarter, from your records . ▶	17
18	Balance due (subtract line 17 from line 16). This should be less than $500. Pay to IRS . . . ▶	18
19	If line 17 is more than line 16, enter overpayment here ▶ $ _____ and check if to be: ☐ Applied to next return or　　☐ Refunded.	

Record of Federal Tax Liability (Complete if line 16 is $500 or more.) See the instructions under rule 4 for details before checking these boxes.
Check only if you made eighth-monthly deposits using the 95% rule ▶ ☐　　Check only if you are a first time 3-banking-day depositor ▶ ☐

Date wages paid	Tax liability (Do not show Federal tax deposits here.)		
	First month of quarter	Second month of quarter	Third month of quarter
1st through 3rd	A	I	Q
4th through 7th	B	J	R
8th through 11th	C	K	S
12th through 15th	D	L	T
16th through 19th	E	M	U
20th through 22nd	F	N	V
23rd through 25th	G	O	W
26th through the last	H	P	X
Total liability for month	I	II	III

IV Total for quarter (add lines **I, II,** and **III**) . . . . ▶

Under penalties of perjury, I declare that I have examined this return, including accompanying schedules and statements, and to the best of my knowledge and belief, it is true, correct, and complete.

Signature ▶　　　　　　　　　　　　Title ▶　　　　　　　　　　　　Date ▶

Form 940
Department of the Treasury
Internal Revenue Service

Employer's Annual Federal Unemployment (FUTA) Tax Return
▶ For Paperwork Reduction Act Notice, see page 2.

OMB No. 1545-0028

Employer identification number

EMPLOYER'S COPY

A Did you pay all required contributions to your state unemployment fund by the due date of Form 940? (See instructions if none required.) . . ☐ Yes ☐ No
If you checked the "Yes" box, enter amount of contributions paid to your state unemployment fund . . . . . ▶ $ _____

B Are you required to pay contributions to only one state? . . . . ☐ Yes ☐ No
If you checked the "Yes" box: (1) Enter the name of the state where you are required to pay contributions . . . ▶ _____
(2) Enter your state reporting number(s) as shown on state unemployment tax return. ▶ _____

C If any part of wages subject to FUTA tax is not subject to state unemployment tax, check the box . . . . ☐

Part I — Computation of Taxable Wages and Credit Reduction (To be completed by all taxpayers.)

1. Total payments (including exempt payments) during the calendar year for services of employees . . . . . . | 1 |
2. Exempt payments. (Explain each exemption shown, attaching additional sheets if necessary.) ▶ _____ | 2 | Amount paid
3. Payments for services of more than $7,000. Enter only the excess over the first $7,000 paid to individual employees not including exempt amounts shown on line 2. Do not use the state wage limitation. | 3 |
4. Total exempt payments (add lines 2 and 3) . . . . | 4 |
5. **Total taxable wages** (subtract line 4 from line 1). (If any part is exempt from state contributions, see instructions.)▶ | 5 |
6. Additional tax resulting from credit reduction for unrepaid advances to the states listed (by two-letter Postal Service abbreviations). Enter the wages included on line 5 above for each state and multiply by the rate shown. (See the instructions.)
   (a) IL _____ x .012= _____   (c) OH _____ x .011= _____   (e) WV _____ x .011= _____
   (b) LA _____ x .009= _____   (d) PA _____ x .012= _____
7. Total credit reduction (add resulting amounts from lines 6(a) through 6(e) and enter here and in Part II, line 2 or Part III, line 4.) . . . . ▶ | 7 |

Part II — Tax Due or Refund (Complete if you checked the "Yes" boxes in both questions A and B and did not check the box in C, above.)

1. FUTA tax. Multiply the wages in Part I, line 5, by .008 and enter here . . . . | 1 |
2. Enter amount from Part I, line 7 . . . . | 2 |
3. Total FUTA tax (add lines 1 and 2) . . . . | 3 |
4. Minus: Total FUTA tax deposited for the year, including any overpayment applied from a prior year (from your records) | 4 |
5. **Balance due** (subtract line 4 from line 3). This should be $100 or less. Pay to IRS . . . . ▶ | 5 |
6. **Overpayment** (subtract line 3 from line 4). Check if it is to be: ☐ Applied to next return, or ☐ Refunded . ▶ | 6 |

Part III — Tax Due or Refund (Complete if you checked the "No" box in either question A or B or you checked the box in C, above. Also complete Part V.)

1. Gross FUTA tax. Multiply the wages in Part I, line 5, by .062 . . . . | 1 |
2. Maximum credit. Multiply the wages in Part I, line 5, by .054 . . . . | 2 |
3. Enter the smaller of the amount in Part V, line 11, or Part III, line 2 . . . . | 3 |
4. Enter amount from Part I, line 7 . . . . | 4 |
5. **Credit allowable** (subtract line 4 from line 3). (If zero or less, enter 0.) . . . . | 5 |
6. **Total FUTA tax** (subtract line 5 from line 1) . . . . | 6 |
7. Minus: Total FUTA tax deposited for the year, including any overpayment applied from a prior year (from your records) | 7 |
8. **Balance due** (subtract line 7 from line 6). This should be $100 or less. Pay to IRS . . . . . . ▶ | 8 |
9. **Overpayment** (subtract line 6 from line 7). Check if it is to be: ☐ Applied to next return, or ☐ Refunded . ▶ | 9 |

Part IV — Record of Quarterly Federal Tax Liability for Unemployment Tax (Do not include state liability.)

Quarter	First	Second	Third	Fourth	Total for Year
Liability for quarter					

If you will not have to file returns in the future, write "Final" here (see general instruction "Who Must File") and sign the return. ▶

Keep This Copy for Your Records—You must keep this copy and a copy of each related schedule or statement for a period of 4 years after the date the tax is due or paid, whichever is later. These copies must be available for inspection by the Internal Revenue Service.

For More Information—See Circular E and **Publication 539**, Employment Taxes, for more information. Household employers should see Publication 503.

SINGLE Persons–WEEKLY Payroll Period

And the wages are–		And the number of withholding allowances claimed is–										
At least	But less than	0	1	2	3	4	5	6	7	8	9	10
		The amount of income tax to be withheld shall be–										
$320	$330	$46	$40	$35	$29	$24	$18	$13	$7	$2	$0	$0
330	340	47	42	36	31	25	20	14	9	3	0	0
340	350	50	43	38	32	27	21	16	10	5	0	0
350	360	53	45	39	34	28	23	17	12	6	2	0
360	370	55	46	41	35	30	24	19	13	8	3	0
370	380	58	48	42	37	31	26	20	15	9	4	0
380	390	61	51	44	38	33	27	22	16	11	5	1
390	400	64	54	45	40	34	29	23	18	12	7	2
400	410	67	56	47	41	36	30	25	19	14	8	3
410	420	69	59	49	43	37	32	26	21	15	10	4
420	430	72	62	52	44	39	33	28	22	17	11	6
430	440	75	65	55	46	40	35	29	24	18	13	7
440	450	78	68	57	47	42	36	31	25	20	14	9
450	460	81	70	60	50	43	38	32	27	21	16	10
460	470	83	73	63	53	45	39	34	28	23	17	12
470	480	86	76	66	55	46	41	35	30	24	19	13
480	490	89	79	69	58	48	42	37	31	26	20	15
490	500	92	82	71	61	51	44	38	33	27	22	16
500	510	95	84	74	64	54	45	40	34	29	23	18
510	520	97	87	77	67	56	47	41	36	30	25	19
520	530	100	90	80	69	59	49	43	37	32	26	21
530	540	103	93	83	72	62	52	44	39	33	28	22
540	550	107	96	85	75	65	55	46	40	35	29	24
550	560	110	98	88	78	68	57	47	42	36	31	25
560	570	114	101	91	81	70	60	50	43	38	32	27
570	580	117	104	94	83	73	63	53	45	39	34	28
580	590	121	108	97	86	76	66	56	46	41	35	30
590	600	124	111	99	89	79	69	58	48	42	37	31
600	610	128	115	102	92	82	71	61	51	44	38	33
610	620	131	118	106	95	84	74	64	54	45	40	34
620	630	135	122	109	97	87	77	67	57	47	41	36
630	640	138	125	113	100	90	80	70	59	49	43	37
640	650	142	129	116	103	93	83	72	62	52	44	39
650	660	145	132	120	107	96	85	75	65	55	46	40
660	670	149	136	123	110	98	88	78	68	58	47	42
670	680	152	139	127	114	101	91	81	71	60	50	43
680	690	156	143	130	117	105	94	84	73	63	53	45
690	700	159	146	134	121	108	97	86	76	66	56	46
700	710	163	150	137	124	112	99	89	79	69	58	48
710	720	166	153	141	128	115	102	92	82	72	61	51
720	730	170	157	144	131	119	106	95	85	74	64	54
730	740	173	160	148	135	122	109	98	87	77	67	57
740	750	177	164	151	138	126	113	100	90	80	70	59
750	760	180	167	155	142	129	116	103	93	83	72	62
760	770	184	171	158	145	133	120	107	96	86	75	65
770	780	187	174	162	149	136	123	110	99	88	78	68
780	790	191	178	165	152	140	127	114	101	91	81	71
790	800	194	181	169	156	143	130	117	105	94	84	73
800	810	198	185	172	159	147	134	121	108	97	86	76
810	820	201	188	176	163	150	137	124	112	100	89	79
820	830	205	192	179	166	154	141	128	115	102	92	82
830	840	208	195	183	170	157	144	131	119	106	95	85
840	850	212	199	186	173	161	148	135	122	109	98	87
850	860	215	202	190	177	164	151	138	126	113	100	90
860	870	219	206	193	180	168	155	142	129	116	104	93
870	880	222	209	197	184	171	158	145	133	120	107	96
880	890	226	213	200	187	175	162	149	136	123	111	99
890	900	229	216	204	191	178	165	152	140	127	114	101
900	910	233	220	207	194	182	169	156	143	130	118	105
910	920	236	223	211	198	185	172	159	147	134	121	108
920	930	240	227	214	201	189	176	163	150	137	125	112
930	940	243	230	218	205	192	179	166	154	141	128	115
940	950	247	234	221	208	196	183	170	157	144	132	119
950	960	250	237	225	212	199	186	173	161	148	135	122
960	970	254	241	228	215	203	190	177	164	151	139	126

MARRIED Persons—WEEKLY Payroll Period

And the wages are—		And the number of withholding allowances claimed is—										
At least	But less than	0	1	2	3	4	5	6	7	8	9	10
		The amount of income tax to be withheld shall be—										
$0	$40	$0	$0	$0	$0	$0	$0	$0	$0	$0	$0	$0
40	42	1	0	0	0	0	0	0	0	0	0	0
42	44	1	0	0	0	0	0	0	0	0	0	0
44	46	1	0	0	0	0	0	0	0	0	0	0
46	48	1	0	0	0	0	0	0	0	0	0	0
48	50	1	0	0	0	0	0	0	0	0	0	0
50	52	2	0	0	0	0	0	0	0	0	0	0
52	54	2	0	0	0	0	0	0	0	0	0	0
54	56	2	0	0	0	0	0	0	0	0	0	0
56	58	2	0	0	0	0	0	0	0	0	0	0
58	60	3	0	0	0	0	0	0	0	0	0	0
60	62	3	0	0	0	0	0	0	0	0	0	0
62	64	3	0	0	0	0	0	0	0	0	0	0
64	66	3	0	0	0	0	0	0	0	0	0	0
66	68	3	0	0	0	0	0	0	0	0	0	0
68	70	4	0	0	0	0	0	0	0	0	0	0
70	72	4	0	0	0	0	0	0	0	0	0	0
72	74	4	0	0	0	0	0	0	0	0	0	0
74	76	4	0	0	0	0	0	0	0	0	0	0
76	78	5	1	0	0	0	0	0	0	0	0	0
78	80	5	1	0	0	0	0	0	0	0	0	0
80	82	5	1	0	0	0	0	0	0	0	0	0
82	84	5	1	0	0	0	0	0	0	0	0	0
84	86	5	1	0	0	0	0	0	0	0	0	0
86	88	6	2	0	0	0	0	0	0	0	0	0
88	90	6	2	0	0	0	0	0	0	0	0	0
90	92	6	2	0	0	0	0	0	0	0	0	0
92	94	6	2	0	0	0	0	0	0	0	0	0
94	96	7	2	0	0	0	0	0	0	0	0	0
96	98	7	3	0	0	0	0	0	0	0	0	0
98	100	7	3	0	0	0	0	0	0	0	0	0
100	105	8	3	0	0	0	0	0	0	0	0	0
105	110	8	4	0	0	0	0	0	0	0	0	0
110	115	9	4	0	0	0	0	0	0	0	0	0
115	120	10	5	1	0	0	0	0	0	0	0	0
120	125	11	6	2	0	0	0	0	0	0	0	0
125	130	11	6	2	0	0	0	0	0	0	0	0
130	135	12	7	3	0	0	0	0	0	0	0	0
135	140	13	7	3	0	0	0	0	0	0	0	0
140	145	14	8	4	0	0	0	0	0	0	0	0
145	150	14	9	4	0	0	0	0	0	0	0	0
150	160	16	10	5	1	0	0	0	0	0	0	0
160	170	17	12	6	2	0	0	0	0	0	0	0
170	180	19	13	8	3	0	0	0	0	0	0	0
180	190	20	15	9	4	0	0	0	0	0	0	0
190	200	22	16	11	5	1	0	0	0	0	0	0
200	210	23	18	12	7	3	0	0	0	0	0	0
210	220	25	19	14	8	4	0	0	0	0	0	0
220	230	26	21	15	10	5	1	0	0	0	0	0
230	240	28	22	17	11	6	2	0	0	0	0	0
240	250	29	24	18	13	7	3	0	0	0	0	0
250	260	31	25	20	14	9	4	0	0	0	0	0
260	270	32	27	21	16	10	5	1	0	0	0	0
270	280	34	28	23	17	12	6	2	0	0	0	0
280	290	35	30	24	19	13	8	3	0	0	0	0
290	300	37	31	26	20	15	9	4	0	0	0	0
300	310	38	33	27	22	16	11	6	1	0	0	0
310	320	40	34	29	23	18	12	7	3	0	0	0
320	330	41	36	30	25	19	14	8	4	0	0	0
330	340	43	37	32	26	21	15	10	5	1	0	0
340	350	44	39	33	28	22	17	11	6	2	0	0
350	360	46	40	35	29	24	18	13	7	3	0	0
360	370	47	42	36	31	25	20	14	9	4	0	0
370	380	49	43	38	32	27	21	16	10	5	1	0
380	390	50	45	39	34	28	23	17	12	6	2	0
390	400	52	46	41	35	30	24	19	13	8	3	0
400	410	53	48	42	37	31	26	20	15	9	4	0
410	420	55	49	44	38	33	27	22	16	11	6	2
420	430	56	51	45	40	34	29	23	18	12	7	3
430	440	58	52	47	41	36	30	25	19	14	8	4

(Continued on next page)

MARRIED Persons–WEEKLY Payroll Period

And the wages are–		And the number of withholding allowances claimed is–										
At least	But less than	0	1	2	3	4	5	6	7	8	9	10
		The amount of income tax to be withheld shall be–										
$440	$450	$59	$54	$48	$43	$37	$32	$26	$21	$15	$10	$5
450	460	61	55	50	44	39	33	28	22	17	11	6
460	470	62	57	51	46	40	35	29	24	18	13	7
470	480	64	58	53	47	42	36	31	25	20	14	9
480	490	65	60	54	49	43	38	32	27	21	16	10
490	500	67	61	56	50	45	39	34	28	23	17	12
500	510	68	63	57	52	46	41	35	30	24	19	13
510	520	70	64	59	53	48	42	37	31	26	20	15
520	530	71	66	60	55	49	44	38	33	27	22	16
530	540	73	67	62	56	51	45	40	34	29	23	18
540	550	74	69	63	58	52	47	41	36	30	25	19
550	560	76	70	65	59	54	48	43	37	32	26	21
560	570	77	72	66	61	55	50	44	39	33	28	22
570	580	79	73	68	62	57	51	46	40	35	29	24
580	590	81	75	69	64	58	53	47	42	36	31	25
590	600	84	76	71	65	60	54	49	43	38	32	27
600	610	87	78	72	67	61	56	50	45	39	34	28
610	620	90	80	74	68	63	57	52	46	41	35	30
620	630	93	82	75	70	64	59	53	48	42	37	31
630	640	95	85	77	71	66	60	55	49	44	38	33
640	650	98	88	78	73	67	62	56	51	45	40	34
650	660	101	91	81	74	69	63	58	52	47	41	36
660	670	104	94	83	76	70	65	59	54	48	43	37
670	680	107	96	86	77	72	66	61	55	50	44	39
680	690	109	99	89	79	73	68	62	57	51	46	40
690	700	112	102	92	82	75	69	64	58	53	47	42
700	710	115	105	95	84	76	71	65	60	54	49	43
710	720	118	108	97	87	78	72	67	61	56	50	45
720	730	121	110	100	90	80	74	68	63	57	52	46
730	740	123	113	103	93	83	75	70	64	59	53	48
740	750	126	116	106	96	85	77	71	66	60	55	49
750	760	129	119	109	98	88	78	73	67	62	56	51
760	770	132	122	111	101	91	81	74	69	63	58	52
770	780	135	124	114	104	94	84	76	70	65	59	54
780	790	137	127	117	107	97	86	77	72	66	61	55
790	800	140	130	120	110	99	89	79	73	68	62	57
800	810	143	133	123	112	102	92	82	75	69	64	58
810	820	146	136	125	115	105	95	84	76	71	65	60
820	830	149	138	128	118	108	98	87	78	72	67	61
830	840	151	141	131	121	111	100	90	80	74	68	63
840	850	154	144	134	124	113	103	93	83	75	70	64
850	860	157	147	137	126	116	106	96	85	77	71	66
860	870	160	150	139	129	119	109	98	88	78	73	67
870	880	163	152	142	132	122	112	101	91	81	74	69
880	890	165	155	145	135	125	114	104	94	84	76	70
890	900	168	158	148	138	127	117	107	97	86	77	72
900	910	171	161	151	140	130	120	110	99	89	79	73
910	920	175	164	153	143	133	123	112	102	92	82	75
920	930	178	166	156	146	136	126	115	105	95	85	76
930	940	182	169	159	149	139	128	118	108	98	87	78
940	950	185	173	162	152	141	131	121	111	100	90	80
950	960	189	176	165	154	144	134	124	113	103	93	83
960	970	192	180	167	157	147	137	126	116	106	96	86
970	980	196	183	170	160	150	140	129	119	109	99	88
980	990	199	187	174	163	153	142	132	122	112	101	91
990	1,000	203	190	177	166	155	145	135	125	114	104	94
1,000	1,010	206	194	181	168	158	148	138	127	117	107	97
1,010	1,020	210	197	184	171	161	151	140	130	120	110	100
1,020	1,030	213	201	188	175	164	154	143	133	123	113	102
1,030	1,040	217	204	191	178	167	156	146	136	126	115	105
1,040	1,050	220	208	195	182	169	159	149	139	128	118	108
1,050	1,060	224	211	198	185	173	162	152	141	131	121	111
1,060	1,070	227	215	202	189	176	165	154	144	134	124	114
1,070	1,080	231	218	205	192	180	168	157	147	137	127	116
1,080	1,090	234	222	209	196	183	170	160	150	140	129	119

SINGLE Persons—MONTHLY Payroll Period

And the wages are—		And the number of withholding allowances claimed is—										
At least	But less than	0	1	2	3	4	5	6	7	8	9	10
		The amount of income tax to be withheld shall be—										
$440	$460	$54	$30	$9	$0	$0	$0	$0	$0	$0	$0	$0
460	480	57	33	11	0	0	0	0	0	0	0	0
480	500	60	36	13	0	0	0	0	0	0	0	0
500	520	63	39	15	0	0	0	0	0	0	0	0
520	540	66	42	18	0	0	0	0	0	0	0	0
540	560	69	45	21	2	0	0	0	0	0	0	0
560	580	72	48	24	5	0	0	0	0	0	0	0
580	600	75	51	27	7	0	0	0	0	0	0	0
600	640	79	55	32	10	0	0	0	0	0	0	0
640	680	85	61	38	14	0	0	0	0	0	0	0
680	720	91	67	44	20	1	0	0	0	0	0	0
720	760	97	73	50	26	6	0	0	0	0	0	0
760	800	103	79	56	32	10	0	0	0	0	0	0
800	840	109	85	62	38	15	0	0	0	0	0	0
840	880	115	91	68	44	20	2	0	0	0	0	0
880	920	121	97	74	50	26	6	0	0	0	0	0
920	960	127	103	80	56	32	10	0	0	0	0	0
960	1,000	133	109	86	62	38	15	0	0	0	0	0
1,000	1,040	139	115	92	68	44	20	2	0	0	0	0
1,040	1,080	145	121	98	74	50	26	6	0	0	0	0
1,080	1,120	151	127	104	80	56	32	11	0	0	0	0
1,120	1,160	157	133	110	86	62	38	15	0	0	0	0
1,160	1,200	163	139	116	92	68	44	21	2	0	0	0
1,200	1,240	169	145	122	98	74	50	27	6	0	0	0
1,240	1,280	175	151	128	104	80	56	33	11	0	0	0
1,280	1,320	181	157	134	110	86	62	39	15	0	0	0
1,320	1,360	187	163	140	116	92	68	45	21	2	0	0
1,360	1,400	193	169	146	122	98	74	51	27	7	0	0
1,400	1,440	199	175	152	128	104	80	57	33	11	0	0
1,440	1,480	206	181	158	134	110	86	63	39	15	0	0
1,480	1,520	217	187	164	140	116	92	69	45	21	2	0
1,520	1,560	228	193	170	146	122	98	75	51	27	7	0
1,560	1,600	239	199	176	152	128	104	81	57	33	11	0
1,600	1,640	251	206	182	158	134	110	87	63	39	16	0
1,640	1,680	262	218	188	164	140	116	93	69	45	21	3
1,680	1,720	273	229	194	170	146	122	99	75	51	27	7
1,720	1,760	284	240	200	176	152	128	105	81	57	33	11
1,760	1,800	295	251	207	182	158	134	111	87	63	39	16
1,800	1,840	307	262	218	188	164	140	117	93	69	45	22
1,840	1,880	318	274	229	194	170	146	123	99	75	51	28
1,880	1,920	329	285	240	200	176	152	129	105	81	57	34
1,920	1,960	340	296	252	207	182	158	135	111	87	63	40
1,960	2,000	351	307	263	218	188	164	141	117	93	69	46
2,000	2,040	363	318	274	230	194	170	147	123	99	75	52
2,040	2,080	374	330	285	241	200	176	153	129	105	81	58
2,080	2,120	385	341	296	252	208	182	159	135	111	87	64
2,120	2,160	396	352	308	263	219	188	165	141	117	93	70
2,160	2,200	407	363	319	274	230	194	171	147	123	99	76
2,200	2,240	419	374	330	286	241	200	177	153	129	105	82
2,240	2,280	430	386	341	297	253	208	183	159	135	111	88
2,280	2,320	441	397	352	308	264	219	189	165	141	117	94
2,320	2,360	455	408	364	319	275	231	195	171	147	123	100
2,360	2,400	469	419	375	330	286	242	201	177	153	129	106
2,400	2,440	483	430	386	342	297	253	209	183	159	135	112
2,440	2,480	497	442	397	353	309	264	220	189	165	141	118
2,480	2,520	511	455	408	364	320	275	231	195	171	147	124
2,520	2,560	525	469	420	375	331	287	242	201	177	153	130
2,560	2,600	539	483	431	386	342	298	253	209	183	159	136
2,600	2,640	553	497	442	398	353	309	265	220	189	165	142
2,640	2,680	567	511	456	409	365	320	276	232	195	171	148
2,680	2,720	581	525	470	420	376	331	287	243	201	177	154
2,720	2,760	595	539	484	431	387	343	298	254	210	183	160
2,760	2,800	609	553	498	443	398	354	309	265	221	189	166
2,800	2,840	623	567	512	457	409	365	321	276	232	195	172
2,840	2,880	637	581	526	471	421	376	332	288	243	201	178

MARRIED Persons–MONTHLY Payroll Period

And the wages are–		And the number of withholding allowances claimed is–										
At least	But less than	0	1	2	3	4	5	6	7	8	9	10
		The amount of income tax to be withheld shall be–										
$0	$160	$0	$0	$0	$0	$0	$0	$0	$0	$0	$0	$0
160	164	1	0	0	0	0	0	0	0	0	0	0
164	168	1	0	0	0	0	0	0	0	0	0	0
168	172	2	0	0	0	0	0	0	0	0	0	0
172	176	2	0	0	0	0	0	0	0	0	0	0
176	180	3	0	0	0	0	0	0	0	0	0	0
180	184	3	0	0	0	0	0	0	0	0	0	0
184	188	3	0	0	0	0	0	0	0	0	0	0
188	192	4	0	0	0	0	0	0	0	0	0	0
192	196	4	0	0	0	0	0	0	0	0	0	0
196	200	5	0	0	0	0	0	0	0	0	0	0
200	204	5	0	0	0	0	0	0	0	0	0	0
204	208	6	0	0	0	0	0	0	0	0	0	0
208	212	6	0	0	0	0	0	0	0	0	0	0
212	216	6	0	0	0	0	0	0	0	0	0	0
216	220	7	0	0	0	0	0	0	0	0	0	0
220	224	7	0	0	0	0	0	0	0	0	0	0
224	228	8	0	0	0	0	0	0	0	0	0	0
228	232	8	0	0	0	0	0	0	0	0	0	0
232	236	9	0	0	0	0	0	0	0	0	0	0
236	240	9	0	0	0	0	0	0	0	0	0	0
240	248	10	0	0	0	0	0	0	0	0	0	0
248	256	11	0	0	0	0	0	0	0	0	0	0
256	264	12	0	0	0	0	0	0	0	0	0	0
264	272	12	0	0	0	0	0	0	0	0	0	0
272	280	13	0	0	0	0	0	0	0	0	0	0
280	288	14	0	0	0	0	0	0	0	0	0	0
288	296	15	0	0	0	0	0	0	0	0	0	0
296	304	16	0	0	0	0	0	0	0	0	0	0
304	312	17	0	0	0	0	0	0	0	0	0	0
312	320	18	0	0	0	0	0	0	0	0	0	0
320	328	19	1	0	0	0	0	0	0	0	0	0
328	336	19	2	0	0	0	0	0	0	0	0	0
336	344	20	3	0	0	0	0	0	0	0	0	0
344	352	21	4	0	0	0	0	0	0	0	0	0
352	360	22	5	0	0	0	0	0	0	0	0	0
360	368	23	6	0	0	0	0	0	0	0	0	0
368	376	24	6	0	0	0	0	0	0	0	0	0
376	384	25	7	0	0	0	0	0	0	0	0	0
384	392	26	8	0	0	0	0	0	0	0	0	0
392	400	27	9	0	0	0	0	0	0	0	0	0
400	420	28	11	0	0	0	0	0	0	0	0	0
420	440	31	13	0	0	0	0	0	0	0	0	0
440	460	34	15	0	0	0	0	0	0	0	0	0
460	480	37	17	0	0	0	0	0	0	0	0	0
480	500	40	19	2	0	0	0	0	0	0	0	0
500	520	43	22	4	0	0	0	0	0	0	0	0
520	540	46	24	6	0	0	0	0	0	0	0	0
540	560	49	26	9	0	0	0	0	0	0	0	0
560	580	52	29	11	0	0	0	0	0	0	0	0
580	600	55	32	13	0	0	0	0	0	0	0	0
600	640	60	36	16	0	0	0	0	0	0	0	0
640	680	66	42	21	3	0	0	0	0	0	0	0
680	720	72	48	25	8	0	0	0	0	0	0	0
720	760	78	54	30	12	0	0	0	0	0	0	0
760	800	84	60	36	17	0	0	0	0	0	0	0
800	840	90	66	42	21	3	0	0	0	0	0	0
840	880	96	72	48	25	8	0	0	0	0	0	0
880	920	102	78	54	31	12	0	0	0	0	0	0
920	960	108	84	60	37	17	0	0	0	0	0	0
960	1,000	114	90	66	43	21	4	0	0	0	0	0
1,000	1,040	120	96	72	49	25	8	0	0	0	0	0
1,040	1,080	126	102	78	55	31	12	0	0	0	0	0
1,080	1,120	132	108	84	61	37	17	0	0	0	0	0
1,120	1,160	138	114	90	67	43	21	4	0	0	0	0
1,160	1,200	144	120	96	73	49	26	8	0	0	0	0
1,200	1,240	150	126	102	79	55	31	13	0	0	0	0
1,240	1,280	156	132	108	85	61	37	17	0	0	0	0
1,280	1,320	162	138	114	91	67	43	21	4	0	0	0

(Continued on next page)

MARRIED Persons—MONTHLY Payroll Period

And the wages are—		And the number of withholding allowances claimed is—										
At least	But less than	0	1	2	3	4	5	6	7	8	9	10
		The amount of income tax to be withheld shall be—										
$1,320	$1,360	$168	$144	$120	$97	$73	$49	$26	$8	$0	$0	$0
1,360	1,400	174	150	126	103	79	55	31	13	0	0	0
1,400	1,440	180	156	132	109	85	61	37	17	0	0	0
1,440	1,480	186	162	138	115	91	67	43	22	4	0	0
1,480	1,520	192	168	144	121	97	73	49	26	9	0	0
1,520	1,560	198	174	150	127	103	79	55	32	13	0	0
1,560	1,600	204	180	156	133	109	85	61	38	17	0	0
1,600	1,640	210	186	162	139	115	91	67	44	22	4	0
1,640	1,680	216	192	168	145	121	97	73	50	26	9	0
1,680	1,720	222	198	174	151	127	103	79	56	32	13	0
1,720	1,760	228	204	180	157	133	109	85	62	38	18	0
1,760	1,800	234	210	186	163	139	115	91	68	44	22	5
1,800	1,840	240	216	192	169	145	121	97	74	50	26	9
1,840	1,880	246	222	198	175	151	127	103	80	56	32	13
1,880	1,920	252	228	204	181	157	133	109	86	62	38	18
1,920	1,960	258	234	210	187	163	139	115	92	68	44	22
1,960	2,000	264	240	216	193	169	145	121	98	74	50	27
2,000	2,040	270	246	222	199	175	151	127	104	80	56	32
2,040	2,080	276	252	228	205	181	157	133	110	86	62	38
2,080	2,120	282	258	234	211	187	163	139	116	92	68	44
2,120	2,160	288	264	240	217	193	169	145	122	98	74	50
2,160	2,200	294	270	246	223	199	175	151	128	104	80	56
2,200	2,240	300	276	252	229	205	181	157	134	110	86	62
2,240	2,280	306	282	258	235	211	187	163	140	116	92	68
2,280	2,320	312	288	264	241	217	193	169	146	122	98	74
2,320	2,360	318	294	270	247	223	199	175	152	128	104	80
2,360	2,400	324	300	276	253	229	205	181	158	134	110	86
2,400	2,440	330	306	282	259	235	211	187	164	140	116	92
2,440	2,480	336	312	288	265	241	217	193	170	146	122	98
2,480	2,520	343	318	294	271	247	223	199	176	152	128	104
2,520	2,560	354	324	300	277	253	229	205	182	158	134	110
2,560	2,600	366	330	306	283	259	235	211	188	164	140	116
2,600	2,640	377	336	312	289	265	241	217	194	170	146	122
2,640	2,680	388	344	318	295	271	247	223	200	176	152	128
2,680	2,720	399	355	324	301	277	253	229	206	182	158	134
2,720	2,760	410	366	330	307	283	259	235	212	188	164	140
2,760	2,800	422	377	336	313	289	265	241	218	194	170	146
2,800	2,840	433	389	344	319	295	271	247	224	200	176	152
2,840	2,880	444	400	355	325	301	277	253	230	206	182	158
2,880	2,920	455	411	367	331	307	283	259	236	212	188	164
2,920	2,960	466	422	378	337	313	289	265	242	218	194	170
2,960	3,000	478	433	389	345	319	295	271	248	224	200	176
3,000	3,040	489	445	400	356	325	301	277	254	230	206	182
3,040	3,080	500	456	411	367	331	307	283	260	236	212	188
3,080	3,120	511	467	423	378	337	313	289	266	242	218	194
3,120	3,160	522	478	434	389	345	319	295	272	248	224	200
3,160	3,200	534	489	445	401	356	325	301	278	254	230	206
3,200	3,240	545	501	456	412	368	331	307	284	260	236	212
3,240	3,280	556	512	467	423	379	337	313	290	266	242	218
3,280	3,320	567	523	479	434	390	346	319	296	272	248	224
3,320	3,360	578	534	490	445	401	357	325	302	278	254	230
3,360	3,400	590	545	501	457	412	368	331	308	284	260	236
3,400	3,440	601	557	512	468	424	379	337	314	290	266	242
3,440	3,480	612	568	523	479	435	390	346	320	296	272	248
3,480	3,520	623	579	535	490	446	402	357	326	302	278	254
3,520	3,560	634	590	546	501	457	413	368	332	308	284	260
3,560	3,600	646	601	557	513	468	424	380	338	314	290	266
3,600	3,640	657	613	568	524	480	435	391	347	320	296	272
3,640	3,680	668	624	579	535	491	446	402	358	326	302	278
3,680	3,720	679	635	591	546	502	458	413	369	332	308	284
3,720	3,760	690	646	602	557	513	469	424	380	338	314	290
3,760	3,800	702	657	613	569	524	480	436	391	347	320	296
3,800	3,840	713	669	624	580	536	491	447	403	358	326	302
3,840	3,880	724	680	635	591	547	502	458	414	369	332	308
3,880	3,920	735	691	647	602	558	514	469	425	381	338	314

Tables for Percentage Method of Withholding

Remember: *The wage amounts on this page are after withholding allowances have been subtracted.*

TABLE 1—If the Payroll Period With Respect to an Employee Is Weekly

(a) SINGLE person—including head of household:

If the amount of wages is:		The amount of income tax to be withheld shall be:	of excess over—
Not over $12		0	
Over—	But not over—		
$12	—$47	11%	—$12
$47	—$335	$3.85 plus 15%	—$47
$335	—$532	$47.05 plus 28%	—$335
$532	—$1,051	$102.21 plus 35%	—$532
$1,051		$283.86 plus 38.5%	—$1,051

(b) MARRIED person—

If the amount of wages is:		The amount of income tax to be withheld shall be:	of excess over—
Not over $36		0	
Over—	But not over—		
$36	—$93	11%	—$36
$93	—$574	$6.27 plus 15%	—$93
$574	—$901	$78.42 plus 28%	—$574
$901	—$1,767	$169.98 plus 35%	—$901
$1,767		$473.08 plus 38.5%	—$1,767

TABLE 2—If the Payroll Period With Respect to an Employee Is Biweekly

(a) SINGLE person—including head of household:

If the amount of wages is:		The amount of income tax to be withheld shall be:	of excess over—
Not over $25		0	
Over—	But not over—		
$25	—$94	11%	—$25
$94	—$671	$7.59 plus 15%	—$94
$671	—$1,063	$94.14 plus 28%	—$671
$1,063	—$2,102	$203.90 plus 35%	—$1,063
$2,102		$567.55 plus 38.5%	—$2,102

(b) MARRIED person—

If the amount of wages is:		The amount of income tax to be withheld shall be:	of excess over—
Not over $72		0	
Over—	But not over—		
$72	—$187	11%	—$72
$187	—$1,148	$12.65 plus 15%	—$187
$1,148	—$1,802	$156.80 plus 28%	—$1,148
$1,802	—$3,533	$339.92 plus 35%	—$1,802
$3,533		$945.77 plus 38.5%	—$3,533

TABLE 3—If the Payroll Period With Respect to an Employee Is Semimonthly

(a) SINGLE person—including head of household:

If the amount of wages is:		The amount of income tax to be withheld shall be:	of excess over—
Not over $27		0	
Over—	But not over—		
$27	—$102	11%	—$27
$102	—$727	$8.25 plus 15%	—$102
$727	—$1,152	$102.00 plus 28%	—$727
$1,152	—$2,277	$221.00 plus 35%	—$1,152
$2,277		$614.75 plus 38.5%	—$2,277

(b) MARRIED person—

If the amount of wages is:		The amount of income tax to be withheld shall be:	of excess over—
Not over $78		0	
Over—	But not over—		
$78	—$203	11%	—$78
$203	—$1,244	$13.75 plus 15%	—$203
$1,244	—$1,953	$169.90 plus 28%	—$1,244
$1,953	—$3,828	$368.42 plus 35%	—$1,953
$3,828		$1,024.67 plus 38.5%	—$3,828

TABLE 4—If the Payroll Period With Respect to an Employee Is Monthly

(a) SINGLE person—including head of household:

If the amount of wages is:		The amount of income tax to be withheld shall be:	of excess over—
Not over $53		0	
Over—	But not over—		
$53	—$203	11%	—$53
$203	—$1,453	$16.50 plus 15%	—$203
$1,453	—$2,303	$204.00 plus 28%	—$1,453
$2,303	—$4,553	$442.00 plus 35%	—$2,303
$4,553		$1,229.50 plus 38.5%	—$4,553

(b) MARRIED person—

If the amount of wages is:		The amount of income tax to be withheld shall be:	of excess over—
Not over $155		0	
Over—	But not over—		
$155	—$405	11%	—$155
$405	—$2,488	$27.50 plus 15%	—$405
$2,488	—$3,905	$339.95 plus 28%	—$2,488
$3,905	—$7,655	$736.71 plus 35%	—$3,905
$7,655		$2,049.21 plus 38.5%	—$7,655

Remember: *The wage amounts on this page are after withholding allowances have been subtracted.*

TABLE 5—If the Payroll Period With Respect to an Employee Is Quarterly

(a) SINGLE person—including head of household:

If the amount of wages is:		The amount of income tax to be withheld shall be:	of excess over—
Not over $160		.0	
Over—	But not over—		
$160	—$610	. . .11%	—$160
$610	—$4,360	. . $49.50 plus 15%	—$610
$4,360	—$6,910	. . $612.00 plus 28%	—$4,360
$6,910	—$13,660	. . $1,326.00 plus 35%	—$6,910
$13,660	. . . . . .	. $3,688.50 plus 38.5%	—$13,660

(b) MARRIED person—

If the amount of wages is:		The amount of income tax to be withheld shall be:	of excess over—
Not over $465		.0	
Over—	But not over—		
$465	—$1,215	. . . 11%	—$465
$1,215	—$7,465	. . . $82.50 plus 15%	—$1,215
$7,465	—$11,715	. . $1,020.00 plus 28%	—$7,465
$11,715	—$22,965	. . $2,210.00 plus 35%	—$11,715
$22,965	. . . . . .	. $6,147.50 plus 38.5%	—$22,965

TABLE 6—If the Payroll Period With Respect to an Employee Is Semiannual

(a) SINGLE person—including head of household:

If the amount of wages is:		The amount of income tax to be withheld shall be:	of excess over—
Not over $320		.0	
Over—	But not over—		
$320	—$1,220	. . .11%	—$320
$1,220	—$8,720	. . $99.00 plus 15%	—$1,220
$8,720	—$13,820	. . $1,224.00 plus 28%	—$8,720
$13,820	—$27,320	. . $2,652.00 plus 35%	—$13,820
$27,320	. . . . . .	. $7,377.00 plus 38.5%	—$27,320

(b) MARRIED person—

If the amount of wages is:		The amount of income tax to be withheld shall be:	of excess over—
Not over $930		.0	
Over—	But not over—		
$930	—$2,430	. . . 11%	—$930
$2,430	—$14,930	. . $165.00 plus 15%	—$2,430
$14,930	—$23,430	. . $2,040.00 plus 28%	—$14,930
$23,430	—$45,930	. . $4,420.00 plus 35%	—$23,430
$45,930	. . . . . .	. $12,295.00 plus 38.5%	—$45,930

TABLE 7—If the Payroll Period With Respect to an Employee Is Annual

(a) SINGLE person—including head of household:

If the amount of wages is:		The amount of income tax to be withheld shall be:	of excess over—
Not over $640		.0	
Over—	But not over—		
$640	—$2,440	. . .11%	—$640
$2,440	—$17,440	. . $198.00 plus 15%	—$2,440
$17,440	—$27,640	. . $2,448.00 plus 28%	—$17,440
$27,640	—$54,640	. . $5,304.00 plus 35%	—$27,640
$54,640	. . . . . .	. $14,754.00 plus 38.5%	—$54,640

(b) MARRIED person—

If the amount of wages is:		The amount of income tax to be withheld shall be:	of excess over—
Not over $1,860		.0	
Over—	But not over—		
$1,860	—$4,860	. . . 11%	—$1,860
$4,860	—$29,860	. . $330.00 plus 15%	—$4,860
$29,860	—$46,860	. . $4,080.00 plus 28%	—$29,860
$46,860	—$91,860	. . $8,840.00 plus 35%	—$46,860
$91,860	. . . . . .	. $24,590.00 plus 38.5%	—$91,860

TABLE 8—If the Payroll Period With Respect to an Employee Is a Daily Payroll Period or a Miscellaneous Payroll Period

(a) SINGLE person—including head of household:

If the amount of wages divided by the number of days in the payroll period is:		The amount of income tax to be withheld per day shall be:	of excess over—
Not over $2.50		.0	
Over—	But not over—		
$2.50	—$9.40	. . .11%	—$2.50
$9.40	—$67.10	. . $0.76 plus 15%	—$9.40
$67.10	—$106.30	. . $9.42 plus 28%	—$67.10
$106.30	—$210.20	. . $20.40 plus 35%	—$106.30
$210.20	. . . . . .	. $56.77 plus 38.5%	—$210.20

(b) MARRIED person—

If the amount of wages divided by the number of days in the payroll period is:		The amount of income tax to be withheld per day shall be:	of excess over—
Not over $7.20		.0	
Over—	But not over—		
$7.20	—$18.70	. . . 11%	—$7.20
$18.70	—$114.80	. . $1.27 plus 15%	—$18.70
$114.80	—$180.20	. . $15.69 plus 28%	—$114.80
$180.20	—$353.30	. . $34.00 plus 35%	—$180.20
$353.30	. . . . . .	. $94.59 plus 38.5%	—$353.30

Social Security Employee Tax Table
7.15% employee tax deductions

Wages at least	But less than	Tax to be withheld	Wages at least	But less than	Tax to be withheld	Wages at least	But less than	Tax to be withheld	Wages at least	But less than	Tax to be withheld
$0.00	$0.07	$0.00	12.66	12.80	.91	25.39	25.53	1.82	38.12	38.26	2.73
.07	.21	.01	12.80	12.94	.92	25.53	25.67	1.83	38.26	38.40	2.74
.21	.35	.02	12.94	13.08	.93	25.67	25.81	1.84	38.40	38.54	2.75
.35	.49	.03	13.08	13.22	.94	25.81	25.95	1.85	38.54	38.68	2.76
.49	.63	.04	13.22	13.36	.95	25.95	26.09	1.86	38.68	38.82	2.77
.63	.77	.05	13.36	13.50	.96	26.09	26.23	1.87	38.82	38.96	2.78
.77	.91	.06	13.50	13.64	.97	26.23	26.37	1.88	38.96	39.10	2.79
.91	1.05	.07	13.64	13.78	.98	26.37	26.51	1.89	39.10	39.24	2.80
1.05	1.19	.08	13.78	13.92	.99	26.51	26.65	1.90	39.24	39.38	2.81
1.19	1.33	.09	13.92	14.06	1.00	26.65	26.79	1.91	39.38	39.52	2.82
1.33	1.47	.10	14.06	14.20	1.01	26.79	26.93	1.92	39.52	39.66	2.83
1.47	1.61	.11	14.20	14.34	1.02	26.93	27.07	1.93	39.66	39.80	2.84
1.61	1.75	.12	14.34	14.48	1.03	27.07	27.21	1.94	39.80	39.94	2.85
1.75	1.89	.13	14.48	14.62	1.04	27.21	27.35	1.95	39.94	40.07	2.86
1.89	2.03	.14	14.62	14.76	1.05	27.35	27.49	1.96	40.07	40.21	2.87
2.03	2.17	.15	14.76	14.90	1.06	27.49	27.63	1.97	40.21	40.35	2.88
2.17	2.31	.16	14.90	15.04	1.07	27.63	27.77	1.98	40.35	40.49	2.89
2.31	2.45	.17	15.04	15.18	1.08	27.77	27.91	1.99	40.49	40.63	2.90
2.45	2.59	.18	15.18	15.32	1.09	27.91	28.05	2.00	40.63	40.77	2.91
2.59	2.73	.19	15.32	15.46	1.10	28.05	28.19	2.01	40.77	40.91	2.92
2.73	2.87	.20	15.46	15.60	1.11	28.19	28.33	2.02	40.91	41.05	2.93
2.87	3.01	.21	15.60	15.74	1.12	28.33	28.47	2.03	41.05	41.19	2.94
3.01	3.15	.22	15.74	15.88	1.13	28.47	28.61	2.04	41.19	41.33	2.95
3.15	3.29	.23	15.88	16.02	1.14	28.61	28.75	2.05	41.33	41.47	2.96
3.29	3.43	.24	16.02	16.16	1.15	28.75	28.89	2.06	41.47	41.61	2.97
3.43	3.57	.25	16.16	16.30	1.16	28.89	29.03	2.07	41.61	41.75	2.98
3.57	3.71	.26	16.30	16.44	1.17	29.03	29.17	2.08	41.75	41.89	2.99
3.71	3.85	.27	16.44	16.58	1.18	29.17	29.31	2.09	41.89	42.03	3.00
3.85	3.99	.28	16.58	16.72	1.19	29.31	29.45	2.10	42.03	42.17	3.01
3.99	4.13	.29	16.72	16.86	1.20	29.45	29.59	2.11	42.17	42.31	3.02
4.13	4.27	.30	16.86	17.00	1.21	29.59	29.73	2.12	42.31	42.45	3.03
4.27	4.41	.31	17.00	17.14	1.22	29.73	29.87	2.13	42.45	42.59	3.04
4.41	4.55	.32	17.14	17.28	1.23	29.87	30.00	2.14	42.59	42.73	3.05
4.55	4.69	.33	17.28	17.42	1.24	30.00	30.14	2.15	42.73	42.87	3.06
4.69	4.83	.34	17.42	17.56	1.25	30.14	30.28	2.16	42.87	43.01	3.07
4.83	4.97	.35	17.56	17.70	1.26	30.28	30.42	2.17	43.01	43.15	3.08
4.97	5.11	.36	17.70	17.84	1.27	30.42	30.56	2.18	43.15	43.29	3.09
5.11	5.25	.37	17.84	17.98	1.28	30.56	30.70	2.19	43.29	43.43	3.10
5.25	5.39	.38	17.98	18.12	1.29	30.70	30.84	2.20	43.43	43.57	3.11
5.39	5.53	.39	18.12	18.26	1.30	30.84	30.98	2.21	43.57	43.71	3.12
5.53	5.67	.40	18.26	18.40	1.31	30.98	31.12	2.22	43.71	43.85	3.13
5.67	5.81	.41	18.40	18.54	1.32	31.12	31.26	2.23	43.85	43.99	3.14
5.81	5.95	.42	18.54	18.68	1.33	31.26	31.40	2.24	43.99	44.13	3.15
5.95	6.09	.43	18.68	18.82	1.34	31.40	31.54	2.25	44.13	44.27	3.16
6.09	6.23	.44	18.82	18.96	1.35	31.54	31.68	2.26	44.27	44.41	3.17
6.23	6.37	.45	18.96	19.10	1.36	31.68	31.82	2.27	44.41	44.55	3.18
6.37	6.51	.46	19.10	19.24	1.37	31.82	31.96	2.28	44.55	44.69	3.19
6.51	6.65	.47	19.24	19.38	1.38	31.96	32.10	2.29	44.69	44.83	3.20
6.65	6.79	.48	19.38	19.52	1.39	32.10	32.24	2.30	44.83	44.97	3.21
6.79	6.93	.49	19.52	19.66	1.40	32.24	32.38	2.31	44.97	45.11	3.22
6.93	7.07	.50	19.66	19.80	1.41	32.38	32.52	2.32	45.11	45.25	3.23
7.07	7.21	.51	19.80	19.94	1.42	32.52	32.66	2.33	45.25	45.39	3.24
7.21	7.35	.52	19.94	20.07	1.43	32.66	32.80	2.34	45.39	45.53	3.25
7.35	7.49	.53	20.07	20.21	1.44	32.80	32.94	2.35	45.53	45.67	3.26
7.49	7.63	.54	20.21	20.35	1.45	32.94	33.08	2.36	45.67	45.81	3.27
7.63	7.77	.55	20.35	20.49	1.46	33.08	33.22	2.37	45.81	45.95	3.28
7.77	7.91	.56	20.49	20.63	1.47	33.22	33.36	2.38	45.95	46.09	3.29
7.91	8.05	.57	20.63	20.77	1.48	33.36	33.50	2.39	46.09	46.23	3.30
8.05	8.19	.58	20.77	20.91	1.49	33.50	33.64	2.40	46.23	46.37	3.31
8.19	8.33	.59	20.91	21.05	1.50	33.64	33.78	2.41	46.37	46.51	3.32
8.33	8.47	.60	21.05	21.19	1.51	33.78	33.92	2.42	46.51	46.65	3.33
8.47	8.61	.61	21.19	21.33	1.52	33.92	34.06	2.43	46.65	46.79	3.34
8.61	8.75	.62	21.33	21.47	1.53	34.06	34.20	2.44	46.79	46.93	3.35
8.75	8.89	.63	21.47	21.61	1.54	34.20	34.34	2.45	46.93	47.07	3.36
8.89	9.03	.64	21.61	21.75	1.55	34.34	34.48	2.46	47.07	47.21	3.37
9.03	9.17	.65	21.75	21.89	1.56	34.48	34.62	2.47	47.21	47.35	3.38
9.17	9.31	.66	21.89	22.03	1.57	34.62	34.76	2.48	47.35	47.49	3.39
9.31	9.45	.67	22.03	22.17	1.58	34.76	34.90	2.49	47.49	47.63	3.40
9.45	9.59	.68	22.17	22.31	1.59	34.90	35.04	2.50	47.63	47.77	3.41
9.59	9.73	.69	22.31	22.45	1.60	35.04	35.18	2.51	47.77	47.91	3.42
9.73	9.87	.70	22.45	22.59	1.61	35.18	35.32	2.52	47.91	48.05	3.43
9.87	10.00	.71	22.59	22.73	1.62	35.32	35.46	2.53	48.05	48.19	3.44
10.00	10.14	.72	22.73	22.87	1.63	35.46	35.60	2.54	48.19	48.33	3.45
10.14	10.28	.73	22.87	23.01	1.64	35.60	35.74	2.55	48.33	48.47	3.46
10.28	10.42	.74	23.01	23.15	1.65	35.74	35.88	2.56	48.47	48.61	3.47
10.42	10.56	.75	23.15	23.29	1.66	35.88	36.02	2.57	48.61	48.75	3.48
10.56	10.70	.76	23.29	23.43	1.67	36.02	36.16	2.58	48.75	48.89	3.49
10.70	10.84	.77	23.43	23.57	1.68	36.16	36.30	2.59	48.89	49.03	3.50
10.84	10.98	.78	23.57	23.71	1.69	36.30	36.44	2.60	49.03	49.17	3.51
10.98	11.12	.79	23.71	23.85	1.70	36.44	36.58	2.61	49.17	49.31	3.52
11.12	11.26	.80	23.85	23.99	1.71	36.58	36.72	2.62	49.31	49.45	3.53
11.26	11.40	.81	23.99	24.13	1.72	36.72	36.86	2.63	49.45	49.59	3.54
11.40	11.54	.82	24.13	24.27	1.73	36.86	37.00	2.64	49.59	49.73	3.55
11.54	11.68	.83	24.27	24.41	1.74	37.00	37.14	2.65	49.73	49.87	3.56
11.68	11.82	.84	24.41	24.55	1.75	37.14	37.28	2.66	49.87	50.00	3.57
11.82	11.96	.85	24.55	24.69	1.76	37.28	37.42	2.67	50.00	50.14	3.58
11.96	12.10	.86	24.69	24.83	1.77	37.42	37.56	2.68	50.14	50.28	3.59
12.10	12.24	.87	24.83	24.97	1.78	37.56	37.70	2.69	50.28	50.42	3.60
12.24	12.38	.88	24.97	25.11	1.79	37.70	37.84	2.70	50.42	50.56	3.61
12.38	12.52	.89	25.11	25.25	1.80	37.84	37.98	2.71	50.56	50.70	3.62
12.52	12.66	.90	25.25	25.39	1.81	37.98	38.12	2.72	50.70	50.84	3.63

Social Security Employee Tax Table
7.15% employee tax deductions

Wages at least	But less than	Tax to be withheld	Wages at least	But less than	Tax to be withheld	Wages at least	But less than	Tax to be withheld	Wages at least	But less than	Tax to be withheld
50.84	50.98	3.64	63.57	63.71	4.55	76.30	76.44	5.46	89.03	89.17	6.37
50.98	51.12	3.65	63.71	63.85	4.56	76.44	76.58	5.47	89.17	89.31	6.38
51.12	51.26	3.66	63.85	63.99	4.57	76.58	76.72	5.48	89.31	89.45	6.39
51.26	51.40	3.67	63.99	64.13	4.58	76.72	76.86	5.49	89.45	89.59	6.40
51.40	51.54	3.68	64.13	64.27	4.59	76.86	77.00	5.50	89.59	89.73	6.41
51.54	51.68	3.69	64.27	64.41	4.60	77.00	77.14	5.51	89.73	89.87	6.42
51.68	51.82	3.70	64.41	64.55	4.61	77.14	77.28	5.52	89.87	90.00	6.43
51.82	51.96	3.71	64.55	64.69	4.62	77.28	77.42	5.53	90.00	90.14	6.44
51.96	52.10	3.72	64.69	64.83	4.63	77.42	77.56	5.54	90.14	90.28	6.45
52.10	52.24	3.73	64.83	64.97	4.64	77.56	77.70	5.55	90.28	90.42	6.46
52.24	52.38	3.74	64.97	65.11	4.65	77.70	77.84	5.56	90.42	90.56	6.47
52.38	52.52	3.75	65.11	65.25	4.66	77.84	77.98	5.57	90.56	90.70	6.48
52.52	52.66	3.76	65.25	65.39	4.67	77.98	78.12	5.58	90.70	90.84	6.49
52.66	52.80	3.77	65.39	65.53	4.68	78.12	78.26	5.59	90.84	90.98	6.50
52.80	52.94	3.78	65.53	65.67	4.69	78.26	78.40	5.60	90.98	91.12	6.51
52.94	53.08	3.79	65.67	65.81	4.70	78.40	78.54	5.61	91.12	91.26	6.52
53.08	53.22	3.80	65.81	65.95	4.71	78.54	78.68	5.62	91.26	91.40	6.53
53.22	53.36	3.81	65.95	66.09	4.72	78.68	78.82	5.63	91.40	91.54	6.54
53.36	53.50	3.82	66.09	66.23	4.73	78.82	78.96	5.64	91.54	91.68	6.55
53.50	53.64	3.83	66.23	66.37	4.74	78.96	79.10	5.65	91.68	91.82	6.56
53.64	53.78	3.84	66.37	66.51	4.75	79.10	79.24	5.66	91.82	91.96	6.57
53.78	53.92	3.85	66.51	66.65	4.76	79.24	79.38	5.67	91.96	92.10	6.58
53.92	54.06	3.86	66.65	66.79	4.77	79.38	79.52	5.68	92.10	92.24	6.59
54.06	54.20	3.87	66.79	66.93	4.78	79.52	79.66	5.69	92.24	92.38	6.60
54.20	54.34	3.88	66.93	67.07	4.79	79.66	79.80	5.70	92.38	92.52	6.61
54.34	54.48	3.89	67.07	67.21	4.80	79.80	79.94	5.71	92.52	92.66	6.62
54.48	54.62	3.90	67.21	67.35	4.81	79.94	80.07	5.72	92.66	92.80	6.63
54.62	54.76	3.91	67.35	67.49	4.82	80.07	80.21	5.73	92.80	92.94	6.64
54.76	54.90	3.92	67.49	67.63	4.83	80.21	80.35	5.74	92.94	93.08	6.65
54.90	55.04	3.93	67.63	67.77	4.84	80.35	80.49	5.75	93.08	93.22	6.66
55.04	55.18	3.94	67.77	67.91	4.85	80.49	80.63	5.76	93.22	93.36	6.67
55.18	55.32	3.95	67.91	68.05	4.86	80.63	80.77	5.77	93.36	93.50	6.68
55.32	55.46	3.96	68.05	68.19	4.87	80.77	80.91	5.78	93.50	93.64	6.69
55.46	55.60	3.97	68.19	68.33	4.88	80.91	81.05	5.79	93.64	93.78	6.70
55.60	55.74	3.98	68.33	68.47	4.89	81.05	81.19	5.80	93.78	93.92	6.71
55.74	55.88	3.99	68.47	68.61	4.90	81.19	81.33	5.81	93.92	94.06	6.72
55.88	56.02	4.00	68.61	68.75	4.91	81.33	81.47	5.82	94.06	94.20	6.73
56.02	56.16	4.01	68.75	68.89	4.92	81.47	81.61	5.83	94.20	94.34	6.74
56.16	56.30	4.02	68.89	69.03	4.93	81.61	81.75	5.84	94.34	94.48	6.75
56.30	56.44	4.03	69.03	69.17	4.94	81.75	81.89	5.85	94.48	94.62	6.76
56.44	56.58	4.04	69.17	69.31	4.95	81.89	82.03	5.86	94.62	94.76	6.77
56.58	56.72	4.05	69.31	69.45	4.96	82.03	82.17	5.87	94.76	94.90	6.78
56.72	56.86	4.06	69.45	69.59	4.97	82.17	82.31	5.88	94.90	95.04	6.79
56.86	57.00	4.07	69.59	69.73	4.98	82.31	82.45	5.89	95.04	95.18	6.80
57.00	57.14	4.08	69.73	69.87	4.99	82.45	82.59	5.90	95.18	95.32	6.81
57.14	57.28	4.09	69.87	70.00	5.00	82.59	82.73	5.91	95.32	95.46	6.82
57.28	57.42	4.10	70.00	70.14	5.01	82.73	82.87	5.92	95.46	95.60	6.83
57.42	57.56	4.11	70.14	70.28	5.02	82.87	83.01	5.93	95.60	95.74	6.84
57.56	57.70	4.12	70.28	70.42	5.03	83.01	83.15	5.94	95.74	95.88	6.85
57.70	57.84	4.13	70.42	70.56	5.04	83.15	83.29	5.95	95.88	96.02	6.86
57.84	57.98	4.14	70.56	70.70	5.05	83.29	83.43	5.96	96.02	96.16	6.87
57.98	58.12	4.15	70.70	70.84	5.06	83.43	83.57	5.97	96.16	96.30	6.88
58.12	58.26	4.16	70.84	70.98	5.07	83.57	83.71	5.98	96.30	96.44	6.89
58.26	58.40	4.17	70.98	71.12	5.08	83.71	83.85	5.99	96.44	96.58	6.90
58.40	58.54	4.18	71.12	71.26	5.09	83.85	83.99	6.00	96.58	96.72	6.91
58.54	58.68	4.19	71.26	71.40	5.10	83.99	84.13	6.01	96.72	96.86	6.92
58.68	58.82	4.20	71.40	71.54	5.11	84.13	84.27	6.02	96.86	97.00	6.93
58.82	58.96	4.21	71.54	71.68	5.12	84.27	84.41	6.03	97.00	97.14	6.94
58.96	59.10	4.22	71.68	71.82	5.13	84.41	84.55	6.04	97.14	97.28	6.95
59.10	59.24	4.23	71.82	71.96	5.14	84.55	84.69	6.05	97.28	97.42	6.96
59.24	59.38	4.24	71.96	72.10	5.15	84.69	84.83	6.06	97.42	97.56	6.97
59.38	59.52	4.25	72.10	72.24	5.16	84.83	84.97	6.07	97.56	97.70	6.98
59.52	59.66	4.26	72.24	72.38	5.17	84.97	85.11	6.08	97.70	97.84	6.99
59.66	59.80	4.27	72.38	72.52	5.18	85.11	85.25	6.09	97.84	97.98	7.00
59.80	59.94	4.28	72.52	72.66	5.19	85.25	85.39	6.10	97.98	98.12	7.01
59.94	60.07	4.29	72.66	72.80	5.20	85.39	85.53	6.11	98.12	98.26	7.02
60.07	60.21	4.30	72.80	72.94	5.21	85.53	85.67	6.12	98.26	98.40	7.03
60.21	60.35	4.31	72.94	73.08	5.22	85.67	85.81	6.13	98.40	98.54	7.04
60.35	60.49	4.32	73.08	73.22	5.23	85.81	85.95	6.14	98.54	98.68	7.05
60.49	60.63	4.33	73.22	73.36	5.24	85.95	86.09	6.15	98.68	98.82	7.06
60.63	60.77	4.34	73.36	73.50	5.25	86.09	86.23	6.16	98.82	98.96	7.07
60.77	60.91	4.35	73.50	73.64	5.26	86.23	86.37	6.17	98.96	99.10	7.08
60.91	61.05	4.36	73.64	73.78	5.27	86.37	86.51	6.18	99.10	99.24	7.09
61.05	61.19	4.37	73.78	73.92	5.28	86.51	86.65	6.19	99.24	99.38	7.10
61.19	61.33	4.38	73.92	74.06	5.29	86.65	86.79	6.20	99.38	99.52	7.11
61.33	61.47	4.39	74.06	74.20	5.30	86.79	86.93	6.21	99.52	99.66	7.12
61.47	61.61	4.40	74.20	74.34	5.31	86.93	87.07	6.22	99.66	99.80	7.13
61.61	61.75	4.41	74.34	74.48	5.32	87.07	87.21	6.23	99.80	99.94	7.14
61.75	61.89	4.42	74.48	74.62	5.33	87.21	87.35	6.24	99.94	100.00	7.15
61.89	62.03	4.43	74.62	74.76	5.34	87.35	87.49	6.25			
62.03	62.17	4.44	74.76	74.90	5.35	87.49	87.63	6.26			
62.17	62.31	4.45	74.90	75.04	5.36	87.63	87.77	6.27			
62.31	62.45	4.46	75.04	75.18	5.37	87.77	87.91	6.28			
62.45	62.59	4.47	75.18	75.32	5.38	87.91	88.05	6.29			
62.59	62.73	4.48	75.32	75.46	5.39	88.05	88.19	6.30			
62.73	62.87	4.49	75.46	75.60	5.40	88.19	88.33	6.31			
62.87	63.01	4.50	75.60	75.74	5.41	88.33	88.47	6.32			
63.01	63.15	4.51	75.74	75.88	5.42	88.47	88.61	6.33			
63.15	63.29	4.52	75.88	76.02	5.43	88.61	88.75	6.34			
63.29	63.43	4.53	76.02	76.16	5.44	88.75	88.89	6.35			
63.43	63.57	4.54	76.16	76.30	5.45	88.89	89.03	6.36			

Wages	Taxes
100	$7.15
200	14.30
300	21.45
400	28.60
500	35.75
600	42.90
700	50.05
800	57.20
900	64.35
1,000	71.50

Assignment 8.2

Payroll

Use the tax table for the wage-bracket method in this chapter to find the withholding income tax for each of the following employees.

	Employee	Gross Salary	Pay Period	Marital Status	Exemptions	Withholding Tax
1.	Boer, L.	$ 482	Weekly	Married	2	$ 54
2.	Cooper, J.	$2,380	Monthly	Single	2	375
3.	Eddy, E.	$3,198	Monthly	Married	5	325
4.	Greer, N.	$ 820	Weekly	Married	3	118
5.	Hardy, S.	$ 957	Weekly	Single	3	212
6.	Hersner, J.	$2,650	Monthly	Single	1	511
7.	Lashua, M.	$3,840	Monthly	Married	4	547
8.	Loftus, K.	$ 928	Weekly	Single	0	240
9.	McDowell, A.	$2,081	Monthly	Married	1	258
10.	Nolan	$2,081	Monthly	Single	4	208

Using the percentage method, find the FIT tax for each of the following employees.

	Employee	Gross Earnings	Pay Period	Marital Status	Exemptions	FIT Tax
11.	Robinson	$ 4,260	Monthly	S	1	$1071.53

Monthly, Single

```
  $4,260.00
- $  158.33   Exemption
  $4,101.67
-    2,303
  $1,798.67   Excess
×       35%
  $  629.5345
+      442.00
  $1,071.53   Tax
```

$1,071.53

continued

Payroll **339**

Assignment 8.2 *continued*

12. Rogers $ 1,910   Semimonthly   M   5   <u>245.54</u>

       $1,910.00 $79.17   Semimonthly, Married
−   <u>395.85</u>   Exemption   ×   <u>   5   </u>
       $1,514.15 $395.85 Exemption allowance
−   <u>1,244   </u>
      $ 270.15   Excess
×   <u>28%</u>
      $ 75.642
+   <u>169.90 </u>   <u>$245.54</u>
      $ 245.54   Tax

13. Rollins $ 840   Biweekly   M   3   <u>77.71</u>

       $840 $73.08   Biweekly, Married
−   <u>219.24</u>   Exemption   ×   <u>   3   </u>
       $620.76 $219.24 Exemption allowance
−   <u>187   </u>
      $433.76   Excess
×   <u>15%</u>
      $ 65.064
+   <u>12.65 </u>   <u>$77.71</u>
      $ 77.71   Tax

14. Roper $ 470   Weekly   S   2   <u>64.39</u>

       $470.00 $36.54   Weekly, Single
−   <u>73.08</u>   Exemption   ×   <u>   2   </u>
       $396.92 $73.08 Exemption allowance
−   <u>335.00</u>
      $ 61.92   Excess
×   <u>28%</u>
      $ 17.3376
+   <u>47.05 </u>   <u>$64.39</u>
      $ 64.3876   Tax

15. Rymar $ 75   Daily   S   0   <u>11.63</u>

       $75.00   Daily, Single
−   <u>67.10 </u>
      $ 7.90   Excess
×   <u>28%</u>
      $ 2.212
+   <u>9.42 </u>   <u>$11.63</u>
      $11.63   Tax

16. Salk $38,000   Annually   S   2   <u>7,600</u>

       $38,000 $1,900   Annually, single
−   <u>3,800 </u>   ×   <u>   2   </u>
       $34,200   Exemption $3,800 Exemption allowance
−   <u>27,640</u>
      $ 6,560   Excess
×   <u>35%</u>
      $ 2,296
+   <u>5,304 </u>   <u>$7,600</u>
      $ 7,600   Tax

continued

Assignment 8.2 *continued*

17. Simins $ 6,580   Monthly   M   6   1,340.47

$6,580.00 $158.33   Monthly, Married
− 949.98 Exemption   ×   6
$5,630.02 $949.98 Exemption allowance
− 3,905.00
$1,725.02 Excess
×   35%
$ 603.757
+ 736.71 $1,340.47
$1,340.467 Tax

18. Sonchez $12,250   Quarterly   M   4   1,087.35

$12,250 $ 475   Quarterly, Married
− 1,900 Exemption   ×   4
$10,350 $1900 Exemption allowance
− 465
$ 9,885 Excess
×   11% $1,087.35
$ 1,087.35 Tax

19. Stevens $ 1,450   Weekly   S   1   423.41

$1,450.00   Weekly, Single
− 36.54 Exemption
$1413.46
− 1051.00
$ 362.46 Excess
×   38.5%
$ 139.5471
+ 283.86 $423.41
$ 423.7071 Tax

20. Swartz $ 1,450   Weekly   M   1   349.34

$1,450.00   Weekly, Married
− 36.54 Exemption
$1413.46
− 901
$ 512.46 Excess
×   35 %
$ 179.361
+ 169.98   349.34
$ 349.34 Tax

For all FICA problems, assume that the FICA earnings limit has not been reached. Using the FICA tables, find the FICA tax for each of the following employees.

Employee	Gross Earnings	FICA Tax
21. Talbot	$ 798.30	57.08
22. Taylor	$3,180.23	227.39

continued

Assignment 8.2 continued

23. Teiger	$ 367.50	26.28	
24. Thayer	$1,724.40	123.29	
25. Trolson	$2,518.72	180.09	

Tri-Manufacturing company has hired eight new employees who started working on January 1. Assume that the FICA tax is 7.15%. Federal income withholding taxes are found using the wage-bracket tables. Complete the following monthly payroll register.

	Name	Marital Status	Exemptions	Salary	Federal Income Tax	FICA	Other Deductions	Net Pay
26.	Foley	S	1	$2,820	567	201.63	$143.27	1,908.10
27.	Geyer	M	3	$2,760	313	197.34	$102.70	2,146.96
28.	Harris	M	6	$3,850	458	275.28	$161.90	2,954.82
29.	Lashell	S	2	$1,870	229	133.71	$ 84.85	1,422.44
30.	Routson	S	0	$2,280	441	163.02	$ 98.41	1,577.57
31.	Shaeffer	M	7	$2,500	176	178.75	$120.64	2,024.61
32.	Smedley	M	0	$2,779	422	198.70	$134.76	2,023.54
33.	Young	M	4	$2,080	187	148.72	$ 86.03	1,658.25
34.	Uber	S	1	$1,520	193	108.68	$ 84.01	1,134.31

Using the percentage method, find the federal income tax withheld for each of the following employees. The pay period is weekly.

	Name	Marital Status	Exemptions	Salary	Federal Income Tax	FICA	Other Deductions	Net Pay
35.	Young	S	2	$ 910	208.93	65.07	$61.88	574.12

FIT

$910.00
− 73.08 Exemption
$836.92
− 532.00
$304.92 Excess
× 35%
$106.72
+ 102.21
$208.93 FIT amount

Section

$36.54
× 2
$73.08 Exemption allowance

continued

Assignment 8.2 *continued*

36. Zabeliski   S   1 $ 530   91.42   37.90 $43.75   356.93
FIT   Section

```
  $530.00
-  36.54 Exemption
  $493.46
- 335.00
  $158.46 Excess
×    28%
  $ 44.3688
+   47.05
  $ 91.4188 = $91.42 FIT amount
```

37. Zachary   M   3 $ 509   52.23   36.39 $56.03   364.35
FIT   Section

```
  $509.00              $  36.54
- 109.62 Exemption   ×       3
  $399.38              $109.62 Exemption allowance
-  93.00
  $306.38 Excess
×    15%
  $ 45.957
+   6.27
  $ 52.227 = $52.23 FIT amount
```

38. Zeller   S   0 $1,340   395.13   95.81 $65.18   783.88
FIT   Section

```
  $1340
- 1051
  $ 289 Excess
× 38.5%
  $ 111.265
+ 283.86
  $ 395.125 = $395.13 FIT amount
```

39. Zilko   M   2 $1,800   459.05   128.70 $67.04   1,145.21
FIT   Section

```
  $1800.00             $36.54
-  73.08 Exemption   ×     2
  $1726.92             $73.08 Exemption allowance
- 901.00
  $ 825.92 Excess
×    35%
  $ 289.072
+  169.98
  $ 459.05 FIT amount
```

40. Zuber   M   4 $ 485   43.15   34.68 $33.73   373.44
FIT   Section

```
  $485.00              $  36.54
- 146.16 Exemption   ×       4
  $338.84              $146.16 Exemption allowance
-  93.00
  $245.84 Excess
×    15%
  $36.876
+   6.27
  $43.146 = $43.15 FIT amount
```

continued

Comprehensive Problems for Chapter 8

Payroll

1. The receptionist at Holiday Motel receives $5.00 an hour for regular pay, time and a half for overtime (nonholiday hours over 40), and double time for holidays. If he worked 43 hours and an additional 5 hours on a holiday this week, what is his gross pay?

   40 × $5.00 = $200.00 Regular
    3 × $7.50 =   22.50 Overtime
    5 × $10.00 = + 50.00 Holiday time
                 $272.50 Gross pay

   $272.50

2. Mrs. Crisp is the personnel manager at Associated Glass Company. She has a salaried position of $820 a week. Each week this month she has worked 48 hours. What is her gross pay at the end of the month? (Assume that this month had exactly four weeks.)

   $820 × 4 weeks = $3,280 Gross pay

   $3,280

3. Glenda Jackson is a salesperson at Millcreek Jewelers. She is paid $8.20 an hour, time and a half overtime, plus a commission of 2% of all sales. What did she earn during a week in which she worked 53 hours and her sales were $36,300?

      40 × $8.20 = $328.00 Regular
      13 × $12.30 =   159.90 Overtime
   $36,300 × 2% = + 726.00 Commission
                   $1,213.90 Gross pay

   $1,213.90

4. The machinist apprentice for Tower Manufacturing Co. is paid on a piecework basis. For each day, his quota pay for 20 units is $7.80 a unit. The bonus pay for all units produced over the quota is $8.20 a unit. Find his gross pay for the week if he produced the following number of units: Monday, 26; Tuesday, 28; Wednesday, 30; Thursday, 29; and Friday, 32.

   100 × $7.80 = $780 Quota pay   6 + 8 + 10 + 9 + 12 = 45 bonus units
    45 × $8.20 = + 369 Bonus pay
                $1,149 Gross pay

   $1,149

5. Melvin Larsen is employed as a marketing representative for Rice Footwear, Inc. He is paid on a graduated commission basis of 2% on the first $40,000 sales, and 3% on sales over $40,000. During the month of August, he had sales of $178,000. What was his commission?

     178,000 Total sales
   − 40,000 @ 2% commission
     138,000 @ 3% commission

    $40,000 × 2% = $ 800
   $138,000 × 3% = 4,140
                 $4,940 Gross pay

   $4,940

continued

Comprehensive Problems *continued*

6. Four Corners Drapery Service pays time and a half for hours over 8 per day and double time for Saturday and Sunday hours. Morgan's time card reads as follows: Monday, 7 hours; Tuesday, 9.5 hours; Wednesday, 8 hours; Thursday, 7.5 hours; Friday, 9 hours; Saturday, 4.5 hours. The hourly rate is $9.10. What is his gross pay?

   38.5 × $9.10 = $350.35 Regular
   2.5 × $13.65 =   34.13 Overtime
   4.5 × $18.20 =   81.90 Double time
                  $466.38 Gross pay

   $466.38

7. Craig Electronics Company pays according to piecework assembled. The scale is as follows:

For the first 80 units	$0.90 a unit
81 to 120 units	$1.25 a unit
121 to 150 units	$1.52 a unit
151 to 180 units	$1.79 a unit
181 to 205 units	$2.02 a unit

   If Kit Saunders work part-time and assembled 202 units, what is her gross pay?

   80 × $ .90 = $ 72.00
   40 × $1.25 =   50.00
   30 × $1.52 =   45.60
   30 × $1.79 =   53.70
   22 × $2.02 = + 44.44
   202 units $265.74 Gross pay

   $265.74

8. Marion Nichols is married and entitled to 3 exemptions. She receives an annual salary of $22,776. Other deductions amount to $41.03 a week. If she is paid on a weekly basis, what are her FICA tax, federal income tax (using the wage-bracket method), and net pay for the week?

   22,776 ÷ 52 = $438 Weekly gross pay
   438 × 7.15% = $31.317 = $31.32 FICA

     $438.00
   −   41.00 FIT (Married, weekly, 3 exemptions)
     $397.00
   −   31.32 FICA
     $365.68
   −   41.03 Other deductions
     $324.65 Net pay

   $324.65

9. Fred Cold works for Star Trophy Company. He is paid weekly at an hourly rate of $11.90, with time-and-a-half pay over 40 hours. He worked a total of 47 hours last week. He is single and has claimed 2 exemptions. What are his FICA tax and federal income taxes (using the percentage method)? If $40 is deducted for medical insurance, $18.20 for optional life insurance, and $9.80 for disability insurance, what is his net pay?

   40 × $11.90 = $476.00
    7 × $17.85 = + 124.95
                  $600.95 Gross pay

continued

Comprehensive Problems *continued*

```
  $600.95              $36.54
-  73.08  Exemption  ×    2
  $527.87             $73.08  Exemption allowance
-  335.00
  $192.87  Excess
×    28%
  $ 54.0036
+   47.05
  $101.0536 = $101.05  FIT
```

$600.95 × 7.15% = $42.9679 = $42.97 FICA

```
  $600.95  Gross pay
   101.05  FIT
    42.97  FICA
    40.00  Medical
    18.20  Life
-    9.80  Disability
  $388.93  Net pay
```
$388.93

10. Linda McKinley works on a salary-plus-commission basis. She is paid monthly and receives a base salary of $400 a month and a commission of 6% on sales. She is single and claims 1 exemption. Her sales amounted to $41,000. Find each of the following.

   a) FICA, FIT (using the wage-bracket method) taxes, and net pay

```
   $41,000 × 6% =  $2,460  Commission
                +    400  Base pay
                  $2,860  Gross pay
   $2,860.00
      581.00  FIT (single, monthly, 1 exemption)
-     204.49  FICA (2860 × 7.15%)
   $2,074.51  Net pay
```
a) $204.49, FICA; $581, FIT; $2,074.51, net

   b) FICA, FIT (using the percentage method) taxes, and net pay

```
   $2,860.00
-     158.33  Exemption allowance
   $2701.67
-  2303.00
   $ 398.67  Excess
×       35%
   $ 139.5345
+    442.00
   $581.5345 = $581.53  FIT

   $2,860.00
      581.53  FIT
-     204.49  FICA
   $2,073.98  Net pay
```
b) $204.49, FICA; $581.53, FIT; $2,073.98, net

continued

Case 1

You are a management consultant currently working with Knoll's Assembly Company, which deals with assembling stereo receivers, tuners, and turntables. The company has been having a problem with the motivation and productivity of its workers. They are paid at an hourly rate of $8.00 with time-and-a-half overtime after 40 hours a week. Prepare a list of items you would need to study before making a recommendation.

Case 2

The Happy Hamburger, a fast-food restaurant, pays its employees on a monthly basis. For each month figure the FICA tax and the income tax withheld using the wage-bracket method. Next fill in the information for the Employer's Quarterly Tax Return.

Name	Marital Status	Exemptions	Wages January	Wages February	Wages March
Eden	M	4	$2,960	$3,123	$3,080
Gray	S	0	$2,146	$1,950	$2,190
La Plante	S	1	$1,870	$1,625	$1,841
Rowan	M	3	$3,880	$3,614	$3,752
Chen	S	2	$1,960	$1,843	$1,856

EMPLOYER'S QUARTERLY TAX RETURN

Number of employees _____

Total taxable wages _____

Income tax withheld _____

FICA taxes (employer and employee) _____

Total taxes _____

Key Terms

Bonus rate
Exemption allowance
Federal income tax
Payroll deductions
Piecework pay

Salary
Salary plus commission
Social security tax
Straight commission
Wages

Key Concepts

- Methods of paying employees include the following.

    Salary: A fixed payment, usually in monthly or annual terms.

    Wages: Payment according to the amount of time spent on the job, usually per hour.

Piecework: Payment based on the number of units prouced.

Commission: Payment based on sales or amount of business generated, usually a percent.

- Payroll deduction = Employee's gross earnings − Net earnings or take-home pay.
- The amount of federal income tax withheld depends on four factors: gross earnings, marital status, number of exemptions, and pay period. This tax is also called a FIT tax.
- Employers can use either of two methods in figuring income tax withheld: the wage-bracket method and the percentage method.
- Another payroll deduction, the social security tax, is based on a percent of an employee's gross wages. This tax is also known as FICA tax.
- *Circular E,* printed by the Internal Revenue Service, contains tables to be used for the federal income tax and social security tax.

9
Interest

Business Takes a Positive Approach

TOYS 'Я' US

There are countless outlets for toys these days, ranging from home parties to local supermarkets and drugstores. One retailer has managed to permeate the marketplace with a different approach, revolutionizing the toy industry in the process. Toys 'Я' Us offers low prices on over 18,000 items for the adult as well as for the child. The company is known for its self-service, free-standing, warehouse-style stores. Its outlets are characterized by bright lighting, long aisles, and supermarket-type checkout counters. The company's private label goods have proven to be very profitable. Interestingly enough, though known as a toy discount house, Toys 'Я' Us maintains a policy of never holding sales. Encouraged by the high performance of its toy outlets, the company has arranged financing and opened a sister chain of apparel stores called Kids 'Я' Us. Expansion does not stop there, however. Toys 'Я' Us has begun successfully opening stores in several foreign countries including West Germany, France, Italy, and Japan. Revenues and profits are increasing steadily. The outlook for the future is encouraging for shoppers and investors alike.

> **Learning Objectives**
>
> After reading and studying this chapter and working the problems, you will be able to:
>
> - Compute simple ordinary interest using either 30-day month time or exact time.
> - Calculate simple exact interest at exact time.
> - Find principal, rate, or time, when the amount of interest earned is given.
> - Determine compound interest either mechanically or by using a compound-interest table.

Interest is a fee charged for the use of money. If a business or an individual borrows some amount, the lending institution charges a percentage of what is borrowed for the privilege of using its funds. At the end of an agreed-upon period of time, both the amount borrowed and the amount of the interest must be repaid to the lender.

Similarly, if money is invested or placed in a savings account, the depositor is entitled to receive interest because the depositor is allowing the funds to be used by someone else.

The **principal** is the amount of money loaned or borrowed. It is the basis on which interest is calculated. The **interest rate** is the percent of interest charged or earned. This rate is figured on an annual, or **per annum,** basis unless otherwise stated.

The interest calculation is:

$$\text{Principal} \times \text{Interest Rate} \times \text{Time} = \text{Interest}$$

> **HOW THE PERCENTAGE FORMULA APPLIES**
>
> Principal = Base
> Interest Rate = Rate
> Interest = Percentage
>
> The time dimension is included in the interest calculation because loans are made over a specific period of days, months, or years. The person or business doing the borrowing must pay interest for the entire time that the money is in use.
>
> Principal × Rate × Time = Interest
> Base × Rate   = Percentage

9.1 Simple Interest

In the case of **simple interest,** which is generally applied to loans of a year or less, the rate is applied only to the principal.

Example 1 Baylor Jones and Company borrows $1,200 for one year at an interest rate of 12%. What amount of interest will the company have to pay at the end of the time period?

Step 1 Set up the formula, identifying its elements.

Principal = $1,200
Rate = 12%
Time = 1 year

Principal × Rate × Time = Interest
$1,200 × 12% × 1 =

Step 2 Multiply.

$$\begin{array}{r}\$1{,}200 \\ \times \quad .12 \\ \hline \$144\end{array}$$

Answer The amount of simple interest is $144.

NOTE: When interest is figured for a one year period, the time factor does not affect the calculation and may be disregarded.

Calculate interest on loans of less than one year by using a fraction of the full year as the time factor. If the time is expressed in months, use a denominator of 12 for the number of months.

Example 2 Petula Kirk borrowed $1,200 to help finance her plastic dinnerware franchise. She took the loan for 6 months at an interest rate of 12%. What amount of interest did she owe at the end of the 6 months?

Step 1 Set up the formula, using 12 months as the base in the time factor.

Principal × Rate × Time = Interest
$1,200 × .12 × $\frac{6}{12}$ =

Step 2 Multiply.

$$\frac{\$1{,}200 \times .12 \times 6}{12} = \$72$$

Answer The amount of interest for 6 months is $72.

Example 3 Jerry Donnelly loans $1,200 to a local business for 7 months. He asks 12% interest. What amount will he receive at the end of the 7 months?

Step 1 Set up the formula.

P × R × T = I
$1,200 × .12 × $\frac{7}{12}$ =

Step 2 Multiply.

$$\frac{\$1{,}200 \times .12 \times 7}{12} = \$84$$

Step 3 Add the amount of interest to the principal to find the total he will receive.

$$\begin{array}{r}\$1{,}200 \\ + \ \$ \quad 84 \\ \hline \$1{,}284\end{array}$$

Answer The amount received after 7 months is $1,284.

NOTE: In performing interest calculations, note what you are asked to find. You may be requested to state the amount of interest due or the total due, as in the example above. This total is called the **maturity value.**

Self-Check

Calculate each of the following.

1. Principal = $300
   Rate = 9%
   Time = 1 year
   Amount of interest = _____

2. Principal = $726
   Rate   = 9.75%
   Time   = 3 months
   Amount of interest =

3. Daisy Quantro, president of La Mode Hosiery, Inc., must borrow $42,568 to meet her monthly payroll. She arranges a loan at 12.3% for 1 month. How much must she pay back?

ANSWERS 1. $27   2. $17.70   3. $43,004.32

NAME _____ DATE _____ SECTION _____

Assignment 9.1

Interest

Round your answers to the nearest cent.

As an employee of Shorecrest Savings and Loan, find the amount of interest and the maturity value for each of the following loans.

	Principal	Rate	Time	Interest	Maturity Value	
1.	$ 650.00	12%	1 year	$ 78.00	$ 728	$650 × .12 × 1 = $78
2.	$1,482.29	11%	1 year	163.05	1,645.34	$1,482.29 × .11 × 1 = $163.0519
3.	$ 763.40	12.5%	1 year	95.43	858.83	$763.40 × .125 × 1 = $95.425
4.	$2,425.36	$11\tfrac{3}{4}$%	1 year	284.98	2,710.34	$2,425.36 × .1175 × 1 = $284.9798
5.	$3,281.44	$13\tfrac{1}{4}$%	1 year	434.79	3,716.23	$3,281.44 × .1325 × 1 = $434.7908
6.	$1,964.28	$12\tfrac{3}{4}$%	1 year	250.45	2214.73	$1,964.28 × .1275 × 1 = $250.4457

7. Valeria Monti, a loan officer at Bardell's Bank, must process a 1-year loan of $3,726 that carries an interest rate of $10\tfrac{3}{4}$%.

   a) What is the amount of interest due?

   $3,726 × .1075 × 1 = $400.545
   = $400.55 Interest due

   $400.55 interest due

   b) What is the maturity value of the loan?

   $3,726.00 Amount of loan
   + 400.55 Interest due
   $4,126.55 Maturity value

   $4,126.55 maturity value of loan

8. You receive an unexpected inheritance of $10,500 from your Aunt Gertrude. If you invest it in a savings certificate paying $6\tfrac{3}{4}$% interest, how much will your inheritance be worth at the end of 6 months?

   $10,500.00 Inheritance
   + 354.38 Interest earned
   $10,854.38 Worth at end 6 months

   $$\frac{10,500 \times .0675 \times 1}{2} = \frac{708.75}{2} = 354.375$$

   $10,854.38 worth of inheritance at end of 6 months

Calculate the interest and the maturity value for each of the following loans.

	Principal	Rate	Time	Interest	Maturity Value	
9.	$ 300.00	12%	2 months	$ 6.00	$ 306	9. $\dfrac{300 \times .12 \times 1}{6} = \$6$
10.	$ 780.00	13%	7 months	59.15	839.15	10. $\dfrac{780 \times .13 \times 7}{12} = \$59.15$
11.	$ 624.56	11.25%	10 months	58.55	683.11	11. $\dfrac{624.56 \times .1125 \times 5}{6} = \$58.55$

continued

Assignment 9.1 continued

	Principal	Rate	Time	Interest	Maturity Value	
12.	$9,726.41	9¾%	8 months	632.22	1,0358.63	12. $\dfrac{9{,}726.41 \times .0975 \times 2}{3}$ = $632.21663

Daniel Young lends money to several business associates. Find the amount of interest due him and the maturity value of each of the following loans.

	Principal	Rate	Time	Interest	Maturity Value
13.	$ 700.00	10%	6 months	$ 35.00	$ 735
14.	$ 450.00	12%	3 months	13.50	463.50
15.	$ 518.00	14%	4 months	24.17	542.17
16.	$ 650.00	12½%	9 months	60.94	710.94
17.	$ 128.65	16⅔%	5 months	8.93	137.58
18.	$ 937.50	13¾%	1 month	10.74	948.24
19.	$1,976.42	12.25%	11 months	221.94	2,198.36

20. Raul McGuire, owner of Midway Developments, borrowed $1,750 for 4 months at 12.5% interest. What was the total amount of interest he owed at the end of the 4 months?

$\dfrac{1750 \times .125 \times 4}{12}$ = 72.9166

$72.92 amount of interest owed

356 Chapter 9

9.2 Ordinary Interest, 30-Day Month Time

Often in your calculations, you must show the time as a fraction in which the numerator represents the number of days the money is in use and the denominator represents the number of days in a full year. You may want to reduce this fraction to lowest terms for convenience in calculating.

One way of figuring interest, called **ordinary interest,** uses 360 to represent the number of days in the year. This is called the business, or **commercial, year.** Each month in it is considered to have 30 days, regardless of the number of days it actually has. The business year is most often used for long-term loans because it simplifies calculation. However, now that computers are in general use, the ordinary-interest method is not as commonly used as it once was.

To figure ordinary interest, 30-day month time:

Step 1   Count the number of months between the one when the loan is made and the month when the loan matures.

Step 2   Multiply this number of months by 30.

Step 3   Determine the difference between the day of the month the loan was made and the day of the month the loan is due. Add this difference to or subtract it from the total found in step 2.

Step 4   Use this figure as the numerator over 360 in your interest calcualtion.

Example 1   On July 6, Mandy DuPrey obtains a business loan of $950 from Fidelity Bank. The interest rate is 9%, and repayment is due on October 16 of the same year. What amount of ordinary interest will Mandy pay?

Step 1   Count the number of months between July 6 and October 6.   3 months

Step 2   Multiply by the standardized 30-day month.

$$\begin{array}{r} 30 \\ \times\ 3 \\ \hline 90\ \text{days} \end{array}$$

Step 3   Determine the number of days between October 6 and October 16. Add this to the number of days found in step 2.

$$\begin{array}{r} 16 \\ -\ 6 \\ \hline 10\ \text{days} \end{array} \qquad \begin{array}{r} 90\ \text{days} \\ +\ 10\ \text{days} \\ \hline 100\ \text{days} \end{array}$$

Step 4   Place this figure over the business year. $\dfrac{100}{360}$

Step 5   Perform the interest calculation. $\$950 \times .09 \times \dfrac{100}{360} = \$23.75$

Answer   The ordinary interest due is $23.75.

Example 2   Joseph Chu took out a loan of $950 on June 25, which is due on August 14 of the same year. If the ordinary-interest rate is 9%, how much interest will Joseph owe?

Step 1   Count the number of months between June 25 and August 25.   2 months

Step 2   Multiply by 30.

$$\begin{array}{r} 30 \\ \times\ 2 \\ \hline 60\ \text{days} \end{array}$$

Step 3   Determine the number of days between August 25 and August 14. Subtract this from the number of days found in step 2.

$$\begin{array}{r} 25 \\ -\ 14 \\ \hline 11\ \text{days} \end{array} \qquad \begin{array}{r} 60 \\ -\ 11 \\ \hline 49\ \text{days} \end{array}$$

Step 4 Place the result over 360. $\frac{49}{360}$

Step 5 Proceed with the interest calculation, rounding the answer to the nearest cent. $950 \times .09 \times \frac{49}{360} = \$11.6375$

Answer The ordinary interest due is $11.64.

Self-Check

Calculate the ordinary interest, using 30-day month time. Round the result to the nearest cent.

1. Principal = $750
   Rate = $9\frac{1}{2}\%$
   Time = March 1 to April 1 of the same year
   Amount of interest = _____

2. Principal = $1,550
   Rate = 13%
   Time = July 28 to December 22 of the same year
   Amount of interest = _____

3. Barbara Sweet borrows $12,000 and agrees to pay $11\frac{1}{4}\%$ ordinary interest. The loan period is from April 15 to June 27 of the same year. How much must Barbara pay back at maturity? _____

ANSWERS 1. Time fraction = $\frac{30}{360}$; interest = $5.94   2. Time fraction = $\frac{144}{360}$; interest = $80.60   3. $12,270

NAME   DATE   SECTION

Assignment 9.2

Interest

Use ordinary interest, 30-day month time. Round the answers to the nearest cent.

Hank Boladaro, an officer at Prudential Trust and Savings, is processing several loans. Help him by finding the number of days, interest due, and maturity value for each of the following.

	Principal	Rate	Time Period	Number of Days	Interest Due	Maturity Value
1.	$600.00	9%	August 13–October 7	54	$8.10	$608.10
2.	$340.00	13%	January 9–February 9	30	3.68	343.68
3.	$294.60	$16\frac{1}{2}$%	March 24–May 9	45	6.08	300.68
4.	$589.42	12.8%	April 14–June 26	72	15.09	604.51
5.	$4,400.00	$8\frac{1}{3}$%	October 10–January 27	107	108.98	4,508.98
6.	$7,500.00	$9\frac{3}{5}$%	July 28–December 23	145	290	7,790

The space below is provided to work problems 1 to 6.

1.   30   13 Aug   60
   × 2 months   − 7 Aug   − 6
   ─────────   ─────────   ─────────
   60 days   6 days   54 days total

   $\frac{600}{1} \times \frac{9}{100} \times \frac{54}{360} = \frac{81}{10} = \$8.10$

2. 1 month = 30 days

   $\frac{340}{1} \times \frac{13}{100} \times \frac{1}{12} = \frac{221}{60} = \$3.68\overline{3}$

3.   30   24   60
   × 2 months   − 9   − 15
   ─────────   ─────────   ─────────
   60 days   15 days   45 days total

   $\frac{294.60}{1} \times .165 \times \frac{45}{360} = \$6.0761$

4.   30   26   60
   × 2 months   − 14   + 12
   ─────────   ─────────   ─────────
   60 days   12 days   72 days

   $\frac{589.42}{1} \times .128 \times \frac{72}{360} = \$15.0891$

5.   30   27   90
   × 3 months   − 10   + 17
   ─────────   ─────────   ─────────
   90 days   17   107 days total

   $\frac{4,400}{1} \times \frac{1}{12} \times \frac{107}{360} = \frac{2942.5}{27} = \$108.981$

6.   30   28   150
   × 5 months   − 23   − 5
   ─────────   ─────────   ─────────
   150 days   5   145 days total

   $\frac{7500}{1} \times .096 \times \frac{145}{360} = \$290$

7. Ann Muldina, an accountant, borrowed $15,000 on May 10, agreeing to pay 14% ordinary interest. She paid off her obligation on August 24.

continued

Assignment 9.2 continued

a) Find the interest Ann owed.

```
    30              24           90
  ×  3 months    − 10          + 14
    90 days        14          104 days total
```

$$\frac{\cancel{15{,}000}^{150\ 15}}{1} \times \frac{14}{\cancel{100}} \times \frac{104}{\cancel{360}_{36}} = 606.666$$

$606.67 interest owed

b) Find the maturity value of her loan.

```
  $15,000.00  Principal
+     606.67  Interest
  $15,606.67  Maturity value
```

$15,606.67 maturity value

Find the number of days for which money is loaned and calculate the ordinary interest and maturity value of each of these loans; all of them have a principal of $11,400.

	Rate	Time	Number of Days	Interest Due	Maturity Value
8.	10%	June 6–August 23	77	$ 243.83	$ 11,643.83
9.	11.5%	January 4–December 31	357	1,300.08	12,700.08
10.	9.3%	July 1–November 3	122	359.29	11,759.29
11.	12.4%	February 15–May 16	91	357.33	11,757.33
12.	13¼%	March 15–October 10	205	860.15	12,260.15
13.	12⅗%	April 1–December 15	254	1,013.46	12,413.46

8.
```
    30            23         60
  × 2 months    −  6       + 17
    60 days       17         77 days total
```
$$\frac{\cancel{11{,}400}^{285}}{1} \times .10 \times \frac{77}{\cancel{360}_9} = 243.833 = \$243.83 \text{ interest}$$
```
  $11,400.00  Loan
+    243.83  Interest
  $11,643.83  Maturity value
```

9.
```
    11 months     31        330
  ×     30      −  4       + 27
    330 days      27        357 days total
```
$$\frac{\cancel{11{,}400}^{285}}{1} \times .115 \times \frac{357}{\cancel{360}_9} = 1{,}300.075 = \$1{,}300.08 \text{ interest}$$
```
  $11,400.00  Loan
+  1,300.08  Interest
  $12,700.08  Maturity value
```

10.
```
    30            3         120
  × 4 months    − 1       +   2
    120 days      2         122 days total
```
$$\frac{\cancel{11{,}400}^{285}}{1} \times .093 \times \frac{122}{\cancel{360}_9} = \$359.29 \text{ interest}$$
```
  $11,400.00  Loan
+    359.29  Interest
  $11,759.29  Maturity value
```

11.
```
    30            16         90
  × 3 months    − 15       +  1
    90 days       1          91 days total
```
$$\frac{\cancel{11{,}400}^{285}}{1} \times .124 \times \frac{91}{\cancel{360}_9} = 357.3266 = \$357.33 \text{ interest}$$
```
  $11,400.00  Loan
+    357.33  Interest
  $11,757.33  Maturity value
```

12.
```
    30            15        210
  × 7 months    − 10      −   5
    210 days      5         205 days total
```
$$\frac{\cancel{11{,}400}^{285}}{1} \times .1325 \times \frac{205}{\cancel{360}_9} = 860.14583 = \$860.15 \text{ interest}$$
```
  $11,400.00  Loan
+    860.15  Interest
  $12,260.15  Maturity value
```

13.
```
    30            15        240
  × 8 months    −  1      + 14
    240 days      14        254 days total
```
$$\frac{\cancel{11{,}400}^{285}}{1} \times .126 \times \frac{254}{\cancel{360}_9} = \$1{,}013.46 \text{ interest}$$
```
  $11,400.00  Loan
+  1,013.46  Interest
  $12,413.46  Maturity value
```

9.3 Exact Time

Since computers are now in general use, many interest transactions today involve **exact time.** Here, the actual number of days during which the money is in use is counted. To do this, you must know the number of days in each calendar month. Each month has the same number of days every year, except for February. Every fourth year, the **leap year,** February has 29 days instead of 28. To decide whether or not you are dealing with a leap year, divide the last two digits of the year by four. If the answer comes out even, it is a leap year: 1988, for instance is a leap year; 1989 and 1990 are not. In working the problems in this text, assume that February has 28 days.

The months and the number of days in each of them are listed below. If you do not already know how many days are in each month, you will want to take time to learn this now.

January—31	May—31	September—30
February—28/29	June—30	October—31
March—31	July—31	November—30
April—30	August—31	December—31

To compute exact time:

Step 1 Subtract the date the loan is made from the number of days in that particular month.

Step 2 Total the number of days in each month up to the one when the loan matures. Add this total to the number of days found in step 1.

Step 3 Add to this total the day of the month in which the loan matures.

Example 1 Federal Savings and Loan lends Perry Browntree some money for his auto repair company on July 6. The loan matures on the following October 16. What is the exact number of days of Perry's loan?

Step 1 Subtract the date the loan is made from the number of days in the month. The money is in use for 25 days in the month of July.

July has 31 days
   31 No. of days
 − 6 Date of loan
   25 days

Step 2 Total the number of days in the months up to the month of maturity, adding the number of days found in step 1.

August has   31 days
September has + 30 days
               61 days
             + 25 days in July
               86 days

Step 3 Add to this the day the loan matures.

   86 days
 + 16 th of October
  102 days

Answer The duration of Perry's loan is 102 days.

Self-Check

Calculate the exact number of days.

1. Date of loan = January 4
   Date due   = March 16

2. Date of loan = May 5
   Date due   = November 23

Interest 361

3. Marge Atkinson borrows money, agreeing to pay exact interest. If she takes the loan on November 15 and pays it back on December 28, how many days has she had the use of the money?

ANSWERS   1.   31 days in January
              − 4 th of January
              ─────────────────
               27 days
               28 days in February
              + 16 th of March
              ─────────────────
               71 days total

2. 202 days   3. 43 days

SIX-PERCENT, SIXTY-DAY METHOD OF INTEREST

You may want to know about the *six-percent, sixty-day method*, once a commonly used way of figuring simple interest. Since the introduction of electronic calculators, this technique is not used nearly as often as in the past. However, in the world of business, you will find yourself working with people who once used this shortcut method every day. It is important that you know about it as a part of your business background and for purposes of estimating.

Sixty days is one-sixth of the business year.

$$\frac{60}{360} = \frac{1}{6}$$

If a loan is made at 6% it is the same as making it at 1% ordinary interest for 60 days. We can show this by cancellation.

$$\frac{1}{\cancel{6}} \times \frac{\cancel{6}}{100} = \frac{1}{100} = .01 = 1\%$$

You can figure interest at 6% for a period of 60 days merely by moving the decimal point in the principal two places to the left, dividing it by .01. (See Section 1.4.)

NAME   DATE   SECTION

Assignment 9.3

Interest

You are a new employee at Bender Bank and Trust. Your supervisor gives you the following dates, asking you to calculate the exact number of days of each loan.

Date of Loan	Date Due	Exact Number of Days
1. September 22	December 4	73
2. July 14	November 14	123
3. March 5	April 6	32
4. June 14	September 18	96
5. January 2	November 29	331
6. February 14	December 30	319
7. April 1	May 23	52
8. August 6	October 4	59
9. May 24	July 6	43
10. October 31	April 15	166

```
1.    30  Sept
    - 22  date of loan
       8  Sept
      31  Oct
      30  Nov
     4th  Dec date due
      73  days exact

2.    31  July
    - 14  date of loan
      17  July
      31  Aug
      30  Sept
      31  Oct
    14th  Nov date due
     123  days exact

3.    31  March
    -  5  date of loan
      26  March
     6th  April date due
      32  days exact

4.    30  June
    - 14  date of loan
      16  June
      31  July
      31  Aug
    18th  Sept date due
      96  days exact

5.    31  Jan
    -  2  date of loan
      29  Jan
      28  Feb
      31  March
      30  April
      31  May
      30  June
      31  July
      31  Aug
      30  Sept
      31  Oct
    29th  Nov date due
     331  days exact

6.    28  Feb
    - 14  date of loan
      14  Feb
      31  March
      30  April
      31  May
      30  June
      31  July
      31  Aug
      30  Sept
      31  Oct
      30  Nov
    30th  Dec date due
     319  days exact

7.    30  April
    -  1  date of loan
      29  April
      23  May date due
      52  days exact

8.    31  Aug
    -  6  date of loan
      25  Aug
      30  Sept
     4th  Oct date due
      59  days exact

9.    31  May
    - 24  date of loan
       7  May
      30  June
     6th  July date due
      43  days exact

10.   31  Oct
    - 31  date of loan
       0  Oct
      30  Nov
      31  Dec
      31  Jan
      28  Feb
      31  March
    15th  April date due
     166  days exact
```

Interest 363

9.4 Exact Interest, Exact Time and Ordinary Interest, Exact Time

Calculating Exact Interest, Exact Time

This method of calculating interest is used for most government loans. In the time fraction, the exact number of days in the loan period is used as a numerator over the actual number of days in the year, 365, except for leap year, which has 366 days. In working the problems in this text, assume that every year has 365 days.

Example 1   Brenda McQueen qualifies for a small-business loan to open her beachwear shop. The loan is for $3,500, and the interest rate is 8%. The time period is from July 1 to November 28 of the same year, at terms of exact interest, exact time. Find the amount of interest Brenda has to pay, rounded to the nearest cent.

Step 1   Find the exact number of days.

```
   31 days in July
-   1 st of July
   30 days
   31 days in August
   30 days in September
   31 days in October
+  28 th of November
  150 days
```

Step 2   Place the number of days over 365, the actual number of days in the year.

$$\frac{150}{365}$$

Step 3   Set up the formula and multiply.

$$\$3{,}500 \times 0.08 \times \frac{150}{365} = \$115.06849$$

Answer   The amount of interest to be paid is $115.07, rounded to the nearest cent.

Calculating Ordinary Interest, Exact Time

The interest on business loans is often figured using the exact number of days in the loan period as a numerator over 360 days. This sometimes simplifies calculation. The smaller denominator also works to the financial advantage of the lender. This method of figuring interest is often used in discounting notes. (See Section 10.2.)

Example 2   To remodel his place of business, Miles Jones takes out a loan at Farmington Bank and Trust for $3,500 at an interest rate of 8%. The time period is July 1 to November 28, and the terms are ordinary interest, exact time. How much interest will Miles owe at the end of the time period?

Step 1   Find the exact number of days. (This calculation was shown in Example 1.)   150 days

Step 2   Place the number of days over 360, the number of days in the business or commercial year.

$$\frac{150}{360}$$

Step 3   Multiply, using the interest formula.

$$P \times R \times T = I$$
$$\$3{,}500 \times 0.08 \times \frac{150}{360} = \$116.66\overline{6}$$

Answer   The amount of interest due is $116.67.

Self-Check

1. Morris Stern, an officer of a government agency, approves a loan of $4,000 at an interest rate of 10%. The terms are exact interest, exact time, and the time period is July 17 to October 2. What is the amount of interest due at maturity, rounded to the nearest cent?

2. Acom Bank, where you are employed, approves a loan for $6,200, ordinary interest, exact time. The loan is to run from January 3 to March 6, and the rate of interest is $13\frac{1}{2}\%$. What amount will the borrower pay back at maturity?

ANSWERS

1.
```
  31  days in July
-  17  th of July
  14  days
  31  days in august
  30  days in September
+  2  nd of October
  77  days
```

Interest = $84.38

2.
```
  $6,200.00
+ $  144.15
  $6,344.15
```

HOW DOES YOUR MONEY GROW?

Compound interest is sometimes called the magic of the banking world. Put a small amount of cash into an interest-earning account and leave it there. Over time, it doubles, triples, and quadruples, building on itself. To find out how many years it will take to double your money in an interest-earning account, just divide 72 by the particular interest rate at which your money is invested. For example, suppose you are saving at 6%. Since

$$\frac{72}{6} = 12,$$

you can see that your money will double in 12 years. Invested at 5%, it will double in 14.4 years, or a little less than 14 years and 5 months.

Assignment 9.4

Interest

Round your answers to the nearest cent.

Reggie Popov, who works in a federal disaster aid office, must calculate interest due on short-term, low-interest loans granted to victims of a volcanic eruption in the state of Washington. Assuming an interest rate of 4.5%, find the number of days in each loan, and figure the interest due and the maturity value.

	Principal	Time	Number of Days	Interest	Maturity Value		
1.	$ 500	January 4–April 1	$ 87	$ 5.36	$ 505.36	1. $500 × .045 × $\frac{87}{365}$	= $5.36030136
2.	726	February 8–March 30	50	4.48	730.48	2. $726 × .045 × $\frac{10}{73}$	= $4.4753424
3.	8,422	April 6–December 31	269	279.31	8,701.31	3. $8,422 × .045 × $\frac{269}{365}$	= $279.31043
4.	6,871	June 12–October 2	112	94.88	6,965.88	4. $6,871 × .045 × $\frac{112}{365}$	= $94.876273
5.	5,928	May 16–August 30	106	77.47	6,005.47	5. $5,928 × .045 × $\frac{106}{365}$	= $77.470027

6. Constance Barton miscalculated and underpaid her federal income tax by $285 on April 15. Finding the error on May 10, she immediately sent a check for the amount of her error plus 12%, figured at exact interest, exact time. What was the amount of her check?

    30 April
  − 15
    15 April
  + 10 May
    25 days

285 × .12 × $\frac{25}{365}$ = 2.3424657

= $2.34 interest   **$287.34 amount of check**

$285.00 Underpayment
    2.34 Interest
$287.34 Amount of check

7. Reid Bandanhower mistakenly paid $2,968 in federal income tax on April 15, rather than $3,864, the amount actually due. On August 1, he sent a check for the difference, including 12% interest, figured at exact interest, exact time. What was the total Reid sent?

  $3,864
− 2,968
$ 896 Underpayment

896 × .12 × $\frac{108}{365}$ = 31.814143

= $31.81 interest

$927.81 amount of check

$896.00 Underpayment
+ 31.81 Interest
$927.81 Amount of check

  30 April
− 15
  15 April
  31 May
  30 June
  31 July
   1 Aug
108 days exact

Barrington Twilp of McPhearson Bank and Trust approves loans to small businesses. Find the number of days in each loan and figure the interest due and the maturity values, assuming ordinary interest, exact time.

continued

Assignment 9.4 *continued*

	Principal	Rate	Time	Number of Days	Interest	Maturity Value
8.	$985.00	$9\frac{3}{4}$%	January 6–February 10	35	$9.34	$994.34

35 days $\quad$ $985 \times .0975 \times \dfrac{7}{72} = 9.3369791$
$\qquad\qquad\qquad\qquad\quad$ = $9.34 interest
$\qquad$ $985 + 9.34 = $994.34 maturity value

9.	$1,000.00	10.2%	March 5–June 15	102	28.90	1,028.90

102 days $\quad$ $1,000 \times .102 \times \dfrac{17}{60} = $28.90 interest
$\qquad$ $1,000 + 28.90 = $1,028.90 maturity value

10.	$1,500.00	8.6%	April 1–July 10	100	35.83	1,535.83

100 days $\quad$ $1,500 \times 0.86 \times \dfrac{5}{18} = $35.83 interest
$\qquad$ $1,500 + 35.83 = $1,535.83 maturity value

11.	$5,280.00	9%	June 15–October 8	115	151.80	5,431.80

115 days $\quad$ $5,280 \times .09 \times \dfrac{23}{72} = $151.80 interest
$\qquad$ $5,280 + 151.80 = $5431.80 maturity value

12.	$3,385.00	11.2%	July 10–December 5	148	155.86	3,540.86

148 days $\quad$ $3,385 \times .112 \times \dfrac{37}{90} = 155.86044$
$\qquad\qquad\qquad\qquad\quad$ = $155.86 interest
$\qquad$ $3,385 + 155.86 = $3,540.86 maturity value

13.	$1,925.80	12%	January 16–May 20	124	79.60	2,005.40

124 days $\quad$ $1,925.80 \times .12 \times \dfrac{31}{90} = 79.599733$
$\qquad\qquad\qquad\qquad\quad$ = $79.60 interest
$\qquad$ $1,925.80 + 79.60 = $2,005.40 maturity value

14.	$2,328.00	11.5%	February 10–December 14	307	228.31	2,556.31

307 days $\quad$ $2,328 \times .115 \times \dfrac{307}{360} = 228.30566$
$\qquad\qquad\qquad\qquad\quad$ = $228.31 interest
$\qquad$ $2,328 + 228.31 = $2,556.31 maturity value

15.	$10,000.00	$12\frac{1}{2}$%	May 9–October 25	169	586.81	10,586.81

169 days $\quad$ $10,000 \times .125 \times \dfrac{169}{360} = 586.80555$
$\qquad\qquad\qquad\qquad\quad$ = $586.81 interest
$\qquad$ $10,000 + 586.81 = $10,586.81 maturity value

16.	$12,264.80	9.25%	August 11–November 30	111	349.80	12,614.60

111 days $\quad$ $12,264.80 \times .0925 \times \dfrac{111}{360} = 349.8023$
$\qquad\qquad\qquad\qquad\quad$ = $349.80 interest
$\qquad$ $12,264.80 + 349.80 = $12,614.60 maturity value

continued

| NAME | DATE | SECTION |

Assignment 9.4 *continued*

17. $26,942.72   10.3%   September 1–December 31   __121__   __932.74__   __27,875.46__

   121 days $26,942.72 × .103 × $\frac{121}{360}$ = 932.74197

   = $932.74 interest

   $26,942.72 × 932.74 = $27,875.46 maturity value

18. Peter Chan, a singer, is performing a benefit concert for the Chinese Benevolent Society. On May 1, he spends $860 on costumes, agreeing to pay the amount due plus 11% interest, figured by ordinary interest, exact time, on December 15, when he expects to receive a royalty check from sales of his first record album.

    a) How much interest will Peter owe?

    $860 × .11 × $\frac{57}{90}$ = 59.913$\overline{3}$

    = $59.91

    __$59.91__ interest owed

    b) What is the total that he must repay?

    $860.00
    + 59.91
    $919.91

    __$919.91__
    total amount owed

18a)   31 May
     − 1
        30 May
        30 June
        31 July
        31 Aug
        30 Sept
        31 Oct
        30 Nov
        15 Dec
       228 days exact

$\frac{228}{360} = \frac{57}{90}$ time

9.5 Principal, Rate, and Time Calculations

Thus far, we have discussed finding the amount of interest generated when principal, interest rate, and time are known. Sometimes the amount of interest earned and two of the other factors are known, and you are asked to find the third. The formulas for doing so are as follows.

$$\text{Principal} = \frac{\text{Interest}}{\text{Rate} \times \text{Time}} \qquad \text{Rate} = \frac{\text{Interest}}{\text{Principal} \times \text{Time}} \qquad \text{Time} = \frac{\text{Interest}}{\text{Principal} \times \text{Rate}}$$

HOW THE PERCENTAGE FORMULA APPLIES

As shown in Section 5.3, you can remember the relationships in the percentage formula by drawing a diagram. Substitute the terms needed in the interest calculation and proceed exactly as you did when using the percentage formula.

Percentage Diagram *Interest Diagram*

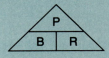

P = Percentage = Interest = I
B = Base = Principal = P
R = Rate = Interest Rate = R
Time = T

Finding Principal

Example 1 Marylou Carter put some money into her savings account and left it there for 90 days. At an ordinary interest rate of 9%, the money earned $22.50 during the time period. How much had Marylou put into the account?

Step 1 Identify the terms and set up the formula.

Rate = 9%
Time = 90 days
Interest = $22.50
Principal = ?

$$P = \frac{I}{RT}$$

$$\frac{\$22.50}{.09 \times \frac{90}{360}}$$

Step 2 Calculate the denominator.

$$.09 \times \frac{90}{360} = .0225$$

Step 3 Divide the numerator by the denominator.

$$\frac{\$22.50}{.0225} = \$1,000$$

Answer The principal that Marylou put into her savings account is $1,000.

This method can also be used in situations involving exact interest.

Example 2 Marylou invested in a new public relations business. The owner agreed to pay her exact interest of $10.00 figured at the rate of 10% if he could use her money for 73 days. How much did Marylou invest?

Interest 371

Step 1	Identify the terms and set up the formula.	$P = \dfrac{I}{RT}$
	Rate = 10% Time = 73 days, exact interest Interest = $10 Principal = ?	$\dfrac{\$10}{.1 \times \frac{73}{365}}$
Step 2	Calculate the denominator.	$.1 \times \dfrac{73}{365} = .02$
Step 3	Divide.	$\dfrac{10}{.02} = \$500$
Answer	The amount that Marylou invested was $500.	
	NOTE: Problems like those above can also be solved directly by using the simple-interest formula and solving for the unknown—in this case, the principal.	$\$10 = P \times .1 \times \dfrac{73}{365}$

Finding Rate

Example 3 Barry Dorkman put $1,000 into his savings account for 90 days. If the money earned $22.50 in ordinary interest, at what rate of interest did the account pay?

Step 1	Identify the terms and set up the formula.	$R = \dfrac{I}{PT}$
	Principal = $1,000 Time = 90 days, ordinary interest Interest = $22.50 Rate = ?	$\dfrac{\$22.50}{\$1,000 \times \frac{90}{360}}$
Step 2	Calculate the denominator.	$\$1,000 \times \dfrac{90}{360} = 250$
Step 3	Divide.	$\dfrac{22.5}{250} = .09$
Answer	The ordinary-interest rate on the account is 9%.	

Example 4 Barry invested $500 in Hankins Hobby Shop. Mr. Hankins agreed to pay him $10 in exact interest for 73 days' use of the money. What rate of interest did Hankins pay?

Step 1	Identify the terms and set up the formula.	$R = \dfrac{I}{PT}$
	Principal = $500 Time = 73 days, exact interest Interest = $10 Rate = ?	$\dfrac{\$10}{\$500 \times \frac{73}{365}}$
Step 2	Calculate the denominator.	$\dfrac{500 \times 73}{365} = \dfrac{36,500}{365} = 100$
Step 3	Divide.	$10.00 \div 100 = .1$
Answer	The rate of interest that Hankins paid was 10%.	
	NOTE: Calculations such as those above can also be viewed as follows:	$\$10 = \$500 \times R \times \dfrac{73}{365}$

Finding Time

Example 5 Benno Marcuse put $1,000 into a savings account that draws 9% ordinary interest. How many days must he keep the money in the account to gain $22.50 in interest?

Step 1 Identify the terms and set up the formula.

Principal = $1,000
Rate = 9%, ordinary interest
Interest = $22.50
Time = ?

$$T = \frac{I}{PR}$$

$$\frac{\$22.50}{\$1,000 \times .09}$$

Step 2 Calculate the denominator.

$1,000 \times .09 = 90$

Step 3 The interest over the denominator represents a fraction or decimal part of the year—in this case, 360 days. Reduce the fraction if convenient.

$$\frac{22.5}{90} = \frac{1}{4}$$

Step 4 Multiply by the number of days in the year to convert the result to days.

$$\frac{22.5}{90} \text{ of } 360 = \frac{1}{4} \times 360 = 90$$

Answer The number of days that the money must be kept in the account is 90.

Example 6 Benno invested $500 in a business that sells plants and seeds. He received $10 in exact interest at 10%. How many days did he have the money invested?

Step 1 Identify the terms and set up the formula.

Principal = $500
Rate = 10% exact interest
Interest = $10
Time = ?

$$T = \frac{I}{PR}$$

$$\frac{\$10}{\$500 \times .1}$$

Step 2 Calculate the denominator.

$500 \times .1 = 50$

Step 3 Set up the fraction and reduce it if convenient.

$$\frac{10}{50} = \frac{1}{5}$$

Step 4 Multiply to convert the fraction to days, remembering that you are working with exact interest.

$$\frac{1}{5} \times 365 = 73$$

Answer The number of days that Benno's money was invested is 73.

NOTE: Calculations such as those above can also be viewed as follows:

$$\$10 = \$500 \times .1 \times T$$

Self-Check

Find the missing factor.

	Principal	Rate	Time in Days	Interest
1.	$ _____	15% ordinary	40	$ 8.33
2.	$4,750	_____ ordinary	120	$190.00
3.	$ 540	8% ordinary	_____	$ 16.20

ANSWERS 1. $499.80   2. 12%   3. 135 days

Assignment 9.5

Interest

Truman Insurance Company hires you to work in its investment department. On your first day there, you are given an information form regarding current investments. Find the missing figures.

	Principal	Rate	Time in Days	Ordinary Interest
1.	$ __120__	5%	72	$ 1.20
2.	$ 500	__8%__	90	$ 10
3.	$2,750	12%	__21__	$ 19.25
4.	$__6,385.26__	9.5%	60	$101.10
5.	$6,500	11.5%	__84__	$174.42

1. $P = \dfrac{I}{RT}$

$\dfrac{1.20}{\frac{5}{100} \times \frac{72}{360}} = \dfrac{1.20}{\frac{\cancel{5}^1}{100} \times \dfrac{\cancel{72}^{\cancel{8}^1}}{\cancel{360}_{\cancel{46}_{\cancel{8}_1}}}} = \dfrac{1.20}{\frac{1}{100}}$

$1.20 \div \dfrac{1}{100}$

$1.20 \times \dfrac{100}{1} = \$120$ principal

check $I = P \times R \times T$

$\dfrac{\cancel{120}^6}{1} \times \dfrac{\cancel{5}^1}{\cancel{100}_1} \times \dfrac{\cancel{72}^1}{\cancel{360}_{5}} = \dfrac{6}{5} = \$1.20$ interest

2. $R = \dfrac{I}{PT} = \dfrac{10}{500 \times \frac{90}{360}}$

$500 \times \dfrac{90}{360} = \dfrac{500}{4} = \$125$

$10 \div 125 = .08 = 8\%$ rate

3. $T = \dfrac{I}{PR} = \dfrac{19.25}{2,750 \times \frac{12}{100}}$

$\cancel{2,750}^{110} \times \dfrac{\cancel{12}^3}{\cancel{100}_{\cancel{25}_1}} = \dfrac{330}{1} = \$330$

$\dfrac{19.25}{330} = .058\tfrac{1}{3}$

$.05833 \times 360 = 20.99$ days $= 21$ days

$.3944397 \times 360 = 141.998 = 142$ days

6. Bramwald Manufacturing Company charges exact interest on its customers' overdue accounts. Morton Retailing Inc., owed $5,400, but paid $5,533.15 as a result of being 75 days overdue. What rate of interest does Bramwald charge?

$5,533.15 Paid
− 5,400.00 Owed originally
   133.15 Interest

$\dfrac{133.15}{5,400 \times \frac{75}{365}} = \dfrac{133.15}{1,109.589} = .1199993$

__12% rate of interest charged__

7. Harry Visconti, an advertising executive, borrowed $3,655 from Happy Heart Finance Company, paying 14¼% ordinary interest. If the interest amounts to $205.44, what is the term of the loan?

$\dfrac{\$205.44}{\$3,655 \times .1425} = \dfrac{\$205.44}{\$520.84} = .3944397$

__142 days__

Sherry Craig works for the telephone company. She has responsibility for a program of loans to business subscribers who are unable to pay their past-due bills. Assist her in calculating each of the following accounts.

	Principal	Rate	Time	Exact Interest	Maturity Value
8.	$ 5,846	__6%__	140	$134.50	$ 5,980.54

$R = \dfrac{I}{PT}$ $\dfrac{\$134.54}{5,846 \times \frac{140}{365}}$ $5,846 \times \dfrac{140}{365} = 2242.3013$

$\$134.54 \div 2242.3013 = .06 = 6\%$ rate
$\$5,846 + 134.54 = \$5,980.54$ maturity value

continued

Assignment 9.5 *continued*

	Principal	Rate	Time	Exact Interest	Maturity Value
9.	$ 8,524	7¾%	180	$325.78	$ 8,849.78

$T = \dfrac{I}{PR}$ $\dfrac{\$325.78}{8,524 \times .0775}$ $8,524 \times .0775 = 660.61$
$\$325.78 \div 660.61 = .4931502$
$.4931502 \times 365 = 179.99 = 180$ days
$\$8,524 + 325.78 = \$8,849.78$ maturity value

10.	$ 7,950	7.8%	12	$ 20.26	$ 7,970.26

$R = \dfrac{I}{PT}$ $\dfrac{20.26}{7,950 \times \frac{12}{365}}$ $7,950 \times \dfrac{12}{365} = 261.36986$
$20.26 \div 261.36986 = .0775146 = 7.8\%$
$\$7,950 + 20.26 = \$7,970.26$ maturity value

11.	$ 9,649.95	4¾%	301	$378.00	$10,027.95
12.	$10,595	6¼%	5	$ 9.07	$10,604.07

13. Pamela Hartman is notified that she owes $126.54 in back taxes. To this is added an interest penalty of $3.58. If the penalty rate is 12%, figured at exact interest, exact time, how many days are Pamela's taxes overdue?

$\dfrac{\$3.58}{\$126.54 \times .12}$ $126.54 \times .12 = 15.1848$

Check: $\$126.54 \times .12 \times \dfrac{86}{365} = \$3.5777884$

86 days overdue

$T = \dfrac{I}{PR}$
$\$3.58 \div 15.848 = .235762$
$365 \times .235762 = 86.05313$
$= 86$ days

Dan Marion is employed by the State Office of Environmental Concerns. He is in charge of a program of low-interest loans for energy conservation projects. Help him figure the following.

	Principal	Rate	Time in Days	Exact Interest	Maturity Value
14.	$ 999.85	6%	78	$12.82	$1,012.67

$P = \dfrac{I}{RT}$ $\dfrac{\$12.82}{.06 \times \frac{78}{365}}$ $.06 \times \dfrac{78}{365} = .0128219$
$\$12.82 \div .0128219 = 999.851 = \$999.85$ principal
$\$999.85 + 12.82 = \$1,012.67$ maturity value

15.	$ 600	8%	46	$ 6.05	$ 606.05

$R = \dfrac{I}{PT}$ $\dfrac{\$6.05}{600 \times \frac{46}{365}}$ $600 \times \dfrac{46}{365} = 75.616438$
$6.05 \div 75.616438 = .080009 = 8\%$ rate
$\$600 + \$6.05 = \$606.05$ maturity value

16.	$1,250	4%	67	$ 9.18	$ 1,259.18

$T = \dfrac{I}{PR}$ $\dfrac{9.18}{1,250 \times .04}$ $\$1,250 \times .04 = \$50$
$\$9.18 \div 50 = .1836$
$.1836 \times 365 = 67.014 = 67$ days
$\$1,250 + \$9.18 = \$1,259.18$ maturity value

continued

Assignment 9.5 *continued*

	Principal	Rate	Time in Days	Exact Interest	Maturity Value
17. $	967.93	5.25%	360	$50.12	$ 1,018.05

$P = \dfrac{I}{RT}$ $\dfrac{50.12}{.0525 \times \frac{360}{365}}$ $.0525 \times \dfrac{360}{365} = .0517808$
50.12 ÷ .0517808 = 967.92633 = $967.93 principal
$967.93 + 50.12 = $1,018.05 maturity value

	Principal	Rate	Time in Days	Exact Interest	Maturity Value
18. $	1,542.05	$6\frac{1}{4}\%$	284	$74.99	$ 1,617.04

$P = \dfrac{I}{RT}$ $\dfrac{74.99}{.0625 \times \frac{284}{365}}$ $.0625 \times \dfrac{284}{365} = .0486301$
74.99 ÷ .0486301 = 1,542.049 = $1,542.05 principal
$1,542.05 + $74.99 = $1,617.04 maturity value

9.6 Compound Interest

So far, we have talked about simple interest, the type most often used for loans of one year or less. Deposits or investments often accumulate **compound interest**. Here, interest is figured on both the principal and the prior interest, which has been converted into, and is treated as, part of the principal. Compound interest is figured annually, semiannually, quarterly, monthly, or daily.

Determining Accumulated Value

Example 1 Bernie Strongbear deposits $1,000 in a savings certificate that draws interest at 9%, compounded annually for 2 years. How much will he have at the end of the 2 years?

Step 1   Find the interest earned in the first year. $1,000 × .09 = $90

Step 2   Add this to the principal.

     $1,000 Principal
     + $ 90 Interest, year 1
     $1,090 Balance, end of year 1

Step 3   Figure the interest for year 2 on the converted principal. $1,090 × .09 = $98.10

Step 4   Add this to the converted principal.

     $1,090.00 Balance, end of year 1
     + $ 98.10 Interest, year 2
     $1,188.10 Balance, end of year 2

Answer   After 2 years, Bernie's certificate is worth $1,18.10.

Computing Interest Earned

Performing the arithmetical computation for compound interest gives you the total that the original investment is now worth, not the amount of interest earned. To find the amount of compound interest, subtract the original principal from the balance at the end of the period. For Example 1 above:

     $1,188.10 Final balance
     − $1,000.00 Original principal
     $ 188.10 Compound interest

After 2 years, Bernie's certificate yields compound interest of $188.10. If he had withdrawn his interest each year, Bernie would have received $90 per year. By allowing it to compound, he earned an additional $8.10.

Calculating Interest on a Several-Times-A-Year Basis

Interest is often compounded more frequently than once a year. The number of times interest is calculated, which is called the **time period,** depends on how it is compounded. For instance,

"Compounded *annually*" means that interest is figured once every year.
"Compounded *semiannually*" means that interst is figured every six months, or twice a year.
"Compounded *quarterly*" means that interest is figured every three months, or four times a year.

Interest   **379**

The interest earned for each time period is found by applying the appropriate time fraction: $\frac{1}{2}$ for semiannual interest, $\frac{1}{4}$ for quarterly interest, and so on. Interest can also be compounded monthly ($\frac{1}{12}$), and, thanks to the use of computers, it is now practical to compound daily ($\frac{1}{360}$ or $\frac{1}{365}$).

Example 2 Bernie Strongbear invests in a $1,000 certificate that draws 9% interest compounded semiannually for 1 year. How much will his investment be worth at the end of the year?

Step 1 Find the interest earned in the first 6 months.

$$P \times R \times T = I$$
$$\$1{,}000 \times .09 \times \frac{1}{2} = \$45$$

Step 2 Add this to the principal.

$$\$1{,}000 + 45 = \$1{,}045$$

Step 3 Find the interest for the second 6 months, using the converted principal found in step 2.

$$\$1{,}045 \times .09 \times \frac{1}{2} = \$47.025$$

Step 4 Add this to the converted principal.

$$\$1{,}045 + \$47.025 = \$1{,}092.025$$

Answer After 1 year, Bernie's certificate is worth $1,092.03.

Self-Check

1. Calculate the amount of interest produced by $2,000 with interest at 9% compounded annually for 2 years.

2. Find (a) the interest and (b) the maturity value on $800 compounded semiannually for 8% for $1\frac{1}{2}$ years.
   (a) _____
   (b) _____

3. What is the amount of compound interest earned on $6,000 at 10% compounded quarterly for 1 year?

ANSWERS 1. $376.20   2. (a) $99.89; (b) $899.89   3. $622.88

FINANCIAL ADVERTISING

Money Market Fund
Annual Rate, 7.01%
Annual Yield, 7.05%

Most banks and savings-and-loan institutions are required by law to list the rate and the yield on interest-bearing accounts. They are, however, under no obligation to explain how these rates are computed.

The rate is the simple-interest rate. The yield, which is usually the larger number, shows the effect of compounding, assuming that no money is taken out of the account for one year. The banking institution also has the option of telling you in its ads whether the interest is compounded daily, monthly, quarterly, or annually.

Assignment 9.6

Interest

Find the results to the nearest cent for all the problems in this assignment.

Maureen O'Connor works at People's National Bank. Help her determine the maturity value and the amount of compound interest for each of the following savings certificates.

	Principal	Rate	Years	Interest Period	Maturity Value	Interest
1.	$ 1,000	8%	2	Annually	$ 1,166.40	$ 166.40
2.	$ 4,000	6%	1	Semiannually	4,243.60	243.60
3.	$ 720	10%	1	Quarterly	794.75	74.75
4.	$ 9,100	9%	4	Annually	12,845.39	3,745.39
5.	$ 8,650	$8\frac{1}{4}$%	2	Quarterly	10,184.64	1,534.64
6.	$10,600	$11\frac{1}{2}$%	2	Semiannually	13,256.45	2,656.45

7. As the result of a business venture, Cynthia Badencort has $24,500 to invest.

   a) What would be the interest on her investment under a plan in which she invests the money at 10% simple interest for 4 years?

   $9,800 simple interest

   b) What would be the interest on her investment under a plan in which she invests it at 8%, compounded annually for 4 years?

   $33,331.98 Maturity value
   − 24,500.00 Orig. invest.
   $ 8,831.98 Interest

   $8,831.98
   compound interest

   7(b).
   24,500 × .08 × 1 = 1,960
   24,500 + 1,960 = 26,460
   26,460 × .08 × 1 = 2,116.80
   26,460 + 2,116.80 = 28,576.80
   28,576.80 × .08 × 1 = 2286.144
   28,576.80 + 2286.144 =
   30862.944
   30,862.944 × .08 × 1 =
   2469.0355
   30,862.944 + 2469.0355 =
   33331.979
   Maturity value = 33,331.98

   c) How much more interest will the better investment yield?

   $9,800.00 Simple interest
   − 8,831.98 Compound interest
   $ 968.02 More interest

   $968.02
   more interest yielded

8. Determine the maturity value on an investment of $15,300 at $11\frac{1}{4}$% compounded semiannually for 2 years.

   15,300 × .1125 × $\frac{1}{2}$ = 860.625
   15,300 + 860.625 = 16160.625
   16160.625 × .1125 × $\frac{1}{2}$ = 909.03515
   16160.625 + 909.08515 = 17069.66
   17069.66 × .1125 × $\frac{1}{2}$ = 960.16835

   17069.66 + 960.16835 = 18,029.828
   18,029.828 × .1125 × $\frac{1}{2}$ = 1014.1778
   18,029.828 + 1014.1778 = 19,044.005
   Maturity value = $19,044.01

   $19,044.01
   maturity value

continued

Assignment 9.6 *continued*

9. Find the compound interest paid for $1\frac{1}{2}$ years on a deposit of $3,600 at 8% if it is:

   a) compounded semiannually.

   $3600 \times .08 \times \frac{1}{2} = 144$
   $3600 + 144 = 3744$
   $3744 \times .08 \times \frac{1}{2} = 149.76$
   $3744 + 149.76 = 3893.76$
   $3893.76 \times .08 \times \frac{1}{2} = 155.7504$
   $3893.76 + 155.7504 = 4049.5104$
   Maturity value = $4,049.51

   $4,049.51 Maturity value
   − 3,600.00 Orig. deposit
   449.51 Interest paid

   $449.51 interest paid

   b) compounded quarterly.

   $3600 \times .08 \times \frac{1}{4} = 72$
   $3600 + 72 = 3672$
   $3672 \times .08 \times \frac{1}{4} = 73.44$
   $3672 + 73.44 = 3745.44$
   $3745.44 \times .08 \times \frac{1}{4} = 74.9088$
   $3745.44 + 74.9088 = 3820.3488$

   $3820.3488 \times .08 \times \frac{1}{4} = 76.406975$
   $3820.3488 + 76.406975 = 3896.7557$
   $3896.7557 \times .08 \times \frac{1}{4} = 77.935112$
   $3896.755 + 77.535112 = 3974.6908$
   $3974.6903 \times .08 \times \frac{1}{4} = 79.493815$
   $3974.6903 + 79.493815 = 4054.1846$

   $4,054.18 Maturity value
   − 3,600.00 Orig. deposit
   $ 454.18 Interest paid

   $454.18 interest paid

10. How much interest should the Brooks Company receive on an investment of $21,000 held for 4 years at 12% compounded annually?

    $21,000 \times .12 \times 1 = 2,520$
    $21,000 + 2,520 = 23,520$
    $23,520 \times .12 \times 1 = 2,822.4$
    $23,520 + 2,822.4 = 26,342.4$
    $26,342.4 \times .12 \times 1 = 3161.088$
    $26,342.4 + 3,161.088 = 29,503.488$

    $29,503.488 \times .12 \times 1 = 3,540.4185$
    $29,503.488 + 3,540.4185 = 33,043.906$
    Maturity value = $33,043.91

    $33,043.91 Maturity value
    − 21,000.00 Orig. invest
    $12,043.91 Interest received

    $12,043.91 interest received

Calculate the maturity value and the amount of compound interest for each of the following situations.

	Principal	Rate	Years	Interest Period	Maturity Value	Interest
11.	$12,300	7%	3	Annually	$15,068.03	$2,768.03
12.	$29,700	$9\frac{1}{2}$%	$1\frac{1}{2}$	Quarterly	34,191.64	4,491.64
13.	$ 7,000	10%	$2\frac{1}{2}$	Semiannually	8,933.97	1,933.97
14.	$13,000	12%	5	Annually	22,910.44	9,910.44
15.	$ 8,000	$11\frac{1}{4}$%	$2\frac{1}{2}$	Semiannually	10,517.77	2,517.77
16.	$19,000	$10\frac{1}{2}$%	$1\frac{1}{4}$%	Quarterly	21,628.15	2,628.15

17. Dean Wittington invested $46,000 at 11% interest, compounded semi-annually, for $2\frac{1}{2}$ years.

    a) What is the maturity value of his investment?

    $60,120.16 maturity value

    (See work on the following page)

continued

Assignment 9.6 *continued*

b) What amount of interest does it earn?

46,000 × .11 × ½ = 2,530
46,000 + 2,530 = 48,530
48,530 × .11 × ½ = 2,669.15
48,530 + 2,669.15 = 51,199.15
51,199.15 × .11 × ½ = 2,815.9532
51,199.15 + 2,815.9532 = 54,015.103
54,015.103 × .11 × ½ = 2,970.8306
54,015.103 + 2,970.8306 = 56,985.933
56,985.933 × .11 × ½ = 3,134.2263
56,985.933 + 3,134.2263 = $60,120.159 maturity value

$60,120.16 Maturity value
− 46,000.00 Orig. investment
$14,120.16 Interest earned

$14,120.16
interest earned

9.7 The Compound-Interest Table

Using the Table to Figure Interest Compounded Annually

Now that you know the mechanics of figuring compound interest, understand that it is generally determined using tables or a computer.

The compound-interest table on the following page shows columns representing interest rates and rows representing time periods.

The figures placed where the columns and rows intersect show the value of one dollar if invested at a specific rate for a specified period of time. You can determine the value of whatever principal is invested by multiplying it by the correct figure from the table. The procedure is as follows:

Step 1 Locate the required number of time periods at the far left or far right of the table (column n).

Step 2 Locate the appropriate interest rate at the top of the table.

Step 3 Find the figure at the point where the column and the row intersect.

Step 4 Multiply this figure—the compounded value of one dollar—by the principal.

Example 1 Use the table to determine the maturity value of Bernie Strongbear's $1,000 certificate at 9% compounded annually for 2 years.

Step 1	Locate the time period.	2
Step 2	Locate the interest rate.	9%
Step 3	Find the figure at the point of intersection.	1.188100
Step 4	Multiply it by the principal.	1.1881 × $1,000 $1,188.10
Answer	Bernie's certificate is worth $1,188.10.	

NOTE: As before, to find the interest earned, subtract the principal from the maturity value.

$1,188.10
− $1,000.00
$ 188.10

In some cases, the result obtained by using the table will differ slightly from that obtained by the arithmetical method, because of rounding.

Self-Check

Find the maturity value and the amount of interest compounded yearly, using the compound-interest table.

	Principal	Rate	Time in Years	Maturity Value	Interest
1.	$5,000	6%	10	a) $_____	b) $_____
2.	$1,250	10%	3	a) _____	b) _____

3. Barry Comanik put $26,000 in a 6-year saving certificate with 12% interest compounded annually. What was his investment worth at the end of the 6-year period? _____

ANSWERS 1. (a) $8,954.24; (b) $3,954.24   2. (a) $1,663.75; (b) $413.75
3. $51,319.40

Compound Interest Table—Future Worth of One Dollar, to 6 Decimal Places

n*	.5%	1%	1.5%	2%	3%	4%	5%	6%	n*
1	1.005000	1.010000	1.015000	1.020000	1.030000	1.040000	1.050000	1.060000	1
2	1.010025	1.020100	1.030225	1.040400	1.060900	1.081600	1.102500	1.123600	2
3	1.015075	1.030301	1.045678	1.061208	1.092727	1.124864	1.157625	1.191016	3
4	1.020151	1.040604	1.061364	1.082432	1.125509	1.169859	1.215506	1.262477	4
5	1.025251	1.051010	1.077284	1.104081	1.159274	1.216653	1.276282	1.338226	5
6	1.030378	1.061520	1.093443	1.126162	1.194052	1.265319	1.340096	1.418519	6
7	1.035529	1.072135	1.109845	1.148686	1.229874	1.315932	1.407100	1.503630	7
8	1.040707	1.082857	1.126496	1.171659	1.266770	1.368569	1.477455	1.593848	8
9	1.045911	1.093685	1.143390	1.195093	1.304773	1.423312	1.551328	1.689479	9
10	1.051140	1.104622	1.160541	1.218994	1.343916	1.480244	1.628895	1.790848	10
11	1.056396	1.115668	1.177949	1.243374	1.384234	1.539454	1.710339	1.898249	11
12	1.061678	1.126825	1.195618	1.268242	1.425761	1.601032	1.795856	2.012196	12
13	1.066986	1.138093	1.213552	1.293607	1.468534	1.665074	1.885649	2.132928	13
14	1.072321	1.149474	1.231756	1.319479	1.512590	1.731676	1.979932	2.260904	14
15	1.077683	1.160969	1.250232	1.345868	1.557967	1.800944	2.078928	2.396558	15
16	1.083071	1.172579	1.268986	1.372786	1.604706	1.872981	2.182875	2.540352	16
17	1.088487	1.184304	1.288020	1.400241	1.652848	1.947901	2.292018	2.692773	17
18	1.093929	1.196147	1.307341	1.428246	1.702433	2.025817	2.406619	2.854339	18
19	1.099399	1.208109	1.326951	1.456811	1.753506	2.106849	2.526950	3.025600	19
20	1.104896	1.220190	1.346855	1.485947	1.806111	2.191123	2.653298	3.207135	20
21	1.110420	1.232392	1.367059	1.515666	1.860295	2.278768	2.785963	3.399564	21
22	1.115972	1.244716	1.387564	1.545980	1.916103	2.369919	2.925261	3.603537	22
23	1.121552	1.257163	1.408377	1.576899	1.973587	2.464716	3.071524	3.819745	23
24	1.127160	1.269735	1.429503	1.608437	2.032794	2.563304	3.225100	4.048935	24
25	1.132796	1.282432	1.450945	1.640606	2.093778	2.665836	3.386355	4.291871	25

n*	7%	8%	9%	10%	11%	12%	13%	14%	n*
1	1.070000	1.080000	1.090000	1.100000	1.110000	1.120000	1.130000	1.140000	1
2	1.144900	1.166400	1.188100	1.210000	1.232100	1.254400	1.276900	1.299600	2
3	1.225043	1.259712	1.295029	1.331000	1.367631	1.404928	1.442897	1.481544	3
4	1.310796	1.360489	1.411582	1.464100	1.518070	1.573519	1.630474	1.688960	4
5	1.402552	1.469328	1.538624	1.610510	1.685058	1.762342	1.842435	1.925415	5
6	1.500730	1.586874	1.677100	1.771561	1.870415	1.973823	2.081952	2.194973	6
7	1.605781	1.713824	1.828039	1.948717	2.076160	2.210681	2.352605	2.502269	7
8	1.718186	1.850930	1.992563	2.143589	2.304538	2.475963	2.658444	2.852586	8
9	1.838459	1.999005	2.171893	2.357948	2.558037	2.773079	3.004042	3.251949	9
10	1.967151	2.158925	2.367364	2.593742	2.839421	3.105848	3.394567	3.707221	10
11	2.104852	2.331639	2.580426	2.853117	3.151757	3.478550	3.835861	4.226232	11
12	2.252192	2.518170	2.812665	3.138428	3.498451	3.895976	4.334523	4.817905	12
13	2.409845	2.719624	3.065805	3.452271	3.883280	4.363493	4.898011	5.492411	13
14	2.578534	2.937194	3.341727	3.797498	4.310441	4.887112	5.534753	6.261349	14
15	2.759032	3.172169	3.642482	4.177248	4.784589	5.473566	6.254270	7.137938	15
16	2.952164	3.425943	3.970306	4.594973	5.310894	6.130394	7.067326	8.137249	16
17	3.158815	3.700018	4.327633	5.054470	5.895093	6.866041	7.986078	9.276464	17
18	3.379932	3.996019	4.717120	5.559917	6.543553	7.689966	9.024268	10.575169	18
19	3.616528	4.315701	5.141661	6.115909	7.263344	8.612762	10.197423	12.055693	19
20	3.869684	4.660957	5.604411	6.727500	8.062312	9.646293	11.523088	13.743490	20
21	4.140562	5.033834	6.108808	7.400250	8.949166	10.803848	13.021089	15.667578	21
22	4.430402	5.436540	6.658600	8.140275	9.933574	12.100310	14.713831	17.861039	22
23	4.740530	5.871464	7.257874	8.954302	11.026267	13.552347	16.626629	20.361585	23
24	5.072367	6.341181	7.911083	9.849733	12.239157	15.178629	18.788091	23.212207	24
25	5.427433	6.848475	8.623081	10.834706	13.585464	17.000064	21.230542	26.461916	25

*n = Number of interest periods

Using the Table to Figure Interest Compounded Several Times a Year

As stated earlier, interest is often compounded more frequently than once a year. It can be figured semiannually (every six months), quarterly (every three months), monthly, or daily. Daily compounding is usually accomplished through use of a computer.

The compound-interest table can be used to derive maturity value for other than annual periods, but some adjustment is required.

Step 1 Divide the annual rate of interest by the number of interest periods per year. In compounding semiannually, for example, divide the annual rate by 2. The result is called the **periodic interest rate.**

Step 2 Multiply the number of years by the number of interest periods per year. In compounding semiannually, multiply the number of years the money is invested by 2. The result is the number of *conversion periods* to be considered.

Step 3 Use the compound-interest table as before, with the periodic rate and the number of conversion periods found in steps 1 and 2.

Step 4 Multiply the number in the table, called the **interest factor,** by the principal.

Example 2 Harry Brencusi invests $1,000 from his real estate firm at 12% compounded quarterly for 2 years. Find the maturity value of this investment.

Step 1 Divide the annual interest by the number of periods per year—in this case, 4.
12% ÷ 4 = 3% periodic rate

Step 2 Multiply the number of years by the number of interest periods per year.
2 × 4 = 8 conversion periods

Step 3 Use the compound-interest table.
8 periods at 3% = 1.266770

Step 4 Multiply by the principal.
```
    1.26677
×   $1000
  $1,266.77
```

Answer The maturity of Harry's investment is $1,266.77.

Self-Check

Find the results to the nearest cent.

	Principal	Rate	Time	Interest Period	Maturity Value
1.	$300	8%	1 year	Semiannually	$ _____
2.	$500	12%	6 years	Quarterly	_____

3. Scintilla Hungate invests $1,000 at 18% compounded monthly for 1 year. What amount must she pay back at maturity? _____

ANSWERS 1. $324.48   2. $1,016.40   3. $1,195.62 (12 periods at 1.5%)

NAME   DATE   SECTION

Assignment 9.7

Interest

Use the compound-interest table to find the results to the nearest cent for all problems in this assignment.

Andrea Holly must calculate maturity value and interest on several long-term investments. The information available to her is shown below. Help Andrea make the necessary calculations by using the compound-interest table. All of these investments are compounded annually.

1. Look up 9% for 11 periods
   $9,468 × 2.580426
   = $24,431.47
   $24,431.47 − 9,468
   = $14,963.47

	Principal	Rate	Time	Maturity Value	Interest	
1.	$ 9,468	9%	11 years	$ 24,431.47	$ 14,963.47	
2.	$11,890	11%	8 years	27,400.96	15,510.96	$11,890 × 2.304538
3.	$ 4,300	8%	21 years	21,645.49	17,345.49	$4,300 × 5.033834

4. Delmar Kennedy of Detroit wins $110,000 in the Michigan Lottery. After paying one third of the gross in taxes, he invests the remainder in a 2-year savings certificate that pays 12% interest compounded monthly. How much will his investment be worth at the end of the 2 years?

   $110,000 × ⅔ = $73,333.33 to invest
   $73,333 × 1.269735 = 93,113.895
                    = $93,113.90 maturity value

   $93,113.90
   maturity value

Mary McVey is a trust officer at Barnard National Bank. For her clients, she makes investments that have various rates and terms. Figure the maturity value and the interest gained on each of the following.

	Principal	Rate	Time	Interest Period	Maturity Value	Compound Interest
5.	$ 2,000	8%	4 years	Quarterly	$ 2,745.57	$ 745.57
	$2,000 × 1.372786					
6.	$ 3,500	12%	1 year	Monthly	3,943.89	443.89
	$3,500 × 1.126825					
7.	$12,000	12%	20 years	Annually	115,755.51	103,755.51
	$12,000 × 9.646293					
8.	$16,550	8%	2 years	Quarterly	19,390.96	2,840.96
	$16,650 × 1.171659					
9.	$16,620	10%	11 years	Semiannually	48,617.84	31,997.84
	$16,620 × 2.925261					

continued

Assignment 9.7 continued

	Principal	Rate	Time	Interest Period	Maturity Value	Compound Interest
10.	$22,336	10%	15 years	Annually	93,303.01	70,967.01

$22,336 × 4.177248

Ben Yang works at a small savings-and-loan company. He approves several investments and now must determine the maturity values and the interest due. Help him to do so by using the compound-interest table.

11. Look up 4% for 20 periods
1,000 × 2.191123 = $2,191.12
$2,191.12 − 1,000 = $1,191.12

	Principal	Rate	Time	Interest Period	Maturity Value	Interest	
11.	$1,000	8%	10 years	Semiannual	$ 2,191.12	$ 1,191.12	
12.	$2,900	10%	12 years	Semiannual	9,352.79	6,452.79	$2,900 × 3.22510
13.	$2,500	10%	5 years	Semiannual	4,072.24	1,572.24	$2,500 × 1.628895
14.	$3,860	12%	2 years	Quarterly	4,889.73	1,029.73	$3,860 × 1.266770
15.	$3,950	16%	1 year	Quarterly	4,620.94	670.94	$3,950 × 1.169859
16.	$4,500	12%	3 years	Quarterly	6,415.92	1,915.92	$4,500 × 1.425761
17.	$5,550	12%	2 years	Monthly	7,047.03	1,497.03	$5,550 × 1.269735
18.	$7,950	18%	2 years	Semiannual	11,222.08	3,272.08	$7,950 × 1.411582
19.	$7,840	12%	5 years	Quarterly	14,159.91	6,319.91	$7,840 × 1.806111
20.	$8,645	18%	1 year	Monthly	10,336.12	1,691.12	$8,645 × 1.195618

Comprehensive Problems for Chapter 9

Interest

1. To start his appliance-repair business, Terry Blodell borrowed $2,500 from his sister, Tessie. One year later, he repaid the loan at 14% ordinary interest. How much did he pay Tessie?

   $2,500 × .14 = 350
   $2,500 + 350 = $2,850

   $2,850 total repaid

2. Bandit Industries, for which you are the accountant, borrows $52,681 to meet its payroll. The rate of ordinary interest is 15%, and the loan is for 1 month. What amount will Bandit Industries pay back at the end of the time period?

   $\frac{52{,}681 \times .15 \times 1}{12}$ = $658.5125
   = $658.51 interest

   $52,681.00 Principal
   658.51 Interest
   $53,339.51 Total paid

   $53,339.51 total paid back

3. Randy Conan plans to invest in tax-free bonds that yield $12\frac{1}{2}\%$ annual ordinary interest. If he invests $11,000, how much will his investment be worth at the end of the 3 months?

   11,000 × $12\frac{1}{2}$% × $\frac{1}{4}$
   $\frac{11{,}000 \times .125 \times 1}{4}$ = $343.75 interest

   $11,000.00 Invested
   343.75 Interest earned
   $11,343.75

   $11,343.75 worth of investments at end of 3 months

As a loan officer, Carol Hyatt must calculate several loans at 12.5% interest. Help her find the interest due on each of them, first using the 30-day month, ordinary-interest method, and then using the exact-interest, exact-time method.

	Principal	Time	Ordinary Interest	Exact Interest
4.	$10,625.00	August 15–December 13	$ 435.33	$ 436.64
5.	$14,294.00	October 11–November 28	233.27	234.97
6.	$12,646.50	September 10–December 21	443.51	441.76
7.	$13,128.48	July 7–September 12	296.30	301.24
8.	$11,242.36	March 5–April 4	113.20	115.50

Ordinary	Exact
4. 118 days	120 days
5. 47 days	48 days
6. 101 days	102 days
7. 65 days	67 days
8. 29 days	30 days

continued

Comprehensive Problems *continued*

9. On April 2, Barry Calmanigi, a fire eater with Murphy and Keller Brothers Circus, purchases pyrotechnic supplies for $955, agreeing to pay for them on September 30, at the close of the summer tour. Assume that he is charged $9\frac{1}{2}\%$ ordinary interest.

   $$\begin{array}{r} 30 \\ \times \ 5 \text{ Months} \\ \hline 150 \text{ Days} \end{array} \quad \begin{array}{r} 30 \\ - \ 2 \\ \hline 28 \text{ Days} \end{array}$$

   $$\begin{array}{r} 150 \\ + \ 28 \\ \hline 178 \text{ Days total} \end{array}$$

   a) What is the amount of interest he will owe?

   $$\frac{\cancel{955}^{191}}{1} \times \frac{\cancel{95}^{19}}{\cancel{1,000}_{\cancel{200}_{40}}} \times \frac{\cancel{178}^{89}}{\cancel{360}_{180}} = \frac{32,981}{7,206} = 44.8584$$

   $44.86 interest owed

   b) What is the total amount he will owe?

   $$\begin{array}{r} 955.00 \text{ Loan} \\ + \ \ 44.86 \\ \hline \$999.86 \text{ Total owed} \end{array}$$

   $999.86 total amount owed

As a financial consultant, Delores Herzog must supply information regarding one of her client's investments. Help her complete the calculations.

	Principal	Rate	Exact Time	Ordinary Interest
10.	$ 9,622	$12\frac{1}{4}\%$	36	$ 117.87

$$\frac{117.87}{9,622 \times .1225} = \frac{117.87}{1178.695} = .1 \times 360 = 36$$

| 11. | $ 1,525 | 12% | 359 | $ 182.49 |

$$\frac{182.49}{1,525 \times \frac{359}{360}} = \frac{182.49}{1520.7638} = .1199989 = 12\%$$

| 12. | $ 7,965.06 | 14.25% | 201 | $ 633.72 |

$$\frac{663.72}{.1425 \times \frac{201}{360}} = \frac{633.72}{.0795625} = 7,965.0589$$

| 13. | $ 10,954.06 | 12.75% | 182 | $ 706.08 |

| 14. | $15,642 | 15.5% | 340 | $2,289.82 |

15. Determine the original principal of your savings certificate if it earns $17.42 ordinary interest at $5\frac{1}{2}\%$ in 120 days.

    $P = \dfrac{I}{RT}$

    $$\frac{\$17.42}{.055 \times \frac{120}{360}} \quad \frac{\cancel{55}^{11}}{\cancel{1,000}_{\cancel{200}}} \times \frac{\cancel{120}^{1}}{\cancel{360}_{3}} = \frac{11}{600} = .01833333$$

    $17.42 \div .01833333 = 950.18354$
    $ = \$950.18$ principal
    Check: $950.18 \times .055 \times \frac{1}{3} = 17.4199$
    $ P \ \times \ R \ \ \times T = \$17.42$ interest

    $950.18 in savings certificate

continued

392 Chapter 9

Comprehensive Problems *continued*

16. Terry Dalla Santa took out several loans to help finance the expansion of her flower shop. Each was for a 1-year time period. The principal and interest rates of the loans were $1,125 at $9\frac{1}{2}$%; $2,400 at 10%; and $1,550 at $11\frac{1}{4}$%. What is the total that Terry owes at the end of the 1-year period?

$1,125 × .095 × 1 = 106.875 = $106.88
$2,400 × .10 × 1 = 240.00 = 240.00
$1,550 × .1125 × 1 = 174.375 = 174.38
$521.26 Total interest owed on 3 separate loans

$1,125.00
2,400.00
+ 1,550.00
$5,075.00 Total principal
521.26
$5,596.26

$5,596.26 total amount owed

For the following problems, use the compound-interest table.

17. Lou Gertner deposits $1,000 in each of three banks. The first, National Trust, pays 6% interest compounded annually; the second, Hometown Bank, 6% compounded semiannually; and the third, Bridgeway Savings, 6% compounded quarterly. Assuming she does not withdraw money in the meantime, what will the amount be in each of Lou's three accounts at the end of five years?

   a) National Trust

   $1,000 × 1.338226 = 1,338.226 = $1,338.23

   $1,338.23

   b) Hometown Bank

   $1,000 × 1.343916 = 1,349.916 = $1,343.92

   $1,343.92

   c) Bridgeway Savings

   $1,000 × 1.346855 = 1,346.855 = $1,346.86

   $1,346.86

18. Mario's Pizza, Inc., invests two amounts of money: (a) $6,000 at 8% simple interest for 5 years and (b) $5,000 at 8% compounded quarterly for 5 years. How much will each investment earn?

   a) $6,000 × .08 × 5 = $2,400 Simple interest

   $2,400 simple interest earned

   b) $5,000 × 1.485947 = 7,429.735
   = $7,429.74 Maturity value
   $7,429.74 − 5,000 = $2,429.74 Compound interest

   $2,429.74 compound interest earned

Sharon Benson must determine the interest earned and the maturity value of several of the investments in her portfolio. Help her, using the following information.

	Principal	Rate, Compounded Annually	Time	Maturity Value	Interest	
19.	$24,500	10%	18 years	$136,217.96	$111,717.96	$24,500 × 5.559917
20.	$19,658	7%	10 years	38,670.25	19,012.25	$19,658 × 1.967151
21.	$22,863	14%	22 years	408,356.93	385,493.93	$22,863 × 17.861039

Case 1

Bill Davidson came to you for advice concerning where he should deposit his savings of $4,860. He planned to deposit the money on January 1 and then withdraw it on November 15 of the same year.

County Bank of Dawson offered a $5\frac{3}{4}\%$ interest rate based at exact interest, exact time. City-View Bank offered a 6% interest rate based on ordinary interest, 30-day month time. Bill's friend, Karl Westfal, offered to hold the money for him and pay 9% interest based on ordinary interest, exact time. Given these three choices:

a. What would you advise Bill to do with his money?
b. Why?

Case 2

Holly Rommel planned to receive $500 in ordinary interest from a business partner who borrowed $9,450 at an interest rate of $11\frac{1}{4}\%$.

a. For how long would the partner be borrowing the money, according to the facts given above?

After the money is returned, Holly plans to invest it in a treasury note that pays 13% interest compounded quarterly.

b. If the money is not withdrawn for $2\frac{1}{2}$ years, what will be the maturity value at the end of that time?

c. What are some things Holly should look at before undertaking these two transactions?

Key Terms

Commercial year
Compound interest
Conversion period
Exact time
Interest

Interest factor
Interest rate
Leap year
Maturity value
Ordinary interest

Per annum
Periodic interest rate
Principal
Simple interest
Time period

Key Concepts

- Interest is a fee charged for the use of money.
- The principal is the amount of money loaned or borrowed.
- The rate is the percent of interest. It is normally calculated on an annual basis.
- The time is the period during which the money is in use, the period for which interest is charged.

- The formula for figuring interest is:

$$\text{Principal} \times \text{Rate} \times \text{Time} = \text{Interest}$$

- In ordinary interest, 30-day month time, the time factor is based on the business year, 360 days. Every month is treated as though it had 30 days.
- In exact interest, exact time, the actual number of days the money is in use is the numerator in the time factor. The denominator is the actual number of days in the year.
- In ordinary interest, exact time, the actual number of days the money is in use is the numerator, and the denominator is 360, the number of days in the business year.
- To find principal, rate, or time when the actual interest earned is known, use one of these formulas:

$$P = \frac{I}{RT} \qquad R = \frac{I}{PT} \qquad T = \frac{I}{PR}$$

- Compound interest is interest figured on the principal plus the interest already accumulated. It is often calculated with the help of a table and can be compounded on an annual, semiannual, quarterly, monthly, or daily basis.

10
Finance

Business Takes a Positive Approach

HONDA

The approach of looking into new areas that others have not explored has been successful for Japanese entrepreneur Sorchiro Honda. Despite cultural differences, government opposition, trade restraints, and a highly competitive market, he insisted that his company become a "master car builder." In doing so, Honda filled a niche in the marketplace left practically untouched by American automobile manufacturers. Since his first concern was for the safety of the driver, Honda's company did not compromise good workmanship for excessive styling or trendy extras. Honda took time to learn about his customers' needs and desires, using his marketing foresight to appeal to them. To stay competitive Honda also offers its own financing for new cars. Among the firm's employees from blue-collar worker to executive, there is an air of mutual respect, and innovation and individual creativity are strongly encouraged. Even today, many years after Sorchiro Honda's retirement, the Honda Motor Company shows his continued influence, tripling its sales over the past decade.

Learning Objectives

After reading and studying this chapter and working the problems, you will be able to:

- Read, analyze, and fill out a promissory note.
- Determine the interest due, the maturity value, and the number of days in the note period of a promissory note.
- Understand the procedure for discounting notes and calculating net proceeds.
- Understand the concepts of personal loans and of installment buying.
- Calculate estimated effective interest rates for consumer loans or installment contracts.
- Use an annual percentage rate table to find the effective interest rate.

Nearly all businesses and many individuals need to borrow money at one time or another. Now that we have considered how interest, the fee for money borrowed, is calculated, let us look at some of the other details of how borrowing is commonly carried out in the business world.

10.1 Promissory Notes

When you borrow money from another person, a business, or a banking institution, you may be required to sign a promissory note. The same is often true when a business borrows from an individual, another business, or a banking institution, or when a business buys merchandise on credit.

The **promissory note,** a common instrument of credit, is a formal indication that a debt is owed, that is, an official I.O.U. It is often **negotiable.** This means that it can be transferred or sold by one person or business to another or to a banking institution.

To be negotiable, the promissory note must meet certain legal requirements:

It must be in writing.

It must include an unconditional promise by the individual or business doing the borrowing to pay the amount due either on demand of the **lender** or by a specified date.

It must be signed by the **borrower.**

It must name the specific individual, business, or institution to whom the money is to be repaid.

Reading a Promissory Note

Example 1

Date loan is made

Term of loan → — Ninety — days after date shown I promise to

The lender, or payee, of note → pay to the order of Bartolth Products Ltd.

Mendleton, Iowa June 1, 19 ___

Amount of loan in numerals → $ 950.00 nine hundred fifty and 00/100 dollars with

interest at 12 % per annum.

Rate of interest charged → Payable at Citizens First Bank

due August 30, 19 ___   Roberta Ritter

Date loan is to be repaid

Amount of loan in words; its face value

The borrower, the **maker,** or **payer** of note

Self-Check

You sign a 60-day promissory note on July 25, 19__, borrowing $9,500 from Manfred Quirt. You agree to pay 14% interest per year and to repay the loan on September 23. Fill out the following note.

Bangor, Maine _____ , 19 ____

_____ days after date shown ____ will pay to the

order of _____ $ _____

_____ dollars with interest

at ____ per year.

Payable at Bangor National Bank, Oakton Branch

due _____ , 19 ____   _____

Finance

ANSWER

> Bangor, Maine July 25, 19 ___
> __Sixty__ days after date shown __I__ will pay to the
> order of __Manfred Quirt__ $ __9,500.00__
> __nine thousand five hundred and 00/100__ dollars with interest
> at __14 %__ per year.
> Payable at Bangor National Bank, Oakton Branch
> due __Sept. 23__, 19 ___   __your name__

Determining Interest Due

To calculate the amount of interest due on a promissory note, use the formula for ordinary interest, exact time (see Section 9.4):

$$\text{Principal} \times \text{Interest Rate} \times \text{Time} = \text{Interest}$$

> **HOW THE PERCENTAGE FORMULA APPLIES**
>
> Principal = Base
> Interest rate = Rate
> Interest = Percentage
>
> The time factor is included in the interest calculation on a promissory note because notes are drawn for a specific period of days, months, or years, and the rate is an annual rate. The maker of the note must pay interest for the entire time the money is in use.
>
> Principal × Rate × Time = Interest
> Base × Rate = Percentage

Example 2 Using the information on the promissory note in Example 1, calculate the amount of interest Roberta Ritter must pay Bartolth Products, Ltd., at the end of 90 days.

Step 1 List the principal, rate, and time.

Principal = Amount of loan
Rate = Rate of interest charged
Time = Term of loan

$P = \$950$
$R = 12\%$ annual
$T = 90$ days

Step 2 Multiply, using the interest formula, including the exact number of days the money is in use over 360 days, the business year.

$P \times R \times T = I$

$$\$950 \times .12 \times \frac{90}{360} = \$950 \times .12 \times \frac{1}{4}$$

$$= \frac{\$950 \times .12}{4}$$

$$= \$28.50$$

Answer The amount of interest due at the end of the loan period is $28.50.

> **PROGRESS IN CALCULATORS**
>
> In 1692, Gottfried Wilhelm von Leibniz, a German, invented a calculating machine that could not only add and subtract but also multiply and divide. It performed these operations by adding and subtracting repeatedly. What's more, Leibniz's amazing invention was also capable of calculating astronomical tables.

Finding Maturity Value

The **maturity value** of a promissory note is the total amount that must be paid by the maker of the note to the lender at the time the note comes due. Some notes are noninterest-bearing. This means that the payee does not require any interest to be charged for the use of the money. The maturity value of a noninterest-bearing note, therefore, is the **face value,** that is, the amount shown on the note. In the case of an **interest-bearing note,** the borrower owes a maturity value that includes **principal** plus interest.

Example 3   What is the total amount Roberta Ritter owes Bartolth Products, Ltd., when the note discussed in Examples 1 and 2 comes due?

Step 1   Calculate the amount of interest, as shown in Example 2.   P × R × T = $28.50

Step 2   Add the interest to the principal, the amount borrowed.

$950.00 Principal
+ $ 28.50 Interest
$978.50

Answer   The maturity value of the note is $978.50.

Self-Check

1. You sign a note on July 25, 19___, borrowing $9,500 from Manfred Quirt. You agree to pay 14% interest per year and to repay the note in 60 days. What amount of interest will you owe when the note is due? _____

2. What is the maturity value of the note described above? _____

3. Jenny Manufacturing Co., borrows $18,500, signing a 45-day note at $12\frac{1}{2}$% interest. How much will the company owe when the note comes due? _____

ANSWERS   1. $221.67   2. $9,721.67   3. $18,789.06

Finance   **401**

Calculating Days in the Note Period

In certain cases, the number of days that a note is in effect is not stated as such. When this is so, count the number of days between the date the note is made and the date it comes due. Interest is not usually charged for the date of issuance, but it is charged for the final day—the due date. (For another discussion of exact dating, see Section 9.3.)

Example 4 Compute the number of days to be used in calculating the interest on the note shown below.

```
                                    Brownell, Idaho  March 18 , 19 ____
I hereby promise to pay to the order of _____
Marilee Sutter Boyd ————————————————  $ 1,500.00
one thousand five hundred and 00/100  dollars with interest at
14% per year          .
Payable at National Bank of Brownell
due  June 5          , 19 ____    Peter Fanington
```

Step 1	Subtract the date the note is drawn from the number of days in that month.	March has 31 days Date of note − 18 th of March 13
Step 2	Add to the result the number of days in each full succeeding month.	13 April has 30 days May has + 31 days 74
Step 3	Add the date in the month the note is due.	74 Due date + 5 th of June 79 days
Answer	The number of days that the note is in effect is 79 days.	

Sometimes the due date is not shown on the note but the number of days the loan is in effect is given. You can determine the due date by checking the date the note is made and using the stated number of days to calculate the date when the note comes due.

Example 5 Bernita Cornell signs a promissory note on May 14, agreeing to pay back the loan in 90 days. What is the actual due date?

Step 1	Subtract the date the note is made from the number of days in that month.	May has 31 days Date of note − 14 th of May 17 days

Step 2   Add the number of days in each succeeding month, not exceeding the term of the note—in this case, 90 days.

```
                    17
June has    30 days
July has  + 31 days
            78 days
```

Step 3   Subtract the result from the total note period, 90 days.

```
   90 days
 − 78 days
   12
```

Answer   The note is due on August 12.

Self-Check

1. Rona Morgan signs a promissory note on December 1, with a due date of the following February 27. What is the term of the note?

2. Parchment Paper Co., Inc., borrows funds on April 26, signing a note due in 60 days. When must the loan be repaid?

ANSWERS
1. Dec. has 31 days
   Dec. − 1
          30 days
   Jan. has 31 days
   Feb. + 27 days
          88 days

2. June 25

NAME _____ DATE _____ SECTION _____

Assignment 10.1

Finance

The following problems are to be worked using the ordinary-interest, exact-time method.

1. Fill in the note form below, given the following: Benno De Lorn, representing De Lorn and Maki, a trucking firm, signs a note on August 18, 19__, agreeing to pay back a loan of $17,650 from Kurt Lambert in 75 days. The annual rate of interest is $13\frac{1}{4}\%$.

   a)

   Villa Nova, Mississippi **Aug. 18**, 19 ____

   75 days after date shown

   De Lorn and Maki will pay

   to the order of **Kurt Lambert** $**17,650.00**

   Seventeen thousand Six hundred fifty and 00/100 dollars with interest of **13¼% per year**

   Payable at Villa National Bank and Trust

   due **Nov. 1**, 19 ____ by **Benno De Lorn**

   b) Calculate the amount of interest due at the end of the loan period on the note shown above.

   $17,650 \times .1325 \times \dfrac{75}{360} = 487.213$

   $= \$487.21$

   $487.21 interest due

   c) Find the maturity value of the note shown above.

   $17,650.00 Principal
   +   487.21 Interest
   $18,137.21 Maturity value

   $18,137.21 maturity value

Having come into a substantial inheritance, Perry Sabley loaned money to several acquaintances, asking each to sign a promissory note. Determine the date due, the amount of interest, and the maturity value for each loan.

Name of Maker	Date Made	Face Value	Term of Note	Annual Interest Rate	Date Due	Amount of Interest	Maturity Value
2. Martha Garger	March 5	$ 456	30 days	14%	a) Apr 4	b) $ 5.32	c) $ 461.32
3. Harry Converse	April 25	$ 637	45 days	$13\frac{1}{2}\%$	a) June 9	b) 10.75	c) 647.75

continued

Finance **405**

Assignment 10.1 *continued*

Name of Maker	Date Made	Face Value	Term of Note	Annual Interest Rate	Date Due	Amount of Interest	Maturity Value
4. Lars Nelson	March 30	$ 826	30 days	$14\frac{2}{7}\%$	a) Apr 29	b) 9.83	c) 835.83
5. Mavis Roseli	July 18	$ 945	75 days	$16\frac{2}{5}\%$	a) Oct 1	b) 32.29	c) 977.29
6. Kari Berger	August 16	$1,068	90 days	$12\frac{2}{3}\%$	a) Nov 14	b) 33.82	c) 1,101.82
7. Mandy Russell	March 28	$2,746	188 days	$14\frac{1}{2}\%$	a) Oct 2	b) 207.93	c) 2,953.93
8. Barton Hargraves	January 16	$3,872	246 days	15%	a) Sept 19	b) 396.88	c) 4,268.88
9. Sandy Chung	October 6	$5,861	38 days	12.2%	a) Nov 13	b) 75.8	c) 5,936.48
10. Ivan Popoff	March 15	$2,987	125 days	18.25%	a) July 18	b) 189.28	c) 3,176.28
11. Bertha Ruedy	January 4	$8,624	150 days	$12\frac{3}{4}\%$	a) June 3	b) 458.15	c) 9,082.15

12. What profit will Perry Sabley make on his total investment, assuming that all of his acquaintances repay him in accordance with the terms of their notes?

$1,419.73 profit on investment (total interest earned)

13. Larry Eng, owner of the Good Luck Fortune Cookie Factory, Inc., buys flour on credit, giving the supplier an interest-bearing note for $8,500. The note is drawn on April 28 and is due on September 14 of the same year. If the supplier asks interest at $15\frac{1}{2}\%$, what total amount will Larry pay back when the note comes due?

$$\$8{,}500 \times .155 \times \frac{139}{360} = \$508.70 \text{ interest due}$$

$9,008.70 maturity value

```
 $8500.00  Principal
+  508.70  Interest
 $9,008.70 Maturity value
    30 April
  - 28
     2 April
    31 May
    30 June
    31 July
    31 Aug
   125
  + 14th Sept
   139 days term of note
```

14. On September 21, Candice Deering, who owns a modeling agency, contracts for presentation photos to be taken of her major models. She signs a note agreeing to pay the photographer $978.60 on December 15 of the same year, with an interest rate of $13\frac{2}{3}\%$. Calculate the amount that she will owe the photographer when the note matures.

$1,010.18 maturity value

```
 $ 978.60  Principal
+   31.58  Interest
 $1010.18  Maturity value
    30 Sept
  - 21
     9 Sept
    31 Oct
    30 Nov
    15th Dec
    85 days term of note
```

10.2 Discounting Notes

Not only are promissory notes often negotiable, they can also be sold. Suppose your business supplies merchandise to several retail stores on credit. The retailers sign promissory notes, agreeing to pay at specified times. Later, but before the notes come due, your business is in need of cash to pay off certain outstanding bills. In other words, you have a cash-flow problem.

When this happens, you might solve the problem by asking your customers to retire, that is, pay off their notes early, understanding that they are not legally obligated to do so. If they are not in a position to retire their loans, you might decide to sell some or all of the notes to a bank, thus gaining the cash you need now.

In buying a note, the banking institution is actually lending you money. You and your business are contingently liable. In other words, should you customer **default**—that is, not pay off the note when it matures—the bank will require you to remit the maturity value of the note.

When the bank buys a note, it discounts it, deducting in advance a discount fee calculated on the maturity value of the original loan. What you receive, once this discount it taken, is called the **net proceeds.**

In determining bank discount and net proceeds, the formula for ordinary interest at exact time,

$$\text{Principal} \times \text{Rate} \times \text{Time} = \text{Interest},$$

is used as follows.

Step 1 Calculate the interest due on the note at maturity:

$$\text{Face value} \times \text{Interest rate} \times \text{Time of note} = \text{Interest}.$$

Step 2 Add this interest to the face value to determine the maturity value.

Step 3 Calculate the **discount period,** that is, the time remaining between the date a promissory note is sold to the bank and the note's maturity date. Note this definition carefully. Do not be confused. The discount period is *not* the time between the date of the note's origin and the date it is taken to the bank.

Step 4 Compute the amount of the bank discount, using this formula:

HOW THE PERCENTAGE FORMULA APPLIES

Maturity value = Base
Rate of discount = Rate
Discount period = Time
Bank discount fee = Percentage

$$\text{Maturity value} \times \text{Rate of discount} \times \text{Discount period} = \text{Bank discount fee}$$
$$\text{Base} \times \text{Rate} = \text{Percentage}$$

Step 5 Determine the net proceeds by subtracting the discount fee from the maturity value.

Example 1 On April 12, Fielding Truck Sales, Inc., accepts a 90-day note for $4,500, at an annual interest rate of 12%. On May 15, the company takes this note to its bank to be discounted. Determine the net proceeds, given a bank discount rate of 14%.

Step 1 Find the interest due.

$$\$4{,}500 \times .12 \times \frac{90}{360} = \$135$$

Step 2 Compute the maturity value.

$$\$4{,}500 + \$135 = \$4{,}635$$

Step 3 Determine the discount period, finding the due date.

```
                April has        30 days
              Date of note    −  12 th of April
                                 18
                May has          31 days
                June has       + 30 days
              Due date = 90  −  79 = 11th of July
```

Then find the discount days.

```
                May has          31 days
              Date of discount − 15 th of May
                                 16
                June has       + 30 days
                                 46
              Due date        + 11 th of July
                                 57 days in discount
                                    period
```

Step 4 Find the amount of the bank discount. Note that 360, the business year, is used as the denominator in the time fraction.

$$\$4{,}635 \times .14 \times \frac{57}{360} = \$102.74$$

Step 5 Calculate the net proceeds.

$$\$4{,}635 − \$102.74 = \$4{,}532.26$$

Answer The net proceeds that Fielding Truck Sales, Inc., receives from the bank is $4,532.26.

Self-Check

1. Abraham Kennedy of Kennedy Brothers Market takes a note to the bank on March 31 to have it discounted. If the note was drawn on March 5 and is for 60 days, what is the discount period? _____

2. If the note Abraham Kennedy has discounted is for $6,500 at an annual interest rate of 13%, and the discount rate at his bank is 15%, what are his net proceeds? _____

ANSWERS 1. 34 days   2. Interest due = $140.83
                         Maturity value = $6,640.83
                         Amount discount = $94.08
                         Net proceeds = $6,546.75

WHERE DID THE AMERICAN DOLLAR COME FROM?

In 1785, the dollar was adopted as the official currency of the United States of America. The new monetary system was based on a version of the decimal system contrived by Thomas Jefferson.

Assignment 10.2

Finance

1. Banachek Advertising, Inc., accepts a $5,000 note from one of its clients on June 12. The note is for 90 days at 14% interest. Banachek turns it over to First National Bank on July 14, to be discounted at a rate of $14\frac{1}{2}\%$. Calculate the net proceeds that Banachek will receive.

   $\$5{,}000 \times .14 \times \dfrac{90}{360} = \$175$ interest $\$5{,}000 + 175 = \$5{,}175$ maturity value

   $\$5{,}175 \times .145 \times \dfrac{58}{360} = \$120.89$ discount

   $\$5{,}175 - 120.89 = \$5{,}054.11$ net proceeds

   $5,054.11 net proceeds

   ```
   30 June
   -12 th
   18 June        90
   31 July       -80
   31 Aug        10th Sept
   80 days        note due
           31 July
           14 th date of discount
           17
           31 Aug
           10 th Sept
           58 day discount period
   ```

2. Mom and Pop's Grocery Store signs a note payable to Big Brother Wholesale Produce. The note is signed on November 3, and it is due on the following April 5. It is in the amount of $3,250 at 11.5% interest. On December 5, Big Brother has the note discounted at the rate of 12.75%. What are its net proceeds?

   $\$3{,}250 \times .115 \times \dfrac{153}{360} = \$158.84$ interest $\$3{,}250 + 158.84 = \$3{,}408.84$ maturity value

   $\$3{,}408.84 \times .1275 \times \dfrac{121}{360} = \$146.08$ discount

   $\$3{,}408.84 - 146.08 = \$3{,}262.76$ net proceeds

   $3,262.76 net proceeds

   ```
   30 Nov
   - 3
   27 Nov
   31 Dec
   31 Jan
   28 Feb
   31 Mar
    5 April
   153 days
           31 Dec
          - 5 date of discount
           26 Dec
           31 Jan
           28 Feb
           31 Mar
            5 April
          121 days discount period
   ```

As an officer of Acom Bank, you are asked to find the discount period on several notes accepted by the institution, according to the following information.

	Date Note is Made	Date of Discount	Loan Period	Discount Period
3.	October 18	December 15	90 days	32 days
4.	September 20	December 30	115 days	14 days
5.	August 15	September 10	60 days	34 days
6.	July 7	August 1	30 days	5 days
7.	June 30	July 20	45 days	25 days
8.	May 2	June 5	60 days	26 days
9.	April 18	August 5	250 days	141 days
10.	March 1	March 20	60 days	41 days
11.	February 4	August 17	300 days	106 days
12.	January 12	January 31	230 days	211 days

Example
```
7.  30 in June
   -30 Note is made
    0 days in June
   31 July
   31 days
   45 days period of loan
   -31
   14 Aug
   31 July
  -20 Date of discount
   11
  +14 Aug
   25 days discount period
```

continued

Assignment 10.2 continued

13. Tandak Corporation holds a $3,450, 12%, 90-day note dated July 15. It sells this note on August 10 at a discount of $14\frac{1}{2}$%. What are its net proceeds?

$3,450 × .12 × $\frac{40}{360}$ = $103.50 interest $3,450 + $103.50 = $3,553.50 maturity value

$3,553.50 × .145 × $\frac{64}{360}$ = $91.60 discount

$3,553.50 − 91.60 = $3,461.90 net proceeds

$3,461.90 net proceeds

```
 81 July
− 15
 16 July
 31 Aug
 30 Sept            90
 77 days          − 77
 31 Aug            13 Oct
− 10
 21 Aug
 30 Sept
 13 th Oct
 64 days discount period
```

14. Maki Meat Packing Company of Ironwood, Michigan, accepts a note on September 12, in exchange for several sides of beef. The note has a face value of $1,200 and is for 70 days at $10\frac{3}{4}$% interest. On October 19, the note is discounted at $12\frac{1}{2}$%. What are Maki's net proceeds?

$1,200 × .1075 × $\frac{70}{360}$ = $25.08 interest

$1,200 + 25.08 = $1,225.08 maturity value

$1,225.08 × .125 × $\frac{33}{360}$ = $14.04 discount

$1,225.08 − 14.04 = $1,211.04 net proceeds

$1,211.04 net proceeds

```
 30 Sept
 12
 18 Sept            70 days
 31 Oct           − 49
 49 days            21 Nov
 31 Oct
 19
 12 Oct
 21 Nov
 33 days discount period
```

15. Martina Nastasi had a $6,000, 40-day, $9\frac{3}{4}$% note discounted at her bank on March 6. If the note was made on March 1 and was discounted at 11%, what were Martina's net proceeds?

$6,000 × .0975 × $\frac{40}{360}$ = $65 interest $6,000 + 65 = $6,065 maturity value

$6,065 × .11 × $\frac{35}{360}$ = $64.86 discount

$6,065 − 64.86 = $6,000.14 net proceeds

$6,000.14 net proceeds

```
 31 March          40 days
−  1             − 30
 30 March          10 April
                   due date
 31 March
−  6
 25 March
 10 th April
 35 day discount period
```

Manfred De Lane, who works at Seaforth National Bank, must compile financial information on several notes discounted by the institution at the rate of $13\frac{3}{4}$%. Help him by filling in the blanks below.

	16.	17.	18.	19.	20.
Date note is made	November 7	January 28	March 8	August 15	July 12
Term of note (days)	30 days	60 days	90 days	60 days	200 days
Face value	$740	$1,500	$33,000	$856	$9,958
Interest rate	12%	13%	$11\frac{1}{2}$%	$12\frac{1}{2}$%	$11\frac{3}{4}$%
Discount date	November 15	March 15	May 15	September 15	December 15
Amount of interest	a) $7.40	a) $27.08	a) $948.75	a) $17.83	a) $650.04
Maturity value	b) $747.40	b) $1,527.08	b) $33,948.75	b) $873.83	b) $10,608.04
Discount period	c) 22 days	c) 4 days	c) 22 days	c) 29 days	c) 44 days
Amount of discount	d) $6.28	d) $2.33	d) $285.26	d) $9.68	d) $178.27
Net proceeds	e) $741.12	e) $1,524.75	e) $33,663.49	e) $864.15	e) $10,429.77

10.3 Consumer Loans

More and more businesses and individuals find themselves needing funds for immediate use beyond those their ongoing incomes provide. They borrow from banks, credit unions, savings-and-loan institutions, finance companies, and individuals.

In today's marketplace, one of the most common uses of the **consumer** or personal **loan** is the charge account, such as VISA or Mastercard. These systems allow the consumer to buy on credit with the option of paying off the amount owed over a period of time—actually making payments on a loan.

Before going into debt, ask yourself some questions.

Can I comfortably meet the payments on a regular basis?

Am I committing too much of my income in advance, money I might need for emergencies?

Is the cost of the loan reasonable?

In 1969, Congress passed the Consumer Credit Protection Act, commonly called the Truth-in-Lending Law. This law requires that the creditor inform you of the cost of credit, that is, the rate of interest. In some states, those without so-called usury laws, which place a ceiling on the rate of interest a creditor can charge, you may be paying interest on personal loans at rates of 18 to 20 percent or higher.

Note that the interest rate originally quoted by the lender may be quite different from and considerably lower than the **effective interest rate**, the actual rate of interest being charged. In some cases, this rate, also called the **annual percentage rate** or APR, may not be disclosed by the lender until the signing of the final loan papers.

Once you as a consumer know certain facts about the terms of the proposed loan, you can use a formula to calculate the effective interest rate. The result will be only a rough estimate. It is usually higher than the actual effective interest rate and is not sufficiently accurate to meet the requirements of the Consumer Credit Protection Act. Nevertheless, it gives you an idea of the rate of interest you will really pay.

To find the estimated effective interest rate:

Step 1 Determine the actual total paid, multiplying the amount per loan payment by the number of payments required.

Step 2 Determine the amount of interest due by subtracting the amount of the loan from the actual total paid.

Step 3 Calculate the effective interest rate by using a formula derived from the formula for computing interest:

$$\text{Interest} = \text{Principal} \times \text{Rate} \times \text{Time}.$$

This derivation is

$$\frac{2 \times \text{Number of payment periods in 1 year} \times \text{Interest}}{\text{Amount of loan} \times (\text{Number of payments} + 1)} = \text{Effective interest rate}$$

NOTE: "Payment periods" in the numerator means the number of payments that could be made in a year. If the loan is to be repaid on a monthly basis, then 12 payments could be made. If repayment is made weekly, 52 payments could be made. This number used in the numerator refers to what is possible, not to the actual number of payments for the particular loan.

Finance

Example 1 To pay the utility bill at his model shop, Peter Kambrick borrows $100 from Waverly National Bank. He agrees to pay off the loan in 4 monthly installments of $26 each. What effective rate of interest is he paying?

Step 1 Find the actual total paid. Multiply the amount per payment by the number of payments.

$26 Amount per payment
× 4 No. of payments
$104 Actual total

Step 2 Find the amount of interest due. Subtract the amount of the loan from the total paid.

$104 Actual total
− 100 Amount of loan
$ 4 Interest

Step 3 Use the formula

$$\frac{2 \times \text{No. of payment periods in 1 year} \times \text{Interest}}{\text{Amount of loan} \times (\text{No. of payments} + 1)}$$

Because payments are to be made monthly, 12 payments are possible in any one year.

$$\frac{2 \times 12 \times \$4}{\$100 \times (4 + 1)} = \frac{96}{500} = .192$$

Answer The estimated effective rate of interest is 19.2%.

Another method of finding effective interest rate, and one that meets federal requirements, is to use annual percentage rate tables. These tables can be obtained from Federal Reserve Banks. They list installment charges on $100 borrowed in a variety of time and interest rate circumstances. Below is a representative exerpt from an APR table.

Annual Percentage Rate

Number of Payments	10.00%	10.25%	10.50%	10.75%	11.00%	11.25%	11.50%	11.75%	12.00%	12.25%	12.50%	12.75%	13.00%	13.25%	13.50%	13.75%
(Finance Charge Per $100 of Amount Financed)															
1	0.83	0.85	0.87	0.90	0.92	0.94	0.96	0.98	1.00	1.02	1.04	1.06	1.08	1.10	1.12	1.15
2	1.25	1.28	1.31	1.35	1.38	1.41	1.44	1.47	1.50	1.53	1.57	1.60	1.63	1.66	1.69	1.72
3	1.67	1.71	1.76	1.80	1.84	1.88	1.92	1.96	2.01	2.05	2.09	2.13	2.17	2.22	2.26	2.30
4	2.09	2.14	2.20	2.25	2.30	2.35	2.41	2.46	2.51	2.57	2.62	2.67	2.72	2.78	2.83	2.88
5	2.51	2.58	2.64	2.70	2.77	2.83	2.89	2.96	3.02	3.08	3.15	3.21	3.27	3.34	3.40	3.46
6	2.94	3.01	3.08	3.16	3.23	3.31	3.38	3.45	3.53	3.60	3.68	3.75	3.83	3.90	3.97	4.05
7	3.36	3.45	3.53	3.62	3.70	3.78	3.87	3.95	4.04	4.12	4.21	4.29	4.38	4.47	4.55	4.64
8	3.79	3.88	3.98	4.07	4.17	4.26	4.36	4.46	4.55	4.65	4.74	4.84	4.94	5.03	5.13	5.22
9	4.21	4.32	4.43	4.53	4.64	4.75	4.85	4.96	5.07	5.17	5.28	5.39	5.49	5.60	5.71	5.82
10	4.64	4.76	4.88	4.99	5.11	5.23	5.35	5.46	5.58	5.70	5.82	5.94	6.05	6.17	6.29	6.41
11	5.07	5.20	5.33	5.45	5.58	5.71	5.84	5.97	6.10	6.23	6.36	6.49	6.62	6.75	6.88	7.01
12	5.50	5.64	5.78	5.92	6.06	6.20	6.34	6.48	6.62	6.76	6.90	7.04	7.13	7.32	7.46	7.60
13	5.93	6.08	6.23	6.38	6.53	6.68	6.84	6.99	7.14	7.29	7.44	7.59	7.75	7.90	8.05	8.20
14	6.36	6.52	6.69	6.85	7.01	7.17	7.34	7.50	7.66	7.82	7.99	8.15	8.31	8.48	8.64	8.81
15	6.80	6.97	7.14	7.32	7.49	7.66	7.84	8.01	8.19	8.36	8.53	8.71	8.88	9.06	9.23	9.41
16	7.23	7.41	7.60	7.78	7.97	8.15	8.34	8.53	8.71	8.90	9.08	9.27	9.46	9.64	9.83	10.02
17	7.67	7.86	8.06	8.25	8.45	8.65	8.84	9.04	9.24	9.44	9.63	9.83	10.03	10.23	10.43	10.63
18	8.10	8.11	8.52	8.73	8.93	9.14	9.35	9.56	9.77	9.98	10.19	10.40	10.61	10.82	11.03	11.24
19	8.54	8.76	8.98	9.20	9.42	9.64	9.86	10.08	10.30	10.52	10.74	10.96	11.18	11.41	11.63	11.85
20	8.98	9.21	9.44	9.67	9.90	10.13	10.37	10.60	10.83	11.06	11.30	11.53	11.76	12.00	12.23	12.46
21	9.42	9.66	9.90	10.15	10.39	10.63	10.88	11.12	11.36	11.61	11.85	12.10	12.34	12.59	12.84	13.08
22	9.86	10.12	10.37	10.62	10.88	11.13	11.39	11.64	11.90	12.16	12.41	12.67	12.93	13.19	13.44	13.70
23	10.30	10.57	10.84	11.10	11.37	11.63	11.90	12.17	12.44	12.71	12.97	13.24	13.51	13.78	14.05	14.32
24	10.75	11.02	11.30	11.58	11.86	12.14	12.42	12.70	12.98	13.26	13.54	13.82	14.10	14.38	14.66	14.95
25	11.19	11.48	11.77	12.06	12.35	12.64	12.93	13.22	13.52	13.81	14.10	14.40	14.69	14.98	15.28	15.57
26	11.64	11.94	12.24	12.54	12.85	13.15	13.45	13.75	14.06	14.36	14.67	14.97	15.28	15.59	15.89	16.20
27	12.09	12.40	12.71	13.03	13.34	13.66	13.97	14.20	14.60	14.92	15.24	15.56	15.87	16.19	16.51	16.83
28	12.53	12.86	13.18	13.51	13.84	14.16	14.49	14.82	15.15	15.48	15.81	16.14	16.47	16.80	17.13	17.46
29	12.98	13.32	13.66	14.00	14.33	14.67	15.01	15.35	15.70	16.04	16.38	16.72	17.07	17.41	17.75	18.10
30	13.43	13.78	14.13	14.48	14.83	15.19	15.54	15.89	16.24	16.60	16.95	17.31	17.66	18.02	18.38	18.74

(Continued)

Annual Percentage Rate

Number of Payments	10.00%	10.25%	10.50%	10.75%	11.00%	11.25%	11.50%	11.75%	12.00%	12.25%	12.50%	12.75%	13.00%	13.25%	13.50%	13.75%
31	13.89	14.25	14.61	14.97	15.33	15.70	16.06	16.43	16.79	17.16	17.53	17.90	18.27	18.63	19.00	19.38
32	14.34	14.71	15.09	15.46	15.84	16.21	16.59	16.97	17.35	17.73	18.11	18.49	18.87	19.25	19.63	20.02
33	14.79	15.18	15.57	15.95	16.34	16.73	17.12	17.51	17.90	18.29	18.65	19.08	19.47	19.87	20.26	20.66
34	15.25	15.65	16.05	16.44	16.85	17.25	17.65	18.05	18.46	18.86	19.27	19.67	20.08	20.49	20.30	21.31
35	15.70	16.11	16.53	16.94	17.35	17.77	18.18	18.60	19.01	19.43	19.85	20.27	20.69	21.11	21.53	21.95
36	16.16	16.58	17.01	17.43	17.86	18.29	18.71	19.14	19.57	20.00	20.43	20.87	21.30	21.73	22.17	22.60
37	16.62	17.06	17.49	17.93	18.37	18.81	19.25	19.69	20.13	20.58	21.02	21.46	21.91	22.36	22.81	23.25
38	17.08	17.53	17.98	18.43	18.88	19.33	19.78	20.24	20.69	21.15	21.61	22.07	22.52	22.99	23.45	23.91
39	17.54	18.00	18.46	18.93	19.39	19.86	20.32	20.79	21.26	21.73	22.20	22.67	23.14	23.61	24.00	24.56
40	18.00	18.48	18.95	19.43	19.90	20.38	20.86	21.34	21.82	22.30	22.79	23.27	23.76	24.25	24.73	25.22
41	18.47	18.95	19.44	19.93	20.42	20.91	21.40	21.89	22.39	22.88	23.38	23.88	24.38	24.88	25.38	25.98
42	18.93	19.43	19.93	20.43	20.93	21.44	21.94	22.45	22.96	23.47	23.98	24.49	25.00	25.51	26.03	26.55
43	19.40	19.91	20.42	20.94	21.45	21.97	22.49	23.01	23.53	24.05	24.57	25.10	25.62	26.15	26.68	27.21
44	19.86	20.39	20.91	21.44	21.97	22.50	23.03	23.57	24.10	24.64	25.17	25.71	26.25	26.79	27.33	27.88
45	20.33	20.87	21.41	21.95	22.59	23.03	23.58	24.12	24.67	25.22	25.77	26.32	26.88	27.43	27.99	28.55
46	20.80	21.35	21.90	22.46	23.01	23.57	24.13	24.69	25.25	25.81	26.17	26.94	27.51	24.08	28.65	29.22
47	21.27	21.83	22.40	22.97	23.53	24.10	24.68	25.25	25.82	26.40	26.98	27.56	28.14	28.72	29.31	29.89
48	21.74	22.32	22.90	23.48	24.06	24.64	25.23	25.81	26.40	26.99	27.58	28.18	28.77	29.37	29.97	30.57
49	22.21	22.80	23.39	23.99	24.58	25.18	25.78	26.39	26.98	27.59	28.19	28.80	29.41	30.02	30.63	31.24
50	22.69	23.29	23.89	24.50	25.11	25.72	26.33	26.95	27.56	28.18	28.80	29.42	30.04	30.67	31.29	31.92
51	23.16	23.78	24.40	25.02	25.64	26.26	26.89	27.52	28.15	28.78	29.41	30.05	30.68	31.32	31.96	32.60
52	23.64	24.27	24.90	25.53	26.17	26.81	27.45	28.09	28.73	29.38	30.02	30.67	31.32	31.98	32.63	33.29
53	24.11	24.76	25.40	26.05	26.70	27.35	28.00	28.66	29.32	29.48	30.64	31.30	31.97	32.63	33.30	33.97
54	24.59	25.25	25.91	26.57	27.23	27.90	28.56	29.23	29.91	30.58	31.25	31.93	32.61	33.29	33.98	34.66
55	25.07	25.74	26.41	27.09	27.77	28.44	29.13	29.81	30.50	31.18	31.87	32.56	33.26	33.95	34.65	35.35
56	25.55	26.23	26.92	27.61	28.30	28.99	29.69	30.39	31.09	31.79	32.49	33.20	33.91	34.62	35.33	36.04
57	26.03	26.73	27.43	28.13	28.84	29.54	30.25	30.97	31.68	32.39	33.11	33.83	34.56	35.28	36.01	36.74
58	26.51	27.23	27.94	28.66	29.37	30.10	30.82	21.55	32.27	33.00	33.74	34.47	35.21	35.95	36.69	37.43
59	27.00	27.72	28.45	29.18	29.91	30.65	31.39	32.13	32.87	33.61	34.36	35.11	35.86	36.62	37.37	38.13
60	27.48	28.22	28.96	29.71	30.45	31.20	31.96	32.71	33.47	34.23	34.99	35.75	36.52	37.29	38.06	38.83

Number of Payments	14.00%	14.25%	14.50%	14.75%	15.00%	15.25%	15.50%	15.75%	16.00%	16.25%	16.50%	16.75%	17.00%	17.25%	17.50%	17.75%
(Finance Charge Per $100 of Amount Financed)															
1	1.17	1.19	1.21	1.23	1.25	1.27	1.29	1.31	1.33	1.35	1.37	1.40	1.42	1.44	1.46	1.48
2	1.75	1.78	1.82	1.85	1.88	1.91	1.94	1.97	2.00	2.04	2.07	2.10	2.13	2.16	2.19	2.22
3	2.34	2.38	2.43	2.47	2.51	2.55	2.59	2.64	2.68	2.72	2.76	2.80	2.85	2.89	2.93	2.97
4	2.93	2.99	3.04	3.09	3.14	3.20	3.25	3.30	3.36	3.41	3.46	3.51	3.57	3.62	3.67	3.73
5	3.53	3.59	3.65	3.72	3.78	3.84	3.91	3.97	4.04	4.10	4.16	4.21	4.29	4.35	4.42	4.48
6	4.12	4.20	4.27	4.35	4.42	4.49	4.57	4.64	4.72	4.79	4.87	4.94	5.02	5.09	5.17	5.24
7	4.72	4.81	4.89	4.98	5.06	5.15	5.23	5.32	5.40	5.49	5.58	5.66	5.75	5.83	5.92	6.00
8	5.32	5.42	5.51	5.61	5.71	5.80	5.90	6.00	6.09	6.19	6.29	6.38	6.48	6.58	6.67	6.77
9	5.92	6.03	6.14	6.25	6.35	6.46	6.57	6.68	6.78	6.89	7.00	7.11	7.22	7.32	7.43	7.54
10	6.53	6.65	6.77	6.88	7.00	7.12	7.24	7.36	7.48	7.60	7.72	7.84	7.96	8.08	8.19	8.31
11	7.14	7.27	7.40	7.53	7.66	7.79	7.92	8.05	8.18	8.31	8.44	8.57	8.70	8.83	8.96	9.09
12	7.74	7.89	8.03	8.17	8.31	8.45	8.59	8.74	8.88	9.02	9.16	9.30	9.45	9.59	9.73	9.87
13	8.36	8.51	8.66	8.81	8.97	9.12	9.27	9.43	9.58	9.73	9.89	10.04	10.20	10.35	10.50	10.66
14	8.97	9.13	9.30	9.46	9.63	9.79	9.96	10.12	10.29	10.45	10.62	10.78	10.95	11.11	11.23	11.45
15	9.59	9.76	9.94	10.11	10.29	10.47	10.64	10.82	11.00	11.17	11.35	11.53	11.71	11.88	12.06	12.24
16	10.20	10.39	10.58	10.77	10.95	11.14	11.33	11.52	11.71	11.90	12.09	12.28	12.46	12.65	12.84	13.03
17	10.82	11.02	11.22	11.42	11.62	11.82	12.02	12.22	12.42	12.62	12.83	13.03	13.23	13.43	13.63	13.83
18	11.45	11.66	11.87	12.08	12.29	12.50	12.72	12.93	13.14	13.35	13.57	13.78	13.99	14.21	14.42	14.64
19	12.07	12.30	12.52	12.74	12.97	13.19	13.41	13.64	13.86	14.09	14.31	14.54	14.76	14.99	15.22	15.44
20	12.70	12.93	13.17	13.41	13.64	13.88	14.11	14.35	14.59	14.82	15.06	15.30	15.54	15.77	16.01	16.25
21	13.33	13.58	13.82	14.07	14.32	14.57	14.82	15.06	15.31	15.56	15.81	16.06	16.31	16.66	16.81	17.07
22	13.96	14.22	14.48	14.74	15.00	15.26	15.52	15.78	16.04	16.30	16.57	16.83	17.09	17.36	17.62	17.88
23	14.59	14.87	15.14	15.41	15.68	15.96	16.23	16.50	16.78	17.05	17.32	17.60	17.88	18.15	18.43	18.70
24	15.23	15.51	15.80	16.08	16.37	16.65	16.94	17.22	17.51	17.80	18.09	18.37	18.65	18.95	19.24	19.53
25	15.87	16.17	16.46	16.76	17.06	17.35	17.65	17.95	18.25	18.55	19.85	19.15	19.45	19.75	20.05	20.36

(Continued)

Annual Percentage Rate

Number of Payments	14.00%	14.25%	14.50%	14.75%	15.00%	15.25%	15.50%	15.75%	16.00%	16.25%	16.50%	16.75%	17.00%	17.25%	17.50%	17.75%
26	16.51	16.82	17.13	17.44	17.75	18.06	18.37	18.69	18.99	19.30	19.62	19.93	20.24	20.56	20.97	21.19
27	17.15	17.47	17.80	18.12	18.44	18.76	19.09	19.41	19.74	20.06	20.14	20.71	21.04	21.37	21.69	22.02
28	17.80	18.13	18.47	18.80	19.14	19.47	19.81	20.15	20.48	20.82	21.16	21.50	21.86	22.18	22.52	22.86
29	18.45	18.79	19.14	19.49	19.83	20.18	20.53	20.88	21.23	21.58	21.76	22.29	22.64	22.99	23.35	23.70
30	19.10	19.45	19.81	20.17	20.54	20.90	21.26	21.62	21.99	22.35	22.72	23.08	23.45	23.81	24.18	24.55
31	19.75	20.12	20.49	20.87	21.24	21.61	21.99	22.37	22.74	23.12	23.50	23.49	24.26	24.64	25.02	25.40
32	20.40	20.79	21.17	21.56	21.95	22.33	22.72	23.11	23.50	23.89	24.28	24.68	25.07	25.46	25.86	26.25
33	21.06	21.46	21.85	22.25	22.65	23.06	23.46	23.86	24.26	24.67	25.07	25.48	25.88	26.29	26.70	27.11
34	21.72	22.13	22.54	22.95	23.37	23.78	24.19	24.61	25.03	25.44	25.86	26.29	26.70	27.17	27.54	27.97
35	22.38	22.80	23.23	23.65	24.08	24.51	24.94	25.36	25.79	26.23	26.66	27.09	27.52	27.96	28.39	28.83
36	23.04	23.48	23.92	24.35	24.80	25.24	25.68	26.12	26.57	27.01	27.46	27.90	28.35	28.80	29.25	29.70
37	23.70	24.16	24.61	25.06	25.51	25.97	26.42	26.88	27.34	27.80	28.26	28.72	29.18	29.64	30.10	30.57
38	24.37	24.84	25.30	25.77	26.24	26.70	27.17	27.64	28.11	28.59	29.06	29.53	30.01	30.40	30.96	31.44
39	25.04	25.52	26.00	26.48	26.96	27.44	27.92	28.41	28.89	29.38	29.87	30.36	30.85	31.34	31.83	32.32
40	25.71	26.20	26.70	27.19	27.69	28.18	28.68	29.18	29.68	30.18	30.69	31.18	31.68	32.18	32.69	33.20
41	26.39	26.89	27.40	27.91	28.41	28.92	29.44	29.95	30.46	30.97	31.49	32.01	32.52	33.04	33.56	34.08
42	27.06	27.58	28.10	28.62	29.15	29.67	30.19	30.72	31.25	31.78	32.31	32.84	33.37	33.90	34.44	34.97
43	27.74	28.27	28.81	29.34	29.88	30.42	30.96	31.50	32.04	32.58	33.13	33.67	34.22	34.76	35.31	35.86
44	28.42	28.97	29.52	30.07	30.62	31.17	31.72	32.29	32.83	33.39	33.95	34.51	35.07	35.63	36.19	36.76
45	29.11	29.67	30.23	30.79	31.36	31.92	32.49	33.06	33.63	34.20	34.77	35.35	35.02	36.50	37.08	37.66
46	29.79	30.36	30.94	31.52	32.10	32.68	33.26	33.84	34.43	35.01	35.60	36.19	36.78	37.17	37.96	38.56
47	30.48	31.07	31.66	32.25	32.84	33.44	34.03	34.63	35.23	35.83	36.43	37.04	37.64	38.25	38.86	39.46
48	31.17	31.77	32.37	32.98	33.59	34.20	34.81	35.42	36.03	36.65	37.27	37.88	38.50	39.13	39.75	40.37
49	31.86	32.48	33.09	33.71	34.34	34.96	35.59	36.21	36.84	37.47	38.10	38.74	39.37	40.01	40.66	41.29
50	32.55	33.18	33.82	34.45	35.09	35.73	36.37	37.01	37.65	38.30	38.94	39.59	40.24	40.89	41.55	42.20
51	33.25	33.89	34.54	35.19	35.84	36.49	37.15	37.81	38.46	39.12	39.79	40.45	41.11	41.78	42.45	43.12
52	33.95	34.61	35.27	35.93	36.60	37.27	37.94	38.61	39.28	39.96	40.63	41.31	41.99	42.67	43.36	44.04
53	34.65	35.32	36.00	36.68	37.36	38.04	38.72	39.41	40.10	40.74	41.48	42.17	42.87	43.57	44.27	44.97
54	35.35	36.04	36.73	37.42	38.12	38.82	39.52	40.22	40.92	41.63	42.33	43.04	43.75	44.47	45.14	45.90
55	36.05	36.76	37.46	38.17	38.88	39.60	40.31	41.03	41.74	42.47	43.19	43.91	44.64	45.37	46.10	46.83
56	36.76	37.48	38.20	38.92	39.65	40.38	41.11	41.84	42.57	43.31	44.05	44.79	45.53	46.27	47.02	47.77
57	37.47	37.20	38.94	39.68	40.42	41.16	41.91	42.65	43.40	44.15	44.91	45.66	46.47	47.18	47.96	48.71
58	38.18	38.93	39.68	40.43	41.19	41.95	42.71	43.47	44.23	45.00	45.77	46.54	47.32	48.09	48.87	49.65
59	38.89	39.66	40.42	41.19	41.96	42.74	43.51	44.20	45.07	45.85	46.66	47.42	48.71	49.01	49.80	50.60
60	39.61	40.39	41.17	41.95	42.74	43.53	44.32	45.11	45.91	46.71	47.51	48.31	49.12	49.92	50.73	51.55

Number of Payments	18.00%	18.25%	18.50%	18.75%	19.00%	19.25%	19.50%	19.75%	20.00%	20.25%	20.50%	20.75%	21.00%	21.25%	21.50%	21.75%
					(Finance Charge for $100 of Amount Financed)											
1	1.50	1.52	1.54	1.56	1.58	1.60	1.62	1.65	1.67	1.69	1.71	1.73	1.75	1.77	1.79	1.81
2	2.26	2.29	2.32	2.35	2.38	2.41	2.44	2.48	2.51	2.54	2.57	2.60	2.63	2.66	2.70	2.73
3	3.01	3.06	3.10	3.14	3.18	3.23	3.27	3.31	3.35	3.39	3.44	3.48	3.52	3.56	3.60	3.65
4	3.78	3.83	3.88	3.94	3.99	4.04	4.10	4.15	4.20	4.25	4.31	4.36	4.41	4.47	4.52	4.57
5	4.54	4.61	4.67	4.74	4.80	4.86	4.93	4.99	5.06	5.12	5.18	5.25	5.31	5.37	5.44	5.50
6	5.32	5.39	5.46	5.54	5.61	5.69	5.76	5.84	5.91	5.99	6.06	6.14	6.21	6.29	6.36	6.44
7	6.09	6.18	6.26	6.35	6.43	6.52	6.60	6.69	6.78	6.86	6.95	7.04	7.12	7.21	7.29	7.38
8	6.87	6.96	7.06	7.16	7.26	7.35	7.45	7.55	7.64	7.74	7.84	7.94	8.03	8.13	8.23	8.33
9	7.65	7.76	7.87	7.97	8.08	8.19	8.30	8.41	8.52	8.63	8.73	8.84	8.95	9.06	9.17	9.28
10	8.43	8.55	8.67	8.79	8.91	9.03	9.15	9.27	9.39	9.51	9.63	9.75	9.88	10.00	10.12	10.24
11	9.22	9.35	9.49	9.62	9.75	9.88	10.01	10.14	10.28	10.41	10.54	10.67	10.80	10.94	11.07	11.20
12	10.02	10.16	10.30	10.44	10.59	10.73	10.87	11.02	11.16	11.31	11.45	11.59	11.74	11.88	12.02	12.17
13	10.81	10.97	11.12	11.28	11.43	11.59	11.74	11.90	12.05	12.21	12.36	12.52	12.67	12.83	12.99	13.14
14	11.61	11.78	11.95	12.11	12.28	12.45	12.61	12.78	12.95	13.11	13.28	13.45	13.62	13.79	13.95	14.12
15	12.42	12.59	12.77	12.95	13.13	13.31	13.49	13.67	13.85	14.03	14.21	14.39	14.57	14.75	14.93	15.11
16	13.22	13.41	13.60	13.80	13.99	14.18	14.37	14.56	14.75	14.94	15.13	15.33	15.52	15.71	15.90	16.10
17	14.04	14.24	14.44	14.64	14.85	15.05	15.25	15.46	15.66	15.86	16.07	16.27	16.48	16.68	16.89	17.09
18	14.85	15.07	15.28	15.49	15.71	15.93	16.14	16.36	16.57	16.79	17.01	17.22	17.44	17.66	17.88	18.09
19	15.67	15.90	16.12	16.35	16.58	16.81	17.03	17.26	17.49	17.72	17.95	18.18	18.41	18.64	18.87	19.10
20	16.49	16.73	16.97	17.21	17.45	17.69	17.93	18.17	18.41	18.66	18.90	19.14	19.38	19.63	19.87	20.11

Chapter 10

Annual Percentage Rate

Number of Payments	18.00%	18.25%	18.50%	18.75%	19.00%	19.25%	19.50%	19.75%	20.00%	20.25%	20.50%	20.75%	21.00%	21.25%	21.50%	21.75%
21	17.32	17.57	17.82	18.07	18.33	18.58	18.83	19.09	19.34	19.60	19.85	20.11	20.36	20.62	20.87	21.13
22	18.15	18.41	18.68	18.94	19.21	19.47	19.74	20.01	20.27	20.54	20.81	21.08	21.34	21.61	21.88	22.15
23	18.98	19.26	19.54	19.81	20.09	20.37	20.65	20.93	21.21	21.49	21.77	22.05	22.33	22.61	22.90	23.18
24	19.82	20.11	20.40	20.69	20.98	21.27	21.56	21.86	22.15	22.44	22.74	23.03	23.33	23.62	23.92	24.21
25	20.66	20.96	21.27	21.57	21.87	22.18	22.48	22.79	23.10	23.40	23.71	24.02	24.32	24.63	24.94	25.25
26	21.50	21.82	22.14	22.45	22.77	23.09	23.41	23.73	24.04	24.36	24.68	25.01	25.33	25.65	25.97	26.79
27	22.35	22.68	23.01	23.34	23.67	24.00	24.33	24.67	25.00	25.33	25.67	26.00	26.34	26.67	27.01	27.34
28	23.20	23.55	23.89	24.23	24.58	24.92	25.27	25.61	25.96	26.30	26.65	27.00	27.35	27.70	28.05	28.40
29	24.06	24.41	24.77	25.13	25.49	25.84	26.20	26.56	26.92	27.28	27.64	28.00	28.37	28.73	29.09	29.46
30	24.92	25.29	25.66	26.03	26.40	26.77	27.14	27.52	27.89	28.26	28.64	29.01	29.39	29.77	30.14	30.52
31	25.78	26.16	26.55	26.93	27.32	27.70	28.09	28.47	28.86	29.25	29.64	30.03	30.42	30.81	31.20	31.59
32	26.65	27.04	27.44	27.84	28.24	28.64	29.04	29.44	29.84	30.24	30.66	31.05	31.45	31.85	32.26	32.67
33	27.52	27.93	28.34	28.75	29.16	29.57	29.99	30.40	30.82	31.23	31.65	32.07	32.49	32.91	33.33	33.75
34	28.39	28.81	29.24	29.66	30.09	30.52	30.95	31.37	31.80	32.23	32.67	33.10	33.53	33.96	34.40	34.83
35	29.27	29.71	30.14	30.58	31.02	31.47	31.91	32.35	32.79	33.24	33.68	34.13	34.58	35.03	35.47	35.92
36	30.15	30.60	31.05	31.51	31.96	32.42	32.87	33.33	33.79	34.25	34.71	35.17	35.63	36.09	36.56	37.02
37	31.03	31.50	31.97	32.43	32.90	33.37	33.84	34.32	34.79	35.26	35.74	36.21	36.69	37.16	37.64	38.12
38	31.92	32.40	32.88	33.37	33.85	34.33	34.82	35.30	35.79	36.28	36.77	37.26	37.75	38.24	38.73	39.23
39	32.81	33.31	33.80	34.30	34.80	35.30	35.80	36.30	36.80	37.30	37.81	38.31	38.82	39.32	39.83	40.34
40	33.71	34.22	34.73	35.24	35.75	36.26	36.78	37.29	37.81	38.33	38.85	39.37	39.89	40.41	40.93	41.46
41	34.61	35.13	35.66	36.18	36.71	37.24	37.77	38.30	38.83	39.36	39.89	40.43	40.96	41.50	42.04	42.58
42	35.51	36.05	36.59	37.13	37.67	38.21	38.76	39.30	39.85	40.40	40.95	41.50	42.05	42.60	43.15	43.71
43	36.42	36.97	37.52	38.08	38.63	39.19	39.75	40.31	40.87	41.44	42.00	42.57	43.13	43.70	44.27	44.84
44	37.33	37.89	38.46	39.03	39.60	40.18	40.75	41.33	41.90	42.48	43.06	43.64	44.22	44.81	45.39	45.98
45	38.24	38.82	39.41	39.99	40.58	41.17	41.75	42.35	42.94	43.53	44.13	44.72	45.32	45.92	46.52	47.12
46	39.16	39.75	40.35	40.95	41.55	42.16	42.76	43.37	43.98	44.58	45.20	45.81	46.42	47.03	47.65	48.27
47	40.08	40.69	41.30	41.92	42.54	43.15	43.77	44.40	45.02	45.64	46.27	46.90	47.53	48.16	48.79	49.42
48	41.00	41.63	42.26	42.89	43.52	44.15	44.79	45.43	46.07	46.71	47.35	47.99	48.64	49.28	49.93	50.58
49	41.93	42.57	43.22	43.86	44.51	45.16	45.81	46.46	47.12	47.77	48.43	49.09	49.75	50.41	51.08	51.74
50	42.86	43.52	44.18	44.84	45.50	46.17	46.83	47.50	48.17	48.84	49.52	50.19	50.87	51.55	52.23	52.91
51	43.79	44.47	45.14	45.82	46.50	47.18	47.86	48.55	49.23	49.92	50.61	51.30	51.99	52.69	53.38	54.08
52	44.73	45.42	46.11	46.80	47.50	48.20	48.89	49.59	50.30	51.00	51.71	52.41	53.12	53.83	54.55	55.26
53	45.67	46.38	47.08	47.79	48.50	49.22	49.93	50.65	51.37	52.09	52.81	53.53	54.26	54.98	55.71	56.44
54	46.62	47.34	48.06	48.79	49.51	50.24	50.97	51.70	52.44	53.17	53.91	54.65	55.39	56.14	56.88	57.63
55	47.57	48.30	49.04	49.78	50.52	51.27	52.02	52.76	53.52	54.27	55.02	55.78	56.54	57.30	58.06	58.82
56	48.52	49.27	50.03	50.78	51.54	52.30	53.06	53.83	54.60	55.37	56.14	56.91	57.68	58.46	59.24	60.02
57	49.47	50.24	51.01	51.79	52.56	53.34	54.12	54.90	55.68	56.47	57.25	58.04	58.84	59.63	60.43	61.22
58	50.43	51.22	52.00	52.79	53.58	54.38	55.17	55.97	56.77	57.57	58.38	59.18	59.99	60.80	61.62	62.43
59	51.39	52.20	53.00	53.80	54.61	55.42	56.23	57.05	57.87	58.68	59.51	60.33	61.15	61.98	62.81	63.64
60	52.36	53.18	54.00	54.82	55.64	56.47	57.30	58.13	58.96	59.80	60.64	61.48	62.32	63.17	64.01	64.86

SPEND NOW—PAY LATER!

Americans apparently love to buy with plastic. The annual credit-card debt in the United States is close to 110 billion dollars. In 1985, total interest paid on credit-card debt was about 12 billion dollars. To understand how our national thinking has changed over the years, consider this comparison. In 1960, the average consumer debt per person in the United States was $3,347. By 1986, this average had grown to $30,125 for every man, woman, and child in the country.

Finance

To determine the effective interest rate using a table, follow these steps. Note that steps 1 and 2 are identical to those for using the formula for effective interest rate.

Step 1 Determine the actual total to be repaid.

Step 2 Determine the amount of interest due.

Step 3 Calculate the loan installment charges by dividing the total borrowed into the amount of interest due.

Step 4 Multiply this figure by 100 to find the installment charges per $100.

Step 5 In the APR table, find the figure nearest the result of your calculations by reading across the row that corresponds to the number of payments for the particular loan.

Step 6 Find the APR that heads the column of the table in which the figure closest to the calculated figure appears.

Example 2 As shown in Example 1, Peter Kambrick borrowed $100 to be paid off in 4 monthly installments of $26 each. Using the APR table, determine his effective rate of interest.

Step 1 Find the actual total to be repaid.

$$\begin{array}{r} \$\ 26 \\ \times\ \ \ 4 \\ \hline \$104 \end{array}$$

Step 2 Find the amount of interest due.

$$\begin{array}{r} \$104 \\ -\ \ 100 \\ \hline \$\ \ 4 \end{array}$$

Step 3 Divide the total borrowed into the amount of interest due.

$$\frac{4}{100} = .04$$

Step 4 Multiply by 100. (Simply move the decimal point two places to the right.)

$$\begin{array}{r} 100 \\ \times\ .04 \\ \hline 4.00 \end{array}$$

Step 5 Find the closest figure in the table. $3.99

Step 6 Find the APR column heading. 19%

Answer The effective interest rate is 19%.

NOTE: When we applied the formula, the answer was 19.2%, higher than the figure above.

Self-Check

At Andrews National Bank, you borrow $450, to be repaid in installments of $28.31 per month for 18 months. Find each of the following.

1. The actual total you are paying _____

2. The amount of interest due _____

3. The approximate effective interest rate using the formula _____

4. The effective interest rate, using the table _____

ANSWERS   1. $509.58   2. $59.58   3. 16.7%   4. 16%

THE FIFTY-CENT PIECE

In 1948 the United States Mint began production of a new half-dollar coin with a profile of Benjamin Franklin on one side and the Liberty Bell on the other. This coin replaced the Liberty half dollar that had been in circulation since 1916. It was in turn superseded by the Kennedy fifty-cent piece in 1964. Because of the country's strong emotional feeling regarding its recently assassinated president, the Kennedy coin became an immediate collector's item.

Assignment 10.3

Finance

As a loan officer at Plainview State Bank, you arrange a number of consumer loans for clients. In each instance, calculate the amount the client actually repays, the amount of interest, and the effective rate of interest using the table.

	Amount of Loan	Number of Monthly Payments	Amount Per Payment	Total to be Repaid	Amount of Interest	Effective Interest Rate
1.	$200	10	$21.72	a) $217.20	b) $17.20	c) 18.25%

$21.72 \times 10 = \$217.20$ to be repaid
$\$217.20 - 200 = \$17.20$ interest
$\dfrac{17.20}{200} = .086 \times 100 = 8.60$ (closest figure in table = 8.55)

2.	$375	10	$40.20	a) 402.00	b) 27.00	c) 15.5%

$40.20 \times 10 = \$402$ to be repaid
$\$402 - 375 = \$27$ interest
$\dfrac{27}{375} = .072 \times 100 = 7.20$ (closest figure in table = 7.24)

3.	$150	8	$20.00	a) 160.00	b) 10.00	c) 17.5%

$\$20 \times 8 = 160$ to be repaid
$\$160 - 150 = \$10$ interest
$\dfrac{10}{150} = .06\overline{6} \times 100 = 6.67$ (in table)

4.	$400	15	$29.10	a) 436.50	b) 36.50	c) 13.25%

$\$29.10 \times 15 = \$436.50$ to be repaid
$\$436.50 - 400 = \$36.50$ interest
$\dfrac{36.5}{400} = .09125 \times 100 = 9.13$ (nearest table figure 9.06)

5.	$5,200	36	$179.00	a) 6,444	b) 1,244	c) 14.5%

$\$179 \times 36 = \$6,444$ to be repaid
$\$6,444 - 5,200 = \$1,244$ interest
$\dfrac{1244}{5200} = .2392307 \times 100 = 23.92$ (in table)

6. Steve Heck borrows $100 from a friend, agreeing to repay it in 8 monthly installments of $14 each. Find each of the following:

   a) The amount to be repaid.

   $\$14 \times \$8 = \$112$

$112 amount to be repaid

continued

Assignment 10.3 *continued*

b) The amount of interest.

$112 - 100 = $12

$12 amount of interest

c) The estimated effective interest rate, using the formula.

$$\frac{2 \times 12 \times \$12}{\$100(8 + 1)} = \frac{\$288}{\$900} = .32$$

32% effective interest rate

7. Penny Greengrass owes $100 on her VISA account. She pays $9 per month for 12 months to retire the debt. Determine what effective rate of interest or annual percentage rate she is being charged:

$9 × 12 = $108
$108 − 100 = $8 interest

$$\frac{2 \times 12 \times \$8}{\$100(12 + 1)} = \frac{192}{1,300} = .1476923$$

a) using the formula. — **14.77%**

b) using the table. — **14.5%**

8. To buy a color television set for the recreation area, the director of Sunnydale Children's Home borrows $750, to be paid back in 26 weekly installments of $32.75 each. What estimated effective rate of interest is he paying? (Use the formula.)

$32.75 × 26 = $851.50 amount to repay
$851.50 − 750 = $101.50 interest

$$\frac{2 \times 52 \times \$101.50}{\$750(26 + 1)} = \frac{10,556}{20,250} = .5212$$

52.1% effective rate of interest

9. In order to furnish her apartment, Patricia Kennedy borrows $300 from her company credit union. She is to repay the loan in 9 monthly payments of $35 each.

a) How much is she actually paying?

$35 × 9 = $315

$315 actual payment

b) What is the cost of the loan (the amount of interest)?

$315 − $300 = $15

$15 cost of loan

Calculate her effective interest rate:

c) using the formula.

$$\frac{2 \times 12 \times \$15}{300(9 + 1)} = \frac{360}{3,000} = .12$$

12% effective rate of interest

d) using the table.

$$\frac{15}{300} = .05 \times 100 = 5$$

11.75% effective rate of interest

10. Harry Conroy loaned Bill Bradford $100. He had Bill sign an agreement to pay the money back in 3 monthly payments of $34.50 each. Determine what effective rate of interest Harry was charging:

$34.50 × 3 = $103.50 amount to repay
103.50 − 100 = $3.50 interest

a) by estimating.

$$\frac{2 \times 12 \times \$3.50}{\$100(3 + 1)} = \frac{84}{400} = .21$$

21% effective rate of interest

continued

Assignment 10.3 *continued*

b) using the table.

$$\frac{3.5}{100} = .035 \times 100 = 3.50$$

20.75% effective rate of interest

---

11. Bonnie Belknap paid Carver Savings and Loan $96 per month for 9 months to retire a loan of $800. Determine what effective rate of interest she was paying:

    $96 × 9 = $864 amount to repay
    $864 − 800 = $64 interest

    a) using the formula.

    $$\frac{2 \times 12 \times \$64}{\$800 \times (9 + 1)} = \frac{1,536}{8,000} = .192$$

    19.2% effective rate of interest

    b) using the table.

    $$\frac{64}{800} = .08 \times 100 = 8$$

    18.75% effective rate of interest

---

12. To purchase a sofa, Jerry Chang arranged to borrow $450. According to his contract, he was to repay in installments of $22.50 per month for 2 years. Determine what effective interest rate he was paying:

    $22.50 × 24 = $540 amount to repay
    $540 − 450 = $90 interest

    a) using the formula.

    $$\frac{2 \times 12 \times 90}{450 \times (24 + 1)} = \frac{2,160}{11,250} = .192$$

    19.2 effective interest rate

    b) using the table.

    $$\frac{90}{450} = .2 \times 100 = 20$$

    18.25%

---

13. If Peter Goodman pays 15 monthly installments of $84.40 each to retire a loan of $1,000, determine his effective interest rate using the formula.

    $84.40 × 15 = $1,266 amount to repay
    $1,266 − 1,000 = $266 interest

    $$\frac{2 \times 12 \times 266}{1,000(15 + 1)} = \frac{6,384}{16,000} = .399$$

    39.9% effective interest rate

---

14. Barry Chew pays off a $400 loan by making 14 monthly payments of $28.50 and one of $28.75. What is the effective interest rate according to the table? (Note: There is a total of 15 payments)

    $28.50 × 14 = $399
    $399 + 28.75 = $427.75 amount to repay
    $427.75 − 400 = $27.75 interest
    27.75 ÷ 400 = .069375 × 100 = 6.94

    10.25% effective interest rate

---

15. Before setting out on a trip across the country, Mary LeTour borrows $500, which she agrees to repay in 16 monthly payments of $35 each and one of $36.50. Calculate her effective interest rate using the formula.

    $35 × 16 = $560
    $560 + 36.50 = $596.50 amount to repay
    $596.50 − 500 = $96.50 interest

    $$\frac{2 \times 12 \times 96.50}{500(17 + 1)} = \frac{2,316}{9,000} = .25733$$

    25.7% effective rate of interest

continued

Assignment 10.3 *continued*

16. To retire a loan of $1,200, Clement Bodeen makes 15 payments of $83.50 per week.

    a) What is the total amount that he will repay?

    $83.50 × 15 = $1,252.50

    $1,252.50 amount to repay

    b) What is the cost of the loan (the amount of interest)?

    $1,252.50 − 1,200 = $52.50

    $52.50 cost of loan

    c) What is the effective interest rate according to the formula?

    $$\frac{2 \times 52 \times 52.50}{1,200 \times (15 + 1)} = \frac{5,460}{19,200} = .2843$$

    28.4% effective interest rate

17. Perdita Moran borrows $500 from her brother, agreeing to retire the loan in 4 monthly payments of $130 each. Determine what effective interest rate her brother is charging:

    $130 × 4 = $520 amount to repay
    $520 − 500 = $20 interest

    a) using the formula.

    $$\frac{2 \times 12 \times 20}{500(4 + 1)} = \frac{480}{2,500} = .192$$

    19.2% effective rate of interest

    b) using the table.

    $$\frac{20}{500} = .04 \times 100 = 4$$

    19% effective rate of interest

18. On a loan of $1,000, Mary Lou Wingate agrees to make 6 monthly payments of $176 per month. Determine the effective interest rate:

    $176 × 6 = $1,056 amount to repay
    $1,056 − 1,000 = $56 interest

    a) using the formula.

    $$\frac{2 \times 12 \times 56}{1,000(6 + 1)} = \frac{1,344}{7,000} = .192$$

    19.2% effective rate of interest

    b) using the table.

    $$\frac{56}{1,000} = .056 \times 100 = 5.60$$

    19% effective rate of interest

19. Jan Hourback borrows $1,500 to buy a used car. She agrees to pay back $90 per month for 18 months. Determine what effective interest rate she is paying:

    $90 × 18 = $1620 amount to repay
    $1620 − 1500 = $120 interest

    a) using the formula.

    $$\frac{2 \times 12 \times 120}{1500 \times (18 + 1)} = \frac{2,880}{28,500} = .1010$$

    10.1% effective interest rate

    b) using the table.

    $$\frac{120}{1,500} = .08 \times 100 = 8$$

    10% effective rate of interest

10.4 Installment Buying

Until the last 30 or 40 years, cash was the major basis of the retail economy. Full payment was often made at the time merchandise was purchased. Now, many purchases—particularly those of major items such as furniture or home appliances—are made on credit or on the **installment-buying** plan.

Under this installment system, you, the buyer, contract to make a series of regular payments—weekly, monthly, or on whatever schedule is established by the merchant—until the merchandise and additional fees are paid off. This has certain advantages. You can purchase more goods by paying over a period of time, during which you have the use of the merchandise. Through the installment plan, you can also manage to buy more expensive merchandise, paying for it in "easy" payments.

Be aware that your installment purchase normally carries with it a conditional sales contract, stating that the seller actually owns the item purchased until you have made all the payments. This means that the seller can reclaim—repossess—the merchandise and keep any payments you have made to date should you fail to make a payment, that is, not live up to the terms of the contract.

Terms you should know in installment buying are:

Down payment: A specified amount of cash given by the buyer to the seller at the time the contract is made.

Carrying charge: A service fee (actually interest) added by the seller to the purchase price to cover such costs as bookkeeping and billing, insurance against bad debts, and fees for credit investigation.

Before agreeing to buy an item on the installment plan, be sure your personal financial situation allows you to keep up the payments to completion. Also, determine whether the extra costs involved in buying the particular item on the installment plan are reasonable. To do this, look at several figures.

Actual Total Cost

Figure this by multiplying the dollar amount of each periodic payment by the number of payments and adding the amount of any down payment.

Example 1 Sylvia Martina purchases a dining room chair on the installment plan. The chair sells for $145, and Sylvia agrees to a down payment of $15, plus 6 monthly payments of $25 each. How much is she really paying for the chair?

Step 1   Multiply the amount of each payment by the number of payments. $25 × 6 = $150

Step 2   Add the amount of the down payment, if any. $150 + $15 = $165

Answer   The actual cost of the chair is $165.

Carrying Charges

Once you have found the actual total cost, you can determine the amount of the carrying charge, or service charge. Do this by subtracting the cash (or retail) price from the actual total cost.

Example 2 What is Sylvia Martina paying in carrying charges on the dining room chair that she purchases on the installment plan?

Solution Subtract the cash price from the total actual cost.

$165
− $145
$ 20

Answer The carrying charge for the chair is $20.

Effective Interest Rate

Once the total actual cost and the carrying charge are known, you can estimate the effective rate of interest using a variation of the formula for personal or consumer loans. (See Section 10.3.) Note that in this case the amount financed is the cash price less the down payment.

$$\frac{2 \times \text{Number of payment periods in 1 year} \times \text{Carrying charge}}{(\text{Cash price} - \text{Down payment}) \times (\text{Number of payments} + 1)}$$

Example 3 What is the estimated effective rate of interest on the chair Sylvia Martina purchases on the installment plan?

Step 1 Find the actual cost of the item. Multiply the amount per payment by the number of payments and add the amount of the down payment.

$150
+ $ 15
$165

Step 2 Find the carrying charge. Subtract the cash price from the actual cost, as in Example 2.

$165
− $145
$ 20

Step 3 Use the formula. Note that these are monthly payments, so 12 are possible in 1 year.

$$\frac{2 \times 12 \times 20}{(145 - 15) \times (6 + 1)} = .527$$

Answer The effective rate of interest is approximately 53%.

NOTE: There will not always be a down payment. When there is none, use the number of payments times the amount per payment minus the cash price as the carrying charge and the cash price times the number of payments plus one as the denominator of the formula. In other words, you proceed exactly as you do in estimating the effective interest rate for a personal loan. (See Section 10.3.)

An APR table like the one shown on pages 412–415 can be used to find the effective interest rate in an installment-buying situation. Remember to take the down payment into consideration as demonstrated above.

Self-Check

Martin Sebring purchases a citizen band radio on the installment plan. The radio retails for $200. Martin pays $35 down and agrees to 9 monthly payments of $20 each. Compute the following:

1. Actual total cost. _____

2. Carrying charges. _____

3. Effective rate of interest. (using the formula) _____

ANSWERS 1. $215   2. $15   3. 21.8%

NAME   DATE   SECTION

Assignment 10.4

Finance

Use the formula to solve these problems.

1. Howard Bargroves uses the time-payment plan to purchase a single waterbed priced at $129.50. He pays $5 down and agrees to 15 monthly payments of $9.10 each. What is the effective rate of interest?

   $15 \times \$9.10 = \$136.50$
   $\$136.50 + 5.00 = \$141.50$
                actual cost
   $\$141.50 - 129.50 = \$12$
              carrying charge

   $$\frac{2 \times 12 \times 12}{(129.50 - 5) \times (15 + 1)} = \frac{288}{1{,}992} = .1445$$

   14.5% effective rate of interest

2. Sensational Skiwear offers a set of boots at $99.50 cash or $5 down and 15 monthly payments of $6.95. If you purchase on the installment plan, what are the following?

   a) Your actual cost.

   $\$6.95 \times 15 = \$104.25$
   $\$104.25 + 5 = \$109.25$

   $109.25 actual cost

   b) The amount of the service charge.

   $\$109.25 - 99.50 = \$9.75$

   $9.75 service charge

   c) The effective rate of interest.

   $$\frac{2 \times 12 \times 9.75}{(99.50 - 5) \times (15 + 1)} = \frac{234}{1{,}512} = .1547$$

   15.5% effective rate of interest

3. A sectional sofa sells for $721. Buying on credit, Mary Lou Chang pays $240 down and makes 12 monthly payments of $45 each. What is the effective interest rate?

   $\$45 \times 12 = \$540$
   $\$540 + 240 = \$780$ actual cost
   $\$780 - 721 = \$59$
             service charge

   $$\frac{2 \times 12 \times 59}{(721 - 240) \times (12 + 1)} = \frac{1416}{6253} = .2264$$

   22.6% effective interest rate

4. Bamburg's Appliances advertises a stereo for $795 cash or $95 per month for 8 months, after a $95 down payment. If you buy the stereo on time, what effective rate of interest will you pay?

   $\$95 \times 8 = \$760$
   $\$760 + 95 = \$855$ actual cost
   $\$855 - 795 = \$60$
             service charge

   $$\frac{2 \times 12 \times 60}{(795 - 95) \times (8 + 1)} = \frac{1{,}440}{6300} = .2285$$

   22.9% effective interest rate

5. Talia Moran purchases a designer suit from La Mode Fashions, paying $84 down and $18 per month for 22 months. If the cash price of the suit is $424, what is the effective interest rate?

   $\$18 \times 22 = \$396$
   $\$396 + 84 = \$480$ actual cost
   $\$480 - 424 = \$56$
             service charge

   $$\frac{2 \times 12 \times 56}{(424 - 84) \times (22 + 1)} = \frac{1{,}344}{7{,}820} = .1718$$

   17.2% effective interest rate

6. Larry Tenowski buys a small diamond pendant for his girlfriend. The cash price is $195. Larry pays $35 down and agrees to 12 monthly payments of $14.50 each. What are the following?

   a) The actual cost to Larry.

   $\$14.50 \times 12 = \$174$
   $\$174 + 35 = \$209$

   $209 actual cost

   continued

Assignment 10.4 *continued*

b) The amount of the service charge.

$209 − 195 = $14   **$14 service charge**

c) The effective interest rate.

$$\frac{2 \times 12 \times 14}{(195 − 35) \times (12 + 1)} = \frac{336}{2080} = .1615$$

16.2% effective interest rate

7. Bonita Terrill buys a used motorcycle priced at $300, agreeing to pay $48 down and $32 a month for 10 months. Find her effective rate of interest.

$$\frac{2 \times 12 \times 68}{(300 − 48) \times (10 + 1)} = \frac{1{,}632}{2772} = .5887$$

58.9% effective interest rate

$32 × 10 = $320
$320 + 48 = $368 actual cost
$368 − 300 = $68 service charge

8. Harry Kennedy sells floor coverings at Bonbilt Department Store. He quotes a customer a cash price of $109.50 and tells her she may make 6 monthly payments of $15 each and a down payment of $25. Find each of the following.

a) Her actual cost.

$15 × 6 = $90
$90 + 25 = $115   **$115 actual cost**

b) The amount of the service charge.

$115 − 109.50 = $5.50   **$5.50 service charge**

c) The effective interest rate.

$$\frac{2 \times 12 \times 5.50}{(109.50 − 25)(6 + 1)} = \frac{132}{591.5} = .2231$$

22.3% effective rate

9. Two customers, Clark Able and Marlynn Munrow, came into Bonbilt Department Store to purchase identical brass floor lamps for a cash price $150 each. Able bought the lamp for $20 down, with 6 monthly payments of $23.50 each. Since Munrow needed more time to pay, she agreed to pay $22 down and to make 15 monthly payments of $10.25 each.

a) Which of the two purchasers has the higher effective interest rate?

Able   29% effective interest rate
Munrow 30.2% effective interest rate

Munrow

b) How much higher is it?

30.2%
− 29.0
1.2% higher

1.2% higher

Able
$23.50 × 6 = $141
$141 + 20 = $161 actual cost
$161 − 150 = $11 service charge

$$\frac{2 \times 12 \times 11}{(150 − 20) \times (6 + 1)} = \frac{264}{910} = .2901$$

Munrow
$10.25 × 15 = 153.75
153.75 + 22 = $175.75 actual cost
175.75 − 150 = $25.75 service charge

$$\frac{2 \times 12 \times 25.75}{(150 − 22) \times (15 + 1)} = \frac{618}{2048} = .3017$$

10. Giddings Bicycle Shop lists a French ten-speed bike at $250. Installment buyers are asked to pay $29 down and $29 a month for 8 months. What effective interest rate is the installment buyer paying?

$$\frac{2 \times 12 \times 11}{(250 − 29) \times (8 + 1)} = \frac{264}{1989} = .1327$$

13.3% effective interest rate

10. $29 × 8 = $232
$232 + 29 = $261 actual cost
$261 − 250 = $11 service charge

continued

Assignment 10.4 continued

Habib Smith is setting up his own apartment. He is buying several items and wants to determine how much greater the installment price is than the cash price in each instance. Help him to do so.

Item	Cash Price	Down Payment	Number of Monthly Installments	Each Installment	Total Price on Installment Plan	Difference
11. TV set	$175.00	$25.00	12	$15.00	a) $205.00	b) $30.00
12. Chair	$140.00	$20.50	10	$14.25	a) 163.00	b) 23.00
13. Vacuum cleaner	$90.00	$15.00	11	$8.00	a) 103.00	b) 13.00
14. Sofa	$242.50	$50.00	21	$10.00	a) 260.00	b) 17.50
15. Recliner	$210.75	$40.75	18	$10.00	a) 220.75	b) 10.00

Find the actual cost on the installment plan, the service charge, and the effective interest rate for each of the following items.

Item	Cash Price	Down Payment	Number of Monthly Payments	Amount per Payment	Actual Cost	Service Charge	Effective Rate of Interest
16. Dinette set	$169.50	$7.50	12	$15.00	a) $187.50	b) $18.00	c) 20.5%
17. Portable TV	$119.00	$25.00	11	$10.00	a) 135.00	b) 16.00	c) 34%
18. Desk	$164.50	$35.00	4	$35.00	a) 175.00	b) 10.50	c) 38.9%
19. Club chair	$235.00	$50.00	6	$33.50	a) 251.00	b) 16.00	c) 29.7%
20. Convection oven	$199.50	$25.00	8	$25.00	a) 225.00	b) 25.50	c) 39%

Comprehensive Problems for Chapter 10

Finance

Mansard Bank and Trust discounts each of the following notes at the rate of 15%. Determine the discount period, the discount amount, and the net proceeds for each of them.

	Date Note is Made	Loan Period	Face Value	Rate	Discount Date	Discount Period	Discount Amount	Net Proceeds
1.	August 18	90 days	$35,000	12%	October 1	a) 46	b) $ 690.96	c) $ 35,359.04
2.	February 28	40 days	$12,500	10%	March 10	a) 30	b) 157.99	c) 12,480.90
3.	July 14	45 days	$ 5,500	13%	August 15	a) 13	b) 30.28	c) 5,559.10
4.	May 6	60 days	$28,100	11½%	May 31	a) 35	b) 417.65	c) 28,220.93
5.	October 13	185 days	$17,500	14¾%	December 30	a) 107	b) 839.35	c) 17,987.13
6.	September 10	65 days	$11,400	12.5%	October 10	a) 35	b) 170.00	c) 11,487.29
7.	May 19	90 days	$12,450	13.5%	June 5	a) 73	b) 391.47	c) 12,478.72
8.	July 12	85 days	$16,250	10¾%	August 3	a) 63	b) 437.39	c) 16,225.07
9.	April 15	170 days	$ 8,750	12.25%	May 30	a) 125	b) 482.09	c) 8,774.07
10.	January 12	200 days	$ 2,955	14⅔%	March 5	a) 148	b) 196.69	c) 2,992.83

11. An antique dealer, Bart Sankowski, borrows $1,300 to pay for a buying trip to Europe. He agrees to repay it over 16 months at $88.15 per month. Find each of the following.

   a) The amount he will actually repay

   $88.15 × 16 = $1,410.40

   $1,410.40 amount to repay

   b) The amount of interest

   $1,410.40 − 1,300 = $110.40

   $110.40 amount of interest

   c) The effective rate of interest using the formula

   $$\frac{2 \times 12 \times 110.40}{1,300 \times (16 + 1)} = \frac{2,649.60}{22,100} = .11989$$

   12% effective rate of interest

12. Queen City Finance Company loaned Martin Feldman $700. He agreed to pay it back in 8 months at $93 per month. What effective interest rate was he paying according to the APR table?

   $$\frac{44}{700} = .0628571 \times 100 = 6.29$$

   $93 × 8 = $744 amount to repay
   $744 − 700 = $44 interest

   16.5% effective rate of interest

continued

Comprehensive Problems *continued*

Below is information on several consumer loans. For each of them, compute the amount of the repayment and the amount of interest. Find the effective interest rate, first using the formula and then using the table.

	Amount of loan	Number of Monthly Payments	Amount per Payment	Total to be Repaid	Amount of Interest	Effective Interest Rate (Formula)	Effective Interest Rate (Table)
13.	$ 225	12	$20.05	a) $ 240.60	b) $ 15.60	c) 12.8%	d) 12.5%
14.	$ 750	20	$41.50	a) 830.00	b) 80.00	c) 12.2%	d) 11.75%
15.	$1,750	35	$58.50	a) 2,047.50	b) 297.50	c) 11.3%	d) 10.75%
16.	$1,500	28	$61.22	a) 1,714.16	b) 214.16	c) 11.8%	d) 11.25%
17.	$1,900	43	$52.85	a) 2,272.55	b) 372.55	c) 10.7%	d) 10%

Find the actual cost on the installment plan, the service charge, and the effective interest rate for each of the following items.

	Item	Cash Price	Down Payment	Number of Monthly Payments	Amount per Payment	Actual Cost	Service Charge	Effective Interest Rate (Formula)
18.	Oriental rug	$2,590.00	$350.00	15	$165.00	a) $ 2,825.00	b) $ 235.00	c) 15.7%
19.	Side chair	$ 165.00	$ 20.00	8	$ 20.00	a) 180.00	b) 15.00	c) 27.6%
20.	Refrigerator	$1,195.00	$225.00	14	$ 75.00	a) 1,275.00	b) 80.00	c) 13.2%
21.	Microwave oven	$ 495.00	$ 60.00	10	$ 47.50	a) 535.00	b) 40.00	c) 20.1%
22.	End table	$ 32.50	$ 5.00	11	$ 3.00	a) 38.00	b) 5.50	c) 40%
23.	Mattress	$ 119.00	$ 10.00	11	$ 11.00	a) 131.00	b) 12.00	c) 22%
24.	Table lamp	$ 109.95	$ 6.95	11	$ 10.50	a) 122.45	b) 12.50	c) 24.3%

Case 1

Michael Beamish, of Beamish Construction, is reviewing some of his financial obligations that fall due within the next month. These include the following.

1. Repayment in full of an interest-bearing note to Henry Baresford. Beamish signed it on April 16, agreeing to pay $750 in 90 days at 12% interest.
2. The first payment on a $1,000 business improvement loan from Cattlemen's Bank. He has agreed to 10 equal monthly payments, and the loan is costing him $100.
3. A building rent payment of $595.50.

In order to raise money to help meet these obligations, Michael sells Cattlemen's Bank two notes that he is holding.

1. The first is a 60-day note made on May 10, for $200 at an annual interest rate of 12%.
2. The second is a 40-day note made on June 15, for $350 at an annual interest rate of $13\frac{1}{2}$%.

If Michael sells the two notes on June 30, and the Cattlemen's Bank uses a discount rate of 15%, will Michael have to raise more money in order to meet the obligations described above?

a. If so, how much more will he have to raise? If not, how much money will he have left after meeting his obligations?

b. If on this or other occasions Beamish is unable to meet his business obligations by selling notes, suggest ways in which he might raise the needed funds.

Case 2

Dora Munro, an attorney, attends a seminar called "Understanding Personal Finance." The instructor recommends that she analyze her personal-loan and installment-purchase obligations to determine the actual, effective rate of interest she is paying.

Dora has the following obligations:

1. A personal loan from Sedgeway Bank and Trust for $1,500. Dora agreed to pay it off in 30 equal monthly installments of $61.50 each.
2. A console television set, purchased on the easy-payment plan. The cash price was $900, and Dora paid $150 down, agreeing to 16 equal monthly payments of $50 each.
3. A used automobile, purchased with a $2,000 loan taken at 12% interest with an additional $55 carrying charge. The loan is to be repaid in 24 equal monthly installments over 2 years.

What effective rate of interest will Dora find for each of these obligations? Use the formula to calculate your answers.

1. _____ %   2. _____ %   3. _____ %

Key Terms

Annual percentage rate (APR)
Borrower
Carrying charge
Consumer loan
Default
Discount Period
Discounting
Down payment
Effective interest rate
Face value
Installment buying
Interest-bearing note
Lender
Maker
Maturity value
Negotiable instrument
Net proceeds
Payee
Payer
Principal
Promissory note
Term of loan

Key Concepts

- A promissory note is an instrument of credit that is a formal indication that a debt is owed. It is often negotiable.
- The maturity value of an interest-bearing note is equal to the interest plus the principal. It is the amount the payer must remit to the payee when the note comes due.
- Discounting a note involves selling it to a banking institution, which deducts in advance a discount fee calculated on the basis of the maturity value of the original loan, the result being the net proceeds.
- A consumer loan is one that can be repaid in regular installments. The true or effective rate of interest may be higher than the stated rate. It can be determined either by using a table or by using this formula:

$$\frac{2 \times \text{Number of payment periods in 1 year} \times \text{Interest}}{\text{Amount of loan} \times (\text{Number of payments} + 1)}$$

- Paying for items on the installment plan involves the same concept that a consumer loan does. Often a down payment is made. The interest is called a carrying charge.
- The formula for estimating an effective interest rate is:

$$\frac{2 \times \text{Number of payment periods in 1 year} \times \text{Carrying charge}}{(\text{Cash price} - \text{Down payment}) \times (\text{Number of payments} + 1)}$$

11
Real Estate

Business Takes a Positive Approach

DISNEY

After Walt Disney's death in 1966, It seemed the corporation he had founded was in deep trouble. Few new ideas were being generated to capture the imagination of the adults who had grown up with Mickey Mouse, Donald Duck, and other famous members of the Disney cartoon family. All this changed when the company modernized its definition of entertainment. Disney released several hit movies aimed at the adult market. It reentered the television market with syndicated series and Saturday morning cartoons, and Disney launched its own successful pay cable channel. The company also became involved in the game-show and business-news program market. It re-released classic films such as *Snow White and the Seven Dwarfs* and *Sleeping Beauty* to theaters as well as marketing them in the form of video cassettes. Disney also updated and expanded its theme parks, even going so far as to sponsor rock concerts at Disneyland. The corporation continued to invest in the building of new hotels, parks, and movie studios. Disney does not limit new development to the United States, however, setting its sights on Europe, China, and Japan as well. The Tokyo version of Disneyland, for example, has proved a huge success. The firm licenses over 8,000 products in 50 countries, including such items as clothing, jewelry, skiis, stationery, and even computer software. The company has also made wise real estate investments. The success of the Disney turnaround is reflected in annual revenues exceeding $2.5 billion. Disney searches continually for new talent, new ideas, and new acquisitions to make its dreams come true.

> **Learning Objectives**
>
> After reading and studying this chapter and working the problems, you will be able to:
>
> - Understand the basic workings of the mortgage-loan process.
> - Determine monthly mortgage payments by using an amortization table.
> - Figure the assessed valuation of property, given the market value and assessment rate.
> - Calculate mortgage-loan repayment schedules.
> - Figure the assessed valuation of property, given the market value and assessment rate.
> - Find property taxes.
> - Express the tax rate in the following forms: tax rate per $1, tax rate per $100, tax rate per $1,000, and mills.
> - Figure assessed value given the amount of taxes to be raised and the rate.
> - Calculate a property-tax rate.

At some time during your life you will probably purchase property as a place to live, as a location for your business, or as an investment. When you do, methods of paying for it and of calculating the taxes on it are major concerns.

11.1 Real-Estate Loans

Perhaps the largest single purchase you ever make will be for real estate, that is, for your home or your business location. It is unlikely that you will be able to accumulate enough cash to buy it outright. Therefore, you will probably agree to make a down payment followed by monthly installments for 30 years or more.

Choosing a Mortgage

The basic instrument in real-estate finance is the **mortgage**. It is a pledge of property to secure financing and is usually accompanied by a promissory note—a written agreement to pay back the money borrowed. (See Section 10.1.)

The mortgage, which is a contract, can be modified or tailored to fit a variety of needs. This characteristic is particularly important in today's changing real-estate market, which requires the use of various creative methods of financing.

In a **conventional mortgage,** only the good credit rating of the borrower and the property itself—the **collateral**—support the note, and there is a fixed rate of interest. Other kinds of mortgages are as follows.

Insured mortgage: Some of these are guaranteed by private mortgage insurance companies. FHA (Federal Housing Administration) and VA (Veteran's Administration) mortgages, both government programs, also fall into this category and are insured by federal funds.

Blanket mortgage: Should you become involved in developing large parcels of land, subdividing them into lots to be sold off separately, you will probably attempt to finance your original purchase with this type of mortgage.

Purchase money mortgage: This type of mortgage provides funding for part of the payment, the buyer's equity and/or cash down payment furnishing the difference.

Variable interest rate mortgage: The interest rate on this type of loan is tied to the prime rate. Thus it may be raised or lowered at intervals, depending on the cost of money to the lender at that particular time.

Graduated payment mortgage: Under this plan, the monthly payment is increased gradually over the term of the mortgage. The theory behind it is that borrowers are able to make higher payments as they become better established financially.

UNDERSTANDING LAND CONTRACTS

The land contract is not, strictly speaking, a mortgage. It does, however, incorporate the major elements of a mortgage and serves much the same purpose. Under this arrangement, the buyer takes possession of the property, but the seller retains title to it until an agreed-upon portion of the purchase price has been paid.

Finding Mortgage Money

Sources of mortgage money include savings-and-loan associations, mutual savings banks, commercial banks, life insurance companies, mortgage companies, real-estate investment trusts, credit unions, pension funds, and, as an alternative, certain individuals.

Amortizing Mortgages

Each monthly mortgage payment includes both money applied to the principal and money applied to the interest. Over the term of the loan, both principal and interest are gradually eliminated. This process is called **amortization.** The appropriate monthly payment is found using an amortization table. Here is a portion of such a table, showing the monthly payment needed to amortize loans of various amounts over 25- and 30-year periods at interest rates of 11%, $11\frac{1}{2}$%, and 12%.

Monthly Payment Necessary to Amortize a Loan

Amount	11% 25 years	11% 30 years	11½% 25 years	11½% 30 years	12% 25 years	12% 30 years
$ 50	$ .50	$ .48	$ .51	$ .50	$ .53	$ .52
100	.99	.96	1.02	1.00	1.06	1.03
500	4.91	4.77	5.09	4.96	5.27	5.15
1,000	9.81	9.53	10.17	9.91	10.54	10.29
10,000	98.02	95.24	101.65	99.03	105.33	102.87
15,000	147.02	142.85	152.48	148.55	157.99	154.30
20,000	196.03	190.47	203.30	198.06	210.65	205.73
25,000	245.03	238.09	254.12	247.58	263.31	257.16
30,000	294.04	285.70	304.95	297.09	315.97	308.59
31,000	303.84	295.23	315.11	307.00	326.50	318.87
32,000	313.64	304.75	325.28	316.90	337.04	329.16
33,000	323.44	314.27	335.44	326.90	347.57	339.45
34,000	333.24	323.74	345.60	336.70	358.10	349.73
35,000	343.04	333.32	355.77	346.61	368.63	360.02
36,000	352.85	342.84	365.93	356.51	379.17	370.31
37,000	362.65	352.36	376.10	366.41	389.70	380.59
38,000	372.45	361.89	386.26	376.32	400.23	390.88
39,000	382.25	371.41	396.43	386.22	410.76	401.16
40,000	392.05	380.93	406.59	396.12	421.29	411.45
41,000	401.85	390.46	416.76	406.02	431.83	421.74
42,000	411.65	399.98	426.92	415.93	442.36	432.02
43,000	421.45	409.50	437.09	425.83	452.89	442.31
44,000	431.25	419.03	447.25	435.73	463.42	452.59
45,000	441.06	428.55	457.42	445.64	473.96	482.88
50,000	490.06	476.17	508.24	495.15	526.62	514.31
55,000	539.07	523.78	559.06	544.67	579.28	565.74
60,000	588.07	571.40	609.89	594.18	631.94	617.17
65,000	637.08	619.02	660.71	643.69	684.60	668.60
70,000	686.08	666.63	711.53	693.21	737.26	720.03
75,000	735.09	714.25	762.36	742.72	789.92	771.46
80,000	784.10	761.86	813.18	792.24	842.58	822.90

Example 1 In buying a house, Mary Sue Wingate takes out a 30-year mortgage for $40,000 at 11½% interest. What is her monthly payment?

Step 1 Using the table, find the amount of the loan in the column to the left.

39,000
→ 40,000
41,000

Step 2 Reading across, find the 11½%, 30-year figure. 396.12

Answer The monthly payment needed to amortize this mortgage is $396.12.

Example 2 Mary Sue's brother, Samuel Butler Wingate, takes out a 25-year, $50,500 mortgage at 12% interest. What is his monthly payment?

Step 1 In the table, find the amount of the loan. In this case, look up both $50,000 and $500.

Step 2 Find the 12%, 25-year figures for $50,000 and for $500 and total them.

$50,000: $526.62
$500: + 5.27
$531.89

Answer The monthly payment is $531.89.

Dealing with Other Costs

In addition to the amount needed to amortize the mortgage, you may be required to pay one-twelfth of the annual property tax (see Section 11.3) and fire insurance premium (see Section 12.3) each month. This is placed in an **escrow account** by the lender, where it is held in reserve to pay taxes and insurance costs on your behalf as they come due.

Example 3 If Mary Sue Wingate's monthly amortization payment is $396.12, the annual taxes on her property are $636.00, and the annual insurance premium is $168.00, what is her total monthly payment?

Step 1 Divide to find the amount of property tax, pro-rated on a monthly basis.

$$\frac{\$\ 53}{12)\overline{\$636}}$$

Step 2 Divide to find the monthly insurance cost.

$$\frac{\$\ 14}{12)\overline{\$168}}$$

Step 3 Total the amortization payment, taxes, and insurance.

```
  $396.12
  $ 53.00
+ $ 14.00
  $463.12
```

Answer The total monthly payment is $463.12.

Self-Check

1. You contract for a mortgage of $42,000 at $11\frac{1}{2}\%$ interest with a 30 year term. What is the monthly payment? _____

2. Mark Rushmore takes out a mortgage for $61,500. It is to run 25 years at an interest rate of 12%. Find his monthly payment. _____

3. In addition to his amortization payment, Mark Rushmore must pay a monthly amount to cover property and school taxes, which come to an annual total of $927, and fire insurance with a yearly premium of $236. What is his total monthly payment? _____

ANSWERS 1. $415.93 2. $631.94 3. $647.75
                        10.54   77.25
                      + 5.27   + 19.67
                        $647.75 $744.67

Real Estate

NAME　　　　　　　　　　　　　　　　　DATE　　　　　　　　SECTION

Assignment 11.1

Real Estate

Maxine Peragreen works for Steele and Fritz Mortgage Company. Using the amortization table, help her find the monthly amounts needed to pay off the mortgages listed below.

	Loan Amount	Interest Rate	Term of Mortgage	Monthly Payment	
1.	$31,000	11%	30 years	$ 295.23	
2.	$43,000	11%	25 years	421.45	
3.	$44,000	11½%	25 years	447.25	
4.	$51,500	11½%	30 years	510.02	$495 + 9.91 + 4.96
5.	$39,250	11.5%	30 years	388.72	$386.22 + 2.50
6.	$85,000	12%	25 years	895.28	$842.58 + (10.54 × 2)
7.	$75,500	12%	25 years	795.19	$789.92 + 5.27
8.	$56,000	11.5%	30 years	554.58	$544.67 + 9.91
9.	$62,500	11%	25 years	612.60	$588.07 + (9.81 × 2) + 4.91
10.	$73,650	12%	30 years	757.60	$720.03 + (10.29 × 3) + 5.15 + 1.03 + .52

Working at Steele and Fritz Mortgage Company, Maxine Peragreen must find the monthly payment due on each of the mortgages below, including the amounts for taxes and insurance. Help her, using the amortization table.

	Amount of Loan	Rate of Interest	Term of Loan	Annual Taxes	Annual Insurance	Total Monthly Payment	
11.	$25,000	11%	30 years	$ 375	$ 56	$ 274.01	Example 11. 238.09 Loan
12.	$36,000	11%	25 years	$ 450	$ 62	395.52	375 ÷ 12 = 31.25 Tax
13.	$40,000	11%	25 years	$ 475	$ 71	437.55	56 ÷ 12 = 4.67 Insurance 274.01 Total Payment
14.	$42,500	11½%	25 years	$ 698	$ 68	495.85	
15.	$43,100	11½%	30 years	$ 795	$ 86	500.25	
16.	$45,150	11½%	30 years	$ 756	$105	518.89	

continued

Assignment 11.1 *continued*

	Amount of Loan	Rate of Interest	Term of Loan	Annual Taxes	Annual Insurance	Total Monthly Payment
17.	$51,500	12%	25 years	$ 925	$128	630.18
18.	$72,550	12%	25 years	$1,050	$130	862.47
19.	$75,650	12%	30 years	$1,225	$180	895.24
20.	$81,750	11%	30 years	$1,560	$195	924.81

11.2 Loan-Repayment Schedules

During the initial years of the term of a real-estate loan, monthly payments are used mainly to pay the interest. Very little is applied to reducing the principal. The amount of interest per payment is gradually diminished, and in the last years of the loan's term most of the payment is applied to retiring the principal.

To clarify this, the lender may provide a **repayment schedule**. This details, for the term of the loan, the amount of each payment applied to the interest and the amount applied to the principal. It also shows the balance of the principal that remains to be repaid.

Once the amount of the monthly amortization payment is established, you can set up a repayment schedule using the following procedure.

Step 1 Multiply the amount of the loan by the interest rate to find the amount of interest for 1 year.

> **HOW THE PERCENTAGE FORMULA APPLIES**
>
> Amount of loan = Base
> Interest rate = Rate
> Annual interest = Percentage
>
> Amount of loan × Interest rate = Annual interest
> Base × Rate = Percentage

Step 2 Divide the interest for 1 year by 12 to find the interest for 1 month.

Step 3 Subtract the interest for 1 month from the monthly payment as found in the amortization table to determine the amount that applies to the principal.

Step 4 Subtract the amount that applies to the principal from the amount of the loan to find the balance of the principal still to be repaid.

Example 1 For one of her company's mortgages, Maxine Peragreen must prepare a repayment schedule for the first month on a loan of $45,000 at 11% for 25 years. According to the amortization table, the monthly payment is $441.06.

Step 1 Amount of loan × Interest rate = Interest for 1 year

$45,000
× .11
$ 4,950

Step 2 $\frac{\text{Interest for 1 year}}{12}$ = Interest for 1 month

$ 412.50
12)$4,950.00

Step 3 Monthly payment − Interest for one month = Payment on principal

$ 441.06
− $ 412.50
$ 28.56

Step 4 Amount of loan − Payment on principal = Balance of principal

$45,000.00
− $ 28.56
$44,971.44

Answer The repayment schedule for the first month is:

Payment Number	Interest Payment	Principal Payment	Balance of Principal
1	$412.50	$28.56	$44,971.44

In figuring the payment for each of the months to follow, use the balance of the principal after the previous payment has been applied as the basis for your calculations.

Example 2 Maxine prepares a repayment schedule for the second month of the loan described in Example 1.

Step 1 Balance of principal × Interest rate = Interest for 1 year

$44,971.44
×   .11
$ 4,946.86

Step 2 $\dfrac{\text{Interest for 1 year}}{12}$ = Interest for 1 month

$ 412.24 rounded
12)$4,946.86

Step 3 Monthly payment − Interest for 1 month = Payment on principal in second month

$441.06
− $412.24
$ 28.82

NOTE: In the second payment, a slightly increased amount, 26 cents more than in the previous month, is going toward the principal.

Step 4 Balance of principal − Payment on principal in second month = Balance of principal

$44,971.44
− $ 28.82
$44,942.62

Answer The repayment schedule for the second month follows.

Payment Number	Interest Payment	Principal Payment	Balance of Principal
2	$412.24	$28.82	$44,942.62

Using the method shown, Maxine could continue to work out a schedule through the entire term of the loan. It is more likely that she would do so, however, using a computer or a table prepared for this purpose.

Self-Check

As an employee of Elkhorn Savings and Loan, prepare a repayment schedule for the first month of this mortgage loan.

Amount of Loan	Interest Rate	Term of Loan
$10,000	12%	30 years

Payment Number	Total Payment	Interest Payment	Principal Payment	Balance of Principal
1	a) _____	b) _____	c) _____	d) _____

ANSWERS (a) $102.87; (b) $100.00; (c) $2.87; (d) $9,997.13

UNDERSTANDING FHA AND VA POINTS

The Federal Housing Administration (FHA) and the Veteran's Administration (VA) do not actually lend money. Instead, they act as the loan guarantors. In cases where the rate of interest is higher than the maximum allowed by the FHA or the VA, points are assessed by the lender. A *point* is equal to one percent of the mortgage principal. Points are paid by the property's seller to the mortgage company of the buyer.

NAME _____ DATE _____ SECTION _____

Assignment 11.2

Real Estate

Perry Mandel and his wife, Joan, take out a mortgage of $50,000 with an interest rate of $11\frac{1}{2}\%$ and a term of 30 years. Prepare a repayment schedule for the first 5 months.

Total monthly payment _____$495.15_____.

Repayment Schedule

Payment Number	Interest Payment	Principal Payment	Balance of Principal
1.	a) $ 479.17	b) $ 15.98	c) $ 49,984.02
2.	a) 479.01	b) 16.14	c) 49,967.88
3.	a) 478.86	b) 16.29	c) 49,951.59
4.	a) 478.70	b) 16.45	c) 49,935.14
5.	a) 478.55	b) 16.60	c) 49,918.54

Example
1. $50,000 × .115 = $5,750 for 1 yr
5,750 ÷ 12 = 479.16̄6 for 1 month
$495.15 − 479.17 = $15.98
$50,000 − 15.98 = $49,984.02

As the mortgage loan officer of First Bank and Trust, you are required to prepare first-month repayment schedules for the following 30-year loans.

	Loan Amount	Interest Rate	Total Payment	Interest Payment	Principal Payment	Balance of Principal
6.	$40,000	11%	a) $ 380.93	b) $ 366.67	c) $ 14.26	d) $ 39,985.74
7.	$45,000	11%	a) 428.55	b) 412.50	c) 16.05	d) 44,983.95
8.	$43,000	11%	a) 409.50	b) 394.17	c) 15.33	d) 42,984.67
9.	$55,000	$11\frac{1}{2}\%$	a) 544.67	b) 527.08	c) 17.59	d) 54,982.41
10.	$39,000	$11\frac{1}{2}\%$	a) 386.22	b) 373.75	c) 12.47	d) 38,987.53
11.	$39,500	12%	a) 406.31	b) 395.00	c) 11.31	d) 39,488.69
12.	$65,000	12%	a) 668.60	b) 650.00	c) 18.60	d) 64,981.40
13.	$70,000	12%	a) 720.03	b) 700.00	c) 20.03	d) 69,979.97
14.	$71,000	$11\frac{1}{2}\%$	a) 703.12	b) 680.42	c) 22.70	d) 70,977.30
15.	$81,500	12%	a) 838.34	b) 815.00	c) 23.34	d) 81,476.66

11.3 Property Taxes

Property taxes are monies collected by local and state governments for general operation and for providing services such as police and fire protection, education, road maintenance, recreation, and so on. The tax can apply to real property, such as land and buildings, and to personal property, such as cars, furnishings, or stock. Once the tax is collected, it is divided among the various strata of government: towns, cities, counties, and the state. Sometimes property taxes are levied separately by these governmental bodies.

Depending on a particular locality's needs, the taxation may be at different levels. Property tax is paid on **assessed valuation,** which can be true market value or a percent of the market value of the property. A tax assessor evaluates what the assessed valuation will be according to law and inspects the property periodically. The assessed valuation can change over time. For example, a business' assessed valuation increases if an addition is built on to an existing building.

Real property is assessed according to a certain percent, called the **assessment rate** of the market value. The assessment rate may vary according to the type of property. For example, the rate for commercial property may be higher than the rate for residential property.

Finding Assessed Valuation Using Assessment Rate

The formula to use in finding assessed valuation is:

$$\text{Market value} \times \text{Assessment Rate} = \text{Assessed valuation}$$

Example 1 What is the assessed valuation of a warehouse with a market value of $210,000 if the assessment rate is 40%?

Solution Multiply the market value by the assessment rate. $210,000 × 40% = $84,000

Answer The assessed valuation is $84,000.

Self-Check

Find the assessed valuation of a home whose market value is $89,000. The assessment rate is 60%.

ANSWER $53,400

Once the assessed valuation is found, three main factors must be applied in order to solve the rest of the problems in this section. These factors are:

> **HOW THE PERCENTAGE FORMULA APPLIES**
>
> Assessed value—the value of the property for tax purposes = Base
>
> Tax rate—the rate at which taxes are determined. This can be expressed as a dollar amount per $1, per $100, per $1,000 of assessed value, or in mills = Rate
>
> Taxes—the actual dollar amount collected. Also referred to as tax revenue, budget, or money to be raised by a locality = Percentage

Finding Property Taxes

The tax to be collected is found by applying the percentage formula.

> **HOW THE PERCENTAGE FORMULA APPLIES**
>
> Assessed valuation = Base
> Tax rate = Rate
> Taxes = Percentage
>
> Assessed valuation × Tax rate = Taxes
> Base × Rate = Percentage

Tax Rate Expressed per $1

Example 2 Find the property tax on Terry Kenmore's property, which is assessed at $53,200. The tax rate is .0215 per $1 of assessed valuation.

Solution Multiply the assessed valuation by the tax rate.

Assessed valuation × Tax rate = Taxes
$53,200 × .0215 = $1,143.80

Answer The property tax is $1,143.80.

Tax Rate Expressed per $100

When the tax rate is expressed per $100, it is necessary to determine how many 100's there are in the assessed valuation. Find this by dividing the assessed valuation by 100.

Example 3 Find the property tax on Terry Kenmore's property, which is assessed at $53,200, if the tax rate is $2.15 per $100 of assessed valuation.

Step 1 Divide the assessed valuation by 100.

$$\frac{\$53,200}{100} = 532$$

Step 2 Multiply the assessed valuation expressed in hundreds by the tax rate.

532 × 2.15 = $1,143.80

Answer The property tax is $1,143.80.

Tax Rate Expressed per $1,000

When the tax rate is expressed per $1,000, it is necessary to determine how many 1,000's there are in the assessed valuation. This is found by dividing the assessed valuation by 1,000.

Example 4 Find the property tax on Terry Kenmore's property, which is assessed at $53,200, if the tax rate is $21.50 per $1,000.

Step 1 Divide the assessed valuation by 1,000.

$$\frac{\$53,200}{1,000} = 53.2$$

Step 2 Multiply the assessed valuation expressed in thousands by the tax rate.

53.2 × 21.50 = $1,143.80

Answer The property tax is $1,143.80.

Tax Rate Expressed in a Combination of Forms

If two or more different tax rates are given, and you are asked to find the total amount of taxes, the tax rates can be added together. However, the tax rates must be expressed in the same terms before you can add them. If one tax rate is expressed per $100 and the other is expressed per $1,000, one rate must be changed by moving the decimal point in the dollar amount of the tax rate. For instance, the tax rate of .0129 per $1 can be changed to the tax rate per $100 by moving the decimal point 2 places to the right, whereas for per $1,000 it is moved 3 places to the right.

$.0129 per $1

$1.29 per $100   (01.29)

$12.90 per $1,000   (012.9)

Example 5 A building in Monroe, Virginia, is assessed at $80,000. If the tax rates are $1.13 per $100 for county tax and $9.50 per $1,000 for city tax, find the total tax.

Step 1 Express the tax rate per $100 in per $1,000 terms by moving the decimal point one place to the right. Note that the decimal point is moved only one place because the rate is already expressed per $100. $1.13 per $100 = $11.3 per $1,000

Step 2 Add the tax rates together.

$11.30 per $1,000
+ $ 9.50 per $1,000
$20.80 per $1,000

Step 3 Divide the assessed valuation by $1,000. $\frac{\$80,000}{\$1,000} = 80$

Step 4 Multiply the assessed valuation expressed in thousands by the combined tax rate. $80 \times \$20.80 = \$1,664$

Answer The total taxes are 1,664.

NOTE: The tax rates could have been changed to per $1, per $100, or per $1,000. If you want to change tax rate per $1,000 to a smaller term, move the decimal point to the left. In this example, $9.50 per $1,000 also could have been expressed as $.95 per $100.
    If a problem asks for the individual taxes for the county and town, there is no need to add the two tax rates together. Instead, each tax can be figured separately.

Tax Rate Expressed in Mills

Mills stands for the thousandths place in decimal form. Mills must be expressed as a decimal before it can be used to find the taxes. This is done by moving the decimal point 3 places to the left, which gives the rate per $1.

Example 6 Harborview Manor is assessed at $450,000. What are the property taxes if the tax rate is 42 mills?

Step 1 Change mills to a decimal per $1.   42 mills = .042

Step 2 Multiply the assessed valuation by this decimal. $450,000 \times .042 = \$18,900$

Answer The property taxes are $18,900.

Self-Check

1. The following properties are given at their assessed valuations. Find the taxes due according to each tax rate.

Property	Assessed Valuation	Tax Rate	Tax Due
a. Land	$31,900	$.0121 per $1	$ _____
b. Building	$78,210	$2.70 per $100	_____
c. House	$93,800	$14.20 per $1,000	_____

2. Find the total taxes for property that is assessed at $68,000. The tax rate is $.005 per $1 for the city and $11.40 per $1,000 for the state. _____

3. A building assessed at $49,800 is charged a tax rate of 18 mills. What is the property tax? _____

ANSWERS 1. (a) $385.99; (b) $2,111.67; (c) $1,331.96 2. $1,115.20
3. $896.40

Finding Tax Rate

A local government determines its **tax rate** by first totaling the assessed valuation of all taxable properties within its boundaries. Next, expenses are figured for operating the government and providing services to the public. A budget is prepared. Taxes are raised in order to meet this budget. The tax rate is determined by applying a variation of the percentage formula.

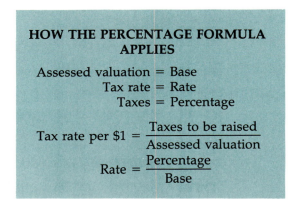

Once the tax rate per $1 is found, it can be expressed per $100 by moving the decimal point 2 places to the right. The rate per $1 can be changed to the rate per $1,000 by moving the decimal point 3 places to the right. The tax rate per $1 can be changed to the mill rate by moving the decimal point 3 places to the right. For instance, the tax rate of:

.0324 per $1 = $3.24 per $100

.0324 per $1 = $32.40 per $1,000

.0324 per $1 = 32.4 mills

Example 7   Note that 32.4 mills is the same as $32.40 per $1,000 because a mill is 1/1000 of a dollar.

Step 1 Find the tax rate per $100 of assessed valuation if the total assessed valuation for Cedar County is $9,720,000. Total taxes to be raised are $101,000.

Find the tax rate per $1 by dividing the amount of taxes to be raised by the assessed valuation.

$$\text{Tax rate per \$1} = \frac{\text{Taxes to be raised}}{\text{Assessed valuation}}$$

$$\text{Tax rate per \$1} = \frac{\$101,000}{\$9,720,000}$$

$$\text{Tax rate per \$1} = .01039$$

Step 2 Change the tax rate per $1 to the tax rate per $100 by moving the decimal point 2 places to the right and rounding.

$0.01039 = \$1.04$ per $100

Answer The tax rate is $1.04 per $100.

Self-Check

1. A town has a budget of $380,600. If the total assessed valuation of the town is $15,340,000, what is the tax rate per $1, rounded to 4 decimal places?

2. If the total assessed valuation is $5,820,000, and taxes needed to be raised are $219,000, find the tax rate in mills to the nearest tenth of a mill.

ANSWERS 1. $.0248 per $1   2. 37.6 mills

Finding Assessed Valuation

A government can figure the total assessed valuation needed by applying the following formula:

> **HOW THE PERCENTAGE FORMULA APPLIES**
>
> Assessed valuation = Base
> Tax rate = Rate
> Taxes = Percentage
>
> $$\text{Assessed valuation} = \frac{\text{Taxes}}{\text{Tax rate per \$1}}$$
>
> $$\text{Base} = \frac{\text{Percentage}}{\text{Rate}}$$

When you apply the tax rate in this formula, it should be in the form of tax rate per $1 so that you can divide without further adjustment.

Example 8 Find to the nearest dollar what assessed valuation will produce $70,000 in taxes if the tax rate is $1.04 per $100.

Step 1 Express the tax rate in per $1 form. $1.04 per $100 = .0104 per $1

Real Estate **451**

Step 2   Divide the total amount of taxes by the tax rate to find the assessed valuation.

$$\text{Assessed value} = \frac{\text{Taxes}}{\text{Tax rate per \$1}}$$

$$\text{Assessed value} = \frac{\$70,000}{.0104}$$

$$\text{Assessed value} = \$6,730,769$$

Answer   The total assessed value is $6,730,769.

Self-Check

1. Determine to the nearest dollar the assessed valuation needed to generate total taxes of $98,000 if the tax rate is .0112 per $1.

2. If the tax rate is $4.21 per $1,000, what is the assessed valuation to the nearest dollar when the budget requirements are $120,000?

ANSWERS   1. $8,750,000   2. $28,503,562

NAME   DATE   SECTION

Assignment 11.3

Real Estate

1. In Washington County, residential property is assessed at 45% of its market value for single-family dwellings and 51% for multi-unit dwellings. Commercial property is assessed at 58% of its market value. Find the assessed valuation for the following properties.

    a) A duplex with a market value of $105,000
    $105,000 × 51% = $53,550
    $53,550 assessed valuation

    b) A gas station with a market value of $150,000
    $150,000 × 58% = $87,000
    $87,000 assessed valuation

    c) A single-family dwelling with a market value of $76,400
    $76,400 × 45% = $34,380
    $34,380 assessed valuation

    d) A fourplex with a market value of $210,000
    $210,000 × 51% = $107,100
    $107,100 assessed valuation

    e) A single-family dwelling with a market value of $92,000
    $92,000 × 45% = $41,400
    $41,400 assessed valuation

Complete the following table of tax rates.

	Mills	Per $1 (accurate to 4 decimal places)	Per $100	Per $1,000
2.	12.6	a) .0126	b) $1.26	c) $12.60
3.	a) 44.9	b) .0449	$4.49	c) $44.90
4.	a) 36.7	.0367	b) $3.67	c) $36.70
5.	a) 18.5	b) .0185	c) $1.85	$18.50
6.	a) 110.2	b) .1102	$11.02	c) $110.20

If property is assessed at $89,000, find the property taxes for each of these situations.

7. The tax rate is $3.15 per $100.

    $\frac{89,000}{100} = 890$
    $890 \times \$3.15 = \$2,803.50$

    $2,803.50 property tax

8. The tax rate is $.0178 per $1.

    $89,000 × .0178 = $1,584.20

    $1,584.20 property tax

continued

Assignment 11.3 *continued*

9. The tax rate is 21 mills.

   $89,000 × .021 = $1,869

   $1,869 property tax

10. The tax rate is $18.40 per $1,000.

    $\frac{89,000}{1,000} = 89$
    $89 × 18.40 = $1637.60

    $1,637.60 property tax

11. If the tax rate in Kingston, New Jersey, is $3.20 per $100 of assessed valuation, what is the tax on property assessed at $78,900?

    $\frac{78,900}{100} = 789$
    $789 × 3.2 = $2,524.80

    $2,524.80

12. The market value of a home in Eatonville, Illinois, is $69,200. The tax rate is $10.40 per $1,000. If the assessed valuation is 46% of market value, find the property tax.

    $69,200 × 46% = $31,832 Assessed value
    31,832 × .0104 = 331.0528
    = $331.05

    $331.05 property tax

13. Last year the property tax rate on a grocery store with an assessed valuation of $143,000 was 12.6 mills. This year the tax rate was raised to $1.31 per $100 of assessed valuation. Find each of the following.

    a) Last year's taxes

    $143,000 × .0126 = $1,801.80

    $1,801.80 last year's taxes

    b) This year's taxes

    $\frac{143,000}{100} = 1,430$
    $1,430 × 1.31 = $1,873.30

    $1,873.30 this year's taxes

    c) The increase in dollars

    $1,873.30 This year's taxes
    − 1,801.80 Last year's taxes
    $ 71.50 Increase in taxes

    $71.50 increase in taxes

14. A piece of land in Lollard County is appraised at $51,000. The county tax rate is $12.90 per $100 and the city tax rate is .0104 per $1. Determine each of the following.

    a) The county tax $6,579 $510 × 12.90 = $6,579
    b) The city tax $530.40 $51,000 × .0104 = $530.40
    c) The total taxes $7,109.40 $6,579 + 530.40 = $7,109.40

    $\frac{51,000}{100} = 510$

continued

NAME   DATE   SECTION

Assignment 11.3 *continued*

Fill in the blanks for the following situations. (Compute to the nearest cent.)

	Market Value	Assessment Rate	Assessed Value	County Tax Rate	City Tax Rate	Total Property Taxes
15.	$120,000	60%	a) $ 72,000	12 mills	10.3 mills	b) $ 1,605.60
16.	$ 90,000	40%	a) 36,000	$2.09 per $100	$8.76 per $1,000	b) $ 1,067.76
17.	$ 58,000	50%	a) 29,000	$.0211 per $1	$9.20 per $1,000	b) 878.70

18. Red Creek County determines that it needs $600,000 to operate for the year. The assessed valuation of property in the county is $15,000,000. Find the necessary tax rate per $1.

$$\frac{600,000}{15,000,000} = .04$$

.04 per $1
necessary tax rate

19. The town of Powell needs to collect $450,000 in taxes. The total assessed valuation of property in the town is $12,600,000.

   a) Find the tax rate in mills to the nearest tenth.

   $$\frac{450,000}{12,600,000} = .0357142$$
   $$= .0357$$

   35.7 mills
   necessary tax rate

   b) Express the tax rate per $1

   .0357142

   .03571 per $1

   c) Express the tax rate per $100

   .0357
   ⌊↑

   $3.57 per $100

   d) Express the tax rate per $1,000.

   .0357142
   .03571
   ↑

   $35.71 per $1,000

20. Jackson City, Wyoming, has assessed the total value of residential property at $5,480,000 and the total value of commercial property at $2,900,000. The city plans to have the following expenses for the year:

Salaries:	$400,000
Road work:	$120,000
Parks and recreation:	$ 40,000
Supplies:	$ 25,000

   $585,000 budget

   $5,480,000 Residential assessed value
   + 2,900,000 Commercial assessed value
   8,380,000 Total assessed value

   a) Find the tax rate per $1 to 4 decimal places.

   $$\frac{585,000}{8,380,000} = .069809$$
   $$= .0698 \text{ per } \$1$$

   .0698
   per $1 tax rate

continued

Assignment 11.3 continued

b) Convert the tax rate per $1 to mills.

.0698

69.8 mills

Fill in the blanks in the following table. Express the tax rate per $1, correct to 4 decimal places.

	Total Market Value	Assessment Rate	Total Assessed Value	Total Taxes	Tax Rate Per $1	Per $100	Per $1,000	In Mills
21.	$13,420,000	60%	a) $ 8,052,000	$ 220,450	b) $ .0274	c) $ 2.74	d) $ 27.40	e) $ 27.4
22.	$72,600,000	80%	a) 58,080,000	$2,348,000	b) .0404	c) 4.04	d) 40.40	e) 40.4
23.	$51,400,000	50%	a) 25,700,000	$ 611,000	b) .0238	c) 2.38	d) 23.80	e) 23.8

24. What is the total assessed valuation to the nearest dollar of the property in Lake County if the tax rate is $.0340 per $1 and total taxes amount to $386,450?

$\dfrac{\$386{,}450 \text{ total taxes}}{.0340 \text{ per \$1 tax rate}} = \$11{,}366{,}176 \text{ assessed value}$

$11,366,176 assessed value

25. Property taxes collected for the Central Medical Building amount to $2,800. If the tax rate is $2.64 per $100, what is the assessed valuation of the property to the nearest dollar?

$\dfrac{\$2{,}800 \text{ taxes}}{.0264 \text{ per \$1}} = 106{,}060.60$

= $106,061 assessed value

$106,061 assessed value (to nearest dollar)

Find the total assessed valuation to the nearest dollar of property for the following counties.

	County	Tax Rate	Total Expenses	Total Assessed Valuation
26.	Boulder	$.0542 per $1	$650,400	$ 12,000,000
27.	San Pedro	22.6 mills	$100,179	4,432,699
28.	North	$1.25 per $100	$ 77,880	6,230,400

continued

Assignment 11.3 *continued*

29. Jill Lynness owns land that is taxed at a rate of 37.5 mills. The property taxes she must pay amount to $970.

  a) What is the assessed valuation of her land to the nearest dollar?

  $\dfrac{\$970}{.0375} = 25{,}866.666$

  $= \$25{,}867$ assessed value

  $\$25{,}867$
  assessed value
  (to nearest dollar)

  b) What is the market value to the nearest dollar if the assessment rate is 88%?

  $25{,}867 \div 88\% = 29{,}394.318$
  $= \$29{,}394$ market value

  $\$29{,}394$
  market value
  (to nearest dollar)

30. Property taxes on a particular home are $688.80. The tax rate is $1.20 per $100. If the assessment rate is 70% of market value, find the market value of the home.

  $\dfrac{688.80}{.012} = \$57{,}400$ assessed value

  $\$57{,}400 \div 70\% = \$82{,}000$ market value

  $\$82{,}000$ market value

Comprehensive Problems for Chapter 11

Real Estate

Arlie Fritz agrees to a mortgage loan of $42,500 at 12% interest for 25 years. Prepare a repayment schedule for the first 4 months of this loan.

Repayment Schedule

	Payment Numbers	Interest Payment	Principal Payment	Balance of Principal
1.	1	a) 425	b) 22.63	c) 42,477.37
2.	2	a) 424.77	b) 22.86	c) 42,454.51
3.	3	a) 424.55	b) 23.08	c) 42,431.43
4.	4	a) 424.31	b) 23.32	c) 42,408.11

5. Happy Homes Realty advertised a home for $85,000 with 10% down and the remainder to be amortized over 25 years at an interest rate of 11%. Find the monthly payment required of the purchaser.

$85,000 × 10% = $8,500 down
$85,000 − 8,500 = $76,500 to be financed
$76,000 at 11% for 25 years
$735.09 + 9.81 + 4.91 = $749.81

$749.81 monthly payment

6. Find the monthly mortgage payment on a loan of $43,000 at 12% interest to be amortized over a 30-year period.

$43,000 at 12% for 30 years

$442.31

As an employee of Martindale Credit Union, Marvin Pinchley must prepare a repayment schedule for the first 3 months on a mortgage loan of $55,000 at $11\frac{1}{2}$% interest for 25 years. Help him to do so.

Repayment Schedule

	Payment Numbers	Interest Payment	Principal Payment	Balance of Principal
7.	1	a) 527.08	b) 31.98	c) 54,963.02
8.	2	a) 526.78	b) 32.28	c) 54,935.74
9.	3	a) 526.47	b) 32.59	c) 54,903.15

continued

Comprehensive Problems *continued*

Ann Banks asks her mortgage company to provide a loan repayment schedule for the first 3 monthly payments of her mortgage loan of $60,000 at 11% interest for 30 years. Figure the schedule for the mortgage company.

Repayment Schedule

Payment Numbers	Interest Payment	Principal Payment	Balance of Principal
10. 1	a) 550	b) 21.40	c) 59,978.60
11. 2	a) 549.80	b) 21.60	c) 59,957.00
12. 3	a) 549.61	b) 21.79	c) 59,935.21

13. Jose and Juana Domingo purchase a house that costs $70,000. They pay 20% down and finance the rest with a conventional mortgage. If the mortgage has a 30-year term and an interest rate of 11.5%, what is the payment per month?

$70,000 × 20% = $14,000 down payment
$70,000 − $14,000 = $56,000 to be financed

$554.58 monthly payment

14. Bill Robinson purchased a home for $76,500. Paying $6,000 down, he agreed to repay the balance at 12% interest over 25 years. What is his monthly payment?

$76,500 − 6,000 = $70,500 to be financed
$70,500 at 12% for 25 years
$737.26 + 5.27 = $742.53 per month

$742.53 monthly payment

Complete the following table of tax rates.

	Mills	Per $1	Per $100	Per $1,000
15.	9.1	a) .0091	b) .91	c) 9.10
16.	a) 21.3	b) .0213	c) 2.13	$21.30
17.	a) 19.4	.0194	b) 1.94	c) 19.40

18. The market value of an office building in Jefferson County is $460,000. The property tax rate for the county is set at 39.1 mills. If the assessment rate is 70%, find the property taxes.

$12,590.20

19. In the township of Gilbert, the total market value of property is $63,900,000. Total taxes to be collected amount to $309,700. If the assessment rate of the property is 45%, figure each of the following.

a) The total assessed value in dollars

$28,755,000

continued

NAME   DATE   SECTION

Comprehensive Problems *continued*

The tax rate expressed per $1, per $100, per $1000, and in mills

b) _____.0108_____   d) _____$10.80_____

c) _____$1.08_____   e) _____10.8_____

20. You own a warehouse in Mill Valley that has a market value of $270,000. The assessed rate for commercial property is 70%. The county tax rate is 19 mills and the city tax rate is $2.12 per $100. Find the total amount of property taxes that you owe.

    $270,000 × 70% = 189,000 assessed value
    19 mills = .019   per $1 County rate
    2.12 per $100 = .0212 per $1 City rate
    　　　　　　　　.0402 per $1 Total tax rate

    $189,000 × .0402 = $7,597.80 total taxes   _____$7,597.80_____

21. The total expenses to be covered by property taxes in Macon County are $207,800. If the tax rate is $11.79 per $1,000, find the total assessed valuation.

    $11.79 per $1000 = $.01179 per $1
    $\frac{207,800}{.01179}$ = $17,625,106 assessed value   _____$17,625,106_____

22. The market value of a building lot in Sunrise Hills is $46,000. The assessment rate is 40%. Find the total amount of property taxes if the county tax rate is $0.042 per $1 and the city tax rate is $1.56 per $100.

    $46,000 × 40% = $18,400 assessed value
    $.042   per $1 County
    .0156 per $1 City ($1.56 per $100 = $.0156 per $1)
    .0576   Total tax rate per $1

    $18,400 × .0576 = $1,059.84   _____$1,059.84_____

23. The market value for property in School District 15 totals $7,250,000. The assessment rate is 60%, and the school budget is $253,000. What is the tax rate per $100 to the nearest cent?

    $7,250,000 × 60% = $4,350,000 assessed value
    $\frac{253,000}{4,350,000}$ = .0581609
    .0581609 = 5.81609 per $100   _____$5.82 per $100_____
    ↰

24. Total expenses of Tulipville, Maine, amount to $374,750. If the tax rate is $65.00 per $1,000, what is the total assessed valuation to the nearest dollar?

    $65 per $1,000 = $.065 per $1
    $\frac{374,750}{.065 \text{ per } \$1}$ Total taxes = 5,765,384.60 assessed value   _____$5,765,385_____

Case 1

Mr. and Mrs. Barry Chumbley decide to sell their home and purchase another in a more fashionable neighborhood. They confer with Marianna Moran of Highland Homes Realty Company. She advises them to use the cash they receive from the sale of their present home as the down payment on the new house. They agree, telling her they owe $22,000 on their present mortgage. Marianna puts their house on the market and begins previewing places they may want to buy.

By the end of the week, Marianna sells the Chumbley home for $65,550. From this amount, she takes her 8% real-estate commission. Another $3\frac{1}{2}\%$ of the total selling price is required to pay taxes and seller's closing costs. When the Chumbleys have satisfied these obligations and paid off their present mortgage, the remainder is theirs to use as a down payment.

Assuming any home the Chumbleys want to buy requires a 20% down payment, what is the most they can afford to pay for it?

Case 2

You are an advisor to the tax commission of Creek County. The assessed valuation of noncommercial property in the county is $5,000,000. The tax rate for noncommercial property is 16 mills. Total market value of commercial property is $12,000,000. The assessment rate for commercial property is 80% and the tax rate is $2.10 per $100.

The problem is that the county must raise a total of $306,600 in property taxes. The tax commission does not want to change the assessment rate or the property tax rate, because there would be a public outcry from both individuals and businesses.

a. How much more money in taxes must be raised?
b. If the additional taxes will come from the commercial sector, how much more assessed valuation to the nearest dollar will be needed?
c. What will the market value of taxable commercial property have to be?
d. How would you advise the council to go about attracting businesses to relocate and build in Creek County in order to have more business property available that can be assessed and taxed?

Key Terms

Amortization
Assessed valuation
Assessment rate
Blanket mortgage
Collateral
Conventional mortgage
Escrow
Graduated payment mortgage
Insured mortgage
Mortgage
Point
Property taxes
Purchase money mortgage
Real estate
Repayment schedule
Tax rate
Variable interest rate

Key Concepts

- A mortgage is a contractual pledge of property to secure financing and can be modified to fit individual and situational needs.

- Mortgages are amortized. Part of each payment applies to the principal and part to interest, with a gradual elimination of both.
- Often, a proration of such yearly costs as property taxes and insurance is included in the mortgage payment. Money collected is held in an escrow account and paid by the lender on behalf of the buyer as obligations come due.
- The lender may provide a loan-repayment schedule to the buyer showing the amount of each payment that goes toward interest, the amount toward principal, and the balance remaining to be paid on the principal.
- Property taxes are collected from property owners by units of government to pay for various services provided by those units of government.
- Property tax is determined by multiplying the assessed valuation of the property times the established tax rate, which can be expressed per $1, per $100, per $1,000, or in mills.

$$\text{Taxes} = \text{Assessed valuation} \times \text{Tax rate}$$

$$\text{Tax rate} = \frac{\text{Taxes to be raised}}{\text{Assessed valuation}}$$

$$\text{Assessed valuation} = \frac{\text{Taxes}}{\text{Tax rate per dollar}}$$

12
Insurance

Business Takes a Positive Approach

KIRK HORSE INSURANCE, INC.

Isn't the insurance market saturated? No. There is still room for enterprising new ideas. A prime example is insurance for horses. Just a few years ago, Ronald and Lori Kirk started a business insuring race horses. Before that time, these animals could be insured only for their cash value. This fluctuated with their performance at the track, a factor that led to lengthy and complicated settlements. The Kirks took a fresh approach. They offered insurance with quick, fixed settlement fees, a concept similar to term life insurance. The annual insurance premium for a thoroughbred race horse can run as high as $400,000. In 1986, Kirk Horse Insurance, Inc., made the list of INC., Magazine's 500 fastest growing private American companies. It insures over $1 billion worth of horses in a worldwide market.

> **Learning Objectives**
>
> After reading and studying this chapter and working the problems, you will be able to:
>
> - Understand four basic types of generally available life insurance policies.
> - Use a premium schedule to compute annual premiums for these types of life insurance.
> - Understand the most commonly recommended types of automobile insurance.
> - Calculate automobile insurance premiums using premium tables.
> - Understand some important concepts of fire insurance, including premium basis, short-rating, and coinsurance.
> - Determine fire insurance premiums and related costs and reimbursements using the appropriate tables.

Businesses and individuals must guard against financial loss resulting from unexpected and/or catastrophic events. Among the losses against which we commonly protect ourselves are those caused by death, automobile accident, and fire. **Insurance** provides this protection.

12.1 Life Insurance

You may have any one of several purposes in contracting for **life insurance.** One of the most common is to ensure economic protection for your dependents in case of your death. While providing for them, you may also want to enhance your own comfort in retirement by taking out a **policy** that offers you a payback after a specified number of years.

Knowledge of life insurance is particularly important if you are a partner in or an owner of a business. Because of your continued efforts to make the business successful, it may suffer or even collapse without your expertise. Lending institutions often require business partners to take out life insurance payable to the institution to ensure that their loans are covered in the event of death. Moreover, your business may be the major asset you have to pass on to your heirs. Without you there to run it, its value can decrease; thus your life insurance, payable to the heirs, helps make up the difference. The term **beneficiary** is used to describe the person or institution you name as the recipient of your life insurance benefits.

Usually, insurance companies pay a lump sum if you elect to discontinue your policy. The amount you receive on turning in the policy is called its **cash surrender value.** It does not generally apply to term insurance, which is explained below.

Selecting a Life-Insurance Policy

There are various types of life insurance available. The most common are the following.

Term insurance: A contract issued to cover a person during a limited period of time—say, for one, five, or ten years after the date the policy goes into effect. If the individual dies at any time during this period, the beneficiary receives the entire face value of the policy. Once the period is over, however, the protection is terminated, and the insured receives nothing in return. Because it is pure insurance, with no savings feature built into it, term life insurance is usually the least costly type.

Ordinary or **straight life insurance:** A contract that requires payment of a premium each year until the insured person dies, at which time the value of the policy is paid to the beneficiary. Straight life is the most common type of life insurance purchased.

Limited-payment life insurance: A contract similar to straight life insurance except that payments are made for a specified number of years—for example, 10, 20 (in which the policy is called **twenty-pay life**), or 30—rather than for the entire life of the person insured, even though coverage at death is assured. Premiums for limited-payment life insurance are usually higher than those for straight life insurance.

Endowment insurance: A contract enabling the insured person to accumulate funds for later use. It pays the face value to the beneficiary in the event of the death of the insured, or pays the insured this amount if he or she is still alive at the end of a specified period, usually 10 to 30 years from the date the policy takes effect.

Universal life insurance: A contract that combines the features of term insurance with a tax-deferred savings program. The cost of the life insurance is deducted on a regular basis from the total amount of premiums collected. The remaining accumulated funds draw interest on an ongoing basis. The cash value eventually reverts to the insured.

Determining the Premium Using a Schedule

The amount of the **premium,** the fee you pay on a regular basis for insurance coverage, is figured from tables compiled by **actuaries,** experts in insurance.

A Typical Premium Table

Premiums differ depending on the insurance company and the particular contract. The following table shows a hypothetical premium schedule for several types of coverage.

Annual Premium Rate Per $1,000 of Life Insurance

Age at time of Purchase	Ten-Year Term	Straight Life	Twenty-Pay Life	Twenty-Year Endowment
20	$ 8.64	$17.26	$27.50	$48.28
21	8.86	17.64	27.98	48.35
22	9.07	18.03	28.48	48.43
23	9.29	18.43	28.98	48.51
24	9.51	18.86	29.51	48.60
25	9.73	19.30	30.05	48.69
30	10.93	21.87	33.02	49.34
35	12.67	25.15	36.54	50.40
40	15.07	29.39	40.80	52.12
45	18.13	34.88	45.95	54.74
50		42.05	52.38	58.78
55		51.53	60.74	65.02
60		64.26	72.04	74.59

These rates apply to males. For females, use three years younger than the actual age.

Figuring Annual Premiums

Example 1 Manfred Quigley, 30, wants to buy 10-year term insurance with a face value of $25,000. What is his annual premium?

Step 1 The premium table shown gives rates per $1,000 of face value. Find the number of thousands in $25,000.

$$\frac{\$25,000}{\$1,000} \text{ or } 25 \text{ thousands}$$

Step 2 Find the rates in the table. Age: 30. Locate 30 in the column at the left of the table. Type of insurance: 10-year term. Locate the rate per $1,000 at age 30.

Age 30, rate per $1,000 = $10.93

Step 3 Multiply the rate per thousand by the number of thousands.

$10.93
× $ 25
$273.25

Answer Manfred's annual premium for 10-year term insurance is $273.25.

Example 2 Perdita Chang, 33, purchases ordinary, or straight, life insurance with a face value of $30,000. Determine her annual premium.

Step 1 Find the number of thousands in $30,000.

30 thousands
$1,000)$30,000

Step 2 Find the rate in the table. Actual age: 33. Because Perdita is a woman, use a table age of 30. Type of insurance: straight life.

Rate per $1,000 = $21.87

Step 3 Multiply the rate per $1,000 by the number of thousands.

$ 21.87
× $ 30
$656.10

Answer The annual premium for straight life insurance is $656.10.

For the convenience of the insured person, life insurance premiums can be paid annually, semiannually, quarterly, or monthly. Paying your premium annually is usually less costly to you than the other payment schedules because it involves less bookkeeping costs for the insurance company.

GROUP LIFE INSURANCE

Businesses with several employees often offer a group life insurance plan as a fringe benefit. This is usually straight, or ordinary, life insurance and applies only for as long as you work for the organization. The group, the people who are employed by the company, are all insured under one policy. No physical examination is required, and, in many instances, the employer pays all or part of the premium. If you as an employee are asked to provide all or part of the premium, you can often arrange to have it withheld from your paycheck.

Self-Check

Find the cost of the annual premium, using the annual premium rate table.

1. You take out a 20-pay life insurance policy with a face value of $20,000. If you are a 25-year-old male, what premium will you pay each year for the next 20 years?

2. Jana O'Malley, 58, buys $35,000 worth of 20-year endowment insurance, for which she will pay a yearly premium for 20 years or until death, whichever comes first. What is the amount of this premium?

ANSWERS   1. Annual premium = $601   2. Annual premium = $2,275.70

Assignment 12.1

Insurance

Use the annual premium rate table on page 467 to solve the following problems.

1. Compute the annual premium for Marvin Mason, age 55, on his 20-pay life-insurance policy of $15,000.

   60.74 × $15 = $911.10 $911.10 per annum

2. Find the annual premium for Janet Meadowcroft, age 43, on her ordinary life insurance policy, face value $22,000.

   29.39 × $22 = $646.58 $646.58 per annum

3. Ms. Anne Titterington contracts for life insurance in the amount of $35,000. If she is 25 years old, and the policy is a 20-year endowment, determine her annual premium.

   48.43 × $35 = $1,695.05 $1,695.05 per annum

4. Perry Danforth, president of Danforth Advertising Company, agrees to take out $50,000 in 10-year term insurance in order to qualify for a Small Business Administration loan. What will be his annual premium if he is 25 at the time he contracts for the policy?

   9.73 × $50 = $486.50 $486.50 per annum

You are an agent for Armstrong Insurance Agency. Figure the annual premium for each of the following clients.

Name and Age	Policy Value	Type of Policy	Annual Premium
5. Anna Hauberg, 26	$10,000	Straight	$ 184.30
6. Paul Maynard, 45	10,000	Ordinary	348.80
7. Andrea Holly, 25	20,000	20-pay life	569.60
8. Susan Kaye, 28	20,000	20-pay life	601.00
9. Bert Bailey, 50	3,500	Ordinary	147.18
10. Debbie Nomaguchi, 48	7,500	10-year term	135.98
11. Betsy Borrow, 23	12,500	20-year endowment	603.50
12. Gertrude Denny, 33	5,600	20-year endowment	276.30
13. Tom Barry, 50	66,000	20-year endowment	3,879.48

12.2 Automobile Insurance

Automobile insurance protects you or your business against high expenses that can result from a motor-vehicle accident.

Understanding Types of Automobile Insurance

Bodily injury: Insurance that covers a person or persons injured by your automobile. In most cases, the amount of bodily injury insurance is indicated by a fraction. For example, 50/100 means the insurance company pays up to $50,000 for injury to one person and up to a total of $100,000 for injury to two or more persons in the same accident.

Property damage: Insurance that pays for the repair of damages caused to the property of others by your automobile.

Collision: Insurance that covers the costs of repair of damage to your car as a result of an automobile accident. To lower your premium, you may want to purchase a $50, $100, or $200 **deductible** policy. Under this type of coverage, you pay the first $50, $100, or $200 of the loss, depending on the terms of your policy, and the insurance company pays the remainder.

Comprehensive damage: Insurance that pays the cost of repairing damage caused to your automobile by such events as vandalism, theft, fire, windstorm, hail, flood, or falling objects. Should yours be an older-model car, but not a classic, you may decide not to carry collision or comprehensive insurance.

Figuring Automobile Insurance Premiums

Your annual premium, the amount you pay to keep your automobile insurance in effect, is determined on the basis of **actuarial tables**. These are compiled from statistics on automobile accidents according to gender, age, location of the mishap, and other variables. The rate classification varies from state to state. Most states now require drivers to carry liability insurance or offer proof of financial responsibility in the event of an accident.

Should you want to lower your automobile insurance premiums, consider the following points.

1. A number of companies offer lower cost policies to people with good driving records.
2. Having drivers in your household who are less than 21 years old raises your premium. If they take a course in driver training or move more than 100 miles away from you, your rate may be lowered.
3. If you have more than one motor vehicle, you might consider insuring all of them with the same company.
4. Perhaps you can reduce the number of miles you drive per year. The fewer miles you drive, the lower your premium.
5. Consider a less expensive car. Collision and comprehensive insurance rates decrease as your car grows older. Repairs to more expensive autos are more costly. Some companies even offer a compact-car discount.
6. Move out of the city. Urban insurance rates tend to be considerably higher than those for small towns or rural areas.

7. Talk to agents of various insurance companies. Some offer the same coverage at a lower price. Shop carefully. Insurance is an important and expensive product.
8. Review your coverage often. Your circumstances can change, and this may affect the premium.
9. Many automobile insurance companies allow payment of premiums on an annual basis. As in the case of life insurance premiums, paying annually is usually less costly to the insured party.

Reading Automobile Insurance Premium Tables

The total annual automobile insurance premium is calculated by taking the sum of the applicable numbers in the following hypothetical tables.

Table 1 Annual Rates for Bodily Injury Insurance

	Amount of Coverage					
	10/20		25/50		100/300	
Age of Insured	Rural	Urban	Rural	Urban	Rural	Urban
Under 25	$175	$300	$185	$315	$195	$332
25 and older	$130	$220	$140	$235	$150	$250

Table 2 Annual Rates for Property Damage Insurance

		Limit $10,000		
Location	Age of Insured	Pleasure Driving	Driving to Work	Business
Rural	Under 25	$105	$117	$123
Rural	25 and older	$ 80	$ 92	$ 98
Urban	Under 25	$150	$162	$168
Urban	25 and older	$115	$127	$133

Table 3 Annual Rates for Collision Insurance for Average-Value Autos

	$50 Deductible		$100 Deductible	
Age of Insured	Rural	Urban	Rural	Urban
Under 25	$229	$399	$155	$230
25 and older	$147	$249	$ 99	$174

Table 4 Annual Rates for Standard Comprehensive Insurance for Average-Value Autos

Age of Insured	Rural	Urban
Under 25	$60	$97
25 and older	$42	$79

Example 1 Tanya Berlitz, 32, lives in Chicago, Illinois. She uses her car to drive to work and buys auto insurance as follows:

25/50 bodily injury;
$10,000 property damage;
$100 deductible collision;
Standard comprehensive.

What is her total annual premium?

Step 1	Find the bodily injury rate, using Table 1. (Over 25, 25/50, Urban)	$235
Step 2	Find the property damage rate, using Table 2. (Urban, Over 25, Driving to Work)	$127
Step 3	Find the collision insurance rate, using Table 3. (Over 25, $100 Deductible, Urban)	$174
Step 4	Find the comprehensive rate, using Table 4. (Over 25, Urban)	$ 79
Step 5	Total the rates for the four types of coverage.	$235 127 174 + 79 $615

Answer   Tanya Berlitz's annual premium is $615.

Self-Check

Determine the annual automobile insurance premium for each of the following clients of Auto-Write Insurance Agency.

Name	Age	Location	Bodily Injury	$10,000 Property Damage	Collision Deductible	Comprehensive
1. John Overton	20	Urban	25/50	Pleasure	Not carried	No
2. Marion Harper	46	Rural	100/300	Business	$ 50	Yes
3. Jill Conway	35	Rural	10/20	Drive to work	$100	Yes

1. _____   2. _____   3. _____

ANSWERS   1. $465   2. $437   3. $363

Insurance   475

NO-FAULT INSURANCE

In recent years, several states have passed no-fault insurance laws. Under the provisions of such laws, the company with which you are insured covers costs associated with an accident, regardless of who caused that accident. This protects you in the event that your vehicle is struck and/or you and your passengers are injured by a vehicle whose owner does not carry insurance. If you live in a state that does not allow for no-fault insurance, you can expect to carry uninsured-driver, or uninsured motorist insurance, which will provide you with the same protection that no-fault insurance does.

Assignment 12.2

Insurance

Use Tables 1-4 on pages 474–475 to solve the following problems.

1. Ms. Willie Fonstead, 25, lives in Atlanta, Georgia, and uses her Mustang for pleasure driving. Find her annual insurance premium if she carries 10/20 bodily injury limits, $10,000 property-damage limits, collision insurance with a $100 deductible, and standard comprehensive insurance.

   $220 BI 10/20
   115 PD
   174 coll.
   + 79 comp.
   $588

   $588 annual premium

2. Pittsville, Wisconsin, where Morris Deanwall, 42, lives, is classified as a rural community. He buys comprehensive automobile insurance, plus a $50 deductible on collision, $10,000 limits on property damage, and 25/50 limits on bodily injury. If Morris uses his Ford pickup principally for business purposes, what is his annual premium?

   $140 BI 25/50
   98 PD
   147 coll.
   + 42 comp.
   $427

   $427 annual premium

3. In an automobile crash, Jerid Malloy injures Matt Gulas and Tandy Warrington, pedestrians. When the case is brought to court, the judge awards damages of $25,000 to Gulas and $12,000 to Ms. Warrington. If Jerid carries bodily injury insurance with limits of 10/20, how much will he have to pay to settle the claims?

   $10,000 Gulas
   + 10,000 Warrington
   $20,000 Total insurance coverage

   $25,000 + $12,000 = $37,000 total awarded
   $37,000 − $20,000 = $17,000 paid by Malloy

   $17,000 to be paid by Malloy

4. In an accident involving Jerry Moran's car and another car, four people in the other car are injured. The court judges Moran to be at fault and awards damages of $10,000 each to the injured. If Moran carries a policy that includes bodily injury limits of 25/50, what is the total his insurance company will pay toward these bodily injury claims?

   25/50 coverage
   4 × $10,000 = $40,000 award

   $40,000 (total award) paid by insurance company under Moran's 25/50 coverage

continued

Assignment 12.2 continued

Randy Polaski is an agent for Appleby Insurance Agency in Carp, Indiana. Help him figure the annual automobile insurance premium for the following clients, all of whom live on farms.

Client Name	Age	Bodily Injury	$10,000 Property Damage	Collision Deductible	Comprehensive	Annual Premium
5. Robert Nichols	24	10/20	Business	$100	Yes	$ 473
6. Frank Howard	21	25/50	Business	$ 50	Yes	597
7. Claudine Palo	36	25/50	Pleasure	Not carried	No	220
8. Ann Gunason	30	100/300	Drive to work	$100	Yes	383
9. Ed Thuma	18	10/20	Pleasure	$ 50	Yes	569
10. David Rohn	19	100/300	Pleasure	$ 50	No	529

Manny Rosell owns Rosell Independent Insurance Agency, Inc. Assurity Limited, one of the automobile insurance companies with which he deals, announces that it is offering a 15% reduction in collision and comprehensive rates for people who have not had an accident in the last five years. What will be the adjusted annual premium for each of the following qualified clients?

	Age	Location	Bodily Injury	$10,000 Property Damage	Collision Deductible	Comprehensive	Adjusted Annual Premium
11.	24	Urban	25/50	Business	$ 50	Yes	$ 904.60
12.	22	Urban	100/300	Pleasure	Not carried	Yes	564.45
13.	43	Rural	10/20	Drive to work	$100	Yes	341.85
14.	36	Rural	10/20	Drive to work	$100	Yes	341.85
15.	29	Urban	25/50	Pleasure	$ 50	No	561.65
16.	23	Rural	100/300	Business	$ 50	No	512.65
17.	72	Urban	25/50	Business	Not carried	Yes	435.15

12.3 Fire Insurance

You can protect your business or residence against fire loss or damage, but you must understand that your coverage applies only to the particular property specified in the policy. For example, the insurance company is not liable for the cost of destroyed clothing, furniture, machines, equipment, and so on, unless they are insured along with the building.

Fire insurance usually applies to damage caused in fighting a fire, such as that from water, chemicals, and breakage by firefighters in the performance of their duty, as well as to destruction caused by the fire itself. It does not cover loss or damage caused by earthquake, tornado, winds, lightning, flood, and other events termed "acts of God," or by crashes into the building by motor vehicles or aircraft, although coverage for these and similar risks can be added to the policy for an increase in the premium.

In the case of loss, the insurance company pays either the amount of the claim or the **face value** of the policy, whichever is less.

Figuring Fire Insurance Premiums

The premium on fire insurance is usually presented in terms of a certain amount for each one hundred dollars' worth of coverage purchased.

Example 1 Tina Huntington takes out a $40,000 fire insurance policy on the building housing her public-relations office. If the annual premium rate is 26 cents per $100, find her annual premium.

Step 1 Divide the coverage amount of the policy by 100 to determine how many hundreds of dollars are involved.

$$\frac{\$40,000}{100} = 400$$

Step 2 Multiply the number of hundreds by the cost per hundred.

$$\begin{array}{r}\$400 \\ \times\ .26 \\ \hline \$104 \end{array}$$

Answer The annual fire insurance premium is $104.

In some instances, the insurance rate is quoted as a percent of the face value of the policy, that is to say, a percent of the maximum coverage.

Example 2 Tina Huntington takes out a $40,000 fire insurance policy on her office building. The annual premium rate is $.2\frac{3}{5}\%$ of the policy's face value. What is her annual premium?

Step 1 Convert the percent rate to a decimal. (Note the relationship to 26 cents per $100 in Example 1.)

$.2\frac{3}{5}\% = .0026$

Step 2 Multiply, using the percentage formula with $40,000 as the base and .0026 as the rate. (See Section 5.3.)

$B \times R = P$
$\$40,000 \times .0026 = \$104$

Answer The annual premium for fire insurance is $104.

Often the insurance company gives a discount if you purchase fire insurance for more than one year. Typical rates are the following.

Period of Time	Rate
2 years	1.85 times the annual rate
3 years	2.7 times the annual rate

Insurance **479**

Because of rising repair and replacement costs, insurance companies rarely provide fire insurance terms of more than 3 years.

Example 3 Tina Huntington decides to purchase the $40,000 fire insurance coverage on her building for 3 years. If the insurance company offers a typical discount, what is the total amount of her premium?

Step 1   Find the premium for 1 year. (See Examples 1 and 2.) $104

Step 2   Increase this 2.7 times by multiplying.

$$\begin{array}{r}\$104\\ \times\ 2.7\\ \hline \$280.8\end{array}$$

Answer   The total fire insurance premium for 3 years is $280.80.

NOTE: What we have done is, in effect, a percentage calculation. Saying that the premium for 3 years is 2.7 times that for 1 year is the same thing as saying it is 270% of the premium for 1 year. The 1-year premium is the base. The 3-year rate percent is the rate. The 3-year premium is the percentage.

Self-Check

1. Clifton Fenster, owner of Fenster Tool and Die Company, takes out a 1-year fire-insurance policy in the amount of $30,000. It carries an annual premium rate of 22.85 cents per $100. What is the annual premium?

2. Mr. and Mrs. Millard Eng purchase fire insurance for their home. The face value of the policy is $76,500, and the rate is $0.45 per $100. If the Engs receive a discount for taking the policy for 2 years, what is their total premium?

3. If you buy a fire insurance policy with a limit of $45,000 coverage, and the premium is at $1\frac{1}{4}\%$ of face value, what is your annual premium?

ANSWERS   1. $68.55   2. $636.86   3. $562.50

AN INSURANCE FIRST

In 1688, Edward Lloyd and a group of merchants and sea captains gathered at Lloyd's London coffeehouse to develop a society to provide marine insurance to the burgeoning British trading industry. Each man agreed to put up a certain amount of money to cover loss in case of shipwreck. Whenever insurance was requested for a particular vessel, members of ther society signed their names at the bottom of the policy along with the amount of money they were prepared to pay in the event of loss. Signatures were added until the full amount required was guaranteed. The term "underwriting" derives from this practice. Lloyds of London operates to this day and maintains a reputation for insuring what other insurance companies consider it impossible to cover.

Assignment 12.3

Insurance

As an agent for Comstead Insurance Company, Don Bodega must determine the premiums on a number of policies. Help him, using the following information.

Policy Number	Face Value	Cost per $100	Payment Period	Total Premium	
1.	$ 22,000	$.31	1 year	$ 68.20	220 × .31
2.	$ 24,000	$.28	1 year	67.20	240 × .28
3.	$ 10,000	$.26	3 years	70.20	100 × .26 × 2.7
4.	$ 55,000	$.44	3 years	653.40	550 × .44 × 2.7
5.	$ 42,500	$.19	2 years	149.39	425 × .19 × 1.85
6.	$101,250	$.24	2 years	449.55	1,012.5 × .24 × 1.85
7.	$ 75,650	$.42	3 years	857.87	756.5 × .42 × 2.7
8.	$ 12,500	$.43	1 year	53.75	125 × .43
9.	$116,650	$.25	1 year	291.63	1,166.5 × .25
10.	$300,000	$.32	3 years	2,592.00	3,000 × .32 × 2.7

11. Kitty Fosdick, owner of Fosdick Fine Foods, is seeking fire insurance for her store, valued at $175,000. Applemen Insurance Agency offers her a yearly policy with a rate of 31.5 cents per $100. Celsen Insurance offers similar coverage at .35% of face value, and will give her a standard discount for 3 years. Assuming Applemen does not offer such a discount, which coverage costs less over the 3-year period?

Applemen on $175,000
31.5¢ per $100 no discount
   1,750 × .315 = $551.25
     551.25 × 3 = $1,653.75 (3 yr)
Celsen .35% of face value
   175,000 × .35% = $612.50
     612.50 × 2.7 = $1,653.75

Both policies cost the same for three years

12.4 Other Aspects of Fire Insurance

Cancellation by the Policyholder

For a variety of reasons, you may want to purchase fire insurance for less than one year's time or to cancel your policy before its one-year term expires. When you do so, the company returns a part of the premium. However, because of its initial costs, such as bookkeeping, the company returns less than the prorated share of the annual premium. This is called **short-rating**. The amount returned to you is determined by a table, such as the following.

Standard Short-Rate Table

Days in Force	% Retained	Days in Force	% Retained	Days in Force	% Retained
1	5	92– 94	36	215–218	68
2	6	95– 98	37	219–223	69
3– 4	7	99–102	38	224–228	70
5– 6	8	103–105	39	229–232	71
7– 8	9	106–109	40	233–237	72
9–10	10	110–113	41	238–241	73
11–12	11	114–116	42	242–246 (8 mos.)	74
13–14	12	117–120 (4 mos.)	43	247–250	75
15–16	13	121–124	44	251–255	76
17–18	14	125–127	45	256–260	77
19–20	15	128–131	46	261–264	78
21–22	16	132–135	47	265–269	79
23–25	17	136–138	48	270–273 (9 mos.)	80
26–29	18	139–142	49	274–278	81
30–32 (1 mo.)	19	143–146	50	279–282	82
33–36	20	147–149	51	283–287	83
37–40	21	150–153 (5 mos.)	52	288–291	84
41–43	22	154–156	53	292–296	85
44–47	23	157–160	54	297–301	86
48–51	24	161–164	55	302–305 (10 mos.)	87
52–54	25	165–167	56	306–310	88
55–58	26	168–171	57	311–314	89
59–62 (2 mos.)	27	172–175	58	315–319	90
63–65	28	176–178	59	320–323	91
66–69	29	179–182 (6 mos.)	60	324–328	92
70–73	30	183–187	61	329–332	93
74–76	31	188–191	62	333–337 (11 mos.)	94
77–80	32	192–196	63	338–342	95
81–83	33	197–200	64	343–346	96
84–87	34	201–205	65	347–351	97
88–91 (3 mos.)	35	206–209	66	352–355	98
		210–214 (7 mos.)	67	356–360	99
				361–365 (12 mos.)	100

Example 1 Tina Huntington sells her public-relations business and cancels her $40,000 one-year fire insurance policy after it has been in effect for 90 days. If the yearly premium is $104, how much will the company return to her?

Step 1 Find in the standard short-rate table the percent of the premium to be retained by the company.

Amount retained after 90 days = 35%

Step 2	Multiply the yearly premium by the percent retained to find the amount retained. Note that you are using the percentage formula.	B × R = P $104 × .35 = $36.40
Step 3	Subtract the amount retained by the company from he total premium.	$104.00 × 36.40 $ 67.60
Answer	The amount returned after 90 days is $67.60.	

Self-Check

1. Arthur La Tour cancels his fire insurance policy after it has been in effect for 40 days. How much will be returned to him by the company if his annual premium is $124.50? _____

2. Anna Taski sells her trucking company. She cancels the fire insurance on the building that houses her office and repair shop. The policy, with an annual premium of $237, has been in effect for 216 days. How much of the premium will be returned? _____

ANSWERS   **1.** $98.36   **2.** $75.84

Cancellation by the Insurance Company

Should a fire insurance company cancel your policy for some reason, the portion of the premium returned to you is usually calculated by multiplying the total premium by the actual number of days the insurance was in effect, divided by 365, the number of days in the year. The result is subtracted from the total premium to determine the amount to be returned. In most states, the insurance company is required to give you a **grace period,** a specified number of days' advance notice, before cancellation. This allows you time to obtain coverage from another company if you so desire.

Example 2   Eino Makinen purchased a one-year policy from Fidelity Fire Insurance Company on November 15, 19___. The premium was $150. Effective February 12 of the following year, Fidelity canceled the policy. What amount did Eino receive as a refund?

Step 1	Find the number of days the coverage was in effect.	30 days in November − 15 th of November 15 31 days in December 31 days in January + 12 th of February 89 days
Step 2	Multiply the annual premium by the part of the year the insurance was in effect divided by the number of days in a year.	$150 \times \dfrac{89}{365} = \$36.58$
Step 3	Subtract the portion of the premium retained by the company from the total premium.	$150.00 − 36.58 $113.42
Answer	The amount of the premium refunded is $113.42.	

Self-Check

1. Effective December 3, Mutual Insurance Company cancels the fire-insurance policy of Mr. and Mrs. Jan Fenwick, returning part of the premium. If the Fenwicks paid an annual premium of $98 on July 12 of the same year as the cancellation, what is the amount of their refund? _____

2. Barney Rumley contracted for a 3-year fire-insurance policy on his business building on April 6, 19__, for which he paid a total premium of $295. The insurance company canceled Barney's policy as of June 25, of the following year. What portion of the premium was retained by the company? _____

ANSWERS   1. $59.34   2. 3 yr = 1,095 days $295 × $\frac{445}{1,095}$ = $119.89

Calculating Coinsurance

Usually applied to fire insurance carried by a business, the term **coinsurance** means that the insured and the insurance company share the cost of losses when they occur. When there is a coinsurance clause in the policy, the insurance company agrees to pay the amount of the face value of the policy in the event of total loss. Complete devastation of property is very rare. In most cases, only a portion of it is destroyed before the fire is extinguished. For this reason, it is common for the insured party to save on the premium by contracting for insurance on a percentage of the property's market value rather than on its full value.

The insurance company sets the percent of coverage the policyholder must maintain to be fully protected. Eighty percent is typical, but any rate may be used. Should coverage be less than this percent, the policyholder bears a prorated share of any loss.

To determine this share, divide the amount of insurance actually carried by the amount needed to meet the rate requirement. Calculate the decimal accurately to at least the third place, and multiply the result by the actual loss. In no case does the company pay more than the face value of the policy.

Example 3 On its main warehouse, Camelite Distributing Company carries a $75,000 fire-insurance policy with an 80% coinsurance clause, even though the building is currently valued at $150,000. If there is a fire at the warehouse resulting in damages of $30,000, how much can Camelite expect to recover from the insurance company?

Step 1 Determine the amount of coverage required to meet the terms of the coinsurance clause.

$150,000
× .8
$120,000

Step 2 Divide the figure into the amount of insurance actually carried.

.625
120,000)75,000

Step 3 Multiply the actual loss by this figure.

$30,000
× .625
$18,750

Answer The amount payable by the insurance company is $18,750.

Example 4 Suppose the loss from the fire at Camelite Distributing Company is $120,000. How much can the insurance company be expected to pay?

Steps 1 and 2 See Example 1.

$150,000 × .8 = $120,000
$75,000 ÷ $120,000 = .625

Step 3 Multiply the actual loss by .625.

$$\begin{array}{r} \$120,000 \\ \times \quad .625 \\ \hline \$\ 75,000 \end{array}$$

Answer The insurance company can be expected to pay the face value of the policy, $75,000.

Example 5 Suppose the loss from the fire at Camelite is $140,000. How much will the insurance company pay?

Steps 1–3 See Examples 1 and 2.

$$\begin{array}{r} \$140,000 \\ \times \quad .625 \\ \hline \$\ 87,500 \end{array}$$

Answer Even though the prorated loss is $87,500, the insurance company will pay only $75,000, the face value of the policy.

Self-Check

1. Marveline de Lorean has a small gift shop. She carries $37,000 in fire insurance with an 80% coinsurance clause. A fire causes a $30,000 loss. Decide the amount to be recovered from the insurance company if the value of the shop was $45,000 at the time of the fire.

2. Badincourt Corporation suffered a fire loss of $30,000. At the time of the fire, the property damaged was valued at $50,000. The corporation had insured the property for $30,000, with an 80% coinsurance clause. What is the amount to be paid by the insurance company?

ANSWERS 1. $30,000. The company pays the full amount of the damage because coverage exceeds 80% of total value of the property.   2. $22,500

Assignment 12.4

Insurance

Parks Sniderman, of Independent Insurance Agency Inc., has several business clients who have decided to cancel their fire insurance policies. Using the short-rate table, help him calculate the refund to which each is entitled.

Client Name	Annual Premium	Number of Days Policy in Effect	Amount Refunded
1. Bargreen Aquarium Sales	$39.40	128	$ 21.28
2. Manwite Service Station	$78.24	240	21.12
3. Guido's Taco Stand	$49.60	218	15.87
4. Stanton Sausage Co.	$28.75	55	21.27
5. Little Finland Sauna	$73.25	43	57.13

Example
1. $39.40 × 46% = $18.12
   $39.40 − $18.12 = $21.28

Constance Rosareo, an employee of Comstock Insurance Company, must determine the refunds due several of her clients, who had their policies canceled by the company for a variety of reasons. Assist her, given the information below.

Policy	Annual Premium	Days Coverage Was in Effect	Premium Refund
6.	$ 54.50	25	$ 50.77
7.	$ 29.35	66	24.04
8.	$134.25	246	43.77
9.	$ 76.30	301	13.38
10.	$105.20	210	44.67

Example
6. $54.50 × $\frac{25}{365}$ = 3.73 retained
   $54.50 − 3.73 = $50.77 refund

Jerry and Angela Young took out a one-year, $80,000 fire insurance policy on their rural home on March 16. They decided to cancel the policy, effective the following July 15. The annual rate of the policy was $.5\frac{1}{2}$% of face value.

11. What was the annual premium for the Youngs' policy?

    $80,000 × .55% = $440 annual premium   **$440 annual premium**

12. What refund should they receive after their cancellation of the policy?

    $440 × 44% = $193.60 retained   **$246.60 refund**
    $440 − $193.60 = $246.60 refund

continued

Assignment 12.4 *continued*

13. Assume instead that the insurance company was the party who canceled the policy. What refund should the Youngs receive?

    $440 \times \dfrac{121}{365} = \$145.86$ retained

    $440 - \$145.86 = \$294.14$ refund

    $294.14 refund

    ```
    31  March
    - 16
      15  March
      30  April
      31  May
      30  June
      15  July
     121  days
    ```

14. Palmer Bowling Lanes had a fire that did $67,000 worth of damage. The building was insured for $130,000 with an 80% coinsurance clause and was valued at $175,000. What amount can the insurance company be expected to pay?

    $175,000 × 80% = $140,000
    $130,000 ÷ 140,000 = .929
    $67,000 × .9 = $62,243 insurance would pay

    $62,243 insurance would pay

15. According to the morning paper, a fire at Kandick and Ross, a candy company, did damage amounting to $36,000. As the agent who sold the company its policy, you know that the building is insured for $45,000 and has a market value of $62,000. If the policy has an 80% coinsurance clause, how much can the insurance company be expected to pay toward the loss?

    $62,000 × 80% = $49,600
    $45,000 ÷ 49,600 = .907
    $36,000 × .907 = $32,652 insurance would pay

    $32,652 insurance would pay

16. Ben Gomez carries $60,000 worth of fire insurance on his office building. There is an 80% coinsurance clause. A flash fire causes a loss of $24,000 to the building, which has a market value of $120,000. What amount can be expected from the insurance company?

    $120,000 × 80% = $96,000
    60,000 ÷ 96,000 = .625
    $24,000 × .625 = $15,000

    $15,000 payment from insurance

17. Assuming the facts in the above situation are the same, what amount can be expected from the insurance company if the loss is $96,000?

    $96,000 × .625 = $60,000

    $60,000 from insurance company

Comprehensive Problems for Chapter 12

Insurance

Use the tables in this chapter where applicable to solve the following problems.

1. On May 1, Bill Kovell, 26, who lives in Los Angeles, California, bought a used Plymouth Fury to drive to his job at Bayon's Cement Plant. He contracted for automobile insurance in these amounts: 25/50 bodily-injury limits, $10,000 property-damage limits, $50 deductible on collision, and standard comprehensive. Discovering after eight months that he could not afford the expense, Bill sold the Plymouth and canceled his insurance. The short-term insurance rate for an eight-month period is 73% of the annual premium. How much did Bill receive as a refund from the insurance company?

   $235 BI 20/50
   127 PD
   249 Coll. 50 Ded.
   + 79 Comp.
   $690 Annual premium

   $690 × 73% = $503.70
   $690 − $503.70 = $186.30 refund

   $186.30 refund

2. Marilee Rush and Barbara Tretor, partners in an insulated underwear manufacturing firm, agree to take out $30,000 straight life insurance policies, declaring one another as beneficiaries. If Marilee is 25 and Barbara is 28, what is the total combined premium?

   $18.03 × 30 = $540.90
   $19.30 × 30 = $579.00
   $540.90 + 579 = $1,119.90

   $1,119.90 total combined premium

3. Judy Chambers, a widow, owns a commercial building that is valued at $375,000. On it, she carries an insurance policy with a face value of $275,000 and an 80% coinsurance clause. If a fire does $220,000 damage to the building, how much reimbursement can Judy expect from the insurance company?

   $375,000 × 80% = $300,000
   $275,000 ÷ 300,000 = .917
   $220,000 × .917 = $201,740 insurance would pay

   $201,740 reimbursement from insurance

How much will it cost Joe's Auto Sales, Inc., in annual premiums to insure each of the following employees with 10-year term nongroup life insurance policies?

	Name	Age	Face Value of Policy	Annual Premium
4.	Ben Moran	30	$10,000	$ 109.30
5.	Thomas Baynon	25	$12,500	121.63
6.	Mary Tudor	24	$11,600	102.78
7.	Eliza Saxon	43	$17,550	264.48

continued

Comprehensive Problems *continued*

8. Elliot Conway, an electrician, has his inventory and tools insured for $10,000, with an 80% coinsurance clause. He suffers a fire that destroys both inventory and tools, a total value of $15,000. Decide how much he will recover from his insurance company.

   $15,000 × 80% = $12,000 meet terms of coinsurance
   $10,000 ÷ 12,000 = .833
   $15,000 × .833 = $12,495 prorated loss

   $10,000 Even though prorated loss is $12,495, the insurance company will pay only $10,000, the face value of the policy.

9. Maria Grossman, 22, of Milwaukee, Wisconsin, buys insurance for her Chevette. She takes out a policy with 10/20 bodily injury limits, $10,000 property-damage limits, $100 deductible on collision, and comprehensive insurance. If Maria uses the Chevette for pleasure driving only, and if her insurance company offers a 20% reduction on collision and comprehensive insurance for compact models, what is her annual premium?

   $300.00   10/20 BI
   150.00   10/PD
   184.00   100 Ded. coll. 230 × 80%
     77.60   Comp. 97 × 80%
   $711.60

   $711.60 annual premium

10. Tom Carlson, owner of a chain of beauty salons, wants to purchase fire insurance to cover all five of his shops, a total value of $1,250,000. Zimbrick Insurance Agency offers him a policy at an annual premium of $.46 per $100. If he contracts for 2 years, Zimbrick offers the standard discount. Abbot Insurance Agency offers him similar coverage at a total annual premium of $.5\frac{1}{2}$% of the face value of the policy. Abbot offers no reduction in rate for a 2-year contract, but will give Harry 10 percent off the premium because he is willing to insure all five of his properties with them. Figuring the total premium for 2 years, what is the cost of coverage by:

    a) Zimbrick Insurance Agency?

    .46 per $100   2 yr standard discount
    $12,500 × .46 = $5,750 per year
    $5,750 × 1.85 = $10,637.50 total premium

    $10,637.50 total premium

    b) Abbot Insurance Agency?

    .5$\frac{1}{2}$% face $1,250,000 less 10%
    $1,250,000 × .55% = $6,875 per year $13,750
    $6,875 × 2 = $13,750   − 1,375
    $13,750 × 10% = 1,375 $12,375 Total premium

    $12,375 total premium

    c) How much will Harry save by taking the less expensive policy?

      $12,375   Abbot
    − 10,637.50   Zimbrick
      $ 1,737.50

    $1,737.50 savings

continued

Comprehensive Problems *continued*

Steve Heck, an agent for Dayton Insurance Agency, must determine the annual premium for each of the clients below. Help him do so by using the premium table.

	Name and Age	Face Value	Type of Life-insurance Policy	Annual Premium
11.	Carl Inman, 21	$16,000	20-year endowment	$ 773.60
12.	Karen Shield, 24	$75,000	Straight	1,323.00
13.	Mavis Rosell, 38	$65,000	Straight	1,634.75
14.	Harold Kean, 60	$42,000	20-pay life	3,025.68
15.	Bill Stern, 40	$ 5,000	20-pay life	204.00

For a group of clients whose fire insurance is canceled by the company in less than one year, calculate refunds on the basis of the following data.

Policy Number	Face Value of Policy	Date Coverage Began	Effective Date of Cancellation	Annual Rate per $100	Premium Refund	
16.	$ 86,000	January 16	February 27	.46	$ 350.08	42 days
17.	9,700	March 1	November 30	.54	13.06	274 days
18.	19,850	May 1	December 15	.36	26.82	228 days
19.	100,000	April 17	June 25	.58	470.36	69 days
20.	94,000	July 20	December 31	.26	134.59	164 days

As an independent auto insurance agent, calculate the annual premium for the following customers, who live in a rural area.

	Name	Age	Bodily Injury	$10,000 Property Damage	Collision Deductible	Comprehensive	Premium
21.	Cynthia Snow	28	100/300	Drive to Work	Not carried	Yes	$ 284
22.	Pamela Diamond	25	10/20	Business	Not carried	Yes	270
23.	Bernice Brady	42	100/300	Pleasure	$ 50	Yes	419

continued

Comprehensive Problems *continued*

	Name	Age	Bodily Injury	$10,000 Property Damage	Collision Deductible	Comprehensive	Premium
24.	Maryann Simons	31	25/50	Business	$100	Yes	379
25.	Diane Dailey	58	25/50	Drive to work	$100	No	331
26.	Richard Warrum	62	10/20	Drive to work	$ 50	Yes	411

Case 1

Perry Brumstine, 35, president of Brumstine and Marsh Accounting, and Ann Marsh, 28, vice president, decided to review the firm's insurance coverage. They found the following:

Life Insurance Policies:

Purpose: Assurance for bank loan

$75,000 ten-year term on Brumstine
$35,000 ten-year term on Marsh

Purpose: Fringe benefit

$50,000 twenty-year endowment on Brumstine
$25,000 twenty-year endowment on Marsh

Insurance on company car (driven by Brumstine in urban area for business purposes only):

Bodily injury, 25/50
Property damages, $10,000
Collision, $50 deductible
Comprehensive, standard

Fire Insurance (on company offices, valued at $100,000):

Annual rate, 28.5 cents per $100
Three-year policy with standard discount

a) Using the tables provided in this chapter, determine the total annual cost of the firm's insurance coverage.

b) What factors should Brumstine and Marsh explore in deciding whether this coverage is adequate for the company's current needs?

Case 2

One snowy night, Bill Parnell and Harry Standish were driving home in Bill's Mustang.
"What kind of insurance coverage do you carry?" Harry asked.
"Ten thousand dollars' worth of property damage, 10/20 bodily injury, $100 deductible collision, and standard comprehensive. Why?"
"No reason. I guess the slippery roads make me think it's a good night for accidents."
Hardly had Harry finished speaking when the car sent into a skid, and Bill lost control. The car spun into the oncoming traffic, where it collided with a Plymouth driven by Mary Sue Kinsley, injuring both her and her mother, who was riding with her. Bill and Harry were not hurt.
It cost $1,236 to repair the Mustang and $1,450 to repair the Plymouth. The following damages were awarded to each of the injured: Mary Sue Kinsley, $10,500; Mrs. Kinsley, $18,550.

a) What was the total cost of the accident?

b) How much did the accident cost Bill after all claims were paid by his insurer?

Key Terms

Actuarial table	Endowment insurance	Policy
Actuary	Face value	Property-damage insurance
Automobile insurance	Fire insurance	Short-rating
Beneficiary	Grace period	Straight life insurance
Bodily-injury insurance	Insurance	Term insurance
Cash surrender value	Life insurance	Twenty-pay life insurance
Coinsurance	Limited-payment life insurance	Universal life insurance
Collision insurance	Ordinary life insurance	
Comprehensive-damage insurance	Premium	
Deductible		

Key Concepts

Life insurance includes several types. The most common are the following.

- Term insurance provides a benefit if death occurs within the limited period of time during which the policy is in effect.
- Ordinary or straight life insurance does not operate within a specified term, and requires payment of a set premium each year while the insured party lives.
- Limited-payment life insurance provides that premiums are paid for a specified number of years, rather than for the duration of the insured party's life.
- Endowment insurance allows the insured party to accumulate funds for later use.

Automobile insurance has four basic categories:

- Bodily injury, which covers the insured party in case another person or persons is injured by the insured's automobile.
- Property damage, which pays for repair of property damaged by the insured's automobile.
- Collision, which covers repair of damage to the insured's automobile that results from an auto accident.
- Comprehensive, which pays for repair of damage to the insured's automobile that results from vandalism, theft, fire, falling objects, or similar events.

Fire insurance protects against fire loss or damage, and coverage applies only to property specifically mentioned in the policy.

- Fire insurance policies may be canceled by either the insured party or the insurance company. If the insured cancels, a short-rate table is used to calculate the portion of the premium to be returned.
- Often, a coinsurance clause is added to a fire insurance policy. Under this arrangement, the insured party agrees to bear part of any loss if the face value of the policy is less than a specified percent of the current market value of the property.

13
Depreciation

Business Takes a Positive Approach
ALCOA ALUMINUM

With the continued decline in the use of aluminum, prospects for growth in the industry appear dim. Instead of resigning itself to defeat, however, Alcoa Aluminum has come up with an enterprising alternative. The company now employs over 1,000 researchers to seek out new materials to replace aluminum in the future. These researchers are also exploring ways of transforming existing production facilities to meet the needs of the changing marketplace. Alcoa has also chosen to acquire companies in fields such as aerospace and defense, where a strong demand exists for new technology in lightweight materials. At the same time, the company is modernizing its current plants to open new avenues for the use of aluminum. By investing in new, advanced equipment, the company is in a position to take excellent advantage of the current Internal Revenue Service's regulations involving depreciation for tax purposes. Alcoa sets an example for business and industry. With foresight and resourcefulness, a company can prove itself successful even in a declining market.

> ## Learning Objectives
>
> After reading and studying this chapter and working the problems, you will be able to:
>
> - Figure the total cost of an asset.
>
> - Calculate the annual depreciation of an asset by using each of the following methods:
>   straight line;
>   units of production;
>   sum of the years' digits;
>   declining balance;
>   accelerated cost recovery system;
>   modified accelerated cost recovery system.
>
> - Determine accumulated depreciation.
>
> - Calculate the book value of an asset.
>
> - Complete a depreciation schedule.

Every business, whether small or large, is concerned with depreciation. When it is said that something depreciates over time, it means that the value of the item has decreased because of such things as physical wear and tear or product obsolescence. If you have ever tried to sell a used car, bicycle, or tennis racquet, you have probably found that the value has depreciated during the time that you have been using it. A company is able to calculate this decrease or "loss" in value of items used in business and label it as a business expense. Simply stated, the process of distributing the cost of an item over its useful life is called **depreciation**.

The items or properties owned by a business are called its **assets**. Assets are divided into two general categories: (1) current assets and (2) long-term assets. **Current assets** are cash and other assets that can be turned into cash quickly or sold or used within a year's time, such as accounts receivable and merchandise inventory. **Long-term assets**, however, are assets that have a useful life of longer than one year, such as those that are used for the production or sale of other assets or services, called **fixed assets**. Some examples of fixed assets are a store's cash register, a lawyer's office furniture, a plumber's tools, a restaurant's oven, or a contractor's dump truck.

According to our tax structure, a business can deduct the cost of fixed assets as an expense over a period of time. The period of time involved depends on the estimated life of the fixed asset. The **book value** of a fixed asset is found by subtracting the amount of accumulated depreciation to date from the original cost of the asset. Depreciation can be computed monthly, quarterly, or annually, depending on how frequently a particular business prepares its financial statements.

For our purposes, computations in this chapter will be concerned with year-end annual reports. It is important to remember, however, that only fixed assets can be depreciated. Although deprecation is based on estimated, not exact figures, the Bureau of Internal Revenue does set some guidelines.

Revisions of the tax law in 1981 and 1986 changed the view of depreciation. Depreciation is called "cost recovery," which means that the entire cost of an asset is recovered through tax deductions over a certain period of time. The actual value of the asset (the **salvage value**) at the end of the period is not taken into account. This new concept of depreciation is really a tax calculation and applies to all fixed assets purchased since January 1981. It is a faster method of recovery, and hence is called the *accelerated cost recovery system* (ACRS).

It is important to study the other methods of depreciation since assets placed in service before 1981 are still being depreciated with these methods. The ACRS and the Modified ACRS of 1986 also use some of the concepts of these earlier methods. In addition, internal accounting procedures in many businesses may use the traditional methods.

Several different methods of depreciation will be covered in this chapter. They are:

1. The straight-line method,
2. The units-of-production method,
3. The sum-of-the-years'-digits method,
4. The declining-balance method,
5. The Accelerated Cost Recovery System [ACRS], and
6. The Modified Accelerated Cost Recovery System [MACRS].

The sum-of-the-years'-digit method and the declining-balance method are known as *accelerated depreciation* methods, because the depreciation is "speeded up" so that larger amounts of depreciation can be written off during the first years and smaller amounts during the last years of the asset's life.

All these methods are applied according to the type of asset, the date the asset is placed in service, the manner in which the asset is used, and the financial situation of the firm. It is important to know the following factors:

Cost of the asset: This includes sales tax, transportation, and expenditures required to place the asset and make it ready to be used.

Salvage value: This is the estimated market value of the asset at the end of its estimated life. It may also be called trade-in value, scrap value, residual value, or liquidation value.

Estimated life: This is the number of years the asset is expected to be used. It can also be expressed in terms of total miles, total hours, total revolutions, and so forth.

13.1 Depreciation by the Straight-Line Method

One of the most common methods of computing depreciation is the **straight-line method**, which is used when the usage of the asset is fairly uniform from year to year during its estimated life. It is called "straight line" because the depreciation is written off in equal amounts for each accounting period during the life of the asset. On a graph, the equal amounts of depreciation would look like a straight line.

The annual depreciation cost for the straight line method is found by subtracting the salvage value from the total cost of the asset and dividing that figure by the estimated life of the asset.

The formula for finding depreciation using the straight-line method is as follows:

$$\text{Annual depreciation} = \frac{\text{Total cost} - \text{Salvage value}}{\text{Life (in years)}}$$

Sometimes the estimated life of an asset is quoted as a rate (percent). This is called the **straight-line depreciation rate** and is found by dividing 100% by the estimated years of an asset's life. For instance, the straight-line depreciation rate for an asset with a life of 4 years is 25% (100% ÷ 4).

Example 1 A paint sprayer with an estimated life of 5 years was purchased for $2,500 plus a transportation charge of $35. What is the yearly depreciation if its salvage value is $300?

Step 1   Find the total cost of the asset

$$\begin{aligned}&\$2,500\\+\,&\underline{\,\,\,\,35}\\&\$2,535\end{aligned}$$

Step 2   Find the amount to be depreciated by subtracting the salvage value from the original total cost.

$$\begin{aligned}&\$2,535\\-\,&\underline{\,300}\\&\$2,235\end{aligned}$$

Step 3   Divide the figure found in step 2 by the estimated life (in years)

$$\frac{\$2,235}{5} = \$447$$

Answer   The yearly depreciation is $447.

Example 2 Allied Glass Company purchased a precision cutting machine for $15,800. The salvage value after the estimated life of 5 years is $1,500. What is the straight-line depreciation rate and what is the annual depreciation using this rate?

Step 1   Determine the straight-line depreciation rate by dividing 100% by the years of the asset's life.

$$\frac{100\%}{5} = 20\%$$

Step 2   Find the total amount to be depreciated during the asset's life.

$15,800 Cost
− 1,500 Salvage
$14,300 Total amount to be depreciated

Step 3   Find the annual depreciation by multiplying the total amount to be depreciated times the straight-line depreciation rate.

$14,300 × 20% = $2,860

Answer   The straight-line rate is 20%. The annual depreciation is $2,860.

NOTE: If you wanted to find the book value of this machine after the first year, you would subtract the annual depreciation from the total cost ($15,800 − $2,860 = $12,940).

Constructing a Depreciation Schedule

A **depreciation schedule** gives a complete picture of the depreciation and book value of an asset over its useful life. In order to set up a depreciation schedule, you need to know:

1. The year of depreciation,
2. The dollar amount of the depreciation for each year,
3. The accumulated depreciation (the total of depreciation amounts for the previous years),
4. The book value, which may also be called the balance (the original cost less the accumulated depreciation).

To illustrate further, let's set up a depreciation schedule for Example 2:

Allied Glass Company Depreciation Schedule

Year	Annual Depreciation	Accumulated Depreciation	Balance (Book Value)
0	$ 0	$ 0	$15,800
1	2,860	2,860	12,940
2	2,860	5,720	10,080
3	2,860	8,580	7,220
4	2,860	11,440	4,360
5	2,860	14,300	1,500

A depreciation schedule can be constructed for any method of depreciation. For the straight-line method, however, note that the amount of annual depreciation remains the same for each year and that the book value at the end of the fifth year is equal to the salvage value. For some methods, like the ACRS method, an asset is depreciated to a value of "0" without using a salvage value at all.

Self-Check

1. A chemical tank that costs $3,900 plus an installation charge of $400 has a useful life of 4 years. What is the annual straight-line depreciation if the salvage value is $300?

2. Using the straight-line method, find the yearly depreciation, the straight-line depreciation rate, and the book value at the end of the first year for a machine that costs $10,600. The salvage value after the estimated life of 5 years is $600.

ANSWERS 1. $1,000   2. $2,000 yearly depreciation; 20% rate; $8,600 book value

NAME   DATE   SECTION

Assignment 13.1

Depreciation

1. Calculate the depreciation and the rate of depreciation for the first year for the following equipment owned by Hendrickson Furniture Manufacturers, Inc. Use the straight-line method. Round to the nearest dollar.

Machine Number	Cost	Life	Salvage	Yearly Depreciation	Rate (%)
1	$14,800	20	$1,300	$ 675	5%
2	$ 3,500	5	$ 250	650	20%
3	$21,100	12	$2,100	1,583	$8\frac{1}{3}$%
4	$36,900	10	$3,400	3,350	10%
5	$ 9,350	8	$ 950	1,050	$12\frac{1}{2}$%

Sample solution for machine 1
1. $14,800 Cost
    − 1,300 Salvage
    $13,500 Depr. Cost

$\frac{100\%}{20 \text{ yr}} = 5\%$ Straight-line rate

$13,500 × 5% = $675 yearly depreciation

2. Broadway Amusement Park purchased a multiunit musical vending machine that cost $4,800. Transportation charges were $460 and the installation charge was $540. The estimated life is 5 years with an estimated trade-in value of $800. Complete the following depreciation schedule using the straight-line method.

Year	Yearly Depreciation	Accumulated Depreciation	Balance (Book Value)
0			$ 5,800
1	$ 1,000	$ 1,000	4,800
2	1,000	2,000	3,800
3	1,000	3,000	2,800
4	1,000	4,000	1,800
5	1,000	5,000	800

$4,800 Cost
  460 Transportation
+ 540 Installation
$5,800 Total cost, book value
− 800 Salvage
$5,000 Depr. cost

$\frac{100\%}{5 \text{ yr}} = 20\%$ Straight-line rate

$5,000 Total depreciation
×   20%
$1,000 Yearly depreciation

continued

Assignment 13.1 *continued*

3. A skiwear factory paid $18,000 for an assembly-line system. After an estimated life of 12 years, the scrap value of the system was $2,300.

    a) What is the annual depreciation to the nearest dollar by the straight-line method?

        $18,000 Total cost
    –   2,300 Salvage
        $15,700 Depr. cost

    $15,700 ÷ 12 = $1,308.33
                   = $1,308

                                          $1,308 annual depreciation

    b) What is the book value at the end of the first year?

        $18,000 Total cost
    –   1,308 Annual depreciation
        $16,692 Book value

                                            $16,692 book value

4. Sales Consultants Employment Agency purchased office cabinets for $4,530. After 5 years' use, the trade-in value in $220. If installation costs were an additional $209:

    a) What is the depreciation using the straight-line method?

        $4,530
    +   209 Installation
        $4,739 Total cost
    –   220 Trade-in
        $4,519 Depr. cost

    $4,519 × 20% = $903.80 depreciation

                                            $903.80 year's depreciation

    b) What is the straight line depreciation rate?

    $\dfrac{100\%}{5 \text{ yr}}$ = 20% depreciation cost

                                            20% depreciation rate

5. The Duke and Duchess Hair Salon purchased hair dryers costing $218 each. Freight and installation expenses amounted to $41 for each dryer. Salvage value after an estimated life of 6 years is $57 for each hair dryer. What is the annual depreciation on 5 hair dryers to the nearest cent using the straight-line method of depreciation?

    $218 × 5 = $1,090
      41 × 5 = +   205 Installation
                    $1,295 Total cost
      57 × 5 = –   285 Salvage
                    $1,010 Depr. cost

    $1,010 ÷ 6 = $168.33 Annual depreciation

                                            $168.33 annual depreciation

13.2 Depreciation by the Units-of-Production Method

The **units-of-production method** is used to depreciate a fixed asset that is not used uniformly throughout its life expectancy. For example, a machine may sit idle for a time and then be used heavily for a period. Thus depreciation is written off according to when the fixed asset is used (producing) rather than equally during its life expectancy.

With this method, the depreciation per unit (or per hour or per mile, depending on the type of fixed unit) is found. This is then multiplied by the number of units (hours or miles) used during the accounting period, according to the following formulas:

$$\text{Depreciation per unit} = \frac{\text{Total cost} - \text{Salvage value}}{\text{Life (in production units)}};$$

$$\text{Amount of depreciation} = \text{Depreciation per unit} \times \text{Number of units produced}.$$

Example 1 A splicing machine that cost $19,000 has a scrap value of $1,000 and an estimated unit of output of 200,000 units. If production during the first year, was 4,600 units, what is the depreciation for that year?

Step 1 Find the amount to be depreciated by subtracting the scrap value from the total cost.

$19,000
− 1,000
$18,000

Step 2 Divide the amount to be depreciated by the number of estimated units of output to find the depreciation per unit of production.

$\frac{18,000}{200,000} = \$.09$ Depreciation per unit

Step 3 Multiply the number of units produced during the year by the depreciation per unit.

4,600 units
× $ .09
$414.00

Answer The depreciation for the first year is $414.00.

Self-Check

1. What is the unit depreciation for equipment that cost $40,700 plus an installation charge of $1,300? The scrap value is $2,000; and the estimated life is 80,000 hours. Use the units-of-production method.

2. Kalico Paints purchased a custom truck for $19,500 with added options that cost an additional $4,500. The estimated life is 200,000 miles with a salvage value of $4,000. If the truck is driven 60,000 miles during the first year, what is the depreciation expense using the units-of-production method?

ANSWERS 1. $.50   2. $6,000

NAME _____ DATE _____ SECTION _____

Assignment 13.2

Depreciation

1. Find the unit and yearly depreciation (to the nearest cent) on the following equipment owned by Coast Concrete Company.

Type	Cost	Scrap Value	Estimated Life	Hours Used During the Year	Unit Depreciation	Year's Depreciation
a) Machine #12A	$24,000	$4,000	80,000 hr	7,000 hr	$ .25	$ 1,750.00

$24,000 Cost
− 4,000 Salvage value
$20,000 Depr. cost

$\dfrac{\text{Depreciated amt.}}{\text{Est. life}} = \dfrac{\$20,000}{80,000 \text{ hr}} = \$.25$ unit depreciation

7,000 × $.25 = $1,750 year's depreciation

b) Machine #8D	$18,000	$1,000	43,000 hr	8,200 hr	.40	3,280.00

$18,000 Cost
− 1,000 Salvage value
$17,000 Depr. cost

$\dfrac{\text{Depreciated amt.}}{\text{Est. life}} = \dfrac{\$17,000}{43,000} = .3953 = .40$ unit depreciation

8,200 × $.40 = $3,280 year's depreciation

2. Highway equipment cost the city of Greenbank $57,000 with a residual value of $7,000. The estimated life is 100,000 miles. If the equipment was driven 2,108 miles last year, what is each of the following? Solve using the units-of-production method.

   a) The depreciation per mile _____$.50_____

   $57,000 Total cost
   − 7,000 Salvage value
   $50,000 Depr. cost

   $\dfrac{\$50,000}{100,000} = \$.50$ depr/mile

   b) last year's depreciation _____$1,054_____

   $.50 × 2,108 = $1,054 depreciation last year

3. Sawdust Supply Company purchased an industrial saw that costs $16,500 and has a scrap value of $1,900.

   a) If the estimated life is 26,000 hours, what is the unit depreciation?

   $16,500 Total cost
   − 1,900 Salvage value
   $14,600 Depr. cost

   $\dfrac{\text{Depr. amt.}}{\text{Est. life}} = \dfrac{\$14,600}{26,000 \text{ hr}} = \$.56$ **$.56 unit depreciation**

   b) If during one year it was used 5,018 hours, what is the depreciation using the units-of-production method?   **$2,810.08 year's depreciation**

   5,018 hr × $.56 = $2,810.08

continued

Assignment 13.2 *continued*

4. Creagan Glass Company purchased new packing equipment for $31,400. Installation was an additional charge of $4,600 and the extra delivery charge was $1,000. The estimated life of the machine is 70,000 hours. It is estimated that it will be used 6,540 hours during its first year. The scrap value is $5,200. Using the units-of-production method, figure each of the following.

   a) The unit depreciation in dollars

   $37,000 Cost
   − 5,200 Salvage value
   $31,800 Total depr.

   $\dfrac{\$31,800}{70,000 \text{ hr}} = .4542 = \$.45$ unit depreciation

   $.45 \rule{2cm}{0.4pt}$

   b) The first year's depreciation in dollars

   6,540 hr × $.45 unit depr. = $2,943

   $2,943 \rule{2cm}{0.4pt}$

5. The City Aquarium bought a new industrial water pump for $2,450. Installation charges amounted to $190. Its estimated life is 28,800 hours, and the scrap value is $102. If it ran for 8,640 hours during the first year, what are the depreciation and the book value at the end of the first year, using the units-of-production method? Round the depreciation per hour to the nearest cent.

   $2,450 Cost
   + 190 Installation
   $2,640 Total cost
   − 102 Salvage value
   $2,538 Depr. cost

   $\dfrac{\$2,538}{28,800} = .088 = \$.09$ unit depr.
   8,640 × $.09 = $777.60 depr.
   $2,640 − $777.60 = $1,862.40 book value

   $777.60 depreciation, end of first year;
   $1,862.40 book value, end of first year

13.3 Depreciation by the Sum-of-the-Year's-Digits Method

The rest of the methods covered in this chapter are accelerated ways of calculating depreciation. The **sum-of-the-year's-digits method** is accelerated because the amount of depreciation is higher in the early years of an asset's life. Actually, most equipment does depreciate more the first year (like new-model cars). Use of this method can be particularly advantageous to a small or new business, since writing off a large share of depreciation expense in the beginning years gives a business a boost toward financial stability. Thus the amount of income tax payable is reduced when the asset is new.

The sum-of-the-years'-digits method is based on the idea that each year an asset depreciates by a certain fraction of its total amount to be depreciated (cost − salvage value). The denominator of the fraction is found by totaling or "summing" the digits of the years of expected life of the asset. For example, if a machine has an expected life of 5 years, the sum of the digits would be $5 + 4 + 3 + 2 + 1$, which equals 15.

The numerator of the fraction changes from year to year and represents the remaining years of life for the asset. In the above example, then, for the first year the numerator would be 5, for the second year 4, for the third year 3, and so on. The fractions in sequence are $\frac{5}{15}, \frac{4}{15}, \frac{3}{15}, \frac{2}{15}, \frac{1}{15}$. These fractions are sometimes called the **depreciable rate**. The depreciation for each year is found by multiplying the total amount to be depreciated by the depreciable rate (which is expressed as a fraction) for that year, according to the following formula:

$$\text{Depreciable rate} = \frac{\text{Number of remaining years of asset's life}}{\text{Sum of years}}$$

$$\text{Amount of depreciation} = [\text{Total cost} - \text{Salvage value}] \times \text{Depreciable rate}.$$

Example 1 J. R. Bottling Company purchased a new capping machine for $16,000. The estimated life is 4 years, and the salvage value is $2,500. Calculate the depreciation for each year by using the sum-of-the-years'-digits method.

Step 1 Find the total amount to be depreciated (cost − salvage value).

```
  16,000
-  2,500
 $13,500
```

Step 2 Find the denominator by summing the digits. $1 + 2 + 3 + 4 = 10$

Step 3 Find the fraction for each year.

1st year: $\frac{4}{10}$

2nd year: $\frac{3}{10}$

3rd year: $\frac{2}{10}$

4th year: $\frac{1}{10}$

Step 4 Multiply the total amount to be depreciated by each year's fraction to find the depreciation for each year.

1st year: $\$13{,}500 \times \frac{4}{10} = \$5{,}400$

2nd year: $\$13{,}500 \times \frac{3}{10} = \$4{,}050$

3rd year: $\$13{,}500 \times \frac{2}{10} = \$2{,}700$

4th year: $\$13{,}500 \times \frac{1}{10} = \$1{,}350$

Answer   The depreciation for each year is $5,400, $4,050, $2,700, $1,350, consecutively.

NOTE: The total amount to be depreciated ($13,500) equals the sum of each year's depreciation ($5,400 + $4,050 + $2,700 + $1,350).

A depreciation schedule for the example above is as follows:

J. R. Bottling Company Depreciation Schedule

Year	Annual Depreciation	Accumulated Depreciation	Balance (Book Value)
0	$ 0	$ 0	$16,000
1	$5,400	$ 5,400	$10,600
2	$4,050	$ 9,450	$ 6,550
3	$2,700	$12,150	$ 3,850
4	$1,350	$13,500	$ 2,500

Note that with this method the book value at the end of the fourth year is equal to the salvage value ($2,500). Also, be aware that the accumulated depreciation at the end of the asset's life ($13,500) is equal to the cost of the asset less its book value ($16,000 − $2,500 = $13,500).

Self-Check

1. Using the sum-of-the-years'-digits method, calculate the fraction to be used each year for figuring depreciation on an asset that has an estimated life of 5 years.

2. Using the sum-of-the-years'-digits method, find the depreciation and the book value after the first year of a stove that costs $980. It has a trade-in value of $140, and its estimated life is 6 years. (*Hint:* Remember that the initial book value equals the total cost of the asset.)

ANSWERS   1. Year 1: $\frac{5}{15}$; year 2: $\frac{4}{15}$; year 3: $\frac{3}{15}$; year 4: $\frac{2}{15}$; year 5: $\frac{1}{15}$ 2. $240 depreciation; $740 book value

THE BIRTH OF A GIANT

Financed by a grant of $5,000,000 from IBM, the first digital computer was built by a mathematics professor at Harvard University in 1944. The machine contained 500 miles of wire and had 760,000 parts. When it came to calculations, it needed 4 seconds to do simple multiplication and 11 seconds for simple division. Besides that, it broke down with great frequency.

Assignment 13.3

Depreciation

1. Alpine Data System purchased a new minicomputer costing $10,300 with a residual value of $2,600 after an estimated life of 4 years. Using the sum-of-the-years'-digits method, determine each of the following.

   a) The first year's depreciation

   $10,300 Total cost
   − 2,600 Salvage value
   $ 7,700 Depr. cost

   1 + 2 + 3 + 4 = 10

   $7,700 × $\frac{4}{10}$ = $3,080 depreciation

   $3,080 first year's depreciation

   b) The book value at the end of the first year

   $10,300 Total cost
   − 3,080 Depreciation
   $ 7,220 Book value

   $7,220 book value, end of first year

2. Prompt Press Printing Company bought a new paper cutter with a scrap value of $600 for $6,200. The estimated life is 7 years for the equipment. Complete the following depreciation schedule to the nearest dollar using the sum-of-the-years'-digits method.

   $6,200 Cost
   − 600 Salvage value
   $5,600 Depr. cost

   Life of 7 years
   1 + 2 + 3 + 4 + 5 + 6 + 7 = 28
   (Initial book value = Total cost)
   $5,600 × fraction = Yearly depreciation

Year	Fraction Used	Yearly Depreciation	Accumulated Depreciation	Balance (Book Value)
0	——	$ ——	$ ——	$ 6,200
1	$\frac{7}{28}$ ——	1,400	1,400	4,800
2	$\frac{6}{28}$ ——	1,200	2,600	3,600
3	$\frac{5}{28}$ ——	1,000	3,600	2,600
4	$\frac{4}{28}$ ——	800	4,400	1,800
5	$\frac{3}{28}$ ——	600	5,000	1,200

continued

Assignment 13.3 *continued*

Year	Fraction Used	Yearly Depreciation	Accumulated Depreciation	Balance (Book Value)
6	$\frac{2}{28}$	400	5,400	800
7	$\frac{1}{28}$	200	5,600	600

3. Clean-Up Janitorial Service bought equipment costing $1,700 with an additional charge of $52 for air freight. The salvage value is $300, and the estimated life is 4 years. Using the sum-of-the-years'-digits method, what is the depreciation expense allowed for the first and second years?

   $1,700
   + 52 Freight
   $1,752 Total cost
   − 300 Salvage value
   $1,452 Depr. cost

   $1 + 2 + 3 + 4 = 10$

   $\$1{,}452 \times \frac{4}{10} = \$580.80$ depr, first year

   $\$1{,}452 \times \frac{3}{10} = \$435.60$ depr, second year

   $580.80 depreciation first year;
   $435.60 depreciation, second year

4. A moving electrical display unit for Carnegie Sports Shop was priced at $3,126. There was an additional charge of $374 for installation. The display is expected to be in service for 5 years, and has a resale value of $500. Figure the depreciation expense in dollars for each year.

   $3126
   + 374
   $3500 Total cost
   − 500 Salvage value
   $3000 Total dep.

   Year 1 $3000 \times \frac{5}{15} = \$1{,}000$

   Year 2 $3000 \times \frac{4}{15} = 800$

   Year 3 $3000 \times \frac{3}{15} = 600$

   Year 4 $3000 \times \frac{2}{15} = 400$

   Year 5 $3000 \times \frac{1}{15} = 200$

   Year 1 = $1000; year 2 = $800; year 3 = $600;
   year 4 = $400; year 5 = $200

5. Utopia Landscaping purchased earth-moving equipment at a total cost of $21,100. The useful life is estimated at 7 years with a salvage value of $3,400. To the nearest dollar, what is the depreciation for the second and fifth years using the sum-of-the-year's-digits method?

   $21,100 Total cost
   − 3,400 Salvage value
   $17,700 Depr. cost

   $1 + 2 + 3 + 4 + 5 + 6 + 7 = 28$

   $\$17{,}700 \times \frac{6}{28} = \$3{,}793$ depr., second year

   $\$17{,}700 \times \frac{3}{28} = \$1{,}896$ depr., fifth year

   $3,793 second year's depreciation,
   $1,896 fifth year's depreciation

13.4 Depreciation by the Declining-Balance Method

Another accelerated method used to show a large depreciation expense during the first years of an asset's estimated life is the **declining-balance method,** so called because the amount of depreciation declines in the later years. A decreasing amount of depreciation is written off every year. This is quite different from the straight line method where the same amount of depreciation is written off each year. A unique feature of this method is that the salvage value is *not* used in determining the amount to be depreciated. Instead, the entire cost of the asset is applied. The Internal Revenue Service closely regulates this method and allows only certain types of assets to be depreciated in this way. One guideline is that the estimated life of the asset must be at least three years.

With this method, the declining book value of the asset is multiplied by a fixed rate (percent). The amount of depreciation steadily decreases or declines each year because the constant rate is applied to each year's declining book value. Depreciation continues until the asset is replaced or disposed of or until the book value *equals* the salvage value of the asset.

An asset cannot be depreciated to less than its salvage value. If the last year's depreciation would make the book value less than the salvage value, then an adjustment must be made. Only part of the depreciation for the final year is then allowed. Example 2 illustrates this situation.

The declining-balance method permits a business to double the rate at which the straight-line method is figured. This is called the **declining-balance rate.** Lower rates do exist depending on the laws that apply for a particular asset. However, the maximum rate permitted is the double rate, 200% (2), and will be used for all examples and problems in this section.

The formula for finding depreciation by the declining-balance method is as follows:

> Declining-balance rate = 2 × Straight-line rate,
>
> Depreciation amount = Book value × Declining-balance rate.

Example 1 Sun & Earth Wallpaper Company purchased a new roller for $18,400. It has an estimated life of 4 years with a salvage value of $1,150. Find the depreciation amount and the book value at the end of the second year using the declining-balance method.

Step 1   Finding the declining-balance rate by multiplying the straight-line depreciation rate by 2.

$\dfrac{100}{4} = 25\%$ Straight-line rate

25% × 2 = 50% Declining-balance rate

Step 2   Find the depreciation for the first year by multiplying the cost of the asset by the declining-balance rate.

$18,400 × 50% = $9,200

Step 3   Find the book value by subtracting the depreciation from the cost of the asset.

```
  $18,400  Cost
-   9,200  Depreciation for year 1
   $9,200  Book value for year 1
```

Step 4   Find the depreciation for the second year by multiplying the book value by the declining-balance rate.

$9,200 × 50% = $4,600

Step 5   Find the book value for the second year by subtracting the depreciation for year 2 from the book value for year 1.

```
   $9,200  Book value for year 1
-   4,600  Depreciation for year 2
   $4,600  Book value for year 2
```

Answer   The depreciation for year 2 is $4,600. The book value for year 2 is $4,600.

Example 2 A sealing machine purchased for $6,100 by Allied Supply Company has an estimated life of 5 years. The salvage value is $500. Set up a depreciation schedule using the declining-balance method.

Step 1 Find the declining-balance rate by multiplying the straight-line depreciation rate by 2.

$$\frac{100\%}{5} = 20\% \text{ Straight-line rate}$$
$20\% \times 2 = 40\%$ Declining-balance rate

Step 2 Find the depreciation for the first year by multiplying the cost of the asset times the declining-balance rate.

$6,100 \times 40\% = \$2,440$

Step 3 Find the book value by subtracting the depreciation from the cost.

$6,100 Cost
− 2,440 Depreciation for year 1
$3,660 Book value for year 1

Step 4 Find the depreciation for the second year by multiplying the book value times the declining-balance rate.

$3,660 \times 40\% = \$1,464$

Step 5 Find the book value for year 2 by substracting the depreciation from the book value for year 1.

$3,660 Book value for year 1
− 1,464 Depreciation for year 2
$2,196 New book value

Step 6 Find the depreciation for the third year by multiplying the new book value times the declining-balance rate.

$2,196 \times 40\% = \$878.40$

Step 7 Find the book value for year 3.

$2,196.00 Book value for year 2
− 878.40 Depreciation for year 3
$1,317.60 Book value for year 3

Step 8 Find the depreciation for the fourth year by multiplying the new book value by the declining-balance rate.

$1,317.60 \times 40\% = \$527.04$

Step 9 Find the book value for year 4.

$1,317.60 Book value for year 3
− 527.04 Depreciation for year 4
$ 790.56 Book value for year 4

Step 10 Find the depreciation for the fifth year by multiplying the new book value by the declining-balance rate.

$790.56 \times 40\% = \$316.22$

Step 11 Find the book value for year 5.

Not allowed {
$790.56 Book value for year 4
− 316.22 Depreciation for year 5
474.34 Book value for year 5

Step 12 Adjust the allowable depreciation for year 5.

$316.22
− 25.66 Amount over salvage value [$500 − $474.34]
$290.56 Adjusted depreciation for year 5

Answer **Allied Supply Company Depreciation Schedule**

Year	Annual Depreciation	Accumulated Depreciation	Balance (Book Value)
0	$ 0	$ 0	$6,100.00
1	$2,440.00	$2,440.00	$3,660.00
2	$1,464.00	$3,904.00	$2,196.00
3	$ 878.40	$4,782.40	$1,317.60
4	$ 527.04	$5,309.44	$ 790.56
5	$ 290.56	$5,600.00	$ 500.00

NOTE: Since the book value at the end of the fifth year is less than the salvage value, only $290.56 depreciation for year 5 will be allowed. Remember that with this method, the book value at the end of an asset's life must equal its salvage value.

When using the declining-balance method, you must be careful to recognize if an adjustment is needed in the final depreciation amount so that the book value will equal the salvage value. Note that this type of adjustment is never needed when you use the straight-line method or the sum-of-the-years'-digits method.

Self-Check

1. Find the declining-balance depreciation rate for equipment that has a useful life of 4 years.

2. Using the declining-balance method, find the depreciation and the book value after the first year for a sealing machine that costs $11,720 plus an installation charge of $280. The salvage value is $1,500 after an estimated life of 5 years.

ANSWERS 1. 50%   2. $4,800 depreciation; $7,200 book value

EXPANDING ON A GOOD IDEA

Because we have grown used to seeing uniform product code stripes (UPC) on items we buy at the supermarket, many of us think that speeding up the checkout process and controlling retail business inventory is its only purpose.

The fact is that the UPC, or the bar code as it is often called, is finding broad acceptance, in both industry and government, anywhere that items must be accounted for on a regular basis. For example, the U.S. Air Force now uses the UPC to inventory the thousands of parts in stock at its many maintenance depots around the country and throughout the world.

NAME   DATE   SECTION

Assignment 13.4

Depreciation

1. Stevens Health Center purchased 6 desks. Each desk has a useful life of 5 years with a trade-in value of $40 each.

   a) If the desks cost $420 each, what is the declining-balance rate?

   $\dfrac{100\%}{5}$ = 20% straight-line rate

   2 × 20% = 40% Declining-balance rate

   40% declining-balance rate

   b) What is the total depreciation expense for all of the desks after the first year, using the declining-balance method?

   $420 × 6 = $2,520 Total cost
   $2,520 × 40% = $1,008 depr.

   $1,008 Total depreciation expense

2. Quality Homes Realty purchased a company car for $9,210 with additional charges for detail painting of $392. The estimated life of the vehicle is 5 years. Using the declining-balance method, calculate each of the following.

   a) The depreciation expense and the book value to the nearest cent at the end of the first year

   $9,210
   + 392 Detail painting
   $9,602 Total cost

   $\dfrac{100\%}{5}$ = 20% straight-line rate

   20% × 2 = 40% declining-balance rate
   $9,602 × 40% = $3,840.80 depreciation
   $9,602 − $3,840 = $5,761.20 book value

   $3,840.80 depreciation expense, $5,761.20 book value

   b) The depreciation expense and the book value to the nearest cent at the end of the second year

   $5,761.20 × 40% = $2,304.48 depreciation
   $5,761.20 − 2,304.48 = $3,456.72 book value

   $2,304.48 depreciation exp., second year; $3,456.72 book value, second year

3. Using the declining-balance method, calculate the depreciation expnse for each of the first 3 years for a machine costing $12,000 with an installation expense of $800. The estimated life is 4 years with a scrap value of $1,900.

   $12,000
   + 800 Installation
   12,800 Total cost
   − 1,900 Salvage value
   $10,900 Depr. cost

   $\dfrac{100\%}{4}$ = 25% straight-line rate

   25% × 2 = 50% declining-balance rate

   $12,800 × 50% = $6,400 depr. first year
   $6,400 × 50% = $3,200 depr. second year
   *$3,200 × 50% = $1,600 not allowed
   $3,200 − $1,900 salvage = $1,300 depr. third year

   *Note: Cannot depreciate less than salvage value.

   $6,400 depr., first year; 3,200 depr. second year; 1,300 depr. third year

continued

Assignment 13.4 *continued*

4. Using the declining-balance method, fill in the following depreciation schedule for a small conveyer belt system that was purchased for $4,500 with an additional installation charge of $500. The system has a trade-in value of $625 and an estimated life of 4 years.

```
  $4,500  Cost
+    500  Installment
  $5,000  Total cost, Book Value
```

$\dfrac{100\%}{4}$ = 25% straight-line rate

25% × 2 = 50% declining-balance rate
$5,000 × 50% = $2,500 depr., year 1
$2,500 × 50% = $1,250 depr., year 2

Year	Annual Depreciation	Accumulated Depreciation	Balance (Book Value)
0			$ 5,000
1	$ 2,500	$ 2,500	2,500
2	1,250	3,750	1,250
3	625*	4,375	625
4	None	4,375	625

*Remember, an asset cannot be depreciated below its trade-in or salvage value for this method.

5. Delta Dairy purchased a new milking machine for $25,000. Installation was an additional $3,400. The trade-in value of the machine is $6,000, and it has a useful life of 5 years. Using the declining-balance method, complete the following depreciation schedule.

$\dfrac{100\%}{5}$ = 20% straight-line rate   20% × 2 = 40% declining-balance rate

```
   $25,000
 +   3,400
   $28,400  Total cost
```

Year 1 $28,400 × 40% = $11,360.00
Year 2 $17,040 × 40% = $6,816.00
Year 3 $10,224 × 40% = $4,089.60
Year 4 $6,134.40 × 40% = $2,435.76*

*Note: Depreciation in year 4 is only $134.40 since depreciation could not be below salvage value.

Year	Annual Depreciation	Accumulated Depreciation	Balance (Book Value)
0	$ ——	$ ——	$ 28,400
1	11,360	11,360	17,040
2	6,816	18,176	10,224
3	4,089.60	22,265.60	6,134.40
4	134.40	22,400	6,000
5	0	22,400	6,000

13.5 Depreciation by the Accelerated Cost Recovery System and the Modified Accelerated Cost Recovery System

Using the ACRS Method of Depreciation

The **Accelerated Cost Recovery System (ACRS),** which can be used only for assets purchased on or after January 1, 1981, was established through the Economic Recovery Tax Act of 1981. The purpose of the act was to stimulate business capital investment. ACRS is concerned with depreciation of tangible property for tax purposes only. **Tangible property** is property that can be seen or touched. It can be real or personal. *Personal property* is property that is not real estate, such as a computer or machinery. *Real Property* is land and anything that is erected on, growing on, or attached to land. The actual land itself, however, is not depreciable. There are numerous guidelines set by the IRS to correctly classify property. Allowable depreciation deductions are based on the type of property or asset depreciated.

Under the ACRS method, all of the purchase cost can be shown as an expense over the life of the asset. This cost is "recovered" over a specific time period as defined by the classification of the asset. The salvage value of the asset is not subtracted first as is done using most of the other methods. The original cost figure is used as the base for depreciation.

The ACRS method is simple to use and allows for a quicker recovery time than the other methods. A certain annual rate of depreciation is allowed. The original cost of the asset is multiplied by that rate to determine the depreciation for that year. The rate varies according to the class or category under which the asset falls. The classes are listed as recovery periods. A **recovery period** is basically the time period allowed to depreciate a particular type of asset. With the ACRS method, the number of years of estimated life of an asset is reduced and grouped into recovery periods. Thus the annual depreciation is in effect increased. This is why the term "accelerated" is used. The recovery periods with their corresponding rates are quoted by the Internal Revenue Service and are monitored closely. The Tax Reform Bill of 1986 regrouped some of the classifications of property and changed some of the applicable rates.

Property is grouped into the following cost-recovery classes: 3-year, 5-year, 10-year, 15-year, 18-year, and 19-year. If an asset falls into the 5-year class, for example, the full cost of the property is written off (depreciated) over a 5-year time period. It is not practical to define each class fully, but for purposes of explanation, the following is a sample of what is included.

3-year class   Assets with a useful life of 4 years or less. Includes property with a short life, such as certain tools, and automobiles, light trucks, and race horses over 2 years old.

5-year class   Assets with a useful life of more than 4 years and less than 10 years. Includes most machinery and office equipment, such as computers, copiers, and typewriters; qualified technological equipment, small power-production facilities; single-purpose agricultural and horticultural structures.

10-year class   Assets that are classified as certain real property such as public utility property. Assets that have a useful life of 12.5 years or less. Includes manufactured mobile homes, amusement and theme parks, and railroad tank cars.

15-year class   Real-property assets placed in service before March 16, 1984, that are not listed in the 10-year class. Includes properties such as buildings, sewage plants, telephone distribution plants, and equipment and data communications. Also includes some low-income housing.

Depreciation   **517**

18-year class   Real-property assets placed in service after March 15, 1984, but before May 9, 1985, with a useful life of more than 12.5 years and not listed in the 15-year class.

19-year class   Real-property assets placed in service after May 8, 1985, and not listed in the other classes.

Another interesting provision of the ACRS method is that an asset in the 3-, 5-, and 10-year classes is depreciated for a whole year even if it was purchased and used for only part of that year. Thus for many properties, the exact month the asset is put into service is not used to figure the depreciation. Also, assets in the same class are grouped together to calculate depreciation.

Using the Recovery Rate for the 3-, 5-, and 10-Year Classes

Once an asset or property is classified, then the rate of depreciation can be found. Table 1 shows the percent of depreciation used depending on the recovery time (year class) allowed for the asset. Note in the table that the rate for the first year in each property class is lower than the rates for the following years. Since the first year is the year of purchase, it is likely that there was not full use of the asset. Thus depreciation in the first year is somewhat less than in the other years.

Table 1 Accelerated Cost Recovery Rates

Year	Property Class		
	3 Year	5 Year	10 Year
1	25%	15%	8%
2	38%	22%	14%
3	37%	21%	12%
4	—	21%	10%
5	—	21%	10%
6	—	—	10%
7	—	—	9%
8	—	—	9%
9	—	—	9%
10	—	—	9%

In Table 1 the point at which the class and year intersect tells you which rate to apply in order to figure the depreciation for an asset. For instance, the rate for an asset in the 5-year class after 3 years of service is 21%. The actual amount of depreciation for that year is found by multiplying the total original cost by the rate shown in Table 1, according to the following formula:

$$\text{Total cost of asset} \times \text{Accelerated cost recovery rate} = \text{Depreciation for a particular year.}$$

HOW THE PERCENTAGE FORMULA APPLIES

This formula is also an application of what you have learned in Section 5.3:

$$\text{Base} \times \text{Rate} = \text{Percentage,}$$
$$\text{Cost of asset} \times \text{Depreciation rate} = \text{Depreciation}$$

Example 1   Network, Inc., purchased new office equipment with a total value of $42,800. Resale value is estimated at $8,000. The ACRS method of depreciation is being used over a 5-year period. What are the amounts of depreciation of the equipment for the first and second years?

Step 1   Locate the depreciation rate in Table 1 for year 1.   Rate = 15%

Step 2   Multiply the cost of the asset by the rate. $42,800 × 15% = $6,420

Step 3   Locate the depreciation rate in Table 1 for year 2.   Rate = 22%

Step 4   Multiply the cost of the asset by the rate. $42,800 × 22% = $9,416

Answer $6,420 is the depreciation for year 1, and $9,416 is the depreciation for year 2.

NOTE: For each year's calculation, the total cost figure of the asset is used. The resale value is not deducted.

Using Example 1, let's complete the depreciation for the remaining years in the 5-year period and construct a depreciation schedule.

Year 3: $42,800 × 21% = $8,988

Year 4: $42,800 × 21% = $8,988

Year 5: $42,800 × 21% = $8,988

Network, Inc. Depreciation Schedule

Year	Annual Depreciation	Accumulated Depreciation	Balance (Book Value)
0	$ 0	$ 0	$42,800
1	$6,420	$ 6,420	$36,380
2	$9,416	$15,836	$26,964
3	$8,988	$24,824	$17,976
4	$8,988	$33,812	$ 8,988
5	$8,988	$42,800	0

You can check your calculations by making sure that the accumulated depreciation at the end of year 5 is equal to the beginning balance (book value) of the asset. Keep in mind that the beginning balance is the original cost of the asset. Also, note that with the ACRS method, the book value at the end of the recovery period is 0 because the salvage value is not used.

Using the Recovery Rate for the 15-Year Class

For recovery periods (class life) of 15, 18, and 19 years, the month the asset is placed in service determines which rate can be used. The IRS prints different schedules for each category and even for specific properties such as low-income housing within a category. For our purposes here, the 15-year real-property table (Table 2) is used.

Table 2 is used in much the same way as Table 1. The point at which the year and the month intersect tells you which rate applies. To use the table, find the month in the tax year that you placed the property in service and use the percents listed under that month for each year of the recovery period.

For instance, for an asset in the 15-year category that was placed in service in March, the recovery rate for the first year is 10% (the point at which month 3 and year 1 intersect). The second year is 11% (the point at which month 3 and year 2 intersect).

Table 2 15-year Real Property (other than low-income housing)

Year	Month Placed in Service											
	1	2	3	4	5	6	7	8	9	10	11	12
1	12%	11%	10%	9%	8%	7%	6%	5%	4%	3%	2%	1%
2	10%	10%	11%	11%	11%	11%	11%	11%	11%	11%	11%	12%
3	9%	9%	9%	9%	10%	10%	10%	10%	10%	10%	10%	10%
4	8%	8%	8%	8%	8%	8%	9%	9%	9%	9%	9%	9%
5	7%	7%	7%	7%	7%	7%	8%	8%	8%	8%	8%	8%
6	6%	6%	6%	6%	7%	7%	7%	7%	7%	7%	7%	7%
7	6%	6%	6%	6%	6%	6%	6%	6%	6%	6%	6%	6%
8	6%	6%	6%	6%	6%	6%	5%	6%	6%	6%	6%	6%
9	6%	6%	6%	6%	5%	6%	5%	5%	5%	6%	6%	6%
10	5%	6%	5%	6%	5%	5%	5%	5%	5%	5%	6%	5%
11	5%	5%	5%	5%	5%	5%	5%	5%	5%	5%	5%	5%
12	5%	5%	5%	5%	5%	5%	5%	5%	5%	5%	5%	5%
13	5%	5%	5%	5%	5%	5%	5%	5%	5%	5%	5%	5%
14	5%	5%	5%	5%	5%	5%	5%	5%	5%	5%	5%	5%
15	5%	5%	5%	5%	5%	5%	5%	5%	5%	5%	5%	5%
16	—	—	1%	1%	2%	2%	3%	3%	4%	4%	4%	5%

Example 2 For $300,000 you have purchased and put into service in June a warehouse that falls into the 15-year class life. Figure the depreciation and the book value for the first and second years, using the ACRS method.

Step 1 Locate the depreciation rate in Table 2 for month 6 and year 1.

Rate = 7%

Step 2 Multiply the cost of the asset by the rate to find the depreciation.

$300,000 × 7% = $21,000

Step 3 Subtract the depreciation from the cost to find the book value.

$300,000 Cost
− 21,000 Depreciation
$279,000 Book value for year 1

Step 4 Locate the depreciation rate in Table 2 for month 6 and year 2.

Rate = 11%

Step 5 Multiply the cost of the asset by the rate.

$300,000 × 11% = $33,000

Step 6 Subtract the depreciation from the previous book value.

$279,000 Book value
− 33,000 Depreciation
$246,000 Book value for year 2

Answer For year 1, the depreciation is $21,000 and the book value is $279,000. For year 2, the depreciation is $33,000 and the book value is $246,000.

Self-Check

1. Allied Transport purchased 3 trucks at a cost of $31,400 each. The ACRS method of depreciation is used under a 5-year classification. Figure the total depreciation for the third year.

2. Using the ACRS method, determine the depreciation and the book value for the second year for light tools that were purchased for $3,860.

3. Harris Properties purchased a small apartment building for $970,000. The property is in the 15-year class and was put into use in September. Determine the book value for year 1 and year 2 using the ACRS method.

ANSWERS 1. $19,782   2. $1,466.80 depreciation; $1,428.20 book value
3. $931,200 book value for year 1; $824,500 book value for year 2

Using the Modified ACRS Method of Depreciation

In order to further stimulate the economy and to make the payment of taxes more equitable, the Tax Reform Bill of 1986 was passed. As a result, the information on the accelerated cost recovery system in the preceding section has been revised to reflect the changes that apply through this new tax bill. In addition, this tax bill provided for a **Modified Accelerated Cost Recovery System (MACRS)**, which applies to tangible property (assets) placed in service after December 31, 1986. One can elect to use either the regular or the modified version of ACRS on tangible property placed in service after July 31, 1986. Some major differences of the MACRS system is that it allows a larger recovery deduction in early years for some classes and it gives a half-year depreciation allowance for the year of disposition or sale of an asset. It also states that residential and nonresidential real property must be depreciated using the straight-line method and the recovery period is extended.

The modified plan changes some of the assets that are included in the recovery periods, as follows:

3-year class   Assets with a life of 4 years or less. Includes tractors and race horses.

5-year class   Assets with a life of more than 4 years but less than 10 years. Includes heavy and light trucks, office machinery, typewriters, computers, and automobiles. However, the depreciation deduction is limited for passenger automobiles. For 1987, the limit is $4,100; for 1988, the limit is $2450; and for each succeeding year, the limit is $1,475.

7-year class   Assets with a life of at least 10 years but less than 16 years. Includes office furniture (desks, files, etc.), agriculture and horticulture structures.

10-year class   Assets with a life of at least 16 years but less than 20 years. Includes water vessels and barges.

15-year class   Assets with a life of at least 20 years but less than 25 years. Includes water treatment plants.

20-year class   Assets with a life of 25 years or more. Includes structures such as farm buildings.

27.5-class   Assets that are residential rental property

31.5 class   Assets that are nonresidential rental property and real property with a life of 27.5 years or more.

Under MACRS, the double (200%) declining-balance method is used for the 3-, 5-, 7-, and 10-year classes. For the 15- and 20-year classes, the one-and-a-half (150%) declining-balance method is used. An adjustment must also be made for the first year's depreciation. For the first year only half of the depreciation is allowed. This is called taking a half-year convention. This half-year convention applies to all property assigned to the 3, 5, 7, 10, 15, or 20-year classes. For property in 27.5 and 31.5 class, the straight-line method of depreciation is used. For the remaining years, the full depreciation amount is allowed. If the property is held for the entire recovery period, the other half year of depreciation is allowed for the year following the end of the recovery period. As with the original ACRS method, salvage value is not used and assets in the same class can be grouped together in order to figure depreciation.

To figure depreciation using ACRS, you must first find the rate of depreciation by dividing the number 1 by the number of years in the recovery period (class life). For instance, if you were finding the rate of depreciation for a tractor, you would be using a recovery period of 3. The basic rate of depreciation is $\frac{1}{3}$, which is $33\frac{1}{3}\%$. For a tractor, this rate is multiplied by the double-declining rate, which is 200%, or 2. The rate allowed in this case is $66\frac{2}{3}\%$ ($33\frac{1}{3}\% \times 2$). To find the actual amount of depreciation for each year, the declining balance (book value) of the tractor is multiplied by $66\frac{2}{3}\%$.

The formula for finding the actual dollar depreciation for each year using the MACRS method is as follows:

$$\text{Book value} \times \text{Declining Balance cost recovery rate} = \text{Yearly depreciation.}$$

The process for figuring the MACRS method of depreciation will be made clearer to you as you follow through each step of the following example.

Example 3 Sun Brite Pool Supply Company purchased a memory typewriter for $5,000 with a salvage value of $900. Find the depreciation and the book value at the end of year 2 using the MACRS method.

Step 1 Look at the schedule on page 521 to find the recovery period (class life) that applies.

Recovery period = 5 years

Step 2 Find the basic depreciation rate by dividing the number 1 by the recovery period.

$\frac{1}{5} = 20\%$

Step 3 Find the declining-balance rate by multiplying the basic rate by 2 (200%). Note that 200% rather than 150%, is used because of the number of years in the recovery period.

$20\% \times 2 = 40\%$

Step 4 Figure the amount of depreciation for year 1 by multiplying the cost of the asset by the declining-balance rate. Disregard the salvage value.

$\$5,000 \times 40\% = \$2,000$

Step 5 Adjust the depreciation for year 1 by multiplying it by $\frac{1}{2}$. Remember, with the MACRS method, only half the depreciation is allowed for the first year.

$\$2,000 \times \frac{1}{2} = \$1,000$

Depreciation for year 1

Step 6 Find the book value for year 1 by subtracting the depreciation from the cost.

$\$5,000$
$- \ \ 1,000$
$\$4,000$ Book value for year 1

Step 7 Find the depreciation for year 2 by multiplying the book value by the declining-balance rate. (See Section 13.4 for a review of the declining-balance method.)

$\$4,000 \times 40\% = \$1,600$
Depreciation for year 2

Step 8 Find the book value for year 2 by subtracting the depreciation for year 2 from the book value for year 1.

$\$4,000$
$- \ \ 1,600$
$\$2,400$ Book value for year 2

Answer   The depreciation for year 2 is $1,600; the book value for year 2 is $2,4000.

Using Example 3, let's complete the depreciation and the book value for the remaining years and construct a depreciation schedule.

Year 3: $2,400 × 40% = $960 $2,400
                                        − 960
Year 4: $1,440 × 40% = $576 $1,440   Book value for year 3
                                        − 576
Year 5: $ 864 × 40% = $345.60 $ 864   Book value for year 4
                                        − 345.60
Year 6: $\begin{cases} \$ \ 518.40 \times 40\% = \$207.36 \\ \$ \ 207.36 \times \frac{1}{2} = \$103.68 \end{cases}$ $ 518.40 Book value for year 3
                                        − 103.68
                                       $ 414.72 Final book value

Note that the depreciation for year 6 is $103.68. Year 6 is after the end of the recovery period. This half depreciation is permitted here because only half of the depreciation was allowed in year 1.

Sun Bright Pool Supply Company Depreciation Schedule

Year	Annual Depreciation	Accumulated Depreciation	Balance (Book Value)
0	$ 0	$ 0	$5,000.00
1	$1,000.00	$1,000.00	$4,000.00
2	$1,600.00	$2,600.00	$2,400.00
3	$ 960.00	$3,560.00	$1,440.00
4	$ 576.00	$4,136.00	$ 864.00
5	$ 345.60	$4,481.60	$ 518.40
6 half year	$ 103.68	$4,585.28	$ 414.72

Note that at the end of the schedule the book value of the typewriter is below the salvage value of $900. This is allowable under the MACRS method. You can also see that with this method, more depreciation is deducted than with the traditional declining-balance method. (*Note:* When figuring depreciation for year 5, you have the option under MACRS to switch to the straight-line method. If you chose to change methods at this point the book value could be brought down to 0 and higher amounts of depreciation would be allowed for the later years. In this way 100% of the cost of depreciation can be recovered. However, for simplicity we will not change methods during the figuring of problems in this section. It is anticipated that the IRS will offer official percentage tables to figure MACRS similar to the tables used for ACRS.)

The MACRS method also allows some depreciation to be figured on a quarterly and monthly basis with many guidelines for different classes of real property. In some cases, the straight-line method of depreciation can also be used with no salvage value.

The preceding information is provided to help you become aware of some of the changes brought about by the Tax Reform Bill of 1986. In the years to come, it is likely that there will be even more changes and new guidelines proposed. It is important to check with the Internal Revenue Service for the most recent rates and laws.

It is also important to know that if you want to change the method of depreciation you are using, you must first obtain permission from the IRS. The only exception is a change from the declining-balance method to the straight-line method. It is interesting to note that the units-of-production method for depreciation remains unchanged and is not affected by the ACRS or Modified ACRS methods.

Self-Check

1. The Lehman Development Company uses the MACRS method of depreciation. Find the declining-balance rate allowed rounded to the nearest hundredth of a percent for each of the follow assets.

   a) Office desk
   b) Wastewater treatment plant
   c) Calculator

   a) _____
   b) _____
   c) _____

2. Right Track Enterprises purchased a small coal barge for $900,000. The salvage value is $86,000. The company uses the MACRS method of depreciation. Find the depreciation and the book value at the end of the second year.

   _____

ANSWERS   1. (a) 28.57%; (b) 10%; (c) 40%   2. $162,000 depreciation; $648,000 book value

Assignment 13.5

Depreciation

1. K&S Construction purchased a mobile home for on-site consulting purposes. The mobile home has a total cost of $37,000. Using the ACRS method, determine the depreciation for the third year and the book value for the end of the third year.

   (Use the 10-year property class.)
   $37,000 × 8% = $2,960 depr. year 1

   $37,000 × 14% = $5,180 depr. year 2

   $37,000 × 12% = 4,440 depr. year 3

   ```
   $37,000
   -  2,960
   $34,041  Book value year 1
   -  5,180
   $28,860  Book value year 2
   -  4,440
   $24,420  Book value year 3
   ```

   $4,440 depr.;
   $24,420 book value

2. Swift Communication, Inc., purchased a computer with a salvage value of $1,500 for $6,000. The company also purchased 3 typewriters for $900 each. Using the ACRS method, determine the depreciation allowed on all the properties for the second year.

   ```
   *$6,000
   + 2,700  (900 × 3)
   $8,700  Total cost (Use 5-year property class.)
   ```

   $8,700 × 22% = $1,914 depr. for year 2

   *Note: Salvage value is not used.

   $1,914 depr.

3. Your company purchased light tools with a salvage value of $500 for $3,000. You also purchased office equipment totaling $11,900. Using the ACRS method, determine each of the following.

   a) The total depreciation allowed for these properties for the third year

   ```
   $3,000 × 37% =    $1,110  (Use 3-year property class.)
   $11,900 × 21% = + 2,499   (Use 5-year property class.)
                     $3,609  Depr. for year 3
   ```

   $3,609 depr.

   b) The book value of the light tools at the end of the second year

   $3000 × 25% = $750 depr. year 1
   $3000 × 38% = $1,140 depr. year 2

   ```
   $3,000
   -   750
   $2,250  Book value year 1
   - 1,140
   $1,110  Book value year 2
   ```

   $1,110 book value

continued

Assignment 13.5 *continued*

4. Wright Enterprises purchased an amusement park in Houston, Texas, for $1,420,000 and another one in Sonoma, Arizona, for $3,650,000. Using the ACRS method, find each of the following.

   a) The total depreciation allowed on both parks for the seventh year

   (Use 10-year property class.)
   $1,420,000
   + 3,650,000
   $5,070,000 × 9% = $456,300 Total depr. for seventh year

   a) __$456,300 depr.__

   b) The total book value of the parks at the end of the third year

   $5,070,000 × 8% = $405,600 depr. year 1

   $5,070,000 × 14% = $709,800 depr. year 2

   $5,070,000 × 12% = $608,400 depr. year 3

   $5,070,000
   −   405,600
   $4,664,400 Book value year 1
   −   709,800
   $3,954,600 Book value year 2
   −   608,400
   $3,346,200 Book value year 3

   b) __$3,346,200 book value__

5. Jonea Designs purchased 2 typewriters for $1,560 each, an electronic calculator for $900, and a copy machine for $2,100. Using the ACRS method, construct a depreciation schedule for the total assets above.

   (Use 5-year for property class.)

   $1,560
   1,560
   900
   + 2,100
   $6,120 Total cost

   $6,120 × 15% = $ 918.00 Depr. year 1
   $61,20 × 22% = $1,346.40 Depr. year 2
   $6,120 × 21% = $1,285.20 Depr. year 3
   $6,120 × 21% = $1,285.20 Depr. year 4
   $6,120 × 21% = $1,285.20 Depr. year 5

   ### Jonea Designs
   #### Depreciation Schedule

Year	Annual Depreciation	Accumulated Depreciation	Balance (Book Value)
0	$ 0	$ 0	$6,120.00
1	918.00	918.00	5,202.00
2	1,346.40	2,264.40	3,855.60
3	1,285.20	3,549.60	2,570.40
4	1,285.20	4,834.80	1,285.20
5	1,285.20	6,120	0

6. Commonwealth Automotive Inc., purchased a 6-car garage, with a salvage value of $62,000 for $850,000. The garage was placed into service in April. The property falls into the 15-year recovery class period. Using the ACRS method, find each of the following.

Assignment 13.5 *continued*

a) The depreciation and the book value for the end of the first year

(Use 15-year recovery rate: Table 2, month 4.)
$850,000 × 9% = $76,500 Depr. year 1

$850,000 × 11% = $93,500 Depr. year 2

$850,000 × 9% = $76,500 Depr. year 3

```
  $850,000
-   76,500
  $773,500  Book value year 1
-   93,500
  $680,000  Book value year 2
-   76,500
  $603,500  Book value year 3
```

a) __$76,500 depr.; $773,500 book value__

b) The depreciation and the book value for the end of the third year.

b) __$76,500 depr.; $603,500 book value__

7. World Wide Services, Inc., uses the MACRS method of depreciation. Figure the recovery period and the declining-balance rate to the nearest hundredth of a percent for each of the following assets.

Asset		Recovery Period		Declining-balance Rate
Office files	a)	7	b)	28.57%
Typewriter	c)	5	d)	40%
Tractor	e)	3	f)	66.67%
Barge	g)	10	h)	20%
Computer	i)	5	j)	40%
Waste water treatment plant	k)	15	l)	10%
Automobile	m)	5	n)	40%
Horticulture structure	o)	7	p)	28.57%
Farm silo building	q)	20	r)	7.5%
Light truck	s)	5	t)	40%

continued

Assignment 13.5 *continued*

8. Pony Express, Inc., purchased a race horse with an estimated salvage value of $50,000 for $750,000. The company uses the MACRS method of depreciation. Determine the depreciation amount and the book value at the end of the first year. (Round the depreciation rate to the nearest hundredth of a percent.)

   (3-year class is used.)
   $$\frac{1}{3} \times 2 = \frac{2}{3} \quad 66.67\% \text{ double-declining rate}$$
   $750,000 \times 66.67\% = $500,025 Full year 1 depr.
   $$\$500,025 \times \frac{1}{2} = \$250,012.50 \text{ depr. year 1}$$

   For year 1 only $\frac{1}{2}$ the depreciation is allowed.

   $750,000.00
   − 250,012.50
   $499,987.50 Book value year 1

   Note to teacher: If student used $\frac{2}{3}$ instead of 66.67%, the answer will be: $250,000 depreciation and $500,000 book value.

   $250,012.50 depr.;
   $499,987.50 book value

9. A water vessel was purchased by Lakefront Resort for $930,000. The vessel has an estimated salvage value of $80,000. Using the MACRS method, find the depreciation amount and the book value for the end of the third year.

   (10-year class is used.)
   $$\frac{1}{10} = 10\% \times 2 = 20\%$$

   $930,000 × 20% = $186,000
   $$186,000 \times \frac{1}{2} = \$93,000 \text{ depr. year 1}$$
   $837,000 × 20% = $167,400 depr. year 2
   $669,600 × 20% = $133,920 depr. year 3

   $930,000 Cost
   −   93,000 Depr. year 1
   $837,000 Book value year 1
   − 167,400 Depr. year 2
   $669,600 Book value year 2
   − 133,920 Depr. year 3
   $535,680 Book value year 3

   Note: Salvage value is not used with MACRS problems.

   $133,920 depr.;
   $535,680 book value

NAME   DATE   SECTION

Assignment 13.5 *continued*

10. Video Software Systems uses the MACRS method of depreciation. The company purchased 2 computers, with a salvage value of $800 each, for $4,600 each and an electronic calculator with a salvage value of $180 for $2,000. Set up a depreciation schedule for the total purchases.

    $4,600 × 2 = $9,200
    $+2,000$
    $$$11,200$ Total cost

    (5-year class is used.)

    $\dfrac{1}{5} = 20\% \times 2 = 40\%$

    $11,200 × 40% = $4,480

    $4,480 × $\dfrac{1}{2}$ = $2,240 depr. year 1

    $8,960 × 40% = $3,584 depr. year 2
    $5,376 × 40% = $2,150.40 depr. year 3
    $3,225.60 × 40% = $1,290.24 depr. year 4
    $1,935.36 × 40% = $774.14 depr. year 5
    $1,161.22 × 40% = $464.49

    $464.49 × $\dfrac{1}{2}$ = 232.24 depr. year 6

    Video Software Systems Depreciation Schedule

Year	Annual Depreciation	Accumulated Depreciation	Balance (Book Value)
0	$ 0	$ 0	$11,200
1	2,240	2,240	8,960
2	3,584	5,824	5,376
3	2,150.40	7,974.40	3,225.60
4	1,290.24	9,264.64	1,935.36
5	774.14	10,038.78	1,161.22
6	232.24	10,271.02	928.98

    Note: The depreciation for year 1 and year 6 is $\frac{1}{2}$ of the full year's depreciation. Also, with the MACRS method, the extra half year (year 6) is allowed for the year following the recovery period.

Comprehensive Problems for Chapter 13

Depreciation

1. Angelique's Pizza Parlor purchased a new specialized oven for $5,000. An additional charge for installation came to $640. The estimated life of the oven is 16,000 hours, and the number of hours of use for the first year is 1,980. If the trade-in value of the stove is $500 and the store uses the units-of-production method of depreciation, determine each of the following.

   a) The unit depreciation in dollars

   $5,000 Price
   + 640 Installation
   $5,640 Total cost
   − 500 Salvage value
   $5,140 Total depreciation

   $\dfrac{\$5,140 \text{ Total depr.}}{16,000 \text{ hrs life}} = .3212 = \$.32 \text{ per hr depr.}$

   $.32 unit depr.

   b) The first year's depreciation in dollars

   1,980 hr × $.32 = $633.60 depreciation

   $633.60 depr.

2. A sprayer with an estimated life of 3 years was purchased by Guard Pest Control for $3,780. The trade-in value is $650. At the end of the first year:

   a) What are the depreciation and the book value by the sum-of-the-years'-digits method?

   $3,780 Cost
   − 650 Trade-in value
   $3,130 Depr. cost

   1 + 2 + 3 = 6

   $\dfrac{3}{6} \times \$3,130 = \$1,565$ depr.

   $3,780 − $1,565 = $2,215 book value

   $1,565 depreciation, end of first year;
   $2,215 book value, end of first year

   b) What are the depreciation and the book value by the declining-balance method? Round to the nearest dollar.

   $\dfrac{100\%}{3} = 33\tfrac{1}{3}\%$ straight-line rate

   $33\tfrac{1}{3}\% \times 2 = 66\tfrac{2}{3}\%$ declining-balance rate
   $3,780 × 66.66% = $2,519.74 = $2,520 (rounded) depr.
   $3,780 − $2,520 = $1,260 Book value

   $2,520 depreciation;
   $1,260 book value

continued

Comprehensive Problems *continued*

3. Alcon Energy purchased a small power production facility for $8,410,000. It has a salvage value of $960,000. Construct a depreciation schedule using the ACRS method of depreciation.

   (5-year property class is used.)
   $8,410,000 × 15% = $1,261,500 depr. year 1
   $8,410,000 × 22% = $1,850,200 depr. year 2
   $8,410,000 × 21% = $1,766,100 depr. year 3, year 4, year 5

   Alcon Energy Depreciation Schedule

Year	Annual Depreciation	Accumulated Depreciation	Balance (Book Value)
0	$ 0	$ 0	$8,410,000
1	1,261,500	1,261,500	7,148,500
2	1,850,200	3,111,700	5,298,300
3	1,766,100	4,877,800	3,532,200
4	1,766,100	6,643,900	1,766,100
5	1,766,100	8,410,000	0

4. Maid-For-You, Inc., purchased an industrial vacuum cleaner for $1,775. A delivery charge of $106 was added. The vacuum has an estimated life of 6 years and a salvage value of $369. Using the sum-of-the-years'-digits method, complete the following depreciation table.

   $1,775
   + 106 Delivery
   $1,881 Total cost
   − 369 Salvage value
   $1,512 Total depr.

   $6 + 5 + 4 + 3 + 2 + 1 = 21$

   $1,512 \times \dfrac{6}{21} = \$432$ $1,512 \times \dfrac{3}{21} = \$216$

   $1,512 \times \dfrac{5}{21} = \$360$ $1,512 \times \dfrac{2}{21} = \$144$

   $1,512 \times \dfrac{4}{21} = \$288$ $1,512 \times \dfrac{1}{21} = \$72$

Year	Annual Depreciation	Accumulated Depreciation	Balance (Book Value)
0	$ 0	$ 0	$ 1,881
1	432	432	1,449
2	360	792	1,089
3	288	1,080	801
4	216	1,296	585
5	144	1,440	441
6	72	1,512	369

Comprehensive Problems *continued*

5. Ready-Mail Company purchased a courier car for $10,340. There was an additional charge of $1660 for specialized shelving. The car is expected to last 5 years and have a trade-in value of $933. Using the declining-balance method, find the amount of depreciation and the book value for the end of the third year.

   $10,340
   + 1,660 Additional
   $12,000 Total cost

   $100\% \times \dfrac{1}{5} = 20\%$ $20\% \times 2 = 40\%$

   $12,000 \times 40\% = \$4,800$ depr. year 1

   $\$7,200 \times 40\% = \$2,800$ depr. year 2

   $\$4,320 \times 40\% = \$1,728$ depr. year 3

   $12,000
   − 4,800
   $ 7,200 Book value year 1
   − 2,800
   $4,320 Book value year 2
   − 1,728
   $2,592 Book value year 3

   $1,728 depr.;
   $2,592 book value

6. Eastern Print Shop purchased a new camera for $8,500. Transportation charges were $80 and the installation charge was $110. The trade-in value at the end of 4 years is estimated at $1,780.

   a) What is the depreciation for the second year by the straight-line method?

   $8,500 Cost
   80 Transportation
   + 110 Installation
   $8,690 Total cost
   − 1,780 Salvage value
   $6,910 Depr. cost

   $6,910 × 25% = $1,727.50 depr.

   $1,727.50 second year's depreciation

   b) What is the depreciation for the second year by the sum-of-the-years'-digits method?

   1 + 2 + 3 + 4 = 10

   $6,910 \times \dfrac{3}{10} = \$2,073$

   $2,073 second year's depreciation

7. Ralph's Roofing Service purchased equipment costing $8,700. The residual value is $900, and the estimated life is 4 years. Determine the following.

   a) The straight-line depreciation rate

   $\dfrac{100\%}{4} = 25\%$

   25% depreciation rate

continued

Comprehensive Problems *continued*

b) The declining-balance depreciation rate

25% × 2 = 50%

50% depreciation rate

c) The depreciation and the book value at the end of the first year using:

1) The straight-line method.

$8,700 Cost
− 900 Salvage value
$7,800 Depr. cost

$7,800 × 25% = $1,950 depr.
8,700 − 1,950 = $6,750 book value

1) $1,950 depr.; $6,750 book value

2) The declining-balance method.

$8,700 × 50% = $4,350 depr.
$8,700 − $4,350 = $4,350 book value

2) $4,350 depr.; $4,350 book value

8. Gemstones, Inc., purchased a polisher for $4211. The additional shipping cost amounted to $289. The salvage value of the polisher is $360, and the estimated life is 5 years. Complete the following depreciation schedule using the declining-balance method.

$4,211
+ 289
4,500 Total cost

$\frac{100\%}{5} = 20\%$ 20% × 2 = 40%

$4,500 × 40% = $1,800 depr. year 1
$2,700 × 40% = $1,080 depr. year 2
$1,620 × 40% = $648 depr. year 3
$972 × 40% = $388.80 depr. year 4
$223.20 depr. year 5

Note: Year 5 depreciation is only $223.20 so that book value will not be below salvage value.

Year	Annual Depreciation	Accumulated Depreciation	Balance (Book Value)
0	$ 0	$ 0	$ 4,500.00
1	1,800.00	1,800.00	2,700.00
2	1,080.00	2,880.00	1,620.00
3	648.00	3,528.00	972.00
4	388.80	3,916.80	583.20
5	223.20	4,140.00	360.00

Comprehensive Problems *continued*

9. Milcreek Tile Manufacturers purchased a machine that cost $9,872 with additional freight and installation charges of $1,621. Its estimated life is a productive capacity of 40,000 units or 5 years with a salvage value of $1,302. During the first year, 9,900 units were produced.

   a) Using the units-of-production method, what is the depreciation for the first year? Round the depreciation per unit to the nearest cent.

   $9,872
   + 1,621 Freight & installation
   $11,493 Total cost
   − 1,302 Salvage value
   $10,191 depr. cost

   $\dfrac{\$10,191}{40,000} = .2547 = \$.25$

   9,900 × $.25 = $2,475 depr.

   $2,475 depreciation, first year

   b) Using the straight-line method, what is the depreciation for the first year?

   $10,191 ÷ 5 yr = $2,038.20 depr.

   $2,038.20 depreciation, first year

10. Mason Marble, Inc., purchased light tools with a useful life of $3\tfrac{1}{2}$ years for $2,100. The company also purchased a copy machine for $4,900 that has a salvage value of $841. Using the ACRS method of depreciation, find each of the following.

    a) The total depreciation allowed on these assets for the second year

    $2,100 × 38% = $ 798 (3-year property class)
    $4,900 × 22% = $1,078 (5-year property class)
    $1,876 Total depreciation

    a) $1,876

    b) The book value of the copy machine at the end of the fourth year

    $4,900 × 15% = $ 735 depr. year 1 $4,900
                                          −   735
    $4,900 × 22% = $1,078 depr. year 2 $4,165 Book value year 1
                                          − 1,078
    $4,900 × 21% = $1,029 depr. year 3 $3,087 Book value year 2
                                          − 1,029
    $4,900 × 21% = $1,029 depr. year 4 $2,058 Book value year 3
                                          − 1,029
                                          $1,029 Book value year 4

    b) $1,029 book value

continued

Comprehensive Problems *continued*

c) The depreciation and the book value for year 2 for a warehouse purchased for $450,000 and put into service in February. The property falls into the 15-year class category.

(Use 15-year property class: Table 2, month 2.)
$450,000 × 11% = $49,500 depr. year 1

$450,000 × 10% = $45,000 depr. year 2

$450,000
− 49,500
$400,500 Book value year 1
− 45,000
$355,500 Book value year 2

c) $45,000 depr.; $355,500 book value

11. Sarah's Interior Landscaping Services purchased office furniture with a total salvage value of $4,000 for $31,600. Find the depreciation and the book value at the end of the third year using the MACRS method. (Round the depreciation rate to the nearest hundredth of a percent.)

(7-year recovery period is used.)

$\frac{1}{7} \times 2 = \frac{2}{7} = 28.57\%$

$31,600 × 28.57% = $9,028.12

$9,028.12 \times \frac{1}{2}$ = $4,514.06 depr. year 1

$27,085.94 × 28.57% = $7,738.45 depr. year 2
$19,347.49 × 28.57% = $5,527.58 depr. year 3

$31,600.00
− 4,514.06
$27,085.94 Book value year 1
− 7,738.45
$19,347.49 Book value year 2
− 5,527.58
$13,819.91 Book value year 3

$5,527.58 depr.; $13,819.91 book value

12. Bill Beal's Insulation Services purchased a light truck with a salvage value of $570 for $8,200. Using the MACRS method, find each of the following.

a) The depreciation and the book value at the end of year 1

b) The depreciation and the book value at the end of year 2

(5-year recovery period is used.)

$\frac{1}{5}$ = 20% × 2 = 40%

$8,200 × 40% = $3,280

$3,280 \times \frac{1}{2}$ = $1,640 depr. year 1

$6,560 × 40% = $2,624 depr. year 2

$8,200
− 1,640
$6,560 Book value year 1
− 2,624
$3,936 Book value year 2

a) $1,640 depr.; $6,560 book value

b) $2,624 depr.; $3,936 book value

Case 1

Skytrek Aviation Company purchased soldering equipment that cost $5,800. After an estimated life of 5 years, the trade-in value is $800. The equipment was purchased January 1, and the accounting year ends December 31.

a) Set up three depreciation schedules using the straight-line, the sum-of-the-years' digits, and the declining-balance methods.

In which circumstances would you want to use each of the three methods?

b) Set up a depreciation schedule for the tax purposes using ACRS method. The equipment falls under the five-year recovery class.

Case 2

The Special Advertising Specialists purchased a printing machine at a cost of $18,037 plus an installation charge of $103. The machine's trade-in value is $1,740. The machine is expected to print 820,000 items. Set up a depreciation schedule for the following years of use showing the depreciation, the accumulated depreciation, and the book value for each year.

Time	Number of Items Printed
Year 1	133,400
Year 2	140,950
Year 3	130,600
Year 4	130,100
Year 5	126,300
Year 6	127,500
Year 7	132,000
Year 8	48,000

Key Terms

Accelerated cost recovery system (ACRS)
Assets
Book value
Cost of an asset
Current assets
Declining-balance depreciation
Declining-balance rate
Depreciable rate
Depreciation
Depreciation schedule
Estimated life
Fixed assets
Long-term assets
Modified Accelerated cost recovery system (MACRS)
Recovery period
Salvage value
Straight-line depreciation
Straight-line depreciation rate
Sum-of-the-years'-digits depreciation
Tangible property
Units-of-production depreciation

Key Concepts

- Depreciation is the process of dividing the cost of an item over its useful life.
- The book value of a fixed asset is found by subtracting the amount of accumulated depreciation to date from the original cost of the asset.

- Three factors must be known in order to determine depreciation and book value:
  1. Total cost of the asset,
  2. Salvage value,
  3. Estimated life.
- There are six methods of depreciation:
  1. Straight line,
  2. Units of production,
  3. Sum-of-the-years' digits,
  4. Declining balance,
  5. Accelerated cost recovery system (ACRS),
  6. Modified accelerated cost recovery system (MACRS).
- Straight-line depreciation $= \dfrac{\text{Total cost} - \text{Salvage value}}{\text{Years of estimated life}}$
- Straight-line depreciation rate $= \dfrac{100\%}{\text{Years of estimated life}}$
- Units-of-production depreciation per unit $= \dfrac{\text{Total cost} - \text{Salvage value}}{\text{Estimated units of output}}$
- Units-of-production depreciation = Depreciation per unit × Number of units produced for an accounting period
- Sum-of-the-years' depreciable rate $= \dfrac{\text{Remaining year of asset's life}}{\text{Sum of years}}$
- Sum-of-the-years'-digits depreciation = (Total cost − Salvage value) × Depreciable rate
- Declining-balance rate = 2 × Straight-line depreciation rate
- Declining-balance depreciation = Book value × Declining-balance rate
- Depreciation continues until the fixed asset is sold or replaced or until the book value equals the salvage value of the asset (except for ACRS and MCRS).
- Accelerated cost recovery depreciation = Total cost of asset × Accelerated cost recovery rate
- Modified accelerated cost recovery depreciation = Book value × Declining balance cost recovery rate

14
Accounting and Analysis

Business Takes a Positive Approach

GREYHOUND

The Greyhound Corporation was in trouble. Its financial statements showed that the company's earnings and profits had fallen. Greyhound found itself fighting for space in a declining market where passenger count fell from 65 million riders to 33 million in less than 10 years. Profound changes were necessary; the firm's top managers reevaluated the company's holdings and sold off more than 14 businesses. The Greyhound Lines itself was sold which ended an era in the transportation industry for Greyhound Corporation. After an intensive search, Greyhound acquired 10 new companies including the U.S. Transit bus-building operations of General Motors. The company retained Greyhound Financial Corporation in order to use real estate financing as a growth vehicle. Today the corporation is mainly a consumer products/services company. It owns Dial Corporation, the Purex line of laundry and household products, Armour Star brand of canned meats, Travelers Express (which includes Quantum—an electronic funds transfer system), and Premier Cruise Lines. There is a stronger emphasis also being placed on new product development, including a variety of microwaveable food products, foods meeting regional taste preferences and natural skincare soaps. Other companies within the Greyhound family include Greyhound Exposition Services, a convention service company; Greyhound Leisure Services, which owns airport gift shops, and travel services; Greyhound Airport Services, which maintains and operates fueling systems and storage facilities for major airports; and Restaura which contracts food service operations. This fresh approach which Greyhound has taken has paid off. The company has over $3 billion in assets and net income has substantially increased. Back on solid ground, Greyhound is racing ahead. John Teets, chief executive officer of Greyhound explained, "However reluctantly, a company has to let go of its past if it is to have a hand free to reach for its future."

Learning Objectives

After reading and studying this chapter and working the problems, you will be able to:

- Explain the difference between a balance sheet and an income statement.
- Prepare the balance sheet in both account and report form.
- Prepare the income statement.
- Calculate the cost of goods sold.
- Perform horizontal and vertical analysis.
- Figure financial ratios.
- Read and prepare bar, pictogram, circle, and line graphs.

Businesses are concerned with both past and present financial records. Analyzing accounting records gives clues to the financial condition and stability of a firm. Financial statements are used by managers, unions, bankers, investors, prospective and present employees, government officials, suppliers, and others. The information obtained can help to answer such questions as: What are the resources of the firm? Is the company a good credit risk? How much of the business is owned by creditors? Are the expenses too high in relation to sales? How many assets can be turned into cash quickly? Are the future prospects for the firm promising? Can the firm afford to hire more salespeople? Should the firm introduce a new product? Are taxes adequate?

Accounting statements give a concise picture of the profitability and financial position of a firm. The two most important are the balance sheet, and the income statement. The balance sheet gives the financial position of a business on a particular date. It deals with the resources of a business. The income statement gives the financial results (profit and loss) of these resources over a period of time.

14.1 Financial Statements

Preparing the Balance Sheet

Before learning more about this financial statement, it would be helpful for you to become familiar with some of the basic terminology used.

Terms for a Balance Sheet

Assets are the economic resources or properties owned by the business. These include the following:

Current assets: Assets that can be turned into cash, sold, or consumed within a short period of time, usually within one year from the date of the balance sheet.

Plant assets: Assets held for more than one year, also called fixed or long-term assets. Where it applies, depreciation is subtracted from plant assets.

Accounts receivable: Amounts owed to a business by customers for goods and services sold to them on credit.

Notes receivable: Promissory notes owed to the business.

Merchandise inventory: Goods or products held for sale by the business.

Cash: Funds on hand or deposits in the bank.

Other examples of assets are equipment, office furniture and supplies, land, buildings, and patents.

Liabilities are the debts of a business, or what a firm owes. These include the following:

Current liabilities: Debts that must be paid within a short time, usually within one year from the date of the balance sheet.

Long-term liabilities: Debts that are due after a long period, usually one year or more.

Accounts payable: Amount owed to creditors for goods and services bought on credit.

Notes payable: Promissory notes owed by the business.

Other examples of liabilities are salaries, wages, commissions owed to employees, taxes payable, mortgage payable, and interest payable.

Capital is the owner's equity and the value of the business after all debts have been paid, that is, the difference between assets and liabilities.

The **balance sheet** gives the financial picture of a business as it stands on one particular day. It can be prepared at any time, but most often balance sheets are prepared at the end of a fiscal year. The balance sheet gives the accounting of the assets, liabilities, and capital of a firm. It makes use of the following accounting equation:

$$\text{Assets} - \text{Liabilities} = \text{Capital}$$
$$(\text{Business owns}) - (\text{Business owes}) = (\text{Business net worth or owner's equity}).$$

The main principle governing the balance sheet is:

$$\text{Total assets} = \text{Total liabilities} + \text{Capital} \quad \text{or} \quad A = L + C.$$

The balance sheet can be prepared in either the account form or the report form. With the **account form,** the balance sheet is written with the assets on the left side and the liabilities and capital on the right side. The totals for the two sides must always be in balance (equal). The account form is a good visual illustration of the accounting equation. A balance sheet in account form is shown here.

Sound Systems Company
Balance Sheet
December 31, 19__

ASSETS		LIABILITIES	
Cash	$ 16,000	Accounts Payable	$190,000
Equipment	120,000	Wages Payable	95,000
Accounts Receivable	109,000	Taxes Payable	50,000
Inventory	110,000		$235,000
		CAPITAL	
		E. John, Owner	$120,000
Total Assets	$355,000	Total Liabilities and Capital	$355,000

The *report form* for the balance sheet lists the assets, liabilities, and capital in a single column. When the information is presented this way, it makes it easier to compare figures to past balance sheets. A balance sheet in report form is shown here.

Sound Systems Company
Balance Sheet
December 31, 19__

ASSETS

Cash	$ 16,000
Equipment	120,000
Accounts Receivable	109,000
Inventory	110,000
	$355,000

LIABILITIES

Accounts Payable	$190,000
Wages Payable	95,000
Taxes Payable	50,000
	$225,000

CAPITAL

E. John, Owner	$120,000
Total Liabilities and Capital	$355,000

Note that the double line means "final total." The total of the assets equals the total of the liabilities and capital. Regardless of which form is used, this basic balance still exists.

Be aware that the liabilities of a business are actually claims against its assets. If a company were to go out of business, all the creditors (liabilities) must be paid first from the sale of the assets. The owner has a residual claim, which means that the owner would receive only the amount left over after all other debts have been paid.

Example 1 McCandles Roofing Supply owns $200,000 in buildings, $80,000 in land, and $150,000 in inventory. The company owes $90,000 in wages, $20,000 in taxes, $30,000 in notes payable, and $80,000 to other companies. Determine its capital.

Step 1 List and total all assets.

```
  $200,000 Buildings
    80,000 Land
+  150,000 Inventory
  $430,000 Assets
```

Step 2 List and total all liabilities.

```
  $ 90,000 Wages
    20,000 Taxes
    30,000 Notes
+   80,000 Creditors
  $220,000 Liabilities
```

Step 3 Subtract total liabilities from total assets to find the capital.

```
  $430,000 Assets
-  220,000 Liabilities
  $210,000 Capital
```

Answer The capital is $210,000.

NOTE: The accounting equation can also be applied to find assets or liabilities:

$$\text{Assets} = \text{Liabilities} + \text{Capital},$$
$$\text{Liabilities} = \text{Assets} - \text{Capital}.$$

Self-Check

1. If the total assets of a firm are $120,000 and the capital is $19,300, what are the liabilities?

2. The liabilities of Roy Chemical Company are $412,400 and the total owner's equity amounts to $167,000. Determine the total assets.

3. Bookworm Books has an inventory valued at $45,000. It also has $16,000 in cash, $12,000 in accounts receivable, $25,000 in wages payable, $90,000 in buildings, $15,000 for taxes due, $40,000 in accounts payable, $20,000 in mortgage payable. Find the amount of capital.

ANSWERS 1. $100,700   2. $579,400   3. $63,000

Preparing the Income Statement

The **income statement** is also referred to as the profit and loss statement. It presents a summary of the revenue condition of a firm over a period of time. While the balance sheet shows the financial condition of a firm on a given date, the income statement shows the flow of the financial resources and net result for a period of time (usually one year). That is, it shows the difference between what the business received in revenue minus all the expenses incurred to operate the business. The difference is either a net profit or a net loss for the year. In simple terms, the income statement shows:

$$\text{Revenues} - \text{Expenses} = \text{Net income}.$$

(A discussion on profit also appears in Section 7.1.)
Some of the terms used for the income statement are the following.

Net sales: The amount received from customers after subtracting sales returns and allowances (refunds and adjustments) from gross sales.

Cost of goods sold: The cost of the items sold by a business—what the business paid for them.

Gross margin: The difference between net sales and the cost of goods sold. Also known as *gross profit* or *markup*.

Operating expenses: The costs involved in running the business. Also called *overhead*. Some examples are employee wages, rent, insurance, utilities, taxes, depreciation, advertising, and so on.

Net income: The difference between all income and all expenses. In accounting terms, the difference between gross margin and total operating expenses. Also referred to in business as "the bottom line."

> The basic relationships for the income statement are:
>
> Net sales − Cost of goods sold = Gross profit,
>
> Gross profit − Expenses = Net income (Profit or loss).

Finding the Cost of Goods Sold

When a company sells merchandise, records are usually kept at the retail price of the goods. When it comes time to prepare the income statement, many businesses use an inventory system to figure the cost of goods sold. Inventory figures at cost are used to figure the cost of goods sold. To use this method, the following facts should be known:

1. The beginning inventory for the period (cost of goods in stock).
2. Net purchases made during the period (at cost price).
3. The ending inventory remaining at the end of the period (at cost price).

The following procedure is used to find the cost of goods sold:

> Beginning inventory
> + Purchases
> Goods available for sale
> − Ending inventory
> Cost of goods sold

For our purposes, we will assume that the inventory and purchase figures are recorded at cost. (For a detailed discussion on evaluating ending inventory, refer to Section 7.6.)

Example 2 Steven's U-Finish Furniture had a beginning inventory of $80,000 and an ending inventory of $70,000. Purchases during the period amounted to $50,000. What is the cost of goods sold?

Step 1   Add the beginning inventory and purchases to find the goods available for sale.

$ 80,000 Beginning inventory
+ 50,000 Purchases
$130,000 Goods available for sale

Step 2   Subtract the ending inventory from goods available for sale to find the cost of goods sold.

$130,000
− 70,000 Ending inventory
$ 60,000 Cost of goods sold

Answer   The cost of goods sold is $60,000.

Self-Check

Atlantic's Short and Small Shop purchased $14,000 worth of clothes during the month of March. The beginning inventory on March 1 is $52,000, and the ending inventory on March 31 is $54,600. Determine the cost of goods sold for the month of March.

ANSWER $11,400

A simplified illustration of a business's income statement is shown here.

Sound Systems Company
Income Statement
For the Year Ended December 31, 19__

Total Sales		$198,000
Less Returns		− 6,500
Net Sales		$191,500
Cost of Goods Sold		
Beginning Inventory	$ 60,000	
Purchases	110,000	
Goods Available for Sale	$170,000	
Ending Inventory	− 50,000	
Cost of Goods Sold		− 120,000
Gross Profit		$ 71,500
Expenses		
Salaries	$ 24,000	
Advertising	6,000	
Rent	3,400	
Utilities	830	
Supplies	1,100	
Total Expenses		− 35,330
Net Income		$ 36,170

If a loss, rather than a profit, is shown for net income, the numbers are put in parentheses. For instance, a $1,200 loss is shown as ($1,200).

Self-Check _____

1. Carla's Ceramic Studio shows net sales of $120,000, cost of goods sold of $64,300, and operating expenses of $42,190. Determine the gross profit and the net income. Was the net income a profit or a loss?

2. Good Earth Garden Supplies showed gross sales of $480,000, operating expenses of $209,980, sales returns of $9,300, and cost of goods sold of $263,000. What are the gross margin and the net income? Was the net income a profit or a loss?

ANSWERS   1. $55,700 gross profit; $13,510 profit   2. $207,700 gross margin; ($2,280) loss

Accounting and Analysis

NAME   DATE   SECTION

Assignment 14.1

Accounting and Analysis

1. Using the accounting equation for the balance sheet, find the missing term for each of the following.

   a) Assets = $60,000; liabilities = $40,000; capital = __$20,000__   Assets − Liabilities = Capital

   b) Owner's equity = $21,000; liabilities = $32,080; assets = __$53,080__   Owner's equity + Liabilities = Assets

   c) Assets = $120,000; capital = $46,400; liabilities = __$73,600__   Assets − Capital = Liabilities

   d) Liabilities = $29,600; capital = $18,000; assets = __$47,600__   Liabilities + Capital = Assets

2. Medeen Muffler Shop owns $150,000 in building, $30,000 in land, and $80,000 in inventory. The company owes $70,000 in taxes, $130,000 to other companies, and $50,000 in wages. What is the capital?

   Assets − Liabilities = Capital
   $260,000 − $250,000 = $10,000

   __$10,000 capital__

   $150,000 Bldg.
     30,000 Land
   + 80,000 Inv.
   $260,000 Total Assets

   $70,000 Taxes
   130,000 A/P
   + 50,000 Wages
   $250,000 Total liabilities

3. Bent Bike Company has a capital value of $23,000. It has cash on hand of $15,000, $80,000 in land and building, and $24,000 in merchandise. What are the total liabilities and total assets?

   Assets − Capital = Liabilities
   $119,000 − $23,000 = $96,000

   __$96,000 total liabilities,__
   __$119,000 total assets__

   $15,000 Cash
   80,000 Land & Bldg.
   + 24,000 Inv.
   $119,000 Total assets

4. County Canopy Company owes $10,000 to suppliers, $4,000 in interest, and $20,000 in wages. Notes payable amount to $7,000. If the total capital amounts to $16,000, what are the total assets of the firm?

   Liabilities + Capital = Assets
   $41,000 + $16,000 = $57,000

   __$57,000 total assets__

   $10,000 A/P
   4,000 Int. payable
   20,000 Wages
   + 7,000 N/P
   $41,000 Total liabilities

5. Redi-Tile Company has accounts receivable of $17,000. Accounts payable are $12,000, and notes payable are $21,000. If the company has $6,000 in cash with an inventory of $35,400, what are the capital, the total liabilities, and the total assets?

   Assets − Liabilities = Capital
   $58,400 − $33,000 = $25,400

   __$25,400 capital,__
   __$33,000 total liabilities,__
   __$58,400 total assets__

   $6,000 Cash
   17,000 A/R
   + 35,400 Inv.
   $58,400 Total Assets

   $12,000 A/P
   + 21,000 N/P
   $33,000 Total liabilities

6. Fisherman's Landing owns $89,900 in buildings and property. Equipment owned amounts to $12,600. The business's inventory amounts to $34,980, and total accounts receivable are $21,430. If the capital amounts to $30,020, what are the total liabilities?

   Assets − Capital = Liabilities
   $158,910 − $30,020 = $128,890

   __$128,890 total liabilities__

   $21,430 A/R
   34,980 Inv.
   12,600 Eqpt.
   + 89,900 Bldg & Prop.
   $158,910 Total assets

continued

Assignment 14.1 continued

7. Prepare a balance sheet in account form for The House of Gifts as of December 31, 19--.

   Accounts receivable $17,000
   Accounts payable $12,000
   Cash on hand $ 5,000
   Inventory $34,000
   K. Bersten, capital $23,000
   Notes payable $21,000

   The House of Gifts
   Balance Sheet
   December 31, 19__

ASSETS		LIABILITIES	
Cash on hand	$ 5,000.00	Accounts payable	$12,000.00
Accounts receivable	17,000.00	Notes payable	21,000.00
Inventory	34,000.00	Total liabilities	$33,000.00
		OWNER'S EQUITY	
		K. Bersten, Capital	$23,000.00
Total Assets	$56,000.00	Total liabilities and owner's equity	$56,000.00

8. In their first year of operation, Milltown Flour Wholesalers had total liabilities of $71,900 with total assets of $111,030. After the second year, it was found that assets had decreased by $1,200 while liabilities increased by $2,611.

   a) What is the capital at the end of the first year?

   Assets − Liabilities = Capital
   $111,030 − $71,900 = $39,130   **$39,130 capital**

   b) What is the capital at the end of the second year?

   Assets − Liabilities = Capital
   $109,830 − $74,511 = $35,319   **$35,319 capital**

   $71,900 Liab., first year
   + 2,611 Increase
   $74,511 Total liab., second year

   $111,030 Assets, first year
   −   1,200 Decrease
   $109,830 Total assets, second year

The following information for problems 9–11 is obtained from income statements. Fill in the missing terms.

9. Sales $23,400
   Cost of goods sold 11,500
   Operating expenses   7,200
   Gross profit $11,900
   Net income $4,700

   $23,400 Sales
   − 11,500 Less CGS
   $11,900 Gross profit
   − 7,200 Less op. exp.
   $ 4,700 Net income

continued

NAME   DATE   SECTION

Assignment 14.1 continued

10. Cost of goods sold $ 6,730 $12,400 Sales
    Operating expenses   4,280   − 6,730 Less CGS
    Sales   12,400 $ 5,670 Gross profit
    Gross profit $5,670   − 4,280 Less op. exp.
    Net income $1,390 $ 1,390 Net income

11. Operating expenses $18,100 $40,000 Sales
    Sales   40,000   − 29,000 Less CGS
    Cost of goods sold   29,000 $11,000 Gross profit
    Gross profit $11,000   − 18,100 Less op. exp.
    Net income $(7,100) loss $(7,100) Net income

12. Johnston Company has a gross margin of $44,998. The net sales are $273,194 with operating expenses of $11,254. If net income amounts to $33,744, what is the cost of goods sold?

    $228,196
    cost of goods sold

    $ 11,254 Op. exp.
    + 33,744 Net inc.
    $ 44,998 Gross profit

    $273,194 Net sales
    − 44,998 Gross profit
    $228,196 CGS

13. Olsen Suppliers show a loss of $2,500. If net sales are $25,000 and the cost of goods sold is $18,750, what are the total operating expenses?

    $8,750
    operating expenses

    $ 25,000 Sales
    − 18,750 CGS
    $ 6,250 Gross profit
    + (2,500) Net inc. (loss)
    $ 8,750 Op exp.

14. Find the cost of goods sold for Arrow Printers if the beginning inventory at cost is $17,400, purchases made are $6,280, and ending inventory at cost is $15,407.

    $17,400 Beginning inventory
    + 6,280 Purchases
    $23,680 Cost of goods avail.
    − 15,407 Less ending inv.
    $ 8,273 Cost of goods sold

    $8,273
    cost of goods sold

15. Associated Fixture Supply had net sales of $219,000, with purchases of $91,600. The beginning inventory at cost was $62,600, and the ending inventory at cost amounted to $54,500. Determine the gross margin.

    Net sales $219,000
      Beg. inv. $ 62,600
      Purchases   + 91,600
      Cost of goods avail. $154,200
      Less end. inv.   − 54,500
      Cost of goods sold   99,700
      Gross margin $119,300

    $119,300
    gross margin

16. What is the ending inventory at cost for Guest Linens Company if the beginning inventory at cost is $18,000, purchases are $80,000, and cost of goods sold is $73,000?

    $25,000
    ending inventory

    $18,000 Beg. inv.
    + 80,000 Purchases
    $98,000 Cost of goods avail
    − 73,000 Less CGS
    $25,000 End. inv.

continued

Assignment 14.1 *continued*

17. For Admiral Dynamics, prepare a complete income statement for the period ending December 31, 19-- using the following figures.

Utilities:	$ 1,200
Advertising:	5,200
Rent:	4,800
Sales returns:	754
Ending inventory:	5,000
Beginning inventory:	6,000
Purchases:	4,000
Gross sales:	29,800

Admiral Dynamics
Income Statement
for the Period Ending December 31, 19__

Gross Sales			$29,800
Less: Sales returns			754
Net sales			$29,046
Cost of goods sold			
Beginning inventory	$ 6,000		
Purchases	4,000		
Cost of goods available	$10,000		
Ending inventory	5,000		
Cost of goods sold			5,000
Gross profit			$24,046
Expenses			
Advertising	$ 5,200		
Rent	4,800		
Utilities	1,200		
Total expenses			11,200
Net income			$12,846

14.2 Comparative Analysis

Although information obtained in a specific financial statement is helpful in understanding the financial condition of a business, it can be even more meaningful to look at statements prepared over a period of time. This helps the reader to become aware of changes, trends, and possible trouble spots or strong areas within the workings of a firm. A **comparative statement** compares a business's financial condition of the current period with the figures for the previous period(s). It can be prepared for the balance sheet and for the income statement.

A comparative statement for the balance sheet is shown here. Following this statement is an explanation of horizontal analysis.

Wood World
Comparative Balance Sheet
December 31, This Year and Last Year

	This Year	Last Year	Horizontal Analysis Amount Increase/(Decrease)	% Change
ASSETS				
Current Assets:				
Cash	$ 7,000	$ 7,500	$(500)	(6.67)
Accounts Receivable	21,000	17,000	4,000	23.53
Inventory	50,000	40,000	10,000	25
Supplies	2,000	1,800	200	11.11
Total Current Assets	$ 80,000	$ 66,300	$ 13,700	20.66
Plant Assets:				
Land	$ 26,000	$ 26,000	$ 0	0
Building	80,000	83,000	(3,000)	(3.61)
Equipment	30,000	33,000	(3,000)	(9.09)
Total Plant Assets	$136,000	$142,000	$(6,000)	(4.23)
Total Assets	$216,000	$208,300	$ 7,700	3.70
LIABILITIES				
Current Liabilities:				
Accounts Payable	$ 26,000	$ 38,000	$(8,000)	(21.05)
Notes Payable	14,000	12,000	2,000	16.67
Total Current Liabilities	$ 40,000	$ 50,000	$(10,000)	(20)
Long-Term Liabilities:				
Mortgage Payable	$ 68,500	$ 72,000	$(3,500)	(4.86)
Total Liabilities	$108,500	$122,000	$(13,500)	(11.07)
CAPITAL				
D. Crocket, owner	$107,500	$ 86,300	$ 21,200	24.57
Total Liabilities and Capital	$216,000	$208,300	$ 7,700	3.70

Performing Horizontal Analysis

Once the figures for two or more balance sheets or income statements are prepared on the comparative statement, the next step is to analyze these figures. This can be done through **horizontal analysis,** which means that the numbers for the different periods are compared from left to right across each horizontal line. The comparison is made in dollar amounts and in percent form. When finding the percent, it is important to use the correct base year. The earliest year is the base year. In the preceding statement, the base year is last year's figures.

Example 1 For Wood World Company, what is the change in cash in amount and in percent form between last year and this year? Is the change an increase or a decrease?

Step 1 Subtract the cash figure for this year from the figure for last year to find the change.

Last year $7,500
This year − 7,000
            $ 500

Step 2 Divide the change by the cash figure for the base year (R = P/B).

$$\frac{\$500}{\$7{,}500} = 6.67\%$$

Step 3 Determine whether the change is a decrease or an increase by looking at the base figure. (Since the base figure is higher, there was a decrease in the figure for the next year.)

Decrease

Answer There was a 6.67% decrease in the cash figure.

NOTE: When showing a decrease in a financial statement in the amount column, enclose the dollar figure and the percent figure in parentheses.

Self-Check

For Wood World, determine the amount and the percent change in each of the following.

a) The accounts receivable figure   _____

b) The accounts payable figures for this year and for last year   _____

Determine whether the change is an increase or a decrease.

ANSWERS (a) $4,000; 23.53%; increase; (b) ($8,000); (21.05%); decrease

Horizontal analysis for the income statement follows the same procedure as horizontal analysis for the balance sheet. Find the difference between each year's figures, and then divide that difference by the base amount. The exception is the case where there is a change from a loss to a profit. If the figures for the base year have a negative amount, the percent change is not determined, because you would be dividing by a negative number. The amount of change can still be found, but it is determined by adding the two amounts instead of subtracting. In fact, whenever one of the amounts to be compared in a statement is negative, the amount change is found by totaling the figure for the differemt time periods. To illustrate further, a shortened version of a comparative income statement is shown on the top of page 553.

In comparing the net income, we see that the amount of change is $1,800 ($1,300 + ($500)). The $500 in April is a loss or a negative number. Since this is the earlier time period, it is the base figure. In the comparative statement, the amount of the change is shown as an increase but no percent change is given.

Columbia Air Conditioning Company
Comparative Income Statement
April and May, 19___

	May	April	Amount Increase or (Decrease)	% Change
Net Sales	$25,000	$21,000	$4,000	19.05
Cost of Goods Sold	− 17,500	− 18,000	(500)	(2.78)
Gross Profit	$ 7,500	$ 4,000	$3,500	87.5
Expenses	− 6,200	− 4,500	− 1,700	37.78
Net Income	$ 1,300	$(500)	$1,800	—

Performing Vertical Analysis

With **vertical analysis,** percents are used to make comparisons for figures on a financial statement for the same period. Each item in the financial statement is compared to a specific dollar figure from the statement. The specific figure to which the figures are compared is called the base. The comparisons are made for items that are recorded for the same time period, instead of for two or more time periods as with horizontal analysis.

For the balance sheet, all the separate asset listings are compared to total assets. Total assets is the base for this section of the statement. All the separate liability listings are compared to the total liabilities and capital. Likewise, each listing under capital is compared to the total liabilities and capital. Note, however, that since the total assets is equal to the total of liabilities and capital, the actual dollar figure used as the base is the same. Often the separate vertical analysis of two or more time periods is given in the same statement so that the percents are even more meaningful. Here is a simplified illustration.

Eastern Farm Supplies
Comparative Balance Sheets and Vertical Analysis
December 31, This Year and Last Year

	This Year Amount	This Year Percent	Last Year Amount	Last Year Percent
ASSETS				
Cash	$ 8,000	7.92	$10,000	10.31
Accounts Receivable	42,000	41.58	39,000	40.21
Inventory	51,000	50.50	48,000	49.48
Total Assets	$101,000	100	$97,000	100
LIABILITIES				
Accounts Payable	$ 23,000	22.77	$30,000	30.93
Wages Payable	45,000	44.55	41,000	42.27
Total Liabilities	$ 68,000	67.33*	$71,000	73.20
CAPITAL				
F. Gray, Owner	$ 33,000	32.67	$26,000	26.80
Total Liabilities and Capital	$101,000	100	$97,000	100

*Notice that because of rounding not all totals will add to exact figures.

Example 2   In the Eastern Farm Supplies statement, fill in the percent for accounts payable for this year.

Solution   Divide the accounts payable by the base, which is the total for liabilities and capital (remember that the base = 100%).

$$\frac{23,000}{101,000} = 22.77\%$$

Answer   The accounts-payable percent is 22.77%.

Self-Check

In the previous statement, find the percents for wages payable and owner's capital for this year.

ANSWERS   Wage payable = 44.55%; owner's capital = 32.67%

Vertical analysis of income statements uses net sales as the base. All individual listings in the statement are compared to the net sales figure and presented in percent form. Comparing percents can point out efficiencies and inefficiencies that otherwise may be difficult to see. Remember that net sales is found by subtracting sales returns and allowances from gross sales. As with the balance sheet, vertical analysis is often done for two periods, which are shown on one comparative statement. An illustration of this type of statement is shown here.

Craig Craft Company
Comparative Income Statement and Vertical Analysis

	This Year Amount	Percent	Last Year Amount	Percent
Gross Sales	$28,000	107.69	$21,500	113.16
Less Returns	2,000	7.69	2,500	13.16
Net Sales	$26,000	100.00	$19,000	100.00
Cost of Goods Sold	18,000	69.23	12,000	63.16
Gross Profit	$ 8,000	30.77	$ 7,000	36.84
Operating Expenses	6,300	24.23	7,400	38.95
Net Income	$ 1,700	6.54	$ (400)	—

Note in the Craig Craft Company statement that no percent is given for net income for last year. This is because the $400 is a loss and negative percents are not shown.

Example 3   In the statement above, find the percent of gross profit for this year.

Solution   Divide the gross profit by the net sales, which is the base (R = P/B).

$$\frac{\$8,000}{\$26,000} = 30.77\%$$

Answer   The percent gross profit is 30.77%.

Self-Check

In the previous statement, find the percent of operating expenses for this year and for last year.

ANSWERS This year: 24.23%; last year: 38.95%

Assignment 14.2

Accounting and Analysis

1. Prepare a horizontal analysis of the balance sheet of the Sunrise Lighting Company. Round to the nearest hundredth of a percent.

Sunrise Lighting Company
Comparative Balance Sheet
December 31, This Year, and December 31, Last Year

	This Year	Last Year	Amount Increase or (Decrease)	% Change
ASSETS				
Current Assets:				
Cash	$ 10,000	$ 12,000	$ (2,000)	(16.66%)
Accounts Receivable	21,000	19,800	1,200	6.06%
Supplies	1,100	900	200	22.22%
Merchandise Inventory	42,000	39,000	3,000	7.69%
Total Current Assets	$ 74,100	$ 71,700	$ 2,400	3.35%
Plant Assets:				
Equipment (less depreciation)	$ 8,000	$ 9,100	$ (1,100)	(12.09%)
Building (less depreciation)	70,000	75,200	(5,200)	(6.91%)
Land	40,000	40,000	∅	∅
Total Plant Assets	$118,000	$124,300	$ (6,300)	(5.07%)
Total Assets	$192,100	$196,000	$ (3,900)	(1.99%)
LIABILITIES				
Current Liabilities:				
Accounts Payable	$ 40,000	$ 49,500	$ (9,500)	(19.19%)
Notes Payable	5,000	8,000	(3,000)	(37.5%)
Total Current Liabilities	$ 45,000	$ 57,500	$ (12,500)	(21.74%)
Long-term Liabilities:				
Mortgage Payable	$ 24,400	$ 27,030	$ (2,630)	(9.73%)
Total Liabilities	$ 69,400	$ 84,530	$ (15,130)	(17.9%)
CAPITAL				
C. Crystal, Capital	$122,700	$111,470	$ 11,230	10.07%
Total Liabilities and Capital	$192,100	$196,000	$ (3,900)	(1.99%)

Percent change $= \dfrac{\text{Increase or (decrease)}}{\text{\$ for base year}}$

Example:
$\dfrac{(\$2,000)}{\$12,000} = (16.66\%)$

continued

Assignment 14.2 *continued*

2. Prepare a vertical analysis for Sunrise Lighting Company for this year's balance sheet. Round to the nearest hundredth of a percent.

Sunrise Lighting Company
Balance Sheet
December 31, This Year

		Percent
ASSETS		
Current Assets:		
Cash	$ 10,000	5.21%
Accounts Receivable	21,000	10.93%
Supplies	1,100	.57%
Merchandise Inventory	42,000	21.86%
Total Current Assets	$ 74,100	38.57%
Plant Assets:		
Equipment (less depreciation)	$ 8,000	4.16%
Building (less depreciation)	70,000	36.44%
Land	40,000	20.82%
Total Plant Assets	$118,000	61.43%
Total Assets	$192,100	100%
LIABILITIES		
Current Liabilities:		
Accounts Payable	$ 40,000	20.82%
Notes Payable	5,000	2.60%
Total Current Liabilities	$ 45,000	23.43%
Long-term Liabilities:		
Mortgage Payable	$ 24,400	12.70%
Total Liabilities	$ 69,400	36.13%
CAPITAL		
C. Crystal, Capital	$122,700	63.87%
Total Liabilities and Capital	$192,100	100%

Percent = $\dfrac{\text{Separate asset listing}}{\text{Total assets}}$

Example:
$\dfrac{\text{Cash}}{\text{Total assets}}$

$\dfrac{\$10,000}{\$192,100} = 5.21\%$

$\dfrac{\text{Separate liability listing}}{\text{Total liabilities and capital}}$

Example:
$\dfrac{\text{A/P}}{\text{Total liabilities and capital}}$

$\dfrac{\$40,000}{\$192,100} = 20.82\%$

$\dfrac{\text{Separate capital listing}}{\text{Total liabilities and capital}}$

continued

Assignment 14.2 continued

3. Carry out a horizontal analysis of the following statement. Round to the nearest hundredth of a percent.

Sunrise Lighting Company
Comparative Income Statement
For the Year Ended December 31, This Year, and December 31, Last Year

	This Year	Last Year	Amount Increase or (Decrease)	% Change
Sales	$84,000	$79,000	$ 5,000	6.33%
Less: Sales returns and Allowances	8,000	12,000	(4,000)	(33.33%)
Net Sales	$76,000	$67,000	9,000	13.43%
Cost of Goods Sold	35,000	32,400	2,600	8.02%
Gross Profit	$41,000	$34,600	6,400	18.50%
Operating Expenses	12,000	14,000	(2,000)	(14.29%)
NET INCOME	$29,000	$20,600	8,400	40.78%

Percent change
$$= \frac{\text{Increase or (decrease)}}{\text{\$ for base year}}$$

Example: $\dfrac{\$5,000}{\$79,000} = 6.33\%$

4. Compute a vertical study for the Sunrise Lighting Company for this year. Round to the nearest hundredth of a percent.

	$	%
Sales	$84,000	110.53%
Less: Sales Returns and Allowances	8,000	10.53%
Net Sales	$76,000	100%
Cost of Goods Sold	35,000	46.05%
Gross Profit	$41,000	53.95%
Operating Expenses	12,000	15.79%
NET INCOME	$29,000	38.16%

Individual listing
Net sales

Example:
$\dfrac{\text{Sales}}{\text{Net sales}} = \dfrac{\$84,000}{\$76,000} = 110.53\%$

continued

Assignment 14.2 continued

5. Prepare a horizontal analysis of the following statement. Also prepare a vertical analysis separately for each year. Round to the nearest hundredth of a percent.

Toro Manufacturing
Comparative Balance Sheet
December 31, This Year, and December 31, Last Year

ASSETS	This Year	Last Year	Horizontal Analysis Amount Increase or (Decrease)	% Change	Vertical Analysis This Year	Last Year
Current Assets:						
Cash	$ 12,000	$ 14,100	$ (2,100)	(14.89%)	3.13%	3.70%
Accounts Receivable	21,000	19,000	2,000	10.53%	5.48%	4.99%
Office Supplies	2,400	2,200	200	9.09%	.63%	.58%
Inventories	63,000	70,500	(7,500)	(10.64%)	16.43%	18.51%
Total Current Assets	$ 98,400	$105,800	$ (7,400)	(6.99%)	25.67%	27.78%
Plant Assets:						
Land	$ 80,000	$ 80,000	$ Ø	Ø	20.87%	21.01%
Building (less depreciation)	139,000	144,000	(5,000)	(3.47%)	36.25%	37.87%
Equipment (less depreciation)	46,000	51,000	(5,000)	(9.80%)	12%	13.39%
Total Plant Assets	$285,000	$275,000	$ 10,000	3.64%	74.33%	72.22%
Total Assets	$383,400	$380,800	$ 2,600	.68%	100%	100%
LIABILITIES						
Current Liabilities:						
Notes Payable	$ 18,000	$ 21,000	$ (3,000)	(14.29%)	4.69%	5.51%
Accounts Payable	74,000	87,400	(13,400)	(15.33%)	19.30%	22.95%
Total Current Liabilities	$ 92,000	$108,400	$ (16,400)	(15.13%)	24%	28.47%
Long-term Liabilities:						
Mortgage Payable	$118,000	$125,300	$ (7,300)	(5.83%)	30.78%	32.90%
Total Liabilities	$210,000	$233,700	$ (23,700)	(10.14%)	54.77%	61.37%
CAPITAL						
P. Atwood, Owner	$173,400	$147,100	$ 26,300	17.88%	45.23%	38.63%
Total Liabilities and Capital	$383,400	$380,800	$ 2,600	.68%	100%	100%

continued

NAME   DATE   SECTION

Assignment 14.2 *continued*

6. Prepare a horizontal analysis for the following comparative income statement. Also prepare a vertical analysis of net sales for each year. Round to the nearest hundredth of a percent.

Toro Manufacturing
Comparative Income Statement
For Year Ending December 31, This Year, and December 31, Last Year

	This Year	Last Year	Horizontal Analysis Amount Increase or (Decrease)	% Change	Vertical Analysis % This Year	Last Year
Gross Sales	$217,000	$199,000	$ 18,000	9.05%	105.60%	110.68%
Less: Returns and Allowances	11,500	19,200	(7,700)	(40.10%)	5.60%	10.68%
Net Sales	$205,500	$179,800	25,700	14.29%	100%	100%
Cost of Goods Sold	100,200	90,000	10,200	11.33%	48.76%	50.06%
Gross Profit	$105,300	$ 80,800	24,500	30.32%	51.24%	44.94%
Expenses						
Salaries	$ 57,480	$ 65,700	(8,220)	(12.51%)	27.97%	36.54%
Advertising	10,610	3,200	7,410	231.56%	5.16%	1.78%
Interest	8,800	9,300	(500)	(5.38%)	4.28%	5.17%
Utilities	2,500	1,980	520	26.26%	1.22%	1.10%
Supplies	3,100	4,600	(1,500)	(32.61%)	1.51%	2.56%
Total Expenses	$ 82,490	$ 84,780	(2,290)	(2.70%)	40.14%	47.15%
NET INCOME	$ 22,810	$ (3,980)	26,790	Ø	11.10%	Ø

14.3 Financial Ratios

In addition to horizontal and vertical analysis of financial statements, another measure for the financial condition of a business is the use of **financial ratios**. A ratio expresses the relationship between two numbers. It can be expressed in fractional form such as $\frac{2}{3}$, or as 2:3, or as a percent. (For a more detailed explanation of ratios, please refer to Chapter 4.)

Financial ratios make use of the amounts given in the balance sheet and the income statement. Although there are many different ratios that can be used, this section will present a few of the more important ones: current ratio, acid-test ratio, ratio of plant assets to long-term liabilities, ratio of owner's equity to liabilities, and ratio of net income to owner's equity. It is very important to realize that a "good" financial ratio varies according to the type of industry and company. Ratios used by themselves are not a realistic financial analysis. Dun & Bradstreet, a credit-reporting service company, publishes a report that gives industry averages for different ratios according to type of business. This can be used as a basis for comparison.

For the ratios used in this section, the amounts are taken from the comparative statements shown here for Brite Art Supply Company.

Brite Art Supply
Comparative Balance Sheet
December 31, This Year, and December 31, Last Year

	This Year	Last Year
ASSETS		
Current Assets:		
Cash	$ 26,000	$ 20,500
Accounts Receivable	39,000	35,300
Merchandise Inventory	57,000	45,000
Total Current Assets	$122,000	$100,800
Plant Assets:		
Building (after depreciation)	$ 89,000	$ 91,000
Equipment (after depreciation)	35,000	36,500
Total Plant Assets	$124,000	$127,500
Total Assets	$246,000	$228,300
LIABILITIES		
Current Liabilities:		
Accounts Payable	$ 26,000	$ 22,600
Notes Payable	19,000	20,400
Wages Payable	15,000	18,000
Total Current Liabilities	$ 60,000	$ 61,000
Long-term Liabilities:		
Mortgage Payable	$ 72,800	$ 75,000
Total Liabilities:	$132,800	$136,000
CAPITAL		
B. Brite, Owner	$113,200	$ 92,300
Total Liabilities and Capital	$246,000	$228,300

Accounting and Analysis

Brite Art Supply
Comparative Income Statement
For Years Ended December 31, This Year,
and Ended December 31, Last Year

	This Year	Last Year
Net Sales	$134,000	$126,000
Cost of Goods Sold	70,000	65,000
Gross Profit	$ 64,000	$ 61,000
Operating Expenses	44,000	43,400
NET INCOME	$ 20,000	$ 17,600

Finding Current Ratio

The **current ratio** is found by dividing current assets by current liabilities. It shows the ability of a firm to meet its current obligations (debts). In general, financial analysts agree that a 2 to 1 current ratio is adequate for debt-paying ability. This means that a business has $2 of current assets for each $1 of current liabilities. An "adequate" ratio, however, really depends on the nature of the business and the type and turnover of current assets. For example, a company that has a small inventory and quickly collectible accounts receivable can perform better with a lower current ratio than a company that has little cash and much money tied into large inventories.

Example 1 Find the current ratio for Brite Art Supply for this year.

Solution Apply the formula $\dfrac{\text{Current assets}}{\text{Current liabilities}}$. $\dfrac{\$122,000}{\$60,000} = \dfrac{2.03}{1}$

Answer The current ratio is 2.03 to 1.

Finding Acid-Test Ratio

The **acid-test ratio** is a more rigorous test of a company's ability to meet its short-term debts. It is also referred to as the *quick ratio* because it is a ratio of "quick assets" to current liabilities. *Quick assets* are those current assets that can be turned into cash quickly. These include cash, notes receivable, accounts receivable, and marketable securities (stocks, bonds, and investments that can be turned into cash quickly). Inventories are not considered quick assets because these items have yet to be sold and it would take a significant amount of time to find buyers for the entire inventory at the stated value.

An acid-test ratio of 1 to 1 is considered satisfactory, but, of course, there may be exceptions depending on the type of business.

Example 2 What is the acid-test ratio for Brite Art Supply for this year?

Step 1 Determine quick assets by adding cash plus receivables.

$26,000 Cash
+ 39,000 Accounts receivable
$65,000 Quick assets

Step 2 Apply the formula $\dfrac{\text{Quick assets}}{\text{Current liabilities}}$. $\dfrac{\$65,000}{\$60,000} = \dfrac{1.08}{1}$

Answer The acid-test ratio is 1.08 to 1.

Finding Ratio of Plant Assets to Long-Term Liabilities

In order to borrow money, companies will often pledge their plant assets as security for a loan. This ratio gives an indication of the ability of the business to borrow additional funds over a long period of time. It can be used as a measure of security of a firm for the mortgage and bondholders, and it is found by dividing plant assets by long-term liabilities. The general "safe" ratio is a ratio of 2:1. This can vary considerably according to the type of plant assets and the business itself. Also, it is important to remember that plant assets are recorded at book value. The amount actually received for them if they had to be sold may not be the same as book value.

Example 3 What is the ratio of plant assets to long-term liabilities for Brite Art Supply for this year?

Solution Apply the formula $\dfrac{\text{Plant assets}}{\text{Long-term liabilities}}$. $\dfrac{\$124,000}{\$72,800} = \dfrac{1.7}{1}$

Answer The ratio of plant assets to long-term liabilities is 1.7 to 1.

Finding Ratio of Owner's Equity to Total Liabilities

Owner's equity has the same meaning as owner's capital. This ratio shows the investment of the owner compared to the investment of the creditors. This ratio is of particular interest to the analyst because owner equity acts as a buffer in absorbing losses. The higher the investment of the owner in relation to creditors, the more losses can be absorbed by the owners themselves before the creditors begin to feel any losses. So, from the creditors' viewpoint, the higher the ratio, the less risk there is in lending money to the company. Of course, keep in mind that ratios are just indicators and do not give a complete analysis of a business by themselves.

Example 4 Determine the ratio of owner's equity to total liabilities for Brite Art Supply for this year.

Solution Apply the formula $\dfrac{\text{Owner's equity}}{\text{Total liabilities}}$. $\dfrac{\$113,200}{\$132,800} = \dfrac{.85}{1}$

Answer The ratio of owner's equity to total liabilities is .85 to 1.

Finding Ratio of Net Income to Owner's Equity

This ratio measures the income yielded on the amount invested by the owner. Usually this ratio is expressed in the form of a percent, which is often referred to as the **rate of return on owner's equity,** or **return on investment (ROI).** This percent then can be compared to current interest rates, stock market figures, yields on other investments, and so on. In this way the owner can compare his or her return on investments to other yields that might have been received if the capital had been invested in another manner. However, this ratio does not measure the potential yield over the years, and this, along with other factors, should be considered when analyzing investments.

Example 5 Find the ratio of net income to owner's equity for Brite Art Supply for this year.

Solution Apply the formula $\dfrac{\text{Net income}}{\text{Owner's capital}}$. $\dfrac{\$20,000}{\$113,200} = \dfrac{.18}{1}$, or 18%

Answer The ratio of net income to owner's equity is 18% (rounded to a whole percent).

Self-Check

Determine each of the following ratios for Brite Art Supply for the year ended December 31, last year.

1. Current ratio
2. Acid-test ratio
3. Ratio of plant assets to long-term liabilities
4. Ratio of owner's equity to total liabilities
5. Ratio of net income to owner's equity (percent form)

ANSWERS 1. $\dfrac{\$100,800}{\$61,000} = \dfrac{1.65}{1}$ 2. $\dfrac{\$20,500 + \$35,300}{61,000} = \dfrac{.91}{1}$ 3. $\dfrac{\$127,500}{\$75,000} = \dfrac{1.7}{1}$ 4. $\dfrac{\$92,300}{\$136,000} = \dfrac{.68}{1}$ 5. $\dfrac{\$17,600}{\$92,300} = 19\%$

INTERNATIONAL COMPETITION

On March 25, 1957, the treaty of Rome was signed. This treaty established the European Common Market, or European Economic Community. Under the terms of the agreement, Belgium, France, West Germany, Italy, Luxembourg, and the Netherlands did away with their mutual tariff barriers. This action was aimed at improving the economies of European nations and at making European goods competitive with those produced by the United States and Great Britain.

ACCOUNTING CROSSWORD PUZZLE

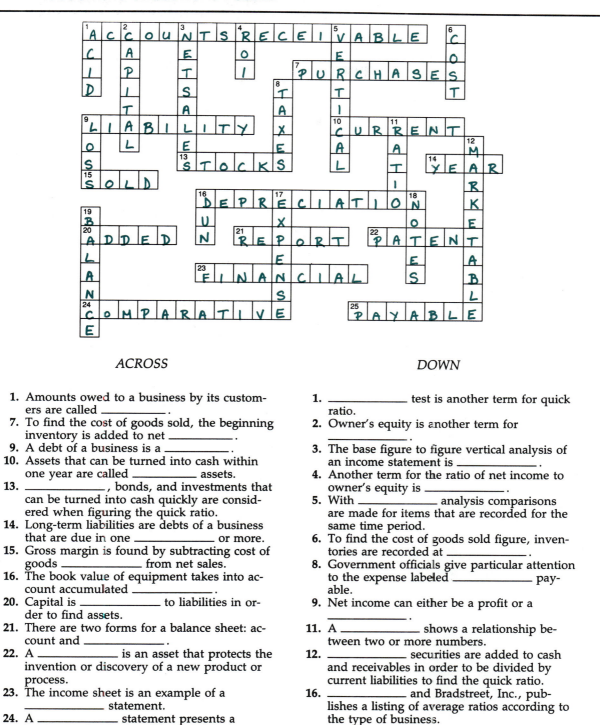

ACROSS

1. Amounts owed to a business by its customers are called _____.
7. To find the cost of goods sold, the beginning inventory is added to net _____.
9. A debt of a business is a _____.
10. Assets that can be turned into cash within one year are called _____ assets.
13. _____, bonds, and investments that can be turned into cash quickly are considered when figuring the quick ratio.
14. Long-term liabilities are debts of a business that are due in one _____ or more.
15. Gross margin is found by subtracting cost of goods _____ from net sales.
16. The book value of equipment takes into account accumulated _____.
20. Capital is _____ to liabilities in order to find assets.
21. There are two forms for a balance sheet: account and _____.
22. A _____ is an asset that protects the invention or discovery of a new product or process.
23. The income sheet is an example of a _____ statement.
24. A _____ statement presents a business's financial condition for the current period and for previous period(s).
25. Amounts owed to creditors for goods and services purchased on credit are accounts _____.

DOWN

1. _____ test is another term for quick ratio.
2. Owner's equity is another term for _____.
3. The base figure to figure vertical analysis of an income statement is _____.
4. Another term for the ratio of net income to owner's equity is _____.
5. With _____ analysis comparisons are made for items that are recorded for the same time period.
6. To find the cost of goods sold figure, inventories are recorded at _____.
8. Government officials give particular attention to the expense labeled _____ payable.
9. Net income can either be a profit or a _____.
11. A _____ shows a relationship between two or more numbers.
12. _____ securities are added to cash and receivables in order to be divided by current liabilities to find the quick ratio.
16. _____ and Bradstreet, Inc., publishes a listing of average ratios according to the type of business.
17. Wages payable is an example of an operating _____.
18. Two types of receivable are accounts and _____.
19. The _____ sheet gives the financial condition of a firm for a particular point in time.

Accounting and Analysis 567

Assignment 14.3

Accounting and Analysis

Figure each of the following financial ratios for this year for Sunrise Lighting Company by using the figures in the financial statements in Assignment 14.2, Questions 1–3.

1. Current ratio — 1.65 to 1 — $\dfrac{\$74{,}100}{\$45{,}000} = \dfrac{1.646}{1}$

2. Acid-test ratio — .69 to 1 — $\dfrac{\$31{,}000}{\$45{,}000} = \dfrac{.688}{1}$

3. Ratio of plant assets to long-term liabilities — 4.84 to 1 — $\dfrac{\$118{,}000}{\$24{,}400} = \dfrac{4.836}{1}$

4. Ratio of owner's equity to total liabilities — 1.77 to 1 — $\dfrac{\$122{,}700}{\$69{,}400} = \dfrac{1.768}{1}$

5. Ratio of net income to owner's equity — .24 to 1 or 24% — $\dfrac{\$29{,}000}{\$122{,}700} = \dfrac{.236}{1}$

For Toro Manufacturing Company, use the figures in the financial statements in Assignment 14.2, Questions 5 and 6, to figure the following ratios for each year:

	This Year		Last Year
Current ratio	6. 1.07 to 1	11.	.98 to 1
Acid test ratio	7. .36 to 1	12.	.31 to 1
Ratio of plant assets to long-term liabilities	8. 2.42 to 1	13.	2.19 to 1
Ratio of owner's equity to total liabilities	9. .83 to 1	14.	.63 to 1
Ratio of net income to owner's equity	10. .13 to 1 or 13%	15.	(.03) to 1 (loss) or (3%) loss

Use the following space to solve Questions 6–15.

6. $\dfrac{\$98{,}400}{\$92{,}000} = \dfrac{1.069}{1}$

7. $\dfrac{\$33{,}000}{\$92{,}000} = \dfrac{.358}{1}$

8. $\dfrac{\$285{,}000}{\$118{,}000} = \dfrac{2.415}{1}$

9. $\dfrac{\$173{,}400}{\$210{,}000} = \dfrac{.825}{1}$

10. $\dfrac{\$22{,}810}{\$173{,}400} = \dfrac{.131}{1}$

11. $\dfrac{\$105{,}800}{\$108{,}400} = \dfrac{.976}{1}$

12. $\dfrac{\$33{,}100}{\$108{,}400} = \dfrac{.305}{1}$

13. $\dfrac{\$275{,}000}{\$125{,}300} = \dfrac{2.194}{1}$

14. $\dfrac{\$147{,}100}{\$233{,}700} = \dfrac{.629}{1}$

15. $\dfrac{(\$3{,}980)}{147{,}100} = \dfrac{(.027)}{1}$

14.4 Bar Graphs and Pictograms

A **graph** is a visual representation of statistical data. Your role in the business world may demand that you prepare material in this way. It will almost surely require that you be able to interpret graphs and understand what they show.

Generally, graphs make complex data easier to grasp, pointing out how one set of facts relates to another. For instance, if six salespeople each sell a different amount of product, you may want to illustrate the comparison by preparing a graph, rather than by simply presenting a column of sales figures. In order to aid the viewer in interpretation, give each graph you prepare a title and label its parts clearly.

Some of the common types of graphs used in business are described below.

Simple Bar Graphs

A **simple bar graph** often charts the relationship among items of the same kind. The length of each bar represents the amount or magnitude of each item being compared. The bars may run either horizontally or vertically.

Example 1 The president of the hardware supply firm for which you work asks you to construct a bar graph comparing the amounts of paint sold by the following salespeople during a 30-day period: Andrews, 350 gallons; Barth, 590 gallons; Carlson, 90 gallons; Dealy; 450 gallons; Earl, 200 gallons; and Firth, 500 gallons.

Step 1   On a piece of graph paper, place the names of the six salespeople down the page, or vertically. Leave an equal amount of space between each name.

Step 2   Horizontally, across the page, indicate numbers of gallons sold, from 0 to 600. Use increments of 50 and space them evenly.

Step 3   Plot the sales volume of each person in the space beside the name, using a darkened bar.

Answer   The completed simple bar graph is shown below.

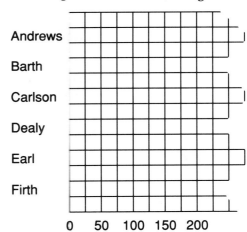

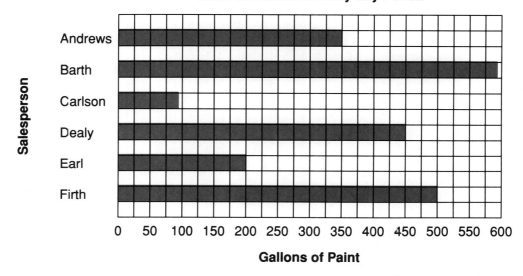

Sales of Paint in a Thirty-day Period

Accounting and Analysis   **571**

Component Bar Graphs

A **component bar graph** divides each bar into parts, allowing you to show relationships *within* a category in addition to those among categories. Generally, the largest value is placed first, nearest the base or left edge of the graph. It is particularly important to provide a key with this type of bar graph to enable the viewer to interpret the graph correctly.

Example 2 Your president at the hardware supply company wants to see on a graph how much of each kind of paint the six salespeople sold during the 30-day period referred to in Example 1. The amounts were: Andrews, 200 gallons latex, 100 gallons high gloss enamel, 50 gallons matte enamel; Barth, 300 gallons latex, 200 gallons high gloss enamel, 90 gallons matte enamel; Carlson, 50 gallons latex, 30 gallons high gloss enamel, 10 gallons matte enamel; Dealy, 300 gallons latex, 90 gallons high gloss enamel, 60 gallons matte enamel; Earl, 100 gallons latex, 60 gallons high gloss enamel, 40 gallons matte enamel; Firth, 250 gallons latex, 200 gallons high gloss enamel, 50 gallons matte enamel.

Step 1 Set up the graph exactly as in Example 1, but do not shade in the bars.

Step 2 Develop a key, choosing a different type of shading or different color for each kind of paint.

Step 3 Shade in the bars, according to type of paint, dividing each bar into components at the same scale as that used at the bottom of the graph where the total number of gallons is shown.

Answer The completed component bar graph is shown below.

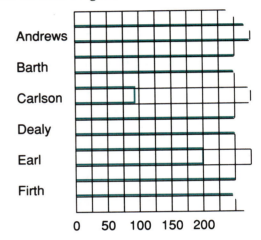

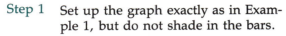

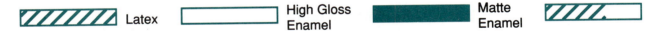

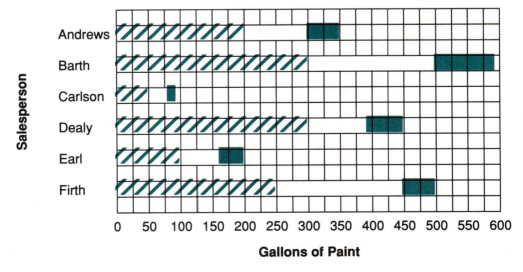

Self-Check

1. Fill in the simple bar graph below, given the following information: The A. C. Robards Company has three assembly plants. Plant One has 50 employees, plant Two has 35 employees, and plant Three has 25 employees.

   Plant: One, Two, Three
   Number of Employees: 0 5 10 15 20 25 30 35 40 45 50 55 60 65 70 75 80 85 90 95

2. At its three plants, A. C. Robards Company employs people of various ages. Show on a component bar graph the following data:

   a) Plant One has 30 employees between 20 and 30 years of age; 10 between 30 and 40; and 10 over 40.

   b) Plant Two has 15 employees between 20 and 30 years of age; 10 between 30 and 40; and 10 over 40.

   c) Plant Three has 10 employees between 20 and 30 years of age; 10 between 30 and 40; and 5 over 40.

   Plant: One, Two, Three
   Number of Employees: 0 5 10 15 20 25 30 35 40 45 50 55 60 65 70 75 80 85 90 95

   Key: ☐ _____ ☐ _____ ☐ _____

ANSWERS

Plant: One (50), Two (35), Three (25)
Number of Employees: 0 5 10 15 20 25 30 35 40 45 50

Plant: One, Two, Three
Number of Employees: 0 5 10 15 20 25 30 35 40 45 50

Key: ☐ 20-30 years ■ 30-40 years ▨ Over 40 years

Accounting and Analysis   573

Pictograms

For purposes of publicity or dramatic effect, a **pictogram** (or **pictograph**) may be used to show data. Each symbol, or picture, represents a specific value.

Example 3 Given the facts about paint sales in the 30-day period described in Example 1, prepare a pictograph for use at your company's annual employee appreciation banquet. The sales were: Andrews, 350 gallons; Barth, 590 gallons; Carlson, 90 gallons; Dealy, 450 gallons; Earl, 200 gallons; and Firth, 500 gallons.

Solution

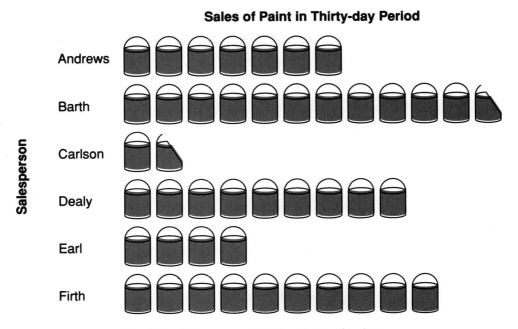

Each bucket represents 50 gallons of paint.

Assignment 14.4

Accounting and Analysis

1. You are an employee of Superspeed Snowmobile Manufacturing Company. To explain the company's operations to its stockholders, prepare a bar graph showing the number of employees in each department.

Executive staff	8	Machinists	20
Clericals	4	Assembly personnel	32
Salespeople	6	Others	5

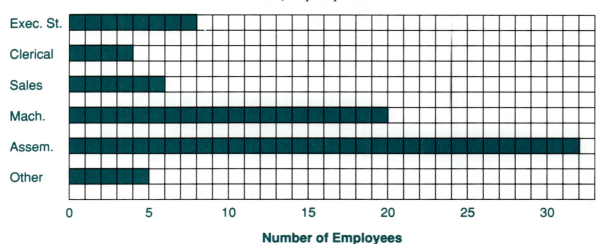

2. Esther Kloppman is preparing a report for the board of directors of Bridge-Riley Department Store. In it, she will show a comparison of sales in several departments for a one-week period. Help her construct a bar graph with the following data.

Department	Sales for One Week
Men's Wear	$55,000.00
Men's Accessories	$12,500.00
Women's Wear	$39,500.00
Women's Accessories	$14,500.00
Children's Wear	$24,000.00
Shoes	$16,000.00

continued

Assignment 14.4 *continued*

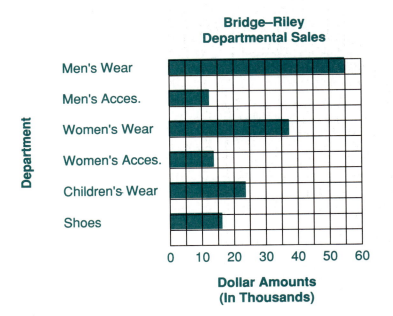

3. The monthly sales of Alberton Kitchenware Company are as follows:

June	$ 550,000
July	$ 580,000
August	$ 490,000
September	$ 650,000
October	$ 840,000
November	$ 990,000
December	$1,200,000

   Design a bar graph to compare these figures.

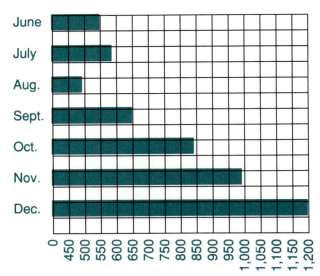

continued

576   Chapter 14

Assignment 14.4 *continued*

4. Power-Ski Inc., manufactures four grades of cross-country skis: standard, deluxe, all-weather, and professional. Using the figures below, design a component bar graph comparing sales for the four quarters of last fiscal year.

	Pairs Sold			
Quarter	Standard	Deluxe	All-Weather	Professional
I	650	550	670	460
II	780	660	840	740
III	770	730	700	600
IV	340	240	320	210

Yearly Sales, Power–Ski Incorporated

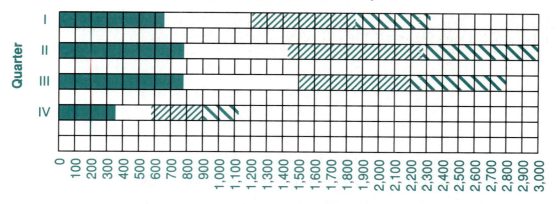

Number of Pairs Sold

Key
- Standard
- Deluxe
- All-weather
- Professional

Accounting and Analysis **577**

14.5 Circle Graphs and Line Graphs

Circle Graphs

To show the parts of a whole in terms of percent, you might draw a **circle graph,** or **pie chart.** Because every circle contains 360 degrees, each one percent of the circle is equal to 3.6 degrees. Drawing lines from the center of the circle to its edges, you can symbolize graphically the parts of any whole, or 100%.

For purposes of clarity, use a larger circle when showing more and smaller parts. If the parts you are comparing are not expressed as percents, you must convert them to percents before constructing the circle graph.

Example 1 Help Mavis Rodrick prepare a circle graph to show the types of investments held by the Buford Charitable Foundation. These investments include real estate, 50%; common stocks, 25%; and municipal bonds, 25%.

Step 1 Multiply each of the percents by 360°, the number of degrees in a circle. Check yourself by totaling the degrees found. They must equal 360°.

$$.5 \times 360° = 180°$$
$$.25 \times 360° = 90°$$
$$.25 \times 360° = 90°$$
$$100\% = 360°$$

Step 2 Draw a cricle. In this case, it will not have to be very large, because you are dividing it into only three areas.

Step 3 Using the center of the circle as your reference point, measure the number of degrees for each segment and draw lines to the edge of the circle.

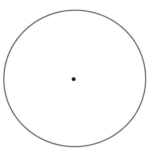

Answer Investments held by the Buford Charitable Foundation:

Self-Check

In preparing a historical report on changes in federal government spending, Igor Pinski must develop a circle graph showing how the federal budget was spent in 1958. Aid him in doing so, on the basis of the following facts: Of each dollar, 59 cents went for national defense, 10 cents for interest on the national debt, 7 cents for veterans' benefits, 7 cents for agriculture, 2 cents toward retirement of the national debt, and the rest for other purposes.

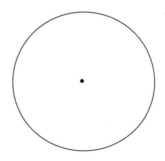

ANSWER

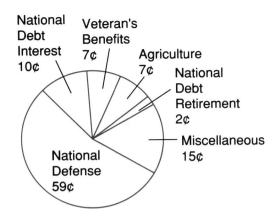

Line Graphs

When there is a limited amount of statistical data to be presented and, particularly, when a time element is involved in a comparison, you will probably use a **line graph.** Prepare it by plotting points on two *axes,* that is, pairs of intersecting lines. One of these intersecting lines is horizontal, the other is vertical, and the place at which they meet is called the **origin.** The points you plot are joined by a continuous line. Although it is not absolutely necessary, you may find it easier to use graph paper in plotting line graphs.

Example 2 Over a ten-month period, January to October, your distributing company had total monthly sales as follows:

January	$ 50,000	June	$ 80,000
February	$ 75,000	July	$ 90,000
March	$ 90,000	August	$100,500
April	$100,000	September	$120,000
May	$ 85,000	October	$130,000

Step 1 At the left side of the graph—on the vertical axis—list sales figures, beginning with an amount below the lowest actual monthly sales and ending at a figure equal to or above the highest actual sales.

$150,000 ⎤

$ 40,000 ⎦

Step 2 On the horizontal axis, starting at the far left—the origin—list the months, leaving equal spaces between each.

JAN   FEB   MAR   APR

Step 3 Plot each monthly sales figure at the appropriate point of intersection.

Step 4 Connect the points of intersection with a straight line.

Answer The completed line graph is shown on the following page.

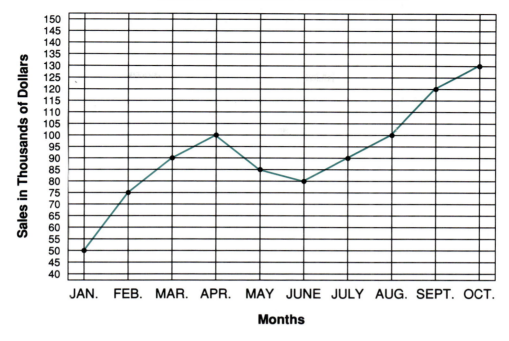

If you are presenting more than one set of figures, use different types of lines, identifying them with a key.

Example 3 Mary Musgrove, president of Musgrove Public Relations, Inc., has her graphics department prepare a line graph comparing weekly business for July with weekly business in June. Construct such a graph on the basis of the information given here.

	Business	
Weeks	June	July
1	$2,500.00	$2,600.00
2	$2,750.00	$2,800.00
3	$2,850.00	$2,650.00
4	$3,000.00	$2,500.00

Step 1   On the vertical axis, list the income figures, beginning with a figure below lowest actual income and ending with a figure equal to or above highest actual income.

Step 2   On the horizontal axis, list the 4 weeks, leaving equal space between them.

Step 3   Plot each month's figures.

Step 4   Connect the points, using a different type of line for each month, and add a key showing the meaning for each type of line.

Answer   The completed line graph is shown on the following page.

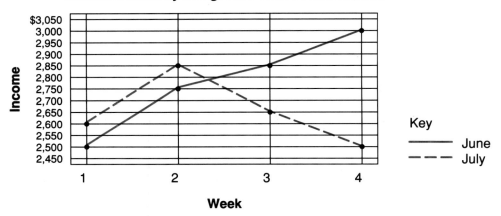

Self-Check

Over a one-week period, your company, Bendamin Auto Sales, ran a competition among its three salespeople. Construct a line graph comparing their performances.

| | | Salesperson | |
Day	Brownell	Harvey	Zek
Monday	$6,000	$4,500	$5,500
Tuesday	$5,200	$4,200	$4,000
Wednesday	$5,000	$4,600	$4,300
Thursday	$4,100	$5,700	$4,600
Friday	$4,500	$5,500	$5,400
Saturday	$4,000	$4,900	$4,600
Sunday	$5,500	$4,500	$4,600

ANSWER

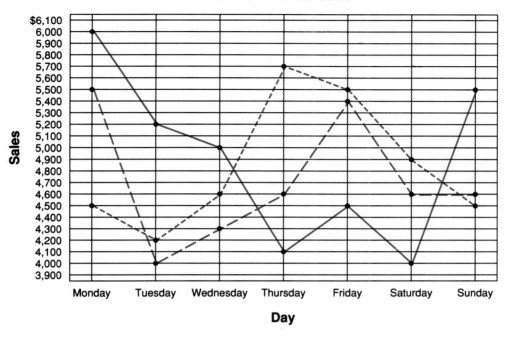

Assignment 14.5

Accounting and Analysis

1. Bernard Riley works in the publicity department of Imperial Film Studios. Help him prepare a circle graph illustrating how each dollar budgeted for publicity is used.

Newspapers	29% = 104.4°	Special events	14% =	50.4°
Billboards	20% = 72°	Press kits	12% =	43.2°
Magazines	10% = 36°	Direct mail	15% =	54°

   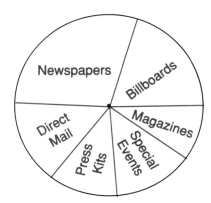

2. The king of Fenwickstein, a tiny country in central Europe, commands his treasury minister to prepare a circle graph showing the source of the country's revenues. Help the minister do so, given these facts about Fenwickstein's annual income: Of each dollar, 50 cents comes from individual income taxes, 30 cents comes from tax on businesses, 12 cents comes from excise taxes, and the remainder comes from various other sources.

   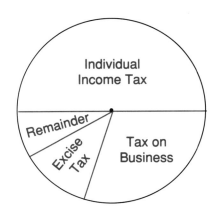

   .50 = 180°
   .30 = 108°
   .12 = 43.2°
   .08 = 28.8°

continued

Assignment 14.5 *continued*

3. Using a circle graph, show how you spend the twenty-four hours of a typical day. Remember that you will have to convert each activity period into a percent of the total day. You may want to limit the graph to five activities or less.

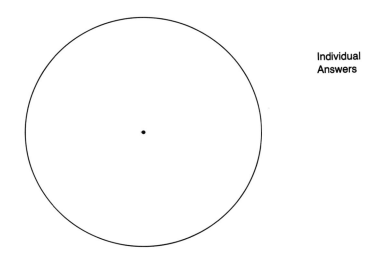

Individual Answers

4. Brownstone Publishing Company made the following amounts in sales to distributors.

January	$12,000	July	$11,000
February	$11,500	August	$10,500
March	$11,000	September	$10,000
April	$12,500	October	$12,000
May	$12,000	November	$11,000
June	$10,000	December	$11,500

Construct a line graph to illustrate these sales figures.

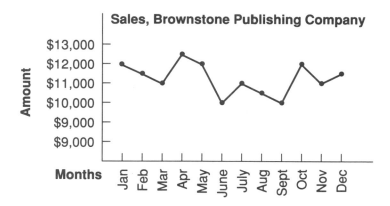

continued

Assignment 14.5 *continued*

5. Pinkly Trust and Savings Bank prepares an annual report showing the new accounts opened during a particular year. Prepare a line graph comparing the data for the four quarters.

Quarter	Individual Checking	Accounts Commercial Checking	Savings
I	45	70	35
II	36	65	30
III	40	42	44
IV	52	60	36

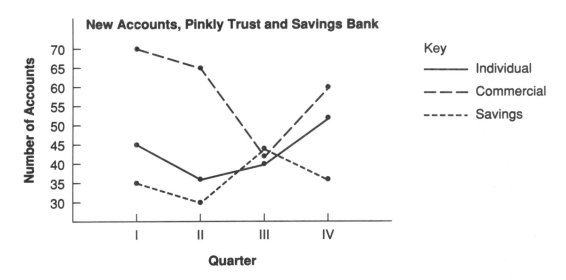

6. During the month of January, average daily temperatures in Bellingham, Washington, were as follows:

Date	Date	Date	Date
1—24°	9—35°	17—28°	25—29°
2—28°	10—30°	18—24°	26—36°
3—29°	11—31°	19—22°	27—40°
4—32°	12—36°	20—28°	28—38°
5—22°	13—28°	21—30°	29—36°
6—25°	14—20°	22—32°	30—35°
7—30°	15—25°	23—25°	31—30°
8—30°	16—28°	24—28°	

Prepare a line graph to illustrate these figures.

continued

Assignment 14.5 *continued*

Use this space to draw the graph for Question 6.

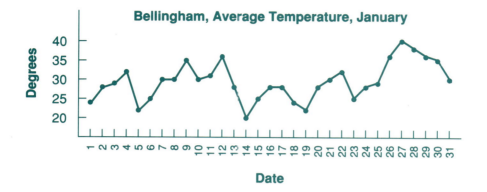

Comprehensive Problems for Chapter 14

Accounting and Analysis

1. Quality Paper has a capital value of $123,000. It has $19,000 in cash on hand, $260,000 in land and building, $77,300 in merchandise, and $45,000 in notes payable. What are the total liabilities and the total assets?

   $\quad\ \ $ $ 19,000 $\qquad\qquad$ $356,300 Assets
   $\quad\quad\ $ 260,000 $\qquad\ \ -$ 183,000 Capital
   $\quad+\ \ $ 77,300 $\qquad\qquad$ $173,300 Liabilities $\qquad$ $356,300 assets
   $\quad\quad\ $ 356,300 Total assets $\qquad\qquad\qquad\qquad\qquad$ $173,300 liabilities
   Note: Notes payable figure is not used.

2. What is the cost of goods sold for a firm that has an ending inventory at cost of $34,500, purchases of $131,000, and a beginning inventory at cost of $37,240?

   $\quad\ \ $ $ 37,240 Beginning inv.
   $\quad+\ $ 131,000 Purchases
   $\quad\quad\ $ $168,240 Cost of goods avail. $\qquad\qquad$ $133,740 cost
   $\quad-\ \ $ 34,500 Less end inv. $\qquad\qquad\qquad\qquad$ of goods sold
   $\quad\quad\ $ $133,740 Cost of goods sold

3. Determine the gross profit and the net income and prepare an income statement for Vance Associated for the period ending December 31, 19__, given the following information.

Gross sales:	$335,000	Cost of goods sold:	$185,600
Selling expense:	$ 64,000	Rent expense:	$ 12,000
Depreciation expense:	$ 9,200	General expenses:	$ 40,000
Salaries expense:	$ 20,000	Sales returns and allowances:	$ 20,000

Vance Associated
Income Statement
For the Period Ending December 31, 19__

Gross Sales		$335,000
Less: Sales returns and allowances		20,000
Net Sales		$315,000
Cost of goods sold		185,600
Gross profit		$129,400
Expenses		
$\quad$Selling expense	$64,000	
$\quad$Depreciation expense	9,200	
$\quad$Salaries expense	20,000	
$\quad$Rent expense	12,000	
$\quad$General expenses	40,000	
Total expenses		145,200
Net loss		$(15,800)

continued

Comprehensive Problems *continued*

4. Murray's Hobby Shop owes $41,270 to its suppliers. The store also has notes payable to $5,100, wages payable of $20,000, and interest payable of $6,334. Total capital amounts to $18,975. If the mortgage due amounts to $72,000, what are the total assets, total liabilities, and total capital?

    Liabilities + Capital = Assets
    $144,704 + $18,975 = $163,679

    $163,679 Total assets,
    $144,704 Total liabilities,
    $ 18,975 Capital

    $ 41,270 A/P
       20,000 Wages
        6,334 Int. payable
        5,100 N/P
    + 72,000 Mortgage due
    $144,704 Total liabilities

5. A profit of $29,143 was declared by Conrad Auto Glass. If operating expenses amounted to $17,643 and cost of goods sold is $126,371, what are the gross margin and the net sales?

    $46,786 gross margin,
    $173,157 net sales

    $ 29,143 Net inc.
    + 17,643 Op. exp.
    $ 46,786 Gross margin
    + 126,371 CGS
    $173,157 Net sales

6. Determine capital and prepare a balance sheet in report form for Kelly's Lawn Care as of December 31, 19__, using the following information.

Salaries payable:	$3,500
Notes payable:	$4,000
Taxes due:	$2,040
Accounts receivable:	$1,870
Equipment:	$6,690
Office furniture:	$ 920

    Kelly's Lawn Care
    Balance Sheet
    December 31, 19__

    Assets

Accounts receivable	$1,870.00
Office furniture	920.00
Equipment	6,690.00
Total assets	9,480.00

    Liabilities

Notes payable	$4,000.00
Salaries payable	3,500.00
Taxes due	2,040.00
Total liabilities	$9,540.00

    Owner's Equity

Kelly, Capital	$ (60.00)
Total liabilities and owner's equity	$9,480.00

continued

Comprehensive Problems *continued*

7. Prepare a horizontal analysis of the following statement. Also, prepare a separate vertical analysis separately for this year.

The Birthday House
Comparative Balance Sheet
December 31, This Year and Last Year

	This Year	Last Year	Horizontal Analysis Amount Increase or (Decrease)	% Change	Vertical Analysis This Year
ASSETS					
Current Assets:					
Cash	$ 22,000	$ 65,100	(43,100)	(66.21%)	2.40%
Accounts Receivable	204,000	191,000	13,000	6.81%	22.27%
Office Supplies	2,700	3,100	(400)	(12.90%)	.29%
Merchandise Inventory	145,000	140,000	5,000	3.57%	15.83%
Total Current Assets	$373,700	$399,200	(25,500)	(6.39%)	40.80%
Plant Assets:					
Land	$120,000	$110,000	10,000	9.09%	13.10%
Building (Less Depreciation)	250,000	279,000	(29,000)	(10.39%)	27.29%
Equipment (Less Depreciation)	172,300	198,400	(26,100)	(13.16%)	18.81%
Total Plant Assets	$542,300	$587,400	(45,100)	(7.68%)	59.20%
Total Assets	$916,000	$986,600	(70,600)	(7.16%)	100%
LIABILITIES					
Current Liabilities:					
Accounts Payable	$260,000	$310,700	(50,700)	(16.32%)	28.38%
Notes Payable	82,400	41,000	41,400	100.98%	9.00%
Total Current Liabilities	$342,400	$351,700	(9,300)	(2.64%)	37.38%
Long-Term Liabilties:					
Mortgage Payable	$310,000	$328,000	(18,000)	(5.49%)	33.84%
Total Liabilities	$652,400	$679,700	(27,300)	(4.02%)	71.22%
CAPITAL					
N. Horn, Owner	$263,600	$306,900	(43,300)	(14.11%)	28.78%
Total Liabilities and Capital	$916,000	$986,600	(70,600)	(7.16%)	100%

continued

Comprehensive Problems *continued*

8. Prepare a horizontal analysis for the following comparative income statement. Also, prepare a vertical analysis of net sales for this year.

The Birthday House
Comparative Income Statement
For Year Ending December 31, This Year, and December 31, Last Year

	This Year	Last Year	Horizontal Analysis Amount Increase or (Decrease)	% Change	Vertical Analysis % This Year
Gross Sales	$423,000	$459,000	(36,000)	(7.84%)	109.87%
Less: Returns and Allowances	58,000	52,000	6,000	11.54%	15.06%
Net Sales	$385,000	$407,000	(22,000)	(5.41%)	100%
Cost of Goods Sold	192,000	221,000	(29,000)	(13.12%)	49.87%
Gross Profit	$193,000	$186,000	7,000	3.76%	50.13%
Expenses					
Salaries	$ 94,700	$ 79,100	15,600	19.72%	24.60%
Advertising	19,000	26,000	(7,000)	(26.92%)	4.94%
Interest	16,500	17,300	(800)	(4.62%)	4.29%
Utilities	2,300	2,100	200	9.52%	.6%
Supplies	4,600	4,300	300	6.98%	1.19%
Total Expenses	$137,100	$128,800	8,300	6.44%	35.61%
NET INCOME	$ 55,900	$ 57,200	(1,300)	(2.27%)	14.52%

9. Use the figures in the financial statements in Questions 7 and 8 to figure each of the following ratios for the Birthday House for this year:

   a) Current ratio

   $$\frac{373{,}700}{342{,}400} = \frac{1.09}{1} \qquad 1.09 : 1$$

   b) Acid-test ratio

   $$\frac{22{,}000 + 204{,}000}{342{,}400} = \frac{226{,}000}{342{,}400} = \frac{1}{.660} \qquad 1 : .66$$

   c) Ratio of plant assets to long-term liabilities

   $$\frac{542{,}300}{310{,}000} = \frac{1.75}{1} \qquad 1.75 : 1$$

continued

Comprehensive Problems *continued*

d) Ratio of owner's equity to total liabilities

$$\frac{263,600}{652,400} = \frac{.4040}{1}$$

.4 : 1

e) Ratio of net income to owner's equity

$$\frac{55,900}{263,600} = \frac{.21206}{1}$$

.21 : 1 or 21.21%

10. In preparing a presentation for the board of directors of Kimball's Department Store, design a line graph comparing the sales in various departments over a three-month period, given the following facts.

Department	June	Sales July	August
Menswear	$16,500	$15,500	$16,000
Sportswear	$14,500	$15,000	$14,500
Children's Clothes	$15,000	$14,300	$14,200
Womenswear	$15,000	$14,600	$15,500

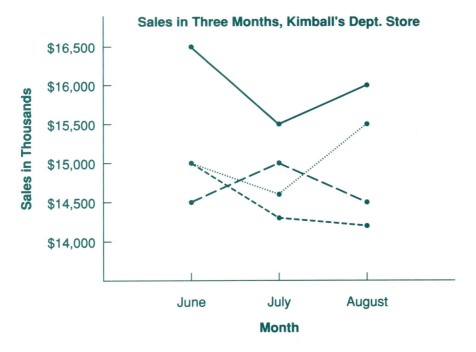

continued

Accounting and Analysis **593**

Comprehensive Problems *continued*

11. The manager of Read-A-Bit Bookstore wants to compare sales by each of her sales personnel for the fiscal year. Help her by preparing a bar graph using the following information.

Salesperson	Total Sales
Dickens	$10,550
Goldsmith	$ 9,650
Hughes	$ 7,925
Keats	$12,600
Shelton	$11,450
Zimbrick	$10,350

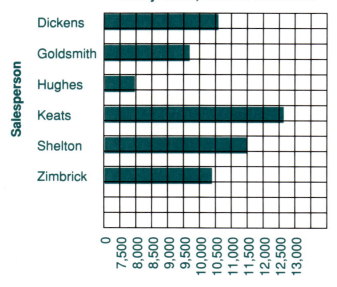

12. Della Tremainian earns $325 a week. Twenty percent of this is withheld for taxes and social security. Della spends $60 for food, $80 for rent, $20 for furniture rental, and $40 for recreation, puts $20 into savings, and uses the rest for miscellaneous expenses. As her budget consultant, prepare a circle graph showing her expense distribution.

    $65 = .20 = 72°   Taxes and Social Security
    $60 = .185 = 66.5° Food
    $80 = .246 = 88.6° Rent
    $20 = .061 = 22.2° Furniture rental
    $40 = .123 = 44.3° Recreation
    $20 = .061 = 22.2° Savings
    $40 = .123 = 44.3° Misc. Expenses

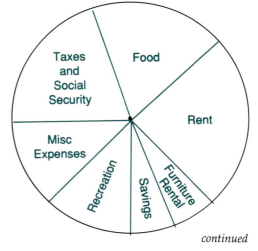

continued

Comprehensive Problems *continued*

13. The Glenvue Health Club has five massuers, all of whom work on an hourly basis. During the month of February, each of them serves both club members and guests. Given the information that follows, prepare a component bar graph comparing the masseurs' work during the month.

	Hours Worked	
Masseur	*Members*	*Guests*
Clinkenburg	120	40
Sullivan	100	30
Bonebender	90	60
Smedly	110	40
Crusherman	80	35

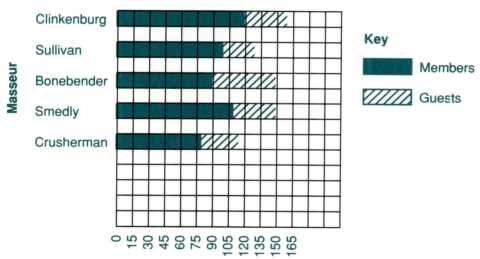

14. As director of the Campout Youth Group, you receive the following information on candy sales for your region: troop A, 420 bars; troop B, 500 bars; troop C, 400 bars; troop D, 610 bars, and troop E, 580 bars. Prepare a pictogram to show sales for your region for this 20-day period.

    Let your students use their imagination with this graph. For the pictogram a variety of images could be used, such as chocolate bars, pennants, tents, hats, etc.

Case 1

You are a financial consultant and have been hired by Quality Frame Shop. The store is considering expanding to more outlets and would like your advice on their operations and on the possibility of obtaining a loan. The first thing you have asked for is an income statement for last year. They have supplied you with the following information:

Gross sales	$112,000
Sales returns	$ 25,000
Beginning inventory at cost	$ 40,000
Ending inventory at cost	$ 49,000
Purchases	$ 60,000
Advertising	$ 10,000
Salaries	$ 18,000
Rent	$ 4,000
Utilities	$ 800

As you can see, the income statement is incomplete and not well organized.

a) Prepare a proper income statement using the figures ab)ve.
b) Carry through with a vertical analysis.
c) List three problem areas in the store's operation that you can see and give suggestions for improving each one.

Case 2

M. Reynolds, the owner of Reynolds Stereo Accessories, asks your help in putting his financial records in good order for December 31 of last year. Given the following information, construct a balance sheet and an income statement and give the following ratio analyses: current ratio, quick ratio, plant assets to long-term liabilities, owner's equity to total liabilities, and ROI.

Ending inventory at cost	$ 49,000
Cash	$ 6,000
Inventory	$ 40,000
Accounts receivable	$ 35,000
Accounts payable	$ 27,000
Equipment (less depreciation)	$ 15,000
Building (less depreciation)	$ 89,000
Mortgage payable	$ 80,000
Notes payable	$ 6,750
Notes receivable	$ 6,000
Beginning inventory at cost	$ 43,000
Interest expense	$ 1,510
Sales returns and allowance	$ 6,000
Interest payable	$ 3,000
Advertising	$ 7,000

Land	$ 30,000
Net purchases	$ 70,000
Wages paid	$ 18,200
Gross sales	$140,000
Salaries paid	$ 22,500
Utilities expense	$ 900
Taxes payable	$ 3,250
M. Reynolds, capital	$101,000

Key Terms

Accounts payable
Accounts receivable
Acid-test ratio
Assets
Balance sheet
Bar graph
Capital
Cash
Circle graph, or pie chart
Comparative statement
Component bar graph
Cost of goods sold
Current assets
Current liabilities
Current ratio
Financial ratios
Graph
Gross margin
Horizontal analysis
Income statement
Liabilities
Line graph
Long-term liabilities
Merchandise inventory
Net income
Net sales
Notes payable
Notes receivable
Operating expenses
Origin
Pictogram, or pictograph
Plant assets
Rate of return on owner's equity, or return on investment (ROI)
Vertical analysis

Key Concepts

- Accounting statements give a concise picture of the financial position of a firm. The two basic financial statements are:
    1. Balance sheet: Gives the financial position of a business on a particular date, showing the assets, the liabilities, and the capital. There are two acceptable forms: the account form and the report form.
    2. Income statement: Gives the operating results of a firm over a period of time, showing revenue, expenses, and a profit or loss.

- The accounting equation used in the balance sheet is:

    $$\text{Assets} = \text{Liabilities} + \text{Capital}.$$

- The basic principle for the income statement is:

    Net sales
    − Cost of goods sold
    Gross profit
    − Expenses
    Net income

- The cost of goods sold is found by the following procedure:

```
    Beginning inventory at cost
  + Purchases
    Goods available for sale
  - Ending inventory at cost
    Cost of goods sold
```

- A comparative statement compares a firm's financial condition of the current period with the figures for previous period(s).
- Horizontal analysis compares the figures for the different periods across each horizontal line in the comparative statement. The comparison is in dollar amounts and in percent form. The base is the earlier year's figures.
- Vertical analysis compares the figures for the same period within the financial statement. The base dollar figure for the balance sheet is total assets. The comparison is in percent form. The base for the income statement is net sales.
- Financial ratios express relationships between numbers in the balance sheet and/or income statement. The basic ratios covered in this chapter are:

$$\text{Current ratio} = \frac{\text{Current assets}}{\text{Current liabilities}}$$

$$\text{Acid test ratio} = \frac{\text{Cash} + \text{Receivables} + \text{Marketable securities}}{\text{Current liabilities}}$$

Ratio of plant assets to long-term liabilities

$$= \frac{\text{Plant assets}}{\text{Long-term liabilities}}$$

Ratio of owner's equity to total liabilities

$$= \frac{\text{Owner's equity}}{\text{Total liabilities}}$$

Ratio of net income to owner's equity

$$= \frac{\text{Net income}}{\text{Owner's capital}}$$

- A graph is a visual representation of statistical data. The common types include:

1. Simple bar graph: A bar represents the amount of each item.
2. Component bar graph: Each bar is divided into parts.
3. Pictogram: A symbol or picture is used to present data.
4. Circle graph: A circle or pie is used to show the whole amount and is then broken into parts.
5. Line graph: Points are plotted on a graph and connected by lines.

15
Annuities and Investments

Business Takes a Positive Approach

MICROSOFT

At a time when many corporations are jumping on the computer software bandwagon, one company stands out above the rest: Microsoft. In 1975 when they were barely out of their teens, Bill Gates, pictured above, and a friend from high school started Microsoft. Gate's genius, persistence, and understanding of the rapidly changing computer market won him the chance to develop the operating system now sold with IBM's personal computers. Because of its wide acceptance, this operating system has become an industry standard. Microsoft continues to develop and market new software programs with one goal in mind, bringing technology to a practical level for the average computer user. The company employs a closeknit group of about 1,500 people. Under Gate's direction, they work in an atmosphere that encourages creativity and camaraderie. Since Microsoft went public in 1986, its stock has quadrupled in value. Gate's share alone is estimated at over a billion dollars. Business analysts predict that Microsoft, with its sharp eye toward the future of the computer industry, will continue to produce soaring revenues and profits.

Learning Objectives

After reading and studying this chapter and working the problems, you will be able to:

- Figure present value.
- Correctly use a present-value table.
- Figure the amount of an ordinary annuity.
- Find the amount of an annuity due.
- Calculate the present value of an annuity.
- Figure a sinking fund.
- Define various types of stocks and bonds.
- Determine stock dividends.
- Find the dividend yield for a stock.
- Accurately read a stock quotation.
- Accurately read a bond quotation.
- Figure bond prices, premiums, and discount.
- Determine bond prices with accrued interest.
- Find the current yield on a bond.

In order for any business or individual to become financially secure, proper money management is essential. Planning for the future involves a realistic examination of the present situation along with the addition of short- and long-term financial goals. You may be asking yourself: How much money should I set aside now in order to meet my goals in the future? Should I plan for an annuity? What is the difference between stocks and bonds? This chapter explores some of the vehicles for investment. There are many options available and it is important to be well informed so that you can make the most productive decisions.

15.1 Present Value

When deciding how much money to invest either as a business or as an individual, it is helpful to consider the value of money over time. You need to know how much money should be invested now in order to have a certain amount available at a later date. **Present value** is the current value of a sum of money that will yield a higher desired amount at a future date. Present value answers the question, "How much must I deposit now to reach a specific amount in the future?" The amount of interest paid determines how high that amount will be.

Present value can be used to determine such things as how much money you need to invest now in order to have a certain sum to open a business in five years, to purchase needed equipment in two years, to be able to have enough money to retire, to vacation comfortably, or to meet business debts that will become due at a future date.

To determine present value, three figures are needed:

1. The rate of compound interest to use in a table,
2. The number of compounding interest periods,
3. The desired amount at the end of a specific time period.

The **rate of compound interest** (to use in the present-value table given in this section) is found by dividing the annual rate given in the problem by the number of times compounding occurs each year. For instance,

$$8\% \text{ compounded annually} = \frac{8\%}{1} = 8\% \text{ in the table,}$$

$$8\% \text{ compounded semiannually} = \frac{8\%}{2} = 4\% \text{ in the table,}$$

$$8\% \text{ compounded quarterly} = \frac{8\%}{4} = 2\% \text{ in the table.}$$

The number of **compounding interest periods** to use in the table is found by multiplying the number of years by the number of times compounding occurs each year. For instance,

4 years compounded annually = 4 × 1 = 4 interest periods in the table,

4 years compounded semiannually = 4 × 2 = 8 interest periods in the table,

4 years compounded quarterly = 4 × 4 = 16 interest periods in the table.

The *desired amount* at the end of a specified time will be used as it is given in the problem.

Actually, finding present value can be compared to a compound-interest problem in which the maturity value is known and you are asked to find the original principal. Using a present-value table to solve these problems is similar to using a compound-interest table. This table gives the present value of $1 at compound interest for a certain number of interest periods. The desired amount is multiplied by the present value of $1 (given in the table in decimal form) to find the total present value.

Example 1 How much money must be invested for 10 years at a rate of 10% compounded semiannually in order to receive $8,000 at the end of the period?

Step 1 Determine the compound-interest rate to use in the table. (In this case, divide the given rate by 2 since it is compounded semiannually.)

$$\frac{10\%}{2} = 5\%$$

Step 2 Determine the number of compound-interest periods. (In this case, multiply the year by 2.)

10 × 2 = 20 Interest periods

Step 3 Find the present value of $1 at 5% for 20 periods by looking at the table.

.376889

Step 4 Multiply the desired amount by the present value of $1 to find how much money must be invested initially.

$8,000 × .376889 = $3,015.11

Answer $3,015.11 must be invested.

This answer can be checked by using the compound-interest table (Section 8.7) and finding the maturity value of $3,015.11 at 10% compounded semiannually for 10 years:

$$\$3,015.11 \times 2.653298 = \$7,999.99$$

The difference of 1¢ in the check answer is because of rounding in the tables.

Self-Check

1. What is the present value of $1,500 compounded annually for 3 years at 7%?

2. Find the present value of $4,800 compounded quarterly for 2 years at 12%.

ANSWERS   1. $1,224.45   2. $3,789.16

Space does not permit showing the entire present-value table. However, should the need arise, there are paperback books available that print the complete present-value and compound-interest tables.

Present-Value Table

Present Value of $1 at Compound Interest (to 6 Decimal Places)

N*	.5%	1%	1.5%	2%	N
1	0.995025	0.990100	0.985222	0.980392	1
2	0.990075	0.980296	0.970662	0.961169	2
3	0.985149	0.970590	0.956317	0.942322	3
4	0.980249	0.960980	0.942187	0.923845	4
5	0.975371	0.951466	0.928260	0.905731	5
6	0.970518	0.942045	0.914542	0.887971	6
7	0.965690	0.932718	0.901027	0.870560	7
8	0.960858	0.923483	0.887711	0.853490	8
9	0.956105	0.914340	0.874592	0.836755	9
10	0.951348	0.905287	0.861667	0.820348	10
11	0.946615	0.896324	0.848933	0.804263	11
12	0.941905	0.887449	0.836387	0.788493	12
13	0.937219	0.878663	0.824027	0.773033	13
14	0.932556	0.869963	0.811849	0.757875	14
15	0.927917	0.861349	0.799852	0.743015	15
16	0.923300	0.852821	0.788031	0.728446	16
17	0.918707	0.844377	0.776385	0.714163	17
18	0.914136	0.836017	0.764912	0.700159	18
19	0.909588	0.827740	0.753607	0.686431	19
20	0.905063	0.819544	0.742470	0.672971	20
21	0.900560	0.811430	0.731498	0.659776	21
22	0.896080	0.803396	0.720688	0.646839	22
23	0.891622	0.795442	0.710037	0.634156	23
24	0.887186	0.787566	0.699544	0.621721	24
25	0.882772	0.779768	0.689206	0.609531	25

N*	3%	4%	5%	6%	N
1	0.970874	0.961538	0.952381	0.943396	1
2	0.942596	0.924556	0.907029	0.889996	2
3	0.915142	0.888996	0.863838	0.839619	3
4	0.888487	0.854804	0.822702	0.792094	4
5	0.862688	0.821927	0.783526	0.747258	5
6	0.837484	0.790315	0.746215	0.704961	6
7	0.813092	0.759918	0.710681	0.665057	7
8	0.789409	0.730690	0.676839	0.627412	8
9	0.766417	0.702587	0.644609	0.591898	9
10	0.744094	0.675564	0.613913	0.558395	10
11	0.722421	0.649581	0.584679	0.526788	11
12	0.701380	0.624597	0.556837	0.496969	12
13	0.680951	0.600574	0.530321	0.468839	13
14	0.661118	0.577475	0.505068	0.442301	14
15	0.641862	0.555265	0.481017	0.417265	15
16	0.623167	0.533908	0.458112	0.393647	16
17	0.605016	0.513373	0.436297	0.371364	17
18	0.587395	0.493628	0.415521	0.350344	18
19	0.570286	0.474642	0.395734	0.330513	19
20	0.553676	0.456387	0.376889	0.311805	20
21	0.537549	0.438834	0.358942	0.294155	21
22	0.521893	0.421955	0.341850	0.277505	22
23	0.506692	0.405726	0.325571	0.261797	23
24	0.491934	0.390121	0.310068	0.246979	24
25	0.477606	0.375117	0.295303	0.232999	25

*N = Number of interest periods

Present-Value Table (*continued*)

	Present Value of $1 at Compound Interest (to 6 Decimal Places)				
N*	7%	8%	9%	10%	N
1	0.934579	0.925926	0.917431	0.909091	1
2	0.873439	0.857339	0.841680	0.826446	2
3	0.816298	0.793832	0.772183	0.751315	3
4	0.762895	0.735030	0.708425	0.683013	4
5	0.712986	0.680283	0.649931	0.620921	5
6	0.666342	0.630170	0.596267	0.564474	6
7	0.622750	0.583490	0.547034	0.513158	7
8	0.582009	0.540269	0.501866	0.466507	8
9	0.543934	0.500249	0.460428	0.424098	9
10	0.508349	0.463193	0.422411	0.385543	10
11	0.475093	0.428883	0.387533	0.350494	11
12	0.444012	0.397114	0.355535	0.318631	12
13	0.414965	0.367698	0.326179	0.289664	13
14	0.387817	0.340461	0.299246	0.263331	14
15	0.362446	0.315242	0.274538	0.239392	15
16	0.338735	0.291890	0.251870	0.217629	16
17	0.316574	0.270269	0.231073	0.197845	17
18	0.295864	0.250249	0.211994	0.179859	18
19	0.276508	0.231712	0.194490	0.163508	19
20	0.258419	0.214548	0.178431	0.148644	20
21	0.241513	0.198656	0.163698	0.135131	21
22	0.225713	0.183941	0.150182	0.122846	22
23	0.210947	0.170315	0.137781	0.111678	23
24	0.197147	0.157699	0.126405	0.101526	24
25	0.184249	0.146018	0.115968	0.092296	25
N*	11%	12%	13%	14%	N
1	0.900901	0.892857	0.884956	0.877193	1
2	0.811622	0.797194	0.783147	0.769468	2
3	0.731191	0.711780	0.693050	0.674972	3
4	0.658731	0.635518	0.613319	0.592080	4
5	0.593451	0.567427	0.542760	0.519369	5
6	0.534641	0.506631	0.480319	0.455587	6
7	0.481658	0.452349	0.425061	0.399637	7
8	0.433926	0.403883	0.376160	0.350559	8
9	0.390925	0.360610	0.332885	0.307508	9
10	0.352184	0.321973	0.294588	0.269744	10
11	0.317283	0.287476	0.260698	0.236617	11
12	0.285841	0.256675	0.230706	0.207559	12
13	0.257514	0.229174	0.204165	0.182069	13
14	0.231995	0.204620	0.180677	0.159710	14
15	0.209004	0.182696	0.159891	0.140096	15
16	0.188292	0.163122	0.141496	0.122892	16
17	0.169633	0.145644	0.125218	0.107710	17
18	0.152822	0.130040	0.110812	0.094561	18
19	0.137678	0.116107	0.098064	0.082948	19
20	0.124034	0.103667	0.086782	0.072762	20
21	0.111742	0.092560	0.076798	0.063826	21
22	0.100669	0.082643	0.067963	0.055988	22
23	0.090693	0.073788	0.060144	0.049112	23
24	0.081705	0.065882	0.053225	0.043081	24
25	0.073608	0.058823	0.047102	0.037790	25

*N = Number of interest periods

Assignment 15.1

Annuities and Investments

Determine the rate per period and the number of periods for each of the following. Use the present-value table to find the present value of $1 (show all places given).

	Rate per Period	Number of Interest Periods	Present Value of $1
1. 6% compounded semiannually for 4 years	3%	8	.789409
2. 12% compounded quarterly for 6 years	3%	24	.491934
3. 8% compounded annually for 9 years	8%	9	.500249
4. 14% compounded semiannually for 12 years	7%	24	.197147
5. 9% compounded annually for 7 years	9%	7	.547034
6. 8% compounded quarterly for 3 years	2%	12	.788493
7. 8% compounded semiannually for 3 years	4%	6	.790315
8. 13% compounded annually for 5 years	13%	5	.542760
9. 10% compounded semiannually for 8 years	5%	16	.458112
10. 6% compounded quarterly for 5 years	1.5%	20	.742470

Using the present-value table, find the present value to the nearest cent for each of the following.

	Maturity Value	Annual Interest Rate	Interest Compounded	Time in Years	Present Value	
11.	$ 8,400	6%	Semiannually	7	$ 5,553.39	11. Look up 3% for 14 periods. $8,400 × .661118 = $5,553.39
12.	$12,000	8%	Quarterly	4	8,741.32	$12,000 × .728446
13.	$16,500	10%	Semiannually	11	5,640.53	$16,500 × .341850
14.	$50,000	11%	Annually	13	12,875.70	$50,000 × .257514
15.	$39,300	12%	Quarterly	3	27,564.23	$39,300 × .701380
16.	$ 5,000	8%	Semiannually	9	2,468.14	$5,000 × .493628
17.	$12,250	6%	Quarterly	4	9,653.38	$12,250 × .788031

continued

Assignment 15.1 continued

Maturity Value	Annual Interest Rate	Interest Compounded	Time in Years	Present Value	
18. $28,000	14%	Semiannually	10	7,235.73	$28,000 × .258419
19. $ 3,500	4%	Quarterly	5	2,868.40	$3,500 × .819544
20. $18,750	13%	Annually	23	1,127.70	$18,750 × .060144

Solve each of the following using the present-value table.

21. Kay Builders plans to buy new equipment that will cost $87,000 in 3 years. Determine the amount that the company should invest now at 8% compounded quarterly in order to buy the equipment.

    Look up 2% for 12 periods.
    $87,000 × .788493 = $68,598.89

    $68,598.89 should be invested

22. Sure Employment Agency wants to have $6,500 in 6 years to purchase new office equipment. How much should the agency invest now at 10% compounded semiannually?

    Look up 5% for 12 periods.
    $6,500 × .556837 = $3,619.44

    $3,619.44 should be invested

23. The Mather family plans to buy a new house in 4 years and figures they will need at least $15,000 for the down payment. At 12% compounded quarterly, how much should they invest now?

    Look up 3% for 16 periods.
    $15,000 × .623167 = $9,347.50

    $9,347.50 should be invested

24. A debt of $8,000 will be due in 5 years. How much should be invested now at 11% compounded annually in order to meet the debt?

    Look up 11% for 5 periods.
    $8,000 × .593451 = $4,747.61

    $4,747.61 should be invested

25. Ace Delivery Company needs $64,500 to buy a new truck in 3 years. How much should the company invest now at 8% compounded semiannually?

    Look up 4% for 6 periods.
    $64,500 × .790315 = $50,975.32

    $50,975.32 should be invested

15.2 Annuities

Annuities are periodic payments of equal sums of money. Some examples are loan and mortgage payments, Social Security payments, retirement payments, and payments or deposits for specialized funds. Annuities can also be used for the regular saving of money for some future obligation or investment. For example, you might save money to buy a car, purchase new equipment for your business, or have a certain amount of money available for expansion or for travel. In business situations, this type of annuity is often referred to as a sinking fund.

There are many different types of annuities. Some involve compound interest; others do not. Also, the compound-interest period may differ from the payment period. Payment might be made at the beginning of each period or at the end of each period. Periodic payments can be made in a variety of intervals: annually, semiannually, quarterly, monthly, and so on. However, the particular period chosen usually does not change during the life of the annuity.

The actual length of time an annuity runs is called the term. The term may be definite or indefinite. For example, annuity payments may be made every month for two years (definite) or every month until death (indefinite).

Annuities generally earn compound interest. Rather than dealing with a lump sum (as, we did in Section 9.6 on compound interest), in this case periodic payments are paid into or out of an account that is earning compound interest. Funds accumulate through periodic payments to which compound interest is added each period.

Finding the Amount of an Ordinary Annuity

The following are some important terms concerning annuities with which you should become familiar.

Amount: The dollar value on deposit at the end of the term. Also referred to as **future value.**

Term: The length of time for the life of the annuity.

Payment period: The time between payments. Also known as **conversion period.**

A type of annuity frequently used in business is called an **ordinary annuity,** where payments are made at the end of each payment period. The interest period and the payment period are the same, and there is a definite term for the annuity.

The following sample problem shows how funds accumulate in an ordinary annuity.

If $1,000 is invested at the end of each year in an account paying interest at 8% compounded annually, what will be the amount of the annuity at the end of the third year?

First year	Beginning balance	$0
	Interest	0
	Deposit at end of year	+ 1,000.00
	Total at end of year	$1,000.00
Second year	Beginning balance	$1,000.00
	Interest ($1,000 × 8%)	80.00
	Deposit at end of year	+ 1,000.00
	Total at end of year	$2,080.00
	Beginning balance	$2,080.00

Third year	Interest ($2,080 × 8%)		166.40
	Deposit at end of year	+	1,000.00
	Total at end of year		$3,246.40

Answer $3,246.40 is the amount of the ordinary annuity at the end of the third year.

As you can see, the calculation of the annuity is similar to a complex compound-interest problem, where the principal is increased by a periodic payment plus interest for each period. To simplify the calculation, there is an ordinary annuity table available. This is used in much the same way as the compound-interest table that appeared in Chapter 9.

The table for finding the amount for an ordinary annuity is shown on pages 614–615. The table value gives you the amount that will accumulate for the periodic payment of $1 at a specific rate of interest and for a specific number of periods. Note that the columns across the top represent the rate of interest per period and the rows to the left represent the number of payment periods.

The formula is:

$$\text{Amount of an ordinary annuity} = \text{Dollar value of a periodic payment} \times \text{Table value}$$

Let's see how the table is used in computing the amount of an ordinary annuity for which interest is compounded annually.

Example 1 Determine the amount of an ordinary annuity if the interest is 8% compounded annually for three years and the periodic payment is $1000 a year.

Step 1 Using the table, determine the value for "N." Since the annuity is annual for 3 years, there are 3 periods.

  3 Years
  × 1 Period
  3

  N = 3

Step 2 Determine the value for "%" in the table. Since it is compounded annually, the rate per period is 8%.

  % = 8%

Step 3 The table value is the place where N (row 3) and % (column 8) intersect.

  Table value = 3.246400

Step 4 Find the amount of the annuity by multiplying the dollar value of the periodic payment by the table value.

  Amount
  = $1,000 × 3.246400
  = $3,246.40

Answer $3,246.40 is the amount of the ordinary annuity.

NOTE: We use the same numbers in Example 1 that we did in the sample problem above, where we did the calculations manually without using the table. The answers are the same. Sometimes, however, when the same problem is worked manually and then figured using the table, there will be a few cents difference between the answers due to rounding.

The table can also be used to find the amount of an ordinary annuity for which interest is compounded either semiannually or quarterly.

Example 2 You made semiannual investments of $1,500 for 6 years in an ordinary annuity at 10%, compounded semiannually. Figure the amount of the annuity and the total amount of interest earned.

Step 1 Using the table, determine the value for N. Since the annuity is semiannual for 6 years, there are 12 periods.

  6 Years
  × 2 Periods
  12

  N = 12

Step 2   Determine the value for % in the table. Since it is compounded semiannually, the rate per period is 5% (10% divided by 2 periods).   % = 5%

Step 3   The table value is the place where N (row 12) and % (column 5) intersect.   Table value = 15.917127

Step 4   Find the amount of the annuity by multiplying the dollar value of the periodic payment by the table value.

Amount
= $1,500 × 15.917127
= $23,875.69

Step 5   Find the total amount of annuity payments by multiplying the dollar amount of each payment by the number of payments. $1500 × 12 = $18,000

Step 6   Subtract the total amount of annuity payments from the amount of the annuity to find the interest.

$23,875.69
− 18,000.00
$5,875.69

Answer $23,875.69 is the amount of the ordinary annuity, and $5,875.69 is the total amount of interest earned.

NOTE: If the annuity were compounded quarterly, the number of years would be multiplied by 4 and the percent of interest would be divided by 4. If the annuity were compounded monthly, the number of years would be multiplied by 12 and the percent of interest would be divided by 12.

Self-Check

1. Ralph Van Dyke deposits $2,500 at the end of every year in an account paying 6%, compounded annually. If he makes these deposits for 4 years, what is the amount of the annuity?

2. Color Graphics invested $4,300 at the end of every quarter for 7 years in a plan that paid 8%, compounded quarterly. Find (a) the amount of this annuity and (b) the total amount of interest earned.

Answers   1. $10,936.54   2. (a) $159,320.20; (b) $38,920.20

Finding the Amount of an Annuity Due

With an ordinary annuity, periodic payments are made at the end of each period. When the payments are made at the beginning of each period, it is called an **annuity due.** Because the investment is made at the beginning of the period rather than at the end, more interest is earned, and the final amount is therefore greater.

The following sample problem shows how funds accumulate in an annuity due.

If $1,000 is invested at the beginning of each year in an account paying 8%, compounded annually, what will be the amount of the annuity due at the end of the third year?

First year
Deposit at beginning of year $1,000.00
Interest   +   80.00
Total at end of year $1,080.00

Annuities and Investments   **611**

	Beginning balance	$1,080.00
Second	Deposit at beginning of year	1,000.00
year	Interest ($2,080 × 8%)	+ 166.40
	Total at end of year	$2,246.40
	Beginning balance	$2,246.40
Third	Deposit at beginning of year	1,000.00
year	Interest ($3,246.40 × 8%)	+ 259.71
	Total at end of year	$3,506.11

Answer $3,506.11 is the amount of the annuity at the end of the third year.

For a comparison, look back at the sample problem on page 609. Both problems use the same figures. The difference between the two answers shows how making the $1,000 payment at the beginning of each period rather than at the end adds more to the final amount.

$3,506.11 Amount of annuity due at the end of 3 years
− 3,246.40 Amount of ordinary annuity at the end of 3 years
$ 259.71 Difference

We can use the same table we did for an ordinary annuity to find the amount for an annuity due, we must make an adjustment. Because the payment is made at the beginning of each period, in effect, one additional period is added to the table calculation. Then, in order to adjust the final answer, you must subtract the dollar amount of one payment.

Example 3 Dixon Manufacturing invested $2,000 at the beginning of every 6-month period for 5 years. Find the value of the investment at the end of the fifth year if it has earned interest at 8%, compounded semiannually.

Step 1 Determine the value for N. There are 2 periods for each year. Add one more period because this is an annuity due.

5 Years
× 2 Periods
10
+ 1 Additional period
11

N = 11

Step 2 Determine the value for %. Since it is compounded semiannually, the rate per period is 4% (8% ÷ 2 = 4).

% = 4%

Step 3 The table value is the point at which N (row 11) and % (column 4) intersect.

Table value = 13.486351

Step 4 Multiply the periodic payment by the table value.

$2,000 × 13.486351
= $26,972.70

Step 5 Subtract the dollar value of one payment from the amount above.

$26,972.70
− 2,000
$24,972.70

Answer $24,972.70 is the amount of the annuity due.

NOTE: If you are asked to find interest for an annuity due, figure it the same way you did for an ordinary annuity.

Self-Check

1. Find the amount of an annuity due if payments of $4,000 are made at the beginning of each year for 7 years and the account pays 10%, compounded annually.

2. Payments of $800 each are invested in an account that pays interest at 12%, compounded semiannually. The payment is made at the beginning of each 6-month period for 4 years. What is the final amount at the end of the fourteenth year? _____

ANSWERS 1. $41,743.55   2. $8,393.05

TABLE 1. Amount of an Ordinary Annuity of $1 per period

Period	Interest Rates Per Period						
N	½%	1%	1½%	2%	2½%	3	3½%
1	1.000000	1.000000	1.000000	1.000000	1.000000	1.000000	1.000000
2	2.005000	2.010000	2.015000	2.020000	2.025000	2.030000	2.035000
3	3.015025	3.030100	3.045225	3.060400	3.075625	3.090900	3.106225
4	4.030100	4.060401	4.090903	4.121608	4.152515	4.183627	4.214943
5	5.050251	5.101005	5.152267	5.204040	5.256328	5.309136	5.362466
6	6.075502	6.152015	6.229551	6.308121	6.387737	6.468410	6.550152
7	7.105879	7.213535	7.322994	7.434283	7.547430	7.662462	7.779407
8	8.141409	8.285671	8.432839	8.582969	8.736116	8.892336	9.051687
9	9.182116	9.368527	9.559332	9.754628	9.954518	10.159106	10.368496
10	10.228026	10.462213	10.702722	10.949721	11.203381	11.463879	11.731393
11	11.279167	11.566835	11.863262	12.168715	12.483466	12.807796	13.141992
12	12.335562	12.682503	13.041211	13.412090	13.795552	14.192030	14.601961
13	13.397240	13.809328	14.236830	14.680332	15.140441	15.617790	16.113030
14	14.464226	14.947421	15.450382	15.973938	16.518952	17.086324	17.676986
15	15.536548	16.096896	16.682138	17.293417	17.931926	18.598914	19.295680
16	16.614230	17.257864	17.932370	18.639285	19.380224	20.156881	20.971029
17	17.697301	18.430443	19.201355	20.012071	20.864730	21.761588	22.705015
18	18.785788	19.614748	20.489376	21.412312	22.386348	23.414435	24.499691
19	19.879717	20.810895	21.796716	22.840559	23.946006	25.116868	26.357180
20	20.979115	22.019004	23.123667	24.297370	25.544656	26.870374	28.279681
24	25.431955	26.973465	28.633521	30.421862	32.349036	34.426470	36.666527
28	29.974522	32.129097	34.481479	37.051210	39.859799	42.930923	46.290626
32	34.608624	37.494068	40.688288	44.227030	48.150275	52.502759	57.334500
36	39.336105	43.076878	47.275969	51.994367	57.301409	63.275944	70.007600
40	44.158847	48.886373	54.267894	60.401983	67.402550	75.401260	84.550274
44	49.078770	54.931757	61.688868	69.502657	78.552318	89.048409	101.238326
48	54.097832	61.222608	69.565219	79.353519	90.859577	104.408396	120.388251
52	59.218031	67.768892	77.924892	90.016409	104.444487	121.696197	142.363229
56	64.441404	74.580982	86.797543	101.558264	119.439686	141.153768	167.580022
60	69.770031	81.669670	96.214652	114.051539	135.991581	163.053437	196.516872
64	75.206032	89.046187	106.209628	127.574662	154.261775	187.701707	229.722573
68	80.751571	96.722220	116.817931	142.212525	174.428650	215.443551	267.826878
72	86.408856	104.709931	128.077197	158.057019	196.689107	246.667242	311.552444
76	92.180138	113.021975	140.027372	175.207608	221.260487	281.809781	361.728537
80	98.067714	121.671522	152.710852	193.771958	248.382692	321.363019	419.306757

TABLE 1. Amount of an Ordinary Annuity of $1 per period

Period	Interest Rates Per Period						
N	4%	$4\frac{1}{2}$%	5%	$5\frac{1}{2}$%	6%	8%	10%
1	1.000000	1.000000	1.000000	1.000000	1.000000	1.000000	1.000000
2	2.040000	2.045000	2.050000	2.055000	2.060000	2.080000	2.100000
3	3.121600	3.137025	3.152500	3.168025	3.183600	3.246400	3.310000
4	4.246464	4.278191	4.310125	4.342266	4.374616	4.506112	4.641000
5	5.416323	5.470710	5.525631	5.581091	5.637093	5.866601	6.105100
6	6.632975	6.716892	6.801913	6.888051	6.975319	7.335929	7.715610
7	7.898294	8.019152	8.142008	8.266894	8.393838	8.922803	9.487171
8	9.214226	9.380014	9.549109	9.721573	9.897468	10.636628	11.435888
9	10.582795	10.802114	11.026564	11.256259	11.491316	12.487558	13.579477
10	12.006107	12.288209	12.577893	12.875354	13.180795	14.486562	15.937425
11	13.486351	13.841179	14.206787	14.583498	14.971643	16.645487	18.531167
12	15.025805	15.464032	15.917127	16.385590	16.869941	18.977126	21.384284
13	16.626838	17.159913	17.712983	18.286798	18.882138	21.495297	24.522712
14	18.291911	18.932110	19.598632	20.292572	21.015066	24.214920	27.974983
15	20.023588	20.784054	21.578564	22.408663	23.275970	27.152114	31.772482
16	21.824531	22.719337	23.657492	24.641139	25.672528	30.324283	35.949730
17	23.697512	24.741707	25.840366	26.996402	28.212880	33.750226	40.544703
18	25.645413	26.855084	28.132385	29.481207	30.905653	37.450244	45.599173
19	27.671229	29.063563	30.539004	32.102670	33.759992	41.446263	51.159090
20	29.778079	31.371423	33.065954	34.868317	36.785591	45.761964	57.274999
24	39.082604	41.689197	44.501999	47.537997	50.815577	66.764759	88.497327
28	49.967583	53.993334	58.402583	63.233509	68.528112	95.338830	134.209936
32	62.701469	68.666246	75.298829	82.677496	90.889778	134.213537	201.137767
36	77.598314	86.163966	95.836323	106.765186	119.120867	187.102148	299.126805
40	95.025516	107.030324	120.799774	136.605610	154.761966	259.056519	442.592556
44	115.412877	131.913843	151.143006	173.572663	199.758032	356.949646	652.640761
48	139.263206	161.587903	188.025393	219.368358	256.564529	490.132164	960.172338
52	167.164718	196.974772	232.856165	276.101196	382.281422	671.325510	1410.429320
56	199.805540	239.174270	287.348249	346.383232	418.822348	917.837058	2069.650567
60	237.990685	289.497957	353.583718	433.450352	533.128181	1253.213296	3034.816395
64	282.661904	349.509890	434.093344	541.311246	677.436661	1709.488966	4447.915685
68	334.920912	421.075236	531.953298	674.931979	859.622792	2330.246977	6516.834354
72	396.056560	506.418243	650.902683	840.464637	1089.628586	3174.781398	9545.938177
76	467.576621	608.191366	795.486404	1045.530574	1380.005601	4323.761154	13980.849085
80	551.244977	729.557709	971.228821	1299.571310	1746.599891	5886.935428	20474.002146

NAME _____ DATE _____ SECTION _____

Assignment 15.2

Annuities and Investment

Find the amount of the annuity for each of the following.

	Payments Made	Number of Interest Periods	Annuity Years	Payment Rate	Amount
1.	$4,000	End of every year	13	10% compounded annually	$ 98,090.85

$i = 10\%, n = 13$
$\$4,000 \times 24.522712 = \$98,090.848$

2.	$1,825	End of every 6 months	8	11% compounded semiannually	44,970.08

$i = 5\frac{1}{2}\%, n = 16$
$\$1,825 \times 24.641139 = \$44,970.078$

3.	$6,200	Beginning of every year	9	8% compounded annually	83,616.68

$i = 8\%, n = 10$
$\$6,200 \times 14.486562 = \quad \$89,816.684$
$\qquad\qquad\qquad\qquad\quad -\quad 6,200.00$
$\qquad\qquad\qquad\qquad\quad\quad \$83,616.684$

4.	$ 150	End of every month	$1\frac{1}{4}$	12% compounded monthly	2,414.53

$i = 1\%, n = 15$
$\$150 \times 16.096896 = \$2,414.5344$

5.	$2,900	Beginning of every 3 months	4	14% compounded quarterly	62,944.54

$i = 3\frac{1}{2}\%, n = 17$
$\$2,900 \times 22.705015 = \quad \$65,844.543$
$\qquad\qquad\qquad\qquad\quad -\quad 2,900.00$
$\qquad\qquad\qquad\qquad\quad\quad \$62,944.543$

6.	$ 500	Beginning of every month	1	6% compounded monthly	6,198.62

$i = \frac{1}{2}\%, n = 13$
$\$500 \times 13.397240 = \quad \$6,698.62$
$\qquad\qquad\qquad\qquad\quad -\quad 500.00$
$\qquad\qquad\qquad\qquad\quad\quad \$6,198.62$

7.	$3,400	Beginning of every 3 months	$3\frac{1}{2}$	10% compounded quarterly	57,568.55

$i = 2\frac{1}{2}\%, n = 15$
$\$3,400 \times 17.931926 = \quad \$60,968.548$
$\qquad\qquad\qquad\qquad\quad -\quad 3,400.00$
$\qquad\qquad\qquad\qquad\quad\quad \$57,568.548$

continued

Assignment 15.2 *continued*

8. $1,000 End of every 6 months 22 8% compounded semiannually 115,412.88

   $i = 4\%, n = 44$
   $\$1,000 \times 115.412877 = \$115,412.877$

9. Fantasy Footworks is setting up a fund for new display fixtures. The business pays $2,800 at the beginning of every quarter into an account that pays 14%, compounded quarterly.

   a) How much will be in the fund at the end of $2\frac{1}{2}$ years?

   $i = 3\frac{1}{2}\%, n = 11$
   $\$2,800 \times 13.141992 = \$36,797.577$
   $ \underline{-\ \ \ 2,800.00}$
   $ \$33,997.577$

   a) $33,997.58

   b) How much total interest will accumulate?

   $\$2,800 \times 10 = \$28,000$

   $\$33,997.58$
   $\underline{-\ 28,000.00}$
   $\$5,997.58$ Interest

   b) $5,997.58

10. You deposit $1,400 at the end of every 6 months into an account that pays 11%, compounded semiannually.

    a) How much will you have at the end of 9 years?

    $i = 5\frac{1}{2}\%, n = 18$
    $\$1,400 \times 29.481207 = \$41,273.689$

    a) $41,273.69

    b) If you made the same payments at the beginning of each period and other factors remained the same, how much would you have at the end of 9 years?

    $i = 5\frac{1}{2}\%, n = 19$
    $\$1,400 \times 32.102670 = \$44943.738$
    $ \underline{-\ \ \ 1,400.00}$
    $ \$43,543.738$

    b) $43,543.74

11. **a)** What is the amount of an annuity of $200 payments made at the end of each month for 5 years compounded monthly at 12%?

    $i = 1\%, n = 60$
    $\$200 \times 81.669670 = \$16,333.934$

    a) $16,333.93

    b) If the interest rate is increased to 18% compounded monthly, how much higher will the final amount be over the same time period?

    $i = 1\frac{1}{2}\%, n = 60$
    $\$200 \times 96.214652 = \$19,242.93$

    $\$19,242.93$ @ $1\frac{1}{2}\%$
    $\underline{-\ 16,333.93}$ @ 1%
    $\$2,909.00$ higher

    b) $2,909

12. As a new parent you decide to put $480 at the beginning of each year into an investment account paying 10%, compounded annually, so that your child can attend college 18 years from now. Over the years college costs are rising and it is estimated that tuition and room and board will cost $12,000 a year at the state university.

continued

Assignment 15.2 *continued*

    a) Approximately how many years of college will the fund cover at the end of the 18-year period?

        $i = 10\%, n = 19$
        $\$480 \times 51.159090 = \$24556.363$
                    $- \ \ \underline{480.00}$ ⎤ approximately
                    $\$24,076.363$ ⎦ 2 yr of college   a) __**2 yr**__

    b) What is the total amount of interest earned?

        $\$480 \times 18 = \$8,640$
        $\$24,076.36$
        $\underline{- \ \ \ 8,640.00}$
        $\$15,436.36$ Interest   b) __**$15,436.36**__

13. A deposit of $3,000 is made at the end of each 6-month period in an account paying 10%, compounded semiannually. The term is 12 years.

    a) What is the amount at term?

        $i = 5\%, n = 24$
        $\$3,000 \times 44.501999 = \$133,505.99$ a) __**$133,505.99**__

    b) If the payments were changed to $1,500 at the end of each 3-month period and interest were 10% compounded quarterly, what would be the amount at the end of the same term?

        $i = 2\frac{1}{2}\%, n = 48$
        $\$1,500 \times 90.859577 = \$136,289.36$ b) __**$136,289.36**__

14. Waterpay Recreation Park plans to invest $4,000 at the beginning of each 6-month period into a fund that pays 16%, compounded semiannually.

    a) How much will be in the account at the end of 3 years?

        $i = 8\%, n = 7$
        $\$4,000 \times 8.922803 = \ \ \$35,691.212$
                                $\underline{- \ \ 4,000.00}$
                                $\$31,691.21$ a) __**$31,691.21**__

    b) How much interest will accumulate at the end of 5 years?

        $i = 8\%, n = 11$
        $\$4,000 \times 16.645487 = \ \ \$66581.948$
                                   $\underline{- \ \ 4,000.00}$
                                     $\$62,581.948$
        $\$4,000 \times 10 = \$40,000$

        $\$62,581.948$
        $\underline{- \ \ 40,000}$
        $\$22,581.948$ Interest   b) __**$22,581.95**__

15. Jan Barger operates a day-care center from her home and plans to set up a fund to replace the playground equipment in 4 years. She plans to deposit $150 at the end of each quarter in an account that pays 14%, compounded quarterly.

continued

Assignment 15.2 *continued*

a) How much will she have personally deposited at the end of term?

$150 × 16 = $2,400

a) $2,400

b) What is the amount of the annuity at the end of 4 years?

$i = 3\frac{1}{2}\%, n = 16$
$150 × 20.971029 = $3,145.6543

b) $3,145.65

c) If she increases her payments to $200 a quarter, what will be the percent increase in the final amount of the annuity?

$200 × 20.971029 = $4194.2058

$4,194.21 Amount @ $200 payments
− 3,145.65 Amount @ $150 payments
$1,048.56 Increase

$\dfrac{\$1,048.56}{\$3,145.65}$ = 33.33% increase

c) 33.33%

16. You plan to attend the graphic arts exhibition in Drupa, Germany, in 2 years. You decide to deposit $600 at the end of every quarter into an account that pays 12%, compounded quarterly. However, after making deposits for $1\frac{1}{2}$ years, you can no longer make the deposits because of unforeseen medical bills. You decide to leave the account untouched for the remaining time. How much money will be in the account at the end of 2 years?

$i = 3\%, n = 6$
$600 × 6.468410 = $3881.046 } for $1\frac{1}{2}$ yr

P × R × T = I
$3,881.05 × 12% × $\frac{1}{4}$ = $116.43
$3,997.48 × 12% × $\frac{1}{4}$ = $119.92

$3,881.05
+ 116.43
$3,997.48   for $1\frac{1}{2}$ yr
+ 119.92
$4,117.40 Total in the account

$4,117.40

15.3 Present Value of Annuities

Finding the Present Value of an Ordinary Annuity

In Section 15.2, we looked at annuities in terms of the future value (amount) after payments were made *into* an annuity. However, payments can also be made *from* an annuity as well. In this case, of course, the largest value of the annuity is at the beginning of the term instead of at the end of the term.

The **present value of an annuity** is the total amount that must be deposited initially in order to allow for periodic, equal payments to be withdrawn from the annuity. The initial deposit is less than the sum of the withdrawals because the balance of the deposit earns interest during the term of the annuity. An example of this type of annuity is a retirement fund. A certain amount is put into an annuity. Then, upon retirement, the retiree is paid a fixed amount on a regular basis from the annuity.

The present value of an annuity is found by using a table similar to those we used earlier in the chapter. The formula is:

$$\text{Present value of an annuity} = \text{Size of each periodic payment} \times \text{Table value}.$$

For the following examples, we will use the table on pages 623–624. Assume that all annuities in this section are ordinary annuities.

Example 1 What is the present value of an annuity if it pays $500 at the end of each quarter for 6 years and the interest is 8%, compounded quarterly?

Step 1 Determine the value for N. Since the payment will be quarterly for 6 years, there are 24 periods.

6 Years
× 4 Periods
24

N = 24

Step 2 Determine the value for %. Since the rate is compounded quarterly, the % per period is 2% (8% ÷ 4 periods a year).

% = 2%

Step 3 The table value is the point where N (row 24) and % (column 2%) intersect.

Table value = 18.913926

Step 4 Find the present value by multiplying the periodic payment by the table value.

$500 × 18.913926 = 9,456.96

Answer $9,456.96 is the present value for the annuity.

Example 2 Lisa Hill is going to a trade show in Japan and plans to stay in the Orient for $1\frac{1}{2}$ years. What will she have to deposit now in an account paying 6%, compounded semiannually, in order to withdraw $5,000 at the end of every six months while she is in the Orient? How much interest will be earned on the money?

Step 1 Determine the value for N.

1.5 Years
× 2 Periods
3

N = 3

Step 2 Determine the value for % (6% ÷ 2 periods a year = 3%).

% = 3%

Step 3 Find the table value.

Table value = 2.828611

Step 4	Calculate the present value, which is the amount that needs to be deposited now. Multiply the payment by the table value.	$5,000 × 2.828611 = $14,143.06
Step 5	Find the total amount of annuity payments. Multiply each payment by the number of payments desired.	$5,000 × 3 = $15,000
Step 6	Subtract the initial deposit from the total amount of annuity payments to find the interest.	$15,000.00 − 14,143.06 $856.94
Answer	$14,143.06 needs to be deposited now, and $856.94 is the interest earned.	

Self-Check

1. Find the present value of an annuity that permits withdrawals of $1,500 at the end of every year for the next 10 years. The money is invested at 8%, compounded annually. _____

2. You want to set up a trust fund that will pay $2000 at the end of every 3 months for the next 3 years.

   a. If the fund is compounded quarterly at 12%, how much do you need to deposit today? _____

   b. How much interest will you receive? _____

ANSWERS 1. $10,065.12   2. (a) $19,908.01; (b) $4,091.99

TABLE 2. Present Value of an Ordinary Annuity of $1 per Period

Period N	\frac{1}{2}%	1%	1\frac{1}{2}%	2%	2\frac{1}{2}%	3	3\frac{1}{2}%
1	0.995025	0.990099	0.985222	0.980392	0.975610	0.970874	0.966184
2	1.985099	1.970395	1.955883	1.941561	1.927424	1,913470	1.899694
3	2.970248	2.940985	2.912200	2.883883	2.856024	2.828611	2.801637
4	3.950496	3.901966	3.854385	3.807729	3.761974	3.717098	3.673079
5	4.925866	4.853431	4.782645	4.713460	4.645828	4.579707	4.515052
6	5.896384	5.795476	5.697187	5.601431	5.508125	5.417191	5.328553
7	6.862074	6.728195	6.598214	6.471991	6.349390	6.230283	6.114544
8	7.822959	7.651678	7.485925	7.325481	7.170137	7.019692	6.873955
9	8.779064	8.566018	8.360517	8.162237	7.970865	7.786109	7.607686
10	9.730412	9.471305	9.222185	8.982585	8.752064	8.530203	8.316605
11	10.677027	10.367628	10.071118	9.786848	9.514208	9.252624	9.001551
12	11.618932	11.255077	10.907505	10.575341	10.257764	9.954004	9.663334
13	12.556151	12.133740	11.731532	11.348374	10.983185	10.634955	10.302738
14	13.488708	13.003703	12.543382	12.106249	11.690912	11.296073	10.920520
15	14.416625	13.865053	13.343233	12.849264	12.381377	11.937935	11.517411
16	15.339925	14.717874	14.131264	13.577709	13.055002	12.561102	12.094117
17	16.258632	15.562251	14.907649	14.291872	13.712197	13.166118	12.651320
18	17.172768	16.398269	15.672561	14.992031	14.353363	13.753513	13.189682
19	18.082356	17.226008	16.426168	15.678462	14.978891	14.323799	13.709837
20	18.987419	18.045553	17.168639	16.351433	15.589162	14.877475	14.212403
24	22.562866	21.243387	20.030405	18.913926	17.884985	16.935542	16.058367
28	26.067689	24.316443	22.726717	21.281272	19.964888	18.764108	17.667019
32	29.503284	27.269589	25.267139	23.468335	21.849177	20.388766	19.068865
36	32.871016	30.107505	27.660684	25.488842	23.556251	21.832252	20.290494
40	36.172228	32.834686	29.915845	27.355479	25.102775	23.114772	21.355072
44	39.408232	35.455454	32.040622	29.079963	26.503849	24.254274	22.282791
48	42.580318	37.973959	34.042554	30.673120	27.773153	25.266707	23.091244
52	45.689747	40.394194	35.928742	32.144950	28.923080	26.166240	23.795764
56	48.737757	42.719992	37.705879	33.504694	29.964857	26.965464	24.409713
60	51.725561	44.955038	39.380269	34.760887	30.908656	27.675564	24.944734
64	54.654348	47.102874	40.957853	35.921415	31.763691	28.306478	25.410974
68	57.525285	49.166901	42.444228	36.993564	32.538311	28.867038	25.817275
72	60.339514	51.150391	43.844667	37.984063	33.240078	29.365088	26.171343
76	63.098155	53.056486	45.164138	38.899132	33.875844	29.807598	26.479892
80	65.802305	54.888206	46.407323	39.744514	34.451817	30.200763	26.748776

TABLE 2. Present Value of an Ordinary Annuity of $1 per Period

Period	Interest Rates Per Period						
N	4%	4½%	5%	5½%	6%	8%	10%
1	0.961538	0.956938	0.952381	0.947867	0.943396	0.925926	0.909091
2	1.886095	1.872668	1.859410	1.846320	1.833393	1.783265	1.735537
3	2.775091	2.748964	2.723248	2.697933	2.673012	2.577097	2.486852
4	3.629895	3.587526	3.545951	3.505150	3.465106	3.312127	3.169865
5	4.451822	4.389977	4.329477	4.270284	4.212364	3.992710	3.790787
6	5.242137	5.157873	5.075692	4.995530	4.917324	4.622880	4.355261
7	6.002055	5.892701	5.786373	5.682967	5.582381	5.206370	4.868419
8	6.732745	6.595886	6.463213	6.334566	6.209794	5.746639	5.334926
9	7.435332	7.268791	7.107822	6.952195	6.801692	6.246888	5.759024
10	8.110896	7.912718	7.721735	7.537626	7.360087	6.710081	6.144567
11	8.760477	8.528917	8.306414	8.092536	7.886875	7.138964	6.495061
12	9.385074	9.118581	8.863252	8.618518	8.383844	7.536078	6.813692
13	9.985648	9.682852	9.393573	9.117078	8.852683	7.903776	7.103356
14	10.563123	10.222825	9.898641	9.589648	9.294984	8.244237	7.366687
15	11.118387	10.739546	10.379658	10.037581	9.712249	8.559479	7.606080
16	11.652296	11.234015	10.837770	10.462162	10.105895	8.851369	7.823709
17	12.165669	11.707191	11.274066	10.864608	10.477260	9.121638	8.021553
18	12.659297	12.159992	11.689587	11.246074	10.827603	9.371887	8.201412
19	13.133939	12.593294	12.085321	11.607653	11.158116	9.603599	8.364920
20	13.590326	13.007937	12.462210	11.950382	11.469921	9.818147	8.513564
24	15.246963	14.495478	13.798642	13.151699	12.550358	10.528758	8.984744
28	16.663063	15.742874	14.898127	14.121422	13.406164	11.051078	9.306567
32	17.873551	16.788891	15.802677	14.904198	14.084043	11.434999	9.526376
36	18.908282	17.666041	16.546852	15.536068	14.620987	11.717193	9.676508
40	19.792774	18.401584	17.159086	16.046125	15.046297	11.924613	9.779051
44	20.548841	19.018383	17.662773	16.457851	15.383182	12.077074	9.849089
48	21.195131	19.535607	18.077158	16.790203	15.650027	12.189136	9.896926
52	21.747582	19.969330	18.418073	17.058483	15.861393	12.271506	9.929599
56	22.219819	20.333034	18.698545	17.275043	16.028814	12.332050	9.951915
60	22.623490	18.929290	18.929290	17.449854	16.161428	12.376552	9.967157
64	22.968549	20.893773	19.119124	17.590965	16.266470	12.409262	9.977568
68	23.263507	21.108236	19.275301	17.704871	16.349673	12.433305	9.984679
72	23.515639	21.288077	19.403788	17.796819	16.415578	12.450977	9.989535
76	23.731162	21.438884	19.509495	17.871040	16.467781	12.463967	9.992852
80	23.915392	21.565345	19.596460	17.930953	16.509131	12.473514	9.995118

Assignment 15.3

Annuities and Investments

Assume ordinary annuities for all the problems in this section.

Find the present value in each of the following situations.

	Periodic Payment	Payments Made	Number of Years	Interest Rate	Present Value
1.	$2,000	Every year	20	8% compounded annually	$19,636.29

$i = 8\%, n = 20$
$2,000 \times 9.818147 = \$19,636.294$

2.	$820	Every 3 months	11	8% compounded quarterly	$23,845.57

$i = 2\%, n = 44$
$820 \times 29.079963 = \$23,845.569$

3.	$1,400	Every 6 months	$6\frac{1}{2}$	11% compounded semiannually	$12,763.91

$i = 5\frac{1}{2}\%, n = 13$
$1,400 \times 9.117078 = \$12,763.909$

4.	$250	Every month	3	12% compounded monthly	$7,526.88

$i = 1\%, n = 36$
$250 \times 30.107505 = \$7,526.8762$

5.	$1,000	Every 6 months	14	9% compounded semiannually	$15,742.87

$i = 4\frac{1}{2}\%, n = 28$
$1,000 \times 15.742874 = \$15,742.874$

6.	$3,300	Every year	4	10% compounded annually	$10,460.55

$i = 10\%, n = 4$
$3,300 \times 3.169865 = \$10,460.554$

7.	$160	Every month	$1\frac{1}{4}$	18% compounded monthly	$2,134.92

$i = 1\frac{1}{2}\%, n = 15$
$160 \times 13.343233 = \$2,134.9172$

8.	$500	Every 3 months	8	14% compounded quarterly	$9,534.43

$i = 3\frac{1}{2}\%, n = 32$
$500 \times 19.068865 = \$9,534.4325$

continued

Assignment 15.3 *continued*

9. You are planning a trip to Europe for $1\frac{1}{2}$ years. What should you deposit now in an account paying 12% compounded monthly in order to withdraw $1,400 at the end of every month while in Europe?

    $i = 1\%, n = 18$
    $1,400 × 16.398269 = $22,957.576   __$22,957.58__

10. a) How much must be deposited today at 14% compounded quarterly that would permit withdrawals of $1,500 at the end of each 3-month period for $4\frac{1}{2}$ years?

    $i = 3\frac{1}{2}\%, n = 18$
    $1,500 × 13.189682 = $19,784.52   a) __$19,784.52__

    b) How much interest is earned?

    $1,500 × 18 = $27,000.00
                      − 19,784.52
                        $ 7,215.48 Interest   b) __$7,215.48__

11. Becaue of seasonal demand, Weber Foundation Company will not be operating for the next 4 months, but will still have to pay $4,800 per month in overhead expenses.

    a) How much should the company put into an account now at 18% compounded monthly in order to pay their expenses for the next 4 months?

    $i = 1\frac{1}{2}\%, n = 4$
    $4,800 × 3.854385 = $18,501.048   a) __$18,501.05__

    b) How much interest will accumulate?

    $4,800 × 4 = $19,200.00
                − 18,501.05
                 $ 698.95 Interest   b) __$698.95__

12. A scholarship fund is planned that would award $2,000 every quarter for 4 years.

    a) How much must be invested now at 10% compounded quarterly in order to set up the fund?

    $i = 2\frac{1}{2}\%, n = 16$
    $2,000 × 13.055002 = $26,110.004   a) __$26,110__

    b) How much total interest will be earned?

    $2,000 × 16 = $32,000
                 − 26,110
                 $5,890 Interest   b) __$5,890__

13. Baxter Parts, Inc., plans to give its 4 salespeople a $500 bonus every 6 months for the next 2 years. How much should the company deposit now at 9% compounded semiannually in order to make the bonus payments?

    $i = 4\frac{1}{2}\%, n = 4$
    $500 × 3.587526 = $1,793.763   __$1,793.76__

continued

Assignment 15.3 *continued*

14. A contract for a new car calls for $2,000 down plus payments of $150 a month for the next 3 years. How much is required to pay off the car today if the contract is written at 18% compounded monthly?

    $i = 1\frac{1}{2}\%, n = 36$
    $150 \times 27.660684 = \$4149.1026$

    $4,149.10 Present value of payments
    + 2,000.00 Down payment
    $6,149.10 Needed to pay for car today $6,149.10

15. Kim Peterson would like to receive $2,500 every quarter for the next $1\frac{1}{2}$ years while she is in training overseas. A mutual fund pays 14% compounded quarterly. Find each of the following.

    a) How much must be deposited now in order to withdraw the payments desired?

    $i = 3\frac{1}{2}\%, n = 6$
    $2,500 \times 5.328553 = \$13,321.382   a) $13,321.38

    b) What will be the total amount of Kim's withdrawals?

    $2,500 × 6 withdrawals = $15,000   b) $15,000

    c) How much total interest will be earned?

    $15,000.00
    − 13,321.38
    $ 1,678.62 Interest   c) $1,678.62

16. Charles Pierce wants to set up an annuity that will pay him a certain amount for the next five years so that he can have extra money to use while retiring. How much does he need to invest now in each of the following situations in order to provide the payments he wants?

    a) Payment desired: $1,800 every six months
       Account: 12% compounded semiannually

    $i = 6\%, n = 10$
    $1,800 \times 7.360087 = \$13,248.156   a) $13,248.16

    b) Payment desired: $900 every three months
       Account: 12% compounded quarterly

    $i = 3\%, n = 20$
    $900 \times 14.877475 = \$13,389.727   b) $13,389.73

    c) Payment desired: $300 every month
       Account: 12% compounded monthly

    $i = 1\%, n = 60$
    $300 \times 44.955038 = \$13,486.511   c) $13,486.51

15.4 Sinking Fund for Annuities

Finding a Sinking Fund

A fund established to receive equal periodic payments in order to accumulate a lump sum for use at a future date is called a **sinking fund**. A sinking fund can be thought of as the reverse of an ordinary annuity. With an ordinary annuity, you know the periodic payment and are looking for the future value. With a sinking fund, you know how much you need for the future, and you want to know what periodic payments you need to make in order to reach that future value.

Sinking funds are used often in business. An individual or a company may have a financial obligation in the future. Instead of raising the entire amount when it is needed, the company may decide it is beneficial to make periodic payments that gain interest over a specific time. The accumulated money can then be used for planned future expenditures such as: buying new equipment, building an extension, or paying off a company debt which may be in the form of bonds that become due.

The calculation for sinking funds is done by using a sinking-fund table shown on pages 631–632, much the same way as the other tables we have discussed in this chapter. By using the table you are able to find out the amount of each periodic payment that is needed. The formula is:

$$\text{Amount of annuity} \times \text{Table value} = \text{Sinking-fund periodic payment}.$$

Example 1 Unit Packing, Inc., will need $80,000 in five years in order to replace a loading dock. (a) How much will the company have to put into an account every 3 months to accumulate the amount needed, if the account pays 8% compounded quarterly? (b) How much interest will be earned?

Step 1 Determine the value for N (Five years with quarterly payments means 20 periods).

    5 Years
    × 4 Periods per year
    20

    N = 20

Step 2 Determine the value for % (8% compounded quarterly means 2% per period, that is, 8% ÷ 4 periods per year).

    % = 2%

Step 3 Locate the table value.

    Table value = .041157

Step 4 Find the periodic payment. Multiply the annuity amount by the table value.

    Payment = $80,000 × .041157
            = $3,292.56

Step 5 Find the total amount of payments. Multiply the dollar amount of each payment by the number of payments.

    $3,292.56 × 20 = $65,851.20

Step 6 Subtract the total amount of payments from the amount of the annuity.

    $80,000.00 Amount
    − 65,851.20 Total payments
    $14,148.80 Interest

Answer $3,292.56 is the amount of each periodic payment, and $14,148.80 is the accumulated interest.

NOTE: The interest on a sinking fund is figured in the same way as the interest on an annuity.

Self-Check

1. Baker Mountaineering Company plans to expand its expeditions to Alaska in three years. The company estimates it will need $94,000 to accomplish this. What will have to be deposited every year at 8%, compounded annually, in order to carry out their plan? _____

2. You want to buy a new car and pay cash for it three years from now. You anticipate that the car will cost $9,000.

    a) How much will you have to put into an account every six months that pays 10% compounded semiannually? _____

    b) How much interest will you have earned at the end of three years? _____

ANSWERS 1. $28,955.20   2. (a) $1,323.15; (b) $1,061.08

TABLE 3. Sinking Fund for an Ordinary Annuity of $1 per Period

Period N	$\frac{1}{2}\%$	1%	$1\frac{1}{2}\%$	2%	$2\frac{1}{2}\%$	3	$3\frac{1}{2}\%$
1	1.000000	1.000000	1.000000	1.000000	1.000000	1.000000	1.000000
2	0.498753	0.497512	0.496278	0.495050	0.493827	0.492611	0.491401
3	0.331672	0.330022	0.328383	0.326755	0.325137	0.323530	0.321934
4	0.248133	0.246281	0.244445	0.242624	0.240818	0.239027	0.237251
5	0.198010	0.196040	0.194089	0.192158	0.190247	0.188355	0.186481
6	0.164595	0.162548	0.160525	0.158526	0.156550	0.154598	0.152668
7	0.140729	0.138628	0.136556	0.134512	0.132495	0.130506	0.128544
8	0.122829	0.120690	0.118584	0.116510	0.114467	0.112456	0.110477
9	0.110891	0.106740	0.104610	0.102515	0.100457	0.098434	0.096446
10	0.097771	0.095582	0.093434	0.091327	0.089259	0.087231	0.085241
11	0.088659	0.086454	0.084294	0.082178	0.080106	0.078077	0.076092
12	0.081066	0.078849	0.076680	0.074560	0.072487	0.070462	0.068484
13	0.074642	0.072415	0.070240	0.068118	0.066048	0.064030	0.062062
14	0.069136	0.066901	0.064723	0.062602	0.060537	0.058526	0.056571
15	0.064364	0.062124	0.059944	0.057825	0.055766	0.053767	0.051825
16	0.060189	0.057945	0.055765	0.053650	0.051599	0.049611	0.047685
17	0.056506	0.054258	0.052080	0.049970	0.047928	0.045953	0.044043
18	0.053232	0.050982	0.048806	0.046702	0.044770	0.042709	0.040817
19	0.050303	0.048052	0.045878	0.043782	0.041761	0.039814	0.037940
20	0.047666	0.045415	0.043246	0.041157	0.391470	0.037216	0.035361
24	0.039321	0.037073	0.034924	0.032871	0.030913	0.029047	0.027273
28	0.033362	0.031124	0.029001	0.026990	0.025088	0.023293	0.021603
32	0.028895	0.026671	0.024577	0.022611	0.020768	0.019047	0.017442
36	0.025422	0.023214	0.021152	0.019233	0.017452	0.015804	0.014284
40	0.022646	0.020456	0.018427	0.016556	0.014836	0.013262	0.011827
44	0.020375	0.018204	0.016210	0.014388	0.012730	0.011230	0.009878
48	0.018485	0.016334	0.014375	0.012602	0.011006	0.009578	0.008306
52	0.016887	0.014756	0.012833	0.011109	0.009574	0.008217	0.007024
56	0.015518	0.013408	0.011521	0.009847	0.008372	0.007084	0.005967
60	0.014333	0.012244	0.010393	0.008768	0.007353	0.006133	0.005089
64	0.013297	0.011230	0.009415	0.007839	0.006482	0.005328	0.004353
68	0.012384	0.010339	0.008560	0.007032	0.005733	0.004642	0.003734
72	0.011573	0.009550	0.007808	0.006327	0.005084	0.004054	0.003210
76	0.010848	0.008848	0.007141	0.005708	0.004520	0.003548	0.002765
80	0.010197	0.008219	0.006548	0.005161	0.004026	0.003112	0.002385

TABLE 3. Sinking Fund for an Ordinary Annuity of $1 per Period

Period N	_____ Interest Rates Per Period _____						
	4%	$4\frac{1}{2}$%	5%	$5\frac{1}{2}$%	6%	8%	10%
1	1.000000	1.000000	1.000000	1.000000	1.000000	1.000000	1.000000
2	0.490196	0.488998	0.487805	0.486618	0.485437	0.480769	0.476190
3	0.320349	0.318773	0.317209	0.315654	0.314110	0.308034	0.302115
4	0.235490	0.233744	0.232012	0.230294	0.228591	0.221921	0.215471
5	0.184627	0.182792	0.180975	0.179176	0.177396	0.170456	0.163797
6	0.150762	0.148878	0.147017	0.145179	0.143363	0.136315	0.129607
7	0.126610	0.124701	0.122820	0.120964	0.119135	0.112072	0.105405
8	0.108528	0.106610	0.104722	0.102864	0.101036	0.094015	0.087444
9	0.094493	0.092574	0.090690	0.088839	0.087022	0.080080	0.073641
10	0.083291	0.081379	0.079505	0.077668	0.075868	0.069029	0.062745
11	0.074149	0.072248	0.070389	0.068571	0.066793	0.060076	0.053963
12	0.066552	0.064666	0.062825	0.061029	0.059277	0.052695	0.046763
13	0.060144	0.058275	0.056456	0.054684	0.052960	0.046522	0.040779
14	0.054669	0.052820	0.051024	0.049279	0.047585	0.041297	0.035746
15	0.049941	0.048114	0.046342	0.044626	0.042963	0.036830	0.031474
16	0.045820	0.044015	0.042270	0.040583	0.038952	0.032977	0.027817
17	0.042199	0.040418	0.038699	0.037042	0.035445	0.029629	0.024664
18	0.038993	0.037237	0.035546	0.033920	0.032357	0.026702	0.021930
19	0.036139	0.034407	0.032745	0.031150	0.029621	0.024128	0.019547
20	0.033582	0.031876	0.030243	0.028679	0.027185	0.021852	0.017460
24	0.025587	0.023987	0.022471	0.021036	0.019679	0.014978	0.011300
28	0.020013	0.018521	0.017123	0.015814	0.014593	0.010489	0.007451
32	0.015949	0.014563	0.013280	0.012095	0.011002	0.007451	0.004972
36	0.012887	0.011606	0.010434	0.009366	0.008395	0.005345	0.003343
40	0.010523	0.009343	0.008278	0.007320	0.006462	0.003860	0.002259
44	0.008665	0.007581	0.006616	0.005761	0.005006	0.002802	0.001532
48	0.007181	0.006189	0.005318	0.004559	0.003898	0.002040	0.001041
52	0.005982	0.005077	0.004294	0.003622	0.003046	0.001490	0.000709
56	0.005005	0.004181	0.003480	0.002887	0.002388	0.001090	0.000483
60	0.004202	0.003454	0.002828	0.002307	0.001876	0.000798	0.000330
64	0.003538	0.002861	0.002304	0.001847	0.001476	0.000585	0.000225
68	0.002986	0.002375	0.001880	0.001482	0.001163	0.000429	0.000153
72	0.002525	0.001975	0.001536	0.001190	0.000918	0.000315	0.000105
76	0.002139	0.001644	0.001257	0.000956	0.000725	0.000231	0.000072
80	0.001814	0.001371	0.001030	0.000769	0.000573	0.000170	0.000049

Assignment 15.4

Annuities and Investments

Assume ordinary annuities for all the problems in this section.

Find the amount of each payment to be made into a sinking-fund account for the following situations.

	Amount of Annuity	Payments Made	Number of Years	Interest Rate	Periodic Payment
1.	$ 63,000	Every three months	15	10% compounded quarterly	$ 463.24

$i = 2\frac{1}{2}\%, n = 60$
$\$63,000 \times .007353 = \$463.239$

2.	$ 8,894	Every year	6	8% compounded annually	1,212.39

$i = 8\%, n = 6$
$\$8,894 \times .136315 = \$1,212.3856$

3.	$120,000	Every six months	$8\frac{1}{2}$	12% compounded semiannually	4,253.40

$i = 6\%, n = 17$
$\$120,000 \times .035445 = \$4,253.40$

4.	$ 2,600	Every month	3	18% compounded monthly	55.00

$i = 1\frac{1}{2}\%, n = 36$
$\$2,600 \times .021152 = \$54.9952$

5.	$ 50,000	Every three months	$4\frac{1}{4}$	12% compounded quarterly	2,135.45

$i = 3\%, n = 18$
$\$50,000 \times .042709 = \$2,135.45$

6.	$ 4,300	Every month	$1\frac{1}{4}$	12% compounded monthly	267.13

$i = 1\%, n = 15$
$\$4,300 \times .062124 = \$267.1332$

7.	$ 7,500	Every six months	2	9% compounded semiannually	1,753.08

$i = 4\frac{1}{2}\%, n = 4$
$\$7,500 \times .233744 = \$1,753.08$

8.	$ 80,000	Every year	20	10% compounded annually	1,396.80

$i = 10\%, n = 20$
$\$80,000 \times .017460 = \$1,396.80$

continued

Assignment 15.4 *continued*

9. Miles City sold bonds that will have a cost to the city of $800,000 in 18 years. A sinking fund paying 9% interest compounded semiannually is established. What payment must the city make every 6 months?

    $i = 4\frac{1}{2}\%, n = 36$
    $800,000 \times .011606 = \$9,284.80$

    $\$9,284.80$

10. You plan to make a down payment on a new house that you want to buy in $1\frac{1}{2}$ years. You need to save $15,000 for the down payment.

    a) How much do you need to put into an account every month, if the account earns interest at 12% compounded monthly?

    $i = 1\%, n = 18$
    $\$15,000 \times .050982 = \$764.73$

    a) $\$764.73$

    b) How much interest is earned at the end of term?

    $\$764.73 \times 18$ payments $= \$13,765.14$

    $\$15,000.00$
    $-\ \ 13,765.14$
    $\$\ \ 1,234.86$ Interest

    b) $\$1,234.86$

11. The Design Depot plans to open a new showroom in 6 years. The showroom is estimated to cost $843,000. A sinking fund is set up to provide for these expense. Deposits will be made every three months.

    a) Find the amount of each deposit if the fund earns 14% compounded quarterly.

    $i = 3\frac{1}{2}\%, n = 24$
    $\$843,000 \times .027273 = \$22,991.139$

    a) $\$22,991.14$

    b) Find the total amount of interest earned.

    $\$22,991.14 \times 24$ payments $= \$551,787.36$

    $\$843,000.00$
    $-\ \ 551,787.36$
    $\$291,212.64$ Interest

    b) $\$291,212.64$

12. Macro Software, Inc., needs $80,000 in three years to expand their business.

    a) What is the amount of the regular payment that must be made every 3 months into an account paying 10% compounded quarterly in order to set up a sinking fund for the needed capital?

    $i = 2\frac{1}{2}\%, n = 12$
    $\$80,000 \times .072487 = \$5,798.96$

    a) $\$5,798.96$

    b) Determine the total amount of interest earned.

    $\$5,798.96 \times 12$ payments $= \$69,587.52$

    $\$80,000.00$
    $-\ \ 69,587.52$
    $\$10,412.48$ Interest

    b) $\$10,412.48$

continued

Assignment 15.4 *continued*

13. Sunshine Dairy purchased new milking machines at a cost of $63,000. The equipment has an estimated life of fifteen years and a salvage value of $11,300. The dairy has set up a sinking fund to replace the machines. The estimated price of the machines in fifteen years is $81,000. The salvage value of the original machines will be used to help offset the future price of the machines. How much should the dairy deposit every three months in an account that is compounded quarterly at 8%?

    $81,000
    − 11,300 Salvage value
    $69,700 Needed

    $i = 2\%, n = 60$
    $69,700 × .008768 = $611.1296   **$611.13**

14. Rory's Rollerskate Rental took out a note for $8,000 with interest at 12% compounded annually. The note is due in five years. The company is planning to set up a sinking fund to pay off the face value of the note plus interest. Deposits will be made every six months into an account earning 9% interest compounded semiannually. Determine the amount of the periodic deposit that must be made.

    P × R × T = I
    $8,000 × 12% × 5 yr = $4,800 Interest
                          + 8,000 Face value
                            $12,800 Maturity value

    $i = 4\tfrac{1}{2}\%, n = 10$
    $12,800 × .081379 = $1,041.6512   **$1,041.65**

15. Harrington Enterprises anticipates that in 4 years it will need $165,000 for new equipment, $40,000 for packaging, and $26,000 for new training. A sinking fund is established. They can make monthly deposits into a securities account that pays 12% compounded annually. How much is each deposit?

    $i = 1\%, n = 48$
    $165,000
    40,000
    + 26,000
    $231,000

    $231,000 × .016334 = $3,773.154   **$3,773.15**

16. Happy Campground plans to open a new campground in two years for an estimated cost of $200,000. There are two possibilities available to set up a sinking fund. Fund A requires yearly payments in an account that pays interest at 8% compounded annually. Fund B requires payments every six months in an account that pays interest at 8% compounded semiannually. Determine each of the following.

continued

Assignment 15.4 *continued*

a) The periodic payment for fund A

$i = 8\%, n = 2$
$200,000 × .480769 = $96,153.80 Fund A

a) $96,153.80

b) The period payment for fund B

$i = 4\%, n = 4$
$200,000 × .235490 = $47,098 Fund B

b) $47,098

c) The difference between the two funds in interest earned.

$96,153.80 × 2 payments = $192,307.60
$200,000.00
− 192,307.60
$ 7,692.40 Interest for Fund A

$47,098 × 4 payments = $188,392

$200,000
− 188,392
$ 11,608 Interest for Fund B.

$11,608.00 Interest for Fund B
− 7,692.40 Interest for Fund A
$ 3,915.60 Difference

c) $3,915.60

In order to raise capital, businesses will issue stocks and bonds. Only corporations can issue stocks. A business need not be a corporation to issue bonds, but the company must be secure financially with a bright potential for the future in order to attract investors to buy the bonds. Stocks and bonds are purchased by individual investors, groups of investors, or other businesses and corporations. The basic difference between a stock and a bond is that a **stock** represents actual ownership of the firm. A **bond,** however, represents indebtedness: It is a written promise by a business to pay a certain amount of money to the bondholder. Although bondholders have a claim against the assets of a firm, no actual ownership takes place.

15.5 Stocks

A corporation must be approved and granted a charter by the state in which it incorporates in order to sell stock. The person who buys the stock becomes the **stockholder** or **shareholder.** The stockholder actually owns a part interest in the whole corporation. The stockholders in turn elect a **board of directors,** which governs the officers of the corporation and decides a general policy. The board of directors also makes decisions about dividends.

When stock is sold, a **stock certificate** is issued. A stock certificate is the evidence of ownership. It shows such information as number of share purchased, type of stock, buyer's name, date, name of corporation, and so on. The stock certificate may include the **par value** of the stock, that is, the value given to each share when stock is first issued. The **market value,** what the stock can actually be sold for, may be above or below par value. A corporation shows the value of its stock on its books at par value. If the stock is issued with no par value, the board of directors usually gives a "stated value" to be shown on its books.

Whether or not a corporation issues par value stock is of particular interest to its creditors.

AN IMPORTANT BEGINNING

In 1792, the government of the United States of America floated shares of stock to pay off the huge debt left by the Revolutionary War. On May 17 of that year, a group of 24 merchants and auctioneers met under a tree to establish a market for trading the new stock. Soon they began to trade shares of insurance company and banking stock as well. These traders were the originators of what was to become the New York Stock Exchange.

Defining Types of Stock

There are two kinds of basic stock issued: *common stock* and *preferred stock*. Each type carries with it certain rights and privileges.

Common stockholders have the right to vote for the board of directors and on other major issues. They have the right to earnings that remain after claims have been met of bondholders and preferred stockholders. These earnings are paid only after the board of directors declares a common-stock dividend. Likewise, if the corporation goes bankrupt, common stock holders do not share in the liquidation of assets until after creditors, bondholders, and preferred stockholders are paid. If a corporation sells only one type of stock, it is common stock.

Preferred stockholders usually cannot vote, but they do have some important privileges. They have a right to dividends before common stockholders and they have a prior claim to a corporation's assets if bankruptcy is declared. Many times, preferred stock sells for a higher price than common stock in the financial marketplace. Dividends are expressed on the stock certificate as a percent of par value or as a specific dollar amount.

There are different types of preferred stock. Some of the major types are the following.

Participating preferred: After the stated dividend and common stock dividend are paid, this stock carries with it the right to share in the remaining additional dividends.

Nonparticipating preferred: Holders of this stock are entitled only to the dividend printed on the stock certificate.

Cumulative preferred: Sometimes the board of directors will not declare a stock dividend for preferred stock. When this happens, the cumulative preferred stock accumulates the value of dividends not paid in one year or more. All these back dividends must be paid before common stockholders receive dividends.

Noncumulative preferred: With this stock, if the dividend stated on the certificate is not paid, it cannot be accumulated and recovered later.

Convertible preferred: Stockholders are entitled to convert this type of preferred stock to common stock if they so desire.

Determining Stock Dividends

A **dividend** is actually a share in the earnings of a corporation. The board of directors declares whether or not a divided will be paid to stockholders. Often all the earnings or net income of a company are not distributed as dividends; some of the earnings are kept to be reinvested in the firm. These are called **retained earnings.** The amount of dividend a stockholder receives depends on the type of stock and the number of shares owned. While the dividends on common stock are paid only after the stated dividends on preferred, sometimes the dividends for common stock are actually higher than for preferred.

For common stock, the dividend for each stock is found by dividing the total dividend declared by the number of common **stock outstanding,** that is, the total number of stocks held by the stockholders. An individual's share of this dividend is found by multiplying the stockholder's number of shares by the dividend per share.

Example 1 Allied Wood Corporation had total earnings last year of $190,000. The board of directors decided to reinvest $50,000 back in the company.

a. What is the dividend per share if there are 90,000 common share outstanding?

b. If Mrs. Webster owns 20 shares of common stock in Allied Wood, how much dividend will she receive?

Step 1   Determine the total dividend for all outstanding common stock.

$190,000 Earnings
−   50,000 Reinvestment
$140,000 Total dividend

Step 2   Find the dividend per share by dividing the total dividend by the number of common shares outstanding. $\dfrac{\$140{,}000}{\$90{,}000} = \$1.56$ Dividend per share

Step 3   Multiply the dividend per share by the number of shares to find the dividend received. $\$1.56 \times 20$ shares $= \$31.20$

Answer   (a) The dividend per share is $1.56. (b) Mrs. Webster will receive a dividend of $31.20.

Preferred-stock dividends are paid according to what is stated on the stock certificate. Dividends are expressed as either a percent or a fixed dollar amount. The percent is based on the par value of the stock. For example, the dividend on an $80 par value preferred stock could be expressed as 5% of par or as a stated dollar amount of $4. Of the two, the percent form is used more often.

Example 2   Mr. Cutley owns 62 shares of 8% preferred stock. The par value of the stock is $100. The board of directors has declared that a dividend be paid to preferred stockholders. How much cash dividend will Mr. Cutley receive?

Step 1   Determine the dividend per share by multiplying the par value by the percent dividend ($B \times R = P$). $100 \times 8\% = \$8$ Dividend per share

Step 2   Multiply the number of shares owned times the dividend per share to find the cash dividend received. $\$8 \times 62$ shares $= \$496$

Answer   Mr. Cutley will receive $496.

Remember that preferred stockholders are paid dividends before the common stockholders.

Example 3   Travel Bureau, Inc., through its board of directors, declares total dividends of $120,000. There are 20,000 shares of outstanding common stock. Stockholders own 12,000 shares of 6% preferred stock that has a par value of $75. Find the dividend per share for each type of stock.

Step 1   Determine the dividend per share for preferred stock by multiplying the par value by the percent dividend. $75 \times 6\% = \$4.50$ Dividend per share for preferred

Step 2   Find the total amount of dividends paid to preferred by multiplying the total number of preferred shares by dividend per share for preferred. $12{,}000$ shares $\times \$4.50 = \$54{,}000$

Step 3   Subtract the total preferred-stock dividend from the total stock dividend declared to find the total common-stock dividend allowed.

$\$120{,}000$ Total dividend
$-54{,}000$ Preferred dividend
$\$66{,}000$ Common dividend

Step 4   Divide the total common dividend by the number of common shares outstanding to find the dividend per share for common. $\dfrac{66{,}000}{20{,}000} = \$3.30$ Dividend per share for common

Answer   The preferred-stock dividend per share is $4.50, and the common-stock dividend per share is $3.30

Self-Check

1. A $30,000 dividend was declared for Jackson Metals Corporation. Common stock

Annuities and Investments

outstanding is 25,000 shares. What is the cash dividend for Ms. Peters, who owns 44 shares of common stock? _____

2. Ms. Lashua owns 18 shares of $150 par value preferred stock. The dividend on the stock is stated as 8%.

   a. What is his cash dividend? _____

   b. If he owns 50 shares of $80 par value preferred stock and the dividend is stated as $4, what is his cash dividend? _____

3. Hudson Baking Co., Inc., declared a total of $115,000 in cash dividend. The preferred stock outstanding is 15,000 shares, which are 5% preferred with a par value of $60. Common stock outstanding is 20,000 shares. Find the dividend per share for each type of stock. _____

ANSWERS 1. $52.80   2. (a) $216; (b) $200   3. Preferred-stock dividend per share = $3.00. Common-stock dividend per share = $3.50.

Finding Dividend Yield

Many investors are interested in learning what the **dividend yield** is on potential stock investments. It is found by dividing the annual dividend by the current market price. The dividend yield is expressed in terms of a percent.

Example 4 Terry Roberts is planning to purchase $30 par A.A.L. stock for $52.40 a share. Annual dividends for the stock amount to $7. Find the dividend yield to the nearest hundredth of a percent.

Solution Divide the annual dividend by the current market value. $\dfrac{\$7 \text{ Dividend}}{\$52.40 \text{ Market value}} = 13.36\%$

Answer The dividend yield is 13.36%.

If an individual is planning to invest in several different stocks, the dividend yield for each type of stock can be found and compared. Note that the dividend yield is not concerned with the reselling of stock. Although the investor may make a profit or a loss when reselling the stock, it does not enter into this calculation.

Self-Check

What is the dividend yield to the nearest tenth of a percent for $100 par value common stock that is currently selling for $94.20? The annual dividend paid $8.70. _____

ANSWER 9.2%

Buying and Selling Stock

Shares of stock are sold by an issuing corporation. Most often, however, they are sold by stockholders. Most investors do not plan to hold on to their stocks forever. Instead, they intend to sell them at some time. In fact, some investors buy and sell stocks on an almost daily basis. In order to make this buying and selling easier, security markets were set up. Two types of security markets are:

Stock exchange: An organization of traders. A trading place is provided for members to buy and sell stocks, bonds, and other securities for their customers. An example is the New York Stock Exchange.

Over-the-counter market (OTC): A network of stock and bond dealers who do not have a specific place to meet but instead buy and sell over the telephone or teletype. OTC usually trades securities issued by lesser known and smaller corporations.

Stockbrokers negotiate the buy and sell prices for their customers. They charge a *commission* based on the total value of the stock and the services performed, such as investment advice and analysis. These fees vary among brokers, and it is wise for investors to compare fees with services provided before choosing a stockbroker.

Besides commission fees, the purchaser may need to add on to the quoted price of stock such items as taxes and *odd-lot fees*. Stocks are traded in round lots (100 shares of stock). An odd lot is less than 100 shares. When stocks are traded in odd lots, an additional fee is charged.

After each day's activities, a listing of trading done is prepared by the major stock exchanges and over-the-counter markets. It is published in most newspapers. The stock quotations list prices for the stocks. They are given in dollar amounts, often with fractional parts of a dollar. For example, $65\frac{7}{8}$ means the market price of the stock is $65.875. (For a review of fractions and their equivalents, see Chapter 2.) A stock quotation taken from a daily newspaper is shown here. The small abbreviation "pf" after the name of the stock means preferred stock. The "u" before the Hi number indicates that that price was a new 52-week high.

Stock & div.	P.E.	Sales 100s	Hi	Low	Close	Net Chg
Cenvill 1.40	5	4	35 $\frac{3}{8}$	35 $\frac{1}{8}$	35 $\frac{3}{8}$	+ $\frac{1}{4}$
Crt-teed .90	..	36	15 $\frac{1}{4}$	15	15 $\frac{1}{8}$	+ $\frac{1}{4}$
Cessair .40	18	342	32 $\frac{1}{8}$	31 $\frac{7}{8}$	32 $\frac{1}{8}$	+ $\frac{1}{4}$
Chmpin 1.48	10	831	u29 $\frac{3}{4}$	29 $\frac{1}{2}$	29 $\frac{3}{8}$	+ $\frac{1}{8}$
Chml pf 1.20	..	12	u29 $\frac{3}{8}$	29 $\frac{3}{8}$	29 $\frac{3}{8}$	+ $\frac{1}{8}$
Chml pf 4.60	..	51	55	55	55	+ $\frac{1}{4}$
ChamSp .80	11	121	10 $\frac{3}{8}$	10 $\frac{3}{8}$	10 $\frac{1}{2}$	− $\frac{1}{8}$
ChartCo 1	9	141	14 $\frac{3}{8}$	13 $\frac{3}{4}$	14	− $\frac{1}{4}$

An explanation of the figures for the first company listed is found on page 642.

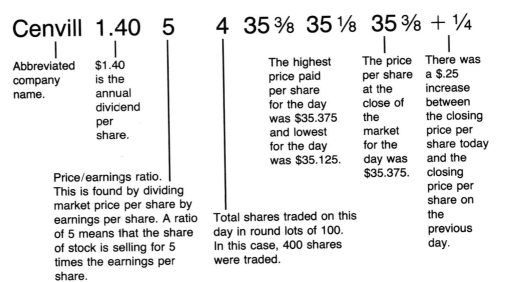

Further analysis of stocks and bonds can be done by referring to publications made available through financial service companies such as Moody's Standard & Poor's, and individual brokerage houses. *The Wall Street Journal, Barron's Forbes,* and *Business Week* can also give insight into the securities market.

Assignment 15.5

Annuities and Investments

Determine the dividends per share to the nearest cent for the following common stock. All the net income is declared as dividends for common stocks. There is no preferred stock.

Corporation	Common Stock Shares Outstanding	Net Income	Dividend Per Share
1. AA Inc.	75,500	$130,000	$ 1.72
2. BB Inc.	8,300	$ 62,000	7.47
3. CC Inc.	180,000	$354,600	1.97
4. DD Inc.	26,400	$ 68,640	2.60
5. EE Inc.	19,200	$ 66,816	3.48

Determine the dividend per share to the nearest cent for the following preferred stock. All of the net income is declared as dividends for preferred stock. No dividend is given for common stock.

Corporation	Preferred Stock Shares Outstanding	Type of Preferred	Net Income	Dividend Per Share
6. FF Inc.	14,680	6%, $80 par	$ 70,464	$ 4.80
7. GG Inc.	367,700	$3, $50 par	$1,103,100	3.00
8. HH Inc.	8,500	7%, $100 par	$ 59,500	7.00
9. II Inc.	12,100	5%, $75 par	$ 45,375	3.75
10. JJ Inc.	103,562	$2, $60 par	$ 207,124	2.00

11. Tim Manning owns 34 shares of 8% preferred stock with a par value of $150 and 21 shares of $3 preferred stock with a par value of $80. Determine his total dividends.

$150 × 8% = $12 div/share

34 × $12 = $408
21 × 3 = 63
$471 Total dividend

$471 Total dividends

continued

Assignment 15.5 *continued*

12. Frederick's Company purchased 184 shares of common stock from Energy National Gas Corporation. The net income for the corporation was $180,000. The board of directors declared a dividend after $75,000 was invested back into the corporation. How much total dividend did Fredericks Company receive if common stock oustanding is 55,000 shares?

    $180,000 Net income
    − 75,000 Retained earnings
    $105,000 Total dividend

    $\frac{\$105,000}{55,000} = \$1.91$ per share

    184 × $1.91 = $351.44 total dividend

    $351.44 Total dividend received

13. Two sisters own 56 shares of Fuller Corporation's common stock. The company announced retained earnings of $40,000. There are 21,000 shares of common stock outstanding. What is the total dividend on their stocks if the net income for the company was $94,600?

    $94,600 Net income
    − 40,000 Retained earnings
    $54,600 Total dividends

    $\frac{\$54,600}{21,000} = \$2.60$ div/share

    $2.60 × 56 = $145.60 total dividend

    $145.60 total dividend

14. Outdoorman Corporation declared a total dividend of $212,250. Outstanding common stock is 63,000 shares and outstanding preferred stock is 41,000 shares. Preferred stock is 3% par $65. Find the dividend per share for each type of stock.

    $65 × 3% = $1.95 div/share preferred
    $1.95 × 41,000 = $79,950 Total div/pref.

    $212,250 Total div.
    − 79,950 Total pref. div.
    $132,200 Total common div.

    $\frac{\$132,300}{63,000} = \$2.10$ common div/share

    **$1.95 preferred div/share,
    $2.10 common div/share**

15. The net income for Simco Corporation is $161,850. There are 15,600 outstanding shares of $2.50 par $100 preferred stock. Common-stock shares oustanding amounts to 32,500. Dividends are declared after retained earnings of $87,100. Determine the dividend per share for common stock and for preferred stock.

    $161,850 Net income
    − 87,100 Retained earnings
    $ 74,750 Total div.
    − 39,000 Total pref. div.
    $ 35,750 Total common div.

    $2.50 × 15,600 = $39,000 total pref. div.
    $\frac{\$35,750}{32,500} = \$1.10$ common div/share

    **$1.10 common div/share,
    $2.50 Preferred div/share**

16. You own 15 shares of common stock and 24 shares of 4%, $75 par preferred stock in Amtex Corporation. The company has retained earnings of $140,500. Common stock outstanding amounts to 31,600 shares. Preferred stock outstanding is 18,700 shares. If the net income for the year is figured at $348,280, what is your share of the total dividends?

    $75 × 4% = $3 pref. div/share
    $3 × 18,700 = $56,100 Total pref. div.

    $348,280 Net income
    − 140,500 Retained earnings
    $207,780 Total div.
    − 56,100 Total pref. div.
    $151,680 Total com. div.

    $\frac{\$151,680}{31,600} = \$4.80$ Common div/share

    15 × $4.80 = $ 72 Common
    24 × 3.00 = $ 72 Preferred
    $144 Total share

    $144 total share of div.

continued

NAME   DATE   SECTION

Assignment 15.5 *continued*

Complete the following table.

Type of Stock	Stock Outstanding	Net Income	Retained Earnings	Dividend Per Share	Number of Shares Held	Stockholder's Dividend for Share Held
17. Common	18,200 common shares	$62,578	$20,900	2.29	68	$ 155.72
18. 2%, $180 par preferred	54,600 preferred shares	$294,560	$98,000	3.60	21	75.60
19. $3, $75 par preferred	7,700 preferred shares	$ 41,500	$18,400	3.00	55	165
20. Common	31,500 common shares	$ 87,110	$26,000	1.94	16	31.04

21. Determine the current yield to the nearest tenth of a percent for stock whose market price is $25\frac{1}{4}$ a share and whose annual dividend is $2.34.

$$\frac{\text{Annual div.}}{\text{Mkt. value}} = \frac{\$2.34}{\$25.25} = .0926$$
$$= 9.3\% \text{ current yield}$$

                                              9.3% current yield

22. Great Midwest Property Inc., has a current market price of $28\frac{1}{8}$ per share. What is the current yield to the nearest hundredth of a percent if annual dividends amount to $1.97?

$$\frac{\$1.97}{\$28.125} = 7\% \text{ current yield}$$
$$(.07004)$$

                                                7% current yield

23. Find the current yield for QT stock whose annual dividend is $3. The current market price is $25 a share.

$$\frac{\$3}{\$25} = 12\% \text{ current yield}$$

                                                12% current yield

continued

Assignment 15.5 *continued*

24. Determine the current yield to the nearest tenth of a percent for Supreme Publishing Co., Inc., when the annual dividend is $5.40. The present selling price is $31.50 a share.

    $\frac{\$5.40}{\$31.50} = .1714$

    = 17.1% current yield

    17.1% current yield

25. What is the current yield to the nearest tenth of a percent for common stock that has an annual dividend of $2.10 and a current market price of $12.50?

    $\frac{\$2.10}{\$12.50} = 16.8\%$ current yield

    16.8% current yield

Complete the matching column for the following terms.

26. __h__ Stockholders
27. __i__ Stated value
28. __j__ Outstanding
29. __k__ Participating preferred
30. __b__ Retained earnings
31. __f__ Market price
32. __n__ Dividend
33. __d__ Board of directors
34. __e__ OTC
35. __a__ Noncumulative preferred

a) Lost dividend cannot be recovered
b) Net income reinvested
c) Number of stocks issued by corporation
d) Declares dividends
e) Type of stock market
f) Selling price
g) Par value
h) Shareholders
i) Given by the board for non-par stock
j) Number of stocks held by stockholders
k) Right to additional dividends
l) Lost dividends can be recovered
m) Entitled only to dividend printed on certificate
n) Share in earnings
o) Stock exchange

15.6 Bonds

Bonds are forms of long-term debt financing. With bonds, capital is raised by borrowing money from an individual or another business. The person or business that buys the bond is called the **bondholder.** Most bondholders are individuals. The company pays the bondholder interest periodically according to a specific interest rate stated on the bond. Interest rates on bonds vary depending on economic conditions as well as on the amount of risk involved for the bondholders. The principal is repaid at a specific maturity date in the future. The principal of a bond is called the *par value,* or *face value,* of the bond. It is usually given as $1,000 or multiples of $1,000.

Yearly or annual interest on a bond is simple interest and is found by multiplying the face value of the bond by the rate of interest stated on the bond certificate. This in turn is multiplied by one year. For instance, the annual interest on a $1,000, 7% bond is:

$$\text{Face value} \times \text{Rate of interest} \times \text{Time} = \text{Interest}$$
$$1{,}000 \quad \times \quad 7\% \quad \times \quad 1 \quad = \quad 70$$

(See Section 9.1 for a discussion of simple interest.)

Most bondholders receive an interest payment twice a year (semiannually). The **semiannual interest payment** is found by dividing the amount of the annual interest by 2. In the situation above the semiannual interest payment is $35.

For some investors bonds are desirable because the interest must be paid on them before any dividends are paid on stocks. Furthermore, dividends for common stock may not be declared at all. Also, if the business were to go bankrupt, the bondholder has a claim on the assets before the stockholder. From a corporation's point of view, issuing bonds is attractive because interest paid to bondholders can be written off as an expense before taxes are paid, whereas dividends to stockholders are not tax deductible. But, if a corporation were struggling financially for a few years, it would not have to declare a dividend for its stockholders. If the corporation failed to pay the interest to its bondholders, though, it may be forced into bankruptcy proceedings.

Defining Types of Bonds

There are many different types of bonds, some of which are listed here.

Secured bonds: Backed up by specific assets; for example, real estate.

Unsecured bonds: Not backed by specific assets but, rather, by the good reputation and strong financial position of a company. Also called **debenture bonds.**

Term bonds: Bonds issued that mature all at the same time.

Serial bonds: Bonds issued that mature at different dates.

Callable bonds: Bonds that can be paid off by the corporation before maturity. This allows the corporation to save money. When interest rates are declining, the corporation could buy back old bonds that were issued at a higher interest rate.

Registered bonds: Bonds that carry the owner's name, which is also is recorded by the corporation. The interest payment is then mailed to bondholders.

Coupon bonds: Bonds that do not carry the owner's name are not registered by the corporation. Negotiable coupons are attached to the bond. The owner must clip the coupons from the bond and submit them for payment at the corporation's bank in order to receive the interest.

Tax-free bonds: Issued by the government. The interest obtained by the bondholder is exempt from federal income taxes.

Convertible bonds: Bonds that can be exchanged or converted for stock at the bondholder's option. These are attractive to investors.

Buying and Selling Bonds

Like stocks, bonds are bought and sold in the marketplace. The degree of risk, economic conditions, maturity date, and financial news about a business will drive bond prices higher or lower. While the purchase price of bonds may fluctuate, the actual face value of the bond remains the same.

An illustration of bond quotations taken from a newspaper is shown here.

Bonds		Cur Yld	Vol	High	Low	Close	Net Chg
ArCk	8s96	12.	5	65½	65½	65⅛	+⅝
AshO	8.2s02	14.	1	60½	60½	60½	−1⅜
AsCp	11s87	13.	65	86⅞	86¾	86⅞	...
AsInv	4¾84	6.0	12	73⅜	73⅜	73⅜	...
AsInv	7⅜88	11.	9	64½	64½	64½	+½
Atchsn	4s95	7.7	2	51¾	51¾	51¾	+⅞
AtlCEl	9¼83	10.	9	92¼	92¼	92¼	+⅛
ARich	8¼00	13.	15	69	69	69	+½

An explanation of the figure for the first company listed is as follows:

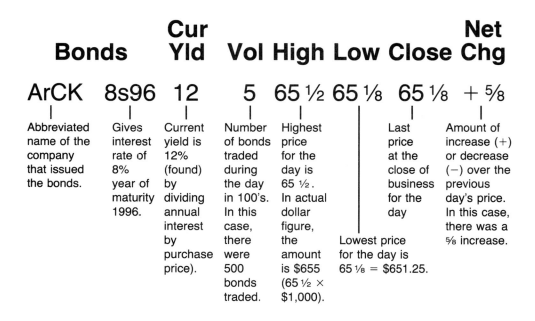

Finding Bond Prices, Premium, and Discount

As shown in the illustration above, bond prices are quoted as a percent of the face value of the bond. For example, a bond with a face value of $1,000 selling at 82 means that the bond is priced to sell at $820 ($1,000 × 82% = $820). A bond with the same face value of $1,000 selling at $101\frac{1}{2}$ means the bond is priced to sell at $1,015 ($1,000 × 101.5% = $1,015).

Bonds sold below face value are said to be sold at a **discount**. The amount of discount equals the face value minus the selling price.

If a bond is sold above face value, it is sold at a **premium**. The amount of premium equals the selling price minus the face value.

Example 1 Lee Madison sells ten bonds with a face value of $1,000 each at $102\frac{1}{2}$. Find the amount of cash received and the amount of discount or premium.

Step 1 Determine the selling price of each bond by multiplying the face value by the bond quote.

$1,000 \times 102\frac{1}{2}\% = \$1,025$

Step 2 Multiplying the selling price by the number of bonds to find the total amount of cash received.

$1,025 \times 10 = \$10,250$

Step 3 Subtract the total face value of the bonds ($1,000 \times 10 = \$10,000$) from the selling price to find the premium.

$10,250 Selling price
− 10,000 Face value
$ 250 Premium

Answer The total cash received is $10,250, and the premium is $250.

The total premium in Example 1 could also have been found in by finding the premium on one bond ($25) and multiplying that by the ten bonds ($25 × 10 = $250 premium).

Self-Check

Mr. Powell sold 5 bonds at $96\frac{1}{2}$. The face value of each bond is $1,000. Determine each of the following.

1. The cash received _____

2. The discount or premium _____

ANSWERS   1. $4,825 cash received   2. $175 discount

Determining Bond Price with Accrued Interest

The buyer of a bond must pay the quoted price of the bond plus any interest that accumulated from the last date interest was paid up to the date of purchase. This accumulated interest is called **accrued interest**. Since most corporations pay interest on a semiannual basis, the new bond buyer will receive interest for the full half year's time even though he or she did not actually hold the bond for the entire time (360 days is used as the base in the time fraction).

Example 2 A $1,000 bond with interest at 8% was purchased for $103\frac{1}{4}$ on September 28. Interest on the bond is paid semiannually on June 30 and December 31. Disregarding all other fees, what is the total cost of the bond?

Step 1 Figure the number of days between the last interest payment (June 30) and the purchase date (September 28).

31 July
31 August
28 September
90 days

Step 2 Figure the interest for 90 days. Ordinary interest, exact time is used. (See Section 9.4.)

Face value × Rate × Time = Interest

$1,000 \times 8\% \times \dfrac{90}{360} = \$20$

Step 3 Determine the price of the bond.

$1,000 \times 103\frac{1}{4} = \$1,032.50$

Step 4	Add the interest to the price of the bond to find the total cost.		$1,032.50 + 20.00 $1,052.50

Answer The total cost of the bond is $1,052.50.

Self-Check

A 9% bond with a face value of $1,000 has interest payments due January 15 and July 15. On February 3, the owner sold the bond at 96. Determine the total cost to the new bondholder.

ANSWER $964.75

Finding Current Yield on Bonds

Another term used for interest is **yield.** If a bond is kept until maturity by the same bondholder, the rate of interest and the rate of yield are the same as what is stated on the bond certificate. However, since bonds can be bought and sold at various prices in the financial marketplace, there is a change of hands, and the new bondholder may want to know what the rate of yield, or **current yield** as it is called, is for the bond. If the bond is sold at a discount or at a premium, the current yield is affected. If the price of the bond is higher than face value, the current yield will be a lower percent than the stated interest rate. Likewise, if the price is lower, the yield will be higher. The rate of current yield is found by dividing the annual interest of the bond by the new price of the bond. The price of the bond is called the market value.

Example 3 Find the current yield on a 9%, $1,000 bond sold at 97.

Step 1 Determine the interest for the bond for one year.
Face value × Rate × Time = Interest
$1,000   × 9% × 1   = $90

Step 2 Find the price of the bond. $1,000 × 97% = $970

Step 3 Find the current yield by dividing the annual interest by the price of the bond.
$\frac{\text{Annual interest}}{\text{Market value}} = \frac{90}{970} = 9.28\%$

Answer The current yield is 9.28%.

Self-Check

Determine the current yield on a $7\frac{1}{2}\%$, $1,000 bond that sold at $103\frac{1}{10}$.

ANSWER 7.27%

STOCKS AND BONDS CROSSWORD PUZZLE

ACROSS

1. With _____ preferred stock, stockholders are entitled only to the dividend printed on the stock certificate.
8. Serial bonds _____ at the same time.
10. A corporation issuing common stock and bonds _____ pays interest on bonds but may not pay dividends on stock.
11. In order to raise _____, businesses will issue stocks and bonds.
13. The price/earnings _____ is found by dividing the market price per share by the earnings per share.
14. The board of directors decides whether or not a _____ will be declared.
15. Dividend _____ is found by dividing the market price by the current market price.
16. Interest on bonds is usually paid on a _____-annual basis.
18. A stock is a _____ in the ownership of a firm.
20. Bonds sold below face value are said to be sold at a _____.
24. The _____ yield for a bond is found by dividing the annual interest by the market value of the bond.
26. _____ preferred stock accumulates the dividends not paid in one year or more.
27. The abbreviation _____ stands for a network of stock and bond dealers who do not have a specific place to meet.
30. A stock _____ can be used as evidence of ownership and shows such things as type of stock, name of corporation, buyer's name, number of shares, and so forth.
32. The _____ value of a bond can also be called the principal.
33. When a bond is sold the _____ interest is called the accrued interest.

DOWN

2. Stock _____ is the number of stocks held by the stockholders.
3. When a stock is first issued a value is given to each share, called the _____ value.
4. With government bonds the holder does not have to pay an income _____ on interest received.
5. _____ preferred stock can be exchanged for common stock at the option of the stockholder.
6. There are two kinds of basic stock issued: common stock and _____ stock.
7. Only a corporation can _____ stock.
9. If a bond is sold above face value, it is sold at a _____.
12. _____-lot fee is charged if less than 100 shares are traded.
17. A bond pays _____ periodically.
19. Net income reinvested in a company is called _____ earnings.
21. The selling _____ of a stock or bond fluctuates with the market.
22. The type of interest figured for bonds is called _____ interest.
23. Bonds sold at below face _____ are said to be sold at a discount.
25. A stock _____ is an organization of traders where a trading place is provided for members to buy and sell stocks and other securities.
28. The abbreviation for preferred is _____.
29. Dividends are paid from the _____ income of a corporation.
31. _____ bonds mature at the same time.
32. A stockbroker charges a commission for his or her services; it is called the broker's _____.

(See crossword boxes on page 652).

STOCKS AND BONDS CROSSWORD PUZZLE

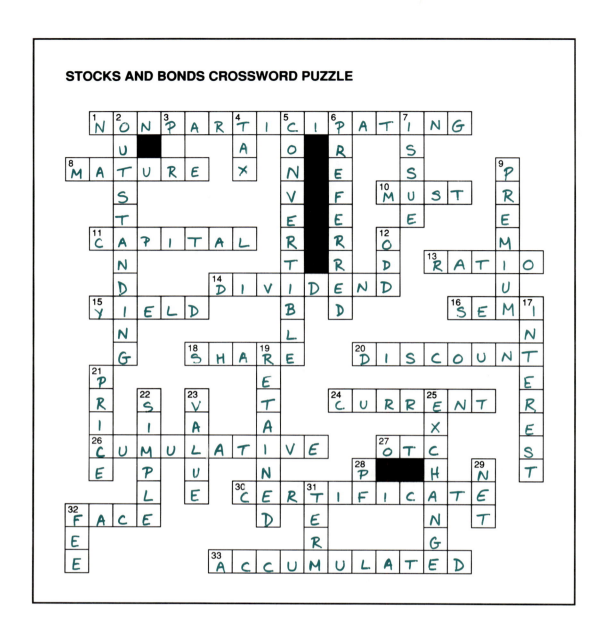

NAME   DATE   SECTION

Assignment 15.6

Annuities and Investments

Complete the following table for bonds that have a face value of $1,000. The interest payment is made twice a year.

	Bond Interest Rate	Bond Life	Annual Interest (to nearest cent)	Interest Payment	Example:
1.	7%	10 years	$ 70.00	35.00	1. $1,000 × 7% × 1 = $70 annual interest
2.	9¼%	8 years	92.50	46.25	$70 ÷ 2 = $35 interest payment
3.	10½%	15 years	105.00	52.50	
4.	6%	5 years	60.00	30.00	
5.	11⅜%	10 years	113.75	56.88	

Determine the price of the following bonds and the amount of discount or premium for each bond. The par value is $1,000.

	Bond	Quote	Price	Discount	Premium	Example:
6.	AdaPg 9¾s 05	85	$ 850.00	150.00		6. $1,000 × 85% = $850 price
7.	BalGA 8⅝ 88	103½	1,035.00		35.00	$1,000 − $850 = $150 discount
8.	EK, NY 2⅝ 86	79⅝	796.25	203.75		
9.	CALLY 9s 08	81	810.00	190.00		
10.	FAirl 5¼ 94	102¼	1,022.50		22.50	
11.	Bexl 10s 90	115½	1,155.00		155.00	
12.	CelC 11¼s 01	92¼	922.50	77.50		
13.	DalC 12s 96	94⅜	943.75	56.25		
14.	ELD 7½s 89	106	1,060.00		60.00	

15. Dan Gossett sold 6 bonds whose face value is $1,000 at 94¼ each. $1,000 × 94.25% = $942.50
                                                                          $1,000 − $942.50 = $57.50
    a) Determine the total amount of cash received. $5,655 total cash received

    $942.50 × 6 = $5,655 total cash received

    b) Determine the total discount or premium.

    $57.50 × 6 = $345 total discount $345 total discount

continued

Assignment 15.6 continued

16. Barbara Middleton sold her $1,000 par value bonds at $103\frac{1}{2}$.

   a) If she sold 12 bonds, how much cash did she receive?

   $1,000 × 103.5% = $1,035 price of one
   $1,035 × 12 = $12,420 total cash received

   $12,420 total cash received

   b) What was the total amount of discount or premium?

   $1,035 − 1,000 = $35 premium on one
   $35 × 12 = $420 total premium

   $420 total premium

17. Dwight O'Brien purchased an 8%, $1,000 bond that pays interest on June 1 and December 1. He purchased the bond on August 5 and the quoted price was 101.3. What is the total purchase price? (Use the business year of 360 days.)

$1,000 × 8% × $\frac{65}{360}$ = $14.44 interest

$1,000 × 101.3% = $1,013 quoted price
$1,013 + 14.44 = $1,027.44 total purchase price

$1,027.44 total purchase price

```
    30
June 1  Int. paid
    29
    31  July
     5  Aug. purchased
    65 days
```

18. On February 15, Rose Ross purchased at $11\frac{1}{4}$%, $1,000 bond that sold at 97. If the bond pays interest on March 1 and September 1, what is the purchase price? (Use the business year of 360 days.)

$1,000 × 11.25% × $\frac{161}{360}$ = $52.19 interest

$1,000 × 97% = $970
$970 + 52.19 = $1,022.19 total purchase price

$1,022.19 total purchase price

```
    30 Sept
 −   1 Sept int. paid
    29
    31 Oct
    30 Nov
    31 Dec
    31 Jan
    15 Feb purchased
   167 days
```

Complete the following table, assuming that this is a 360-day business year. The face value of the bonds is $1,000 and interest is paid on April 1 and October 1.

	Quoted Price	Bond Interest Rate	Date of Purchase	Number of Bonds Purchased	Total Purchase Price
19.	102	$8\frac{1}{2}$%	May 15	10	$10,303.90
20.	97	$10\frac{1}{4}$%	December 20	23	22,833.94
21.	$96\frac{1}{2}$	7%	January 1	8	7,863.12
22.	88	$9\frac{3}{8}$%	September 10	30	27,665.70
23.	$103\frac{1}{4}$	12%	June 22	16	16,957.28

24. What is the current yield to the nearest hundredth of a percent on a $10\frac{1}{2}$%, $1,000 bond, that sold at $103\frac{1}{4}$?

$1,000 × 10.5% × 1 = $105 interest
$1,000 × 103.25% = $1,032.50 market value

$\frac{\text{Annual interest}}{\text{Market value}} = \frac{\$105}{\$1,032.50} = .10169$

= 10.17% current yield

10.17% current yield

Assignment 15.6 *continued*

25. A $9\frac{1}{4}\%$, $1,000 bond sold at 97. Determine the current yield to the nearest tenth of a percent.

$1,000 × 9.25% × 1 = $92.50 interest
$1,000 × 97% = $970 market value

$$\frac{\$92.50}{\$970} = .0953 = 9.5\% \text{ current yield}$$

9.5% current yield

26. Find the current yield to the nearest hundredth of a percent on an $8\frac{1}{2}\%$, $1,000 bond selling at $88\frac{3}{8}$.

$1,000 × 8.5% = $85 interest
$1,000 × 88.375% = $883.75 market value

$$\frac{\$85}{\$883.75} = .09618 = 9.62\% \text{ current yield}$$

9.62% current yield

27. An $11\frac{1}{4}\%$, $1,000 bond sells at $104\frac{1}{2}$. What is the current yield to the nearest hundredth of a percent?

$1,000 × 11.25% × 1 = $112.50 interest
$1,000 × 104.5% = $1,045 market value

$$\frac{\$112.50}{\$1,045} = .10765 = 10.77\% \text{ current yield}$$

10.77% current yield

Complete the matching column for the following terms.

28. __h__ Term
29. __g__ Interest
30. __j__ Face value
31. __d__ Semiannually
32. __c__ Callable
33. __e__ Debenture
34. __b__ Serial
35. __f__ Coupon

a) Owner registered
b) Mature at different times
c) Right to pay off bond
d) Bond payments usually made
e) Unsecured bonds
f) Owner not registered
g) Business expense
h) Mature at the same time
i) Secured bonds
j) Par value

Comprehensive Problems for Chapter 15

Annuities and Investments

1. You must repay $12,000 to Conrad Equipment Company in three years. How much should you invest now at 8% compounded quarterly in order to meet your debt?

   Rate per period = 2%
   Periods = 12
   Present value of $1 = .788493
   $12,000 × .788493 = $9,461.92

   $9,461.92

2. In four years Spectrum Color will need $7,000 to purchase new light tables, $4,000 for a new training program, and $24,000 for a new camera. How much should be invested now at 6% compounded semiannually in order to have enough funds for the future plans?

   $7,000
   24,000
   + 4,000
   $35,000 Needed

   Rate per period = 3%
   Periods = 8
   Present value of $1 = .789409
   $35,000 × .789409 = $27,629.32

   $27,629.32

Find the dollar amount of each payment to be made into an ordinary-annuity, sinking-fund account for each of the following.

	Amount	Payment Made	Number of Years	Interest Rate	Payment
3.	$45,000	Every 6 mos.	16	11% compounded semiannually	$544.28
4.	$26,300	Every year	24	8% compounded annually	$393.92
5.	$900	Every month	$1\frac{1}{2}$	12% compounded monthly	$45.88
6.	$8,700	Every 3 mos.	5	10% compounded quarterly	$340.58

3. $i = 5\frac{1}{2}\%, n = 32$
   $45,000 × .012095 = $544.275

4. $i = 8\%, n = 24$
   $26,300 × .014978 = $393.9214

5. $i = 1\%, n = 18$
   $900 × .050982 = $45.8838

6. $i = 2\frac{1}{2}\%, n = 20$
   $8,700 × .039147 = $340.5789

continued

Comprehensive Problems *continued*

Find the amount of the annuity for each of the following.

	Periodic Payment	Payments Made	Number of Years	Interest Rate	Amount
7.	$ 3,250	At the end of every 6 months	4	9% compounded semiannually	$ $30,485.05

$i = 4\frac{1}{2}\%, n = 8$
$3,250 \times 9.380014 = \$30,485.045$

8.	$15,400	At the beginning of every year	5	8% compounded annually	97,573.30

$i = 8\%, n = 6$
$15,400 \times 7.335929 = \quad \$112,973.30$
$\qquad\qquad\qquad\qquad\quad - \quad \underline{15,400.00}$
$\qquad\qquad\qquad\qquad\qquad \$\ 97,573.30$

9.	$ 350	At the beginning of every month	$1\frac{1}{2}$	18% compounded monthly	7,278.85

$i = 1\frac{1}{2}\%, n = 19$
$350 \times 21.796716 = \quad \$7,628.8506$
$\qquad\qquad\qquad\qquad\ - \quad \underline{350.00}$
$\qquad\qquad\qquad\qquad\quad \$7,278.8506$

10.	$ 1,600	At the end of every 3 months	12	14% compounded quarterly	192,621.20

$i = 3\frac{1}{2}\%, n = 48$
$1,600 \times 120.388251 = \$192,621.20$

11.	$ 8,700	At the end of every 6 months	$3\frac{1}{2}$	10% compounded semiannually	70,835.47

$i = 5\%, n = 7$
$8,700 \times 8.142008 = \$70,835.469$

Find the present value of the ordinary annuity for each of the following.

	Periodic Payment	Payments Made	Number of Years	Interest rate	Present Value
12.	$ 800	Every 6 mos.	24	9% compounded semiannually	$ 15,628.49

$i = 4\frac{1}{2}\%, n = 48$
$800 \times 19.535607 = \$15,628.485$

13.	$7,000	Every year	10	10% compounded annually	43,011.97

$i = 10\%, n = 10$
$7,000 \times 6.144567 = \$43,011.969$

continued

Comprehensive Problems *continued*

	Periodic Payment	Payments Made	Number of Years	Interest rate	Present Value
14.	$ 200	Every month	$1\frac{1}{2}$	12% compounded monthly	3,279.65

$i = 1\%, n = 18$
$\$200 \times 16.398269 = \$3,279.6538$

15.	$1,730	Every 3 mos.	$4\frac{1}{2}$	10% compounded quarterly	24,831.32

$i = 2\frac{1}{2}\%, n = 18$
$\$1,730 \times 14.353363 = \$24,831.317$

16. Prime Electronic, Inc., needs to replace a $43,000 laser cutter after 11 years of use. Because of inflation, the corporation plans to set up an ordinary-annuity, sinking-fund account of $55,000 to replace the cutter at the end of its estimated life. Determine each of the following.

   a) The deposit required every three months in a fund that pays interest at 8% compounded quarterly

   $i = 2\%, n = 44$; sinking fund for an annuity
   $\$55,000 \times .014388 = \$791.34$

   a) $791.34

   b) The total amount of interest earned

   $\$791.34 \times 44$ payments $= \$34,818.96$
   $\$55,000.00$
   $- 34,818.96$
   $\$20,181.04$ Interest

   b) $20,181.04

17. You are the volunteer financial adviser for the regional Boy Scout troop. The troop plans to invest $125 at the end of every three months in a mutual fund that pays 18% compounded quarterly.

   a) What is the amount of the annuity at the end of 2 years?

   $i = 4\frac{1}{2}\%, n = 8$; amount of annuity
   $\$125 \times 9.380014 = \$1,172.5017$

   a) $1,172.50

   b) If the payments were changed to $40 at the end of every month in an account that pays 18% compounded monthly for the same term, find the annuity account.

   $i = 1\frac{1}{2}\%, n = 24$
   $\$40 \times 28.633521 = \$1,145.3408$

   b) $1,145.34

18. E. F. Cummings is setting up a trust fund in the form of an ordinary annuity for his nephew, who will be attending law school. The nephew will be able to withdraw $1,800 every 3 months for the next four years. If the fund earns 10% compounded quarterly, find each of the following.

continued

Comprehensive Problems *continued*

a) The amount that Cummings must invest now

$i = 2\frac{1}{2}\%$, $n = 16$; present value of an annuity
$1,800 \times 13.055002 = \$23,499.003$

a) $\underline{\$23,499}$

b) The total amount of interest earned at the end of 4 years

$1,800 \times 16$ payments = $\$28,800$
$\underline{-23,499}$
$\$5,301$ Interest

b) $\underline{\$5,301}$

19. Glen Howard plans ahead for his small-business expansion. He deposits $1,300 at the beginning of every six months in an account that pays 12% compounded semiannually. After 8 years he stops making deposits, but the account is left untouched for another year.

a) How much is in the account after nine years?

$i = 6\%$, $n = 17$; amount of annuity
$\$1,300 \times 28.212880 = \$36,676.744$
$\underline{-1,300.00}$
$\$35,376.744$

P × R × T = I
$\$35,376.74 \times 12\% \times \frac{1}{2} = \$2,122.60$
$\$37,499.34 \times 12\% \times \frac{1}{2} = \$2,249.96$

$\$35,376.74$
$\underline{+2,122.60}$
$\$37,499.34$
$\underline{+2,249.96}$
$\$39,749.30$ in the account

a) $\underline{\$39,749.30}$

b) How much total interest is earned?

$\$1,300 \times 16$ payments = $\$20,800$
$\$39,749.30$
$\underline{-20,800.00}$
$\$18,949.30$ interest

b) $\underline{\$18,949.30}$

20. You plan to have $21,000 in the bank at the end of 4 years so that you can invest in a photo franchise. You want to set up an ordinary-annuity sinking fund.

a) How much must you deposit every six months in an account that pays 9% compounded semiannually?

$i = 4\frac{1}{2}\%$, $n = 8$; sinking fund for an annuity
$\$21,000 \times .106610 = \$2,238.81$

a) $\underline{\$2,238.81}$

b) If you decide to make quarterly deposits in an account paying 8% compounded quarterly, what would be the difference in interest earned between the two accounts?

$i = 2\%$, $n = 16$
$\$21,000 \times .053650 = \$1,126.65$
$\$1,126.65 \times 16$ payments = $\$18,026.40$
$\$21,000.00$
$\underline{-18,026.40}$
$\$2,973.60$ Interest, situation B

$\$2,238.81 \times 8$ payments = $\$17,910.48$

$\$21,000.00$
$\underline{-17,910.48}$
$\$3,089.52$ Interest, situation A

$\$3,089.52$
$\underline{-2,973.60}$
$\$115.92$ Difference in interest

b) $\underline{\$115.92}$

continued

Comprehensive Problems *continued*

21. Find the amount of the annuity in each of the following situations if deposits are made at the end of each period and the term is 6 years.

    a) Deposits of $600 made every six months; interest rate is 12% compounded semiannually

        $i = 6\%$, $n = 12$, deposit = $600; amount of an annuity
        $600 × 16.869941 = $10,121.964

        a) $10,121.96

    b) Deposits of $300 made every three months; interest rate is 12% compounded quarterly

        $i = 3\%$, $n = 24$, deposit = $300
        $300 × 34.426470 = $10,327.941

        b) $10,327.94

    c) Deposits of $100 made every month; interest rate is 12% compounded monthly

        $i = 1\%$, $n = 72$, deposit = 100
        $100 × 104.709931 = $10,470.993

        c) $10,470.99

22. Congratulations! You are the grand prize winner in a cereal sweepstakes and are offered a choice of the following prizes:

    Prize 1: You will receive payments of $5,000 at the end of every year for 20 years.

    Prize 2: You will receive $80,000 cash now.

    a) The money for prize 1 will be held in an account that pays 10% compounded annually. How much "cash now" does prize 1 represent?

        $i = 10\%$, $n = 20$; present value of an annuity
        $5,000 × 8.513564 = $42,567.82

        a) $42,567.82

    b) Which prize will you choose? Why?

    Individual answers and reasons.

    c) If you wanted to have $100,000 in 20 years, how much would you have to deposit at the end of every year in a fund that pays 10% compounded annually?

        $i = 10\%$, $n = 20$; sinking fund for an annuity
        $100,000 × .017460 = $1,746

        c) $1,746

23. Citrus Growers, Inc., had total earnings last year of $1,420,000. The board of directors voted to reinvest $850,000 back in the company. Figure each of the following.

    a) The dividend per share if there are 70,000 shares outstanding.

        $1,420,000
      −   850,000
        $570,000 ÷ 70,000 shares = $8.14 dividend per share

        a) $8.14

    b) The dividend you will receive if you own 27 shares of common stock in the company.

        $8.14 × 27 shares = $219.78

        b) $219.78

continued

Comprehensive Problems *continued*

24. You are planning to buy preferred stock in New Genetics, Inc., for $146.25 a share. The par value of the stock is $100. Annual dividends amounted to $16.09. Determine the dividend yield to the nearest whole percent.

$$\frac{\$16.09}{\$146.25} = .110017 = 11\%$$

11%

25. Find the current yield to the nearest hundredth of a percent on an $8\frac{1}{4}\%$, $1,000 bond selling at $91\frac{3}{8}$.

$1,000 × 8.25% = $82.50 interest
$1,000 × $91\frac{3}{8}$% = $913.75 market value

$$\frac{\$82.50}{913.75} = .0902872 = 9.03\%$$

9.03%

26. The net income for Ampex Design, Inc., is $55,200. There are 17,000 shares outstanding of $2, $75 par preferred stock. Common-stock shares outstanding amount to 30,000. Retained earnings are $13,600, and dividends have been declared by the Board. Figure each of the following.

a) The dividend per share for common stock

```
      $55,200
    -  13,600
      $41,600  Total dividends
```

$2 × 17,000 shares = $34,000 preferred dividend

```
      $41,600
    -  34,000
30,000 shares | $ 7,600 left for common dividend
      $.25333 dividend per common share
```

a) $.25

b) The dividend per share for preferred stock

$2, $75 par preferred stock means that the dividend per share is $2 per preferred share.

b) $2

27. Terry Boldizar sells 25 bonds with a face value of $1,000 each at $104\frac{1}{2}$. Find each of the following.

a) The amount of cash received

$1,000 × $104\frac{1}{2}$% = $1,045
$1,045 × 25 = $26,125 cash received

a) $26,125

b) The amount of discount or premium

```
  $26,125
-  25,000
  $ 1,125 premium
```

b) $1,125 premium

28. Mrs. Otha Benson owns 211 shares of 6%, $75 par preferred stock in Health Products, Inc. The board of directors declared a dividend for preferred stockholders. The company earned $3,400,000 and $500,000 of this was reinvested in the corporation. Find the amount of Mrs. Benson's dividend.

$75 × 6% = $ 4.50 dividend per share
         ×   211 shares
             $949.50

$949.50

continued

Comprehensive Problems *continued*

29. A $1,000 bond with interest at 7% was purchased for $102\frac{1}{4}$ on October 3. Interest on the bond is paid semiannually on June 30 and December 31. Disregarding all other fees, what is the total cost of the bond?

```
31  July
31  Aug
30  Sept
 3  Oct
95  days
```

$P \times R \times T = I$
$1,000 \times 7\% \times \dfrac{95}{360} = \$18.47$

$1,000 \times \$102.25 = \quad \$1,022.50$
$\qquad\qquad\qquad +\quad\underline{\quad 18.47}$ Interest
$\qquad\qquad\qquad\quad\ \ \$1,040.97$ Total cost

$1,040.97

30. The board of directors of Video Occasions, Inc., declared a total dividend of $971,000. Stockholders own 120,000 shares of 3%, $80 par preferred stock. There are 350,000 shares of outstanding common stock. Figure each of the following.

a) The dividend per share for common stock

$80 \times 3\% = \$2.40$ dividend per share for preferred stock
$2.40 \times 120,000$ shares $= \$288,000$ total preferred dividend

$971,000 Total dividend
$-\ \underline{\ 288,000}$ Preferred
$683,000 Left for common

$683,000 \div 350,000 = \$1.95$ dividend per share for common stock

a) $1.95

b) The dividend per share for preferred stock

3% $80 par preferred stock has a dividend of 3% of $80, which is $2.40.

b) $2.40

Case 1

The Mitchell family owns the following stocks and bonds:

Air Control Corp.: 26 shares of common stock,

Air Control Corp.: 11 shares of 3%, $75 par preferred stock,

American Chemical: 8 bonds, $10\frac{1}{2}$%, $1,000 par 6-year bonds.

Air Control Corp. had total earnings of $68,255. Common stock outstanding is 12,600 shares and preferred stock outstanding is 8,300 shares. The board of directors announced that $26,900 will be held for retained earnings and the rest of net income will be divided into dividends.

The current purchase price for Air Control Corp. common stock is $20\frac{1}{4}$. American Chemical bonds' current market value is 96.

a) What was the Mitchell family's total income from stocks and bonds for the year?

b) Find the dividend yield to the nearest hundredth of a percent for the common stock.

c) Determine the current yield to the nearest hundredth of a percent on American Chemical bonds.

Case 2

A friend of yours has decided that she will need to buy a car in 2 years and wants to have at least $4,000 saved for the purchase. She wonders how much she needs to invest now at her credit union at 6% compounded semiannually in order to have the savings she wants. She knows you are studying business math and asks for your advice.

a) How much should she invest now? She also wondered if she should invest in stocks and/or bonds instead.

b) Give three advantages and disadvantages of investing in stock.

c) Give three advantages and disadvantages of investing in bonds.

d) Would you recommend setting up an annuity instead? Why or why not?

Key Terms

Accrued interest
Amount
Annuities
Annuity due
Board of directors
Bond
Bondholder
Callable bond
Compound-interest period
Conversion period
Convertible bond
Dividend
Dividend yield
Future value
Market value
Noncumulative preferred stock
Nonparticipating preferred stock
Ordinary annuity
Over-the-counter market
Par value
Rate of compound interest
Registered bond
Retained earnings
Secured bond
Semiannual interest payment
Serial bonds
Sinking fund
Stock
Stockholder, or shareholder

Convertible preferred stock
Coupon bonds
Cumulative preferred stock
Current yield
Discount
Participating preferred stock
Payment period
Premium
Present value
Present value of an annuity
Stock certificate
Stock exchange
Stock outstanding
Tax-free bonds
Term
Term bonds
Unsecured bonds
Yield

Key Concepts

- Stocks and bonds are issued by a business in order to raise capital.
- A stock is a share of ownership in a corporation. There are two kinds: common and preferred.
- A stock certificate is evidence of ownership of a stock.
- The board of directors is elected by the stockholders and guides corporate officers and general policy.
- Par value is the value given to each stock when it is issued and is printed on the stock certificate.
- Dividend is the stockholder's share in a corporation's earnings.
- Stock outstanding is the number of shares held by the stockholders.
- Dividend per share = $\dfrac{\text{Total dividend}}{\text{Stock outstanding}}$
- Stockholder's total dividend = Dividend per share × Number of shares held
- Dividend yield on stock = $\dfrac{\text{Dividend per share}}{\text{Current market price per share}}$
- A security market provides a convenient means for selling stocks. There are two types: stock exchange and over-the-counter market (OTC).
- Bonds represent capital raised by borrowing money from individuals and other businesses. There are many different types of bonds.
- The principal of a bond is called the face value, or par value. It is usually $1,000. Interest is paid periodically during the life of the bond. Annual interest on a bond is found by the formula: Principal × Rate × Time = Interest, where time = 1 year.
- Bond prices are quoted as a percent of the face value of the bond.
- Face value − Selling price = Discount
- Selling price − Face value = Premium
- If a bond is purchased between interest periods, the purchaser must pay the accrued interest earned from the date of the last interest payment to the date of purchase.
- Current yield on a bond = $\dfrac{\text{Annual interest}}{\text{Current market value}}$
- Present value is the current value of a sum of money that will yield a higher amount at a future maturity date. To use a present-value table, the rate per period and number of periods must be known.
- Rate per period = $\dfrac{\text{Annual rate}}{\text{Number of times compounding occurs}}$
- Number of periods = Years × Number of times compounding occurs

- Amount of an ordinary annuity = $\dfrac{\text{Dollar value of a}}{\text{periodic payment}} \times$ Table value

- Amount of an annuity due = $\left(\dfrac{\text{Dollar value of a}}{\text{periodic payment}} \times \dfrac{\text{Table}}{\text{value}}\right) - \dfrac{\text{Value of}}{\text{one payment}}$

- $\dfrac{\text{Present value of}}{\text{an annuity}} = \dfrac{\text{Size of each}}{\text{periodic payment}} \times$ Table value

- $\dfrac{\text{Sinking-fund}}{\text{periodic payment}} =$ Amount of annuity $\times$ Table value

Appendix A
The Metric System

The Metric System

The most widely used system of weights and measures in the civilized world is the *metric system*. In fact, the United States of America is the only major nation to resist adopting it.

Metrics offer major advantages over the system we use at present, the English system. First, it is logical, using a basic unit of measure for each of the different types of measurement: linear, volume, weight, and temperature. Second, it is based on tens, making it a decimal system and, therefore, easy to use in computation.

Developed in France after the revolution of 1789, the metric system is already used by certain segments of American society. Medical dosages are administered according to metric standards, for example, and scientific experiments are conducted using the metric system.

Using Metric Prefixes

Part of the reason for the metric system's convenience is its use of prefixes before each basic unit of measurement to indicate powers of ten. Noting the prefix, we can simply multiply or divide the particular unit by the appropriate power of ten to indicate the actual length, volume, or weight.

The commonly used metric prefixes are:

Prefix	*Abbreviation*	*Power of 10*	
milli-	m	.001	or thousandth
centi-	c	.01	or hundredth
deci-	d	.1	or tenth
deca-	da	10	or ten
hecto-	h	100	or hundred
kilo-	k	1,000	or thousand

Defining Metric Units

The *meter* is the basic metric unit of length. It was meant to equal one ten-millionth the distance from the Earth's pole to its equator. Because the original calculation of this distance was inaccurate, that is not strictly true. The meter is slightly longer than a yard, 39.37 inches as opposed to 36 inches. Meter is expressed by the abbreviation *m*.

Dividing a meter into 10 equal parts gives decimeters. Dividing it into 100 equal parts gives centimeters, and so on. A kilometer, on the other hand, equals 1000 meters—one meter multiplied a thousand times.

Example 1   Pedro Ortega is an architect in Mexico City, where the metric system is in use. For part of a large apartment complex, he designs a tiled walkway 2 meters wide. The tiles he intends to recommend for use are each 1 decimeter wide. How many tiles across will the walkway be, not allowing for grouting joints?

Step 1   A decimeter is smaller than a meter: one tenth of a meter. $1 \text{ m} = 10 \text{ d}$

Step 2   Multiply the number of meters by 10 to find the number of decimeters. $2 \text{ m} \times 10 = 20 \text{ d}$

Answer   The walkway will be aproximately 20 tiles wide.

NOTE: In multiplying and dividing metric units, dealing with powers of ten, remember the technique of moving the decimal point. (See Sections 1.3 and 1.4.)

Self-Check

1. Pedro is traveling to his ranch outside Mexico City. It is 38.5 kilometers out into the countryside. How many meters is this?

2. Marilee Rushman, a geographer, wants to express a measurement of 65 meters in terms of hectometers. How many hectometers will there be?

ANSWERS   1. $1 \text{ k} = 1,000 \text{ m}$ 2. $1 \text{ h} = 100 \text{ m}$
38 500.   .65
↑   ↑
38,500 meters   .65 hectometers

The *liter* is the basic metric unit of volume. It is equal to the volume of a cube that is one tenth of a meter—one decimeter—on each side. Again, the prefixes are used.

1 centiliter = $\frac{1}{100}$ (.01) of a liter

1 milliliter = $\frac{1}{1000}$ (.001) of a liter

1 kiloliter = 1,000 liters

Liter is abbreviated "l."

The *gram* is the basic metric unit of weight. It equals the weight of the amount of distilled water that can be contained in a cube one hundredth of a meter—one centimeter—on each side. Gram is expressed by the abbreviation "g."

Example 2   Fatima Marada, a gourmet chef in Vancouver, British Columbia, is making hot sauce. The recipe calls for .5 liter of tomato sauce and 2 grams of chili powder. Express these measurements as centiliters and centigrams.

Solution   The metric prefix "centi-" stands for hundredths. Therefore, in each instance you multiply by 100.
$.5 \text{ l} \times 100 = 50$ or
$.5 = 50$ centiliters

$2 \text{ g} \times 100 = 200$ or
$2 = 200$ centigrams

Answer   The recipe calls for 50 centiliters of tomato sauce and 200 centigrams of chili powder.

Self-Check

1. In his job at the U.S. Mint, Kingsley Troutman finds that a nickel weighs 5 grams. What is the weight in kilograms of the metal needed to manufacture 1,000 nickels? _____

2. Marilyn Bradley, a nurse, must administer an IV that contains 150 centiliters of fluid. How much is this in liters? _____

ANSWERS   1. 5 kilograms   2. 1.5 liters

Degrees Celsius is the metric measure of temperature. On the Celsius scale, 0° Celsius is the temperature at which water freezes, and 100° Celsius is the temperature at which it boils. To convert a temperature reading from Fahrenheit (abbreviated F and the measure currently in general use in the United States) to Celsius (abbreviated C), do the following:

Step 1   Subtract 32 from the Fahrenheit figure.

Step 2   Multiply the result by 5.

Step 3   Divide the product by 9.

Example 3   Nurse Marilyn Bradley takes a patient's temperature, finding it to be 98 degrees Fahrenheit. What is this in degrees Celsius?

Step 1	Subtract 32.	98° − 32 = 66
Step 2	Multiply by 5.	66 × 5 = 330
Step 3	Divide by 9.	330 ÷ 9 = 36.67°

Answer   The patient's temperature in Celsius is 36.67 degrees.

To convert from Celsius to Fahrenheit, reverse the procedure shown above.

Step 1   Multiply the Celsius figure by 9.

Step 2   Divide the product by 5.

Step 3   Add 32.

Example 4   Nurse Bradley is using a thermometer calibrated in degrees Celsius. Her patient's temperature registers $36\frac{2}{3}$°C. What is this in Fahrenheit?

Step 1   Multiply by 9.

$$36\frac{2}{3} = \frac{110}{3}$$

$$\frac{110}{\cancel{3}} \times \cancel{9}^{3} = 330$$

Step 2   Divide by 5.

$$\begin{array}{r} 66 \\ 5\overline{)330} \\ \underline{30} \\ 30 \\ \underline{30} \end{array}$$

Step 3   Add 32.   66 + 32 = 98°

Answer   The patient's temperature in Fahrenheit is 98 degrees.

Self-Check

1. Convert 100°F to Celsius.
2. Convert 25°C to Fahrenheit.

ANSWERS   1. 37.78°C   2. 77°F

Performing Metric Conversions

As we have done with temperature on two scales, you can convert English-system measures of distance, volume, and weight to metric units and metric to English. In the future this will not be necessary. The English system will be of historical interest only, and people will visualize and think in terms of meters, liters, and grams just as we think in feet, quarts, and pounds.

In the meantime, you need to know how to convert from one system to the other. The following table shows various relationships between common units of measurement.

Metric Conversion Table

Type of Measure	Metric to English			English to Metric		
	Metric	Multiply By Conversion Factor	Equals English	Multiply By Conversion Factor	Equals Metric	
	M	× ____	= E	× ____	= M	
Distance	meters meters meters kilometers	39.37 3.28 1.09 .62	inches feet yards miles	.0254 .305 .914 1.609	meters meters meters kilometers	
Volume	liters liters liters	2.12 1.06 .264	pints quarts gallons	.473 .946 3.785	liters liters liters	
Weight	grams kilograms	.0022 2.2	pounds pounds	454 .454	grams kilograms	
Temperature	**Celsius to Fahrenheit** Fahrenheit = $\frac{9 \times \text{Celsius}}{5} + 32$			**Fahrenheit to Celsius** Celsius = $\frac{5 (\text{Fahrenheit} - 32)}{9}$		

Example 1   Marvin Bennett of Buffalo, New York, is touring Canada in a rented car. A road sign tells him that Calgary, Alberta, is 50 kilometers ahead. How many miles is he from Calgary?

Step 1   Locate the conversion factor for kilometers to miles in the table.

Step 2   Multiply the number of kilometers by this factor to find the number of miles.   It is .62.

Answer   The distance to Calgary is 31 miles.   50 × .62 = 31

Example 2 René Martine of Calgary, Alberta, is driving through the United States. Nearing Buffalo, New York, he sees a sign stating that the city is 50 miles ahead. What distance is this in kilometers?

Step 1 Find the conversion factor for miles to kilometers in the table.

Step 2 Multiply the number of miles by this factor to find kilometers. It is 1.609.

Answer The distance to Buffalo is 80.45 kilometers. $50 \times 1.609 = 80.45$

Self-Check

1. Working as a technician in a testing laboratory, Maria Chung must prepare a report for the lab's board of directors in which she translates metric measurements into English-system measurements. Help her by converting the following.
   a) 5 meters to inches
   b) $6\frac{1}{2}$ liters to quarts
   c) 516 grams to pounds
   d) 3.1 kilograms to pounds

2. Perry Whiteside must modify the label on one of his company's products so that it can be sold in Europe. Help him by converting these English-system amounts to metric figures.
   a) 2.6 feet to meters
   b) $2\frac{1}{2}$ pints to liters
   c) 5 gallons to liters
   d) 4.25 pounds to grams

ANSWERS 1. (a) 196.85 inches; (b) 6.89 quarts; (c) 1.14 pounds; (d) 6.82 pounds
2. (a) .79 meter; (b) 1.18 liters; (c) 18.93 liters; (d) 1929.5 grams

Assignment A.1

Metrics

Pierre Decorte works in a French candy factory. In the course of his work, he must convert metric measurements from one level to another. Calculate each of the following, using the rules governing multiplication and division by powers of ten.

1. 46 cl to l ___.46___ 46 × .01
2. 3,524 g to kg ___3.524___ 3,524 ÷ 1,000
3. 35 kg to g ___3,500___ 35 × 1,000
4. 495 cl to l ___4.95___ 495 × .01
5. .955 kg to g ___955___ .955 × 1,000
6. 4.65 kg to g ___4,650___ 4.65 × 1,000
7. 4,600 g to kg ___4.6___ 4,600 ÷ 1,000
8. 56 dl to l ___5.6___ 56 × .1
9. 5,967 ml to l ___5.967___ 5,967 × .001
10. 67 l to cl ___6,700___ 67 ÷ .01

Donna Love is a tool and die maker. One of her assignments is to convert metric measurements to larger or smaller units. Help her with the following.

11. 85 cm to m ___.85___ 85 × .01
12. 6.75 m to cm ___675___ 6.75 ÷ .01
13. 5,645 mm to m ___5.645___ 5,645 × .001
14. 2.47 m to mm ___2,470___ 2.47 ÷ .001

Donna plans a trip to Europe, during which she will tour on a motorcycle. In preparation, she is practicing using metrics and making metric conversions. Help her calculate the following.

15. 3.5 km to m ___3,500___ 3.5 ÷ .001
16. 9,436 m to km ___9.436___ 9,436 × .001
17. 156 km to mi ___96.72___ 156 × .62
18. 956 mi to km ___1,538.204___ 956 × 1.609
19. 54 m to yd ___58.86___ 54 × 1.09
20. 48.4 m to yd ___52.756___ 48.4 × 1.09
21. 75 yd to m ___68.55___ 75 × .914
22. 1.65 m to ft ___5.412___ 1.65 × 3.28
23. 48 m to ft ___157.44___ 48 × 3.28
24. 98.5 ft to m ___30.0425___ 98.5 × .305

As an employee of the U.S. Weather Service, you are assigned to convert some temperatures from Fahrenheit to Celsius as a means of acquainting the public with the metric system. Compute each of the following.

25. Enid, Oklahoma, 98°F = ___36.67°C___   25. $\frac{5(98-32)}{9} = 36.6\overline{6}$
26. Tulsa, Oklahoma, 94°F = ___34.4°C___   26. $\frac{5(94-32)}{9} = 34.4\overline{4}$
27. Flint, Michigan, 63°F = ___17.2°C___   27. $\frac{5(63-32)}{9} = 17.2\overline{2}$
28. Hurley, Wisconsin, 60°F = ___15.56°C___ 28. $\frac{5(60-32)}{9} = 15.5\overline{5}$

continued

Assignment *continued*

29. Victoria, Texas, 108°F = __42.22°C__   29. $\frac{5(108-32)}{9} = 42.2\overline{2}$

30. Terre Haute, Indiana, 79°F = __26.1°C__   30. $\frac{5(79-32)}{9} = 26.1\overline{1}$

31. Bend, Oregon, 65.5°F = __18.61°C__   31. $\frac{5(65.5-32)}{9} = 18.6\overline{1}$

32. Spokane, Washington, 86°F = __30°C__   32. $\frac{5(86-32)}{9} = 30$

Another of your duties at the Weather Service is to convert the temperatures of various European cities from Celsius to Fahrenheit.

33. Helsinki, Finland, 0°C = __32°F__   33. $\frac{9 \times 0}{5} + 32 = 32$

34. Oslo, Norway, 2°C = __35.6°F__   34. $\frac{9 \times 2}{5} + 32 = 35.6$

35. Rome, Italy, 20°C = __68°F__   35. $\frac{9 \times 20}{5} + 32 = 68$

36. Madrid, Spain, 28°C = __82.4°F__   36. $\frac{9 \times 28}{5} + 32 = 82.4$

37. Paris, France, 25°C = __77°F__   37. $\frac{9 \times 25}{5} + 32 = 77$

38. Naples, Italy, 30°C = __86°F__   38. $\frac{9 \times 30}{5} + 32 = 86$

39. Zurich, Switzerland, 23°C = __73.4°F__   39. $\frac{9 \times 23}{5} + 32 = 73.4$

40. Cannes, France, 27°C = __80.6°F__   40. $\frac{9 \times 27}{5} + 32 = 80.6$

41. Determine your weight in grams.   individual answer
    lb × 454

42. Find your weight in kilograms.   individual answer
    lb × .454

43. Compute your height in centimeters.   individual answer
    (ft × .305) ÷ .01

44. Calculate your height in meters.   individual answer
    ft × .305

45. Stanley Kandrick has a Mustang that gets 18.5 miles to the gallon. The gas station where he works converts its pumps to the metric system, selling gas in liters. How many miles does the Mustang get per liter?
                                              __70.02 miles per liter__

    18.5 × 3.785 = 70.0225

Appendix B

The Electronic Calculator

Using The Calculator

The pocket calculator is a fact of modern life. Few electronic tools have swept the market and carved a place for themselves so quickly. In 1973, these instruments cost from $50 to $100 each. Compare that to the price today. The vast volume of sales has brought the cost down to a fraction of what is was only a few years ago, attesting to the immense popularity of the electronic calculator with the public. Engineers have abandoned the slide rule. Nearly every desk in every business office boasts a calculator, as does many a purse or briefcase. Most computers also have calculator capability. The calculator is here to stay, and it can work for you.

A Typical Calculator Face

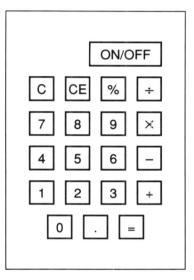

Your calculator may be equipped exactly as the one shown here, its keys may be located in some other configuration, or it may have additional features, such as a memory or a square root key. Read the instructions that came with your calculator to acquaint yourself with its specific features.

There is a key for each arithmetic operation. The button for *addition* is imprinted with a plus sign [+], the one for *multiplication* with a times sign [×], and so on.

The calculator also has keys marked with numbers from 0 to 9, a button for the *decimal point* [.], a *clear* button [C], and a *clear entry* button [CE]. In some cases, the clear key and the clear entry key are combined as one [CE/C].

When you switch your calculator on, a zero followed by a decimal point will appear at the far right of the display window. Try a basic calculation.

Example 1 Add 9 and 5.

	Key	Display Will Read
Step 1	Push the clear button. This is always the first step in any calculation. It guarantees that numbers entered earlier will be erased and will not affect the present operation.	[C]	0.

		Key	Display Will Read
Step 2	Push the 9 button.	9	9.
Step 3	Push the button for addition.	+	9.
Step 4	Push the 5 button.	5	5.
Step 5	Push the equals button.	=	14.
Answer	The display should read 14.		

NOTE: Should you enter an incorrect number, press the clear-entry button. The number just entered, not the entire calculation, will be erased.

Unless your calculator is an old model, it probably has a *floating decimal*. This means it can accept both whole numbers and numbers with decimal points. The decimal point will automatically be positioned correctly in the result.

Example 2 Multiply 9 by 1.23.

		Key	Display Will Read
Step 1	Press clear.	C	0.
Step 2	Press 9.	9	9.
Step 3	Press the multiplication key.	×	9.
Step 4	Press keys to enter the digits of the multiplier, including the decimal point.	1	1.
		.	1.
		2	1.2
		3	1.23
Step 5	Press the equals key.	=	11.07
Answer	The display should read 11.07.		

Example 3 You jot down the mileage—26,381—on the day you have your car's gas tank filled. Later, when you have it filled again, you record the mileage as 26,599. At this second filling, the car takes 8.5 gallons of gasoline. Using your calculator, figure out how many miles you are getting per gallon.

		Key	Display Will Read
Step 1	Clear the calculator.	C	0.
Step 2	Enter the mileage at the second fill: 26,599.	2	2.
		6	26.
		5	265.
		9	2659.
		9	26599.
Step 3	Press the minus key and enter the mileage at the first fill: 26,381.	−	26599.
		2	2.
		6	26.
		3	263.
		8	2638.
		1	26381.
Step 4	Press the division key and enter the number of gallons of gasoline purchased: 8.5.	÷	218.
		8	8.
		.	8.
		5	8.5

Step 5 Press the equals key. | = | | 25.647058 |

Answer Rounding the result, you find that the mileage is 25.6 miles per gallon.

Example 4 Suppose the balance on your bank statement reads $321.66. Looking at your check register, you see that since the date of the statement you have made deposits totaling $196.45. You also have outstanding checks in the amount of $406.55. What is your current balance?

Key	Display Will Read
Step 1 Clear the calculator.	C	0.
Step 2 Enter the statement balance: $321.66.	3	3.
	2	32.
	1	321.
	.	321.
	6	321.6
	6	321.66
Step 3 Press the addition key and enter the total of new deposits: $196.45.	+	321.66
	1	1.
	9	19.
	6	196.
	.	196.
	4	196.4
	5	196.45
Step 4 Press the minus key and enter the total of any outstanding checks: $406.55.	−	518.11
	4	4.
	0	40.
	6	406.
	.	406.
	5	406.5
	5	406.55
Step 5 Press the equals key.	=	111.56

Answer The checkbook balance should be $111.56.

Example 5 According to a recent study, 45% of the 1,260 students attending Crestview Community College expressed interest in a career in business. How many students is this?

Key	Display Will Read
Step 1 Clear the calculator.	C	0.
Step 2 Enter the total number of students: 1,260.	1	1.
	2	12.
	6	126.
	0	1260.
Step 3 Press the multiplication key and enter the percent: 45%.	×	1260.
	4	4.
	5	45.

The Electronic Calculator **B-3**

Step 4   Press the percent key. |%| | 567.|

Answer   The number of students interested is 567.

> **NOTE:** On some calculators, you must press the equals key after pressing the percent key in order to get the final answer.

Appendix C
Glossary

accelerated cost recovery system (ACRS) A method of figuring accelerated depreciation that uses recovery periods with corresponding rates for particular types of assets. Introduced by the Economic Recovery Act of 1981, this method is used for assets purchased on or after January 1, 1981.

accounts payable Amounts owed to creditors for goods and services bought on credit.

accounts receivable Amounts owed to a business by customers for goods and services sold to them on credit.

accrued interest On a bond, the interest accumulated from the last date interest was paid until the date the bond is actually sold.

acid-test ratio A ratio of quick assets to current liabilities.

actuarial table A statistical compilation based on appropriate variables and used to calculate insurance premiums.

actuary An expert who determines insurance premiums.

addends The numbers to be summed in an addition problem.

addition The process of combining two or more numbers into a total.

adjusted balance The actual amount in a checking account after reconciliation. Also known as *current balance*.

amortization The gradual elimination of both principal and interest over the course of a mortgage loan.

amount The percentage added to the base. In an annuity, the dollar value on deposit at the end of the term.

annual percentage rate (APR) The rate of interest charged annually, a commonly used method of quoting interest for personal loans and installment buying.

annuities Periodic payments of equal sums of money.

annuity due The type of annuity where the payments are made at the beginning of each period.

assessed valuation The value of property for tax purposes.

assessment rate The percent of market value used to assess real property.

assets The economic resources or properties owned by a business.

automobile insurance A plan of protection against financial loss resulting from a motor-vehicle accident.

average An estimate of the most common or normal among a series of numbers.

average inventory Total inventory divided by the number of times inventory has been taken during the year.

average-cost method A method of valuing inventory whereby the average cost of total purchases for a period is multiplied by the number of units in the ending inventory.

balance brought forward The amount remaining in a checking account after previously written checks have been subtracted.

balance forward The difference between the total in a checking account and the amount of the check being written.

balance sheet A statement that gives the financial condition of a business on a particular date. It uses the equation: Assets = Liabilities + Capital.

bar graph A graph that charts the relationship among items of the same kind, using bars as a visual representation.

base The whole quantity, that is, the number that is the basis for comparison.

beneficiary The individual or institution named as the recipient of life insurance benefits.

blanket mortgage A real-estate loan involving several properties under one contract.

board of directors Persons elected by the stockholders of a corporation to govern and decide general policy.

bodily-injury insurance A type of automobile insurance protecting owners in the event that others are injured by their vehicle.

bond A method of raising capital by using a long-term debt with a stated interest rate.

bondholder Person or business who purchases a bond.

bonus rate The rate of pay for pieces finished above a certain quota. Also known as *differential*.

book value The difference between the original cost of an asset and its accumulated depreciation.

borrower The business or individual borrowing funds on the basis of a promissory note. Also known as *maker* or *payer*.

callable bonds Bonds that can be paid off by the corporation before maturity.

capital In a business, the owner's equity; the difference between assets and liabilities.

carrying charge In installment buying, an interest charge or service fee added to the cash price of an item to cover certain costs incurred by the seller.

cash Funds on hand or deposits in a bank.

cash discount The amount subtracted from the net price if a buyer pays an invoice within a specified amount of time.

cash surrender value The amount received by the insured from the insurance company after discontinuing a life insurance policy other than term insurance.

cent A monetary unit equal to one hundredth part of a dollar.

check A written notice to a financial institution that payment should be made.

check register An ongoing record of checks written on and deposits made to a checking account.

Glossary **C-1**

check stub An attachment to a check, used to keep a record of activity in the account.

checking account A vehicle by which funds are deposited with a financial institution for disbursement as indicated by the use of checks.

circle graph A graph that uses a circle to chart the relationship of parts to a whole.

coinsurance A type of fire insurance in which a portion of the risk is assumed by the insured party.

collateral Property used as security against the repayment of a mortgage loan.

collision insurance A type of automobile insurance covering repairs to the insured's vehicle in the event of an accident.

commercial year A time factor used to calculate ordinary interest that is based on 360 days. Also known as *business year*.

comparative statement An analysis of a business' financial condition of the current period with figures for the previous period(s). Can be vertical or horizontal.

complex decimal A decimal number that has a proper fraction in its final place.

component bar graph A graph that uses bars to chart relationships within a category in addition to those among categories.

compound interest Interest calculated on both principal and interest already accumulated.

compound-interest period The number of times compounding occurs each year.

comprehensive-damage insurance A type of automobile insurance that pays for damage caused to the vehicle by fire, vandalism, theft, and so on.

consumer loan A lending situation set up to allow the borrower to pay off the amount owed by making periodic payments. Also known as *personal loan*.

conventional mortgage A real-estate loan with a fixed interest rate in which the property itself is the only collateral.

conversion period The number of years for which interest is compounded times the number of interest periods. In an annuity, the time between payments. Also known as *payment period*.

convertible bonds Bonds that can be exchanged for stock.

convertible preferred stock A type of preferred stock that can be changed to common stock if desired by the stockholder.

cost The retail price minus the markup. Also known as *wholesale price*.

cost of an asset The purchase price of an asset plus any other expenditures required to place the asset and make it ready to be used (such as delivery and installation).

cost of goods sold A figure on an income statement that is found by subtracting the ending inventory at cost from the cost of goods available for sale. It represents the cost of the items sold by a business.

coupon bonds Bonds that have negotiable coupons attached to them.

cumulative preferred stock A type of stock in which the value of dividends not paid in one year or more accumulate and are paid before common stockholders receive dividends.

current assets Assets that can be turned into cash, sold, or consumed within a short period of time, usually one year from the date of the balance sheet.

current liabilities Debts that must be paid within a short time, usually within one year from the date of the balance sheet.

current ratio A ratio found by dividing current assets by current liabilities.

current yield The rate of interest of a bond based on the market value of that bond.

decimal A number that describes part of a whole or a unit in terms of tenths, hundredths, thousandths, and so on.

decimal point The symbol (.) distinguishing a whole number, which appears to its left, from a decimal, which appears to its right.

decimal system A method of numbering based on 10 and powers of 10.

declining-balance depreciation A method of figuring accelerated depreciation in which a different amount of depreciation is deducted yearly. The depreciation rate is applied toward a declining balance each year.

declining-balance rate A rate that is commonly double the straight line depreciation rate.

deductible Expenses that must be paid by the insured party before the insurance company is liable for reimbursement.

default Failure to pay off a promissory note at maturity.

denominator The second term in a fraction, or the number below the line.

deposit An amount of money placed in or added to a checking account.

deposit slip The record of a deposit into a checking account.

depreciation The process of distributing the cost of an asset over its useful life.

difference The percentage subtracted from the base. In a subtraction problem, the answer, or the *remainder*.

discount When a bond is sold below face value.

discount period The time remaining between the date a promissory note is sold to a bank and the note's maturity date.

discounting The act of selling a promissory note to a bank before its date of maturity.

dividend A share in the earnings of a corporation that is paid out to the stockholders. In a division problem, the number that is being divided by another number, the divisor.

dividend yield A percent that measures the annual yield of a dividend compared to the market value of the stock.

division The process of discovering how many times one number is contained within another number.

divisor In a division problem, the number doing the dividing, that is, the number that goes into the dividend.

dollar A monetary unit equal to one hundred cents.

down payment A cash payment made by the buyer when entering into an installment buying contract.

effective interest rate The true or actual percent of interest charged in a consumer-loan or installment-buying situation.

end-of-month dating A method of finding the amount of cash discount allowed that does not begin to count time until the end of the month of the date of the invoice.

endowment insurance A type of life insurance allowing the insured individual to accumulate funds for later use.

equivalents Numbers or fractions that are equal to one another.

escrow Money placed and held in an account until specified conditions are met.

estimated life The number of years an asset is expected to be used.

exact time The actual number of days in a loan period.

exemption allowance A certain amount of money that is allowed to be deducted from gross pay before federal income tax is figured.

extra dating A method of finding the amount of cash discount allowed by including a specified number of extra days in which to pay an invoice.

face value The amount of insurance agreed on in a particular policy. The amount of a loan as shown on a note.

factors The numbers or *terms* in a multiplication problem.

federal withholding tax The tax on income collected by the employer and sent to the Internal Revenue Service. It is usually the largest deduction from an employee's paycheck. Also known as the *FIT tax*.

FIFO A method of valuing inventory that assumes that the first units purchased were the first units sold.

financial ratios Ratios that express relationships between numbers in a balance sheet and/or income statement.

fire insurance A plan of protection against financial loss resulting from damage by fire.

fixed assets Long-term assets having a useful life of more than one year.

fraction Two numerals, separated by a line, used to describe part of a whole number.

future value The dollar amount on deposit at the end of an annuity's term. Also known as *amount*.

grace period A specified number of days of advance notice by the insurance company to the insured party before cancellation of a policy.

graduated payment mortgage A real-estate loan with payments that increase gradually over the term of the loan.

graph A visual representation of statistical data.

gross margin The difference between net sales and cost of goods sold. Also known as *gross profit* or *markup*.

horizontal analysis A method of analysis using percents to compare figures on a financial statement for different periods. The numbers for the different periods are compared across each horizontal line in the financial statement.

improper fraction A fraction whose numerator is equal to or larger than its denominator.

income statement A statement that shows the operating results of a business over a period of time. It uses the equation: Revenues − Expenses = Net income.

insured mortgage A real-estate loan guaranteed by a third party.

installment buying A method of purchasing merchandise that allows the buyer to spread payments over an agreed-upon period of time.

insurance Protection against financial loss resulting from unexpected and/or catastrophic events.

interest A fee charged for its use when money is loaned or borrowed.

interest factor A number representing the value of one dollar plus accumulated interest.

interest rate A percent of the principal charged for its use when money is loaned or borrowed.

interest-bearing note A promissory note in which an interest charge is applied to the principal.

invoice A business form that details the merchandise purchased and acts as a record of sale.

land contract A real-estate arrangement whereby the seller retains title to the property until a predetermined portion of the purchase price has been paid.

leap year A 366-day annual period, occurring every fourth year (on years evenly divisible by four).

lender The individual or institution lending money and receiving payment on a promissory note. Also known as *payee*.

level of accuracy A degree of mathematical precision that varies according to the situation.

liabilities Debts of a business.

life insurance A plan of protection against financial loss resulting from the death of the insured party.

LIFO A method of valuing inventory that assumes that the last units purchased were the first units sold.

limited-payment life insurance A type of coverage under which premiums are paid only for a specified number of years.

line graph A chart that plots points on two axes with intersecting lines.

list price The price of merchandise printed on a price sheet or catalogue.

long-term liabilities Debts that are due after a long period, usually one year or more.

lowest, or least, common denominator The lowest whole number into which the denominators of a group of fractions can be divided equally.

maker See *borrower*.

markdown The difference between the original retail price and the new retail price.

markdown percent The rate of markdown based on the original price.

market value What a stock can actually be sold for.

markup The difference between the retail price and the cost. Also known as *gross margin* or *gross profit*.

maturity value An amount equal to face value plus interest that must be repaid by the borrower when a note comes due.

mean The sum of several items divided by the number of items.

median The number located at the midpoint when a series of items is arranged in numerical order.

merchandise inventory Goods or products held for sale by a business.

minuend The number in a subtraction problem from which another number is subtracted.

mixed number A number that includes both a fraction and a whole number.

mode The number that appears most often in a list of numbers.

modified accelerated cost recovery system (MACRS) An optional method of depreciation used for tangible assets placed in service after December 31, 1986. It applies a version of the declining-balance method without using salvage value.

mortgage A temporary transfer of property as security against repayment of a debt.

multiplicand In a multiplication problem, the number that is being multiplied.

multiplication The process of increasing one number by another.

multiplier In a multiplication problem, the number by which the multiplicand is multiplied.

negotiable instrument A document that can be transferred legally from one person or institution to another.

net income The difference between all income and all expenses. Also the difference between gross margin and total operating expenses. Also known in business as the "bottom line."

net price The list price less any trade discount(s).

net proceeds The amount of money received by the seller from the bank for a promissory note.

net profit The difference between the gross profit (gross margin) and expenses. There is a net profit only if the gross profit is higher than expenses; otherwise, there is a *net loss*.

net sales The amount received from customers after subtracting sales returns and allowances from gross sales.

net-price percent The net price stated in terms of a percent rather than in dollars.

new retail price The amount at which merchandise is priced after it has been marked down.

noncumulative preferred stock A type of stock in which a dividend that has not been paid cannot be accumulated and recovered later.

nonparticipating preferred stock A type of stock that entitles the holder only to the dividend printed on the stock certificate.

nonterminating decimal A decimal number that does not divide out evenly. It ends either in a proper fraction or in inaccurate, rounded form.

notes payable Promissory notes owed by a business.

notes receivable Promissory notes owed to a business.

numerator The first term in a fraction, or the number above the line.

operating expenses Costs involved in running a business. Also known as *overhead*.

ordinary annuity A type of annuity where the payments are made at the end of each period.

ordinary interest A method of determining interest based on the premise that every month has 30 days and every year 360 days.

ordinary life insurance See *Straight life insurance*.

ordinary-dating method A common method of finding the amount of cash discount allowed. The time is counted from the date of the invoice until the date paid.

origin The place where two intersecting lines meet on a graph.

original retail price The amount at which merchandise is marked when first offered for sale.

over-the-counter market A network of stock and bond dealers who trade over the telephone or teletype and do not have a specific trading location.

par value The value given to each share of stock when it is first issued.

participating preferred stock A type of stock that carries the right to share in any remaining dividends after the stated dividend and common stock dividend have been paid.

payee See *lender*.

payer See *borrower*.

payment period The time between annuity payments. Also known as *conversion period*.

payroll deductions The difference between gross earnings and net earnings.

per annum On the basis of a year.

percent Hundredths; equivalent to a fraction with a denominator of 100. The symbol "%" represents two decimal places.

percentage A portion or part of the base; the product of the base times the rate.

percentage formula Base × Rate = Percentage.

periodic interest rate The annual interest rate divided by the number of interest periods per year.

pictogram A graph that uses pictures or symbols to chart information.

piecework pay Earnings that are based on the number of units produced.

plant assets Assets held for more than one year. Also called *fixed* or *long-term assets*.

point An amount equal to one percent of the mortgage principal.

policy A contract detailing the agreement between an insurance company and the insured party.

premium The fee, usually annual, charged by the insurance company for coverage. In bonds, when the bond is sold above face value.

present value The current value of a sum of money that will yield a higher desired amount in the future. In an annuity, the total amount that must be deposited now in order to allow for periodic equal payments to be withdrawn.

principal An amount of money originally loaned or borrowed.

product The result, or answer, in a multiplication problem.

promissory note A negotiable document in which a business or an individual agrees to repay a loan by a certain date and at a specified rate of interest.

proper fraction A fraction whose numerator is smaller than its denominator.

property-damage insurance Coverage to pay for repair of damages caused to the property of others by the insured's vehicle.

property taxes Monies collected by local and state governments and levied on property owners.

proportion A statement that two ratios or fractions are equivalent.

purchase money mortgage A real-estate loan that provides funding for only a portion of the payment.

quarterly interest payment Payment found by dividing

the amount of annual interest by 4.

quotient The result, or answer, in a division problem.

rate Determines how large the percentage will be. It is usually in percent form and multiplies the base.

rate of compound interest A rate to use in a present-value table found by dividing the annual rate by the number of times compounding occurs during the year.

rate of return on owner's equity A ratio that measures the income yielded on the amount invested by the owner of a business. Also known as *return on investment* (ROI).

ratio An expression of a relationship or a comparison between two or more numbers. A ratio can be a like ratio, an unlike ratio, or a comparison-to-one ratio.

real estate Land owned as property, along with its resources and permanent buildings.

receipt-of-goods dating A method of finding the amount of cash discount allowed by counting time from the date the goods are received by the buyer until the date paid.

reconciliation The act of comparing a checking account statement against the records of the depositor.

recovery period A time period allowed to depreciate an asset using the ACRS method of depreciation.

registered bonds Bonds that carry the owner's name printed on the bond certificate.

remainder In a subtraction problem, the result, or difference. In a division problem, the amount left when the calculation does not come out even.

repayment schedule A statement showing the portion of a mortgage payment going to interest, the portion to principal, and the balance remaining until the loan is paid off.

restricted endorsement The words "For deposit only" on the back of a check, followed by the depositor's legal signature.

retained earnings Earnings kept by the corporation to be reinvested in the firm.

rounding off The process of converting a number with several decimal places into one with fewer decimal places, thus decreasing its accuracy.

rule of proportion The principle used to test whether two ratios are equal.

salary Earnings that are a fixed payment, usually referred to in monthly or annual terms.

salary plus commission Earnings that include a minimum salary as well as a commission based on total sales.

salvage value The estimated market value of a fixed asset at the end of its useful life. Also known as *scrap value*.

secured bond A bond backed by specific assets.

selling price The retail price; that is, the cost plus the markup.

semiannual interest payment Payment found by dividing the amount of annual interest by 2.

serial bonds Bonds issued that mature at different dates.

series of discounts More than one trade discount. Also known as *chain discount*.

service charge A fee charged by the financial institution for services rendered.

share account An account similar to a checking account offered by a credit union or savings and loan institution.

short-rating The practice of returning less than the prorated share of the premium to the insured after cancellation of the policy.

simple interest Interest paid or collected only on the principal.

single equivalent trade-discount percent A single percent that is equal to a series of discount percents.

sinking fund A fund set up to receive equal periodic payments in order to have a lump sum in the future.

social security tax A tax withheld from the employee's paycheck that is matched by the employer and paid into a fund. Also known as FICA (Federal Insurance Contribution Act).

stock A method of raising capital that is a share in the ownership of a corporation. It can be common or preferred.

stock certificate Evidence of ownership of stock in a corporation.

stock exchange An organization of traders of stocks, bonds, and securities that has a trading place provided by and for its members.

stock outstanding The total number of shares of stock held by the stockholders.

stock turnover The number of times the average inventory is sold and replaced during a certain time period (usually one year). Also known as *stockturn*.

stockholder A person who buys and takes ownership of stock. Also known as *shareholder*.

straight commission Earnings that are a fixed percent of total sales.

straight life insurance A category of coverage in which the insured pays a premium each year until death to keep the policy in effect. Also known as *ordinary life insurance*.

straight-line depreciation A method of depreciation in which the depreciation is written off in equal amounts during each year of an asset's life.

straight-line depreciation rate A rate determined by dividing 100% by the number of years of estimated life of an asset.

subtraction The process of taking one number or quantity away from another.

subtrahend In a subtraction problem, the number being taken away or subtracted.

sum The answer or result in an addition problem. Also known as *total*.

sum-of-the-years'-digits depreciation An accelerated method of depreciation in which an asset is depreciated by a decreasing fraction of its cost each year.

tangible property Depreciable property that can be seen or touched.

tax-free bonds Bonds issued by the government and exempt from federal income taxes.

tax rate The rate at which property taxes are determined.

term The actual length of time that an annuity runs.

term bonds Bonds issued that mature all at the same time.

term insurance A type of life insurance offering coverage for a specific, limited period of time and building no cash value.

term of loan The length of time, that is, the number of days, weeks, or months, until a promissory note is due.

terminating decimal A decimal number that divides out evenly and is therefore accurate.

terms The two numerals that make up a fraction.

time period The number of times that compound interest is calculated in a particular situation.

total Another name for the sum in an addition problem.

trade discount A price adjustment downward from the list price.

twenty-pay life insurance A type of life insurance in which premiums are made for twenty years rather than for the entire life of the insured individual.

uninsured-driver/motorist insurance A type of automobile insurance providing coverage in the event that the insured's vehicle is struck by an uninsured vehicle.

units-of-production depreciation A method of depreciation in which the depreciation is written off according to how much the fixed asset is used.

universal life insurance A type of insurance combining life insurance with a tax-deferred savings program.

unsecured bonds Bonds backed only by the good reputation and strong financial position of a company. Also known as *debenture bonds*.

variable interest rate mortgage A real-estate loan in which the interest rate may be raised or lowered at periodic intervals.

vertical analysis A method of analysis using percents to compare figures on a financial statement for the same period. Each item in the financial statement is compared to a specific dollar figure from the statement.

wages Earnings that are paid according to the amount of time spent on the job.

whole numbers One or more full units; the digits to the left of the decimal point.

yield Another term for interest.

Appendix D

Answers

(Even-numbered answers to assignments and comprehensive problems)

CHAPTER 1

Assignment 1.1
2. Thirty-nine and one hundred nineteen thousandths
4. Two and nine hundred eight thousandths
6. Four hundred thirteen and eight thousandths
8. Eight hundred twelve and two hundred thirty thousandths
10. Sixteen and seventy thousand eight hundred thousandths
12. Eight hundred sixteen and six thousandths
14. Seven and eight thousand seven ten thousandths
16. 33.1   20. 4.05   24. 9,700.80   28. 48.00084
18. 9.015   22. 1.111   26. .002   30. 100.0001

Assignment 1.2
2. 83.428   16. 134,439   30. 31.515
4. 980.4316   18. 827   32. 5,206
6. 1,224.531   20. 27,939,846   34. 71,911
8. 919.215   22. 9.049   36. 10,985
10. 527.8429   24. 5.876   38. 121,458
12. 11   26. .04   40. 5,608,045
14. 180   28. 25.101

Assignment 1.3
2. 360   12. 6,048   22. 4,655,768   32. 25
4. 351   14. 16,146   24. 5,723,905   34. 54,000
6. 711   16. 67.2525   26. .017057   36. 743,760
8. 888   18. .0475   28. .366588   38. 6,532.8
10. 4,416   20. 32,448   30. .00777096   40. 47,600

Assignment 1.4
2. 144   12. 314r74   22. .01   32. 254r8
4. 624   14. 1470r10   24. .37   34. 25
6. 951r2   16. .75   26. .58   36. .004
8. 56   18. 70.14   28. 2.36   38. .07281
10. 23   20. 149.60   30. 9.86   40. .583125

Assignment 1.5
2. 20   16. 2,900,000   30. 11.626
4. 900   18. 84,600,000   32. 65.0074
6. 300   20. 4,178/4,200   34. .7075
8. 6,100   22. 31,744/31,800   36. 8.65
10. 3,000   24. 3.1   38. 95.60
12. 31,000   26. 51.4   40. 10.00
14. 39,000   28. .075

Assignment 1.6
2. 7,844   6. $266,652   10. $30,240   14. 8
4. $14,111,596   8. 3,302   12. $8

Assignment 1.7
2. 1,976   10. 8
4. 210   12. $41,464
6. 28   14. (a) $11,730; (b) $11,750; (c) $12,500
8. 17   16. $5,000

Comprehensive Problems, Chapter 1
2. Nine million, nine hundred eighty-six thousand, nine hundred seven dollars
4. Seven hundred ninety-three million, five hundred thousand dollars
6. 210,076   26. 1,200   46. 57.54
8. 800,860   28. 819,000   48. 956.005
10. 73,020,501   30. 3,943,260,000   50. 77.177
12. 18,200   32. 53.468   52. $6,001.28
14. 1,132.4338   34. .73$\overline{3}$ 54. $8,388
16. 2,090,922   36. 4,280   56. $75.10
18. 3.813   38. 710   58. 3.6
20. 31.4718   40. 82   60. $8,103
22. .840826   42. 245,835/250,000   62. 235.39
24. .00002432   44. 228.46

CHAPTER 2

Assignment 2.1
2. Twenty-three twenty-fifths, 23 ÷ 25 or 25)$\overline{23}$
4. Forty-six thirteenths, 46 ÷ 13 or 13)$\overline{46}$
6. $4\frac{23}{25}$ 12. 27   18. 5   24. $\frac{2}{3}$ 30. $\frac{5}{7}$
8. 2   14. 5   20. 12   26. $\frac{1}{7}$ 32. $\frac{3}{4}$
10. 6   16. 33   22. $\frac{1}{2}$ 28. $\frac{1}{3}$

Assignment 2.2
2. $\frac{7}{24}, \frac{9}{24}, \frac{10}{24}, \frac{4}{24}$ 10. $11\frac{31}{40}$ 18. $\frac{11}{36}$ 26. $\frac{5}{6}$
4. $\frac{28}{42}, \frac{35}{42}, \frac{16}{42}, \frac{30}{42}$ 12. $51\frac{9}{18}$ 20. $\frac{13}{18}$ 28. $39\frac{11}{16}$
6. $\frac{5}{30}, \frac{4}{30}, \frac{9}{30}, \frac{20}{30}$ 14. $187\frac{7}{8}$ 22. $\frac{33}{56}$ 30. $\frac{3}{16}$
8. $\frac{10}{17}$ 16. $\frac{1}{3}$ 24. $\frac{11}{52}$

Assignment 2.3
2. $\frac{5}{32}$ 10. $27\frac{1}{2}$ 18. $9\frac{3}{32}$ 26. $1\frac{1}{8}$
4. $\frac{75}{8}$ 12. $25\frac{7}{8}$ 20. $\frac{6}{11}$ 28. $210\frac{6}{7}$
6. $\frac{85}{16}$ 14. $74\frac{1}{4}$ 22. $\frac{1}{16}$ 30. 42
8. $\frac{3}{4}$ 16. (a) 11; (b) $42.90   24. $10\frac{5}{16}$

Assignment 2.4
2. .4   12. 13.083   22. $\frac{11,907}{25,000}$ 32. $\frac{1}{7}$
4. .14   14. $\frac{9}{25}$ 24. $28\frac{137}{250}$ 34. $\frac{109}{775}$
6. .95   16. $\frac{213}{500}$ 26. $101\frac{10,001}{100,000}$ 36. $\frac{1,911}{8,000}$
8. .917   18. $5\frac{1}{5}$ 28. $\frac{5}{6}$ 38. $\frac{1,141}{2,125}$
10. 3.545   20. $127\frac{141}{200}$ 30. $\frac{43}{50}$

Comprehensive Problems, Chapter 2
2. $\frac{101}{12}$
4. $\frac{3}{16}$
6. $206.67
8. (a) $\frac{11}{40}$; (b) 25,600; (c) 12,800
10. $\frac{2}{3}$
12. $\frac{347}{12}$
14. 9¢
16. $\frac{3}{5}$ 18. $\frac{36}{65}$ 20. $\frac{150}{30}$
22. (a) $100,000; (b) $300,000; (c) $150,000
24. $211.94
26. (a) $342.83; (b) $324.82

CHAPTER 3

Assignment 3.1
2. Bal. Bro't. For'd. $259.33
   Deposits   236.21
                       1.78
   Total   497.32
   This Check   121.36
   Bal. For'd.   375.96
4. Bal. Bro't. For'd. 470.64
   Total   470.64
   This Check   6.73
   Bal. For'd.   463.91
6. 567.63

Assignment 3.2
2. $938.17
4. $753.76
6. $868.88
8. $2,593.41

Comprehensive Problems, Chapter 3
2. Bal. Bro't. For'd. 1,453.60
   Total   1,453.60
   This Check   194.36
   Bal. For'd.   1,259.24
4. Bal. Bro't. For'd. 834.24
   Deposits   431.54
   Total   1,265.78
   This check   1,034.29
   Bal. For'd.   231.49
6. Bal. Bro't. For'd   1.39
   Deposits   556.30
   Total   557.69
   This Check   52.28
   Bal. For'd.   505.41
8. 5.41
10. $110.47
12. $-42.73 (Negative Balance)
14. Client in problem 12 is overdrawn by $42.73.

CHAPTER 4

Assignment 4.1
2. 1 : 3
4. 8 : 3
6. 25 : 1
8. (a) $\frac{3}{7}$; (b) $\frac{3}{4}$
10. (a) $\frac{27}{32}$; (b) $\frac{2}{5}$; (c) $\frac{21}{32}$
12. $\frac{1.3}{1}$
14. $\frac{5}{1}$
16. $164,000; $123,000; $205,000

Assignment 4.2
2. incorrect
4. correct
6. correct
8. 7
10. 2
12. 80
14. 46
16. $7,000
18. $18
20. 8
22. (a) 21; (b) 56
24. 3

Comprehensive Problems, Chapter 4
2. 11 : 4
4. 13 : 17
6. 42 : 1
8. correct
10. incorrect
12. 7.65
14. 9
16. 63.9
18. 54,000
20. $10,800; $16,200; $37,800
22. 180 min. or 3 hrs.
24. $2.16
26. 280; 224; 392; 168
28. $2.40
30. 520
32. $136
34. 3 : 1
36. 32

CHAPTER 5

Assignment 5.1
2. .37
4. 2.74
6. 4.26
8. 5.28
10. .1
12. .000101
14. .00004
16. $\frac{43}{100}$
18. $\frac{19}{25}$
20. $2\frac{31}{50}$
22. $\frac{47}{400}$
24. $\frac{29}{200}$
26. $\frac{4,733}{10,000}$
28. $\frac{1}{200}$

Assignment 5.2
2. $37\frac{1}{2}\%$
4. $83\frac{1}{3}\%$
6. .1%
8. 85%
10. $12\frac{1}{2}\%$; $\frac{1}{8}$
12. 5%; $\frac{1}{20}$
14. .875; $\frac{7}{8}$
16. $62\frac{1}{2}\%$; .625
18. .25%; $\frac{1}{400}$
20. 65%; $\frac{13}{20}$
22. 5%; .05
24. 140%; 1.4

Assignment 5.3
2. $4.62
4. .8046
6. 47%
8. 50%
10. 11.11%
12. $22\frac{1}{2}\%$
14. 8.39%
16. 3,000
18. 2,270
20. 582
22. 5.5
24. 6,680
26. $264.60
28. 50%
30. $8\frac{1}{3}\%$
32. 84
34. $225
36. $16\frac{2}{3}\%$
38. 52.31%
40. $.585
42. 1,500
44. 41
46. $3\frac{1}{2}\%$
48. 152
50. 60%
52. $66\frac{2}{3}\%$

Assignment 5.4
2. $87.50
4. 18
6. $4,320
8. 252
10. $2,643
12. 4,584

Assignment 5.5
2. 16%
4. 43.26%
6. $16\frac{2}{3}\%$
8. 14.27%
10. 82.54%
12. 44.5%; 24.8%
    11.8%; 18.9%

Assignment 5.6
2. $430
4. $320
6. 2,542
8. 978,440
10. $61.18
12. 861,000

Assignment 5.7
2. 199.75
4. 1,578
6. 6,435.66
8. 1,110
10. $148,000
12. $543.20
14. 26
16. 90
18. (a) $216.60; (b) $68.40
20. $403,200
22. $13.69

Comprehensive Problems, Chapter 5
2. 606
4. $68
6. 4,850.7
8. 55%
10. 100%
12. 23.1%
14. 62.5%
16. .163
18. 100
20. 2,000
22. .5% or $\frac{1}{2}\%$
24. 20%
26. $9,000
28. 20%
30. 1.5
32. 655.18
34. 16.57%
36. $59,166.29
38. 16.37%
40. $2,058.82
42. 85.73%
44. $875
46. $13,236.98
48. 2.63%
50. $560
52. $70
54. 12.4%
56. (a) 43,700; (b) 7,866
58. 4,210.5
60. $30,000

CHAPTER 6

Assignment 6.1
2. $193; $386
4. $47.50; $1,852.50
6. $4.33; $48.15
8. $217.69; $653.06
10. $170.03; $774.57
12. 31.6%
14. 82.94%
16. .2875; .7125
18. .3875; .6125
20. .264; .736
22. $1,062.72; $9,737.28
24. $110.13; $521.37
26. $172.10; $380.40
28. $53.94; $318.06

30. $18.80; $68.95
32. $1,044 NP; $406 TD
34. $646.35 TD; $2,188.65
36. $315 TD; $810 NP
38. $425.86
40. $1,351.45

Assignment 6.2
2. Nov. 20, Jan. 4
4. Nov. 24, Dec. 14
6. Dec. 16, Jan. 30
8. Dec. 22, Feb. 10
10. Jan. 4, Jan. 29
12. (a) $113.14; $5,543.66
    (b) $56.57; $5,600.23
    (c) $56.57; $5,600.23
14. $36.33
16. $82.50
18. $2,358.23
20. $2,586.28
22. $5,455.75
24. $2,924.16
26. $1,368.32
28. $3,821.95

Assignment 6.3
2. June 10, July 30
4. April 7, April 27
6. Dec. 24, Jan. 13
8. Nov. 16, Dec. 31
10. Oct. 15, Dec. 4
12. (a) April 10; (b) $9,633.96;
    (c) April 15; (d) $9,938.19;
    (e) April 30; (f) $10,141.01
14. None; $836.42
16. None; $95.44
18. None; $1,234.38
20. $65.67; $3,217.59
22. $56.42; $5,585.98
24. $365.14
26. (a) 28%; (b) $684; (c) $266; (d) $20.52; (e) $663.48
28. (a) 44%; (b) $42.45; (c) $33.35; (d) $.85

Assignment 6.4
2. $570.97
4. $164.22
6. $815.79
8. $436.08
10. $59.29

Comprehensive Problems, Chapter 6
2. $14.33; $53.09; None; $53.09
4. $39.29; $85.03; $.85; $84.18
6. $167.34; $256.96; $7.71; $249.25
8. $142.64; $408.08; None; $408.08
10. $164.51; $711.92; None; $711.92
12. (a) $986.85; (b) $632.87; (c) $6.33; (d) $626.54
14. $628.35
16. $778.95
18. $209.47
20. $410.83
22. $271.13
24. $566.52
26. $5,498.22

CHAPTER 7

Assignment 7.1
2. $25,500 GM; $9,804 P
4. [$4,810] GM; $35,570 L
6. (a) profit; (b) $342; (c) 9%
8. (a) 60%; (b) $8\frac{1}{3}$%
10. 77%

Assignment 7.2
2. $40; 33%; 50%
4. $160; 38%; 60%
6. $1,200; 29%; 42%
8. $27; 41%; 69%
10. $280; 54%; 117%
12. 50%
14. 68%
16. $33\frac{1}{3}$%
18. 67%

Assignment 7.3
2. $64.80
4. $110.34
6. $38.25
8. $22.55
10. $89.60 C; $128 R
12. $112.50
14. $80
16. $4,687.50 R; $937.50 M
18. $.31
20. $5,255.70

Assignment 7.4
2. (a) $45; (b) $7,620
4. $472.50
6. $157.50; $2,870
8. (a) $19.50; (b) $461.50

Assignment 7.5
2. $68,428.57
4. (a) 2; (b) 2.4
6. 3.1
8. 3.1
10. (a) 11.7; (b) $54,600
12. 5.9

Assignment 7.6
2. $3,713
4. $1,291.41
6. $1,263.36
8. $3,333.70
10. $3,512.88
12. $1,013.48

Comprehensive Problems, Chapter 7
2. (a) $283.33; (b) $333.33
4. $150
6. (a) $13.71; (b) $502.81
8. 47%
10. $357
12. 77%
14. (a) $39,285.71; (b) 4.0
16. (a) $35.70; (b) $4,813.20
18. (a) $69,200; (b) 7.01; (c) 7.03
20. (a) $1,200; (b) 17.22%; (c) 38.71%
22. (a) $16,209.30; (b) $18,129.45; (c) $17,168.18

CHAPTER 8

Assignment 8.1

2.	13 hrs.	$61.75
4.	19 hrs.	$95
6.	18.25 hrs.	$144.18
8.	16.25 hrs.	$87.75
10.	12.25 hrs.	$58.80

	Reg. Hours	OT Hours	Reg. Pay	OT Pay	Gross Pay
12.	40	5	$376	$70.50	$446.50
14.	40	1.75	484	31.76	515.76
16.	40	4.25	331.20	52.79	383.99

	Total Pieces	Quota Earning	Bonus Earning	Gross Pay
18.	78	$507.50	$60.80	$568.30
20.	52	364	118.80	482.80
22.	73	507.5	22.80	530.30
24.	86	507.50	121.60	629.10
26.	62	364	217.80	581.80

	Commission	Base Salary	Gross Earnings
28.	2,312.50	400	2,712.50
30.	1,225	400	1,625

Assignment 8.2
- **2.** $375
- **4.** $118
- **6.** $511
- **8.** $240
- **10.** $208
- **12.** $245.54
- **14.** $64.39
- **16.** $7,600
- **18.** $1,087.35
- **20.** $349.34
- **22.** $227.39
- **24.** $123.29

	Federal Income Tax	FICA	Net Pay
26.	567	201.63	1908.10
28.	458	275.28	2954.82
30.	441	163.02	1577.57
32.	422	198.70	2023.54
34.	193	108.68	1134.31

	Federal Income Tax	FICA	Net Pay
36.	91.42	37.90	356.93
38.	395.13	95.81	783.88
40.	43.15	34.68	373.44

Comprehensive Problems, Chapter 8
- **2.** $3,280
- **4.** $1,149
- **6.** $466.38
- **8.** $324.65
- **10.** (a) $204.49 FICA, $581 FIT; $2,074.51 Net

CHAPTER 9

Assignment 9.1
- **2.** (a) $163.05; (b) $1,645.34
- **4.** (a) $284.98; (b) $2,710.34
- **6.** (a) $250.45; (b) $2,214.73
- **8.** $10,854.38
- **10.** (a) $59.15; (b) $839.15
- **12.** (a) $632.22; (b) $10,358.63
- **14.** (a) $13.50; (b) $463.5
- **16.** (a) $60.94; (b) $710.94
- **18.** (a) $10.74; (b) $948.24
- **20.** $72.92

Assignment 9.2
- **2.** (a) 30; (b) $3.68; (c) $343.68
- **4.** (a) 72; (b) $15.09; (c) $604.51
- **6.** (a) 145; (b) $290; (c) $7,790
- **8.** (a) 60; (b) $243.83; (c) $11,643.83
- **10.** (a) 120; (b) $359.29; (c) $11,759.29
- **12.** (a) 210; (b) $860.15; (c) $12,260.15

Assignment 9.3
- **2.** 123   **4.** 96   **6.** 319   **8.** 59   **10.** 166

Assignment 9.4
- **2.** (a) 50; (b) $4.48; (c) $730.48
- **4.** (a) 112; (b) $94.88; (c) $6,965.88
- **6.** $287.34
- **8.** (a) 35; (b) $9.34; (c) $994.34
- **10.** (a) 100; (b) $35.83; (c) $1,535.83
- **12.** (a) 148; (b) $155.86; (c) $3,540.86
- **14.** (a) 307; (b) 228.31; (c) 2,556.31
- **16.** (a) 111; (b) 349.80; (c) 12,614.60
- **18.** (a) $59.91; (b) $919.91

Assignment 9.5
- **2.** 8%
- **4.** 6,385.26
- **6.** 12%
- **8.** (a) 6%; (b) 5,980.54
- **10.** (a) 7.8%; (b) 7,970.26
- **12.** (a) 5; (b) 10,604.07
- **14.** (a) $999.85; (b) $1,012.67
- **16.** (a) 67; (b) $1,259.18
- **18.** (a) $1,542.05; (b) $1,617.04

Assignment 9.6
- **2.** (a) $4,243.60; (b) $243.60
- **4.** $12,845.39; (b) $3,745.39
- **6.** (a) $13,256.45; (b) $2,656.45
- **8.** 19,044.01
- **10.** $1,204.91
- **12.** (a) $34,191.64; (b) $4,491.64
- **14.** (a) $22,910.44; (b) $9,910.44
- **16.** (a) $21,628.15; (b) $2,628.15

Assignment 9.7
- **2.** (a) $27,400.96; (b) $15,510.96
- **4.** $93,113.90
- **6.** (a) $3,943.89; (b) $443.89
- **8.** (a) $19,390.96; (b) $2,840.96
- **10.** (a) $93,303.01; (b) $70,967.01
- **12.** (a) $9,352.79; (b) $6,452.79
- **14.** (a) $4,889.73; (b) $1,029.73
- **16.** (a) $6,415.92; (b) $1,915.92
- **18.** (a) $11,222.08; (b) $3,272.08
- **20.** (a) $10,336.12; (b) $1,691.12

Comprehensive Problems, Chapter 9
- **2.** $53,339.51
- **4.** (a) $435.33; (b) $436.64
- **6.** (a) 443.51; (b) 441.76
- **8.** (a) 113.20; (b) 115.50
- **10.** 36
- **12.** 7,965.06
- **14.** 15.5%
- **16.** $5,596.26
- **18.** (a) $2,400 (b) $2,429.74
- **20.** (a) $38,670.25; (b) $19,012.25

CHAPTER 10

Assignment 10.1
- **2.** (a) Apr. 4; (b) $5.32; (c) $461.32
- **4.** (a) Apr. 29; (b) $9.83; (c) $835.83
- **6.** (a) Nov. 14; (b) $33.82; (c) $1,101.82
- **8.** (a) Sept. 19; (b) $396.88; (c) $4,208.88
- **10.** (a) July 18; (b) $189.28; (c) $3,176.28
- **12.** $1,419.73
- **14.** $1,010.18

Assignment 10.2
- **2.** $3,262.76
- **4.** 14
- **6.** 5

8. 26
10. 41
12. 211
14. $1,211.04
16. (a) $7.40; (b) $747.40; (c) 22; (d) $6.28; (e) $741.12
18. (a) $948.75; (b) $33,948.75; (c) 22; (d) $285.26; (e) $33,663.49
20. (a) $650.04; (b) $10,608.04; (c) 44; (d) $178.27; (e) $10,429.77

Assignment 10.3
2. (a) $402; (b) $27; (c) 15.5%
4. (a) $436.50; (b) $36.50 (c) 13.25%
6. (a) $112; (b) $12; (c) 52%
8. 52.1%
10. (a) 21%; (b) 20.75%
12. (a) 19.2%; (b) 18.25%
14. 10.25%
16. (a) $1,252.50; (b) $52.50; (c) 28.4%
18. (a) 19.2%; (b) 19%
20. 10.1%

Assignment 10.4
2. (a) $109.25; (b) $9.75; (c) 15.5%
4. 22.9%
6. (a) $209; (b) $14; (c) 16.2%
8. (a) $115; (b) $5.50; (c) 22.3%
10. 13.3%
12. (a) $163; (b) $23
14. (a) $260; (b) $17.50
16. (a) $187.50; (b) $18.00; (c) 20.5%
18. (a) $175.00; (b) $10.50; (c) 38.9%
20. (a) $225.00; (b) $25.50; (c) 39%

Comprehensive Problems, Chapter 10
2. (a) 30; (b) $157.99; (c) $12,480.90
4. (a) 35; (b) $417.65; (c) $28,220.93
6. (a) 35; (b) $170.00; (c) $11,487.29
8. (a) 63; (b) $437.39; (c) $16,225.07
10. (a) $148; (b) $196.69; (c) $2,992.83
12. 16.5%
14. (a) $830.00; (b) $80.00; (c) 12.2%; (d) 11.75%
16. (a) $1,714.16; (b) $214.16;(c) 11.8%; (d) 11.25%
18. (a) $2,825.00; (b) $235.00; (c) 15.7%
20. (a) $1,275.00; (b) $80.00; (c) 13.2%
22. (a) $38.00; (b) $5.50; (c) 40%
24. (a) $122.45; (b) $12.50; (c) 24.3%

CHAPTER 11

Assignment 11.1
2. $421.45	8. $554.58	14. $495.85	18. $862.47
4. $510.02	10. $757.60	16. $518.89	20. $924.81
6. $895.28	12. $395.52		

Assignment 11.2
2. (a) $479.01; (b) $16.14; (c) $49,967.88
4. (a) $478.70; (b) $16.45; (c) $49,935.14
6. (a) $380.93; (b) $366.67; (c) $14.26; (d) $39,985.74
8. (a) $409.50; (b) $394.17; (c) $15.33; (d) $42,984.67
10. (a) $386.22; (b) $373.75; (c) $12.47; (d) $38,987.53
12. (a) $668.60; (b) $650.00; (c) $18.60; (d) $64,981.40
14. (a) $703.12; (b) $680.42; (c) $22.70; (d) $70,977.30

Assignment 11.3
2. (a) 0.126; (b) $1.26; (c) $12.60
4. (a) 36.7; (b) $3.67; (c) $36.70
6. (a) 110.2 (b) .1102; (c) $110.20
8. $1,584.20 property tax
10. $1,637.60 property tax
12. $331.05 property tax
14. (a) $6,579; (b) $530.40; (c) $7,109.40
16. (a) $36,000; (b) $1,067.76
18. .04 per $ necessary tax rate
20. (a) .0698 per $1 tax rate; (b) 69.8 mills
22. (a) $58,080,000; (b) .0404 (c) $4.04; (d) $40.40; (e) 40.4
24. $11,366.176 assessed value
26. $12,000,000
28. $6,230,400
30. $82,000 market value

Comprehensive Problems, Chapter 11
2. (a) 424.77; (b) 22.86; (c) 42,454.51
4. (a) 424.31; (b) 23.32; (c) 42,408.11
6. $442.31
8. (a) $526.78; (b) 32.28; (c) 54,935.74
10. (a) $550; (b) $21.40; (c) $59,978.60
12. (a) 549.61 (b) 21.79; (c) 59,935.21
14. $742.53
16. (a) 21.3; (b) .0213; (c) $2.13
18. $12,590.20   22. $1,059.84
20. $7,597.80   24. $5,765,385

CHAPTER 12

Assignment 12.1
2. $646.58	6. $348.80	10. $135.98
4. $486.50	8. $601.00	12. $276.30

Assignment 12.2
2. $427	6. $597	10. $529	14. $341.85
4. $40,000	8. $383	12. $564.48	16. $512.65

Assignment 12.3
2. $67.20	6. $449.55	10. $2,592.00
4. $653.40	8. $53.75	

Assignment 12.4
2. $21.12	6. $50.77	10. $44.67	14. $62,243
4. $21.27	8. $43.77	12. $246.60	16. $15,000

Comprehensive Problems, Chapter 12
2. $1,119.90
4. $109.30
6. $102.78
8. $10,000
10. (a) $10,637.50; (b) $12,375; (c) $1,737.50
12. $1,323.00	16. $350.08	20. $134.59	24. $379
14. $3,025.68	18. $26.82	22. $270	26. $411

CHAPTER 13

Assignment 13.1

2.
Yr.	Yr. dep.	Accum. dep.	Book value
0	$ 0	$ 0	$5,800
1	1,000	1,000	4,800
2	1,000	2,000	3,800

2. (continued)

Yr.	Yr. dep.	Accum. dep.	Book value
3	1,000	3,000	2,800
4	1,000	4,000	1,800
5	1,000	5,000	800

4. (a) $903.80; (b) 20%

Assignment 13.2
2. (a) $.50; (b) $1,054
4. (a) $.45; (b) $2,943

Assignment 13.3

2.

Yr.	Fraction used	Yr. dep.	Accum. dep.	Book value
0		$ 0	$ 0	$6,200
1	7/28	1,400	1,400	4,800
2	6/28	1,200	2,600	3,600
3	5/28	1,000	3,600	2,600
4	4/28	800	4,400	1,800
5	3/28	600	5,000	1,200
6	2/28	400	5,400	800
7	1/28	200	5,600	600

4. $1,000; $800; $600; $400; $200

Assignment 13.4
2. (a) $3,840.80; $5,761.20
(b) $2,304.48; $3,456.72

4.

Yr.	Yr. dep.	Accum. dep.	Book value
0	$ 0	$ 0	$5,000
1	2,500	2,500	2,500
2	1,250	3,750	1,250
3	625	4,375	625
4	None	4,375	625

Assignment 13.5
2. $1,914
4. (a) $456,300; (b) $3,346,200
6. (a) $76,500; $773,500; (b) $76,500; $603,500
8. $250,012.50; $499,987.50

10.

Yr.	Yr. dep.	Accum. dep.	Book value
0	$ 0	$ 0	$11,200
1	2,240	2,240	8,960
2	3,584	5,824	5,376
3	2,150.40	7,974.40	3,225.60
4	1,290.24	9,264.64	1,935.36
5	774.14	10,038.78	1,161.22
6	232.24	10,271.02	928.98

Comprehensive Problems, Chapter 13
2. (a) $1,565; $2,215; (b) $2,520; $1,260

4.

Yr.	Yr. dep.	Accum. dep.	Book value
0	$0	$ 0	$1,881
1	432	432	1,449
2	360	792	1,089

4. (continued)

Yr.	Yr. dep.	Accum. dep.	Book value
3	288	1,080	801
4	216	1,296	585
5	144	1,440	441
6	72	1,512	369

6. (a) $1,727.50; (b) $2,073

8.

Yr.	Yr. dep.	Accum. dep.	Book value
0	$ 0	$ 0	$4,500
1	1,800	1,800	2,700
2	1,080	2,880	1,620
3	648	3,528	972
4	388.80	3,916.80	583.20
5	223.20	4,140	360

10. (a) $1,876; (b) $1,029; (c) $45,000; $355,500
12. (a) $1,640; $6,560 (b) $2,624; $3,936

CHAPTER 14

Assignment 14.1
2. $10,000
4. $57,000
6. $128,890
8. (a) $39,130; (b) $35,319
10. $5,670; $1,390
12. $228,196
14. $8,273
16. $25,000

Assignment 14.2
2.

Sunrise Lighting Company
Balance Sheet
December 31, This Year

ASSETS		Percent
Current Assets:		
Cash	$ 10,000	5.21%
Accounts Receivable	21,000	10.93%
Supplies	1,100	.57%
Merchandise Inventory	42,000	21.86%
Total Current Assets	$ 74,100	38.57%
Plant Assets:		
Equipment (less depreciation)	$ 8,000	4.16%
Building (less depreciation)	70,000	36.44%
Land	40,000	20.82%
Total Plant Assets	$118,000	61.43%
Total Assets	$192,100	100%
LIABILITIES		
Current Liabilities:		
Accounts Payable	$ 40,000	20.82%
Notes Payable	5,000	2.60%
Total Current Liabilities	$ 45,000	23.43%
Long-term Liabilities:		
Mortgage Payable	$ 24,400	12.70%
Total Liabilities	$ 69,400	36.13%
CAPITAL		
C. Crystal, Capital	$122,700	63.87%
Total Liabilities and Capital	$192,100	100%

4. 110.53% Sales
   − 10.53% Less returns
   100   % Net sales
    46.05% Cost of G.S.
    53.95% Gross profit
    15.79% Expenses
    38.16% Net income

6.

	Toro Manufacturing Comparative Income Statement For Year Ending December 31, This Year, and December 31, Last Year						
			Horizontal Analysis Amount Increase or (Decrease)	% Change	Vertical Analysis % This Year		Last Year
	This Year	Last Year					
Gross Sales	$217,000	$199,000	$ 18,000	9.05%	105.60%		110.68%
Less: Returns and Allowances	11,500	19,200	(7,700)	(40.10%)	5.60%		10.68%
Net Sales	$205,500	$179,800	25,700	14.29%	100%		100%
Cost of Goods Sold	100,200	90,000	10,200	11.33%	48.76%		50.06%
Gross Profit	$105,300	$ 80,800	24,500	30.32%	51.24%		44.94%
Expenses Salaries	$ 57,480	$ 65,700	(8,220)	(12.51%)	27.97%		36.54%
Advertising	10,610	3,200	7,410	231.56%	5.16%		1.78%
Interest	8,800	9,300	(500)	(5.38%)	4.28%		5.17%
Utilities	2,500	1,980	520	26.26%	1.22%		1.10%
Supplies	3,100	4,600	(1,500)	(32.61%)	1.51%		2.56%
Total Expenses	$ 82,490	$ 84,780	(2,290)	(2.70%)	40.14%		47.15%
NET INCOME	$ 22,810	$ (3,980)	26,790	∅	11.10%		∅

Assignment 14.3
2. .69 : 1
4. 1.77 : 1
6. 1.07 : 1
8. 2.42 : 1
10. .13 : 1
12. .31 : 1
14. .63 : 1

Assignment 14.4
2.
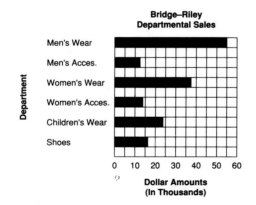

4.
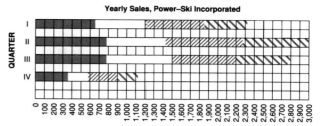

Assignment 14.5
2. .50 = 180°
   .30 = 108°
   .12 = 43.2°
   .08 = 28.8°

4.
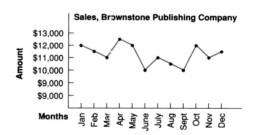

6.
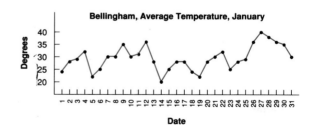

Comprehensive Problems, Chapter 14

2. $133,740
4. $163,679 A; $144,704 L; $18,975 C
6.

```
                Kelly's Lawn Care
                   Balance Sheet
                 December 31, 19__

                      Assets
Accounts receivable                        $1,870.00
Office furniture                              920.00
Equipment                                   6,690.00
  Total assets                              9,480.00

                    Liabilities
Notes payable                              $4,000.00
Salaries payable                            3,500.00
Taxes due                                   2,040.00
  Total liabilities                        $9,540.00

                  Owner's Equity
Kelly, Capital                             $  (60.00)
  Total liabilities and owner's equity     $9,480.00
```

8.

The Birthday House
Comparative Income Statement
For Year Ending December 31, This Year, and December 31, Last Year

	This Year	Last Year	Horizontal Analysis Amount Increase or (Decrease)	% Change	Vertical Analysis % This Year
Gross Sales	$423,000	$459,000	(36,000)	(7.84%)	109.87%
Less: Returns and Allowances	58,000	52,000	6,000	11.54%	15.06%
Net Sales	$385,000	$407,000	(22,000)	(5.41%)	100%
Cost of Goods Sold	192,000	221,000	(29,000)	(13.12%)	49.87%
Gross Profit	$193,000	$186,000	7,000	3.76%	50.13%
Expenses					
Salaries	$ 94,700	$ 79,100	15,600	19.72%	24.60%
Advertising	19,000	26,000	(7,000)	(26.92%)	4.94%
Interest	16,500	17,300	(800)	(4.62%)	4.29%
Utilities	2,300	2,100	200	9.52%	.6%
Supplies	4,600	4,300	300	6.98%	1.19%
Total Expenses	$137,100	$128,800	8,300	6.44%	35.61%
NET INCOME	$ 55,900	$ 57,200	(1,300)	(2.27%)	14.52%

10.

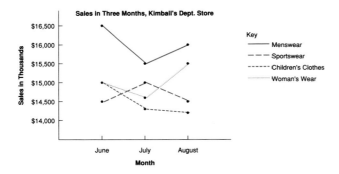

12. $65 = .20 = 72° Taxes & Soc. Sec.
    $60 = .185 = 66.5° Food
    $80 = .246 = 88.6° Rent
    $20 = .061 = 22.2° Furn. Rental
    $40 = .123 = 44.3° Recreation
    $20 = .061 = 22.2° Savings
    $40 = .123 = 44.3° Misc. Exp.

14. individual answers

CHAPTER 15

Assignment 15.1
2. 3%; 24; .491934
4. 7%; 24; .197147
6. 2%; 12; .788493
8. 13%; 5; .542760
10. 1.5%; 20; .742470
12. $8,741.32
14. $12,875.70
16. $2,468.14
18. $7,235.73
20. $1,127.70
22. $3,619.44
24. $4,747.61

Assignment 15.2
2. $44,970.08
4. $2,414.53
6. $6,198.62
8. $115,412.88
10. (a) $41,273.69; (b) $43,543.74
12. (a) 2; (b) $15,436.36
14. (a) $31,691.21; (b) $22,581.95
16. $4,117.40

Assignment 15.3
2. $23,845.57
4. $7,526.88
6. $10,460.55
8. $9,534.43
10. (a) $19,784.52; (b) $7,215.48
12. (a) $26,110; (b) $5,890
14. $6,149.10
16. (a) $13,248.16; (b) $13,389.73; (c) $13,486.51

Assignment 15.4
2. $1,212.39
4. $55
6. $267.13
8. $1,396.80
10. (a) $764.73; (b) $1,234.86
12. (a) $5,798.96; (b) $10,412.48
14. $1,041.65
16. (a) $96,153.80; (b) $47,098; (c) $3,915.60

Assignment 15.5
2. $7.47
4. $2.60
6. $4.80
8. $7.00
10. $2.00
12. $351.44
14. $1.95 pr.; $2.10 com.
16. $144
18. $3.60; $75.60
20. $1.94; $31.04
22. 7%
24. 17.1%
26. h
28. j
30. b
32. n
34. e

Assignment 15.6
2. $92.50; $46.25
4. $60; $30
6. $850; $150 Dis.
8. $796.25; $203.75 Dis.
10. $1,022.50; $22.50 Pre.
12. $922.50; $77.50 Dis.
14. $1,060; $60 Pre.
16. (a) $12,420; (b) $420 Pre.
18. $1,022.19
20. $22,833.94
22. $27,665.70
24. 10.17%
26. 9.62%
28. h
30. j
32. c
34. b

Comprehensive Problems, Chapter 15
2. $27,629.32
4. $393.92
6. $340.58
8. $97,573.30
10. $192,621.20
12. $15,628.49
14. $3,279.65
16. (a) $791.34; (b) $20,181.04
18. (a) $23,499; (b) $5,301
20. (a) $2,238.81; (b) $115.92
22. (a) $42,567.82; (b) individual answers; (c) $1,746
24. 11%
26. (a) $.25; (b) $2
28. $949.50
30. (a) $1.95 (b) $2.40

APPENDIX A

Metrics Assignment
2. 3.524
4. 4.95
6. 4,650
8. 5.6
10. 6,700
12. 675
14. 2,470
16. 9.436
18. 1,538.204
20. 52.736
22. 5.412
24. 30.0425
26. 34.4°C
28. 15.56°C
30. 26.1°C
32. 30°C
34. 35.6°F
36. 82.4°F
38. 86°F
40. 80.6°F
42. individual answer
44. individual answer

Index

Accelerated Cost Recovery System, 517
Account form, 541
Accounting and analysis, 540
   comparative analysis, 551
      horizontal analysis, 552
      vertical analysis, 553
   financial ratios, 563
      acid test ratio, 564
      current ratio, 564
      ratio of net income to owner's equity, 565
      ratio of owner's equity to total liabilities, 565
      ratio of plant assets to long-term liabilities, 565
   financial statements, 540
      balance sheet, 540
         terms for balance sheet, 540
      income statement, 543
         cost of goods sold, 544
         terms for income statement, 543
Accounting equation, 541
Accrued interest, bond, 649
Acid test ratios, 564
Actuarial tables, 467
Actuaries, 467
Addends, 7
Addition, 7
Alcoa Aluminum, 495
Amortization of mortgages, 435
Amount, 197
Amount of annuity due, 611
Amount of ordinary annuity, 609
Annual depreciation cost, 497
Annual percentage rate (APR), 411
   APR table, 412
Annuities, 609
Annuity Tables, 614, 623, 631
   amount, 614
   present value, 623
   sinking fund, 631
Assessed valuation, 447
Assets, 540
Automobile insurance, 473
Average cost method, 294
Average inventory, 285
Averages, 37
Avon, 215

Balance sheet, 540
Bank records, 98
   checks, 98
   deposit slips, 105
   deposits, 98, 104
   electronic banking, 107
   interest-bearing checking, 106
   reconciliation, 115
   records of checks and deposits, 100
   share accounts, 106
Bankers trust, 97
Bar graphs, 571
Base, rate, and percentage, 155
   amount, 198
   base, 171
   finding base using amount and difference, 172
   base narrative problems, 191
   conversion to percents, 156
      decimal to percent, 163
      fraction to percent, 163
   difference, 199
   percentage, 168
   percentage formula, 167
   percentage narrative problems, 180
   percents, 156
      converting a percent to a decimal, 156
      converting a percent to a fraction, 157
      finding percent more than and less than, 170
   rate, 221
   rate narrative problems, 185
Basic processes and decimals, 2
   addition, 7
   averages, mean, median, mode, 37
   division, 19
   estimation and rounding, 27
   multiplication, 13
   narrative problems, 31
   reading numbers, 2
   subtraction, 8
Beneficiary, 466
Board of directors, 637
Bodily injury insurance, 473
Bonds, 647
Bonus rate, 314
Book value, 496

Campbell Soup, 1
Capital, 541
Carrying charges, 423
Cash discounts, 229
   credit for partial payments, 241
   ordinary dating, 229
   other dating methods, 233
   reading terms, 229
   returns, 241
Cash surrender value, 466
Chain discount, 220
Check register, 102
Check stub, 101
Checks, 98
Circle graphs, 579
Circular E, 320
Coinsurance, 485
Collision insurance, 473
Commercial year, 357
Common stock, 638
Comparative accounting statement, 551
Complex decimal, 83
Component Bar Graph, 572
Compound interest, 379
Comprehensive insurance, 473
Consumer Credit Protection Act, 411
Consumer loans, 411
Conversion period, 387
Cost of asset, 497
Cost of goods sold, 257, 544
Current ratio, 564

Decimals, 2
Declining Balance Rate, 511
Denominator, 52
Deposits, bank, 98, 104
Depreciation, 496
   accelerated cost recovery system, 517
   declining balance method, 511
   modified accelerated cost recovery system, 521
   straight line method, 497
   sum-of-the-years' digits method, 507
   units of production method, 503
Depreciable rate, 498
Depreciation schedule, 498
Difference, in percentage, 199
Difference, in subtraction, 8
Differential piece rate, 314
Discount period, 407
Discounting notes, 407
Disney, 433
Dividend, in division, 19
Dividend, stock, 638
Dividend yield, 640
Division, 19
Divisor, 19
Down payment, 423

Effective interest rate, 411, 424
Electronic banking, 107
Electronic calculator, Appendix B-1
Employer's Returns, 325
End of month dating, 233
Endorsements, 106
Ending Inventory, 293
Endowment insurance, 467
Equivalents, decimal-fraction, 84
Escrow accounts, 436
Estimation, 27
Exemption, 319
Extra dating, 234

Index **I-1**

Face value, 401
Factors, 13
FIFO Method, 293
Finance, 398
  consumer loans, 411
  discounting notes, 407
  installment buying, 423
  promissory notes, 398
    days in note period, 402
    interest due, 400
    maturity value, 401
Financial ratios, 563
Financial statements, 540
Fire insurance, 479
Fixed assets, 496
Fractions, 52
  addition, 61
  cancellation, 71
  conversion, 81
  decimal-fraction equivalents, 84
  division, 74
  equivalent fractions, 55
  law of fractions, 54
  lowest common denominator, 61
  multiplication, 71
  raising, 55
  reducing, 55
  rules of divisibility, 56
  subtraction, 64

Graphs, 571
Greyhound Corporation, 539
Gross margin, 257, 543

Honda, 397
Horizontal analysis, 552

Improper fractions, 53
Income statement, 543
Installment buying, 423
Insurance, 466
 automobile, 473
 fire, 479
    cancellation, 483
    coinsurance, 485
 life, 466
Interest, 352
  compound, arithmetical, 379
    using a table, 385
  simple, 352
    exact interest, exact time, 365
    finding principal, 371
    finding rate, 372
    finding time, 373
    ordinary interest, 357
      exact time, 365
      thirty-day month time, 357
Interest-bearing checking, 106
Inventory, 287, 293
Investments, 637
  bonds, 647
    accrued interest, 649
    bond prices, 648
    buying and selling, 648
    current yield, 650
    types of bonds, 637
  stocks, 637
    buying and selling stock, 641

    dividend yield, 640
    dividends, 638
    types of stock, 637
Invoices, 216

Kirk Horse Insurance, Inc., 465

Lands' End, 311
Liabilities, 541
Life insurance, 466
Limited payment life insurance, 467
LIFO Method, 294
Line graphs, 580
List price, 218
Liz Claiborne, Inc., 51
Lowest common denominator, 61

Markdown, 281
Markup, 265, 271
Maturity value, 353, 401
Mean, 37
Median, 37
Metric system, Appendix A-1
Microsoft, 601
Mills, 449
Minuend, 13
Mixed numbers, 53
Mode, 37
Modified Accelerated Cost Recovery System, 521
Mortgage loans, 434
Multiplicand, 13
Multiplication, 13
Multiplier, 13

Narrative problems, explanation, 31, 179
Negotiable instrument, 398
Net price, 218
Net proceeds, 407
Net profit, 257
Net profit percent, 257
Net sales, 281
New retail price, 281
Nordstrom, 255
Numerator, 52

Odd-lot fee, 641
Operating expenses, 257
Ordinary Annuity, 609
Ordinary dating method, 229
Ordinary interest, 357
Ordinary life insurance, 467
Original retail price, 281
Over the counter market, 641
Overtime pay, 313

Par value, bond, 647
Par value, stock, 637
Partial payment, 241
Partial product, 13
Payroll, 311
  compensation, 312
    commission, 315
    overtime, 313
    piecework, 314
    salary, 312
    wages, 313

  deductions, 319
    federal income tax, 319
    social security tax, 323
  employer's returns, 325
  tables, 328, 336
    federal income tax, 328
    social security tax, 336
Per annum, 352
Percent of markup, 265, 266
Percent increase or decrease in profit, 258
Percentage, definition, 168, 180
Percentage formula, 167
Percentage method, federal income tax, 321
Percents, 156
Periodic interest rates, 387
Pictogram, 574
Pie charts, 579
Polaroid, 155
Powers of ten, 15, 22
Preferred stock, 638
Premium, bond, 648
Premium, insurance, 467
Present value, 602
  present value table, 605
Present value annuity, 621
Pricing, 265
Principal, 352, 400, 441
Procter & Gamble, 131
Product, 13
Profit, 256
Promissory notes, 398
Proper fractions, 53
Property damages, insurance, 473
Property taxes, 447
Proportion, 141

Quick assets, 564
Quick ratio, 564
Quotient, 19

Rate, 169, 185
Ratio, 133
  applying ratios, 134
  comparison of more than two, 134
  comparison to one, 133
  unlike quantities, 133
  writing and reading ratios, 133
Ratios, financial, 563
Real estate, 434
  mortgages, 434
    amortization, 435
    loan repayment schedules, 441
    prorating, 436
  property taxes, 447
    assessed valuation, 447, 451
    tax rate, 450
Real property, 517
Receipt of goods dating, 234
Reconciliation of checking accounts, 115
Recovery period, 517
Recovery rate for 15 year class, 519
Remainder, 8, 19
Report form, balance, sheet, 542
Retail merchandising, 255
  cost, retail, markup, 271

cost when markup is on retail, 271
cost and markup when markup is on cost, 275
markup in dollars when markup is on retail, 273
retail and markup when markup is on cost, 274
retail price when markup is on cost, 276
retail price when markup is on retail, 272
markdown, 281
markdown based on original retail price, 281
merchandise inventory, 287
average inventory, 287
converting average inventory, 289
ending inventory, 293
stock turnover, 288
pricing and markup, 265
percent of markup based on cost, 266
percent of markup based on retail, 265
profit, 256
Retail price, 265
Retained earnings, 638

Return on investment, 565
Returned merchandise, 241
Rounding, 27
Rule of Proportion, 141

Salary plus commission, 315
Salvage value, 497
Selling price, 265
Series of discounts, 220
Share accounts, 106
Short-rate tables, insurance, 483
Simple interest, 352
Sinking fund for annuities, 629
Stock certificate, 637
Stock exchange, 641
Stock outstanding, 638
Stock turnover, 288
Stockholder, 637
Stocks, 637
Straight commission, 315
Straight life insurance, 467
Straight line depreciation rate, 497
Straight piecework method, 314
Subtraction, 8
Subtrahend, 8
Sum, 7

Sum-of-the-years' digits depreciation, 507

Tangible property, 517
Term insurance, 466
Terms of fractions, 52
Toys 'Я" Us, 351
Trade discounts, 215
invoices, 216
single equivalent trade discount percent, 221
understanding trade discounts, 218
Truth in Lending Law, 411
Turnover, 288
Twenty-pay life insurance, 467

Units of production depreciation, 503
Universal life insurance, 467

Valuing ending inventory, 293
Vertical analysis, 553

Wage bracket method, federal income tax, 320
W4 Form [sample], 320

Yield, bond, 650
Yield, stock, 640